National Intelligencer Newspaper Abstracts 1857

Joan M. Dixon

HERITAGE BOOKS
2009

HERITAGE BOOKS
AN IMPRINT OF HERITAGE BOOKS, INC.

Books, CDs, and more—Worldwide

For our listing of thousands of titles see our website at
www.HeritageBooks.com

Published 2009 by
HERITAGE BOOKS, INC.
Publishing Division
100 Railroad Ave. #104
Westminster, Maryland 21157

Copyright © 2009 Joan M. Dixon

All rights reserved. No part of this book may be reproduced or transmitted in any form or by any means, electronic or mechanical, including photocopying, recording or by any information storage and retrieval system without written permission from the author, except for the inclusion of brief quotations in a review.

International Standard Book Numbers
Paperbound: 978-0-7884-4794-5
Clothbound: 978-0-7884-8063-8

NATIONAL INTELLIGENCER NEWSPAPER
WASHINGTON, D C
1857

TABLE OF CONTENTS

Daily National Intelligencer, Washington, D C, 1857: pg 1

Acts of Congress passed by last Congress-1856: 90-92
American Hostilities in China: 68-69
Appointments by the President: see index
Appointments in the Navy: 97; 103-104
Appropriations made during 3rd Session of 34th Congress: 211-216
Army Orders: 108
Assassination of Dr Vogel: 131
Atlantic Telegraph: 326; 332; 334
Blue Ridge Tunnel: 84
Breach of Promise: 137
British Gov't-pensions: 306
British Peerage: 388
Buchanan Inauguration: 51-53; 88; 89
Cadet Appointments: 77
Candidates for Congress in Ky: 242
Candidates for Congress in Tenn: 238
Chicago conflagration: 418
Col Sam Colt: 415
Columbia Fire Co: 6
Columbia Typographical Society: 468

Commencements: Academy of Visitation-Gtwn: 268; 270-271
                Columbian College: 244
                Gtwn College: 265; 271-272
                Harvard College: 282
                St Mary's, Chas Co, Md: 324-325
                Washington College, Va: 290

Com'rs appointed in Kansas Territory: 474
Cmte of Elections-affidavits: 296-297
Continental Congress officer's pay: 10-11
Crabbe's expedition-casualties: 233

i

Death of Lt Albert Allmand: 206; 274
Death of John Bell: 196
Death of Hon Preston S Brooks: 41
Death of Hon Andrew P Butler: 197
Death of Archibald Campbell, age 101 years: 307
Death of George Washington Custis: 403; 406
Death of Midshipman R W Meade Graham: 32
Death of Richd Graham: 313
Death of Capt Henry Henry: 295
Death of John Campbell Henry: 147
Death of David Hume: 90
Death of Dr Kane, Artic explorer: 78
Death of Hesther Maria Viscountess Keith: 181
Death of A H Lawrence: 102-103
Death of Purser Thos P McBlair: 106
Death of Hon Louis McLane: 401
Death of Gen Sir Chas J Napier: 139
Death of Cmdor John T Newton: 295
Death of Thos Petigru: 114
Death of Dr Benj Robinson: 95
Death of Mgr Sibour: 38
Death of Hon Andrew Stevenson: 43
Death of Lt Arthur Donaldson Tree: 94
Death of Col Wm Turnbull: 470
Death of Gen John DeBarth Walbach: 225-226

Dept of State-clerks: 276
Descendants of Thos Lewis: 113
Dry Good Merchants: 208
Electric Telegraph: 341-342
English Royalty: 177
Florida-Indian Wars: 19; 107; 337
Gaslights: 320
Gen Walker-returned filibusters: 308-310
Gen Walker's men: 174-175; 450; 488
Headquarters of U S Army: 444-446
Heirs of Elizabeth Spencer [extensive information]: 353-359
Jamestown Society: 168
Jury, Washington City: 85-86; 122; 230; 467; 468
Koran: 13
Ladies Benevolent Society, Washington: 490
Letter from Sir John Franklin: 173
Lt Wm Henry Allen: 456
Longevity: 188

Lord Lyndhurst: 304
Lord Howe: 192
Loss of steamer Rainbow: 458
Loss of steamship Opelousas: 448; 455; 459
Lost in fire in Balt, Md: 148
Massacre of Missionaries: 304; 420
Methodist Episcopal Appointments: 104-105
Metropolis disaster: 323
Missionaries killed in India: 472
Naval Academy Candidates: 190; 399-400
Naval Academy Graduates: 233
Naval Officers: 483-484
Officers of Utah Expedition: 451-452

Officers of the: Dale: 176
                   Falmouth: 337
                   Fulton: 350
                   Minnesota: 199
                   Niagara: 451
                   Powhatan: 460
                   Plymouth: 446

Packet Cataract disaster: 453
Portraits of George Washington: 245
Presidential Vote: 1; 3
Promotions and Appointments in the Army: 224-225; 279-282
Revolutionary Reliques: 261
St Patrick's Church Cmte: 179
Sale of the property of late Gen Jas Thompson, Gtwn, D C: 158
Sale of Easby property: 160-161
Served under Gen Walker: 253-255
Sir John Franklin: 479-480
Steamer Central America disaster: see index
Steamer Scott disaster: 164
Steamship Louisiana disaster: 219-220
Surviving soldiers of the War of 1812: 236
Synod of Virginia: 423
Tax Collector sale, Gtwn, D C: 377
Trial of Col Edwin V Sumner: 415
Tristam Coffin-family record: 351
U S Supreme Court: 467
Valuable Table: 85
Virginia Certificates: 22-23
Walker deserters: 281-282
Washington Corp nominations: 298

Washington Corp police officers: 432
West Point Academy-first class: 222
West Point promotions: 234
Westmoreland Co, Va: 187
Will of Wm Easby: 75

Index: pg 491

Dedicated to the memory of my uncle,
Wm August Neff B. 1881, Md
D. 1938, Wash, D C;
Mrd 1907, Wash, D C,
Emma M Weingart, B. 1886, Wash, D C,
D. 1918, Wash, D C.

PREFACE
Daily National Intelligencer Newspaper Abstracts
1857
Joan M Dixon

The National Intelligencer & Washington Advertiser is hereafter the Daily National Intelligencer. It was the first newspaper printed in Washington, D C; Samuel H Smith, the originator. The same was transferred to Jos Gales, jr on Aug 31, 1810; on Nov 1, 1812, the paper was under the firm of Jos Gales, sr, & Wm W Seaton. The Library of Congress has microfilm of the paper from the first issue of Oct 31, 1800 thru Jan 8, 1870, the final paper. The Evening Star Newspaper of Jan 10, 1870 reports: The Intelligencer is discontinued: the proprietor, Mr Alex Delmar, says that having lost several thousand dollars, & being in poor health, he has resolved to discontinue its publication.

Included in the abstracts are advertisements; appointments by the President; Hse o/Rep petitions; passed Acts; legal notices; marriages; deaths; mscl notices; social events; military promotions; court cases; deaths by accident; prisoners; & maritime information-officers-crews. Items or events which might be a clue as to the location, age or relationship of an individual are copied.

No attempt has been made to correct the spelling. Due to the length of some articles, it was necessary to present only the highlights of same. Chancery and Equity records are copied as written.

The index contains all surnames and *tracts of lands/places*. Maritime vessels are found under barge, boat, brig, frig, schn'r, ship, sloop, steamboat, tugboat, yacht or vessel.

ABBREVIATIONS:

AA CO	ANNE ARUNDEL COUNTY
CMDER	COMMANDER
CMDOR	COMMODOR
ELIZ	ELIZABETH
ELIZA	ELIZA
MONTG CO	MONTGOMERY COUNTY
PG CO	PRINCE GEORGES CO
WASH	WASHINGTON
WASH, D C	WASHINGTON, DISTRICT OF COLUMBIA

BOOKS IN THE NATIONAL INTELLIGENCER NEWSPAPER SERIES: 1800-1805/1806-1810/1811-1813/1814-1817/1818-1820/1821-1823/1824-1826/1827-1829/1830-1831/1832-1833/1834-1835/1836-1837/1838-1839/1840/1841/1842/1843/1844/1845/1846/1847/ 1848/1849/ 1850/1851/1852/1853/1854/1855/1856/1857. SPECIAL: CIVIL WAR 2 VOLS, 1861-1865

DAILY NATIONAL INTELLIGENCER NEWSPAPER
1857

THU JAN 1, 1857
David A Baird, Upholsterer & Paperhanger, has removed from 491 8th st, near Pa ave, to 498 9th st, a few doors north of Pa ave, Wash.

Equity No 1,139: Circuit Court of D C. The U S against Selden, Withers & Co. On Dec 22, 1856, the above cause coming on to be heard, on exceptions by the Fred'k Co Bank to the Auditor's report, the Court decreed: that the claims embraced in the list signed by A Wylie & S S Baxter be referred to the Auditor to take testimony in regard to the same. The claims embraced in the list referred to in the 4th ruling of the Court are the following:

C Wendell: $6.55
J C Connolly: $10.00
H Polkinhorn: $16.18
D Rowland: $20.24
Jas Beers: $94.50
A A Nicholson: $61.66
G H Montserrat & Co: $166.14
Page & Bacon: $380.14
Page, Bacon & Co: $406.29
Bayne, Latham & Co: $181.21
J P Dulany: $9645.95
Hon H Dodge: $10,100.00
J T Neely: $200.00
P Stevens: $34.00
U S Agricultural Soc: $2,149.13
Chesapeake & Ohio Canal Co: $550.00
Va & Tenn R R Co: $3,757.33

In Equity-Circuit Court of D C. W S Herriman & others against the heirs at law & administrator of Thos J Davis. The above cause coming before the Court on the mandate of the Supreme Court, upon the appeal of Jas L Ranson, affirming the decision of the Circuit Court, which over-ruled his exceptions to the Auditor's report & dismissed his petition; & the sum of $636.34 having been left in the trustees' hands to await the result of the said appeal, & the same being subject to the further order of the Court, the cause was referred to the Auditor on the 29th instant to inquire & report upon the distribution of the said sum. Parties interested are to attend at my ofc in the City Hall, Wash, on Jan 23 next, at 11 o'clock. –W Redin, auditor

The popular vote for President:
Buchanan: 1,828,022   Fremont: 1,437,625
Fillmore: 870,358
The electoral votes will stand: for Buchanan & Breckinridge, 174; for Fremont & Dayton, [less Wisc, 6,] 108; & for Fillmore & Donelson, 8.

Agency for American & Foregin Claims: -Alfred Schucking, 18 La ave, Wash.

The case of Richd Chambers vs Carter was lately argued by Judge Chambers & Senator Pearce for the cmplnts, & Madison Brown & P B Hopper, jr, for the dfndnts. Judge Hopper on Tue last filed his opinion, deciding that the devises in the will of Catharine Chambers to the Salem & Spaniard's Neck Methodist Episcopal Churches were valid devises, & ordered the bill to be dismissed with costs. It may, however, go to the Court of Appeals. –Centreville [Md] Times

Teacher wanted in a private family. I wish to engage the services of a young lady, qualified to teach the English branches, French, Latin, & Music. Address B Shumate, Catlett's Station, Fauquier Co, Va.

The family of Mr Abraham Clark, of 6th st, between G & H sts, feel much uneasiness on account of his unexplained absence from home since Sunday evening last. He had on when he left a block cloth over & under coat, velvet vest, black pantaloons, & a silk hat. Any information respecting him will be thankfully received by Mrs Clark & children.

Mrd: on Dec 31, in Wash City, at the Fourth Presbyterian Church, by Rev J C Smith, Harrison J Dawes, of Boston, Mass, to Mary E, daughter of Eden Beall, of Montg Co, Md.

Mrd: on Dec 22, in Christ Church, Raleigh, Dec 22, by Rev Dr Mason, John C Winder, of N Y, to Miss Octavia M, daughter of Hon John H Bryan.

Mrd: on Nov 27 last, at the Navy Yard, Mare Island, Bay of San Francisco, Calif, by Right Rev Bishop Kip, Dr John M Browne, U S Navy, to Miss Alice Key, daughter of the Hon Danl Turner.

Died: on Dec 30, in Wash City, Christiana Ida, daughter of Jas C & the late Janet Dellett, in her 3rd year.

Died: on Dec 28, at the residence of Wm E Hamill, in Frankford, near Phil, Geo J Pepper, in his 57th year.

Died: on Dec 30, near Piscataway, PG Co, Md, Mr John B Spalding, aged 64 years.

The funeral of Maj J Randall Hagner, Paymaster U S Army, will take place on Jan 2 at 12 o'clock, from the residence of his mother.

From Europe: the marriage of Prince Frederick of Prussia with the Princess Royal of England was fixed for Nov 21.

St Louis, Dec 31. E C Davis, late Superintendent of Public Schools, has been arrested, charged with forgeries to a large amount of the names of various persons on a banking-house at St Joseph's.

The friends of Buchanan & Breckinridge to meet at Temperance Hall, E st, between 9th & 10th sts, on Jan 6, to make arrangements for the Inauguration & a Nat'l Ball.

Hon A G Brown
Hon Henry A Edmundson
Hon L M Keitt
Hom H S Bennett
Geo Parker
Cornelius Boyle
Lucien Peyton
Johnson Hellen
Thos J Fisher
Jas McSherry
Thos Hagner, S C
J H Woodford, Ind
H H Woodley
Hon Jas C Jones
Hon F G Davidson
Hon P S Brooks
Hon Saml Caruthers
Thos Parker
Walter Lenox
Jos B Bryan
Alex'r Provost
Chas J Wallach
Aug R Sparks
N E Welch, Mich
H A Street
& other citizens

John D Barrow & Henry Holmes are this day admitted as partners in the Banking House of Chubb Brothers. The firm will be composed of Chas St J Chubb, John D Barrow & Henry Holmes. The House in Davenport, Iowa, is composed of Chas St J Chubb, Wm H Dougal, & Alex'r H Barrow, under the firm of Chubb Brothers, Barrow & Co.

SAT JAN 3, 1857
Mrd: on Jan 1, by Rev Mr Rodgers, Wm Chase to Margaret E Linkens, all of Wash City.

Mrd: on Christmas Day, at Dayton, Ohio, by Rev Jas H Brookes, Mr Geo W Houk to Miss Eliza P Thruston.

Mrd: on Jan 1, at St Patrick's Church, by Rev F X Boyle, W W Tyler, of Va, to Miss Mary L McNerhany, of Wash City.

Mrd: on Dec 31, by Rev Jas Donelan, E F Ruth, of Memphis, Tenn, to Eliza Virginia, eldest daughter of Prof Alex'r Dimitry, of Louisiana.

Died: on Jan 2, in Wash City, Mrs Ellen E Fergusson, in her 65th year, wife of E D Fergusson. Her funeral will take place from the residence of her husband, on 4½ st, [Island,] this afternoon at 3 o'clock.

Died: on Jan 2, Henry S Wood, in his 77th year. His funeral will be on Sunday afternoon, at 2 o'clock, from R F Wood's residence, 663 N J ave.

Criminal Court-Wash: 1-The old man Jacob Briebach, found guilty of stealing a horse, was sentenced yesterday to 4 years in the penitentiary.

Massachusetts State Prison: another murder: Mr Solon H Tenny was murdered on Monday by a prisoner named Chas L Decatur. When Mr Tenny was walking through the upholsterer's shop, where Decatur was at work, Decatur jumped upon his back & thrust a sharp pointed shoe knife entirely through his neck, severing both jugular veins. Decatur was placed in irons & solitary confinement. Mr Tenney was removed to the hospital where he died immediately.

Senate: 1-Ptn from Wm Aiken, Jas Kelly, & others who served in the Japan expedition, asking to be allowed extra pay. 2-Ptn from Thos Lyons, a soldier in the war of 1812, asking to be allowed a pension. 3-Cmte on Pensions: asked to be discharged from the consideration of the bill for the relief of Jos Richards, of Berks Co, Pa, & that it be referred to the Cmte on Private Land Claims: agreed to. Same cmte: bill for the relief of John Mitchell, of the Dist of Columbia. 4-Bill for the relief of Martin Millett, of Iowa: referred to the Cmte on Private Land Claims.

House of Reps: 1-No objection made to the following bills-relief: of Jos White; of Cmder John L Saunders; of Jas P Fleming, of Augusta, Ga; of the heirs of Capt Thos Gill; of Peter Grover; of the sureties of Danl Winslow; of Thos B Steele, passed assist surgeon of the U S Navy; of John C McConnell; of A S Bender; of Jesse Morrison, of Ill; of Antoine Robedeaux; & of Wm Kendall. Also: granting bounty land to Jared L Elliott; & to reimburse the estate of Jos McClure, a paymaster in the war of 1812. Bill to authorize the Postmaster Gen'l to execute a contract with Messrs Garman, Weigle, & Benford, for carrying the mail from Cumberland, Md, to Greensburg, Pa.

Jos Crispin Reklewski is requested to return immediately to Paris, where his brother is waiting. In want of money, write to E Jamiszkiewiez, 3 rue des Sausages, a Paris, & name the banker.

Birth: Nov 11, at Boa Nova, Madera, the wife of Robt Bayman, of a son.

Death: Nov 11, at Boa Nova, Madeira, Ernest, 2nd son of Robt Bayman.

MON JAN 5, 1857
Household & kitchen furniture at auction on: Jan 7, at the House-furnishing store of A H Lee, 23 K st, between 7th & 8th sts. -A Green auct

Hon John A King was inaugurated as Govn'r of the State of N Y on Jan 1; in the Legislative Chamber, at Albany. The oath of ofc was also administered to Lt Gov'r Henry R Selden. A salute of 100 guns followed.

Mr Chas A Peabody, the successful horticulturist of Columbus, Ga, has originated a new & beautiful seedling of the strawverry to which he has given the name: Peabody's New Hautbois Strawberry.

Wash City Ordinance: 1-Act for the relief of Alex'r Borland: to reimburse him $13.13, for money paid for lot 3 in square 214, which was sold at tax sale on Apr 12, 1854, he having become the purchaser; &, the said lot having been improperly described in the advertisement, the Corp could not convey the proper title. –Approved, Dec 31, 1856.

Distressing casualty in the family of Judge Daniel, of the Supreme Court. On Sat last, in Franklin Place, Wash City, Mrs Daniel was in her chamber when a lighted candle fell & set her robe on fire. Mrs Daniel was severely burnt & after suffering 4 hours, she expired. She leaves an inconsolable husband & 2 young children.

Criminal Court-Wash. 1-Wm Robins was acquitted on a charge of larceny. 2-Robt Cross was convicted of an assault & battery, & sentenced to 2 weeks in jail. 3-Jacob Briebach, for horse-stealing, sentenced to 2 years in the penitentiary, instead of 4, as we stated on Sat. 4-John Kenny, for stealing a horse & buggy, has been sentenced to 4 years in the penitentiary.

We learn from Texas advices of the death of Maj Hagner, Paymaster, U S Army, for that district. He died at **Fort Brown** on Dec 6. He was well known in this city, & his numerous personal friends will deeply mourn his loss. –Charleston Courier

Died: on Dec 11, at **Ravenswood**, PG Co, Md, at the residence of John Bowie, Chas L Gantt, in his 70th year.

Died: on Jan 1, at Richmond, Va, Mr Patrick Lyddane, in his 57th year. He was a native of Wash City, but for several years a resident of Richmond, where he was greatly respected for his many good qualities.

Died: on Jan 3, in Wash City, William Gilkeson, son of Wm A & Frances A Brown, late of Winchester, Va, aged 21 months & 14 days.

Died: on Dec 29, John Robbin, infant son of Maria & Morris Dubois, aged 16 months.

New Drug Store on the corner of 7th & H sts. –Tyson & Shoemaker, Pharmacists

Columbia Fire Co, ofcrs elected for the ensuing year on Jan 2nd: Jas A Tait, Pres; Jas A Brown, V Pres; Jas Adams, Treasurer; Jas McDermott, Sec; P J Ennis, Corr Sec; Thos Goldsmith, Librarian; H Prenot, Capt of the Engine Division; Isaac Beers, Capt Hose Division; 1st Engine Division, H Sage; 2nd Assist, J Martin; 3rd Assist, F Martin; 1st Assist Hose Division, P J Ennis; 2nd Assist, Wm E Tucker; 3rd Assist, John S Boots; Delegates to United Fire Dept, Jas A Brown, Thos Marche, Jas McDermott, F Beers, & F Martin.

The firm of Birchett & Downing is this day dissolved by mutual consent. All business now in their hands will be jointly prosecuted to completion.
-R T Birchettt, C W Downing

TUE JAN 6, 1857
Senate: 1-Ptn from Edw Greenman, asking remuneration for sufferings & privations endured by him during his impressment into the British naval service in the war of 1812. 2-Ptn from Sterritt Ramsey, U S navy, asking to be allowed the difference between leave of absence pay & full pay, to which he was entitled while on duty. 3-Ptn from Ignatius Lucas & other watchmen in the ___y Dept, asking compensation for extra service. 4-Ptn from Jeffry T Adams, asking compensation for services as one of the clerks of the U S court in the Territory of Minnesota. 5-Cmte on Pensions: bill for the relief of Mary Clark: recommended its passage. Same cmte: bill for the relief of Mrs Minerva Catlett, widow of Dr Hanson Catlett, surgeon of the U S Army. Same cmte: adverse report on the petition of Geo W Pittman. 6-Bill for the relief of Mary Reeside: asked its immediate consideration: which was agreed to. 7-Following bills were referred:-relief-of Jos White; of Jas P Fleming, of Augusta, Ga; of the heirs of Capt Thos Hill; of the sureties of Danl Winslow; of Thos B Steele, passed assist surgeon U S Navy; of John C McConnell; of Jesse Morrison, of Ill; of Wm Kendall; & of Antoine Robedeau. Act to reimburse the estate of Jos McClure, a paymaster in the war of 1812.

Died: on Jan 4, suddenly, Eliz H, wife of Judge P V Daniel, of the Supreme Court, & youngest daughter of Dr Thos Harris, U S Navy. Her funeral is on Jan 6 at 12 o'clock, from the residence of Judge Daniel, 313 I st. [Jan 7th newspaper: The funeral of Mrs Daniel took place yesterday. Her remains were accompanied to their resting place in **Oak Hill Cemetery**, Gtwn, by a numerous array of mourning friends. The Pres of the U S, members of the Cabinet, Judges of the Supreme & other Courts of the District, & ofcrs of the Army & Navy were amongst the attendants at the funeral.]

Died: on Dec 6, in Wash City, Annie C, wife of Phineas B Bell, in her 43rd year.

Mount Welby for sale: a beautiful estate, opposite Alexandria, Va, commanding a view of **Mount Vernon**, **Fort Washington**, & the Potomac river; 240 acres of rich land. Price $40 an acre. Apply to C B Adams, Library House of Reps, Wash, D C.

Icehouse for sale or rent, on 9th st, between H & I, Island. Inquire of Eliz Walker, 11 C st, Island.

Orphans Court of Wash Co, D C. Letters of administration on the personal estate of Ellen West, late of Wash Co, deceased. –John H Studer, adm

WED JAN 7, 1857
Household & kitchen furniture at auction on: Jan 10, in front of the Auction Rooms, the effects of John Mason, deceased. –L H Brown, adm -Jas C McGuire, auct

Wm Blaisdell, alias Chas E Harding, indicted on 8 charges of altering 8 counterfeit bills of the Elm City Bank, New Haven, was lately sentenced at Hartford to 16 years in the State Prison. –Boston Journal, Jan 3.

Mrd: on Jan 5, in Wash City, in the Wesley Chapel, by Rev W Krebs, Henry O Noyes to Emily L Collison, both of Wash City.

Mrd: on Jan 4, in Wash City, by Rev S A H Marks, Saml Williamson to Miss Mary A Menzeisheimer.

Mrd: on Jan 6, in Wash City, by Rev S A H Marks, Wm Henry Barret to Miss Rebecca Allen, both of PG Co, Md.

Mrd: on Jan 5, in Wash City, by Rev Andrew Carothers, Mr G Alfred Hall to Miss Sallie A M Miller, both of Wash City.

Died: on Jan 6, in Wash City, T Grosvenor King, son of T G & C R King, aged 2 years & 7 months. His funeral will be on Jan 8 at 12 o'clock, from the residence of his grandfather, Dr Philip Smith, 394 Mass ave.

Died: on Jan 5, in Wash City, Mr John Tabler, aged 67 years. His funeral will take place today from the Foundry Chapel, at 3 o'clock P M.

Died: on Jan 2, Miss Mary E Roberts, of Gtwn, D C, daughter of Thos & Eliz Roberts, deceased, of Queen Anne's Co, Md.

Died: on Jan 5, in Wash City, Chas E Rosenthal, aged 54 years, a native of Prussia, but for the last 22 years a resident of Wash City. His funeral is today at 2½ o'clock P M, from his late residence, Pa ave, between 19th & 20th sts. The friends of the family & members of the R A Chapter & the Masonic Order are invited to attend.

Criminal Court-Wash-Mon. 1-Aaron Coakley, colored, acquitted for larceny. 2-A youth, Geo Thompson, tried for larceny at the store of Richmond & Co, was acquitted.

House of Reps: 1-Ptn of Wm Ireland, Jacob Early, & other soldiers of the war of 1812, over 60 years of age, asking that pensions may be granted to the surviving ofcrs & soldiers of that war. 2-Memorial from Capt Henry Wharton, stationed at *Fort Kearny*, in Nebraska Territory, on behalf of himself, the ofcrs & soldiers under his command, praying Congress that the benefit of the 2 acts granting extra compensation to the troops serving in Calif, Oregon, New Mexico, & also at *Fort Laramie*, be extended to the company stationed at *Fort Kearny*.

Senate: 1-Ptn from Joshua P Todd, a lt in the navy, asking to be allowed the pay of a master for services rendered in that capacity while a passed midshipman. 2-Ptn from Chas F Bruckner, adm of Wm White, a soldier of the Revolution, asking to be allowed arrearages of pension. 3-Ptn from Wm Marshall, a soldier in the war of 1812, asking to be allowed arrearages of pension. 4-Ptn from Lt-Col Augustus Moor, of the 4th regt of Ohio volunteers in the war with Mexico, asking compensation for property lost in that war. 5-Ptn from the children & heirs-at-law of Thos Hazard, a Revolutionary soldier, asking remuneration for the expenses paid by their ancestor in raising & subsisting a company of men for service. 6-Ptn from Jas B Weeks, asking that the pension due to his father, John Weeks, a Revolutionary soldier, may be paid to his heirs. 7-Ptn from John Rooney, a U S pensioner, asking an increase in pension. 8-Ptn from the heirs & legal reps of Louis Pellerin, asking the confirmation of their title to certain lands in the State of Louisiana, claimed under a French grant. 9-Ptn from the heirs of Jean Antoine Bernard Dauterive, asking the confirmation of their title to certain lands in the State of Louisiana. 10-Additional papers submitted in relation to the claims of the adm of Fulwer Skipwith, deceased. 11-Court of Claims to return to the Senate the papers relating to the claim of Pierre Menard & Louis Valle, referred to that Court by an order of the Senate on Aug 14 last.

A fire on Tue broke out in a frame dwlg on N, between 12th & 13th sts, inhabited by Mr Wood, a poor laboring man, who, whilst endeavoring to extricate some portion of his property, became unable to retreat, & the consequence was his own destruction. He leaves a wife & child.

THU JAN 8, 1857
Senate: 1-Ptn from Geo W Flood, asking compensation for services performed by him as a clerk in the ofc of the Bureau of Topographical Engineers while employed as a laborer in that ofc. 2-Ptn from Cmder Thos J Page, of the Navy, asking to be allowed a credit for certain items rejected in the settlement of his accounts as acting purser while in command of the expedition for the exploration & survey of the La Plata river & its tributaries. 3-Ptn from H W Fanning & other ofcrs of the police of the District of Columbia, asking the enactment of a law to reform & improve police systems of said District. 4-Mr Hunter gave notice that he would introduce a joint resolution to amend the act entitled "An act for the relief of Fred'k Vincent, adm of Jas Le Caze, survivor of Le Caze & Mallet.

Appointments by the Pres: 1-Robt W Adams, Surveyor of the Customs at New Orleans, in place of Wm E Starke, resigned. 2-S Prioleau Hamilton, Naval Ofcr for Savannah, vice Thos Lynch Hamilton, resigned. 3-Oscar F Dickinson, Collector for Dunkirk, N Y, vice Henry P Whallon, resigned.

Circuit Court of Wash Co, D C-in Chancery, Oct Term, 1856. Saml Strong vs Alanson Sweet, Levi Blossom, Chas James, & Hon Jas Guthrie. The object of this suit is to procure an injunction & to recover $5,000, charged to be due the cmplnt, in & by virtue of a certain contract entered into between the cmplnt & Alanson Sweet, dfndnt. The bill states that the cmplnt, in Apr, 1853, as the successful bidder with the U S Gov't for the bldg of a custom-house in the city of Mobile, Ala; that after the contract was awarded to cmplnt the said Alanson Sweet, acting by his atty, Chas James, purchased of cmplnt all benefit of the same for the sum of $5,000, one moiety payable when said custom-house should be roofed & the balance when the last payment should become due under said original contract; which purchase money of $5,000 was declared to be payable specifically out of the moneys to become due by the Govn't under said original contract, all of which is particularly described in the bill & its accompanying exhibits; that said Sweet has been requested to execute the further assurance agreed on, & that, although admitting his obligation, refused to execute the same. The bill further states that cmplnt, before making his bid aforesaid, incurred much labor & expense in this behalf; that said Sweet was duly received & recognized by the Gov't as assignee of the cmplnt; that said Sweet gave the Gov't as security for the faithful performance of his contract Levi Blossom; that said Sweet, alleging want of means to perform said contract, assigned & transferred the same to said Blossom; that said Blossom has been received & recognized by the Gov't as the assignee of said contract; that said Blossom, before the said assignment to him, had notice of the arrangements between complnt & said Sweet; that, notwithstanding which notice, said Blossom has refused to recognize the claim of cmplnt; that the said $5,000 has not, nor any part, been paid; that the moneys payable under said contract with the Gov't are payable by Hon Jas Guthrie, Sec of the Treasury of the U S, & that the said Alanson Sweet is a non-resident. The absent dfndnt is to appear in this Court, in person or by solicitor, on or before the 4th Mon of May next. —Jno A Smith, clerk

Criminal Court-Wash-Tue: 1-John Maloney, Silvester Shilley, & Noah Garrity convicted of being parties to a fray in the 1st Ward: each fined $8 & costs. 2-Richd Davidson guilty of larceny: sentenced to 2 years' hard labor in the penitentiary, to commence on Wed next. 3-Wm Mullen & Wm Delaney sentenced to 3 months' imprisonment in the county jail for riot, on the Island. 4-Wm & Chas Hesslinger & H Carman were tried for an assault on Edw Hessey. The first 2 were convicted & fined $10 each; Carman was acquitted.

John Farris, a native of Nova Scotia, who did extensive business in forged checks & drafts on the Boston banks in Oct, has been arrested in Boston. He completed a term of 5 years in the State prison for forgery in Jan last.

We quote from the proceedings of the <u>Continental Congress</u> of May 27, 1778, fixing the monthly pay for the ofcrs & soldiers of the Continental lines. This <u>rate of pay</u> was continued to the end of the war, & formed the basis of the settlements with the ofcrs for their commutation of 5 years' full pay. It will be perceived that this only relates to the pay proper, & does not include emoluments of any kind.

<u>Infantry-per month:</u>
Col & Capt-$75.   Maj & capt-$50.
Lt-Col & capt-$60.   Capt-$40.
<u>Paymaster-$25-to be taken from the line</u>
Adj:$16-to be taken from the line
Quartermaster-$16: to be taken from the line.
Surgeon-$75.   Drum-major-$10.41
Surgeon's mate-$50.   Capt –L-$26.66
Sgt-maj-$11.25.   Lt-$26.66
Qrtrmaster sgt-$11.25.   Ensigns-$20
Fife-major-$10.41.
<u>In addition to their pay as ofcrs in the line:</u>
Drum-major-$9.   Cpl-$7.33
Fife-major-$9.   Private-$6.66.
Drum & fife-$7.33.
Each of the field ofcrs' commanded a company, & the lt of the colonel's company had the rank of captain-lt.
<u>Artillery:</u>
Colonel-$100.   Major-$62.50.
Lt-Col-$75.   Capt-$50.
Paymaster-$25.-to be taken from the line
Adjutant-$16.-to be taken from the line
Qrtrmaster-$16.-to be taken from the line.
Surgeon-$75.
Surgeon's mate-$50.   Drum Major-$10.41.
Sgt-major-$11.25.   Capt-lt-$33.33
Qrtrmaster sgt-$11.25.   1st Lt-$33.33.
Fife-major-$10.41.   2nd Lt-$33.33
<u>In addition to their pay as ofcrs in the line:</u>
Sgts-$10   Gunners-$8.66.
Bombardiers-$9.   Drums & fife-$8.66.
Cpls-$9.   Matrosses-$8.33.
<u>Cavalry:</u>
Colonel-$93.75   Major-$60.
Lt-col-$75.   Capt-$50.

Paymaster-$25.-to be taken from the line.
Adjutant-$15.-to be taken from the line.
Qrtrmaster-$15.-to be taken from the line.
Surgeon-$60.
Surgeon's mate-$40.
Saddler-$10.
Tumpet-major-$11.
In addition to their pay as ofcrs in the line.
Qrtrmaster's sgt-$15.
Trumpeters-$10.
Sgts-$15.
Provost:
Captain of provosts-$50.
Lts-$33.33.
Clerk-$33.33.
Qrtrmaster sgt-$15.
Trumpeters-$10.

Farriers-$10.
Lt-$33.33
Cornets-$26.66
Riding-master-$33.33

Cpls-$10.
Dragoons-$8.33.

Sgts-$15.
Cpls-$10.
Provosts or privates-$8.33
Executioners-$10.

The corps was mounted on horseback & armed & accoutred as light dragoons.
Engineers:
Capt-$50.
Lts-$33.33.
Sgts-$10.

Cpls-$9.
Privates-$8.33

The discoveries of Dr Livingstone in Africa are of great commercial value. He lived with a tribe of Bechuanas for 8 years, &, in co-operation with Mr Oswald, discovered Lake Ngami. He traced by himself the course the great river Zamhesi, in Eastern Africa, & extending 2,000 miles.

Five young men of Portland, who have been convicted of incendiarism in consequence of one of their associates, named Worcester, turning State's evidence, have received their sentence as follows: John Burns & Isaac B Pendergast, 7 years in the State prison; Saml Burns, 5 years; Luke Makin, 3 years; Gould, 1 year.

FRI JAN 9, 1857
Convention of survivors of the war of 1812-the Dist of Columbia Association, met yesterday: Gen Henderson, of the Marine Corps, furnished the services of the Marine band. Hon Joeb B Sutherland, of Pa, was appointed to the Chair. Prayer was offered by Rev Mr Hamilton, of Balt. The Pres named the following gentlemen as members of the cmte: Gen Leslie Combs, Dr Danl Bemas, Jas M Porter, Isaac W Mickle, Geo McNeir, Jos P Leclere, Thos Brownell, Andrew Hooton, Col H Raymond, John S Strother, & John Shaw.

Died: on Jan 7, in Gtwn, of dysentery, Mr Geo Battersby, of London, Eng, in his 44th year. His funeral will be from his late residence, 38 Fayette st, Sunday at 3 o'clock.

Circuit Court of Wash Co, D C-in Chancery. Jas F Haliday, Chas F Lowrey & Anne Maria Lowrey his wife, vs Thos J Haliday, Saml Cockrell & Martha I Cockrell his wife, Henry Haliday & Mary Haliday his wife, Otis W Marsh & Harriet E Marsh his wife, & David H Hanlon, Saml C Hanlon, heirs at law of Thos Haliday, Anna Haliday, Wm W Haliday, & Lydia J Hanlon, deceased. Chas S Wallach, the trustee, reported that at the sale made by him in Sep, 1854, Jas F Haliday, became the purchaser of lot 16 in square 779, for $966.29; lot 4 in square 779, for $366.40; lot 5 in square 779, for $237.50; lot 6 in square 779, for $195.94; & lot 7 in square 779, for $214.65; & Henry Haliday became the purchaser of lot 16 in square 703, for $191.76; & of part of lot 3 in square south of square 825, for $214.65; & Wm Doyle became the purchaser of part of square 905 & improvements for $550; that the said several purchasers have complied with the terms of said sales. –Jno A Smith, clerk

Mr Robt Carter Nicholas died at his plantation in Terrebonne, La, on Dec 24. He was a captain in the U S army during a part of the war of 1812, being attached to the division stationed on the Canada frontier & afterwards promoted to the rank of colonel. He was for 12 years a Senator in Congress, which post he filled with honor. He was sent as Charge d'Affaires to Naples by Gen Jackson. He was also Sec of the State of Louisiana; & later, Superintendent of Public Education.

Death of a genius in humble life. Mr Geo Troup Wells, of Ythau Forgue, Scotland, who was born in 1774, died on Dec 24. At age 10 he entered upon the world as a farm servant; at 15 he studied astronomy; at age 30 he bound himself as an apprentice to a mason, & it was while following that occupation that he learned the art of dialing an art in which we question if ever he was excelled by a dialist in the North of Scotland. –Scotch paper

Indian massacre in Florida. Peter Sheves, with his wife & 2 children, was recently murdered & his house fired by Indians 8 miles from Smyrna, Florida, on Dec 19. Sheves was found in the field some 60 yards from the house with 2 bullet holes through his head & his body cut with an axe; his wife & little girl were shot at the water's edge, in front of the house, & the remains of their boy, age 10 years, were found among the burning ruins of the house. Mr Sheves was from Pa, & had been in Florida only a short time.

Criminal Court-Wash-Thu. 1-Jas Sumby, [colored,] was found guilty of simple assault on H McGee: fined $10. 2-John Moriarty was sentenced to 2 years' hard labor in the penitentiary, to take effect after Jan 19, for manslaughter on his own son. [Jan 19th newspaper: on Sat John Moriarty was fully pardoned by the President.]

Martin Hampton, of Lawrence Co, Ohio, having gone partially blind, went to Cincinnati, where an oculist totally destroyed his sight in attempting to restore it. The patient returned home & committed suicide by hanging himself with a handkerchief.

Rev Dr Livingstone arrived at Marseilles from Tunis on Jan 6, & was then in good health. His left arm is, however, broken & partley useless, it having been torn by a lion. When he was taken on board her Majesty's ship **Frolic**, on the Mazambique coast, he had great difficulty in speaking a sentence of English, having disused it so long while traveling in Africa. He had with him a native from the interior of Africa, who was so excited with the steamers & various wonders of civilization that he went mad, & jumped into the sea & was drowned. Dr Livingstone has been absent from England 17 years; he is rather a short man, with a pleasing & serious countenance; remarkable for his modesty & unassuming manners. A herd of lions broke into the tribes camp at night & the Dr shot a lion, which dropped wounded. It afterwards sprang on him & caught him on the arm. The arm was not set properly, & he suffered excruciating agony in consequence. –London Times, Dec 11.

Elder J T Johnson died at Lexington, Mo, on Dec 18. He was a brother of the late Vice Pres, Richd M Johnson, of Ky, & formerly a Judge of the Court of Appeals for that State, & for 4 years a member of Congress. For 30 years he has been a preacher of the Gospel without fee or salary.

Mrd: on Jan 7, by Rev Mr Buck, Jas R C Oldham, of Phil, to Eliza, daughter of Wm H Dundas, of Wash City.

Wash City Ordinances: 1-Act for the relief of Wm A Wilson: to pay him $7.37, for taxes erroneously paid. 2-Act for the relief of Chas Stewart: to pay him $95.81 for repairing alleys. 3-Act for the relief of Alex'r Adams: to pay him $10, for a license he erroneously paid for. –Approved, Jan 8, 1857.

The **Koran** was written about A D 610. Its general aim was to unite the professions of Idolatry & the Jews & Christians in the worship of one God, whose unity was the chief point inculcated-under certain laws & ceremonies, exacting obedience to Mahomet as the prophet. It was written in the Koreish Arabic. Mahomet asserted that the Koran was revealed to him, during a period of 23 years, by the Angel Gabriel. Mahomet admitted the divine mission both of Moses & Jesus Christ. According to Gibbon, the leading article of faith which Mahomet preached is compounded of an eternal truth & a necessary fiction, namely, that there is only one God, & that Mahomet is the apostle of God. The Koran was translated into Latin in 1143, & into English & other European languages about 1763. It is a rhapsody of 3,000 verses, divided into 114 sections.

SAT JAN 10, 1857
The Martinsburg [Va] American: on Jan 2 the dwlg house of Mr Geo Couchman, in Berkeley Co, was burnt to the ground. Mr C, who had been insane for some time, & as a means of safety & mercy was kept chained, was burnt to death. It is supposed that the fire originated in his room. The rest of the family escaped with their lives.

The Charlestown [Va] Free Press says: we are pained to learn that Capt T J Manning, U S Navy, [retired list,] residing about 2 miles from town, was on Jan 5 most horribly burnt. Is appears that Capt Manning was subject to occasional fits, & during one of these attacks was so unfortunate as to fall into the fire. Death ensued from the injuries he had sustained on Tue last. Capt M was 57 years of age, & leaves a wife & 3 children.

Senate: 1-Ptn from Sarah Foy, widow of John Foy, asking indemnity for injury to her property & business by the improper construction of a bridge across the *Tiber* by the late Com'r of Public Bldgs, Mr Easby. 2-Ptn from Dr S S Coudon, asking renumeration for medical services for certain volunteers for the State of Illinois in the Mexican war, & to be allowed traveling expenses while in the public service. 3-Ptn from John Hollohan, asking compensation for finishing a carved cap in the Capitol extension, under the direction of the Com'r of Public Bldgs. 4-Ptn from Sarah B Webber, widow of John A Webber, late military storekeeper at the U S arsenal at Watertown, Mass, asking compensation for the use by Gov't of an improvement of her late husband in the construction of gun carriages. 5-Cmte on the Post Ofc & Post Roads: bill to execute a contract with Messrs Garman, Wigle, & Benford for carrying the mail from Cumberland, Md, to Greensburg, Pa: passed. 6-Cmte on Revolutionary Claims: asked to be discharged from the consideration of the ptn of memorials of Chas F Buckner, adm of Wm White; of C A Graham & Sarah T Hazard, heirs of Thos Hazard: & that they be referred to the Cmte on Pensions: which was agreed to. 7-Cmte on the District of Columbia: joint resolution in favor of J W Nye: recommending its passage. 8-Cmte on Naval affairs: bill for the relief of Jas D Johnson. Same cmte: bill for the relief of Thos B Stelle, passed assist surgeon of the U S Navy: recommended its passage. 9-Bill introduced for the relief of Dr Chas D Maxwell, a surgeon in the U S navy, was recommitted to the Cmte on Naval Affairs.

The clipper ship **Neptune's Car**, Capt Jacob Patten, sailed from N Y for San Francisco about Jul 29th last. The captain was attacked with brain fever & subsequent blindness. The chief mate having been deposed from duty previous to the capt's illness, & the 2nd mate being incompetent to navigate the vessel, the captain's wife, who happened providentially to be on board & who had been taught navigation by her husband, took charge of the ship & brought it safely into port. -Boston Transcript

Mrd: on Jan 8, in Wash City, by Rev Andrew G Carothers, Mr Geo W Crown to Miss Jane Amelia Bradley, both of Wash City.

On Jan 1, 3 of Mr T Finley's children, of Norfolk, Va, were burnt. The eldest boy poured some powder from his father's flask into the fire, when the contents exploded, burning the children in a shocking & probably fatal manner.

House of Reps: 1-Cmte of Claims: bill for relief of Benj Sayre: committed. Same cmte: bill for the relief of Thos Crown: committed. Same cmte: bill for relief of the legal reps of Rinaldo Johnson & of Ann E Johnson, deceased, & the bill of the same body for relief of Wm G Ridgeley & Hodges & Lansdale, or their legal reps, with the recommendation that they do not pass. Same cmte: adverse reports on the several ptns of Jos Janney; of Geo W Biscoe; of the reps of the late Gen Robt Young, & of Christopher Neale, for indemnity for tobacco lost in the war of 1812.
Same cmte: bill for relief of Jos M Kennedy: committed. 2-No objection being made, the following bills were recommended to pass:-relief-of Hannah F Niles; of Mary Burgher, widow of Jeremiah Burgher, deceased, a Revolutionary soldier; of Letty Griggs, widow of Simeon Griggs, a Revolutionary soldier; of surviving children of John Gilbert, a Revolutionary soldier; of Richd Phillips; of Wm Craig; of Geo W Whitten; of Edw Rumery; of Cornelius H Latham; of Robt H Stevens; of Isaac P Washburne; of Henry Stewart; of Isaac Langley; of Jonathan Cilley; of Roxana Kimball; of Wm Pool; of Randolph Clay; of Geo F Baltzell, assignee of Jas P Roan; & of the heirs-at-law of Sarah Crandall, deceased, with an amendment striking out heirs-at-law, & inserting surviving children. Also, granting a pension to Thos Allcock, of Rochester, N Y. 3-The Senate bill for relief of heirs at law of Sarah Crandall, deceased, was passed. 4-Memorial of Henry Dmockowski Saunders, formerly of Poland, offering to Congress 2 life-like busts, in marble, of his countrymen, Gen Kosciusko & Count Pulaski: referred. 5-Ptn of Jas A Tutt & others, citizens of Henry Co, Mo, praying that entries of land made under the graduation act be legalized.

The very sudden death of Mr Jas M Dorsett on Thu morning, in G st, was a striking example of the uncertainty of human life. He was proceeding to his place of business, [Mr Harrover's stove warehouse, on 7th st, where he acted as clerk,] when he began to feel ill. He called to a colored man across the street, but before he could be helped, he fell & shortly expired. Mr Dorsett's physician testified that he had for 18 months past been affected with disease of the heart. He was 39 years of age, & has left a widow & 4 small children to bewail his loss.
+
Died: on Jan 8, suddenly, in Wash City, Mr Jas M Dorsett, son of Mr Fielder R Dorsett, in his 39th year. His funeral will be from his father's residence, on N Y ave, between 17th & 18th sts, near the War Dept, on Sunday, Jan 11, at 2 o'clock.

MON JAN 12, 1857
Capt Casey, ofcr of the army, long Indian agent for South Florida, died at Tampa on Dec 25. He graduated at West Point in 1827 & entered the 2nd regt of artl; appointed commissary of subsistence on Jul 7, 1838, & served under Gen Taylor in Mexico; but the elevated position of Monterey being very unfavorable to his disease, he was compelled to seek a residence nearer the level of the sea, & selected Tampa. In 1849 he was appointed U S Agent for removing the Seminole Indians, the duties of which post he continued to perform, with the exception of a short interval, until his death.

Senate: 1-Bill for the relief of Jesse Haynes: referred. 2-Cmte of Claims: bill for the relief of the heirs of Wm Easby, deceased: committed. 3-Cmte on Private Land Claims: bill for the relief of Jos Irish & others: committed. 4-Cmte on Military Affairs: bill for the relief of John Shaw, a soldier in the war of 1812, & a bill authorizing the return of certain arms to the State of Tenn: committed. Same cmte: bill for the relief of the ofcrs & soldiers of the U S army who sustained loss by the disasters to the steamship **Winfield Scott** & the steamship **San Francisco**: committed. Same cmte: bill for the relief of Richd D Alexander, late a major in the first Tenn regt in the Mexican war: committed. Same cmte: adverse report on the memorial of A R Potts, praying for pay of assist commissary of subsistence, with the rank of captain. Same cmte: adverse reports on the ptns of Lorenzo D Oatman, of J M Bennett, & of Jedediah Grey. 5-Cmte on Territories: bill for the relief of Oliver P Hovey: committed. 6-Cmte on Invalid Pensions: bill for the relief of K K Russell; of Henry Sanford; of R W Caulk; of Danl Drain; & of Elmira White, widow of Capt Thos R White: committed. 7-Cmte on Revolutionary Pensions: bill for the relief of the children of Danl Coit; & of the children of Jas Kiss, a Revolutionary soldier: committed. Also committed-relief of Reuben J Champion, only child & heir of Reuben & Rhoda Champion; of Jane Vreeland; & of the heirs of Wm York; & to increase the pension of Peter Van Buskirk, of Wash, D C: committed. 8-Bill for the relief of Joshua Knowles, jr, & others, owners of the schnr **Garnet**, of Truro: recommended that it pass. 9-Court of Claims: adverse reports in the cases of Robt Roberts; of Saml M Puckett; of John P McElderry; of Louis G Thomas & others; of Cyrus H McCormick; of Wm W Cox; of J D Holman, exc of Jesse B Holman, deceased; & of John C Hale: recommendation that the opinions of the Court be confirmed.

Four years ago a young man named Michl McCarthy, of Hudson, N Y, was found dead in a field, murdered. Monday last a young man, Denny Cummings, of Johnstown, while intoxicated, told McCarthy's father that he was present at the affray, & that Michl had been struck down by one Andrew Dolan. The parties have been arrested to undergo an examination.

Mrs Dasher, wife of Wm Dasher, residing near Springfield, Effingham Co, Geo, prematurely lost her life a few days ago, when her dress took fire while baking cakes, on Dec 24. She died on the 4th day after the accident. Mrs Bankston, wife of Wm R Bankston, clerk of the Superior & Inferior Courts of Butts Co, Geo, came to her death a few days since in a similar manner.

Midshipman Richd W Graham, attached to the U S sloop-of-war **Constellation**, died recently at Constantinople, & was buried in the **Kara Protestant cemetery** with military honors. He was from the District of Columbia & entered the Naval Academy in 1854.

By virtue of an order of distrain from Wm L Green against the good & chattels of Woodburne Potter & to me directed, I have seized sundry goods of Potter, to be sold at public auction, on Jan 15, 1857, at the house of Wm L Green, s w corner of 8th & E sts, to satisfy rent due & in arrears to the said Green. –J F Wollard, Bailiff

Mrd: on Dec 31, at St Luke's Church, Phil, by Rev Dr Howe, Mr Clinton Rice, of N Y C, to Miss Ada W Smith, daughter of the late Capt Geo Smith, formerly of Boston, Mass.

Mrd: Dr Robt H Dalton, of Mississippi, to Mrs Virginia Lindsay. [This notice was too light to read & the above is all that could be copied. It is a recent item in the marriage listing.]

Nashua, N H, Jan 9. Wm Saunders, John Sullivan, & John Undine were placed in the lock-up, under the City Hall, last evening for drunkenness. After being confined for awhile they set fire to the place, & the whole 3 were smothered to death. The bldg was not much damaged. [Jan 13th newspaper: Hon Josephus Baldwin, ex-Mayor of the city, & others, rushed in & brought out the bodies. Tim Sullivan & John Hudine were Irishmen, & Wm Saunders, an American. Saunders was a police ofcr who was addicted to intemperance, & being found drunk by his brother policeman, was thrust into the lobby. –Manchester [N H] American.]

U S Patent Ofc, Wash, Jan 8, 1857. Ptn of T Perkins, of Zanesville, Ohio, & W McMahon, of Phil, Pa, praying for the extension of a patent granted to them on Apr 10, 1843, for an improvement in case iron wheels for locomotives, for 7 years from the expiration of said patent which takes place on Apr 10, 1857. –Chas Mason, Com'r of Patents

TUE JAN 13, 1857
Landon Seminary at trustee's sale: by deed of trust, executed by John R Jones for the benefit of his creditors, I will offer at public sale, at the City Hotel, in Fred'k, Md, on Jan 29, all the right, title, & interest of said John R Jones, of, in, & to that valuable property known as *Landon Seminary*, situated on the Gtwn road, adjoining Urbana, containing 23 acres of land, more or less; improvements consist of a large frame house 2 stories, with attic, contains 18 rooms, with a basement containing 7 rooms. Possession given immediately. –John L Mines, trustee -L Vanfossen, auctioneer, Fred'k, Md.

Bernard Mooney was convicted of rape & sentenced to 10 years' imprisonment in the N Y State prison. After a service of 26 months he was liberated by Gov Clark. On New Year's day, a few days after his liberation, Bernard Mooney murdered Wm Dunn, at 27th st & Broadway. –N Y Mirror

Mrd: on Jan 8, at McKendry Chapel, by Rev Mr Hildt, Wm H Delano, of Balt, Md, to Miss Anna Maria Johnson, only daughter of John Johnson, of Wash City.

Senate: 1-Ptn from S G Pinkham & other owners of the fishing schnr **St Lawrence**, of Cape Porpoise, Maine, asking to be allowed the bounty they would have been entitled to had their schnr been inspected previous to her first voyage this season: referred. 2-Ptn from John M Nourse, asking that execution on the judgment against him as security on the bond of the late purser Wm P Zantzinger may be stayed. [The memorialist states that all Mr Zantzinger's indebtedness to the Gov't for which this judgment was obtained arose subsequent to his protest to the Sec of the Navy against his going to sea, & to order a new bond.] 3-Ptn from Martin Hubbard, asking indemnity for the loss of a vessel owned by him which was run into by the U S steamer **Engineer** in consequence of the captain mistaking the light of the schnr for the light on Point Lookout. 4-Ptn from Wm Brien, asking to be allowed a pension on account of injuries received while in the military service of the U S. 5-Ptn from Jennie D Hoskins, widow of the late Chas Hoskins, who fell dead at the battle of Monterey, asking the continuance of the pension heretofore allowed her. 6-Cmte on Pensions: to inquire into the expediency of granting a pension to Jas Baldwin for his military services. 7-Mr Seward gave notice of his intention to introduce "a bill to reimburse to Elisha W B Moody the moneys paid by him, as owner of the British barque **Sarah**, in the rescue of the passengers & crew of the American ship **Caleb Grimshaw**." 8-The following bills from the House of Reps were referred-relief: of Maria Burger, wife of Jeremiah Burger, deceased, a Revolutionary soldier; of Letty Griggs, widow of Simeon Griggs, a Revolutionary soldier; of the surviving children of John Gilbert, a Revolutionary soldier; of Richd Phillips; of Wm Craig; of Geo W Whitten; of Edw Rumery; of Cornelius H Latham; of Robt H Stevens; of Isaac P Washburne; of Henry Stewart; of Isaac Langley; of Jonathan Cilley; of Roxana Kimball; of Wm Pool, & of Geo F Baltzell, assignee of Jas P Roan. Also, granting a pension to Thos Allock, of Rochester, N Y.

Presbytery of Balt meeting on Jan 15, at 12 o'clock M, in the lecture room of the 2nd Presbytery Church, Wash. –Septimus Tustin, Moderator

A portion of the land attached to the *Fauquier White Sulphur Springs* for sale: by deed of trust executed by Thos Green, dated Mar 24, 1854, recorded in Fauquier Co, Va. Public auction so much, by acre, of the tract of land, constituting a portion of the property formerly belonging to the Fauquier White Sulphur Springs Co, & a part of said springs tract as shall be sufficient to discharge the sum of money, $15,725.68, with interest, [now due & unpaid to said company,] & the costs attending the execution of this trust. The land offered for sale lies along the road leading from the Springs to Fayetteville, & borders on the portion of said Spring tract heretofore sold to P E Hollman. –Isham Keith, B H Shackelford, trustees

For sale, the splendid farm owned by Jno McKelden, containing 116 acres, on the Rockville turnpike, 4 miles from Gtwn, D C: with 2 dwlgs, 5 barns, granary, icehouse, carriage & wood-house. Apply to Dr O A Daily, 352 Pa ave, Wash City; or of A Curtis, on the premises.

Died: on Jan 13, at the Wash Infirmary, Chas J Crossfield, in his 23rd year. His funeral will take place from the infirmary this afternoon at 3 o'clock.

WED JAN 14, 1857
The Florida Indians: letter from Capt Casey, late Indian Agent, written 2 days before his death. Tampa Bay, Fla, Dec 23, 1856. Sir: I have the honor to transmit herewith, for the information of your Excellency, 'official information,' just received, of an attack on the U S troops in the Big Cypress, south of the Caloosahatchee, by the Indians. The Seminoles, finding no alternative left but emigration or hostilities, have chosen the latter. Although a different result was strongly hoped for, yet, in anticipation of this decision, the Gov't has had & has a large force in the Indian country. I hope the troops will occupy the attention of the Indians near their homes, so as to leave them but few warriors to spare for depredation on our frontier; but in the mean time, & with the sanction of Col Munroe, [commanding U S troops in Florida,] I would respectfully suggest the propriety of promptly placing say 2 companies of volunteers in position on Pea river, to give confidence & protection to the extreme frontier settlers. With great respect, your obedient servant, John C Casey, Captain U S Army. [To His Excellency Jas E Broome, Gov of Florida.] [Feb 14th newspaper:*Fort Brooke*, Fla, Jan 29, 1857. Messrs Editors: this letter, with a false date, has been imposed upon you, either through ignorance or design, as Capt Casey on the 23rd of Dec, 1856, was as incapable physically to indite a letter as he was incapable at all times of giving circulation to erroneous statements. This letter of Capt Casey, if geniuine at all, was probably written one year before his death & at the opening of Indian hostilities in 1855. The last attack of the Indians upon troops in Florida was made upon a small party of volunteers on Pease Creek in Jun last. Your obedient servant, Francis N Page, Assist Adj Gen U S A.]

Books at auction: this evening, at store 370, under Browns' Hotel, lately occupied by T Galligan & Co. Wall, Barnard & Co, aucts

An old man named Gregg, who has been confined in Fauquier Co jail since Oct 1, 1846, for debt, under the old law, was released on Christmas day by Jailor Cross, there being nothing left in the hands of the law to pay his jail expenses. We learn that this man had property enough to pay the debt against him, but that he preferred spending his weary hours within the walls of the gloomy county prison.

Mgt Crimmins & Mary Haverty were suffocated to death on Fri night at N Y, by fumes of burning charcoal proceeding from a furnace which the deceased incautiously left burning in their room with closed doors.

Senate: 1-Memorial from Geo T Parry, inventor of Parry's anti-friction box, for diminishing the friction incident to heavy revolving bodies, setting for the merits of said invention: referred to the Cmte on Naval Affairs. 2-Memorial from Sallie Grola Renneau, urging upon the attention of Congress the great subject of female education, & earnestly entreating that a grant of the unappropriated public lands of Mississippi may be made for the purpose of endowing & permanently establishing the State Female College of Mississippi: referred. 3-Ptn from Wilcox Jenkins, sec to the cmder in chief of the Brazil squadron, asking to be compensated for his services as acting purser from Jan 1, 1856, to Apr 30, 1856: referred. 4-Ptn from Franklin Buchanan, asking to be allowed the difference of pay between a captain & cmder during the time he was in command of the frig **Susquehanna** in her recent cruise in the East India, China, & Japan seas: referred. 5-Ptn from E G & L F Rogers & Co, asking to be released from their contract for carrying the mail between New Orleans & Key West, Fla, in consequence of meeting with misfortunes beyond their control: referred. 6-Ptn from John M Gardener, the purchaser & assignee of certain bounty land warrants which were located by him & for which he alleges he cannot obtain patents, asking the passage of a law to enable him to procure the same: referred. 7-Ptn from S S Lee & other ofcrs in the navy, asking to be allowed compensation for performing duties of purser in addition to those appertaining to their proper grades: referred. 8-Ptn from Alex'r Montgomery, assist quartermaster in the army, asking to be allowed a credit in the settlement of his accounts for certain items rejected by the accounting ofcrs of the Treasury for want of vouchers which were accidentally lost. 9-Ptn from Jos Verbiski, asking to be allowed an increase of pension: referred. 10-Ptn from John A Bryan, receiver, & Benj H Mooers, register of the land ofc at Menosha, Wisc, asking an increase of compensation, on the ground that their labors have been more than quadrupled within the last 2 years: referred. 11-Cmte on Revolutionary Claims: asked to be discharged from the consideration of the bills for the relief of Maria Burgher, widow of Jeremiah Burgher; & for the relief of Letty Griggs, widow of Simeon Griggs, a Revolutionary soldier: to be referred to the Cmte on Pensions: agreed to. 12-Bill introduced to reimburse to Elisha W B Moody the moneys paid by him as owner of the British barque **Sarah** in rescuing passengers & crew of the American ship **Caleb Grimshaw**. 13-Bill for the relief of the heirs-at-law of Sarah Crandall, deceased: returned to the House with amendments: passed. 14-Bill for the relief of Mary Reeside: this bill proposes to pay to Mary Reeside, as excx of her husband, Jas Reeside, upwards of $180,000, with interest from Dec 6, 1841. This claim was bottomed on a verdict in favor of Reeside for that amount, with interest, obtained in one of the courts of Pa, & which had been allowed by the Court of Claims, had passed the House of Reps, & received the sanction of the Cmte of Claims of the Senate: passed.

Orphans Court of Wash Co, D C. In the case of Caesar A Brown, adm of John T Neal, deceased: the administrator & Court have appointed Feb 7 next, for the final settlement of the personal estate of said deceased, of the assets in hand.
–Ed N Roach, Reg/o wills

The Presbyterian Genr'l Assemblies have been disputing for a long time concerning the propriety of a man marrying his deceased wife's sister. The highest authority in the State said it is proper for a man to marry his mother-in-law. Ellen Bell married Saml Bell, her son-in law. Mr Bell died, leaving the interesting widow, & also several children by his first wife, whose grand-mother was at the same time their step-mother. These children refused to grant the old lady her dower, & hence the suit. Judge Pryer, decided that the marriage was void, as the parties were within the degree of relationship fixed by the statute of 1798. An appeal was taken & the lower Court was reversed. The Court of Appeals decided that there was no prohibition to such a marriage by the statute of 1798-that marriage within the **Levitical degree** are not void, though voidable. Accordingly, if any man desires to marry his mother-in-law, he can go ahead. The law is on his side. –Louisville Journal

Mrd: on Dec 25, in Wash City, by Rev Dr Sunderland, Miss Caroline Grace Marshall, only daughter of Wm Marshall, to R F Paige, of N H.

Mrd: on Jan 12, at St Dominick Church, by Rev Mr Clarkson, Mr Jas F Moore to Miss Sarah C Wise, all of Wash City.

At San Francisco Jose y Limantour has been arrested for an attempt to defraud the U S of lands in the city by means of forged papers & perjury.

House wanted: for a private residence, a good brick or stone house, in Washington, with at least 9 or 10 rooms. Address through the Star ofc. –Palus Varez

THU JAN 15, 1857
House of Reps: 1-Bill for the relief of Lucien B Adams, surviving executor of Jas Adams, deceased: introduced. 2-Bill for the relief of the legal reps of Abram Stallings: introduced. 3-Bill for the relief of Wm McDaniel: introduced. 4-Bill for the relief of John B Rose, of Wabash Co, Indiana: introduced.

Wash, Jan 5, 1857. I have, at the request of Mr Thos Green, read the advertisement of sale of the *Fauquier White Sulphur Springs* property, published in the Alexandria Gaz, by Messes Isham Keith & B H Shackelford; I have examined the deed connected with the title to said property. My opinion is that such a sale cannot be made against Mr Green's consent unless decreed by the court. –Saml Chilton

Died: on Jan 14, in Wash City, Mrs Mary Ann McNantz, aged 74 years & 8 months, relict of the late Neal McNantz. She was a native of Montg Co, Md, & for the last 62 years a resident of Washington. Her funeral will be on Jan 16 at half past 9 o'clock, from her late residence, 374 B st, Capitol Hill. Mass will be celebrated at St Peter's Church.

Died: on Jan 3, at Black Friars, J Edw F Shaw, of St Mary's Co, Md, in his 22nd year. Having but a short time before retired from his Alma Mater with honor & distinction, he had entered upon the study of a profession which was well calculated to display to advantage the superior order of talents & acquirements which he possessed. The consolation of his family & friends is in the reflection that but few have died with better prospects of a blessed immortality.

Senate: 1-Ptn of Jas McDonnel, carpenter in the navy, asking to be allowed full pay while superintending repairs on board U S steamer **Michigan**: referred. 2-Ptn from Jedediah H Lathrop, late navy agent, asking that he & his sureties on his official bond may be released from certain judgments obtained against them by the U S. 3-Ptn from J Wall Wilson & others, who were engaged in the Arctic expedition in search after Sir John Franklin under Dr Kane, asking extra pay. 4-Cmte on Foreign Relations: bill for relief of Alex'r I Atocha, with a report. 5-Cmte on Pensions: bill for relief of Mary W Thompson, widow of the late Lt Col Alex'r R Thompson, of the U S Army, submitted an adverse report on same. 6-Cmte on Pensions: adverse report on ptn of Eliza Henley, widow of Capt John D Henley, late of the U S Navy.

Redemption of Va 5½% debt: passed on Mar 26, 1853, will proceed on Mar 2, 1857, to redeem the said certificates at the Treasury of the Commonwealth aforesaid.
1845: Diana Talbot, of Norfolk: $1,000.
1845: Francis M Lewis, of Norfolk: $700.
1845: Conway Whittle, of Norfolk: $300.
1846: Saml Ford, of Richmond: $800.
1847: Jos H Travis: $3,000.
1848: Hill Carter: $200.
1849: Dr Jefferson Hancock, of Chesterfield: $100.
1850: Miss Judith C Applewhaite, of Norfolk; $1,000.
1850: Henry W Hunter, of Norfolk: $1,900
1850: John Stewart, of Richmond: $200.
1851: Mary T Chapman: $700.
1851: Jonathan Cowdery, of Norfolk: $500.
1852: Conway Whittle, of Norfolk: $1,000.
1852: Tazewell Taylor, exc & trustee of U Beall, deceased: $1,360.
1852: Juliet J Drew: $700.
1853: John V Wilcox, of Petersburg: $3,000.
1853: R Butler, Treasurer of Va, for the Bank of Winchester: $1,700.
1853: David Henry Reed, of Richmond: $630.
1853: Jane A Griffin, excx: $500.
1853: Miss Helen M Southall, of Wmsbrug, Va: $500
1853: Addison Dodd: $300.
1854: Wm W Justice, guardian of Luther W Moore: $500.
1855: Sally S Upshur: $250.
1855: Richd Rowzie, receiver: $370.

1855: John Richardson, of Louisa: $200.
1855: E M Todd: $400.
1855: Wm D Simms: $1,000
1855: John H Wingfield, of Norfolk: $4,500.
1848: John Southgate, of Norfolk: $5,000.
1850: John Southgate: $1,000
1855: Mrs Fanny P Rowan, excx of M Rowan, dec'd, of Middlesex Co, Va: $900.
1856: Richd L Page, of Norfolk: $600.
1837: Thos Stevenson, of Richmond: $2,500.
1837: Norman Stewart, of Richmond: $5,000.
1840: Mrs Ann Newton Kilby, of Nansemond: $2,000.
1844: Cmdor Jesse Wilkinson, U S Navy: $3,000.
1845: H Hancock, of Chesterfield Co, Va: $500.
1846: Chas A Grice, of Portsmouth, Va: $1,000.
1847: John Scott, of Orange Co: $1,000.
1848: Robt B Cunningham & Ann H his wife: $1,150.
1848: Chas H Poor & Mattie L his wife: $1,150.
1848: S C Rowan & Mary B his wife: $1,150.
1848: John L Ring & Emily J his wife: $1,150.
1848: Geo W Richardson, exc of Edw Govan, deceased: $1,700.
1848: Andrew Johnson, of Richmond: $200.
1848: John McClelland, of Rockbridge: $1,800.
1851: Edmund Wilkins, trustee for Wm F Dandridge & Susan C Dandridge his wife & her 9 children: $2,300.
1851: Richd Archer, jr, of Amelia: $1,000.
1852: R W Flournoy, adm of E H Moseley.
1852: Richd Rowzie, receiver of the fund arising from the sale of the Glebe land in St Anne's parish, Essex Co: $200.
1853: Alex'r J Broadnax, of Brunswick Co: $2,500.
1853: Eliz V Wallace, of Stafford: $300.
1853: Lucilla Wallace, of Fredericksburg: $500.
1853: Mary Hill, Mgt Tyler, Eliz Hill, to be held by them as trustee: $300.
1853: Addison Dold: $100.
1853: J B Stovall, treasurer; interest for Monticello Bank: $8,000.
1854: Richd W Flournoy, adm of Edw H Moseley, deceased: $2,800.
1855: Rev C W Petherbridge: $1,400.
1855: Rev R C Moore, of N J; $100.
1855: Josiah C Wilson, of Kennon's, Chas City Co: $2,500.
1855: John S Walker, guardian of Amandus N Walker: $7,500.
1855: John T Leitch, of Stafford: $100.
1856: Wm D Sims: $1,600.
1856: Mary & Eliz D Vass: $200.
1856: Dr Saml Patterson; $200.
1856: Powhatan Robinson: $1,000

Mrd: on Tue, in Wash City, by Rev John C Smith, Mr Wm A Fouble, of Balt, to Miss Kate B Creamer, of Wash City.

Dissolution by mutual consent of the firm of John Purdy & Son. –John Purdy, H C Purdy. Parties indebted to the above firm will please call & settle at an early period. -John Purdy

FRI JAN 16, 1857
Household & kitchen furniture at auction on: Jan 23, at the residence of J A Sheehan, on 4th st, between Indiana ave & E st. -Jas C McGuire, auct

Senate: 1-Ptn from Jean Lafever, Robt Mallon, & Alex'r McLain, asking for a Gov't exploration & survey of the Pigeon & Arrow rivers, of Lake Superior, & of the route from the mouth of those streams to Rainy Lake, on the U S boundary line, with estimates of the cost of so improving by locks & canals the communication between those waters to make navigation practicable. 2-Ptn from Moses Olmstead, an invalid pensioner, asking to be allowed arrears of pension. 3-Ptn from Wm Roddy, asking to be allowed some gratuity, in land or money for injury received while employed as a mechanic at the Wash navy yard. 4-Ptn from the heirs of John S Frantz, who died while in the military service of the U S, asking to be allowed a pension. 5-Ptn from Mary B Renner, admx of Danl Renner, asking to be allowed further compensation for hemp & cordage destroyed by the enemy in 1814. 6-Cmte on Naval Affairs: bill for the relief of Dr Chas D Maxwell, a surgeon in the U S navy: passed. 7-Cmte on Pensions: bills for the relief of Lyman N Cook; & for the relief of Sally T Matthews: reported that the cmte had disagreed to the amendment. 8-Cmte on Roads & Canals: asked to be discharged from the consideration of the memorial of David M Dryden in relation to a plan for improving the navigation of the falls of the Ohio river: which was agreed to. 9-Bill for the relief of J W Nye: passed. 10-Settlement of the accounts of Luther Jewett, late collector of the district of Portland & Falmouth, in Maine: passed. 11-Bill for the relief of Chas McCormick, assist surgeon U S army: passed. 12-Bill for the relief of Chas L Denman: passed. 13-Bill for the relief of Edw Harte, allowing him $274.80 for papers prepared by direction of the Comr' of Patents illustrative of the progress of agriculture in the U S during 10 years, & also an article entitled Railroads of the U S in 1850.

Waveland for sale: having determined to move to the West, I offer for sale my farm, ***Waveland***, in Upper Fauquier, & well known as the late residence of Gov Bedford Brown, & previously of W J Morgan, containing 866 acres: the dwlg is very large & commodious, nearly new, & the out-bldgs are excellent. –Jas Rogers

Orphans Court of Wash Co, D C. In the case of Joanna M Thompson, excx of Geo W Thompson, deceased, the excx & Court have appointed Feb 7 next, for the final settlement of the personal estate of said deceased, of the assets in hand. –Ed N Roach, Reg/o wills

Orphans Court of Wash Co, D C. Letters testamentary on the personal estate of Maj J R Hagner, late of the U S Army, deceased. –A B Hagner, D R Hagner, excs

Mrd: on Jan 25, by Rev Dr Sunderland, Miss Caroline Grace Marshall, only daughter of Wm Marshall, to K F Page, of N H.

Died: on Jan 14, in Wash City, after a residence of 47 years, G C Grammer, in his 70th year. His funeral will be on Jan 17 at 11 o'clock A M, from his late residence, 4½ & C sts. [Jan 22nd newspaper: He engaged at an early age in mercantile business in Wash City, to him a new country, whose language was in part to be learned, with no capital but a sound understanding of business. He was a tender & lovable husband & father. He died after a long illness.]

Died: on Jan 13, in Wash City, John Walker, in his 45th year. His funeral will take place this evening, at 3 o'clock, from his late residence, N J ave, between M & N sts.

Died: on Jan 15, in Wash City, Mrs Ann Boteler, in her 48th year. Her funeral will be from the residence of her husband, on D st, between 14th & 15th sts. [No date of time given for the funeral.]

Montpelier, Vt, Jan 15. Hon Saml Prentiss, Judge of the U S District Court, & for many years U S Senator from Vt, died here this afternoon.

SAT JAN 17, 1857
Senate: 1-Ptn from John J Glasson, a lt in the U S Navy, asking compensation for performing the duties of purser in the U S schnr **Falcon** during the late war with Mexico. 2-Cmte on Foreign Relations: adverse report on the memorial of the excs of John Armstrong. 3-Cmte of Claims: bill for the relief of the sureties of Danl Winslow: recommended its passage. 4-Cmte of Claims: bill for the relief of the heirs of Saml R Thurston, late delegate from the Territory of Oregon, reported it without an amendment. Same cmte: bill for the relief of Geo A O'Brien. 5-Cmte on Public Lands: asked to be discharged from the consideration of the memorials of Walter M Rockwell & Co, & of the citizens of Iowa, relating to the Pacific railroad: which was agreed to. 6-Bills passed-relief: of Chas Lucas or his legal reps; of the heirs & legal reps of Pierre Cazelar, deceased; of Santiago E Arguello; of Lt Fred'k Chatard, U S Navy; of Catharine V R Cochran, sole surviving child of the late Gen Philip Schuyler; of John Scott, Hill W House, & Saml O House; of Laurant Millaudon; of Jas M Lindsay; of Moses Noble; of John Dick, of Fla; of Andrew A H Knox & Jos O Campbell, of the State of Louisiana; of John Temple, of Louisiana; & of Amos B Corwine. Bill to vest the title to certain warrants for land in Geo M Gordon: passed. Bill to continue the half-pay heretofore paid to Mary C Hamilton, widow of Capt Fowler Hamilton, late of the U S Army: passed.

House of Reps: 1-Cmte of Claims: bill for the relief of John Hastings, collector of the port of Pittsburg: committed. Same cmte: bill for the relief of Brvt Maj H L Kendrick: committed. Same cmte: bill for the relief of W F Wagner: committed. 2-Cmte on Commerce: bill for the relief of Isaac S Smith, of Syracuse, N Y: committed. 3-Cmte on the Judiciary: bill for the relief of Adam D Stewart: committed. 4-Cmte on Revolutionary Claims: discharged from the consideration of the ptn of the heirs of Capt Jas Mugford: laid on the table. Same cmte: asked to be discharged from the consideration of the ptn of the heirs of Hudson Martin; of Saml Gray; of the widow of Wm Tees; & of the heirs of Willis Wilson: & that they be referred to the Court of Claims. 5-Cmte on Private Land Claims: bill for the relief of the heirs or legal reps of Wm Conway, deceased. Same cmte: bill for the relief of Regis Loisel or his legal reps; & a bill for the relief of Manuel D Liza & Joachim D Liza or their legal reps: committed. Same cmte: bill for the relief of Jesse Haymes: committed. Same cmte: discharged from the consideration of the ptn of Hugh Stevenson: laid on the table. 6-Cmte on Military Affairs: bills for the relief of Jas B Wood; of Simeon Steadman; & of Mary Ann Williams: committed. Same cmte: adverse reports in the cases of Geo W Smith; of Esther Wilson; of R A Wainwright; of Horatio Groomes; of A W Desmak; & of Julia A Magan. Same cmte: bill for the relief of Mrs Eliz M Churchill, widow of the late Capt Wm H Churchill, of the U S Army. Same cmte: adverse reports in the cases of Jas E Stewart; & of Terry Runnells. Same cmte: adverse report in the case of Kerr, Bracely & Co. 7-Cmte on Revolutionary Pensions: bills committed-relief: of Thos Moody; of Nancy Weeks, widow of Francis Weeks, a Revolutionary pensioner; of the children of Wm Humphrey; of the children of Ira Johnson, a Revolutionary soldier; of the heirs of Robt McNeill; of the children of Hannah Wilcox, the late widow of David White, a Revolutionary soldier; of the children of Tonsant Lavainway; of Jacob Jero for arrears of pension due to his father, Baptist Jero, for services in the Revolutionary war. Joint resolution relative to the services of Brig Gen Andrew Pickens, of S C, in the war of the Revolution: committed. 8-Cmte on Invalid Pensions: bills for the relief of Eliz E V Field; of Eliz Monroe; & of Mary W Thompson: committed. 9-Cmte on Patents: adverse report in the case of Wm W Woodworth. 10-Act for the relief of Edw Harte: referred. 11-Recommended the following bills pass-relief: of John L Vattier; of the heirs of Jacques Godfroy; of Saml S Haight; of Tarrence Kirby; of John Drout; of Wm L Oliver; of Mary F Swan; of John Houser; & of Benj B Gantt. Pension to Martha Elliott, widow of Saml Elliott, a soldier of the war of 1812; & pension to Franklin W Armstrong, of Hardin Co, Ky. 11-Court of Claims: adverse report in the case of H L Thistle; of of Jacob Hall: laid aside. .

C Maitland James has been convicted at Chicago of being concerned in fraudulent banking, & sentenced to the State prison for 10 years. It was proved on trial that the bills issued purporting to be issued by the American Exchange Bank of Gtwn, D C, were fraudulent, there being no such institution, nor has such ever existed.

Household & kitchen furniture at auction on: Jan 21, at the residence of Mr W S Clary, 438 H st, between 10th & 11th sts. Wall, Barnard & Co, aucts

In the London Illustrated News: some months since there appeared an obituary of Miss Eliz Gray, teacher, who died in Edinburgh in Apr, 1856, at the **age of 108**, having been born in May, 1748, who at the census of 1851 was then the oldest person in that city, & at her death was considered the oldest in Scotland. Her oldest brother died in 1728, 20 years before her birth, & her father in 1755. So that she survived her father 101 years, & [which is so much more extraordinary that it may not again occur in a century] her brother died 128 years before her. She long taught school in her native city, & a gentleman, now resident in London, stated that he attended it 71 years ago.

Mrd: on Jan 15, in Wash City, at Trinity Church, by Rev Mr Cummins, Jas B Shaw, of Texas, to Mary, daughter of the late Prof Bonnycastle, of the Univ of Va.

Mrd: on Jan 15, in Wash City, in the Methodist Protestant Church, 9th st, by Rev P Light Wilson, Mr Saml Barron Cooper to Miss Mary Jane Birkhead, both of Wash City.

Died: on Jan 16, in Gtwn, Lt Edw C Moore, 2nd regt infty, U S Army. His funeral will take place tomorrow at 3½ o'clock, from the residence of his parents, 153 West st, Gtwn.

Died: on Dec 28, at **Belair**, PG Co, Md, Mrs Anna Maria Ogle, relict of Benj Ogle, in her 80th year.

MON JAN 19, 1857

Hurricane, lasting 24 hours, occured at Vera Cruz on Dec 30th, causing the loss of the steamer **Iturbide**, which broke to pieces when she lost 2 of her anchors & another ship was thrown against her. She disappeared with 89 persons on board, beneath the waves. Of all those on board only 17 were saved. The North American schnr **Nenuphar**'s pilot suddenly died, probably from a fit of apoplexy. She was one of the sailing packets of the N Y line.

Mrd: on Jan 14, at Wilmington, Del, in Trinity Chapel, by Rev Chas Breck, Mr Jas R Booth, of New Castle, Del, to Miss Mary E Driver, of Wilmington, Del.

Died: on Jan 16, James, son of James & Martha Riordan, in his 10th year. His funeral will take place on Monday at 10 o'clock.

Died: on Jan 18, Adeline Howell, daughter of Sidney & Mary J DeCamp, aged 5 years & 3 months. Her funeral will be tomorrow at 3 o'clock, from the residence of her father, 281 Pa ave.

Dr Villard, Dentist, [late of Chicago,] is now prepared to perform all operations in his profession. Ofc 250 Pa ave, adjoining Gautier's.

House of Reps: 1-Cmte of the Whole: bill for the relief of the heirs of Maj Gen Arthur St Clair: passed. 2-Bill for the relief of Fred'k Stevens: referred. 3-Cmte on Revolutionary Claims: bill for the relief of Philip Lightfoot: committed. Same cmte: discharged from the consideration of the ptn of Sgt Thos Adams, of the Mass line: laid on the table. 4-Cmte on Private Land Claims: bill for the relief of John B Rose, of Wabash Co, Indiana: committed. Same cmte: discharged from the consideration of the ptn of Danl Davis, of the State of N Y: laid on the table. 5-Cmte on Military Affairs: adverse on the ptn of Jas Sweet. 6-Cmte on Invalid Pensions: bill for the relief of Adam D Gardiner: committed. Same cmte: bill for the relief of Jas Morton: committed. 7-Court of Claims: bill for the relief of Asbury Dickins, reported from the Cmte of the Whole: recommended that it do not pass. 8-Memorial from Capt Saml Mercer, of the U S Navy, representing that he officiated as Cmdor of the U S squadron on the coast of Brazil, by order of the Navy Dept, from Apr 22 to Nov 29, 1856, & praying Congress to award him such compensation for the period specified as ofcrs of that grade are entitled to receive by law: referred. 9-Memorial from Peter D Ankeny, a lt in the war with Mexico, asking that his pension may be increased from that of a private to that of a lt: referred.

Orphans Court of Wash Co, D C. In the case of Eliz Whittlesey, admx of Oliver Whittlesey, deceased, the administratrix & Court have appointed Feb 10 next, for the final settlement of the personal estate of the deceased, with the assets in hand. -Rd N Roach, Reg/o wills

Sleighs, Sleighs, Sleighs: only a few of those very superior Northern Cutters left & for sale at A J Joyce's Coach Factory, corner of 14th & E sts.

Good garden farm for sale: known as the **Hunter Farm**, containing near 20 acres, a short distance west of Gtwn, on the Potomac river. Apply to Rd Smith.

TUE JAN 20, 1857
The Univers quotes a letter from Hong Kong, addressed by a missionary of the name of Arnal to Fr Cazencuve, of the congregation of the Fathers of Mercy at Bordeaux, mentioning the execution of another missionary, M Chapdelaine, in the province of Quang-vi, China. He was beheaded by order of the chief mandarin, after undergoing the most excruciating tortures. His head was then suspended from a tree, & children were allowed to throw missles at in. The liver & heart were fried in a pan & eaten up by the Chinese, under an impression that it would render them invulnerable. The head was subsequently carried off & secreted by a pious Christian. A young man & woman were put to death with the missionary for having embraced Christianity.

Senate: 1-Bills for the relief of Jas Lindsay, & for the relief of Salvador Accardi: postponed indefinitely.

Last evening Mrs Becker, wife of Wm P Becker, constable of the 11th Ward, was filling a fluid lamp, when her clothing took fire. She was burnt in such a shocking manner that her recovery is deemed hopeless. –Phil Bulletin

On Tue there was a large assemblage at Hempstead, Long Island, to celebrate the 97th birthday of Rev Zachariah Greene, who for 67 years has been the pastor of the Presbyterian Church in Setauket, Long Island. The celebration took place at the residence of his daughter, Mrs B F Thompson. Mr Greene was born in Stafford, Conn, in Jan, 1760, & is now in his 98th year. He suffered much during the war of the Revolution. He was addressed by Rev Mr Oakey, of Jamaica. –N Y Com Adv

Mrd: on Jan 15, at Albany, N Y, Wm B Gale, of Marlboro, Mass, to Ann, daughter of Nicholas Quackenbush, of Wash.

Died: on Jan 18, in Wash City, Wm Smith, in his 29th year. His funeral will be from the residence of his brother, Geo B Smith, 3rd & N sts south, on Wed, at 2 o'clock.

Died: on Jan 11, at Middleway, Va, Saml Scollay, M D, aged 76 years.

N Y, Jan 19. The ship **Java**, from Glasgow, which has been ashore for some days on the West Bank, went to pieces last night. Two men were lost.

Boston, Jan 19. The ship **Welsford**, from St John [N B] for Liverpool, was wrecked on Dec 25. Capt Hatfield & 26 of the crew were lost.

WED JAN 21, 1857
Trustee's sale: by deed of trust from John C Harkness & John C Smith, trustees, dated Mar 23, 1852, recorded in Liber J A S No 119, folios 161, of the land records of this county: public auction on Feb 6 next, on the premises, that valuable property on Capitol Hill, composed of lots 1, 2, & 18, in square 761, on B st south; with a fine 3 story brick dwlg. –Walter S Cox, Trustee -J C McGuire, auct

House of Reps: 1-Mr Sapp, of Ohio, gave notice of his intention to introduce a bill for the relief of the heirs of Jas Cisne, deceased.

Appointment by the Pres, by & with the advice & consent of the Senate. Geo C Whiting, who was commissioned during the recess of the Senate, to be Com'r of Pensions, vice Josiah Minot, resigned.

Boarding: Mrs Mary Adams, Pa ave, between 6th & 7th sts, has several unoccupied rooms, & is prepared to accommodate families or single gentlemen with board.

N Y, Jan 20. The ship **California**, at Gloucester from Surinam, dragged out of the harbor yesterday, & was driven ashore on Cohassett rocks, a total loss. Crew saved.

Senate: 1-Ptn from Thos Rosser & the heirs of Wm Reed, asking to be allowed the value of certain pre-emption claims under the Cherokee treaty of 1835. 2-Ptn from J C Tucker, asking the re-imbursement of certain expenses incurred & additional compensation for services performed by him as commercial agent of the U S to the Republic of Honduras. 3-Ptn from Dempsey Pittman, asking the passage of an act amendatory of the act for his relief passed Aug 16, 1856. 4-Cmte on Foreign Relations: asked to be discharged from the consideration of the memorial of Geo W Fletcher, & that it be referred to the Cmte on Commerce. Same cmte: asked to be discharged from the consideration of the memorials of V G Audubon; of R S Field; & also of Philo S Shelton. 5-Cmte of Claims: bill for the relief of the heirs -at-law of Abigail Nason, adm & devisee of John Lord, deceased. 6-Cmte on the Post Ofc & Post Roads: bill for the relief of Jas P Fleming, of Augusta, Ga: passed. 7-Cmte of Claims: asked to be discharged from the consideration of the memorial of Thos J Page, & that it be referred to the Cmte on Naval Affairs: agreed to. 8-Cmte on Revolutionary Claims: asked to be discharged from the consideration of the following memorials: David Dorrance; Saml Logan; John Belknap; David Suezy; Jonathan A Dunning; Sarah P Green; John McClean; Saml B Sawyer; David Tomlinson; Uriah Forrest; Danl Littlefield; Wm M Brooks; Wm Brent; Geo P Frost; John & Eliz Bellinger; Jas Campbell; Francis Lavainway; John Hinkley; Simeon Summers; Jas Hook; Richd T Spottswood, together with numerous others, alleging that persons from whom the said memorialists claim were ofcrs in the Revolutionary army, & were entitled to, but never received the commutation due under the resolution of 1783. The cmte ask that the memorialists have leave to withdraw their papers for the purpose of presenting them to the Court of Claims, if they think proper to do so: which was agreed to. 9-Cmte of Claims: bill for the relief of Jos C G Kennedy. 10-Cmte on Pensions: bill for the benefit of Wm L Oliver, reported it back without amendment, & asked its immediate consideration; but, objection being made, the motion could not be entertained.

Died: yesterday, in Wash City, Andrew R, son of Sarah M & the late Andrew R Locke, aged 23 years, 8 months & 5 days. His funeral will take place on Thu next, at 2 o'clock P M, from the City Hall.

Mrd: on Jan 7, in Wash City, at Wesley Chapel, by Rev John Bear, of Balt, Chas E Walker to Arabella W, eldest daughter of Rev Geo Hildt, all of Wash City.

THU JAN 22, 1857
Henry F Koss was committed to jail on Sat last on a charge of theft, & fully committed. Mr Farnham estimates what was taken from him at $108.

Letters of administration on the estate of Jos Drayton, deceased, having been granted the undersigned, all persons having claims against the said deceased, or indebted to the said estate, are to meet on or before Dec 5, 1857.
—Geo F Lewis, 23 south 3rd st, Phil.

Senate: 1-Ptn from J T Wright, asking compensation for a vessel destroyed by fire while employed in the public service under a contract with the Gov't: referred. 2-Ptn from Geo Charpenning, jr, contractor for carrying the mail on routes 5,066 & 12,801, from Calif to Salt Lake, asking remuneration for losses sustained in Indian depredations & for extra services rendered. 3-Cmte on Revolutionary Claims: bill for the relief of Wm L Davidson. Same cmte: adverse report on the memorial of the legal reps of Col Ethan Allen. 4-Cmte on the Judiciary: adverse report on the bill for the relief of Wm J Appleby, clerk of the Supreme & First District Courts in Utah Territory. Same cmte: asked to be discharged from the consideration of the memorial of Geo E Hand: which was agreed to. 5-Cmte on Foreign Relations: bills for the relief of Anton L C Portman; & of John H Wheeler. 6-Cmte on the District of Columbia: asked to be discharged from the consideration of the memorial of Jno Holohan, & that it be referred to the Cmte on Public Bldgs: which was agreed to. Same cmte: adverse report on the memorial of Thos Fitman, late warden of the penitentiary, asking to be remunerated for money paid to a messenger of said penitentiary. 7-Cmte on Territories: asked to be discharged from the consideration of the memorial of E M Joslin, & that it be referred to the Cmte on Manufactures: which was agreed to. Same cmte: asked to be discharged from the consideration of the memorial of Hezekiah Miller, & that it be referred to the Cmte on Military Affairs: which was agreed to. 8-Resolved, that the memorial of Philo S Shelton, which was referred the last session of Congress to the Cmte on Foreign Relations, asking for the action of Congress in the Aves or Shelton's Isle case, together with the accompanying depositions & papers, be printed with the correspondence of said case transmitted by the Pres to the Senate.

The Hagerstown Mail states that Mr John F Dulaney, of Sharpsburg, Md, was accidentally shot by the discharge of a revolver in the hands of a man named Sowders a few days ago. It appears that Mr Sowders did not think the revolver was loaded. Part of the contents entered Mr Dulaney's back, near the kidneys. The wound is not considered mortal.

Mrd: on Jan 20, in Wash City, by Rev Mr Clarkson, Mr Wm H H Towers to Miss Agnes Virginia Irving, all of Wash City.

Mrd: in Wash City, at the Assembly's Church, by Rev Andrew G Carothers, Mr Weston B Turner to Miss Ellen V Essex, daughter of Josiah Essex, both of Wash City. [No marriage date given-current item.]

Died: on Jan 19, Wm Thos Carroll, jr, in his 24th year. He was prostrated for several years of his life by an agonizing malady, which he bore with Christian patience. His funeral will take place from the residence of his father, F & 18th sts west, on Jan 23, at 1 o'clock P M.

Died: Jan 21, in Wash City, at his residence on 13th st, Francis Masi, in his 86th year.

Obit-died: on Nov 19, 1856, on board the U S sloop-of-war **Constellation**, at Constantinople, aged 19 years & 4 months, Midshipman R W Meade Graham, of the U S Navy, 2nd son of Lt Col Jas D Graham, of the U S Army. He entered the Naval Academy at Annapolis in Oct, 1851, & in Jun, 1855, he passed his examination with a high standing in his class. After a happy sojourn with his family at Chicago of about 5 weeks, he repaired under orders to Norfolk, Va, & early in Aug, 1855, he joined the **Constellation** for duty in the Mediterranean, & continued to serve on board this ship until the day of his death. His disease was an epidemical typhoid fever. He was consoled in his illness, at his own request, by Rev Mr Dwight. His remains were interred in the ***Frank Cemetery***, on a hill at the back of Petra, overlooking the Bosphorus, & a marble momument was ordered to be erected over them by his brother ofcrs as a testimonial of their respect & affection. -Union

Boston, Jan 21. Marine disasters: 1-The ship **Orissa**, from Calcutta, was wrecked on Sunday at Cohasset: mate & 3 seamen were drowned. 2-The barque **A G Cochran**, from Apalachicola, bound to Boston, is ashore near Race Point. Crew saved. 3-The schnr **Bonetta** is ashore at the same place. Two men frozen to death. 4-The schnr **Granite State** & the schnr **Panama** are ashore on the s w ground. 5-The barque **Chester**, from Phil, has drifted to sea. 6-Six bodies have floated ashore from the wreck of the barque **Tedesco**. 7-The brig **Geneva**, from Gtwn, S C, went ashore on Monday at Scituate, & is a total loss. Four seamen were drowned.

Teacher wanted. The Trustees of Allegany County Academy, Cumberland, Md, are desirous of obtaining the services of a gentleman to take charge of their Institution as Principal about Feb 6 next. –Thos J McKaig, Pres of the Board of Trustees

FRI JAN 23, 1857
Mrd: on Jan 21, by Rev S D Gurley, DD, Mr Jas M Witherow to Miss Amanda Hilton, all of Wash City.

Mrd: on Jan 22, by Rev Mr Boyle, Thos W Miller to Julia A Ridgway, both of Wash City.

Died: on Jan 22, in N Y, after a painful illness of 2 weeks, Wm A Dick, of Wash, in his 20th year.

The Western papers announce the death of Elder J T Johnson, one of the most distinguished divines of the Western States. He was a brother of Col Richd M Johnson, Vice Pres of the U S, & was at one time, before entering the ministry, one of the Judges of the Court of Appeals in Ky. He served for 4 years, 1821 to 1825, as one of the Reps in Congress from the State of Ky, & in other depts. of public duty, always with the highest repute. He leaves hosts of friends throughout the Western & Southern States.

Tigers in Florida. Capt Saml Somers recently killed near his residence, on the river St John, an old tigress & two half-grown tigers. He also came in sight of the old male tiger several times, but was afraid to shoot him. [Feb 9th newspaper: The tiger is not a native of this continent, I presume these animals must have been cougars or panthers. Will some gentleman in Florida give us a more minute description of them? -L K Willie, Oxford, N C, Feb 5, 1857]

Hon Wm H Bissell was installed into the ofc of Govn'r of the State of Illinois on Jan 12, 1857.

Senate: 1-Memorial from Sallie'Eola Renneau, urging upon Congress the prompt adoption of measures for the education of the daughters of America by the charter & endowment of The Nat'l Female University of America: referred. 2-Ptn from Marshall O Roberts, Horace F Clark, & Ellwood Fisher, trustees under contract between A G Sloo & the Gov't for mail service between N Y, New Orleans, Havana, & Chagres, asking to be allowed additional compensation: referred. 3-Ptn from John S Van Dyke, wounded in the war of 1812, asking to be allowed arrears of pension. 4-Ptn from Chas G Brown & other watchmen on board the steamer **Minnesota** while lying at the navy yard at Wash, asking to be allowed additional compensation. 5-Additional paper relating to the claim of Geo Whitman to compensation for losses sustained in consequence of the failure of Gov't agents to pay a draft drawn in his favor by the Post Ofc Dept. 6-Ptn from W H Benham, administrator of John McNeil, asking the confirmation of title to certain lands. 7-Cmte on Naval Affairs: asked to be discharged from the consideration of the memorial of T Dana Shaw, & that he have leave to withdraw his papers: which was agreed to. 8-Cmte on Revolutionary Claims: bill for the relief of Eliz Montgomery, heir of Hugh Montgomery. 9-Cmte on Indian Affairs: bill for the relief of John Shaw.

The funeral of Francis Masi will take place on Jan 24 at half past 10 o'clock, from his late residence, 402 13th st. The friends of the family are invited to accompany his remains to St Patrick's Church, where solemn High Mass will be offered.

Charleston, Jan 18. The steamer **Carolina** has arrived, with Jacksonville dates to Jan 15. Gen Harney had withdrawn all the flags of truce, & declared war against the Indians.

On Tue last, Dr Arnold, in attending a little boy of Mr John Eckart, aged about 5 years, left a prescription which was taken to the drug store kept by Ernest Leffer, who compounded the prescription, but instead of putting chloride of potash, as directed, put into it cyanuret of potash, a deadly poison. There was also added some lemon syrup, which made the compound still more deadly, as its addition set free the hydroceanic acid, making a poison more deadly than strychnine. The child took some in the evening and supposedly spit it out. He ate a good breakfast the next morning. His mother remarked there was no use paying for medicine unless they used it, & gave the child a teaspoon full, & he died in a few minutes. Dr Arnold came & tasted some of the mixture & became sick & took a powerful emetic. He was carried home. Mr Leffer, the apothecary, when the medicine was brought back to the shop by Dr Arnold, asserted it was harmless & immediately drank a portion of it, & in 3 minutes after was a corpse. He was a German by birth, about 40 years of age, & leaves a wife & family. –Balt Clipper

SAT JAN 24, 1857
Senate: 1-Ptn from Saml Mercer, a captain in the navy, asking to be allowed the pay of a cmder of a squadron during the time he acted in that capacity. 2-Cmte on Revolutionary Claims: adverse report on the bill for the relief of the heirs of Capt Thos Gill. Same cmte: asked to be discharged from the consideration of the bill for the relief of the surviving children of John Gilbert, a Revolutionary soldier, & that it be referred to the Cmte on Pensions: which was agreed to. 3-Cmte on the Judiciary: asked to be discharged from the consideration of the memorial of Saml P Todd & John Debree, & that it lie on the table: which was agreed to. 4-Cmte of Claims: bill for the relief of Mathew G Emery: recommended its passage. Same cmte: bill for the relief of Geo Phelps. 5-Cmte on Military Affairs: bill for the relief of Adam D Stewart & Alex'r Randall, exc of Danl Randall. 6-Act for the relief of John McConnell; of Wm Kendall; & to reimburse the estate of Jos McClure, a paymaster in the war of 1812. 7-Cmte of Claims: memorial of Geo M Weston, with a bill to provide for quieting certain land titles in the late disputed territory in the State of Maine, & for other purposes. 8-Bill introduced granting bounty land to Mary Felch, widow of Rev Cheever Felch: referred to the Cmte on Public Lands.

Mr Jas Maher, of the Union Hotel, requests us to say that here is no serious truth in an evening paper that a person was yesterday burnt to death in his house. Neither John E Kake, an Indian, nor an Indian Johnny cake came to any such disaster yesterday.

Mrd: Jan 22, in Wash City, in the Thirteenth st Baptist Church, Rev Dr Teasdale, Mr Wm J Church, of Pittsburgh, Pa, to Miss Emma H Teasdale, of Wash City.

Jeffersonton Academy: the 21st session of this School will commence on Sep 1 & end on Jun 29. I have employed a graduate of the Univ of Va to assist me.
-Caleb Brunley, Principal -W M Fischback, Assist. Jeffersonton, Culpeper Co, Va.

House of Reps: 1-No objection to the following bills: recommended that they pass: relief: of Van Rensselaer Hall; of Lt John Guest, U S Navy, & others; of the children of Jas Phelps, a Revolutionary soldier; of the heirs of Mary Hooker; of Wm Walton, a soldier of the war of 1812; of Chas Parish, a soldier of the war of 1812; of the surviving children of Sarah Van Pelt, widow of John Van Pelt, a Revolutionary soldier; of the heirs or legal reps of Jos Bindon, deceased, a Revolutionary ofcr; of Elijah Close, of Tenn; of Eliz Riker; of Amos Armstrong, of Ohio; of John Huff, of Texas; of John H Horne; of Capt Thos Duncan, of the U S Army; of the legal reps of Edmund H McCabe, assignee of Antoine Soulard; of Henry T Mudd, of Missouri; of the heirs & legal reps of Jeremiah Bryan; of Mary Woodbury, Eliz Odell, & others; of Thos J Churchill; of Jas Belger, of the U S Army; & of Israel B Bigelow. Also, directing the pension due Jas Huey, deceased, & Jan Huey, his widow, deceased, to be paid to their sole heir, Alex'r B Huey, of Georgia. 2-Bill for the relief of Horatio J Perry; & of Francis Dainese: referred to the Court of Claims. 3-Bill for the relief of Wm B Trotter: recommitted to the Cmte on Indian Affairs. 4-Memorial of Geo W Hutch, in regard to the cultivation of the Terra Japonica: referred.

On Jan 9, near Tilghmantown, Wash Co, Md, Mrs Mahala Rohrer, the mother of 2 children, ages 3 years & the other 4 months, left the house to get a bucket of water, & locked the children in. The elder child played with fire, & the house was burnt to the ground. The children could not be saved from a terrible death.

Lord Napier has been appointed British Minister to Washington. The London Times objects to his appointment on the ground that, though well fitted by diplomatic experience to represent the country in the East, at any despotic & military Courts in Contintental Europe, he is not the right man for a mission to Washington. [Jan 26th newspaper: Napier is unmarried & his age is only about 35 years. His father, Lord Napier, was British Plenipotentiary to China, & died, about 8 or 10 years ago, at Hong Kong.]

MON JAN 26, 1857
Senate: 1-Act for the relief of the reps of John Donelson, Stephen Heard, & others: amended & passed.

Balt American: on Wed Mrs Reinecker & her 3 children, living near Soller's Point, were found dead in their house. Their bodies were found frozen in the house, having perished with the cold. Mr Reinecker left the city on Sunday last for his home, & has not since been seen or heard from.

U S Patent Ofc, Wash, Jan 21, 1857. Ptn of Danl Fitzgerald, of N Y C, praying for the extension of a patent granted to him on Jun 1, 1843, for an improvement in Fire-proof Chests & Safes, for 7 years from the expiration of said patent, which takes place on Jun 1, 1857. –Chas Mason, Com'r of Patents

In England & Scotland a wide sensation has been created by Hugh Miller's death, a suicide now proved by the tenor of the note left to his wife: "Dearest Lydia: My brain burns. I must have walked; & a fearful dream arises upon me. I cannot bear the horrible thought. God & Father of the Lord Jesus Christ have mercy upon me. Dearest Lydia, dear children, farewell. My brain burns as the recollection grows. My dear, dear wife, farewell. Hugh Miller" -Edinburgh journal. For some months past his overtasked intellect had given evidence of disorder. He was engaged at this time with a treatise on the Testimony of the Rocks, upon which he was putting out all his strength, working at his topmost pitch of intensity. That volume will in a few weeks be in the hands of many of our readers. The pistol used by Miller was taken by a friend to the gunsmith in order to ascertain how many shots were fired & how many charges remained in the chamber. The foreman of the shop, Thos Leslie, while looking into the chamber & turning it around, accidentally let the hammer fall, when a charge exploded, &, penetrating his head by the right eye, killed him instantly.

House of Reps: 1-Resolved, That Jos L Chester be discharged from the custody of the Sgt-at-Arms after he shall have appeared before the select cmte appointed on Jan 9 & fully answered all such proper questions as may be put to him by said cmte. 2-Cmte of Claims: resolutions for the relief of Hall Neilson; & of Jas Young: both committed. 3-Cmte on the Post Ofc & Post Roads: joint resolution for the relief of W W Wimmer, pastmaster at West Zanesville, Ohio, & a bill for the relief of John H Shepherd & Walter K Caldwell, of Pike Co, Missouri: committed. 4-Cmte on the Judiciary: bill for the relief of the sureties of Chas W Cutter, navy agent at Portsmouth, N H: committed. Same cmte: bill for the relief of Roswell W Haskins, of Buffalo; & bill for the relief of Adam D Stewart: committed. 5-Cmte on Revolutionary Claims: discharged from the consideration of the memorials of the heirs of Sarah Aylott; Sarah Ann Dye; Col Wm G Mumford; Capt John McAdams; Thos Shweatt; Wm Royal; & Mary B Davis: & they were referred to the Court of Claims. Same cmte: bill for the relief of the legal heirs of Moses Elmer, deceased: committed. 6-Cmte on Indian Affairs: bill for the relief of Anson Dart: committed. 7-Cmte on Military Affairs: bills for the relief of Ephraim Hunt & of Chas McCormick, assist surgeon in the U S Army: committed. Same cmte: bills to increase the pension of Wm Nash; & for the relief of the heirs of Jas Cisne, deceased: committed. Same cmte: adverse reports on the ptn of Wm Bishop & other operatives in the ordnance dept for bounty land, & on the ptn of Urbano Peretz. Same cmte: adverse reports in the cases of Robt Johnson & Capt Wm Black's company of Florida volunteers. 8-Cmte on Naval Affairs: bill for the relief of Oscar F Johnston, a passed midshipman in the U S Navy: committed. Same cmte: adverse report in the case of John Salter. Same cmte: bill for the relief of Dr Chas D Maxwell, a surgeon in the U S Navy: committed. 9-Cmte on Foreign Affairs: bill for the relief of Wm K Jennings & others, with an amendment: committed. Same cmte: adverse reports in the case of Mgt Heap, widow of the late consul at Tunis; & of Thos L L Brent. Same cmte: bill for the relief of Jos Graham: committed. 10-Cmte on Invalid Pensions: bill for the relief of John W Cox: committed. Same cmte:

adverse report on the ptn of John McGraw for an invalid pension. Same cmte: bill for the benefit of Anthony Devit, late sgt in the 3rd artl of the U S Army: passed. Same cmte: bill for the relief of John Duncan; of Henry Taylor; of Saml Goodrich, jr; of Chove Chase, of N Y; of Thos Berry; of Simon Record; of Jas O Bean; & of Allen Smith. Same cmte: bills for the relief of Jos Bailey & of Elijah Dailey, invalid soldiers of the war of 1812: committed. 11-Cmte on Revolutionary Pensions: bill for the relief of the surviving children of Basil Mignault, an ofcr of the Revolutionary war; & for the relief of John Montey, a soldier of the war of the Revolution: committed. 12-Cmte of Claims: bill for the relief of Geo W Biscoe: committed. 13-Cmte of the Whole: bill for the relief of Charlotte Turner: passed.

Died: on Jan 24, in Wash City, Thomas B Stanley, only son of Jos & Susanna Stanley, aged 4 years, 11 months & 17 days. His funeral is this afternoon at 3 o'clock, from 41 4½ st, between Pa ave & Missouri ave.

Late severe weather: Marlboro [Md] Gaz: on Monday last Miss Virginia, daughter of Mr Thos Clagett, residing near that place, & a negro girl were frozen to death. It appears that the deceased was on a visit to her brother-in-law, Mr Wm I Berry, &, having been informed of the illness of a servant woman in one of the quarters, some distance from the dwlg, she determined to go & see after the sick, &, accompanied by a negro girl, started; but had not gone far before they were completed surrounded by heavy drifts & blinded by the wind & falling snow; & when found they were standing erect, almost entirely covered in the drift, & life was extinct. Miss Clagett was a very amiable young lady, beloved by all who knew her. She was in her 24th year.

TUE JAN 27, 1857
The undersigned have entered into partnership, under the firm of Gardner & Place, for the purpose of carrying on Coachmaking in all its branches. Their Factory is at 553 12th st, south of Pa ave, the stand formerly occupied by P J Gardner.
-Thos J Gardner, Jonah W Place

On Dec 30, at the prison for debt, in the Rue de Clichy, Mr Chas Morey, of Boston, who was confined therein, while standing at a window over-looking the court yard, was deliberately shot dead by a sentinel. The sentinel stated that, having ordered Mr Morey to leave the window & not being obeyed, he fired & killed him. Mr Morey was possessor of the Goodyear patents for England & France & leaves a young wife & family, being himself only 32 years of age. Mr Morey had been adjudged to have been illegally arrested, & was to have been liberated that very day. Mr Mason, the American Minister in France, was investigating the matter. [Mar 14th newspaper: Jos Morel, the sentinel who shot Mr Chas Morey, was acquitted, on the ground that he only obeyed his orders to shoot any prisoner who should appear at a window, & who did not withdraw when 3 times cautioned.]

New weekly paper: National Gazette & Congressional Reporter, intended chiefly for the German portion of our population. Publisher & editor: Mr Magnus Gross.

Ice Cream & Water Ices of the best Phil make: $150 per gallon. –J Fussell & Co, corner of F & 12th sts.

House of Reps: 1-Bill for the relief of Geo Cassady, of the State of Ohio: passed.

Paris, Jan 6, 1857. On Jan 3 the Archbishop of Paris, Mgr Sibour, whilst officiating in the church of St Etineen-de-Mont, was stabbed & murdered by a priest of the diocese of Meaux, named Verges, as he was walking in a procession. Verges had been 4 or 5 times reprimanded for misconduct, & some months back was interdicted for having preached against the dogma of the Immaculate Conception. Mgr Sibour was born on Apr 4, 1792, at St Paul-Trois-Chateaux, in the diocese of Valence, & had nearly attained his 65th year. He was name Bishop of Digne on Sep 30, 1839, & was consecrated on Feb 25, 1840. He was named Archbishop of Paris on Aug 10, 1848. On Oct 12 he took possession of the see by deputy, & was duly installed on the 16th. Verges, the assassin, is the son of a tailor at Neuilly. He was of a very violent temper, & wherever he lived he quarreled with those around him.

Senate: 1-Ptn from John W Phillips, claiming indemnity for the loss of the schnr **Two Brothers**, by reason of her having been dismantled & broken up by the U S troops at Brasos Santiago Jul 3, 1846. 2-Ptn from Jaze B Evans, widow of & excx of the late Cadwalader Evans, inventor & patentee of an apparatus known as Evans' Safety Guard, remonstrating against the provisions of the 9th section of the act now pending before Congress proposing to adopt plugs of pure tin instead of fusible alloys, to prevent the explosion of steam boilers. 3-Cmte on Naval Affairs: bill for the relief of Cmder John L Shaw&; & a bill for the relief of Thos Ap Catesby Jones. Same cmte: asked to be discharged from the consideration of the memorials of Rufus Porter; of Wm M Storm; of Wm D Young; & of John Hughes: which was agreed to. 4-Cmte on Patents: adverse report on the memorial of Wm G Nevins, asking an extension of his patent for cutting crackers. 5-Cmte on Naval Affairs: bill for the relief of Hiram Paulding. 6-Bills referred-relief: of Anthony Devit, late a sgt in the 3rd artl of the U S army; & of John Duncan. 7-Bill for the relief of Charlotte Turner: passed.

Mrd: on Jan 22, in N Y, by Rev Dr Bellows, Maj Robt S Garnett, U S Army, to Marianna Easton, only daughter of Geo S Nelson, of Wash City.

Died: on Sat last, in Annapolis, at the residence of her son-in-law, Alex Randall, Mrs Eliz W Wirt, widow of the late Hon Wm Wirt, in her 73rd year. Her remains will be brought here this morning in the train from Balt to arrive at 11 o'clock, at which time the friends of the family are requested to attend the funeral, from the depot to the **Congressional Burying Ground.**

Died: on Jan 23, in Wash Co, D C, at the residence of her son-in-law, W H Dundas, Mrs Mary W Hesselius, in her 79th year.

Died: on Jan 24, in his 5th year, after a brief illness, Daniel S, youngest child of Daniel S Harkness. His funeral will be this afternoon at 3 o'clock, from his father's residence on H st, between 11th & 12th sts.

Died: on Jan 25, in Wash City, of scarlet fever, Sarah Adelaide, youngest daughter of Thos B & Mary M Entwisle, aged 4 years & 4 months. Her funeral will take place this morning at 11 o'clock, from their residence, 258 H st, between 18th & 19th sts.

Died: on Jan 24, in Wash City, Thomas Tabbs, son of Dr Barton Tabbs, of St Mary's Co, Md.

Died: on Jan 23, in Wash City, Joseph Miller, infant son of Wm P & Virginia Parke, aged 2 years, 11 months & 21 days.

WED JAN 28, 1857

Senate: 1-Memorial from Horatio Hubbell, stating that he was the original projector of the transatlantic ocean telegraph, & that he presented a memorial to Congress in relation to the same in 1849,in which document the great project was first announced & promulgated, with a statement of the means by which it could be effected & the spot where it could be carried through; that the scheme, when presented, was pronounced a piece of madness by all except Jefferson Davis, then a member of the Senate, who said "that the world was not yet prepared for it, but might be soon." The memorialist says the time has now arrived & an organized company is asking for assistance from the Gov't to carry it through; that his rights have been wholly ignored by the company. Mr Brodhead expressed the hope that the company would recognize the rights of Mr Hubbell, who was an intelligent & excellent citizen of the State of Pennsylvania. Appended to this memorial would be found that which he presented to the two Houses of Congress in 1849: referred. 2-Ptn from Amos Kendall, Geo W Riggs, & others, asking an act of incorporation for the Columbia Institution for the instruction of the deaf & dumb & blind: referred. 3-Three memorials from Jas Young, from Jos Chase, & Alex'r Keep, prisoners in Dartmore during the last war with Great Britain, asking to be allowed bounty land: referred. 4-Ptn from Peter B Templeton, asking compensation for services rendered by him in reporting the proceedings of the late trial of Dr Geo A Gardner: referred. 5-Ptn from Edw Gallup, adm of Christian Clemens, an ofcr of the war of 1812, asking to be allowed the pay & emoluments of said Clements during the time he was a prisoner of war: referred. 6-Papers relating to the claim of Richd L Gorton for remuneration for injuries received while in the military service of the U S: referred. 7-Cmte on Revolutionary Claims: bill for the relief of the legal reps of Gustavus B Horner, reported it back with an amendment. 8-Cmte on Naval affairs: bill for the relief of Thos J Page, U S Navy, asking compensation for services as purser; bill for the relief of the petty ofcrs & seamen of the late U S frig **Missouri**. Same cmte: adverse report on the memorials of Asa R Ford, adm of Augustus Ford; of Franklin Buchanan; of J W A Nicholson; of Louis J Williams; of Algernon S Taylor; & of Jas McDonnell.

Died: on Jan 25, in Wash City, at the residence of his sister, Mrs Sarah M Bowers, Mr John Suter, in his 62nd year, after a protracted illness.

In Chancery-No 1,226. Thos Reddin vs John Ratrie et al. The object of the above suit is to procure the sale of lots 2 & 4 in square south of square 999, & lot 1 in square 881, all in Wash City, & a distribution of the proceeds, after satisfying a mortgage debt, among the devisees of Jas Ratrie. The bill of cmplnt sets forth: That Jas Ratrie, then deceased, by his last will & testament, duly made & executed on Sep 17, 1853, devised all his real estate to said cmplnt & John Ratrie as tenants in common; that at the date of said will he was the owner of certain property in Wash City, D C, viz. lots 2 & 4 in square south of square 999, & lot 1 in square 881; that on Sep 28, 1752, he mortgaged lot 1 in square 881 to John Harilland to secure the payment of his promissory note, payable to said Harilland 5½ years after date, with interest, for the sum of $335; that the same is held by said Harilland, who is willing that his debt should be paid now; that said lots are not susceptible of a division between said devisees; & if a partition of said premises was decreed, & a sum certain directed to be paid by either said cmplnt or said Ratrie for equality of partition, neither of them would have the means to pay the same except by selling his portion of said property; & it appearing to the satisfaction of the Court that John Ragrie, one if the dfndnts, resides beyond the District of Columbia. He is notified to appear at the ofcr of the Clerk of this Court on the 1st Monday of Jun next.
–Wm M Merrick, A J -Jno A Smith, clerk

Mrd: at Cromwell, Orange Co, N Y, by Rev Mr Wile, Stephen W Wood, of Wash City, to Catharine Caroline Bell, daughter of the late Capt J C Cunningham.
[No marriage date given-current item.]

Died: on Jan 25, at his residence, in Annapolis, Md, Rev Hector Humphreys, D D, aged 59 years, Pres of St John's College. He presided over this institution for more than a quarter of a century. His bereaved family & friends have lost more than can be told; but there is left to them the memory of his virtues & the beautiful example of his holy life. He was a profound scholar, a warm friend, & a noble model of the true Christian gentleman.

Columbia Institute for Young Ladies: 446 11th st, between G & H sts, Wash City. Prof Geo H Stueckrath, Principal; Miss Eliz L Williams, Vice Principal. Rev Dr Cummins will deliver an address on the opening of the High School. The Second Term will commence on Feb 2 next.

Hon Preston S Brooks, a Rep in Congress from the State of S C, died last evening. He had been unwell but two or three days, when he suddenly died. His disease was a severe cold, which terminated in a violent croup. [Jan 29th newspaper: the funeral of Hon Preston S Brooks will take place from the Capitol today, Jan 29, at 1 o'clock, from Browns' Hotel, the late residence of the deceased. Pall Bearers: Messrs H A Edmundson, Alex H Stephens, A K Marshall, B B Thurston, J Glancy Jones, W W Valk, A Rust, J Scott Harrison. At 2 o'clock the funeral will move from the hall of the House of Reps to the Congressional Cemetery.] [Jan 30th newspaper: the body was conveyed to a vault in the *Congressional Cemetery*, to await the further direction of the bereaved family & friends. Mr Brooks was born in Edgefield district, S C, in Aug, 1819. His father was Whitfield Brooks, a son of Z S Brooks, who had gone through the sufferings & gathered some of the honors of our Revolutionary struggle. His mother was Miss Mary P Carroll. He was educated at the S C College, which he left in 1839, receiving one of its distinctions. In May, 1843, he was admitted to its bar, & in Nov, 1844, elected to the Gen Assembly of the State. In 1846, when troops were called for by the Fed Gov't to repel the invasion of Mexico upon our soil, his native district, Edgefield, furnished a company to the Palmetto regt, of which he was elected captain, & was mustered into the service in Dec of that year. He shared the earlier & later events of the campaign between Vera Cruz & the city of Mexico, having been recalled home by a severe attack of illness. He was an ofcr of that gallant Palmetto regt which in March formed its line of 1,000 men on the beach at Vera Cruz, & which, when, 6 months afterwards, its flag, soiled by the smoke of battle, was planted on the gates of Mexico, could muster but 300 men fit for duty. Its brave cmder, Col Pierce Butler, who fell on the gory field of Churubusco, was the blood kinsman of the deceased. Its second field ofcr, Lt Col Dickinson, having fallen in the same field, & its major, Gladden, severely wounded at the Belen gate, the command devolved on Capt Dunovant, the brother-in-law of the deceased. Five of the relatives of the late Capt Preston S Brooks fell in the last battles of Mexico, he himself had been compelled by severe illness to return home, & did not rejoin his regt until after the capture of the imperial city. At the close of the war he withdrew from the bar & devoted himself to the pursuits of agriculture.]

Elected ofcrs of the Washington United Fire Dept on Jan 26:
Pres: Thos Marche, of the Columbia
1st Vice Pres: J T Halleck, of the Northern Liberties
2nd Vice Pres: W W Grant, of the Perseverance
3rd Vice Pres: T W Cook, of the Anacostia
Sec: Tyler Southall, of the Union
Treas: J T Chauncey, of the Metropolitan Hook & Ladder
Standing cmte:
Columbia: J A Brown, B F Beers, Fayette Martin
Union: W H Hines, Jas Kelly, John Corcoran
Anacostia: Wm Dobyns, S W Cook, Alex'r Eaton
Perseverance: W W Grant, R Grimes, H S Harvey, jr

Northern Liberties: Jas Ward, J H Goddard, jr, T J Dawson
Metropolitan Hook & Ladder: J T Chauncy, W S Baird, & T Stone
American Hook & Ladder: W F Garrett, J Thompson, Jas Kenton
Western Hose: R Mastin, F N Holtzman, Wm Riggles

THU JAN 29, 1857
Col Nathan Boone, youngest son of the celebrated Danl Boone, died a few days since at Springfield, Missouri, in his 76th year.

Senate: 1-Cmte on Naval Affairs: bill for the relief of Jedediah H Lathrop, late navy agent at Wash, to be relieved from the effect of certain judgments against him & his sureties. 2-Cmte on Military Affairs: memorial of Hezekiah Miller to be referred to the Cmte of Claims. Same cmte: bill for the relief of brvt Maj Jas Belger, U S Army, recommended its passage: passed. 3-Cmte on Military Affairs: recommended the passage of the bills for the relief: of C B R Kennerly; of Jesse Morrison, of Ill; of Anthony Devit, late a sgt of the 3rd artl of the U S Army; & of Isaac B Bigelow. 4-Cmte on Pensions: bill for the relief of John Ryley, an Indian, who served in the war of 1812. Same cmte: bill granting a pension to Jonathan Painter, a black man, who acted as a spy in behalf of the Americans during the war of 1812-the ptn of citizens of Sandusky, Ohio, asked that he might be granted a pension. Same cmte: ptn of the heirs of Francis Jacobs, a waiter in the military family of Geo Washington during the time of the Revolution, submitted a report, with a bill for the relief of Catharine Jacobs, of the State of N Y. 5-Additional papers were presented relating to the claim of Eldridge Lawton, assist engineer in the U S Navy, asking extra compensation for services while acting as chief engineer on board the steamer **John Hancock** in the late surveying expedition to Behring's Straits & the China seas.

Pianos, household & kitchen furniture at auction on Feb 4, at the seminary & residence of Rev Wm J Clarke, on E st, between 8th & 9th sts. -Jas C McGuire, auct

Hon John Barney died in Wash City on Monday last, of pneumonia, after a short illness. He was a son of the late Cmdor Joshua Barney, distinguished in the annals of the Revolution & the war of 1812. He served one term as a Rep in Congress from Balt: 1825 to 1827. Up to within a few days of his death Mr Barney appeared to be enjoying, beyond ordinary example, the advantages of a green old age.

Mr Hoffman, one of the millers employed by Mr Vincent Taylor at the Canal Mills in Gtwn, was yesterday engaged in preparing the waterwheel of the mill for the admission of water from the canal, his feet slipped, precipitating him on a beam & then into the cogpit below. He sustained much injury in the breaking of several ribs, & lies in critical condition.

Among the distinguished strangers now in Washington we perceive Brvt Lt Col Hardee, U S A, commandant at the West Point Military Academy, & Ex-Govn'r Bouck, of N Y.

Yesterday on the Metairie Ridge, a duel was fought between Mr Geo W White, a bookkeeper in a large hardware establishment-the challenger, & his antagonist, who was killed, Mr Pakenham LeBlanc, a deputy sheriff who attended to the Supreme Court. The parties met yesterday with double-barrelled guns, at 15 paces. Mr LeBlanc was shot through the heart. His body was carried to his residence on Bourbon st. What became of Mr White after the fatal issue we have not learned. –New Orleans Picayune, 20th.

The Petersburg Express of Wed gives account of 4 persons of that city who perished in the snow storm last week: Dr J E Cox & Mr Traylor started to visit the farm of the former, but were stopped by the drift all night. They were found in the morning; Dr Cox died & at last accounts Mr Traylor's recovery was perfectly hopeless, every limb being utterly frozen. John Brown, aged 23 years was so frozen in the streets of Petersburg that he died. R S Edwards was frozen to death opposite his stall.

Mrd: on Jan 27, in Wash City, by Rev W Krebs, G W Taylor to Eliz Cloud, both of Bladensburg.

Died: on Jan 19, at Petersburg, Va, David Guthrie McCreary, publisher of the Petersburg Gaz, in his 34th year.

FRI JAN 30, 1857
The Charlottesville Advocate announces the death of Hon Andrew Stevenson. He died at *Blenheim*, his residence in Albemarle, on Sunday night last. His remains were interred yesterday in the *Enniscorthy burying grounds*. The death of Mr Stevenson was not unexpected, for many months his health has been gradually failing, & more recently a prostration of his entire nervous system, rendered the more painful by an injury last fall to a nerve of his head. The immediate cause of his death was an attack of pneumonia. We think he was in his 74th year. He was a distinguished man of Virginia who commenced public life at an early age as a member of the Va Legislature in 1804; presided over the House of Reps; & was our Minister to the Court of St James. He was rector of the Univ of Va at the time of his death. Peace to his ashes! [Feb 4th newspaper: We observe in the Charlottesville papers some corrections of the obituary notice of the late Andrew Stevenson: he was in his 72nd year & he entered the Va Legislature in 1810, not 1804.]

The Marlboro Gaz announces the death of Col Saml Hamilton, a prominent citizen of PG Co, Md. He represented that county in the Legislature during several sessions. [No death date given-current item.]

Andrew Wylie has removed his Law Ofc to 8 4½ st, near the City Hall, Wash.

The Pensacola Times announces the sudden death, on Jan 18, of Hon Walker Anderson, a native of Va, but for many years a resident of Florida, & one its most prominent & distinguished citizens, for a time filling the ofc of Chief Justice of the Supreme Court.

Mrs Maj Delafield, wife of of the commandant at West Point, narrowly escaped a fatal accident last week. She was riding down to the ferry wharf, when her horse took fright, rushed down the hill, struck his head against a wall, killing himself instantly, & threw Mrs Delafield, & the orderly who was driving, 10 or 15 feet over into the water, fortunately doing neither any serious harm. Boatmen from the ferry boat rendered prompt assistance.

Orphans Court of Wash Co, D C. Letters testamentary on the personal estate of Gottlieb C Grammer, late of Wash Co, deceased. –Chr Grammer, Julius E Grammer, excs

Mrd: on Jan 27, in Wash City, by Rev G W Samson, Mr Ignatius Clements to Mrs Jane Cunningham, both of Gtwn.

Mrd: on Jan 29, in Wash City, by Rev G W Samson, Mr Logan Precise, of Petersburg, Va, to Miss Catherine Smith, of Leesburg, Va.

Died: on Jan 19, at Parkersburg, Va, David Guthrie McCreary, publisher of the Parkersburgh Gaz, in his 34th year.

Died: on Jan 28, in Wash City, Miss M A Pearce, aged 15 years & 5 months, a native of Va. Her funeral will take place from her brother's residence, 409 G st, this evening at 2 o'clock.

SAT JAN 31, 1857
Toronto Globe of Jan 20. The dwlg house of Mr David Gorman, [a carpenter,] on Front st, was blown up by gas yesterday. Mr Gorman was seriously injured. His family consisted of 10 persons, & all were seriously burnt. His mother of 70 winters received a cut on her head. His 18 year old daughter sustained severe injury.

Orphans Court of Wash Co, D C. Letters testamentary on the personal estate of Chas G Rosenthal, late of Wash Co, deceased. –Augusta S Rosenthal, excx

Mrd: on Jan 27, at Cedar Hill, Fauquier Co, Va, by Rev R C Leachman, Wm H Morrison, of Wash, D C, to Miss E A Rixey, of the former place.

Senate: 1-Ptn from J Horsford Smith, late U S consul at Beyrout, in Syria, asking to be allowed the same salary as that given to consuls in the Chinese & Ottoman empires, under the law of Aug 11, 1848, during his term of service. 2-Ptn from Johnson K Rogers, a Cherokee Indian, asking that provision may be made for paying the claims of Eastern Cherokee for spoliations, subsistence, & removal arising under the treaty of 1855-56 between the U S & the Cherokee Indians. 3-Ptn from Martha Noble Hutchins, protesting against the passage of the bill from the House of Reps now pending in the Senate relinquishing the claims of the U S to certain property of which Elijah King died seised & possessed in the District of Columbia, under certain specified conditions. 4-Ptn from Alex'r Jones, an invalid pensioner, asking an increase of pension. 5-Ptn from Chas R Iliff, asking that his patent instrument for projecting geometrio lines may be adopted by the Gov't, & that he may be allowed a reasonable compensation for the right to use the same. 6-Ptn from John A Monroe, clerk of the district court of the U S for the district of Ky, asking the repeal of the 11th section of the act of Aug, 1856, to regulate the fees & costs to be allowed clerks. 7-Cmte on Naval Affairs: bill for the relief of Edw Lloyd Winder; of Lt Joshua D Todd, U S Navy; & of Danl Ammen, Lt U S Navy. 8-Cmte on Military Affairs: bill for the relief of Capt Alex'r Montgomery, an assist quartermaster in the U S Army; & relief of Jas G Benton, E B Babbitt, & Jas Longstreet, of the U S Navy. Same cmte: bill to authorize an increase of pension to Jos Verbiski. 9-Cmte of Claims: bill for the relief of Henry Hubbard. 10-Cmte on Indian Affairs: asked to be discharged from the consideration of the memorial of Reuben H Grant: which was agreed to.

House of Reps: 1-Cmte of Claims: adverse report on the ptn of Edw Mattingly for additional compensation for services as inspector of customs at Gtwn, D C. Same cmte: adverse reports on the ptn of Eleanor Gardiner, widow of Piney Gardiner; & on the claim of Jas E Kilgour for indemnity for property destroyed by the British in 1814 in consequence of the occupation of his premises by the American forces. 2-Cmte on the Judiciary: bill for the relief of Saml M Puckett, a citizen of the State of Mississippi: which was committed. 3-Cmte on Private Land Claims: bill for the relief of Chas Lucas or his legal reps, & for other purposes: passed. Same cmte: asked to be discharged from the consideration of the ptn of Abraham Long, of Green Co, Ky: laid on the table. Same cmte: bills to vest the title to certain warrants for land in Geo M Gordon; & for the relief of John Dick, of Florida: committed. Same cmte: asked to be discharged from the consideration of the memorials of citizens of Columbis Co, Fla; of Jos E Griffith, of Texas; of Peter Bellinger; & of the ptn of Wm H McNain. Same cmte: bill for the relief of the legal reps or assignees of Jas Lawrence: committed. Same cmte: bills for the relief of John Temple, of Louisiana; of the heirs & legal reps of John Temple, of Louisiana; of the heirs & legal reps of Pierre Cazelar, deceased; & of Laurent Millandon: & they were committed. Same cmte: discharged from the consideration of the bill for the relief of Andrew A H Knox & Jos O Campbell: laid on the table, as the matter had already been acted upon. 5-Cmte on Commerce: bill for the relief of Geo L Bowne & Wm Curry: committed. 6-Cmte on Military Affairs: adverse report on the ptn of Jas Monroe for remuneration for a horse lost in the war of 1812. Same cmte: adverse report on the ptn of Fred'k Stevens for compensation for services in the war of 1812. Same cmte: bill for the relief of Sylvestor Churchill, of the U S Army: committed. Same cmte: bill for the relief of the legal reps of Danl Mallory, deceased: committed. 7-Cmte on Naval Affairs: adverse report on ptn of Harrison Hough. 8-Cmte on Revolutionary Pensions, reported bills for the following, which were committed: for the relief of Rachel Fox; of Saml Winn, only surviving child of Gen Richd Winn, a Revolutionary soldier; of the surviving children of John Neal, deceased; of the heirs of Col Benj Wilson, late of Harrison Co, Va, deceased; & of Jos B Royal for the services of his father, John B Royal, a soldier of the war of the Revolution. 9-Cmte on Invalid Pensions: bill for the relief of Zenia Williams, of N Y: committed. 10-Cmte of Claims: adverse reports on the Senate bills from the Court of Claims for the relief of Ernest Fiedler & for the relief of Stirges, Bennet & Co, merchants of N Y; & on the bill for the relief of Henry & Fred'k W Meyer, merchants of N Y C; & for the relief of Jas Beatty's personal reps: said bills were laid on the table. 11-Cmte on Invalid Pensions: bill to continue the pension heretofore paid to Mary C Hamilton, widow of Capt Fowler Hamilton, late of the U S Army: committed. 12-Bill for the relief of John W Skidmore: introduced. 13-Ptn of Wm B Martin & Eliz his wife for a grant of public land: referred. 14-Ptn from the owners of the barque Ann Elizabeth for registry as an American vessel: referred. 15: Ptn of Dr Jas Higgins, State agricultural chemist of Md, praying that nitrate of soda & other chemical salts forming component parts of Peruvian guano & other agricultural fertilizers may be admitted duty free.

Died: on Jan 24, at the residence of his son, Hon Henry W Hilliard, in the city of Montgomery, Ala, Wm Hilliard, in his 78th year.

Died: on Jan 30, in Wash City, after a long & painful illness, John S Haw, in his 24th year. His funeral will take place on Feb 1st at 3 o'clock, from Browns' Hotel, to which the attendance of the friends of the deceased & of his family is respectfully requested.

Mr Tilghman Hillery, of Bladensburg district, was found frozen in a snow drift on Thu of last week. On the same day a negro man belonging to the above was found dead in a snow drift. We also learn that Clement Hill, residing near this place, lost 2 valuable servants, a man & a woman, during the past week from freezing. A negro man belonging to the estate of the late Col Cross was found in a snow drift on Monday of last week frozen to death. A negro woman belonging to the estate of the late Gov Sprigg, of Bladensburg district, was frozen to death on Thu last.
-Marlboro Gaz [Feb 16th newspaper: Clement Hill requests us to state that no such loss was sustained by him.]

Died: on Jan 25, at the residence of Mrs Mary Fox, King Wm Co, Va, Minta E, wife of Wm H Pleasants, & youngest daughter of the late Saml Smoot, of Wash City.

Lands for sale in Carter & Washington Counties, Tenn: the subscriber has it in contemplation, with a view to the more convenient practice of his profession as a lawyer, to remove from Jonesboro to Knoxville, Tenn, & will sell at private sale the following real estate: the tract upon which I now live, containing about 311 acres, with dwlg house & several out houses. Also, the house & lots near the public square in Jonesboro, now occupied by Messrs McEwen & Dosser & Mr J M Hoss. Also, 5,000 acres of unimproved mountain land, in the s e corner of Carter Co, adjoining the N C line & the line of Wash Co, Tenn. Also, an undivided moiety of 5,000 acres of mountain land near the Doe River Cove, in Carter Co. Also, about 2,700 acres of mountain land in Carter Co, lying between Elizabethton & Blountville. Also, my undivided interest, being about the fifty-third part, of various leases of Copper Lands in Carroll Co, Va. The property in & about Jonesboro will be shown, in the event of my absence on my circuit, by Dr Danl Kenney, of the Eutaw House; & that in Carter Co by C W Nelson, of Elizabethton. –Thos A R Nelson

Died: on Jan 24, at *Cottage Hill*, PG Co, Md, Col Saml Hamilton, aged 72 years, 4 months & 12 days. Regretted by a large circle of relatives & friends, he leaves a widow to mourn his loss. Col Hamilton was a soldier of the war of 1812 & served in almost every capacity in the routine of country offices, & in riper years was twice elected to the House of Delegates.

MON FEB 2, 1857
Movement of the troops. The steamboat **Red Wings** arrived at New Orleans on Dec 12, from **Fort Smith**, bringing 2 companies of U S artl, 120 men, under command of Capt John Lendram. They were bound for **Fortress Monroe**, Va.

Mr Geo Peabody, the London Banker, an American citizen, for many years a successful merchant in Gtwn & Balt, & whose unstinted hospitality to Americans visiting London has made him known every where, was handsomely received & entertained by the Md Historical Society on Fri last. J H B Latrobe addressed the honored guest in a very happy & appropriate speech. [You refer to me as a soldier of the war of 1812. In that year I enrolled myself in a volunteer artillery company in Gtwn, commanded by Col Peter, & for a short time, while expecting an attack from the British fleet, in 1813, was stationed at **Fort Washington**. The author of the Star Spangled Banner was a private in the same mess with myself. On moving to Balt I became a member of the United Volunteers, under Capt Wm Cooke, still among you, hale & hearty at 80.] Thos Swann, Mayor of the City, addressed the assemblage. Pertinent addresses were also made by Mr Kimmel, of Fred'k Co, Mr Z Collins Lee, & Mr Benj Deford, of Balt. The cmte of arrangements consisted of Gen John Spear Smith, Hon John P Kennedy, Rev Geo W Burnap, Capt Robt Leslie, Wm McKim, Wm E Mayhew, Wm Geo Brown, J D Pratt, & S F Streeter.

Trustee's sale of valuable property at auction: on Feb 9, in front of the premises, by deed of trust from Saml S Noland & wife to the subscriber, dated Jan 26, 1854, recorded in Liber J A S No 89, folios 324 & 325, of the land records for Wash Co, D C: sale of that parcel of land in said city known as square 522, with improvements thereon belonging. –Hugh B Sweeny, trustee -A Green auct

A difficulty at Hampden Sidney College on Tue, between 2 students, E A Langhorne, of Lynchburg, & a son of Dr Edie, of Christianburg. They met on the 29th ult in a passage of the college, & Edie was stabbed to the heart & died in a few minutes. Langhorne was arrested.

Wm H Ellis, who was accidentally shot in the back of the head last Monday, near Richmond, by the premature discharge of a fowling piece in the hands of a friend while engaged in a hare hunt, died on Wed night.

Senate: 1-Ptn from Sarah S Hine, widow of a lt in the revenue cutter service who was lost in the revenue cutter **Hamilton**, asking to be allowed a pension. 2-Ptn from John Johnson, asking permission to locate on any unappropriated public land in Florida, a quantity of land equal to a tract claimed by him embraced within a previous grant. 3-Cmte on Naval Affairs: asked to be discharged from the consideration of the memorial of S P Lee & O H Berryman, in behalf of themselves & other ofcrs engaged in the explorations & surveys: which was agreed to.

Died: on Sunday, in Wash City, Dr Josiah Deane Weston, of Dalton, Mass, aged 47 years. Dr Weston had been sojourning here for 2 or 3 months with the hope of benefit to his health, which had been precarious for some years. He was the Democratic candidate in the 11th district of Mass at the late campaign for Congress. His remains will be carried to the Depot at 4 o'clock P M today for removal to his late home.

Died: on Jan 24, in Newport, N H, Mrs Frances Ann Burke, wife of Hon Edmund Burke, late Com'r of Patents. Her last illness was severe, & with full consciousness of her approaching death she parted with her husband & only child in the hope of the Christian.

Died: on Jan 14, in Edenton, N C, Mrs Harriet W Hoskins, wife of Thos S Hoskins, in her 38th year, leaving her husband, 5 children, & numerous relatives & friends to mourn her death. She was a worthy & consistent member of the Protestant Episcopal Church.

N Y, Feb 1. Dr Harvey Burdell, a well-known dentist, was found dead in his ofc yesterday. His body contained 15 stabs & marks of strangulation. There were no signs of any robbery having been committed.

Columbus, Jan 30. Yesterday Mr Slough was expelled from the House, for striking Mr Caldwell, by a vote of 70 to 35. All the Democrats opposed Mr Slough's expulsion with the exception of Mr Corry. Mr Slough left for Cincinnati today.

TUE FEB 3, 1857
House of Reps: 1-Cmte of the Whole: bill for the relief of John Shaw, a soldier in the war of 1812: passed. 2-On the bill for the relief of Sallie T Matthews: passed. 3-Cmte of the Whole: was discharged from the consideration of the bills for the relief of Shadrach Rice, of Jackson Co, Va; & of Jos Bailey, an invalid soldier of the war of 1812: they were passed. 4-Cmte on Patents: adverse report on the ptn of Phineas Emmons & other heirs of Uriah Emmons.

Letter dated Havana, Jan 23, says: "Dr Kane is fast recovering. His mother is now here, & under her gentle nursing there are strong hopes entertained of his ultimate restoration to perfect health."

Senate: 1-Cmte on Private Land Claims: bills for the relief of Benj R Gantt & of John L Vattier: recommended their passage. Same cmte: bill for the relief of Capt Thos Duncan: passed. Same cmte: bill for the relief of the heirs of Jacques Godfroy, & for the relief of the heirs or legal reps of Jeremiah Bryan, severally reported them with a recommendation that they pass. 2-Cmte of Claims: bill for the relief of John Huff, of Texas: recommended that it be passed. 3-Cmte on Public Lands: bill releasing to the legal reps of John McNeil, deceased, the title of the U S to a certain tract of land. Same cmte: bill authorizing Mrs Jane Smith to enter certain lands in the State of Alabama. 4-Cmte on Naval affairs: bill for the relief of Dr Jas Morrow. 5-Cmte on Private Land Claims: bill for the relief of Geo F Baltzell, assignee of Jas P Road: recommended its passage. 6-Cmte on Pensions: bill for the relief of Wm Poole: recommended its passage. 7-Cmte on Military Affairs: bill for the relief of Wm F Russel: passed. 8-The decision of the Court of Claims is in favor of the following claims: of O H Berryman & others; of Nahum Ward; of David Wood; of John Michell; of Collier H Minge; of Phillip T Elicott & Lucretia A Brodie, admx of Chas Brodie; of Atkinson Rollins & Co; of Aymar & Co; of Wolfe & Co; of Starwood & Reed; of Saml A Way; of J D & M Williams; of Udolpho Wood; of Alfred Atkins; of Geo W Wales & of T B Wales & Co: accompanied by bills. Also, an opinion adverse to the claim of Johnson R Rogers. On motion by Mr Brodhead, these cases were severally referred to the Cmte of Claims.

To the heirs at law of Jacob Dull, sr, deceased, who lately died intestate in Augusta Co, Va. By direction of a decretal order of the Circuit Court of Albemarle Co, Va, lately made by said Court in the Chancery suit of Jacob Dull et al vs Geo Baylor, adm of Jacob Dull, sr, deceased, et al, "I hereby give you notice to make yourselves known to me, at my ofc in Staunton, Va, on or before Sep 15, 1857, furnishing your respective names & residences, together with definite proofs of your relationship to said intestate. –John N Hendrew, Com of the Court aforesaid.

Sheppard Insane Asylum of Balt: Moses Sheppard, our venerable fellow-citizen, died on Sunday morning. He was born in the summer of 1773, & was in his 84th year. He is supposed to have been born in the vicinity of Phil, but, in his own language, "the first I knew of myself was on an earthen floor in a log hut near Balt." His parents were poor. He came to Balt before 1800, & entered a grocery establishment kept on Cheapside by John Mitchell, in which he ultimately became clerk, then a partner, & then conducted the business for many years on his own account, retiring in the meridian of life with a princely fortune. He was a quiet unobtrusive citizen, a member of the Society of Friends; took a prominent & active part in the African Colonization movement, & was always the unwavering friend of the black man. He had no early educational advantages, but was possessed of great natural intellectual capacity. For some years past Mr Sheppard proposed to found an Insane Asylum, to be located near Balt; at his death; the charter for which was, on his application, granted by the Legislature of Md 4 years since. His will, which amounted to over $600,000, with the exception of a few small legacies to friends & relatives, was devoted to philanthropic purpose. –Balt American

Died: on Feb 1, in Wash City, John Edwards, son of John E & Catharine B Baker, aged 3 years, 1 month & 11 days, of pneumonia, after 8 days of suffering. His funeral is this evening at half-past 2 o'clock, from 651 7th st, Island.

Blowing up of a steam war frigate in the harbor of Naples: universal panic produced by the awful occurrence; confusion was indescribable, & was vainly attempted to be quelled by his Majesty's brother, Price Luigi. With the exception of the King & Queen, most of the members of the Royal family were present. Within the Palace such was the force of the shock that no fewer than 3,678 panes of glass were destroyed. The Queen, whose accouchement is shortly looked for, fainted. The vessel went down almost immediately, & property to the amount of about a quarter of a million of ducats has been sacrificed by her destruction. It is not at present easy to ascertain with precision the actual loss of life, as only two of the sufferers have been found, one of whom was Capt Masseo, who was dreadfully mutilated, having lost his head from the jaw upwards, & both his arms; his remains were interred on Monday last. He leaves a wife & 2 children. Her cmder, Lt Col Fausse, fell down in something very much resembling an apoplectic fit. Great as has been the sacrifice of human life, it would have been much larger but for the prompt assistance rendered by Capt Farquhar, the ofcrs & crew of the ship **Malacca**, who picked up 25 survivors. [No date given-current item.]

WED FEB 4, 1857
Orphans Court of Wash Co, D C. In the case of Thos Carbery & Wm H Ward, excs of Rev Wm Matthews, deceased, the excs & Court have appointed Feb 28 for the final settlement of the personal estate of said deceased, of the assets in hand.
–Rd N Roach, Reg/o wills

Senate: 1-Ptn from the heirs of Francois Chobert Loncairne, asking that their title to certain lands may be confirmed, & that they may be authorized to locate the same on any unappropriated lands. 2-Cmte on Private Land Claims: bill for the relief of Martin Millet, of Iowa: passed. 3-Cmte on Pensions: adverse report on the ptn of Roldophine Claxton, widow of Capt Alex'r Claxton, U S N, asking arrears of pension due her late husband. 4-Cmte on Revolutionary Claims: act for the relief of Fred'k Vincent, adm of Jas L Case, survivor of Le Case & Mallet: reported back with an amendment. 5-Cmte on Private Land Claims: adverse report on the bill for the relief of Napoleon B Gill, of Perry Co, Mo. Same cmte: bill to confirm the title of Benj E Edwards to a certain tract of land in the Territory of New Mexico: recommended that it pass. 6-House bills referred: relief of Jos Bailey, an invalid soldier in the war of 1812; of Shadrach Rice, of Jackson Co, Va; & of John Shaw, a soldier in the war of 1812. 7-Bill for the relief of Jonathan Painter, a black man, who had been taken prisoner when a child by the Wyandot Indians, & had been identified with them in all their feeling & habits. He was living at Upper Sandusky at the time of the war, & was one of the few Wyandots that aided the American cause. He is now old, poor, & helpless. Bill was passed without a disserting voice.

House of Reps: 1-Ptn of John Hood & Benj T Reeley, of Wash, D C, for relief: referred. 2-Ptn of the owners of the barque **Ann Elizabeth**, for registry as an American vessel: referred.

Alfred Taylor, son of Brvt Lt Col Taylor, 1st artl, U S Army, was thrown from his horse at Brownsville, Texas, & so injured that he died of his wounds on the 15th ult.

Buchanan Inauguration: after the ceremony the marshals, assistant marshals, & aids, will, as the final ceremony, escort the President & his attendants to the Executive mansion. Marshals: Col W Hickey, commandant of the military, or the senior ofcr on duty.

Capt Danl Radcliffe	Chas Dodge, Gtwn	Col S L Lewis
Capt H B Tyler	Col E B Robinson	Capt John Rainbow
Dr A Y P Garnett	Gen John Tyler	Henry Dunlap, Phil
Dr Wm Jones	Robt Ould, Gtwn	Col D M Bull, Phil
Maj A O P Nicholson	Dr Aaron W Miller	Dr Benj King
Maj J N Barker	H Caperton, Gtwn	Col Saml C Stambaugh
Maj Arnold Harris	Henry S Davis	

Assistant Marshals selected from the District:

Elisha Riggs	Jas F Scott	Thos J Fisher
Chas Abert	Abel P Upshur	Wm Handy
Andrew Carroll	Walter Lenox	Hopkins Lightner
Lt H A Wise	Nicholas Bidder	Ferdinand Jefferson
Col J W Irwin	Maj G F Lindsay	Maj Jas McGuire
Thos Bartlett	Capt H L Shields	E Kingman
Alex J Atocha	Dr Chas Frailey	Col Alex Provost

S Y McNair	M W Cluskey	Fr McNerhany
W H Selden	G H Varnell	Chas Miller, jr
Walter T Brooke	John C Rives	Geo W Talburt
Wm Miller	Thos L Smith	Ph Otterback
John McCullom	Dr J C Hunter	Th Champion
Jerome Digges	Thos Berry	Th Altemus
John C Bowyer	John T Hollohan	Richd Henderson
Zephaniah Jones	Chas S Wallach	John R Queen
Dr F B Culver	P M Key	J B Boisseau
Alfred Shucking	Dr W J C Duhamel	Hugh McCaffrey
C G Wagner	B B Curran	Valentine Conner
Dr Saml A Houston	Jas Owner	John Pettibone
Dr Henry Haw	F M Spencer	Geo E Kirk
Merit Jordan	J A McGowen	Saml Pumphrey
G W Jones	Th Hutchinson	John H Simmes
Col W H Woodley	John Pic	John Martin
Jas M Carlisle	J A Hunnicut	Jas Espey
Geo Parker	Theodore Mosher	D B Clark
Andrew Coyle	J J Mulloy	J L Lancaster
W Maury	Francis Reilly	Geo Mattingly, jr
J A Kennedy	W J Wheatly	
F A Kimmel	John Devlin, jr	

Assist Marshals, selected from the States & Territories:

Hon John Appleton, Maine	J N Carpenter, Ark
Col John H George, Concord, N H	Ch S D Jones, Iowa
D A Smalley, Burlington, Vt	H Madden, Wisc
Capt John S Slocum, Providence, R I	A C Bradford, Calif
Col Ch G Green, Boston, Mass	John Thaw, Calif
Gen Hiram Walbridge, N Y C	Hermann H Heath, Mich
O J Keiger, N Y C	R J Warden, Mich
Byron G Daniels: N Y C	H A Cook, Miss
Hon Geo Read Riddle, Wilmington, Del	Hon Geo Vail, N J
	Geo Hackett, N J
C J M Gwinn, Balt, Md	Chas H Jones, Pa
Beverly Tucker, Va	G A Swarzman, Pa
Col John Minor, Va	Fr S Schulze, Pa
John Hart, Charleston, S C	Jos M Howell, Louisiana
Col J R Powell, Alabama	L H Rickard, Conn
Fielding A Patterson, Fla	Thos D Rusk, Texas
Hon F B Stanton, Tenn	Maj Benj McCulloch, Texas
Dr S V Hunter, Ky	Wesley Jones, N C
Col J B Steedman, Ohio	Maj A J Dorn, Missouri
Gen M McConnell, Ill	Hon Smith Miller, Ind
Col J J Stirman, Ark	Hon Thos A Hendricks, Ind

J M Caldwell, Ind
Thompson Allen, Ga
W K de Graffenried, Ga
Col W W Irwin, Minn Terr
R R Nelson, Minn Terr
Assistant Marshals at Large:
Thos J McCalmont, Pa
Stephen Anderson, Pa
Chas W Carrigan, Phil
Hon Wm White, Phil
Andrew Potts, of Ark
J Rind, of Gtwn, D C
Aids to the Marshal-in-Chief:
Gen John Tyler
Dr A Y P Garnett
Capt Henry B Tyler
Capt W W Hunter

Hon Bird B Chapman, Neb Terr
Hon John W Whitfield, Kansas Terr
Hon J Patton Anderson, Wash Terr
Hon Miguel A Otero, New Mexico
Hon J M Bernhisel, Utah

Esau Pickrell, of Gtwn, D C
Walter H S Taylor, of Gtwn, D C
Jas Roache, of Alexandria Co, Va
Col Montague, of Com for Relations, H R

Dr Thos Miller
Wm Flinn
Capt John Rainbow
Maj W W Russell

Desirable business stand for rent in Gtwn: desirable Storeroom & Cellar, 130 Bridge st, between High & Congress sts, Gtwn, for many years occupied by Myers & Bro as a dry good house, & at present occupied by Seldner & Co, as a clothing store; possession given on & after Mar 12 next. –Jas Fullalove, Gtwn, or E S Wright, auct.

Mrd: on Tue, in Wash City, by Rev John C Smith, Mr Rexford Hatch to Miss Sophia J Matthews, both of Fairfax Co, Va.

Died: on Feb 2, in Wash City, after a protracted illness, Miss Mary Ellen Coleman, in her 24th year. Her funeral will take place today at 2 o'clock, from the residence of her brother, Jas Coleman, 2nd st east, near Pa ave.

Died: on Feb 1, in Wash City, Katie Estelle, aged 1 year, 4 months & 1 day, daughter of C S & Kate S Wynkoop.

Died: on Jan 28, in Balt, of scarlet fever, John Bozman Kerr, elder of the sons of John B & Lucy Hamilton Kerr, in his 4th year. He was born at the city of Leon, Central America, Palm Sunday, Mar 20, 1853.

THU FEB 5, 1857
Died: on Feb 4, in Wash City, Danl Simonds, in his 78th year. His funeral will be on Feb 6 at 2 o'clock P M, from the residence of his son, Stephen Simonds, 4th & L sts, Navy Yard.

Prize Beef: the advertiser will have at his Stalls, Nos 5 & 7, Western Market, on Fri, & at Stall 66 Centre Market on Sat, some of the finest beef ever offered in this city. They were brought here by Jacklin Smith from Va. –Wm Linkins

A shocking calamity occurred at the house of Rev E H Havens, a Wesleyan Methodist clergyman, residing about 4 miles south of this village, on Wed, the 12th instant, whereby 3 persons were killed & a 4th injured beyond recovery. It appears that Mr Havens was engaged in making a balsam, of which the principal ingredient was spirits of turpentine. An exposion took place, scattering the burning fluid over the persons of himself, his wife, & 3 children. Mrs Havens died the same day; the youngest daughter died on the 22nd, & the father on the same day. The son still lingers, but with no hope of recovery. Two other children were at school, & are now deprived of father & mother. –Steubenville [Ohio] Farmers Advocate of the 28th ult.

Mrd: on Feb 3, in Wash City, by Rev Fr Alig, Mr Augustus Shaffer to Miss Susana A Lynch, all of Wash City.

Mrd: on Feb 3, in Wash City, by Rev P D Gurley, Mr Armistead B Curtis, of Hanover, Va, to Miss Geraldine Wells, of Wash City.

Mrd: on Feb 3, in Wash City, by Rev P D Gurley, Mr Jas G Long to Miss Virginia Stone.

Mrd: on Feb 2, in Wash City, by Rev Dr Duncan, Mr Robt Johnson to Miss Laura R, daughter of Josiah Egleston, both of Wash.

Dr Benj H May died at his residence on Bank st, in this city, on Jan 31, after an illness of nearly 2 weeks, caused more immediately by his exposure to the severe storm of snow on the 18th whilst engaged in the discharge of his professional duties. Dr May was the brother of the late Judge May, whom he has followed to the grave in less than 7 months, the Judge having died in Jul last. He was in his 69th year. The funeral of the late Dr B H May took place at 11 o'clock A M yesterday from St Paul's Church. The remains were accompanied to **Blandford Cemetery** by a large procession. –Petersburgh Intel, Feb 2

Senate: 1-Ptn from David Ogden & others, asking that moneys illegally exacted from the owners of ships or vessels by the collectors of customs for constructive permits for the examination & landing of the baggage of passengers arriving in the U S may be refunded: referred. 2-Ptn from J C Cutter & other sureties of C W Cutter, late navy agent at Portsmouth, N H, asking to be released from a judgment against them by the U S, & that the amount paid by them on the same may be refunded: referred. 3-Ptn from Franklin S Myers, a justice of the peace for Wash Co, asking that police magistrates & constables may be allowed fees in cases of misdemeanor as well as felony: referred. 4-Ptn from Henry L Goodwin, asking that the rates of postage to &

from Calif may be reduced: referred. 5-Ptn from F McNerhaney, naval storekeeper at the Wash Navy Yard, asking an increase of compensation. 6-Cmte on Pensions: adverse report on the ptn of Anthony Bayard. Same cmte: bill for relief of Michl Kinney. Same cmte: adverse report on ptn of Philip Wilhoit. Same cmte: bill for relief of Jeremiah Pendergast. 6-Cmte on Judiciary: asked to be discharged from the consideration of the memorial of P M De Ridley, & moved it be referred to the Cmte on Private Land Claims: agreed to. 7-Cmte on Naval Affairs: bill for relief of J Wilcox Jenkins. 8-Cmte on Revolutionary Claims: bill for relief of the legal reps of Chas Porterfield. 9-Bill for relief of David Ogden, Andrew Foster, & other shipowners: introduced.

FRI FEB 6, 1857
We are authorized to say that the *President's Mansion* will be open this evening, the health of Mrs Pierce having so far improved as to justify the usual public reception.

Hon Henry Winter Davis & Miss Nannie H, daughter of Jno B Morris, of Balt, were united in marriage on Tuesday last.

Senate: 1-Cmte on Public Lands: bill granting bounty land to Mary Felch, widow of Rev Cheever Felch, deceased: recommended its passage. Same cmte: bill to authorize bounty land to Jos Chase, Jas Young, & Alex'r Keep, certain prisoners in Dartmoor during the war of 1812. 2-Cmte on Military Affairs: bill for the relief of Wm B Belden, adm of Ebenezer Belden: bill was passed over.

Herr Emanuel Leutze, an American artist residing at Dusseldorf, has just finished a new picture, "The Last Court Evening of Charles the Second of England," which is declared by the German art-journals not only to be a worthy pendant to the former works of the same painter, especially to his canvas of "**Washington Crossing the Delaware**", but to surpass them with regard to composition as well as execution. -German correspondent of the Atheneum

Robt C Boden, in Saville township, Pa, has discovered a cave near 250 feet long, adorned with the most curiously formed stalactites.

Died: on Feb 5, in Wash City, Hon Wm D Merrick, of Md, aged 63 years. His funeral will take place on Sat at 3 o'clock, from the residence of his son, Judge Merrick, on F st, between 6th & 7th sts. [Feb 7th newspaper: the funeral of Wm D Merrick is postponed [the members of his family not having all yet reached the city] until Sunday afternoon, at 2½ o'clock.]

Died: on Feb 4, in Wash City, at the residence of his niece, [Mrs M A Spalding,] Mr Timothy Cleary, aged 73 years. May he rest in peace! His funeral will take place this morning at St Patrick's Church, at 10 o'clock.

Died: on Feb 4, in Wash City, in her 39th year, Barbara A, wife of David Hedrick. Her funeral will be at 10 o'clock A M, from the corner of N & 4th sts, Northern Liberties. [No date given for the funeral-assume it is today.]

Died: on Feb 5, in Wash City, after a long pulmonary complaint, John B Floyd, in his 37th year. His friends & the friends of the family, & of his father-in-law, I Beers, are requested to attend the funeral on Feb 7 at 2 o'clock, at 479 E st. [Feb 7th newspaper: the funeral of John B Floyd is unavoidably postponed from today until tomorrow afternoon, at 2 o'clock, from the residence of Mr Isaac Beers.]

Died: on Feb 4, in Wash City, Henry Taylor, in his 43rd year. His funeral will be next Sunday at 2 o'clock P M, from his late residence, on 8th st, between G & H sts.

Died: on Jan 9, at Plaquemine Brutee, La, in her 37th year, Mrs Mary T, wife of Dr Jas Donovan, formerly of Wash City, & daughter of the late Capt Anthony Hodgkinson, of Alexandria, Va. May she rest in peace!

Died: on Feb 3, in Balt, Md, Electius Middleton, of the U S Navy, in his 45th year, a native of Alexandria, Va.

SAT FEB 7, 1857

Senate: 1-Cmte on Military Affairs: bill for the relief of J T Wright. Same cmte: bill for the relief of Capt Alex'r Montgomery, an assist quartermaster in the U S Army. 2-Cmte of Claims: bills for the relief of Collins Boomer, Saml S Haight, & Robt Davis: recommended their passage. 3-Cmte on Pensions: bill for the relief of Moses Olmstead, of Ohio: passed. 4-Cmte on Patents & the Patent Ofc: adverse report on the memorial of Aza Arnold for a renewal of his patent for a machine called a double speeder. Same cmte: adverse reports in each case, to the memorials of Adolphus Allen & of Geo G Henry. 5-Cmte on Private Land Claims: bill for the relief of John W Cheevis, of Louisiana. 6-Bill introduced for the relief of Wm James. 7-Bill for the relief of Mary Reeside: passed. 7-Bill for the relief of Jedediah Lathrop, late Navy Agent at Wash: passed. 8-Bill for the relief of Chas Newbold's heirs. [This bill was for a grant of 12 sections of land as a reward for the invention of a certain cast-iron plough by said Newbold.] Bill was rejected by a vote of 24 to 14. Senate adjourned.

Burning of the **National Theatre** yesterday afternoon. The theatre has been under the direction of Miss Fanny Morant, for a few weeks, though Messrs Kunkel & Co continued to be the lessees. The Mayor, in view of the menacing condition of the naked walls, early gave orders for their demolition, which was done.

A matrimonial alliance of an uncommon character has lately been effected in Fluvana Co, Va, Mr Robt Gray, the gallant groom, is 95 years of age, & the late Mrs Catherine Reilly, [now Mrs Gray,] 92 years of age.

House of Reps: 1-No objection to the following bills-recommended they pass-relief: of Eliz Martin; of the heirs of Amos Oney, a Revolutionary soldier; of the children & heirs of Levi & Mary Stone; of Leonard Lilly; of Jos D Beers, of N Y C; of Benj W Smithson; of Thos M Newell; of Isaac Swain; of Thos Jenkins; of Jos M Kennedy; of the heirs of Wm Easby; & of Jos Irish, Wm Sturgis, & Bartholomew Baldwin. Also, increasing the pension of Danl Denver; & increasing the pension of Isaac Phillips. 2-Bill for the relief of Katharine M Hamer, widow of the late Gen Thos L Hamer, was laid aside with the recommendation that it do not pass. 3-Bill for the relief of Brvt Capt Fred'k Steele, of the U S Army: was passed over.

H J Gardner, Postmaster at Hingham, died on Sat last in consequence of a fall on the ice in the early part of the week. He was 46 years of age, & had held the ofc 3 years, to the entire satisfaction of his townsmen.

John T Sandford, late Postmaster at Florence, N Y, pleaded guilty to the charge of robbing the mail & was sentenced to 10 years' imprisonment.

Mrd: on Feb 3, by Rev G W Samson, Mr C P Webster, of Ill, to Miss Mary E Walker, of Wash City.

Mrd: on Feb 3, by Rev P D Gurley, Mr Jas G Long, of Ill, to Miss Virginia Stone.

Died: on Feb 6, John U Moulder, aged 36 years, son of the late John N Moulder, of Wash City. His funeral is tomorrow at 3 o'clock, from his late residence, 11th st, south of Md ave.

Died: on Feb 6, in Wash City, Lucy A, wife of Augustus H Voss. Her funeral will be on Feb 8 at 2 o'clock P M, from her late residence, near the corner of H & 7th sts.

MON FEB 9, 1857
Hon Preston King, U S Senator elect, has resigned his appointment in the N Y Harbor Commission, & the Govn'r has filled the vacancy with Mr Bradford R Wood, of Albany.

An imposter, passing himself off as Dr J J Stevenson, has been cutting an imposing figure in Petersburgh, Va, recently, & was about to marry a member of a highly respectable & wealthy family, when it was established that he was a penitentiary convict from York, Pa, who had served a full 3 years term at the weaving business in the East Pa Institution devoted to such diplomas. –Balt American

Died: on Feb 3, in Wash City, Henry T Weightman, in his 62nd year.

Died: on Feb 8, at Gtwn, D C, Jeremiah Williams, in his 83rd year. His funeral is on Tue next at 3 o'clock, at his late residence on Dunbarton st.

Died: on Feb 1, at *Spring Grove*, near Dranesville, Fairfax Co, Va, Mr Edw Bates, in his 74th year.

Died: on Feb 2, at Alexandria, Eliza Frances, widow of the late Wm C Gardner, & eldest daughter of the late Anthony Chas Cazenove.

Phil, Feb 8. Geo W Watson, proprietor of Concert Hall, committed suicide this morning. He had been insane more than a year, & was a patient in the Pa Hospital.

Senate: 1-Ptn from Nancy Madison & others, widows of Revolutionary ofcrs & soldiers, asking to be allowed arrears of pension, under the 2nd section of the act of Mar 3, 1853. 2-Ptn from Fabius Stanley, a lt in the navy, asking to be allowed the pay of a cmder for the time he acted as such at the navy yard in San Francisco. 3-Ptn from Wm B Draper, asking additional compensation for his services in managing the magnetic telegraphic dept of the Japan expedition under Com Perry. 4-Cmte on Military Affairs: bill for the relief of Maj Benj Alvord, paymaster in the U S Army. Same cmte: bill for the relief of Dempsy Pittman, approved Aug 10, 1856. Same cmte: bill for the relief of John Shaw: recommended its passage. 5-Cmte on the Judiciary: asked to be discharged from the consideration of the memorial of the members of the bar of Wisc & of Jas Harrison, clerk of the district court of the U S for the district of Missouri. 6-Cmte of Claims: bill for the relief of Nahum Ward: recommended its passage. 7-Bills from the House referred to appropriate cmtes:-relief-of Eliz Martin; of the heirs of Amos Oney, a Revolutionary soldier; of the children & heirs of Levi & Mary Stone; of Leonard Lilly; of Benj W Smithson; of Thos M Newell; of Isaac Swain; of Thos Jenkins; of Brvt Capt Fred'k Steele, of the U S Army; of Jos M Kennedy; of the heirs of Wm Easby; & of Jos Irish, Wm Sturgis, & Bartholomew Baldwin. Also, to increase the pension of Danl Denver; & increase the pension of Isaac Phillips.

Equity Docket-No 63. Bill of Revivor. Circuit Court of PG Co, Md, sitting as a Court of Equity. Basil R Spalding, next friend of Henry St John Clements, & others, against Josias Clements & Mgt E Clements. The bill of revivor states that the cmplnt filed his bill of cmplnt in this court on Nov 10, 1853, as the next friend of Henry St John Clements, Francis Clements, Virginia Clements, & Emily Clements, the infant children & heirs-at-law of Francis H Clements, deceased, against the said Josias Clements & Mgt E Clement, the widow of said Francis H Clements, praying, among other thing, for a decree by this honorable court for the sale of the real estate in the said bill of cmplnt mentioned, which belonged to their said father at the time of his death, [which took place in May, 1851,] & of which said real estate the said children were seized in fee at the time of the filing of said original bill, their said father having died intestate; & also that dower might be assigned out of said real estate to the said Mgt E; that the pretended sheriff's sale spoken of in the said original bill of cmplnt as made to the said Josias [if any such was made, which is not admitted]

should be declared utterly null & void; & that the said Josias Clements should be required to account for the rents & profits of said real estate while the same was in his possession; that said dfndnts have answered the said bill of cmplnt on Mar 19, 1855, & that since the filing of his answer & before the cause was brought to a hearing the said Josias Clements departed this life intestate, & leaving his codefendant, Mgt E, of full age, & John T Clements, Francis J Clements, Mary L Clements, Eliz Clements, & Josias Clements, infants under the age of 21 years, his children & heirs-at-law; that letters of administration on his personal estate have been duly granted to Saml H Berry, of said county. The bill further prays that the said heirs & reps may be made parties dfndnt to the said suit; & that the same may be revived & restored to the condition in which it was at the death of said Josias; & that an order of publication may be passed against the non-resident dfndnts named in said bill of revivor, to wit: Mgt C Clements, Mary L Clement, Eliz Clements, & Josias Clements, residents of Wash City; & they are to appear in this court by the 2nd Mon in Jul next, & show cause why the said suit should not be revived as aforesaid.
–Chas S Middleton, Clerk of the Circuit Court for PG Co [Md]

The following record of American nomenclature is given in the memorials of Wm Shattuck, lately published in Boston: Simon Shattuck, of Fitchburg, named 3 sons Shadrack, Meshach, & Abodnego; Abel Shattuck, of Coleraine, named the male of a pair of twins Truman & the female Truly; this Truman Shattuck named a girl Truly Ann, & Truly Shattuck named a girl Emeline Truly; Moses Shattuck, of Brooklyn, named 4 sons, since 1800, Asia, Africa, Europe, & America. Other odd names in the volume are Al, Philiahasse, Seraph, Sayneda, Sarada, & Thisby Athalia.

TUE FEB 10, 1857
Desirable residence in Gtwn at private sale, situated on Beale st, first door west of Christ's Church. Price $7,000, on easy terms, at 10%, off for cash. Inquire of Jas A Magruder, West st, Gtwn.

Trustee's sale of valuable real property in the city & county of Wash: by deed of trust from Estwick Evans & his wife, dated Feb 7, 1856, recorded in the land records of Wash Co, in Liber J A S No 110, folios 160: sale on Feb 23, of lot 16 in square 184; also, a tract of land in Wash Co, containing 31 acres, 1 rood, & 17 perches, beginning at the end of the 4th line of the tract called *New Seat*. –W B Webb, trustee
-J C McGuire, auct

Died: last evening, in Wash City, at the residence of his father, after a lingering illness, Gales Seaton, in his 40th year, son of W W Seaton.

For rent, a valuable grocery store on the corner of 12th & B sts, near the Canal, formerly occupied by Messrs Sengstack & Clarke. Apply to Francis Hanna, the subscriber, 355 K st, between 12th & 13th sts.

By the will of the late Mrs Mary Hill, of Fredericksburg, Va, all the slaves belonging to her estate, numbering 36, have been set free, with the choice of going either to Liberia or to a free State.

Mrd: on Feb 5, in Wash City, by Rev Smith Pyne, Lt Frank Wheaton, 1st Regt Cavalry, to Miss Maria Mason, daughter of Col Saml Cooper, U S Army.

Died: on Feb 9, in Gtwn, Colin P Harrison, aged 18 years, youngest daughter of Eliz T & the late Gustavus Harrison. His funeral is on Wed afternoon, at 3½ o'clock.

WED FEB 11, 1857
Senate: 1-Ptn from Wm H De Forrest & others, asking appropriations for the further survey & exploration of the La Plata river & its tributaries. 2-Ptn from Alpheus Rice, asking to be allowed bounty land for his services as a soldier in the U S army against hostile Indians. 3-Ptn from Walter M Gibson, asking that his claim for indemnity for illegal imprisonment & consequent loss of property in the East Indian Archipelago, at the hands of the Dutch authorities, may be enforced by the U S against the Gov't of Holland, & that the rights of American citizens in those seas may be properly protected. 4-Ptn from Sarah Ann Roose, widow of Sgt John J Roose, of the regt of voltiguers, asking that her pension may be increased. 5-Ptn from Jas Duane Doty & 19 other citizens of the State of Wisc, asking an appropriation of $5,000 for the purpose of a harbor & canal survey at Sturgeon Bay, in Wisc. 6-Ptn from Jas Maney & other descendants of Cherokee Indians, asking that all reservees & their descendants entitled to a distributive share under the Cherokee treaty of 1835 may be allowed per capita the sum provided by the 8th section of the Indian appropriation act of Jul, 1854. 7-Cmte on Private Land Claims: bill for the relief of Jos Irish, Wm Sturgis, & Bartholomew Baldwin: recommended its passage. 8-Cmte on Pensions: asked to be discharged from the consideration of the ptn of Mary Bennett, widow of Chas W Bennett: which was agreed to. Same cmte: adverse report on the House bill for the relief of Roxana Kimball. Same cmte: asked to be discharged from the consideration of the ptn of the heirs of Thos Hazard, & that it be referred to the Cmte of Claims: which was agreed to.

Died: on Feb 5, at the Mansion House, in Alexandria, in her 71st year, Mrs Hetty W Hall, relict of the late Maj John Hall, of the U S Marine Corps. Honored & loved through a long life, she laid down peacefully to rest in its evening; &, though her death was sudden & unexpected, it is a sweet consolation to her children, relatives, & friends to know that she died in the faith & hope of a Christian.

John C Rheinhardt, aged 96 years, died at Phil on Fri last. He was born in Baden in 1759, & in 1776 came to this country, & subsequently, in company with Lafayette, participated in many battles of the Revolution.

THU FEB 12, 1857
M de Stoeckl, who for some time past has officiated as Russian Charge d'Affaires at Washington, has been raised to the rank of full Minister near our Gov't.

The cmte with the remains of the late Hon Preston S Brooks, left Wash City on Tue in the steamer **Powhatan**, & reached Richmond the same evening by the Richmond, Fredericksburg, & Potomac railroad. The body was escorted to the Capitol, where it was deposited for the night in the Senate chamber. The cmte were taken by the citizens as their guests & quartered at the Exchange Hotel.

Va Historical Society: annual meeting held in Richmond. The following ofcrs of the society were elected: all of them being re-elections, with the exception of Mr Grigsby, who fills the offices made vacant by the death of Wm Maxwell: Hon Wm C Rives, Pres; Hon Jas M Mason, Wm H Macfarland, & Hon John Y Mason, Vice Presidents; Hugh Blair Grigsby, Corr Sec & Librarian; Andrew Johnston, Rec Sec; Jaquelin P Taylor, Treasurer. Reappointments made by the ofcrs after their election: Conway Robinson, chairman; Gustavus A Myers, Thos T Giles, Arthur A Morson, Thos H Ellis, Geo W Randolph, H Coalter Cabell, members of the executive cmte. [No date given for the meeting-current item.]

Dr Purrington offers his professional services to the citizens of Wash. He has had much experience in the treatment of disease. Ofc: 255 G st, near the State Dept.

Mrd: on Feb 3, in Columbus, Ohio, by Rev Henry Davis, Mr A B Laurens, of that city, to Mary Jane, daughter of the late Mr Chas Bell, of Wash City.

Died: on Feb 11, in Wash City, Mrs Eliz A Bell, wife of Saml P Bell, of N Y, aged 28 years. Her funeral will take place tomorrow at 3½ o'clock, from the house of Mrs Williams, on 8th st near Pa ave. St John's Lodge, Wash Chapter, & friends are respectfully invited.

Died: on Feb 11, in Wash City, at Navy Yard Hill, Laura V Berry, daughter of A F & Henrietta L Berry, aged 8 months.

Died: on Jan 25, in Jacksonville, Fla, of consumption, Capt R W M Johnston, late of the U S Army, & a native of Fredericksburg, Va, aged 34 years. He had lately removed to Jacksonville for the benefit of its more genial climate. Capt Johnston was in nearly every hard fought battle in the Valley of Mexico, & was distinguished for his gallantry & good conduct, the command of his regt having devolved upon him after his superior ofcrs were disabled.

We the undersigned, Wm D Bell & Edmund J Ellis, having associated ourselves together in the Butchering business, will always be found at the present old Stands in the Centre Market & the Northern Liberties Market.

FRI FEB 13, 1857
Senate: 1-Cmte on Commerce: bill to reimburse Elisha W B Moody the money paid by him as owner of the British barque **Sarah** in the rescue of the passengers & crew of the American ship **Caleb Grimshaw**, reported it without amendment & recommended its passage. Same cmte: asked to be discharged from the consideration of the memorial of Aaron Haight Palmer: it was referred to the Cmte of Claims. 2-Cmte on Public Lands: memorial of Tench Tilghman, asking remuneration for losses sustained in consequence of the consulate to which he had been appointed having been destroyed by the Spanish Gov't, reported a bill for his relief. 3-Cmte on Commerce: asked to be discharged from the consideration of some papers relating to the case of Geo Whitman, & that they be referred to the Cmte on the Judiciary: which was agreed to. 4-Cmte on Naval Affairs: adverse reports on the following memorials of naval ofcrs asking for extra pay, viz of Wm Mervine & other ofcrs attached to the Pacific squadron; of J M Brooke & others exployed in a survey of the North Pacific; of Cmder Thos J Page & ofcrs of the steamer **Water Witch**, & on the memorial of Wm Aiken & Jas Kelly & 90 others employed in the Japan expedition. Same cmte reported back the House bill relinquishing the claim of the U S to certain property of which Elisha King died seized & possessed in the District of Columbia upon certain conditions without amendment, & recommended its passage. 5-Adverse report on the following bill: relief of Thos Jenkins.

House of Reps: 1-Cmte on Invalid Pensions: bill for the relief of Lt Robt Cunningham for an invalid pension: committed. 2-Cmte on Foreign Affairs: bill for the relief of Ralph King, late U S Consul at Bremen: committed.

Mr Geo Lewis, of Long Branch, N J, hung himself in his own barn, on Fri last. He left a widow & 8 children.

Hon Albion K Parris died on Feb 11, at his residence in Portland, Maine, in his 71st year. He filled at different periods the several ofcrs of Rep & Senator in Congress, Judge of the U S Court for the District of Maine, Govn'r of the State of Maine, &, lastly, 2nd Comptroller of the Treasury of the U S. He was an active member of the Congregational church in Portland. His death is a sad blow to his family.

Died: on Feb 12, in Wash City, Mrs Sarah Waters, aged 64 years, widow of the late David S Waters, sr, after an excruciating bodily pain, which she bore with submissive patience & Christian fortitude. Her funeral will be on Feb 14 at 3 o'clock, from her late residence, on N Y ave, between 6th & 7th sts.

Died: on Feb 12, in Wash City, of consumption, Col Henry E Baldwin, aged 41 years, formerly of N H, & for the past few years a resident of Wash City, holding the position of Assist Sec of the Pres to sign Land Patents. His funeral is this afternoon at half past 3 o'clock, at 417 Pa ave.

Mrd: on Feb 4, at Woodstock, Powhatan Co, Va, by Rev Thos Ambler, Mr Thos P McDowell, of Va, to Miss L Constance, daughter of Mr Wm S Warwick.

Dubuque, Feb 12. On Sat last Odd Fellows' Hall was crushed by the weight of the snow & ice upon the roof, killing S S Foss & his wife.

Equity-No 1,066. Agnes M Easby, against Horatio N & John W Easby, W R Smith & Wilhelmina his wife, Henry King & Marian E C his wife, & Cecilia J Hyde. Horatio N Easby, John W Easby, & Agnes M Easby reported they sold lot 13 in square 559 to John, Michael, & Bridget Kenney for nine & a half cents per square foot, the purchase money amounting to $570.38. –Jno A Smith, clerk

Equity-No 1,066. Agnes M Easby, vs Horatio N & John W Easby, W R Smith & Wilhelmina his wife, Henry King & Marian E C his wife, & Cecilia J Hyde. Wm B Webb, Jos H Bradley, jr, & Richd H Clarke, the trustees in the above cause, reported to the Court that they sold the following: part of lot 1 in square 559 to J D Reynard for $192. Part of lot 10 in square 559 to J D Reynard, for $122.40; & that said Reynard has assigned the same to Geo A Duvall. *Haddock's Hills Farm*, to Horatio A Easby, for $7,050. Parts of lots 7 & 8 in square 728 to Henry King for $4,400. –Jno A Smith, clerk

SAT FEB 14, 1857
Jas Watson was indicted on Wed last in the Court of Gen Sessions at N Y for assaulting on Jan 3 last, Fernando Casfang, & stealing a watch from him, valued at $30. Veridct, guilty; sentence, State prison for 10 years & 3 months.

Senate: 1-Ptn from John M Hinton, mail contractor from Norfolk, Va, to Edenton, N C, asking additional pay to indemnify him for losses sustained on consequence of the prevalence of yellow fever at Norfolk in 1855: referred. 2-Cmte of Claims: bill for the relief of John Erickson; of Isaac Swain; of J M Kennedy; of the heirs of Wm Easby, deceased; & of Thos M Newell. 3-Cmte of Claims: bill for the relief of Jas Maccaboy. 4-Cmte on Pensions: bill for the relief of Wm W Spencer. Same cmte: adverse report on the ptn of Geo Colvin. 5-Bill for the relief of Geo A Magruder, from the Court of Claims: postponed indefinitely.

$50 reward for runaway negro girl Mary Smith, about 12 years old. Her father & mother, free negroes, live in Gtwn. –John P Waring, living near Benning's Bridge, D C.

The daughter of Mr Fred'k Cook, who was accidentally shot by a pistol in the hands of her little brother, died on Wed from the effects of the wound. She lingered in an insensible condition about 40 hours. She was about 11 years of age, a bright & beautiful child, the favorite of the whole neighborhood. –Balt American

House of Reps: 1-Cmte of Claims, reported from the Court of Claims for the relief of Collier H Ming, Philip T Ellicott, & Lucretian A Broadie, admx of Chas Broadie, with the recommendation that it pass; & it was committed. Same cmte: bill for the relief of Mathew G Emery: committed. 2-Cmte on Public Lands: Lewes A Ruse to have leave to withdraw his papers: which motion was agreed to. 3-Cmte on the Post Ofc & Post Roads: bill for the relief of John Scott, Hill W House, & Saml O House: committed. Same cmte: adverse report in the case of E G & L F Rogers. Same cmte: bill authorizing the settlement of the accounts of Frank S Holland, late postmaster at Oregon City, Oregon: committed. Same cmte: asked to be discharged from the consideration of case of J F Caldwell, praying interest on money withheld from him by the Post Ofc Dept, & that the same be referred to the Court of Claims: which was agreed to. Same cmte: adverse reports on the ptns of Jas M Harris, of Darien, Ga, & of the citizens of Alabama in the case of A B McCarty, a mail contractor in said State. Same cmte: bill for the relief of Francis DeP Leonard: committed. Same cmte: bill for the relief of Wm A Forward: committed. 4-Cmte on Revolutionary Claims: bill for the relief of Catherine V R Cochrane, sole surviving child of the late Gen Philip Schuyler: committed. Same cmte: bill for the relief of the heirs of Abraham Buskirk, & a bill for the relief of the heirs of Capt Thos Hazard: committed. 5-Cmte on Private Land Claims: bill for the relief of Danl Whitney: committed. Same cmte: bill for the relief of Martin Millett, of Iowa: passed. Same cmte: adverse report on the ptn of Wm B Allen, of La, for the confirmation of certain lands. Same cmte: bill for the relief of the heirs & legal reps of Pierre Broussard, deceased: committed. 6-Cmte on Military Affairs: adverse report on the ptn of Col A W Doniphan & others. Same cmte: bill for the relief of Thos Phoenix, jr: committed. Same cmte: bill for the relief of Jonathan Painter, a black man who acted as a spy in the war of 1812: passed. Same cmte: adverse report on the ptn of Danl Treadwell, of Mass, praying an appropriation to enable him to test the practicability of constructing cannon of great caliber. 7-Cmte on Naval Affairs: adverse reports on the ptns of Dawson Phoenix, a midshipman in the service of the U S; of Hon Mr Dick, of Pa, for the establishment of a navy yard; & of Chas Alcott, of Medina Co, Ohio. 8-Cmte on Foreign Affairs: bill for the relief of Wm Rich: committed. 9-Cmte on Revolutionary Pensions: bill for the relief of Mary Harris, wife of Newsam Harris, deceased, & to place the name of Zephaniah Halsey, of N Y, on the pension roll, under the act of Jun 7, 1832: committed. Same cmte: bills committed-relief of: the surviving children of Sarah Swartwout; of Eliz Ausman; of the surviving children of Susannah Scott, deceased, late of N Y; & of Mary Bell, of Pa. Same cmte: bill for the relief of Aurelia Fish, widow of Nathl Stowell, a sgt of the Revolution, & a bill for the relief of the children of Elnathan Sears, an ofcr of the Revolution: committed. 10-Cmte on Invalid Pensions: bill for the relief of Wm Sutz; of Isaiah W Green, of N Y; & of Lt Thompson H Crosby: committed. Same cmte: bill for the relief of Wm Thompson, for an increase of pension: committed. Same cmte: bill for the relief of Danl Wacaser & for the relief of Sampson Hayes, a soldier in the Mexican war: passed. Same cmte: bills for the relief of Elkanah English & of Michl Hanson: committed. Same cmte: discharged from the consideration of the ptn of Wm T Broadis: laid on the table. 11-Cmte on Patents: bill for the relief of Nathl Hayard. 12-Bills referred-relief: of John W Cheevis, of La; of Moses Olmstead, of Ohio; of Puig, Mir & Co, of New Orleans; & of Jean B & Pelagie Farribault. 12-Cmte of Claims: bill for the relief of John Robb: laid aside with an unfavorable recommendation. 13-Bills taken up with a recommendation that they pass: relief of J H F Thornton, Lawrence Taliaferro, & Hay T Taliaferro, sureties of D M F Thornton, late a purser in the U S Navy; & a bill for the relief of the legal reps of Jos Nourse, deceased. Also, a bill to allow the legal reps of Saml Jones, of the 11th Va regt on continental establishment, 5 years' full pay as a capt of infty, in lieu of half-pay for life. 14-Bill for the relief of the legal reps of Wm Austin, deceased: pending. 15-Bill granting 160 acres of land to Richd Smith, of Coshocton Co, Ohio, for his services in the expedition against the Rickaree Indians.

Mrd: on Feb 3, in Fauquier Co, Va, by Rev Mr J Landstreet, Mr Louis Fred'k Weber, of Wash City, to Miss Lydia A Rector, of said county.

Died: on Feb 13, in Wash City, William, infant son of Hugh & Jane Lochrey.

Died: on Feb 12, Mrs Hannah Colbert [colored,] aged 24 years, daughter of Jane Butler. Her funeral will be on Sun afternoon at 3 o'clock, from the place of her late residence.

MON FEB 16, 1857
Senate: 1-Ptn from Lt G P Welsh, U S Navy, & other junior ofcrs of the La Plata expedition, asking that the same allowance may be made to them as was made to the acting masters & lts of the Behring's Straits expedition for the time they were on said La Plata expedition & acting as lts. 2-Ptn from Jos C G Kennedy, asking compensation for injury done to his property while rented by the Gov't as an ofc for the Superintendent of the Census. 3-Cmte on Private Land Claims: bill for the administrator of John F Wray: passed. 4-Cmte of Claims: bill for the relief of John R Nourse, asking a suspension of an execution on the judgment obtained against him as security of the late Purser Wm P Vanzant. 5-Bill introduced for the relief of Danl Whitney. 6-Bills referred-relief: of Brvt Capt Fred'k Steele, U S Army; of Danl Wacaser; & of Sampson Hays, a soldier in the Mexican war. 7-An act to entend the provisions of the act entitled "An act in addition to certain acts granting bounty lands to certain ofcrs & soldiers who have been engaged in the military service of the U S" to the ofrcrs & soldiers of Maj Danl Bailey's btln of volunteers of Cook Co, Ill: referred.

Dr Jack Shackleford died at Courtland, Ala, on Tue of last week, in his 66th year. He participated in the Texas struggle for independence; was captain in that band under Col Fannin which was defeated at Goliad & massacred by Santa Anna. His life was spared because he was a physician, that his services might be made available in the Mexican army.

Hon A J Donelson was robbed on Feb 5 on the steamboat **Danl Boone**, from Nashville, of a draft on New Orleans of $4,000 & a gold watch.

Health Report: Ofc of the Com'r of Health. Wash, Feb 14, 1857. Monthly report of deaths in Wash City for Jan, 1857: 63. –Chas F Force, Com'r of Health

N Y, Feb 15. The Coroner's jury in the Burdell investigation case have found a verdict against Mrs Cunningham & Eckel as principals, & Snodgrass as an accessory to the murder of Dr Burdell.

Orphans Court of Wash Co, D C. Letters testamentary on the personal estate of Henry Taylor, late of Wash Co, deceased. –E G Handy, exc

Orphans Court of Wash Co, D C. Letters of administration on the personal estate of Chas K L Good, late of Wash Co, deceased. –Wm Noyes, adm

Orphans Court of Wash Co, D C. Letters of administration on the personal estate of Eliza James, late of Wash Co, deceased. –Christopher Ingle, adm

Orphans Court of Wash Co, D C. In the case of Isabella Johnston, excx of Thos J Johnston, deceased: the executrix & Court have appointed Mar 10 next for the final settlement of the personal estate of said deceased, of the assets in hand.
–Ed N Roach, Reg/o wills

TUE FEB 17, 1857
Yesterday the steam boiler connected with an engine used by T D Barton, in pumping the water out of his section of the canal enlargement at Black Rock, exploded killing John Stoughton, engineer; John Rider, fireman; & Jas Cronyn, John Hagerty, John Devit, Danl Foaren, & Cornelius Downing, laborers. Thos Flanegan was probably fatally injured. –Buffalo Commercial, Thu

Died: on Feb 15, in Wash City, Mrs Mary Echardt, aged 62 years. Her funeral will be this evening at 2 o'clock, on L, near 15th st.

Died: on Feb 16, in Gtwn, D C, Beckie, infant daughter of Dr F S & Rebecca M Barbarin.

Boarding: Mrs Turpin, 375 Pa ave, has several double & single rooms for boarders.

In the matter of the ptn of the heirs of Wm & Matilda Ratcliff, deceased. The Com'rs appointed have returned their report to the Court making a division of the Real Estate among the heirs, & the same being duly examined, it is hereby ordered that the said report be ratified & confirmed. –Jno A Smith, clerk

Senate: 1-Ptn from Danl Kerr, heir of Jno D Kerr, an ofcr of the war of 1812, killed in battle, asking that the amount standing on the books of the Treasury against said Kerr may be cancelled, so as to enable his heirs to receive the arrears of pay to which he was entitled. 2-Cmte on Pensions: bill for the relief of Emma A Wood, widow of the late Brvt Maj Geo W F Wood, of the U S Army. 3-Act for the relief of the surviving children of Sarah Van Pelt, widow of John Van Pelt, a soldier of the Revolutionary army; & an act for the relief of the children of Jas Phelps, a soldier of the Revolution. 4-Cmte on Pensions: act for the relief of Geo Cassady; & an act for the relief of Chas Parish, a soldier of the war of 1812. Same cmte: act for the relief of Terrance Kirby; of the surviving children of John Gilbert, a Revolutionary soldier. Same cmte: bill for the relief of Wm Craig: passed. 5-Cmte on Naval Affairs: asked to be discharged from the consideration of the bill for the relief of Wm James & the memorials of Thos Howard & of Wm Roddy: which was agreed to. Same cmte: adverse report on the memorial of A S Taylor, an ofcr on board the U S steamer **Missouri**, for indemnification for losses by fire in the destruction of said steamer. 6-Cmte on Indian Affairs: asked to be discharged from the consideration of the memorial of Jas Maney & other descendants of Cherokee Indians. 7-Resolved, That the Cmte of Claims return to the Senate the papers in the case of Rebecca Burdsall, widow of Ira Burdsall, agent of the U S. 8-Bill for the relief of Dr Jas Morrow: passed.

Potomac lands for sale: the undersigned will sell privately, in a body or separately, 3 contiguous tracts of land, containing 800, 700, & 300 acres, lying upon the Potomac river & Nomoni creek: upon each tract is a small dwlg house & out-bldgs. Address A Brown, Westmoreland Court-House, or R L T Beale, Rices Store, Westmoreland Co, Va. –A Brown, R L T Beale

Valuable real estate in Wash for sale: part of lot 11 & 12 in square 20, improved. Part of lot 19 in square 36; lot 21 in square 51; & lot 12 in square 544. Apply to L Clifton Hellen, at ofc of Saml Chilton, cor 5th & D sts.

WED FEB 18, 1857

Capt Abraham Bigelow, U S Navy, now in command of the Brooklyn Navy Yard, has resigned.

Senate: 1-Ptn from Geo H Giddings, mail contractor on the route from Santa Fe, New Mexico, to San Antonio, Texas, asking the passage of a law to compel the Postmaster Gen to allow & pay to him the amount to which he is entitled under the provisions of the bill making appropriations for the Post Ofc Dept. 2-Court of Claims: in favor of the following cases: of Geo Ashley, adm of Saml Holgate; of Thos Eggleston & Jos Bartell; of Jane Smith & of Lucinda Rolinson, with bills in each case. Adverse to the claim of Courtlandt Palmer.

Tyre Maupin is to become editor of the Berkeley [Va] American, an old & excellent newspaper.

Orphans Court of Wash Co, D C. Letters of administration on the personal estate of John Tabler, late of Wash Co, deceased. –Danl S Harkness, adm

Mobile papers: effort will soon be made to raise a sufficient amount, by subscription, to defray the expenses of procuring a suitable monument to place over the grave of Maj Gen Gaines.

Mrd: on Feb 16, at Richmond, Va, by Rev C Minnigerode, D D, Lt Col Jas D Graham, of the U S Army, to Miss Frances Wickham, daughter of the late John Wickham, of that city.

Died: on Feb 17, in Wash City, after a brief illness, Mrs Catharine Stone, in her 23rd year, consort of John H Stone. Her funeral will take place this day at 3 o'clock, from her late residence, corner of 7th & L sts.

THU FEB 19, 1857
American hostilities in China: General orders were given to the cmders, ofcrs, seamen, & marines of the U S ships **Portsmouth**, **San Jacinto**, & **Levant**. In the midst of peace you have been called upon to redress an assault upon the flag of your country. San Jacinto, at Whampa, China, on Dec 6, 1856-Jas Armstrong, Cmder-in-chief of U S naval forces in the East Indies & Chinese Seas. [It was on Nov 15 that the pinnace of the U S ship **Portsmouth**, bearing of course the U S flag, & having on board Capt Foote, on his way from Whampoa to Canton for the purpose of withdrawing the American marines stationed in the foreign factories, was fired upon by the Chinese while passing the Barrier forts.]

Of the steam-frig **San Jacinto**:
Killed: Edw Mullen, coxswain; Jas Hoagland, carpenter's mate; Wm Mackin, seaman; Alfred Turner, coxswain; Jos Gibbons, Boatswains' mate.
Wounded: Smith Benjamin, ordinary seaman; Jas McGreevy, seaman; John Brow, seaman; Wm Johnson, coxswain; Thos Robinson, ordinary seamen; F B Petro, landsman; John Mitchell, ordinary seaman; John Stanton, ordinary seaman; Wm Vanhouten, apprentice boy; Thos Pantony, coal heaver; Nicholas Dillon, coal heaver; a McIntosh, capt forecastle.

Of the sloop-of-war **Portsmouth**:
Killed: Lewis Hetzel, apprentice boy; Thos Crouse, do; Chas Beam, seaman; Edw Hughes, do. Wounded: Patrick Melvin, private marine; John Thompson, do; Thos Gaynor, ordinary seaman; John Lake, Boatswains' mate; Jas Lines, cpl marines; Richd Crosby, ordinary seaman; Jas Corlace, do.

Of the sloop-of-war **Levant**:
Killed: Edw Riley, ordinary seaman

Wounded: Earl English, lt, severe contusion; Jonathan Murray, boatswains' mate, severely; John Russell, ordinary seaman, severely; Wm Boyce, marine, severely; Patrick Mohan, marine, severely; Jos O'Neill, marine, slightly. The gentleman who furnished the above account mentions the following ofcrs with great praise: Cmder Foote, of the **Portsmouth**; Cmder Bell, of the frig **San Jacinto**; & Cmder Smith, of the **Levant**. Also, Lts Lewis, Watmough, Guthrie, Davenport, English, Carter, & Simpson, in charge of the boats. Also, Lt Belknapp, with Adams & Shepard, masters, in charge of the field-pieces, [called in the American service howitzers;] & Capt Sims & Lts Kirkland & Tyler, in command of the marines.

Groceries, Household & kitchen furniture at auction on: Feb 25, at the grocery store & residence of Mr T Shannon, 262 20th st, between L & M sts. -A Green auct

Jas Daly died some time ago in Cincinnati, leaving a considerable fortune. In a recent suit it appeared that over 30 years ago he married in Ireland, & lived with his wife till she was the mother of 4 children. He then came to the U S, intending to send for her. In 1831 he married in Cincinnati, & lived with his 2nd wife & had several children. A few years before he died his first wife heard that he was living in Cincinnati & came out from Ireland. He was terribly perplexed by his 2 wives, yet admitted his first marriage. The 2nd wife succeeded in inducing him to convey all his property to trustees for her benefit. The first wife brought suit for dower, & the court awarded it to her.

Harris C Legg, an estimable citizen of Kent Island, Queen Anne's Co, Md, committed suicide by hanging himself in the woods near his residence on Tue of last week. The Centreville Times says he was 45 years of age, & no cause can be assigned for the act.

Senate: 1-Ptn from Catharine Wilkie, daughter of Jos Paine, asking relief on account of the military services & sufferings of her father during the Revolutionary war. 2-Cmte on Revolutionary Claims: adverse report on the memorial of the heirs of Capt Jos Packwood. Same cmte: asked to be discharged from the consideration of the memorial of Thos Gregory Smith. 3-Cmte on Naval Affairs: asked to be discharged from the consideration of the memorial of John J Glasson, & that he have leave to withdraw his papers: which was agreed to. 4-Cmte on Military Affairs: bill for the relief of Benj Smithsop. Same cmte: bill for the relief of Antoine Robedeau: recommended that it do not pass. 5-Cmte of Claims: bill for the relief of Alfred G Benson.

Paris, Fri, Jan 30. Verger was executed this morning at 8 o'clock on the Place de la Roqquette. He was supported by Abbe Hugon on one side & the executioner on the other side. On reaching the platform Verger fell upon his knees.

Notice: the subscriber, surviving partner of C K L Good, late of Gtwn, deceased, has charge of the stock of goods & book of accounts of his late partner, & will prepare the accounts for collection. –H Benton

Orphans Court of Wash Co, D C. Letters of administration with the will annexed on the personal estate of Ann Jenkins, late of Wash Co, deceased.
–Js Walters, sen, adm w a

Mrd: on Feb 17, in Wash City, by Rev Mr O'Toole, Mr Jas L Barbour to Miss Annie E Moore, both of Wash City.

Died: on Feb 14, in Wash City, in her 36th year, Mrs Eliz Trail, consort of Richd Trail, formerly of Montg Co, Md.

House of Reps: 1-Cmte of the Whole: bill for the relief of W W Wimmer, late postmaster at West Zanesville, Ohio: passed. 2-Bill for the relief of the heirs of the late Col John Hardin: passed.

FRI FEB 20, 1857
Senate: 1-Court of Claims:papers in the case of Rebecca Burdsau: laid on the table. 2-Ptn from Eleonoire Miorton, widow of a citizen of the U S, asking indemnity for the destruction of her husband's property in the city of Mexico in 1823.

Died: on Jan 26, in Indianola, Kansas, after a brief illness, Andrew Johnson, formerly of Wash City, in his 33rd year.

Died: on Feb 19, of consumption, after a long & painful illness, Mrs Lucinda L Smith, in her 51st year. Her funeral will be on Feb 21 at 2 o'clock P M, from her late residence, s w corner of 8th & K sts.

Died: on Feb 18, at his residence [Frankland] near Piscataway, PG Co, Md, after an illness of nearly 2 years of paralysis, Col Richd L Jenkins, in his 66th year.

Augusta, Feb 18. A duel occurred at Savannah on Monday between Danl Elliott & Thos Daniel. Daniel was killed at the first fire.

SAT FEB 21, 1857
25,000 fruit trees at auction on Feb 25, the entire stock of the nursery of the late John H King, near Gtwn. Catalogues can be obtained at the ofc of W Albert King, or of the auctioneer. –Edw S Wright, auct, Gtwn

Having sold my farm, I now offer my bldgs, with 4, 8, or 17 acres of land lying immediately without the Corp line of the thriving village of Warrenton, Va. The house contains 7 rooms. –Sam B Fisher, Warrenton, Va

In the House of Reps on Thu last, 6 distinct reports were submitted by the Select Cmte appointed to investigate certain alleged corrupt combinations of Members of Congress. These separate reports are as follows:
1-Report in the case of Wm A Gilbert, a member from the State of N Y, presented by Mr Henry Winter Davis, of Md.
2-Report in the case of Wm W Welch, a member from the State of Conn, presented by Mr Henry Winter Davis, of Md.
3-Report in the case of Francis S Edwards, a member from the State of N Y, presented by Mr David Ritchie, of Pa.
4-Report in the case of Orsamus B Matteson, a member from the State of N Y, presented by Mr Hiram Warner, of Ga.
5-Views of the minority in the foregoing cases, signed & presented by Mr Wm H Kelsey, of N Y.
6-General report & evidence, as presented by Mr Kelsey, & signed by the entire cmte.

Gilbert: unwritten contract was entered into between the author of a book, F F C Triplett, & the member of Congress, Wm A Gilbert. Resolved, That Wm A Gilbert did cast his vote on the Iowa land bill, depending heretofore before this Congress, for a corrupt consideration, consisting of 7 square miles of land & some stock given or to be given to him. Resolved, That Wm A Gilbert, a member of this House from N Y, be forthwith expelled from the House

Welch: Resolved, That Wm W Welch did corruptly combine with Wm A Gilbert, a member of this House from N Y, to procure the passage of a resolution or bill through this House for the purcase of certain copies of the work of F F C Triplett on the pension & bounty land laws, for a share in the money to be paid to the said Gilbert on its passage. Resolved, That Wm W Welch, a member of this House from Conn, be forthwith expelled from this House.

Edwards: Resolved, That Francis S Edwards, a member of this House from the State of N Y, did, on Dec 23 last, attempt to induce Robt T Paine, a member of this House from the State of N C, to vote contrary to the dictates of his judgment & conscience, on a bill making a grant of lands to aid in the construction of a railroad in the Territory of Minnesota, by holding out a pecuniary consideration to the said Paine for his support of the said bill. Resolved, That the said Francis S Edwards be & he is hereby expelled from this House. [In answer to a question by the cmte, Mr Edwards said he & his brother owned 40 acres in Minnesota Territory, at a point opposite La Crosse, & 17 miles from that point on the way to Milwaukee, some 3,000 acres in Wisc. This is the sum total of the lands owned by them to be benefited by the proposed road.]

Matteson: Resolved, That Orsamus B Matteson, in declaring that a large number of the members of this House had associated themselves together & pledged themselves each to the other not to vote for any law or resolution granting money or lands unless they were paid for it, has falsely & willfully assailed & defamed the character of this House, & has proved himself unworthy to be a member thereof. Resolved, That

Orsamus B Matteson, a member of the House from the State of N Y, be & is hereby expelled therefrom.

Simonton: Resolved, That Jas W Simonton be expelled from the floor of this House as a reporter. –Henry Winter Davis, Jas L Orr, Hiram Warner, David Ritchie [Mr Sweeney who was witness before the House Investigating Cmte is not our fellow-citizen H B Sweeny, of the Wash banking-house of Sweeny, Rittenhouse, Fant & Co, as some at a distance imagine, but a citizen of the interior of the State of N Y.]

Senate: 1-Private bills of which a large number were passed-relief: of Wm Heine; of John T Wright, of the ship **Steamer of America**; of the heirs of Robt McConnell; of Livingston, Kinkead & Co; of Maurice K Simons; of Susannah T Lea, widow of & admx of Jas Maglenen, late of the city of Balt, deceased; of John Rogers; of Thos Rhodes & Jeremiah Austill; of Jas D Johnston; of Geo A O'Brien; of the heirs at law of Abigail Nason, sister & devisee of John Lord, deceased; of Jos C G Kennedy; of Wm L Davidson; of Anton L C Portman; of Eliz Montgomery, heir of Hugh Montgomery; of John Shaw; of Matthew G Emory; of Geo Phelps; of Adam D Steuart & of Alex'r Randall, excs of Danl Randall; of Hiram Paulding; of Cmder Thos J Page, U S navy; of Catharine Jacobs, of the State of N Y; of Henry Hubbard; of Jas G Benton, E B Babbitt, & Jas Longstreet, of the U S army; of Edw Lloyd Winder, lt U S navy; of Lt Joshua D Todd, U S navy; of Michl Kinny, late a private in co I, 8th regt, U S army; of Jeremiah Pendergast, of D C; of the legal reps of Chas Porterfield, deceased; of J Wilcox Jenkins; of John P Brown; of Cranston Laurie; of Wm W Belden, adm of Eenezer Belden; of Maj Benj Alvord, paymaster U S army; & of Mary W Winship, widow of Oscar F Winship. Bill to issue land warrants to Jos Chase, Jas Young, & Alex'r Keef; bill granting bounty land to Mary Felch, widow of Rev Cheever Felch, deceased; bill for the legal reps of John McNiel, deceased, the title of the U S to a certain tract of land; bill authorizing Mrs Jane Smith to enter certain lands in the State of Ala; & bill to confirm the title of Benj E Edwards to a certain tract of land in the Territory of New Mexico. 2-Bills indefinitely postponed: relief of Mary W Thompson, widow of the late Lt Col Alex'r R Thompson, of the U S army; bill making compensation to Geo P Marsh for extraordinary services & expenses on a special mission to the Greek Gov't, & for negotiating a treaty between the Gov't of the U S & Persia; & of the relief of Wm J Appleby, clerk of the supreme & first district court of Utah Territory.

Christ Church, in St John's parish, PG & Chas Counties, Md, destroyed by fire on Christmas eve, is to rise from its ruins at once, enlarged & beautified. The Marlboro Advocate states that $2,500.00, the sum required, has been subscribed.

Mrd: on Feb 17, in the parish church of Chestertown, Kent Co, Md, by Rev Mr Stokes, Hon Wm W Vald, of N Y, to Miss Anna Gordon, eldest daughter of Emory Sudler, of **Locust Hill**, near Chestertown.

Mrd: on Jan 29, in Cadiz, Ky, at the residence of R D Baker, by Elder G P Street, Dr Wm F McReynolds to Miss Rubine, daughter of J W Allen, of Lagrange, Ga.

Mrd: on Feb 10, at Cleveland, King Geo Co, Va, 1st Lt Chas W Field, 2nd Cavalry U S Army, to Miss Monimia Mason, daughter of Roy Mason.

Mrd: on Feb 19, by Rev Mr Register, of the M E Church, Robt S Wharton, of Wash, to Penelope G, widow of the late Hon John Test, of Indiana.

Died: on Feb 20, Mr Thompson Brooke Edwards, in his 25th year. His funeral will take place from the residence of his father, Jas L Edwards, corner of F & 12th sts west, this afternoon at half-past 3 o'clock. [Feb 27th newspaper: Mr Edwards was the son of Col Jas L Edwards, of Wash City; graduated at the Columbia College in Wash City 5 years ago; not long after he emigrated to the West & settled in Joliet, Ill; just 2 months before is death he appeared in perfect health; he returned 5 weeks ago in hope of recruiting his health. The parents of the deceased delighted to dwell on the excellencies he exhibited.]

Died: on Feb 14, at the residence of her father, in Anne Arundel Co, Md, Anna Mary Hall, in her 15th year, eldest daughter of Abasom A & Julia Hall.

Died: on Feb 16, in Winchester, Va, at the residence of her father, Thos B Campbell, Mrs Mary Ellen Wells, wife of Dr Richard A Wells, of Jefferson City, Mo.

Fatal duel at Screven's Ferry, near this city, yesterday, Feb 16, between Danl S Elliott & Thos S Daniel, both citizens of Savannah. The weapons used were rifles, distance 25 paces. We are pained to record the melancholy result. Mr Daniel fell at the first fire & expired immediately, the ball having penetrated his heart.
-Savannah Republican of the 17th.

MON FEB 23, 1857
Executor's sale of a valuable farm: execs of the last will & testament of the late Wm Easby, will sell at public auction, on Mar 17 next, at the auction rooms of J C McGuire: **Chillon Castle Manor**, containing in all 62 acres of land, more or less: with a small frame dwlg house & a large well built & nearly new barn; about 3 miles from the center Market. –Agnes M Easby, Horatio N Easby, John W Easby, excs -J C McGuire, auct

Died: at Louisville, Ky, in his 72nd year, Geo Gilliss, for many years a resident of Wash City. [No death date given-current item.]

For sale, that valuable farm, **Melrose**, containing 190 acres; within 2 miles of Bladensburg, & adjoining the farms of Chas B Calvert, Carrol Stevens, & others. Apply to Pollard Webb, 512 7th st, 2nd story, Wash.

Senate: 1-Introduced: a preamble & resolutions in favor of indemnifying the widow & heirs of Richd Chaney for losses sustained in consequence of the land on which he had settled & made improvements having been wrested from him under an act of Congress. 2-Cmte of Claims: bill for the relief of Jane Smith, of Clermont Co, Ohio: passed. Same cmte: bills passed-relief: of Geo Ashley, adm of Saml Holgate; & for Lucinda Robinson, of Orleans Co, Vt. 3-Cmte on Commerce: memorial of Geo W Fletcher: passed. Same cmte: adverse report on the memorial of Atkins Eldridge. 4-Cmte on Public Lands: bill for the relief of Theresa Dardenne, widow of Abraham Dardenne, deceased, & their children. 5-Cmte on Private Land Claims: bill to provide for the final settlement of the land claim of the heirs of John Underwood, of Fla. 6-Cmte on Pensions: bill for the relief of Jos Bailey, an invalid soldier of the war of 1812: recommended its passage. 7-Cmte on Private Land Claims: bill to authorize the purchase of certain lands belonging to Francis Gardere: recommended its passage. 8-Resolved, That the memorial & papers of the reps of Robt B Carter be withdrawn from the files & referred to the Court of Claims. 9-Bill for the relief of Mary B Winship, widow of Oscar F Winship: passed. [This distinguished ofcr died on the frontier in the discharge of his duty.] 10-Bill to continue a pension to Christine Barnard, widow of Brvt Maj Moses J Barnard, U S Army. The husband of this lady was killed in battle while gallantly defending his country's rights, & the widow was left in a destitute condition, with children to support. Bill passed, so amended as to give her $30 per month. 11-Ptn from A S H White, asking remuneration for his services as superintendent of the bldg occupied by the Interior Dept: referred. 12-Ptn from Fred'k A Beelen, sec of legation to Santiago de Chili, asking that his salary at the time of his appointment may be restored, & that he may be allowed the amount of the reduction made in his pay by the act of Mar, 1855. 13-Cmte on Pensions: bill for the relief of Shadrac Rice, of Jackson Co, Va, reported it back without amendment & recommended its passage.

Obit-died: on Jan 24, 1857, at the residence of Hon Alex Randall, in the city of Annapolis, Mrs Eliz Washington Wirt, relict of the late Wm Wirt, Atty Gen of the U S, in her 73rd year. She was the daughter of Col Robt Gamble, of Richmond, Va, & was born on Jan 30, 1784. In 1802 she was married to Wm Wirt. Two little ones, taken as tender buds; 3 grown children, did Mr Wirt live to follow to the grave. On Feb 18, 1834, his own sacred remains were laid in their last resting place. One after another were beloved ones taken from her, until the parent stem was surrounded by but few of the younger branches. Nor was this all. Sweet & beautiful children were taken away. Until Sep last she was able to pursue the quiet & even tenor of her life. On the 14th she occupied her place in the house of God. On the very next day her last sickness came upon her; long & painful, with no permanent improvement. On Jan 11 her disease increased in violence. On Jan 24 her spirit was borne by the angels, & on Jan 27th we laid her down to rest beside her beloved ones.
–Annapolis Republican

S & H T Noble, with their ladies, have just returned from a short drive of nearly 800 miles to St Paul & Minneapolis, Minn, & back to Dixon. They were about 3 weeks, having good sleighing all the while, with no interruption from storms.
-Dixon [M T] Telegraph, Jan 17

Died: on Feb 21, in Wash City, Howard Carroll, in his 6th year. His funeral will take place from the residence of his father, corner of F & 18th sts west, on Feb 23 at 3 o'clock P M.

Died: on Thu last, in PG Co, Md, Hon Edmund Key, in his 87th year. The deceased was for many years one of the Judges of the Circuit Court, & in all the relations of life was highly esteemed & respected. As a father, friend, & citizen, he was kind, generous, trustworthy, & his memory will be long cherished by those who knew him

Orphans Court of Wash Co, D C. Letters testamentary on the personal estate of Francis Masi, late of Wash Co, deceased. –Vincent Masi, exc

Orphans Court of Wash Co, D C. Letters of administration on the personal estate of John B Floyd, late of Wash Co, deceased. –Isaac Beers, adm

For sale or rent: in consequence of the recent death of Mr Peters, his new 3 story brick house & 2 story frame attached, on D st, between 21st & 22nd sts west, have just been vacated & are now for sale or rent. Apply to Mr Hitz, Swiss Consul Gen, in his ofc, on 7th st; or of Mr E Fuller, who lives near the premises.

The undersigned excs of the last will & testament of Wm Easby, deceased, in conformity with the directions contained in said will, & under & by virtue of the decree of the Circuit Court of D C, sitting in Chancery, supplemental to the decree heretofore passed by said court in a cause, No 1,066, wherein Agnes M Easby is cmplnt, seeking an admeasurement of dower & other relief in equity, & Horatio N Easby, & John W Easby, Henry King & Marian his wife, Cecilia J Hyde, Wm R Smith & Wilhelmina his wife, are dfndnts, will proceed to sell at auction on Mar 17 next, on each successive day thereafter until all are disposed of, numerous parts of parcels of real estate: 54 lots or parts of lots, in Wash. –Agnes M Easby, Horatio N Easby, John W Easby, excs -A Green auct

TUE FEB 24, 1857
Dr Jas L Tyson, who for the past 3 years has filled the chair of Materia Medica & Therapeutics in the Medical College of this city, has resigned his Professorship.
-Phil Journal

The Louisville Courier learns that Thos Cotton, a young man resident of Wash Co, Ky, was shot dead at a house near Springfield about the first of the month. The perpetrator, a young man, fled & has not yet been arrested.

Senate: 1-Ptn from Wm D Nutt, a clerk in the Treasury Dept, asking compensation for extra services. 2-Cmte on Indian Affairs: asked to be discharged from the consideration of the ptn of memorials of the heirs of Wm Reid, of Johnson K Rodgers, of the Legislature Assembly of New Mexico respecting Indian depredations in that Territory, of Hutchinson & other residents of the Stockbridge Indian Reserve: which was agreed to. Same cmte: bill for the relief of Mary Woodell, Eliz Woodell, & others: recommended that it do not pass. 3-Cmte on Pensions: bill for the relief of Jas Huey, deceased, & Jane Huey, his widow, deceased, to be paid to their sold heir, Alex'r B Huey, of Ga: recommended that it do not pass.

In the Circuit Court for PG Co, sitting as a Court of Equity. Isaac Gibson & wife & others, vs Abraham Wingerd, Mgt J Wingerd, Stephen G R Wingerd, Virginia F Wingerd. The object of this suit is to procure a decree for the sale of the real estate of which the late John P Wingerd died seized & possessed. The bill states that a certain John P Wingerd died some time in the year ___, [blank] seized & possessed of a certain tract of land in said county, described in the said bill; that he left a widow surviving him, who has since departed this life, & the following children, his heirs at law, via: Ab S Gibson, wife of Isaac Gibson, Mary E Wingerd, Eliza V Wingerd, Abraham Wingerd, Mgt J Wingerd, Virginia F Wingerd, & Stephen G R Wingerd are non-residents of this State, living in Gtwn, D C, & that the said Mgt J Wingerd, Virginia F Wingerd, & Stephen Geo Rosel Wingerd are minors, under the age of 21 years, & that it would be for the interest of all the parties, dfndnts as well as cmplnts, that the said real estate should be sold & the proceeds of sale distributed amongst the parties. It is therefore, on motion of Shelby Clarke, Solicitor for cmplnts, adjudged & ordered that the cmplnts appear in this Court, in person or by solicitor, on or before the second Mon of Jul next. –Chs J Middleton, clerk of the Circuit Court for PG Co, Md.

Hon E A Maxwell has been appointed Navy Agent at Pensacola, effective Mar 4. The ofc became vacant by the death of Judge Anderson. –Savannah Georgian

Mrd: on Feb 21, in Wash City, by Rev P L Wilson, David H Stick, of Balt, to Laura V, daughter of Geo Davis, of Wash City.

Mrd: on Feb 19, by Rev Alfred Holmead, Mr Jno A Stewart, of Balt, to Miss Josephine, 3rd daughter of Jas S Magee, of Wash City.

Phil, Feb 23. Mr Buchanan will arrive here tomorrow to meet Mr Breckinridge, who is here, & they will proceed to Wash the next day in company with Senator Bigler. [Feb 25th newspaper: Lancaster, Feb 24. Mr Buchanan will not leave here until Monday, when he will be escorted by the Lancaster Fensibles, & will proceed to Wash, via N Y & Balt.]

Died: on Feb 20, in her 65th year, Harriet Rumsey, daughter of the late Maj Abraham Broom, of Wash City.

Shirley Female Institute, Urbana, Fred'k Co, Md: the second term will commence on Feb 1 & close on the last of June. -Geo G Butler, A M, Urbana, Fred'k Co, Md.

A tract of land containing 120 acres for sale: within 3 miles of the Navy Yard Bridge, & adjoining the lands of Messrs Young, Wankowietez, & Capt Gibson. For terms apply to S B Boarman, at the Bank of Wash. Letters to the undersigned at Surratsville, PG Co, Md, will meet with prompt attention. –John H Surratt

WED FEB 25, 1857
Senate: 1-Ptn from Jabez M Woodward, claiming to be the originator of the steam mail service between the Atlantic & Pacific States, & asking that the contract for carrying the mail for the next 10 years from N Y to San Francisco may be awarded to him. 2-Ptn from Oliver E Woods, asking an appropriation to enable him to put his plan for the safe & speedy delivery of letters to a floating population in full operation. 3-Ptn from Albert Boschke, asking that a number of copies of his topographical map of the city of Washington may be purchased for the use of Gov't. 4-Cmte on pensions: recommended the passage of the bills for the relief-of Wm L Oliver; of Isaac P Washburne; of Wm Walton, a soldier of the war of 1812; & granting a pension to Franklin W Armstrong, of Hardin Co, Ky. 5-Cmte on Pensions: adverse report on the ptn of Nancy Fisher, one of the heirs of John & Sarah Chisom. 6-Cmte on Revolutionary Claims: adverse report of the memorial of the heirs of Danl Trueheart, to be indemnified for property destroyed by the enemy during the war of the Revolution. The case has been before Congress for the last 12 or 13 years. Same cmte: adverse report in the case of Nathan P Swan for relief for the services of his father in the Revolution, & asked, in order to save future trouble, that it might also be agreed to; & it was agreed accordingly. 7-Bill for the relief of Whitemarsh B Seabrook & others: referred to the Cmte on Military Affairs. 8-Bill for the relief of Jos Richard, of Berks Co, Pa: postponed.

Cadet Appointments at Large: following Cadet appointments made by the Pres, & appointees are directed to report at West Point between the 1st & 20th of Jun, 1857:
1-Alfred Mordecai, son of an ofcr of the army.
2-John T O'Brien, son of a deceased ofcr of the army.
3-Henry H Humphreys, son of an ofcr of the army.
4-Lawrence S Babbitt, son of an ofcr of the army.
5-Jos P Farley, son of a late ofcr of the army.
6-Benj King, son of a Surgeon of the army.
7-Wm F Niemeyer, nephew of a Surgeon Gen of the army.
8-J Bayard Whittemore, grandson of a navy ofcr.
9-John Lane, son of an ofcr of the Mexican war.
10-Richd M Hill, grandson of a late ofcr of the army.

A late Paris letter says: "The great French painter, Horace Vernet, has left for the U S to execute the contract offered him by the American Congress for the new Capitol at Washington."

The death of Dr Kane, whose fame since his Arctic expedition has become world-wide, took place at Havana on Feb 16. It was an event by no means unexpected. He was a son of Judge Kane of Phil. He was 34 years of age, having been born in Phil in 1822; received his classical education at the Univ of Va & his medical education at the Univ of Pa, where he graduated as a doctor of medicine in 1843.
+
New Orleans, Feb 23. The corpse was brought here on the ship **Cahawba**, & now lies in State at the City Hall. It will be escorted tomorrow by the military on board a steamboat bound to Louisville, & thence to proceed to Phil, where his father, Judge Kane, & family reside. [Mar 11th newspaper: Balt, Mar 10-The remains of Dr Kane arrived at the depot of the Balt & Ohio railroad today, & this afternoon were escorted by an immense procession to the hall of the Md Institute, where they are now lying in State.] [Mar 13th newspaper: Phil, Mar 12. The remains of Dr Kane were interred today. The body was borne by the crew of the exploring brig **Advance**, surrounded by the pall-bearers previously selected. The religious services took place in the Second Presbyterian Church.]

THU FEB 26, 1857
The new Cabinet of the Pres Elect, [Buchanan] is to consist of:
Sec of State: Lewis Cass, of Mich
Sec of Treasury: Howell Cobb, of Ga
Sec of War: John B Floyd, of Va
Sec of Navy: Aaron V Brown, of Tenn
Sec of Interior: Jacob Thompson, of Miss
Postmaster Gen: *Gen: J Glancey Jones, of Pa
Atty Gen: Isaac Toucey, of Conn
*There is a rumor to the effect that Mr Jones having declined the ofc of Postmaster Gen, it has been offered to Mr Wm C Alexander, of N J, who has accepted the compliment.

The Mormon Church has lost one of its main pillars by the sudden death of Jedediah M *_rant, 2nd counselor of Brigham Young, Mayor of the city of Salt Lake, & member elect of the Legislature. He died on Dec 1, at about 40 years of age. [*The paper is creased at this point-could be Grant/Brant.]

Naval: The Navy Dept has received intelligence of the death of Brvt Maj N S Waldron, U S Marine Corps, at Portsmouth, Va, on Feb 21.

Furniture to be sold out to close: A Rothwell, 7th st, next Odd Fellows' Hall.

Senate: 1-Ptn from A G Sloo, asking that authority may be given to the Postmaster Gen to contract with him for carrying the mail across the isthmus of Tehuantepec. 2-Ptn from J W Cochran, asking that he may be allowed an opportunity to exhibit & explain before a cmte of the Senate an improvement invented by him in the construction of wrought-iron tunnels for railways under rivers. 3-Ptn from Bassal D Pinkham, contractor for carrying the mail between Bangor & Calais, in Maine, asking remuneration for losses sustained in the execution of his contract, or that said contract may be canceled. 4-Ptn from L Patterson & others, of Mich, asking the establishment of a mail route from Boston to Greenville, Mich. 5-Ptn from Jos Paul, a soldier of the war of 1812, asking to be allowed a pension. 6-Cmte on Foreign Relations: bill for the relief of Chas S Todd, late Minister of the U S to Russia. 7-Cmte on Pensions: bill for the relief of Sarah A Watson, widow of the late Lt Col Wm H Watson, who was killed at Monterey, Mexico. Same cmte: adverse reports on the following bills-relief: of John Duncan; of Letty Griggs, widow of Simeon Griggs, a Revolutionary soldier; of Albro Tripp; of Isaac Langley; & of Saml McDougal & of Micajah Owen. 8-Cmte on Naval Affairs: bill for the relief of Edw D Reynolds. 9-Cmte on Pensions: adverse report on the bill for the relief of Wm James: indefinitely postponed. Same cmte: adverse report on the bill for the relief of Eliz Martin; & of the ptn of L A Latil. 10-Cmte on the Post Ofc & Post Roads: memorial of Henry L Goodwin, reported a bill in relation to the duties of postmasters

Wanted, an Assist Barkeeper, who can render himself useful, to wait at table & carry dinners out when required. Also, a competent oyster oyster shucker & assist housekeeper, & a competent & qualified cook, & a keeper for the same. Inquire at the bar of the subscriber: J Boulanger, G st, n w of War Dept.

The American Board of Commissioners of Foreign Missions have received the intelligence of the death of Rev Eli Smith, D D, one of their most prominent missionaries in Syria. The deceased had been suffering for a long time with cancer.

Ofc of Chief of Police, Wash, Feb 25, 1857. The owners of <u>Hogs & Geese</u> running at large in Wash City after Feb 26, are informed that the law in relation to such nuisances will be enforced, & the Police ofcrs have been directed to seize all such Hogs & Geese & convey them to the Wash Asylum. –J W Baggott, Chief of Police

Mrd: on Feb 24, at the residence of Capt J H Goddard, in Wash City, by Rev Mr Stanley, Mr B S Nicholl, of PG Co, Md, to Miss Eliza Ellen Pumphrey, of Wash City.

Mrd: on Feb 24, in Wash City, by Rev G D Cummins, Wm A Maury to Bettie H, eldest daughter of Lt M B Maury, U S Navy.

Mrd: on Feb 17, in Balt, at the residence of Caesar A Gantt, by Rev Fr Foley, Geo B Simpson, of Oregon Territory, to Miss Louisa Jane Preuss, of Wash.

Died: on Feb 25, in Wash City, in his 61st year, Jos Welch. His funeral is on Thu at 4 o'clock, from Mr Knott's, 252 G st, near 15th st.

Died: yesterday, in Wash City, Marion Pursell, infant son of Thos H & M Cornelia Havenner. His funeral is this morning at 10 o'clock, without further notice.

Died: last evening, in Wash City, of croup, after a few days' illness, aged 15 months & 6 days, Lucy Lyons, daughter of Mary Frances & Wm J Stone, jr.

FRI FEB 27, 1857
Catalogue sale of valuable books: on Mar 2, by order of the Orphans Court of Wash Co, D C, the private library of the late John B Floyd, comprising about 300 volumes of miscellaneous books, a select library. Also, a large lot of piano, violin, flute, & other music. Terms cash. -A Green auct
+
Sale by order of the Orphans Court of Wash Co, D C: on Feb 28, the personal effects of John B Floyd, deceased: excellent assortment of clothing; trunks; revolving pistol, one of Colt's best, & case complete; superior violin & case & bow complete; 10 very fine new bedsteads; & 6 dozen new chairs. -A Green auct

Eustace Conway, of Fredericksburg, has been elected Judge of the 8th judicial circuit of Va, to succeed Judge Lomax, resigned.

The Reeside claim which has been so long before Congress & the Court of Claims, under the management of its leading counsel, Jos B Stewart, of Ky, was on Thu paid at the Treasury Dept in full, principal & interest. -Star

Sale of elegant furniture, large mirrors, pair of carriage horses, & household & kitchen furniture at auction on: Mar 10, at the residence of Hon Jas Guthrie, on F, between 13th & 14th sts. –C W Boteler, auct

Senate: 1-Cmte on Private Land Claims: bill for the relief of Danl Whitney, without amendment. 2-Cmte on Pensions: bill for the relief of Leonard Lilly: recommended its passage. Same cmte: bill for the relief of Huldah Butler.

The Legislature of Mississippi has declined to grant the request of Richd S Graves, the State treasurer, who became 14 years ago, a defaulter, to be permitted to return to Mississippi, on condition that the pay the State $4,000 a year until the balance against him $45,000, should be liquidated. He has been 14 years an exile in Canada West; says that his head is silvered over with trouble & age, that his wife is gradually sinking into the grave, & all she asks is to return to the South & die.

Mrd: on Feb 24, by Rev P L Wilson, Mr Chas A Sears to Miss Eliza S Mathews, all of Wash City.

Died: on Feb 26, in Wash City, Augusta Matilda Hines, aged 26 years, consort of C M Hines, & daughter of Benj Bohrer. Her funeral will take place from Union Chapel, M E Church, this Fri, at 3 o'clock.

Died: on Feb 25, in Wash City, Wm Joy, in his 46th year, late of Newport, Chas Co, Md, leaving a wife & 5 children to mourn his loss.

Died: on Feb 26, in Wash City, James Buchanan, only son of John F C & the late Mahala Ann Offutt, aged 4 months & 14 days.

Died: on Feb 25, Lucy Lyons Stone, daughter of Mary Frances & Wm J Stone, jr. Her funeral will take place from **Mount Pleasant**, this morning, at 12 o'clock. Hacks will be in waiting at the residence of Dr R K Stone, corner of F & 14th sts.

Died: on Jan 28, in Balt, of scarlet fever, John Bozman Kerr, son of J B Kerr. He was born at the city of Leon, Central America, on Palm Sunday, Mar 20, 1853.

The partnership existing between the undersigned in the renting of Holmes' Island, or Jackson city, has this day been dissolved by mutual consent. –Thos Hughes, Jacob Gooding, Peter Gooding

Orphans Court of Wash Co, D C. Letters testamentary on the personal estate of Arthur Boscow, late of Wash Co, deceased. –Emma Boscow, excx

SAT FEB 28, 1857
Valuable farm in Alexandria Co for sale: by deed of trust from Peter Davis & wife, dated Jul 2, 1855: public auction, the tract of land upon which said Peter Davis now resides, containing about 120 acres, lying about 3 miles from the Long Bridge, in said county. The improvements consist of a good & substantial dwlg house, barn & stabling. –Lawrence B Taylor, trustee

Mrd: on Feb 26, in Wash City, by Rev John C Smith, Mr John T Gettings to Miss Mary Ann Wood, all of Wash City.

Died: in Harmony, Somerset Co, Maine, Capt John Morrill, aged 82 years. He leaves a widow aged 80 years, with a family of 13 children, 9 sons & 4 daughters, to mourn the loss of a kind father. It is doubtful whether any family have ever lived in the U S to so great an age without death in the family circle, the youngest son & child being 35 years of age. [No death date given-current item.]

Died: on Thu last, at Gtwn, D C, Purser Edw Fitzgerald, U S N, the senior Purser in the service, leaving a large circle of relatives & friends to mourn his loss.

Died: on Feb 25, in Wash City, of croup, after a few hours' illness, Mary Sophia Theresa Horstkamp, aged 5 years, 9 months & 9 days.

Senate: 1-Cmte on Pensions: asked to be discharged from the consideration of the ptn of Chas F Buckner: which was agreed to. Same cmte: bill for the relief of Robt H Stevens; & a bill increasing the pension of Danl Denver: recommended their passage. 2-Cmte of Claims: bill for the relief of John B Johnson & Thos Johnson, of the State of Arkansas. 3-House bills passed-relief: of Rebecca Smith; of Geo Schellinger; of Mary Ann Clark; of Thos B Steele, passed assist surgeon of the U S navy; of Lyman N Cook; of Richd Phillips; of the heirs of Saml R Thurston, late delegate from Oregon; of John C McConnell; of Wm Kendall; of Cmder John L Saunders; of Jessie Morrison, of Ill; of C B R Kennerly; of Anthony Devit, late a sgt in the 3rd infty of the U S army; of Israel B Bigelow; of John L Vattier; of Benj R Gantt; of Geo F Baltzell, assignee of Jas P Roan; of Wm Poole; of Henry T Mudd, of Missouri; of John Huff, of Texas; of the heirs of Jacques Godfroy; of Collins Boomer; & of Saml S Haight. 4-Resolution to pay the pension due Parmelia Slavin, late wife of John Blue, deceased, to her administrator: passed. 5-Act to reimburse the estate of Jos McClure, a paymaster in the war of 1812: passed. 6-Resolution allowing Cmder Henry S Hartstene, of the U S navy, Lt S D Tranchard, Master Morrison, & the petty ofcrs & crew of the steamer **Vixen**, to accept certain tokens of acknowledgment from the Govn't of Great Britain: passed.

Application will be made to the Pension Ofc for a duplicate of Land Warrant No 49,465, for 160 acres, paid in favor of Henry Green, on Dec 2, 1856, & sent to the Wash City Post Ofc, to Thos J Williams, which has never come to hand. Persons are hereby warned against receiving the said warrant. –Thos J Williams

MON MAR 2, 1857
Fatal duel: Mr Jacob P Hegnrick, of Columbus, Ga, who was wounded in a duel with Mr O S Kimbrough, of the same place, on Monday, is reported to have died on Tue. It appears that the weapons used were rifles, & they fought at 40 paces distance. Upon the second fire Mr Hegnrick fell mortally wounded.

Senate: 1-Cmte on Commerce: adverse report on the bill for the relief of David Ogden, Andrew Foster, & other ship-owners. 2-Bill for the relief of John Shaw, a soldier of the war of 1812: passed. 3-Bill for the relief of Whitemarsh B Seabrook & others: passed.

From Calif: J R Barton, Sheriff of Los Angeles Co, Wm H Little & Chas R Baker, constables of Los Angeles City, & Chas Daly, a blacksmith, were murdered by a band of robbers near the San Juan hills, about 60 miles from Los Angeles, on the 23rd ult, whom they had gone out to arrest. The robbers were some 50 strong.

In Semken's Jewelry Store, on Pa ave, between 9th & 10th sts, may be seen a genuine & somewhat amusing relic of the babyhood of Govn'r Hancock, which every antiquary should go to see. It is nothing else than the identical baby's rattle shaken & bitten by the infant Govn'r in 1737-shaken by the same hand that wrote John Hancock so bodly in the Declaration of Independence. We observe it is on sale; & it certainly would be a choice addition to any collection of relics, even our Nat'l Gallery.

Died: on Feb 28, in Wash City, Mrs Sarah Holmead, relict of the late Anthony Holmead, sr, in her 82nd year. Her funeral will be today at 2 o'clock, from the residence of J D James, 288 F st, between 12th & 13th sts.

Died: on Feb 27, in Wash City, Henrietta Stewart, in her 87th year, wife of the late Reizin Stewart, of Balt City.

House of Reps: 1-Memorial of Empson Hamilton, praying that a pension may be granted him in consequence of wounds received in the privateer service during the war of 1812. 2-Memorial of Dr Henry Kalufsowski, for an exchange of books with 4 Polish libraries.

I offer my farm & country seat for sale, situated on the heights of Gtwn, adjoining the residences of Mrs Barnard, Mrs Morton, Mrs Boyce, Messrs Linthicum, Adler, & Eliason, containing 40 acres of land, improved with a frame dwlg, gardner's house, cow & horse stable. –Henry Gildemeister

Something new. The only silver manufactory in Wash. I am now just finishing some very fine standard Silver Ware. Please call at 338 Pa ave, sign of the Large Spread Eagle. –H O Hood

Orphans Court of Wash Co, D C. Letters of administration on the personal estate of Jos Welch, late of Wash Co, deceased. –John Welch, adm

Orphans Court of Wash Co, D C. In the case of Isaac Beers, adm of Seth M Leavenworth, deceased, the administrator & Court have appointed Mar 24 next, for the final settlement of the personal estate of said deceased, of the assets in hand. –Ed N Roach, Reg/o wills

TUE MAR 3, 1857
Mr Buchanan, Pres Elect, arrived last evening in the Northern train of cars. He is now at the Nat'l Hotel in excellent health & spirits. Mr Breckenridge, the Vice Pres elect, has not yet arrived.

Mrd: on Feb 24, in Wash City, by Rev Wentworth L Childs, Wm T Keneman to Emily Rowland, both of PG Co, Md.

The **Blue Ridge Tunnel**, on the Va central railroad, is completed, but we do not learn that the railroad track through it is yet laid. Length of tunnel 4,284 feet; dimensions of section, 21 feet high & 16 feet wide; dimensions arched, 700 feet; cubic contents, 50,000 yards; cubic contents per lineal foot, 11.7; cubic yards masonry laid, 2,750; inclination of grade, 70 feet per mile; total cost, $464,000; cost per foot, $108.31; total cost per cubic yard, $8,80; cost for excavation alone, $6.50; time of construction, 7 years. The usual force employed upon this work was 200 men & 15 horses. The work proceeded night & day, the men being relieved every 8 hours. There are no shafts, as it is 700 feet below the top of the ridge.

Senate: 1-Cmte on Pensions: bill for the relief of the heirs of Mary Hooker: recommended that it pass. Same cmte: adverse report on the House bill granting a pension to Martha Elliott, widow of Saml Elliott, a soldier of the war of 1812. Same cmte: adverse reports on the following ptns: of Sarah Ann Roose; of Geo V Vandirer; & of Sarah S Hine. Same cmte: bill for the relief of John Drant: reported it back without amendment. 2-Bill from the House to authorize the issue of a register to the barque Ann Elizabeth was read & passed.

Notice: To all whom it may concern that the Levy Court for Wash Co, D C, intend surveying & laying out a county Road near to & along the northern line of the tract of land claimed by the heirs & reps of the late Chas J Queen, lying in said county, which part so intended to be surveyed & laid out extends from the eastern line of Mrs Ann McDanniel, & the west end of the road left by will for the use of the congregation of Queen's Chapel. In case any owner of said land through which said Road will pass shall require compensation therefore, he or she shall within 2 weeks after Apr 14, 1857, apply to the Levy Court, who may agree with him, her, or them for the purchase thereof. –Geo McNeir, Geo W Riggs, Jas A Kennedy, Cmte on the part of the Levy Court.

Sale of valuable real estate in PG Co & Anne Arundel Co, Md. In execution of powers contained in a deed of trust, dated Nov 19, 1855, recorded in Liber N H G, No 5, folios 128, of the land record books for Anne Arundel Co, & Liber C S M, No 1, folios 30, of the land records of PG Co, from Margaretta Nicols & R Nicols Snowden to the undersigned, who is prepared to offer for sale *Fairland Estate*, on which said Margaretta now resides, containing nearly 1,200 acres of land. This land has been recently surveyed & platted by John Duvall, & divided into Farms & Lots to suit the views of almost every class of purchasers. On the home farm is a large brick dwlg, nearly new, a large barn, a 2 story dwlg for a manager, & other suitable out houses in good repair. Private sale up to Mar 25, & if not sold, will be offered at public auction. –Frank H Stockett, Annapolis, Md [Jul 7th newspaper: *Fairland Estate*, on which Snowden resides, is advertised at private sale up to Jul 24.]

Valuable Table:
1607: Va settled by the English
1614: N Y settled by the Dutch
1624: Massachusetts settled by the Puritans
1628: Delaware settled by Swedes & Finns
1633: Connecticut settled by the Puritans
1635: Maryland settled by Irish Catholics
1636: Rhode Island settled by Roger Williams
1659: North Carolina settled by the English
1670: South Carolina settled by the Huguenots
1682: Pennsylvania settled by Wm Penn
1782: Georgia settled by Gen Oglethorpe
1791: Vermont admitted into the Union
1792: Kentucky admitted into the Union
1796: Tennessee admitted into the Union
1802: Ohio admitted into the Union
1811: Louisiana admitted into the Union
1816: Indiana admitted into the Union
1817: Mississippi admitted into the Union
1818: Illinois admitted into the Union
1819: Alabama admitted into the Union
1820: Maine admitted into the Union
1821: Missouri admitted into the Union
1836: Michigan admitted into the Union
1836: Arkansas admitted into the Union
1845: Florida admitted into the Union
1845: Texas admitted into the Union
1846: Iowa admitted into the Union
1848: Wisconsin admitted into the Union
1850: California admitted into the Union

For sale: the splendid farm formerly owned by Jno C McKelden, containing 116 acres, lying on the Rockville turnpike, 4 miles from Gtwn, D C: with 2 dwlg houses, 4 barns, granary, ice house, carriage & wood house. Apply to Dr O A Daily, 352 Pa ave, Wash City; or of A Curtis, on the premises.

<u>Criminal Court-Wash: Grand Jury:</u>

Peter Force	Thos Berry	Richd Jones
Stanislaus Murray	Benedict J Semmes	Hamilton
Chas L Coltman	Easu Pickrell	Loughborough
Selby Scaggs	Edw C Dyer	Robt Bell
Jos Bryan	Wm F Bayly	Robt White
Valentine Harbaugh	Peter F Bacon	Jas B Dodson
Chas H Wiltberger	Saml Drury	Wm R Riley

Jonathan T Walker
Petit Jury:

Michl Coombs	Jas Barnard	Jno Knight
Bernard Brien	Reuben Browne	Kno S Wiltberger
Jas Lusby	John S Devlin	Edw F Brown
Thso B Brown	Francis Murphy	Edw Tolson
Thos R Brightwell	Braxton B Jeffries	John Scrivenner
Edwin Knowles	Rich B Owens	Elijah Edmondston
Chas Fitman	Geo D Spencer	Jas Hull
Thos Cornack	Wm a Kennedy	Jno M Thornton
Henry Thorn	Geo B Smith	Terence Drury
David Fowble	Geo W Bray	Thos Riggles

Died: on Mar 1, in Wash City, Mrs Frances Bebb, widow of the late Capt Thos Bebb, formerly of Fredericksburg, Va, in her 74th year. Her funeral will be from the residence of H H Hazard, on N st west, between 14th & 15th sts, today at 3 o'clock.

WED MAR 4, 1857
House of Reps: 1-Cmte on Military Affairs: bill for the relief of Emily R Hoe, widow of Capt Hoe, who died of disease contracted in the service: passed. 2-Cmte of the Whole: bill for the relief of Geo Chorpenny, jr: passed. 3-Bill for the relief of Jefferson Wilson, adm, with the will annexed, of John F Wray, deceased: passed. 4-Mr Trafton, of Mass, moved a suspension of the rules to obtain the consideration of the resolution for the relief of J W Aye, assignee of Peter Bargy,jr, & Hugh Stewart; which motion was negatived. 5-Cmte on Military Affairs: bill for the relief of Capt Alex'r Montgomery, assist quartermaster in the U S Army: passed. 6-Cmte on Invalid Pensions: bill for the relief of Martin Jewell, of Ky: passed. 7-Bill for the relief of J H F Thornton, Lawrence Taliaferro, & Hay T Taliaferro, sureties of D M F Thornton, late a purser in the U S Navy: passed. 8-Resolution allowing Cmder Henry J Hartstene, of the U S Navy, Lt S D Trenchard, Master Morrison, & the petty ofcrs & crew of the steamer **Vixen**, to accept certain tokens of acknowledgment from the Gov't of Great Britain: passed. 9-Cmte of the Whole: bill for the relief of Jos Graham: passed. 10-Bill for the relief of Jas D Johnston: passed. 11-Bill for the relief of Marten Fenwick: passed. 12-Bill for the relief of the heirs of Alex'r Stevenson, a soldier of the Revolutionary war: passed. 13-Cmte of the Whole: bills for the relief of Thos Rhodes & Jeremiah Austill; of Moses Noble; of Mathew G Emery; of Collier H Minge; Philip T Ellicott; & Lucretia Brodie, admx of Chas Brodie: passed. Same cmte: bill to confirm to Chas Waterman his title to certain lots in Milwaukie, Wisc: passed.

On Mon the clerk in a drug store in Oswego, by mistake gave poison for medicine, which resulted in the death of a child of J B Wallace, to whom it was administered.

Senate: 1-Cmte on Pensions: bill for the relief of Amos Oney, a Revolutionary soldier, submitted an adverse report on the same. Same cmte: adverse report on the ptn of Mgt McClure. Same cmte: increase of pension to Isaac Phillips; & relief of the children & heirs of Levi & Mary Stone; relief of Geo Bond; & relief of Richd L Murray, a soldier of the Seminole war in 1818: recommended their passage. Same cmte: adverse report on the bill for the relief of Robinson Gammon. Same cmte: bill for the relief of Ames Armstrong, of Ohio; relief of Danl Wacaser; of Claiborn Vaughn; & of Sampson Hays, a soldier in the Mexican war. 2-Bill for the relief of Joshua Knowles, jr, & others, owners of the schnr **Garnet**, of Truro: referred. 3-Act for the benefit of John W Cox: referred. 4-Cmte on Foreign Relations: adverse report on the memorial of J G Tucker. 5-Cmte on Commerce: bill for the relief of Townsend Harris. Same cmte: adverse report on the memorial of Edmund W Holmes & others, asking that a register may be issued for the British-built vessel **Lee**. 6-Cmte on Revolutionary Claims: adverse report on the memorial of Jacob Schenck. Same cmte: asked to be discharged from the consideration of the memorial of Jos Holman: which was agreed to. 7-Cmte of Claims: bill for the relief of the legal reps of John D Kerr, deceased. 8-Bill for the relief of Wm Burdell, Saml Medary, & Wm T Martin, adms of the estate of Edgar Gale, deceased: referred.

Walter Crook, jr, 220 Balt st, Balt, Md: Upholstery & Furniture Establishment.

Mrd: on Mar 2, by Rev J R Eckard, John T Clements, jr, to Miss Mary S Brush, all of Wash City.

House of Reps: 1-Cmte on Indian Affairs: bill for the relief of John Ryley, an Indian of the State of Michigan: passed. 2-Cmte of the Whole: discharged from the consideration of the bill for the relief of Mrs Mary Gay: read a third time & passed.

THU MAR 5, 1857
Died: Mar 4, in Wash City, Owen Bestor, in his 45th year, after a short illness. His funeral will take place on Fri at 3 o'clock P M, from his late residence on G st, between 12th & 13th sts.

Senate: 1-House bills disposed of-relief: of Robt Davis; Mark & Richd H Bean, of Arkansas; of Matthew G Emery; of Collier H Minge, Philip T Ellicot, & Lucretia A Brodie, admx of Chas Brodie; of Thos Rhodes & Jeremiah Austin; of Moses Noble; of Henry Steuart; of Betsey Nash; of Shadrac Rice, of Jackson Co, Va; of Jos Bailey, an invalid soldier of the war of 1812; of Benj W Smithson; of Jos Irish, Wm Sturgis, & Bartholomew Baldwin; of Jos M Kennedy; of Isaac Swain; of the children of Jas Phelps, a Revolutionary soldier; of Chas Parrish, a soldier of the war of 1812; of Chas Cassady; of the heirs of Wm Easby, deceased; of the surviving children of John Gilbert, a Revolutionary soldier; of the surviving children of Sarah Van Pelt, widow of John Van Pelt, a Revolutionary soldier; of Wm L Oliver; of Isaac P Washburne; of Wm Walton, a soldier of the war of 1812; of Leonard Lilly; of Robt H Stevens;

of the children & heirs of Levi & Mary Stone; of Geo Bond; of Richd J Murray, a soldier in the Seminole war of 1818; of Anne Armstrong, of Ohio; of Danl Wacaser; of Claiborne Vaughn; & of Sampson Hays, a soldier in the war with Mexico. Act for the benefit of Robt S Wimberly; confirm Chas Waterman his title to certain lots in Milwaukee, Wisc; pension to Franklin W Armstrong, of Hardin Co, Ky; & increase of pension to Isaac Philips. 2-House bills postponed indefinitely-relief: of Robinson Gammon; of the heirs of Amos Aneya, a Revolutionary soldier; of Isaac Langley; of Letty Griggs, widow of Simeon Griggs, a Revolutionary soldier; of Albro Tripp; of Roxana Kimball; of Thos Jenkins; of Antoine Robedeau; of Mary Woodbury, Elisha Odell, & others; & of John Duncan. An act granting a pension to Martha Elliott, widow of Saml Elliott, a soldier of the war of 1812: postponed.

Inauguration ceremonies yesterday signalized the Inauguration of Jas Buchanan, 15th Pres of the U S. No public pageant was ever favored with a more propitious sky. The city was astir at an earlier hour than usual; by 9 o'clock all the avenues & streets leading to & from Wash City were alive with vehicles, horsemen, & pedestrians tending to a common center. About 11 o'clock the military halted at Willard's Hotel, where Pres Pierce & the Pres Elect were to join them. The procession arrived at the north end of the Capitol. The oath of ofc was administered by Hon Jas M Mason, Pres of the Senate pro tempore, to the Hon John C Breckenridge, Vice Pres elect. The Pres & Pres Elect proceeded to the platform erected on the eastern portico of the Capitol. The Pres Elect commenced his Inaugural Address. At the conclusion of his address, he turned towards the Chief Justice of the Supreme Court, who administered the oath of ofc, the Pres reverently kissing the book. After the Pres had reached his official residence, the doors were thrown open to the vast multitudes of people of both sexes who were in attendance, & with the Pres exchanged friendly greetings with all who presented themselves for introduction.

FRI MAR 6, 1857
Mr Roger A Pryor, lately of Richmond, Va, proposes to publish a daily & semi-weekly paper in that city entitled The South. Mr Pryor, though quite a young man, has acquired prominence in the editorial ranks.

The Inauguration Ball on Wed evening, for magnitude & splendor, eclipsed every thing of the kind that ever preceded it. The grand saloon in Judiciary Square, was built for the festival. The people were there, their wives & daughters, as fair, as gay, as happy as the occasion could made them. Pres Buchanan appeared accompanied by Senator Jones, of Tenn, & Cmdor Lavallette, commandant of the Wash navy yard. Mr Breckenridge, the Vice Pres, was attended by Mayor Magruder. Ex-Pres Pierce also honored the occasion with his presence. The Pres stayed about an hour, & left soon after midnight.

Ex-Pres Pierce on Wed removed his family to the residence of ex-Sec of State Marcy, designing to bid Washinton farewell so soon as his arrangements & weather will permit him to proceed North with his wife. –Star

Mrd: on Mar 4, by Rev Andrew G Carothers, Mr Geo A C Smith, of N H, to Miss Eliza A Robinson, daughter of Capt J G Robinson, of Wash City.

Mrd: on Mar 5, in Wash City, by Rev John C Smith, Mr Henley Piper to Miss Emma A Hickman, all of Wash City.

Mrd: on Dec 30, 1856, in Phil, by Rev Geo A Latimer, Mr Jas G Nokes, of Wash City, to Marienne, eldest daughter of John S Slade.

Died: on Mar 5, Mrs Ann Eliza Crossfield, widow of the late Jehiel Crossfield, in her 63rd year. Her funeral will be from 478 9th st, between D & E sts, at 3½ o'clock this afternoon.

Died: on Mar 5, in Wash City, after a protracted illness, Sarah C Gallagher, in her 20th year. Her funeral will take place at 9½ o'clock on Mar 7, from the residence of her brother-in-law, John Wise, corner of 4½ & C sts, Island.

SAT MAR 7, 1857
The new Cabinet of Pres Buchanan:
Sec of State: Lewis Cass, of Mich
Sec of Treasury: Howell Cobb, of Ga
Sec of Interior: Jacob Thompson, of Miss
Sec of War: John B Floyd, of Va
Sec of Navy: Isaac Toucey
Postmaster Gen: Aaron V Brown, of Tenn
Atty Gen: Jeremiah S Black, of Pa

At Bangor last week a man named Curran was sentenced to the State prison for life for setting fire to the barn of Abraham A Lewis, of Orono, it being connected with a dwlg house in which were a family.

While at Balt on Mar 4, on his way to attend the Inauguration, Mr Saml Butterworth, the Superintendent of the Branch Mint in N Y, was severely wounded by the accidental discharge of a pistol in the overcoat pocket of his friend & traveling companion, Isaac V Fowler, Postmaster of N Y C. The weapon went off as Mr Fowler was taking off his coat, & the ball entering Mr Butterworth's thigh ranged upwards. Though but a flesh wound it is said to be severe.

Three days from Europe. Earl of Ellesmere died at Bridgewater House on Feb 18.

The merchants of Alexandria, in Corn Exchange assembled, having recently lost a valued friend & brother merchant in the sudden death of David Hume. We deeply sympathize with the family & friends of the deceased. The Mayor of Alexandria had a meeting on Mar 2, 1857, in regard to the death of the late fellow-citizen. Mr Geo P Wise was called to the chair & Mr Edgar Snowden, jr, appointed sec. Resolved, That in the death of David Hume, who fell by the hands of Doddridge C Lee, a clerk in the Pension Ofc in Wash City, whilst vindicating his character from a foul & false charge in the most forbearing & honorable spirit, this community is called upon to mourn the loss of one of her most useful, upright, & honorable citizens; & that we denounce & deplore the fatal act which had hurried to an untimely grave, in the prime of life, a man endeared to us all by his noble & generous qualities. A copy of the proceedings to be forwarded to his family.

MON MAR 9, 1857
The following List of Acts passed at the late Session of Congress has been carefully prepared & is believed to be entirely correct: 1-For the relief of: Geo K McGunnelge, surviving partner of the late firm of Hill & McGunnegle, of St Louis, Mo.
2-Heirs of the late Col John Hardin
3-Mrs Charlotte Turner, of Louisiana
4-Jas P Fleming, of Augusta, Ga
5-Sureties of Danl Winslow
6-Mary B Winship, widow of Oscar F Winship
7-Capt Thos Duncan, U S Army
8-Legal reps of Edmund H McCabe, assignee of Antoine Soullard.
9-Heirs of Maj Gen Arthur St Clair
10-Surviving children of Sarah Crandall, deceased.
11-Heirs or legal reps of Jeremiah Bryan
12-Brvt Maj Jas Belger, U S Army
13-Lt John Guest, U S Navy, & others
14-Jonathan Painter, a black man, a spy in the war of 1812
15-Thos J Churchill, late a lt in the 1st Ky regt of volunteers
16-Anthony Devit, late a sgt in the 3rd artl U S Army
17-Geo F Baltzell, assignee of Jas P Roan
18-Heirs of Saml R Thurston, late delegate from Oregon
19-Mary B Winship, widow of Oscar F Winship
20-John Shaw, a soldier in the war of 1812
21-Emilie R Hooe, of Prairie du Chien, Wisc
22-Wm Walton, a soldier of the war of 1812
23-John Ryley, an Indian of the State of Michigan
24-Adam D Steuart & Alex'r Randall, exc of Danl Randall
25-Capt Alex'r Montgomery, an assist quartermaster in the U S Army
26-Wm W Belden, adm of Ebenezer Belden
27-Jefferson Wilson, adm with the will annexed of John F Wray, deceased.
28-John B Rose, of Wabash Co, Indiana

29-Increase pension of Danl Denver
30-Collier H Minge, Philip T Ellicot, & Lucretia A Brodie, admx of Chas Brodie
31-Act relinquishing the claim of the U S to certainproperty of which Elijah King died seized & possessed in D C upon certain specified conditions
32-J H F Thornton, Lawrence Taliaferro, & Hay T Taliaferro, sureties of D M F Thornton, late a purser in the U S Navy
33-Surviving children of John Gilbert, a Revolutionary soldier
34-Confirm Chas Waterman his title to certain lots in Milwaukee, Wisc.
35-Surviving children of Jas Phelps, a Revolutionary soldier
36-Jos Irish, Wm Sturgis, & Bartholomew Baldwin
37-Surviving children of Sarah Van Pelt, wid/o John Van Pelt, a Revolutionary soldier
38-Sampson Hays, a soldier in the Mexican war
39-Pension due Parmelia Slavin, late wide of John Blue, deceased, to her administrator Whitemarsh B Seabrook & others
40-Richd J Murray, a soldier in the Seminole war of 1818
41-Shadrac Rice, of Jackson Co, Va
42-Heirs of Wm Easby, deceased
43-Jos Bailey, an invalid soldier of the war of 1812
44-Chas Parrish, a soldier of the war of 1812
45-Thos B Steele, passed assist surgeon of the U S Navy
46-Jededicah H Lathrop & his securities
47-Settle the claim of Wm Cary Jones for certain services
48-Accepting portrait of John Hampden, presented to Congress by John McGregor.
49-Jared L Elliott-granted bounty land
50-Wm Burdell, Saml Medary, & Wm T Martin, adm of estate of Edgar Gale, deceased.
51-Increase pension to Isaac Phillips
52-To reimburse the estate of Jos McClure, a paymaster in the war of 1812
53-Act in addition to certain acts granting bounty land to certain ofcrs & soldiers who have been engaged in the military service of the U S to the ofcrs & soldiers of Maj David Bailey's btln of Cook Co, Ill, volunteers.

54-Heirs of Jacques Godfroy
55-Brvt Capt Fred'k Steele, U S Army
56-Geo Schellinger
57-Lyman N Cook
58-Mary Ann Clark
59-Wm Kendall
60-Jesse Morrison, of Ill
61-Donn Piatt
62-Wm L Davidson
63-Tarrance Kirby
64-John C McConnell
65-Benj W Gantt
66-Richd Phillips
67-Wm Poole
68-Israel B Bigelow
69-Saml S Haight
70-John L Vattier
71-John Hugg, of Texas
72-Henry T Mudd, of Mo
73-Collins Boomer
74-Martin Millett, of Iowa
75-John Mitchell, of D C

76-John H Horne
77-Jas Harrington
78-Peter Grover
79-Hannah F Niles
80-A S Bender
81-J Randolph Clay
82-Sally T Matthews
83-Amos B Corwine
84-Wm Craig
85-Dr Jas Morrow
86-Ransdell Pegg
87-Geo W Torrence
88-Chas L Denman
89-Cmder John L Saunders
90-John Drout
91-Dolly Empson
92-Mrs Mary Gay
93-Jas D Johnston
94-Adam D Stewart
95-Jos Graham
96-Martin Fenwick
97-Thos Crown
98-John W Cox
99-Geo Chorpenning, jr
100-Jonathan Cilley
101-Betsey Nash
102-Robt Davis
103-Robt H Stevens
104-Geo Bond
105-Mark & Richd H Bean
106-Thos M Newell
107-Danl Wacaser
108-Isaac P Washburne
109-Jos M Kennedy
110-Robt S Wimberly
111-Claiborne Vaughn
112-Henry Stewart
113-Leonard Lilly
114-Wm L Oliver
115-Geo Cassady
116-Benj W Smithson
117-Mary Hooker
118-Matthew G Emery
119-Isaac Swain
120-Thos Rhodes & Jeremiah Austill
121-Barton Jewell, of Ky
122-Amos Armstrong, of Ohio

Capt C L Killburn, of the U S Army, has been appointed Indian agent in Florida, vice Capt J C Casey, deceased.

On Thu evening a delegation of 6 Delaware Indians arrived here from Kansas, on business with the Indian Bureau. They took up their lodgings at Mr Maher's Hotel. The next afternoon one of them, Jem Shewannuc, aged about 50 years, died. He had been sick for nearly a year.

Died: on Mar 7, in Wash City, Mrs Eliza M Wilson, wife of Jos S Wilson. She was an exemplary Christian & discharged all the duties of wife & mother to the last moment of life. Her funeral will be from the residence of her husband, 455 13th st, on Mar 11, at 2 o'clock.

Died: on Mar 7, in his 3rd year, Andrew, the 4th child of Edw M & Jane S Clark.

Farm for sale: 100 acres of land, lying about half a miles from the Little Fall's Bridge, across the Potomac river, 4 miles from Wash; improved by a new frame dwlg house, well built. The Farm is in Fairfax Co, Va, convenient to both Gtwn & Washington markets. Apply to B Bayliss, Real Estate Agent.

TUE MAR 10, 1857

Household & kitchen furniture & piano-forte, at auction on: Mar 16, at the residence of A Bennett, 360 north D, between 9th & 10th sts west. –A Green auct

Appointments by the Pres:
Saml Treat to be Judge of the U S Court for the eastern [new] district of Missouri.
M M Parsons to be U S Atty for the western district of Missouri.
Thos H Duval to be Judge of the U S Court for the western district of Texas.
Wm C Young to be marshal of the U S for the western district of Texas.
Richd B Hubbard to be U S Atty for the same district.
Jas L Jones, of Missouri, to be U S Marshal for the western district of Missouri.

John Wentworth was elected Mayor of Chicago on Tue last by 1,100 majority.

The Arctic dog brought home by Dr Kane has strayed away off in Allegany. He has become the property of Jas McArthur, timber dealer in Oramel. The recently cold weather has kept this large black, shaggy animal in high spirits. Mr McArthur calls him Eskimo [Esquimaux] not a very smooth name, but charactistic. To look Esk in the face you see almost a likeness of a black bear. –Newark [N J] Advertiser

Four murderers escaped from the Michigan penitentiary during the night of Mar 2. They dug themselves out around a large pipe that ran through their cells. Handbills have been issued offering a reward of $2,000 for their arrest & return, or $200 for any one of them. They are described as follows:
Saml Ulum, 45 years old, 5 feet 7½ inches high, two toes of each foot, next the big toe, grown together, stout built.
Gabriel Lappan, 40 years old, light complexion, 5 feet 3½ inches high, a scar in India ink on the right hand, stout built.
John M Reynolds, left arm crooked, scar on back of right wrist, scar over left eye, on back of left thumb, & a large scar on right instep, 30 years old, 6 feet half inch high.
Fred'k Haynes, 30 years old, 5 feet 10½ inches high, scar on right leg.

Rev John Howard, the pastor of the Presbyterian Church at Woodstock, Va, recently exhibited decided symptoms of insanity, & was taken to the asylum at Staunton, where he committd suicide soon after his arrival.

Mollie Jennings died recently in Pittsylvania Co, Va, at the age of 107 years. She was a grown woman before the declaration of independence. There died at Laurens Co, Ga, on Dec 22, Mrs Pilate, aged 116 years. She was a wife during the Revolution.

Died: on Mar 7, in Gtwn, of typhoid fever, Saml Groom Osborn, eldest son of the late Wm McK Osborn, age 19 years.

Died: on Feb 15, at **Fort Reiley**, Kansas Territory, Lt Arthur Donaldson Tree, of the U S Dragoons. Lt Tree, at an early age, imbibed a passion for military life, & has been in the dragoon service about 20 years. His saddle was his rocking chair, the prairies his parlor, the chapperal his bed-chamber, & the untrodden forest his hunting park. He won his way successively through subordinate grades to the rank of a commissioned ofcr upon his merit alone. He was in every battle in the Mexican war except one, & was wounded in his bridle arm at Milino del Rey. Lt Tree has left a large circle of friends & relatives in Wash City.

Obit-died: The announcement of the decease of Mrs Eliza M Wilson, wife of Jos S Wilson, of the Gen Land Ofc, has been received by the people of this community with more than ordinary interest & concern, for there are few to whom this lady was not known & endeared by the remembrance of the many qualities that so richly adorned her life.

Obit-died: The steamship **Persia** brings the sad news of the death of Sir Francis Egerton, Earl of Ellesmere, whose visit to this country in the summer of 1853, as one of the Queen's Commissioners, is fresh in the memory of our citizens. We believe that the first public speech he made in this country was made at the festival of the Boston school children, in Faneuil Hall, Jun 26, 1853. The degree of Dr of Laws was conferred upon him by Harvard college, at the Commencement, Jul 20, 1853. He was in his 57th year of his age. –Boston Daily Advertiser

Masonic: Hiram Lodge No 10 meeting this evening at 7 o'clock. –Wm H Dietz, sec

The Boston papers refer to an aged couple residing in Middleboro, Mass who are supposed to be the longest married of any State. They have lived together 75 years, having been respectively 20 & 17 years of age when married. The gentleman's name is Moses Thompson, a merchant.

For sale: 100 acres of **Mount Pleasant**, including $2/3^{rds}$ of the front line on Boundary st, the dwlg & 24 acres having been reserved. Address W J Stone, sen, **Mount Pleasant**, Wash City.

WED MAR 11, 1857

First class residence at public auction: on Mar 20, on the premises, that superior & commodious dwlg lately occupied by Ruel Keith: the lot fronts 60 feet on Dunbarton st, near Congress, & runs back 120 feet. There are beautiful horse-chestnut trees on the front lot. –Barnard & Buckey

The Naval Court of Inquiry yesterday disposed of the case of Lt Lawrence Pennington, being the first case on its calendar. The decision of the Court is not yet known. The next case in order is that of Lt R W Meade.

Four brothers, sons of Mr Lawson McCloud, of Barrington, Ill, were returning from school, when the eldest aged 13 broke through the ice of a slough; the next eldest, aged 11, went to bring assistance, & also broke through; then the next, aged 9 followed, & likewise broke through. The youngest boy then ran for his father, but when he returned all 3 of the boys were drowned.

Lewis Ellen, of Fauquier Co, Va, had the misfortune to break his leg just above the ankle, in Wash City, on Inauguration day. He was coming down one of the slopes in the Capitol grounds, when he slipped & fell. –Alex Gaz

Criminal Court-Wash-Monday. The trial of Jas Keilay, on the charge of mayhem in having deprived Wm Ready of an eye in Oct last: not guilty.

For sale, by virtue of distrain for rent due & in arrears by L R Peck to F Dodge, [Guardian,] & to me directed, I have levied & distrained upon one carpenter shop, on G st, between 9th & 10th sts, known as lot 2, in square 373, Davidson's subdivision, in Wash City, to satisfy the said rent due & in arrears. Sale, for cash, on Mar 13, on the premises. –A E L Keese, Bailiff

THU MAR 12, 1857
Senate: 1-Saml W Lecompt has leave to withdraw his memorial & papers. 2-Papers in relation to the claim of Wm A Cameron to be taken from the files & referred to the Cmte of Claims.

Superior household & kitchen furniture, family carriage, buggy, harness, & horse at auction on: Mar 17, at the residence of Gov Fish, on H st, between 17th & 18th sts. -Jas C McGuire, auct

Gen Pierce, accompanied by Mr Sidney Webster, left Wash City yesterday to visit his old friend in Va, Hon Mr Taylor, of Caroline. He returns to Wash on Thu. -Union

Obit-died: from the Fayetteville Observer of Mar 9. Dr Benj Robinson departed this life at **Monticello**, his residence in this vicinity, yesterday at the ripe old age of 81 years, of which about 52 had been spent here in the practice of his profession & in the performance of the various duties of a patriotic & public spirited citizen & magistrate. He was a skilful physician & surgeon; as a magistrate, an unflinching supporter of law & order. His faculties were providentially preserves. Within the last 10 days he had gone his daily rounds. A severe attack of sickness prostrated him about 6 days ago. Dr Robinson was formerly of this town & marshal of the U S for Florida. In 1825 he was appointed by Mr Adams one of 3 com'rs to treat with the Southern Indians. He was born at Bennington, Vt, Feb 11, 1776, & removed permanently to Fayetteville about 1804.

Gen Felix Huston, one of the leaders of the Texan revolution, died a few days ago at Washington, Mississippi, in his 57th year.

Died: on Feb 21, in Berryville, Clarke Co, Va, Dr Saml Taylor, aged 82 years. He was a native of Dover, Dela, & settled as a practitioner of medicine in Berryville in 1796, & with only a short interval he has been a resident of that village ever since.

For rent, the residence at present occupied by Hon Jas Thorington, 486 11th st, between E & F sts; with all modern improvements. Apply on the premises.

Bailiff's sale: by an order of distress, & to me directed, for house rent due & in arrears by P G Murray to John Sinon: sale of furniture & sundry items, on Mar 17, on the premises, known as part of the Murray House, or formerly as the Empire Hotel, on Pa ave, between 3rd & 4½ sts, to satisfy said rent due. –A E Keese, Bailiff

THU MAR 13, 1857
Household & kitchen furniture at auction on Mar 14, by order of the Orphans Court of Wash Co, D C; belonging to the estate of the late John B Floyd. -A Green auct

Household & kitchen furniture at auction on Mar 16, at the residence of Mr J W Allen, 600 I st, near 4th st. -Jas C McGuire, auct

Superior household & kitchen furniture at auction on Mar 18, at the residence of Hon Israel Washburn, jr, Blagden's Row, between 3rd & 4½ sts. –C W Boteler, auct

Trustee's sale of valuable Pa ave property: by deed of trust from Christopher R Byrne & wife, dated Mar 30, 1857, in front of the premises, all the said grantor's interest & estate in two undivided third parts of the property on the corner of Pa ave & 10th sts west, in square 380, in Wash, D C. I will also offer for public sale, at the same time, the remaining undivided third part of said premises, being the interest & estate of said owner. –Hugh Caperton, trustee -Wall, Barnard & Co, aucts

Mrd: on Mar 10, at Rock Creek Church, by Rev Mr Buck, Albert J De Zeyk to Eliz M Whittlesey, of Wash City.

Senate: 1-Mr Kennedy moved that A H Kilty have leave to withdraw his papers: which was agreed to.

The late Joshua Sears prided himself upon never having paid money to lawyers during his life. The lawyers find his will so loosely drawn as to furnish endless questions for the courts. It is calculated that if the son lives to be 50 years of age, & if the wishes of the testator are in every respect carried out, the property will amount at that time to $20,000,000. The son can, at no time of his life, receive more than $10,000 a year out of the income. –Boston Journal

SAT MAR 14, 1857
Appointments by the Pres. by & with the advice & consent of the Senate.
Felix Livingston, Collector for Fernandina, Fla.
Jos Genois, Naval Ofcr of New Orleans, reappointed.
Wm P Reyburn, additional Appraiser Gen at New Orleans.
J J McCormick, Assist Appraiser for New Orleans, vice Wm P Reyburn.
F H Hatch, Collector of New Orleans, vice Thos C Porter, resigned.
Wm M Lowry, of Tenn, reappointment as U S Marshal for Eastern District of Tenn.
Jos S Smith, Wash Territory, reappointed Atty for said Territory, vice Henry R Crosbie.
J C Ramsey, of Tenn, reappointment as Atty for Eastern District of Tenn.
Hampden McClanahan, of Tenn, reappointment as Marshal for Western District of Tenn.
Jesse B Clements, of Tenn, reappointment as Marshal for Middle District of Tenn.
Richd R Crawford, District of Columbia, to be Justice of the Peace.
Henry C Lowell, of Minn, to be Register of the Land Ofc at Faribault, Minn, vice Diedrich Upham, removed.
Jas U Nesmith, of Oregon, to be Superintendent of Indian Affairs for Wash & Oregon.
J Harralson, Surveyor of port of Selma, Alabama.
Owen L Cochrane, Postmaster at Houston, Texas.
John L Bunch, Postmaster at Tuscumbia, Ala.
Alex'r H McKessack, of Ark, to be Indian Agent for the Wichetas & neighboring tribes west of the Choctaws & Chickawaws.
John Walker, of Tenn, an Indian Agent in New Mexico.
Wm E Murphy, of Kansas, to be Indian Agent for the Pottawatomie Indians.
Jas L Collins, of New Mexico, Superintendent of Indian Affairs in New Mexico.
Flavius J Lovejoy, of Miss, to be Atty for the Northern District of Miss.
Elias S Dennis, of Ill, to be Marshal for Kansas.

Trustee's sale of valuable bldg lots at auction: on Mar 30, by two deeds of trust from Estwick Evans to the subscriber, dated Jun 20, 1854; & Aug 15, 1854: part of lot 13 in square 494, & part of lot 15 in square 368. –Hugh B Sweeny, trustee
-A Green auct

Appointments in the Navy: recently confirmed by the Senate:
Lewis J Williams & Marius Duvall, to be Surgeons in the Navy.
A C Gorgas & A M Veddar, to be Assist Surgeons in the Navy.
Chas W Abbott, to be a Purser in the Navy.
Henry Wood, to be a Chaplain in the Navy.
W A T Maddox & Wm B Slack, to be Capts in the Marine Corps.
Jas Wiley, Geo R Graham, & J R F Tattnall, to be 1st Lts in the Marine Corps.
R A Whittier & P H W Fontaine, to be 2nd Lts in the Marine Corps.
Augustus E Maxwell, to be Navy Agent at Pensacola, Fla.

Four men: Bernard Ford, Edmund E Price, Martin Hart, & Henry Finnegan, have been arrested, charged with being implicated in a prize fight which took place in Essex Co, Mass, on Thu. The contest was for $200.

Geo Knight, who has been on tiral at Auburn, Me, for the murder of his wife, was found guilty, on Tue, of murder in the 1st degree. The convict is a farmer in Poland township, Androscoggin Co, Maine, & prior to this charge of murder bore a respectable character. His wife, Mary Knight, was found on the morning of Oct 7 last, lying dead in her bed, with her throat cut & another fatal stab wound. She was much older than her husband, & it was suspected that he wished to get rid of her in order to marry another woman.

Died: on Mar 13, in Wash City, Capt Jos Smoot, U S Navy. His funeral will take place tomorrow at 3 o'clock P M, from his late residence, in **Franklin Row**, at which time & place the ofcrs of the Navy in Wash & the friends of the family are invited.

Senate-special session: 1-Cmte of Claims: asked to be discharged from the consideration of the memorial of Wm A Cameron: agreed to. 2-Papers withdrawn from files: of Nolle Hutchins; of Wm A Bartlett; of Martin Fenwick; of Azel Spaulding; & of Cornelius O'Flynn.

My grateful thanks are given to the Farmers' & Mechanics' Ins Co, [ofcs Pa ave & 17th st,] for the prompt adjustment & immediate payment of my loss sustained by the fire in I st, between 14th & 15th sts, this morning, Mar 13, 1857. I am thus enabled to resume my business at once. –Ellen O'Keefe

Annual Commencement of the Medical Dept of Gtwn College took place on Thu in the lecture room of the Smithsonian Institute. Mr Maguire conferred on the graduates their diplomas, constituting them doctors in medicine, as follows: to Messrs John A Wilcox, of D C; Geo McCoy, of Ireland; F Matthews Lancaster, of Md; Danl B Clarke, of D C; Jos S Smith, of D C; T J C Kennon, of Ohio; Thos A Wonderly, of Va; & Silas L Loomis, of Conn

Rev B F Bittinger was installed Pastor of the 7th st Presbyterian Church on Mar 12 by the Presbytery of Balt.

Criminal Court-Wash-Thu. 1-Jas O'Connell was convicted of stealing a pair of gloves, valued at $3, from Dr Howard: sentenced to 6 months in jail. 2-Wm F Johnson convicted of stealing $37.50 in gold & silver from Mrs Keeth: motion in arrest of judgment. 3-Wm Moore, Geo W Hines, John Murdock, & Marcellus Holtzman were indicted for riot in the 1st Ward on Christmas day; not guilty. 4-John Roberts alias Robinson, was found guilty of stealing brass from the Gtwn Gaslight Co. 5-Pink Coakley [colored] tried for stealing pocket book & $8 from Roberta Knoxville.

The undersigned offers his services as Gardener, rural & otherwise. Apply at 428 14th st. –Henry Cassidy

Toronto, C W, Mar 12. The train which left Toronto this afternoon for Hamilton, on the Great Western railroad, ran off a bridge at or near that city. The locomotive & baggage car passed over the bridge in safety, but the two rear cars, containing 120 passengers, fell through into the water, a distance of 40 feet. Sixty or eighty persons are supposed to have been killed on the spot; among whom were Saml Zimmerman, the banker & contractor, & Mr Street, the millionaire, of Niagara Falls, together with his sister & mother-in-law. Fifty corpses of men, women, & children are laid out on the floor of an out-house. [Mar 17th newspaper: Few were admitted to view the bodies; the first we remarked was that of poor Donald Stuart; next lay the Brantford contractor, Mr Russell, on whose person was money to the amount of several thousand dollars; in the row opposite was Saml Zimmerman, & near him 2 children, ages 1 & 3, & she whom seemed to be their mother.] [Mar 20th newspaper: Every person in the first passenger car, except Owen Doyle, Jas Barton, of Stratford, & 2 children between 8 & 9 years of age, perished. They were a brother & sister. Their mother, father, & uncle perished, & Owen Doyle, who saved himself, is their uncle. Doyle had his brother, & sister-in-law, 2 cousins, & a cousin's wife, & 2 nieces all killed or drowned. Barton's father was also lost. Richardson, Mr Urquart, of the express, the mail-conductor, & the baggage-master also escaped. In the second car the persons saved were the conductor, Mr Barret, the deputy superintendent, Mr Muir, & Mr Jessop, an auditor.]

Fauquier land for sale: I am authorized to sell privately **Bellevue**, the residence of W Winter Payne, in said county, adjoining the **Oakwood farm** of Robt E Scott, & the **Clifton farm**, lately owned by Arthur M Payne. This farm contains 364 acres, & a very large well planned brick house with 9 rooms, & numerous out-bldgs. Address the undersigned at Warrenton. –Wm H Payne

MON MAR 16, 1857
The remains of Wm T Sherrard, who was recently killed at Lecompton, Kansas, at the close of an exciting meeting, arrived at his family residence in Winchester, Va, on Mar 6, & were interred in **Mount Hebron Cemetery**, attended by a long procession of sympathizing friends. He was the son of Jos H Sherrard, Mayor of Winchester, who was greatly respected. He settled in Kansas in Sep, 1856, & was appointed sheriff by the county court of Douglas Co on Dec 16 last; but Gov Geary refused to issue his commission, & thence arose the feud which terminated in the death of Mr Sherrard.

We regret to learn that Hon Samson W Harris, an esteemed member of Congress from Alabama, lies dangerously ill at his lodgings in this city [Wash City,] of inflammation or congestion of the lungs.

Appointments by the Pres. confirmed by the Senate:
Isaac H Sturgeon to be Assist Treasurer at St Louis.
Philip Clayton to be Assist Sec of the Treasury.
J Patton Anderson, of Wash Territory, to be Govn'r of said Territory.
Turner Nelson, of Indiana, to be Superintendent of Indian Affairs in the Territory of Utah.
Geo H Jones, of Va, to be Sec to the Pres to sign patents.
Wm Weer, of Kansas, to be Atty for Kansas.
Lewis W Sifford to be Marshal for the Southern district of Ohio, vice Thos K Smith.
Jacob Frontman to be Postmaster at Hamilton, Ohio.
Abner Pratt, of Mich, to be Consul at Honolulu.
Wm E Venable, of Tenn, to be Minister resident at Guatemala.
J Page Hopkins, of Va, to be Consul at Tabasco.
Joel W White, of Conn, to be Consul at Lyons.
Francis A Thornton, of N C, to be Consul at Aspinwall, New Granada.
Peter Sanzeneau, of Louisiana, to be Consul at Matamoros.
G A Johnson, of Rhode Island, to be Consular Beirut.
Chas G Baylor, Consul at Manchester, England.
Eugene M Wilson to be Atty for Minnesota.
Henry B Andrews to be Postmaster at Galveston, vice John B Root, removed.
Navy Ofcrs:
Theodorus Bailey, Hugh Y Purviance, Wm F Lynch, Henry W Morris, & Francis B Ellison to be Capts in the Navy.
Alex M Pennock, Geo F Emmons, Edw Middleton, Thos T Hunter, Gustavus H Scott, David McDougal, & Chas F McIntosh, to be Cmders in the Navy.
Dr Grasse Livingston, Wm E Fitzhugh, Trevett Abbot, Benj P Loyall, Chas H Cushman, Oscar F Stanton, Wm H Cheever, Henry A Adams, Geo Brown, Chas E Hawley, Bushrod B Taylor, Wm H Ward, Robt L May, John W Dunnington, Hudson M Garland, Jas W Shirk, Jesse Taylor, Jas P Maxwell, Henry Erben, Francis E Shepperd, Thos P Pelot, Edw P McCrea, & Edw C Stockton, to be Lts in the Navy.
John S Cunningham, of S C, to be Purser in the Navy, vice Edw Fitzgerald, deceased.
Delavan Bloodgood, of N Y, to be an Assist Surgeon in the Navy, vice E K Kane, deceased.
Geo P Turner, of Va, to be a 2nd Lt in the Marine Corps.
Allen Ramsay, of the District of Columbia, to be a 2nd Lt in the Marine Corps.

We see it stated that a Bounty Land Warrant has been issued by the Pension Ofc to Mr Geo Peabody, the London banker, now in Wash City, for 160 acres of land, for his service as a volunteer private in the war with England in 1812.

Died: on Mar 3, at Fond du Lac, Wisc, after a few day's illness, Mrs Abby L Tallmadge, wife of Hon N P Tallmadge, in her 54th year.

Died: on Sat last, at Dexter's Hotel, in Wash City, of pneumonia, Hon David T Disney, of Ohio, formerly a prominent member of Congress from Ohio. His family had left him in good health only a few days before on their return home to Ohio, & the morning he expired a telegraphic dispatch was received here announcing their safe arrival-a dispatch of affection which his eyes were never to behold.

Died: on Mar 14, in Wash City, Mrs Mary A Nally, in her 41st year, relict of the late Richd B Nally, leaving 2 aged parents, with 3 children, together with a large circle of friends, to mourn their irreparable loss. Her funeral will take place from her late residence, on G, near 9th, this morning at 10 o'clock.

Died: on Feb 15, at Pine Bluff, Ark, of consumption, Mrs Mary C Dent, wife of Walter C Dent, formerly of Chas Co, Md.

Died: on Mar 14, in Wash City, Joseph, infant son of John W & Eliz R Nairn. His funeral will be from the residence of his parents, corner of 15th & N Y ave, this morning at 10 o'clock.

Criminal Court-Wash-Fri. 1-Pink Coakley guilty of stealing a pocket book & contents: sentenced to 1 year in jail. 2-John McMahon convicted of assault on Jas Mason. 3-Jas Bennett, tried on the same charge as McMahon, but acquitted. 4-Jas Norris for larceny, not guilty. 5-Wm Cropsey convicted of larceny on the property of John O'Meara. 6-John H Martgan & Martin Dowell, for assault, were under trial when we left the court.

Mount Pleasant farm for sale: located half a mile from Friend's Meeting House & the Post Ofc of Sandy Springs, Montg Co, Md; contains 152 acres; with a substantial brick dwlg 44 by 36 feet; barn & all needful outhouses. Apply to Gerard H Reese, 207 Pratt st, or to the subscriber on the premises, Olive Scott, Sandy Spring Post Ofc, Montg Co, Md.

Handsome 4 story brick house & lot at private sale: located on north G, between 4th & 5th sts west, lot 2 in square 518, the house being No 514. Apply to the subscriber on the premises, or at Mr A Lee's ofc, Pa ave, between 4½ & 6th sts. –D C Reed

Orphans Court of Wash Co, D C. Letters of administration on the personal estate of Ann Martin, late of Wash Co, deceased. –Eliz Vigal, admx

Orphans Court of Wash Co, D C. Letters of administration on the personal estate of John D Scott, late of Wash Co, deceased. –Jane H Scott, John H Semmes, adms

TUE MAR 17, 1857
Household & kitchen furniture at auction on: Mar 19, at the residence of Lt Ives, U S N, 491 7th st, between H & I sts. -J C McGuire, auct

Household & kitchen furniture at auction on: Mar 20, at the residence of Mrs Gage, at the Webster House, on La ave. -A Green auct

Capt J W Rickets, of Mexico, Anderson Co, Mo, formerly of Rappahannock Co, Va, was lately murdered by his wife's brother, near the town of Mexico, in that State.

Dr Pope, Homoeopathic Physician & Surgeon, has removed his ofc & residence to de Menou or Chain Bldgs, formerly occupied by Gov Pennington, 376 H st, between 13th & 14th sts.

Died: on Mar 16, in Wash City, Mrs Harriet P Fontaine, youngest daughter of John & Christiana Underwood. Her funeral will be from her father's residence, Capitol Hill, today, at 11 o'clock.

Died: on Mar 14, in Wash City, at the residence of Jas Little, on L st south, near the Navy Yard, of consumption, John Sutton, in his 63rd year.

Calif: 1-The Calif Legislature impeached Dr Bates, the State Treasurer, & G W Whitemen, Comptroller, for misappropriating State funds to the amount of $250,000. Bates resigned, & Jas English, of Sacramento, succeeded him. 2-Twelve of a band of robbers who recently murdered Sheriff Barton have been hung by the people of San Diego. 3-An Affray took place at San Francisco between F A Cohen, the banker, & Thos King, editor of the Bulletin & brother of the late Jas King. Cohen was the aggressor, & was shot through the jaws. Both were arrested, but King was discharged.

WED MAR 18, 1857
In consequence of the death of the late A H Lawrence, a meeting of the Judges, Members of the Bar, & Ofcrs of the Courts of this District will be held this morning at 9 o'clock at the court-room.
+
Died: on Mar 16, in Wash City, Alex'r H Lawrence, aged 46 years; a Christian, lawyer & gentleman, whose brief career at the bar of the Supreme Court & of Wash City had marked him as no ordinary man, & whose loss will be widely felt & deeply lamented. His funeral will take place from Trinity Church at 3 o'clock today. [Mar 21st newspaper: Mr Lawrence came to Wash City in 1834, when he took charge of the Western Academy, on H st, between 17th & 18th sts; the bldg was destroyed by fire a few years since. He received an appointment as clerk, I believe, in the Gen Land Ofc; he visited at my father's; he was a remarkable sweet singer & performer on several instruments; he married, his choice a wise one. He was admitted to the bar in 1845, & was a member of the Protestant Episcopal Church. -A] [Mar 23rd newspaper: Tribute to the memory of the late A H Lawrence: meeting of the Wardens & Vestry of Trinity Parish, held on Mar 20; resolution presented by Mr

D W Middleton; motion of Mr Wm B Todd, unanimously adopted; this Vestry has special reason to mourn for a member so wise in counsel, so pure in life; we mingle our grief with the deeper anguish of his bereaved family. –G D Cumminns, Rector; Fred Koones, Register]

Died: on Mar 16, in Wash City, Robert, son of Jas & Mattie E Steele, aged 7 months & 9 days.

Died: on Mar 17, in Wash City, Margaret Albertus, infant daughter of John & Bridget Wise. Her funeral is this afternoon at 4 o'clock, from the residence of her parents, 103 4½ st, [Island.]

Died: in Eliz City, N C, Marion, youngest child of Alex'r S & Helen Wadsworth, aged 8 months.

Orphans Court of Wash Co, D C. Letters of administration on the personal estate of Jacob Hunsberger, late of Wash Co, deceased. –Geo W Utermahle, adm

House to let: the large 4 story brick house, with back bldg, on Pa ave, between 3rd & 4½ sts, formerly occupied by Mrs Beveridge. The house has long been known as a boarding house. Apply to Walter Godey, corner of High & Prospect sts, Gtwn.

THU MAR 19, 1857
Appointments in the Navy, confirmed by the Senate:
Captains:
Theodore Bailey, from Dec 15, 1855, vice Capt Joel Abbott, deceased.
Hugh Y Purviance, from Jan 28, 1856, vice Capt Chas Morris, deceased.
Wm F Lynch, from Apr 2, 1856, vice Capt Isaac McKeever, deceased.
Henry W Morris, from Dec 27, 1856, vice Capt Bladen Dulany, deceased.
Francis B Ellison, from Mar 2, 1857, vice Capt A Bigelow, resigned.
Commanders:
Alex'r M Pennock, from Dec 15, 1855, vice Cmder T Bailey, promoted.
Geo F Emmons, from Jan 28, 1856, vice Cmder H Y Purviance, promoted.
Edw Middleton, from Apr 2, 1856, vice Cmder Wm F Lynch, promoted.
Thos T Hunter, from Dec 23, 1856, vice Cmder S Larkin, deceased.
Gustavus H Scott, from Dec 27, 1856, vice Cmder H W Morris, promoted.
David McDougal, from Jan 24, 1857, vice Cmder J H Rowan, dismissed.
Chas F McIntosh, from Mar 2, 1857, vice Cmder F B Ellison, promoted.
Lts:
De Grasse Livingston, from Nov 18, 1855, vice Lt A McRae, deceased.
Wm A Fitzhugh, from Dec 15, 1855, vice Lt A M Pennock, promoted.
Trevett Abbott, from Jan 7, 1856, vice Lt Geo E Morgan, deceased.
Benj P Loyall, from Jan 28, 1856, vice Lt G F Emmons, promoted.
Chas F Cushman, from Feb 8, 1856, vice Lt E Middleton, promoted.

Wm H Cheever, from May 11, 1856, vice Lt John K Millson, resigned.
Henry A Adams, from May 11, 1856, vice Lt E H Oakley, resigned.
Geo Brown, from Jun 2, 1856, vice Lt T C Eaton, deceased.
Chas E Hawley, from Jun 26, 1856, vice Lt E Brinly, resigned.
Bushrod B Taylor, from Jul 31, 1856, vice Lt G V Fox, resigned.
Wm H Ward, from Sep 9, 1856, vice Lt Thos Young, resigned.
Robt L May, from Sep 26, 1856, vice Lt J S Biddle, resigned.
John W Dunington, from Oct 16, 1856, vice Lt Jas Parker, jr, resigned.
Hudson M Garland, from Oct 17, 1856, vice Lt Chas W Aby, deceased.
Jas W Shirk, from Nov 5, 1856, vice Lt Jos S Day, deceased.
Jesse Taylor, from Nov 26, 1856, vice Lt John T Walker, deceased.
Jas G Maxwell, from Dec 23, 1856, vice Lt T T Hunter, promoted.
Henry Erben, from Dec 27, 1856, vice Lt G H Scott, promoted.
Francis E Shepperd, from Jan 1, 1857, vice Lt Jas Higgins, resigned.
Thos P Pelot, from Jan 1, 1857, vice Lt J G Heileman, resigned.
Edw P McCrea, from Jan 24, 1857, vice Lt D McDougal, promoted.
Edw C Stockton, from Feb 7, 1857, vice Lt C E Fleming, dismissed.

The Rockford [Indiana] Herald of Mar 13 states that a dwlg-house near Houston, Jackson Co, occupied by Jas Taylor, was consumed by fire on the night of Mar 5, & that Mrs Taylor & 3 children were burnt to death. The husband was absent at the time of the calamity.

Household & kitchen furniture at auction on: Mar 27, at the residence of the Hon Jefferson Davis, corner of 18th & G sts. -Jas C McGuire, auct

Extensive sale of very superior furniture, piano forte, billiard table, oil paintings, wines & brandy, horses, carriages, & harness at auction: on Mar 30, at the residence of Elisha Riggs, on 223 North G, between 17th & 18th sts. -A Green auct

Criminal Court-Wash-Wed. 1-John L Crown, of Gtwn, was convicted of receiving a quantity of eggs, knowing them to have been stolen: sentenced to 8 months in jail. 2-Jas Wilson, a young man from N Y, convicted of 3 robberies on Mar 4, was found guilty & sentenced to 2 years of hard labor in the penitentiary in each case, making 6 years in all, to take effect tomorrow.

<u>Methodist Episcopal Appointments: the Conference just closed in Balt, Md.</u>
<u>Balt District:</u> Wm Hamilton, P E. Balt City Station, W B Edwards, R L Dashiell; Fielder Israel, Jas Sewell; Chas st, B F Brooke; City Mission, Jas M Clarke; Fayette st, John S Martin, Mayberry Gohen, Thos Sewall; South Balt, John Thrush, J W Bull, sup; Columbia st, Thos Myers; Seaman's Bethel, Geo G Brooke; Sharpe st & John Welsey, Wm H Laney; Asbury & Orchard sts, Isaac Collins; Balt Circuit, John Poisal, W M Showalter, A J Myers, sup, J L Gibbons, sup P O.

Potomac District: John Lanahan, P E. Alexandria: L F Morgan, Theodore Carson, Alfred Griffith, sup; Princess st, J L Gardiner; Gtwn: B N Brown, W R White, sup; West Gtwn & Tenallytown: John N Coombs; Wash-Foundry: Saml Regester; Wesley Chapel, Wm Krebs; Capitol Hill, R R S Hough, M A Turner, sup; McKendree & Fletcher Chapel, Dabney Ball; Ebenezer, Wm H Chapman; Ebenezer Mission, to be supplies; Ryland Chapel, John S Deal; Gorsuch Chapel: Henry N Snipes; Union Chapel: Saml Rogers, Wm O Lumsden, sup; Asbury & Mount Zion: John W Hoover; Fairfax: John W Tongue, Saml Dickson, post ofc Fairfax Co, Va; Stafford Mission: W Gwynn Coe, R R Murphy, post ofc Brentsville, Prince Wm Co, Va; Fredericksburg: Ezra F Busey; St Mary's: J W Lambeth, J H Wolff, J Bunting, sup, post ofc Chaptico, St Mary's Co, Md; Bladensburg: C G Linthicum, one to be supplied; Woodville: John H Ryland, post ofc Horsehead, PG Co, Md; Charles: Bennett H Smith, F A Mercer, post ofc Piscataway, Chas Co, Md; Rockville: Wm G Eggleston, P B Smith, B Barry, sup; Montgomery: Wm P Eggleston, P B Smith, B Barry, sup, post ofc Clarksburg, Montg Co, Md; Pohick to be supplied.
Winchester District: Wm Hirst, P E. Winchester: N J B Morgan; Winchester Circuit: S McMullin, L Watson Berry, P O N T Stephensburgh, Fred'k Co, Va; Jefferson: Norval Wilson, Wm S Edwards, P O Charlestown, Jefferson Co, Va; Berryville: Wm Prettyman, one to be supplied, P O Wadesville, Clarke Co, Va; Shannondale: to be supplied, P O Unison, Loudon Co, Va; Martinsburg: John Landstreet, J T Eakin, sup; Berkeley: F H Richey, J T Trone, T T Wysong, sup, P O Hedgesville, Berkeley Co, Va; Berkeley Springs: J W Start, one to be supplied, P O Berkeley Springs, Morgan Co, Va; Capon, J H Lemon, P O Paw Paw, Morgan Co, Va; Wardensville: S H Griffith, Edw F Hitrick, P O Bloomery, Hampshire Co, Va; Springfield: Wm H Champion, one to be supplied, C Parkison, sup; Shepherdstown: Jas H March; Harper's Ferry & Bolivar: Jos T Phelps; Hillsboro: Wm S Baird, J C Dice, S S Roszel, sup; Leesburg: Elisha D Owen; Rehoboth, to be supplied, P O Lovettsville, Loudoun Co, Va; East Loudoun: R M Lipscomb, T E Carson, P O Middleburg, Loudoun Co, Va; West Loudoun: J Hoffman Waugh, Geo V Leech, P O Paris, Fauquier Co, Va; Warrenton: David Thomas, Wm H Holiday.

The paper mill about 5 miles from Tennallytown was burnt on Tue. The mill was the property of Mr Geo Hill, jr, of Gtwn, & had lately been repaired & supplied with new machinery. The fire first exhibited itself near the roof.

Died: on Mar 18, in Wash City, Mrs Mgt Lenox, relict of Peter Lenox, aged 77 years. Her funeral will take place from her late residence on E st north, between 10th & 11th sts, tomorrow at 11 o'clock. [Mar 28th newspaper: Tribute to Mrs Margaret Lenox: Catholic in spirit; bereaved of her children after they had attained maturity, she mourned them with a deep & abiding sorrow. A few hours before her death, she said, "I rejoice, yea, I do rejoice. Her children will miss the precious tones of love they've heard for many a year. –W T]

Died: yesterday, after a lingering illness, S L W Montgomery, son of Capt J B Montgomery, U S Navy, aged 20 years & 6 months. His funeral will take place today at 3½ o'clock P M, from his father's residence, on I st.

I will sell my house & lot, in the upper part of the village of Bladensburg, situated opposite the residence of C C Hyatt. The house is perfectly new, & the lot contains about 1½ acres of land; with necessary out-houses. Apply to D Benj Berry, Bladensburg, Md. [Jul 8th newspaper: the above property will be at private sale until Jul 23; if not sold by that time it will, on that day, be offered at public sale on the premises. Immediate possession given. –Benj Berry, M D]

Public sale: by order of the Orphans' Court of Chas Co, Md: public auction of *The Refuge*, at the late residence of Col Wm D Merrick, deceased, on Apr 7 next; the personal estate of said Wm D Merrick, consisting of a large quantity of household & kitchen furniture, farming implements, 2 double carriages & one buggy, a large stock of horses & mules; also, a large number of young & valuable negroes of both sexes. -Geo Brent, R H Edelen, adms with the will annexed of W D Merrick.
+
Sale of valuable real estate in Chas Co, Md: by virtue of the trusts contained in a deed, dated Aug 22, 1844, from Wm D Merrick to Henry H Dent, & also a deed, dated Nov 9, 1852, from same to Wm Brent, both duly recorded among the land records of Chas Co: public sale, on the premises, on Apr 8, one of the most desirable farms in the county, *The Refuge*, on which the late Col Wm D Merrick resided; contains 400 acres; dwlg is conveniently arranged, containing 9 rooms. Mr Geo C Merrick, now residing there, will show the property. –Geo Brent

FRI MAR 20, 1857
Purser Thos P McBlair, U S Navy, died on Feb 17 on board the U S steam frig **Merrimac**, in the Gulf. His disease is said to have been of the heart. His remains were buried on the next day in the Episcopal cemetery at Santa Cruz, with the military honors due to his rank.

The Buffalo Express of Tue says: "A series of forgeries were discovered here yesterday to the extent of some $12,000, & the forger, Fred'k A McKnight, was arrested." He would purchase a draft for $35 and then fill in the hundred making the amount $3,500. Then he would make his own check for some small sum dated ahead, & go to the bank & get it certified. This he would alter in its denomination, say a $25 check to $2,500, until he was detected at one of our banks in such a performance.

SAT MAR 21, 1857
Mrd: on Mar 19, in Wash City, by Rev F A Ciampi, Col John Williams, of Wash, to Mrs Leonora M Coolidge, eldest daughter of Cmdor Stephen Cassin, U S Navy.

Phil appointments: Col Jos B Baker, of Lancaster Co, Collector; Gideon G Westcott, of Phil, Postmaster; Chambers McKibben, of Phil, Naval Ofcr; John Hamilton, jr, of Phil, Surveyor ofcr; John Hamilton, jr, of Phil, Surveyor of the port; Wm Badger, of Phil, Navy Agent; & Jacob Yost, of Montgomery, Marshal.

The Indian War in Florida. A letter dated **Fort Dallas** on Mar 10th says: "We are up to the eyes in hostilities. All our command, except N C staff & band, have been out since the 7th ult scouting & burning up Key Largo & the adjacent Keys. Gen Harney's whole force is operating & many of them suffering dreadfully. Maj Pembertons' command, consisting of companies E, F, & K, of the 4th, arrived here last night, after having lost their way & been starved for 4 days. They ate a horse valued at $210 five days ago for breakfast, &, in the interim, until their arrival here had nothing else to eat. The campaign promises to be a squally one."

Criminal Court-Wash-Thu. 1-Jas Thompson was convicted, but recommended to the mercy of the Court on a charge of larceny in stealing penknives from the store of Mr Jos L Savage. Sentenced to 3 months in jail. 2-John Moran, convicted of an aggravated assault & battery, sentenced to 4 months in jail & fined $10. 3-Jas Higgins was acquitted of an assault on a boy, Norris, whilst cutting ice on the river. 4-The grand jury yesterday indicted Dr Platt H Skinner in 8 several cases for assaults on the mute & blind children under his charge. A bench warrant was issued for the arrest of Skinner, who is understood to have left Wash City. 5-D C Lee was arrested for the murder of David Hume & is now in jail for trial. [Apr 8th newspaper: the case of Dr Platt H Skinner: Mrs E D E N Southworth saw the children at dinner & all they were allowed was one large or two small potatoes at a meal. A little girl, Mary Donaldson, had bitterly complained of the treatment she had received. Miss Alice Adams instanced several cases of cruel treatment of the children with fist, horsewhip, & by kicking. The children complained of hunger almost every day. Mrs Raymond deposed to Skinner's severity towards the children, to the insuffieiency & poor quality of the food, & their general bad treatment by their keeper. Dr Storrow saw Dr Skinner inflict punishment of a merciless character on a small boy. Mr Seys had a child at the institution, & deposed unfavorably of its treatment for cruelty & privation by Dr Skinner. Mr O Olds was quite unfavorable to Dr Skinner. Mr Burrows was the last witness examined.]

Died: on Mar 14, at Hoboken, N J, Matilda Stewart Chilton, 2nd daughter of the late Geo Chilton, of N Y.

Rev Calvin Colton died at Savannah, Ga, on Fri last, & his remains have been sent to Massachusetts for interment. He graduated at Yale College in 1812, ordained a Presbyterian clergyman in 1815, & was settled at Batavia, N Y, until 1836, when he partially lost the use of his voice. This induced him to devote his time to writing for periodicals.

Died: on Mar 18, in N Y C, Rev Thos Callan, Catholic Pastor of Malone, Franklin Co, N Y.

Appointments by the Pres: Collectors of Customs:-all reappointed:
Wm F Colcock, Charleston   O S Dewey, Ocracoke, N C
Minott A Osborn, New Haven   John Adair, Oregon
Geo T Wright, Tappahannock, Va

Army Orders, general order No 3, Headquarters of the Army, N Y, Mar 19, 1857. 1-Brvt Maj Gen John E Wool will assume command of the Dept of the East. Headquarters Troy, N Y. 2-Brvt Maj Gen David E Twiggs will, about May 1, repair to & assume command of the Dept of Texas. 3-Brvt Brig Gen Newman S Clarke, Col 6th Infty, will, in anticipation of a future movement of his regt, repair to Calif & assume command of the Dept of the Pacific. Headquarters San Francisco. 4-The Headquarters of the Dept of the West will in future be St Louis, Mo.
-L Thomas, Assist Adj Gen

Dr Champney [age 27,] died at his residence in Brooklyn, N Y, on Mar 13, from poison received while making a post mortem examintation. On Monday, at the request of Coroner Redding, the deceased assisted in the post mortem examination of the body of John Elders, alleged to have died from violence at the hands of garroters. While engaged at this he pricked his finger & died after suffering intense agony.

Gov Gardner, of Mass, has appointed Apr 16th next to be observed by the people of the State as a day of public fasting, humiliation, & prayer.

Trustee's sale: by deed of trust from Leonard Albrecht & wife, recorded in Liber J A S No 94, folios 162-165, of the land records of Wash Co, D C: sale on Apr 6 next: part of lot 4 in square 844, with a 2 story brick house. –Chas Walter, trustee

Wash City Ordinance: 1-Act for the relief of Ann E Bryan: pay her $4.91, the amount for taxes erroneously. 2-Joint resolution authorizing Wm L Langley to weigh hay, straw, & fodder, on the scales at the corner of East Capitol st & 1st st.

MON MAR 23, 1857
Died: on Mar 22, Emmeline Sophia Macleod, wife of Jas Mandeville Carlisle. Her funeral will take place from the house, on D st, tomorrow, Tue, at 10 o'clock. [Mar 26th newspaper: the late Mrs Emmeline Carlisle was a devoted wife, a judicious mother, a tender daughter, loving sister, & a kind neighbor. Heartfelt is the sympathy offered by many friends to those who weep the departure of so much excellence. –J]

Appointments by the Pres.
John Bigler, of Calif, to be Envoy Extraordinary & Minister Plenipotentiary to the Republic of Chile, vice David A Starkweather.
Watson Freeman, U S Marshal for the district of Mass, reappointed.
Chas Levi Woodbury, U S Atty for the district of Mass, vice B F Hallet, whose commission has expired.
Arthur W Austin, Collector of the Customs for the district of Boston & Charlestown, Mass, vice Chas H Peaslee, whose commission has expired.
Peter White, Register of the land ofc at Marquette, Mich, vice Ebenezer Warner, whose term of ofc has expired.
Robt J Graveraet, Receiver of Public Moneys at Marquette, Mich, vice Wm A Pratz, whose term of ofc expired.
John C Blanchard, Register of the land ofc at Ionia, Mich, vice Alex F Bell, whose commission has expired.
Wm A Caruthers, Register of the land ofc at Sauk Rapids, Minn Territory, vice Geo W Sweet, removed.
Wm E Rucker, Register of the land ofc at Plattsburg, Mo, vice Jas H Birch, removed.
J Adams Allen, Receiver of Public Moneys at Kalamazoo, Mich, vice Lawrence Van DeWalker, whose term of ofc has expired.
Geo F Kidder, Register of the land ofc at Kalamazoo, Mich, vice Thos S AtLee, whose term of ofc has expired.

Calif Appointments:
B F Washington, Collector at San Francisco, vice Latham.
Franck Tilford, Naval Ofcr, vice Dameron.
Wm B Dameron, Surveyor of the Port, vice Voorhees.
Andrew Lester, Collector at San Joaquin, vice Scofield.
Jose Cavarrugras, Collector at San Diego, vice Wetherby.

Mrd: on Feb 26, at the residence of the bride's mother, by Rev Robt Morrison, Mr Wm M Morrison, Principal of the Bullitt Academy, Shepperdsville, Ky, to Miss Sallie E Benthall, of Bullitt Co, Ky.

Died: Mar 22, John T Preston, in his 31st year. His funeral will take place today at half-past 3 o'clock P M, from the residence of his mother, on 12th st, between E & F.

Died: on Mar 18, after a lingering illness, near Indianapolis, Indiana, Hon Wm J Brown, for several years a member of Congress, Assist Postmaster Gen during Mr Polk's Administration, & for the last 4 years special agent of the Post Ofc Dept for Indiana & Illnois.

U S Patent Ofc, Wash, Mar 21, 1857. Ptn of E A Stillman, adm of Alfred Stillman, deceased, of N Y, N Y, praying for the extension of a patent granted to said Stillman for an improvement in evaporating saccharine juices, for 7 years from the expiration of said patent, which takes place on Aug 17, 1857. –Chas Mason, Com'r of Patents

$300 reward for runaway negro boy Chas Batson, 18 or 19 years of age.
–W O Reeder, Oakhill, St Mary's Co, Md.

Orphans Court of Wash Co, D C. Letters of administration on the personal estate of Arthur D Tree, late of the U S Army, deceased. –Lambert Tree, adm

TUE MAR 24, 1857
Appointments by the Pres:
Jas S Dougherty, Receiver of Public Moneys for the district of land subject to sale at St Louis, Mo, vice Richd B Dallam, whose term of ofc has expired.
Jacob Beeson, Receiver of Public Moneys at Detroit, Mich, vice Elisha Taylor, whose term of ofc will expire Apr 3 next.
Chas F Hyerman, Register of the land ofc at Detroit, Mich, vice Danl J Campau, whose term of ofc expires on Apr 3 next.
Moses B Hess, Register of land ofc at East Saginaw, Mich, vice Wm M Fenton, whose term of ofc has expired.
Wm P Little, Receiver of Public Moneys at East Saginaw, Mich, vice Russell Bishop, whose term of ofc will expire on Mar 30.

The New Orleans papers record the death of Philemon C Wederstrandt, aged 78 years. The deceased was a native of Queen Anne's Co, Md, & first visited Louisiana in command of a naval force dispatched by the Federal Gov't to intercept & arrest Aaron Burr on his contemplated expedition. He resided in the parish of Plaquemine for a period of 40 years. -Sun

Excellent piano-forte & household & kitchen furniture at auction on: Mar 31, at the residence of Capt T J Lee, on north F st, near 19th. -J C McGuire, auct

$20 reward for runaway light mulatto boy, John Henry, about 13 years old.
-Christian Grammar, Julius E Grammar, excs, near the City Hall.

Disease has made its appearance about the latter part of Jan at the Nat'l Hotel. According to Dr Cornelius Boyle the attack came on in the morning with vomiting or diarrhoea. The proprietors, Messrs Guy & Briggs, have done everything to remove the cause. Mr Thos McDowell states that he ate & drank at the hotel without being made sick; he slept with an open window. Jos Gautier, chief cook, & Alf F Goss, steward, both testified that the copper vessels were perfectly clean & all was in perfect order. Chas Watson, barber, & C H Phelps, operation in House's telegraph ofc, were sometimes affected with a peculiar form of diarrhoea. Mr Amos Davis also had similar attacks. Mr Randolph Coyle, civil engineer, was concerned with the street sewers. A cmte has been formed to consider the sewerage of the city & the proper ventilation of the public hotels.

Orphans Court of Wash Co, D C. In the case of Catherine Engle, admx of Theikman Engle, deceased, the administratrix & Court have appointed Apr 14 next, for the final settlement of the personal estate of said deceased, of the assets in hand.
–Ed N Roach, Reg/o wills

Died: on Mon, in Wash City, Noah Fletcher, aged 71 years. His funeral is this afternoon at 3½ o'clock, from his late residence.

Died: on Mar 8, at his residence, near *Grandcato, La, Dr Robt E Smith, formerly of St Mary's Co, Md. At an early period of his life he removed to Louisiana, where he entered upon the practice of medicine, & became eminently successful in his profession, amassing a handsome fortune. He leaves a family of 6 children to mourn his premature death. [*One letter was light. Grandca_o.]

Farm at private sale: the subscriber offers his farm, containing 50 acres of land, on Sligo Branch, 6 miles from Wash, on the 7th st road. The bldgs are in good condition. Apply on the premises, or address him at Cottage Post Ofc, Montg Co, Md. –Jos Tingle

A new evening paper: the subscriber will commence the publication of a new Evening Paper on Apr 1 next, to be called The Times. Subscription price, 6½ cents per week. –John P Heiss. Ofc No 2 Todd's Bldg, west end of Brown's Hotel.

WED MAR 25, 1857
Appointments by the Pres:
Augustin Olivera, Receiver of Public Moneys at Los Angeles, Calif, vice Andreas Pico, whose term of ofc expires on Mar 29, 1857.
John K Henry, Register of the Land Ofc at Greenville, Ala, vice Eldridge Gardner, whose commission expires on Apr 4, 1857.
Wm W Gift, reappointed, to be Register of the Land Ofc at Benicia, Calif, his previous term of ofc having expired.
Jos B Baker, Collector of the Customs for the district of Phil, vice Chas Brown, whose commission expires on Mar 30, 1857.
Chambers McKibbin, Naval Ofcr for the district of Phil, vice Nathl B Eldred, whose commission expired on Mar 30, 1857.
John Hamilton, jr, Surveyor of the customs for the District of Phil, vice Reuben C Hale, whose commission expires on Mar 29, 1857.
Robt E McHatton, Postmaster of New Orleans, La, vice Arthur S Nevitt, removed.

To the customers of the late John Walker. Mrs Walker is now doing business in her own name, at her Stalls Nox 27 & 29, in the Centre Market, where she will see that the best meat & the most obliging salesman will always be found.
–Hannah M Walker

For sale: Pew No 48 in Trinity Church. Apply to B Bayliss, Missouri ave, between 4½ & 6th sts.

Farm for sale, within 1 miles of Beltsvile, Md, containing 188 acres, more or less. Apply to Geo R Ruff, of Wash City, or to Wm Garner, living upon the premises.

Orphans Court of Wash Co, D C. Letters of administration on the personal estate of Jos Fox, late of Wash Co, deceased. –Alice Fox, adm

Mrd: on Mar 24, in the Fourth Presbyterian Church, by Rev John C Smith, Wm A Coburn to Miss Annie R, daughter of Alex'r Elliott, all of Wash City.

Mrd: on Mar 24, in Wash City, by Rev Mr Deale, Mr Jas M Maddox to Miss Matilda Fugitt, all of Wash City.

Died: on Mar 11, at Stockwood, Elkridge, the residence of her grandfather, Dr R G Stockett, Mrs Margaret A Dorsey, eldest daughter of Geo L & Christiana W Stockett, in her 35th year.

Died: on Mar 15, at St Augustine, Fla, whither he had gone for the benefit of his health, Wm Stubbs, brother of Edw Stubbs, of Wash City, in his 62nd year. He was born in Dublin, Ireland, came to the U S in 1807, & for many years was a resident of Michigan. May he rest in peace.

Obit-died: on Mar 6, in New Orleans, D S Stacy, of the Parish of Concordia, aged about 52 years. He won a distinguished position among the ablest lawyers of the State. He was a native of Maine. In 1839 he married Miss King, of Claiborne Co, Miss, a niece of Cmdor Armstrong. In 1841 he formed a partnership with Gen Edw Sparrow. In 1853 his wife died suddenly in child-bed. It was a blow from which he never recovered. Wealth they had, & they were preparing to enjoy it. His wife is in the grave, his children are sent away, the little ones to be nursed & the older to be educated. His house was left unto him desolate. He brooded over his heart; his mind began to fail; but fortunately a stroke of apoplexy closed the scene. He leaves 6 children, 3 daughters at school in Lexington, Ky, & 2 sons & a daughter with their grandmother, Mrs Neely, in Claiborne Co. -Natchez Courier

Trustee's sale: by deed of trust from Geo B Armstrong & Julia St W, his wife, dated Dec 13, 1854: public auction on Apr 1 next of lots 23 & 24 in square 584; lot 24 being at the intersection of Va ave & 1st st; & lot 23 adjoining, fronting on Va ave. On Apr 2, on the premises, part of lot 10 in square 481, fronting 17 feet on 5th st; & lost 6 in square 777, containing 9,900 square feet. –Chas Myers, trustee
Wall, Barnard & Co, aucts

THU MAR 26, 1857
In Chancery. Com'r Bernard's Ofc, Petersburgh, Va. Thos W Gee & others, plntfs, against Wm C Banister, adm of Harriet B Harrison, deceased, dfndnts. The object of this suit is to obtain a sale of the real estate & negroes of which the late Mrs Harriet B Harrison died seized & possessed, & a distribution of the proceeds amongst those who may be entitled as her heirs at law. Mrs Harrison died intestate, unmarried, & without father, mother, brother or sister, or the descendant of either living at the time of her death; she had no paternal kindred within the decree specified by the Assembly regulating the course of descents living at the time of her death, as far as is known to the parties now before the court. Her maternal kindred living at the time of her death were:
I-The children or descendants of Thos Lewis, deceased, a brother of the mother of Mrs Harrison, namely:
1-Mary C Banister, wife of W C Banister.
2-Virginia Rives, wife of John E Rives.
3-The children of Ann Eliza Gee, deceased, who were Thos W Gee & Caroline Bowden, wife of Wm Bowden.
II-The children or descendants of Ann Quinichett, deceased, who was a sister of Mrs Harrison's mother, viz:
1-Ann Agnes Pucci, her daughter, &
2-John W Quinichett, the only child of her son Vivant Quinichett, deceased.
III-The children of John Lewis, deceased, who was a brother of Mrs Harrison's mother, viz:
1-Mrs Rebecca Raincock.
2-Mrs Mary Ann Schoolfield.
IV-The children of Wm Lewis, deceased, who was a brother of Mrs Harrison's mother, viz:
1-Mary Worsham or her descendants, she having married Edw Worsham, who is dead.
2-Sarah Lester or her descendants, she having married B W Lester.
3-Anne Green, who married Abraham Green, who is dead, or her descendants.
4-Eliza Coleman, who married J H Coleman, who is dead, or her descendants.
5-Thos Lewis or his descendants.
6-Edwin Lewis or his descendants.
7-Jas J W Lewis or his descendants.
8-Louisa F Stith, who married Robt Stith, or her descendants.
Mrs Harrison's estate will be worth, after the payment of the costs of administration & the few debts which she had, about thirty seven or eight thousand dollars. Address your communications to the undersigned com'r, or to David May, who is the counsel managing the cause. –D M Bernard, Com'r

Household & kitchen furniture at auction on: Apr 1, at the residence of E C Eddie, 2 Union Row, on F st, near 7th. -Jas C McGuire, auct

Brvt Maj Sterne H Fowler, capt 5th infty, has resigned his commission, to take effect on Apr 1 next.

Mr Wm Owens, aged about 30 years, was accidentally killed at Phil on Mon. Being present, with his wife & child, at a ball given at Sansom st Hall, he raised one of the windows & sat down upon the window seat, & by some mischance soon afterward fell out upon the pavement, some 30 feet, fracturing his skull & breaking his neck.

Obit-died: on Mar 6, in Wash City, Thos Petigru, of S C, planter, late a cmder in the U S Navy, in his 64th year. He entered the navy in 1812; was twice wrecked & once a prisoner in the hands of the enemy; ever ready to sacrifice ease or expose his life for his country-that county which, after 40 years, without cause shown, turned him adrift. Being possessed of a handsome competency, he was entirely independent of the Federal Treasury, & his disconsolate widow is left with far more of this world's good than she will ever require. But to him & to her all was as trash in comparison with the good name which the action of the Naval Board was calculated to degrade. Childless now, that exemplary widow, whose devotion to his honor & to himself was so touching, mourns his untimely end in the midst of a community which respects his memory & sympathizes with her grief. -K

Appointments by the Pres:
Isaac V Fowler, postmaster at N Y, reappointed.
Edw A King, postmaster at Dayton, Ohio, reappointed.
Henry Sanderson, postmaster at New Brunswick, N J, reappointed.
Jas W Keys, postmaster at Springfield, Ill, vice Isaac R Diller.
Austin Brooks, postmaster at Quincy, Ill, reappointed.
Peter Sweat, postmaster at Peioria, Ill, reappointed.
John H Maier, postmaster at **Fort Wayne**, Ind, reappointed.
The following new post ofcs have been established, for which the persons named have been appointed postmaster:
Hallowell, Dodge Co, Minn: D H Shaw.
Crab Apple Grove, Vermillion, Ill: Jesse Burke.
Haws, Jackson Co, Ohio: Solomon Norris.
Sageland, Henderson Co, Ill: J B Golden.
El Paso, Woodford Co, Ill: M M Jenkins.
Shirley, McLean Co, Ill: Rufus W Dibble.
Etna, Lafayette Co, Wisc: Jona Hoffman.
Mount Alvis, Blount Co, Ala: Jas J Land.
The site & name of the post ofc at Prigmore's Store, Marion Co, Tenn, has been changed to Crown Point, & P A Mitchell has been appointed postmaster, vice J K Prigmore, resigned.

Willis P Bocock, Atty Gen of Va, has resigned his ofc, & Gov Wise has issued a proclamation for an election to fill the vacancy on May 4.

On Mar 15 a young man, Clarke Wiley, of Lexington, Ky, was accidentally shot by a son of Mr Augustus Hall, while the two were out bird hunting, from the effects of which he died in about 18 hours.

Died: on Mar 25, in Wash City, Mr David Ridgely, formerly of Annapolis, Md, in his 65th year. His funeral will take place tomorrow afternoon, at 2 o'clock, from his residence, Pa ave, between 19th & 20th sts.

FRI MAR 27, 1857
Appointments by the Pres:
Isaiah Rynders, Marshal for the Southern district of N Y.
Jacob S Yost, Marshal for the Eastern district of Pa.
Augustus Schell, Collector of Customs at port of N Y, vice H J Redfield, resigned.
Emantel B Hart, Surveyor at the port of N Y.
Land Ofcrs:
Benj Lloyd, Receiver at Greenville, Ala, vice Wm W Fambro.
Jas N B Dodson, Register at Warsaw, Mo, vice Asa C Marvin.
Jas C Tappan, reappointed Receiver at Helena, Ark.
John B Cloutier, reappointed Register at Natchitoches, La.
Edw Conner, reappointed Receiver at Springfield, Ill.
John Connelly, sen, reappointed Register at Springfield, Ill.
Wm W Lewis, reappointed Register at Batesville, Ark.
Chas L Emerson, Surveyor Gen of the U S for the district of Minnesota.
Walter H Harvey, Register at Los Angeles, Calif, vice Hilliard P Dorsey.
Jos P Ament, reappointed Receiver at Palmyra, Mo.
Thos J Bishop, Receiver at Springfield, Mo, vice Henry Fulbright.
Henry J Wilson, Receiver at Ionia, Mich, vice Fred'k Hall.
Postmasters:
G G Westcott, at Phil, vice John Miller.
Geo F Hambright, at Rockford, Ill, vice C H Horsemann, removed.
Edw L Strohecker, at Macon, Ga, vice Jas A Nisbet, resigned.
Jos McCormick, at Baton Rouge, reappointed.
Richd Elward, at Natchez, reappointed.
C R Dickson, at Jackson, Miss, reappointed.
Wm H Carroll, at Memphis, Tenn, reappointed.
Augustus Gassaway, at Annapolis, reappointed.
R L Clow, at Princeton, N J, reappointed.
W A Benjamin, at Trenton, reappointed.
Chas T Gray, at Newark, reappointed.
Mrs Mary Berard, West Point, N Y, reappointed.
Douglas A Danforth, at Burlington, Vt, reappointed.
Jas Atkinson, at Newport, vice Jos Joslin.
Jason Case, at Circleville, Ohio, reappointed.
John L Tuthill, at Lancaster, Ohio, reappointed.

Died: on Mar 17, at Morgantown, Va, Matthew Gay, aged 78 years. He was a native of Ireland, but had been a citizen of Morgantown more than 50 years. He was for many years the Commonwealth's atty for the county, & for the last 15 years Pres of the Branch Bank of Wheeling, in that place. He leaves a widow & 7 children.

Died: on Mar 26, in Wash City, Hannah, wife of Peter Force, in her 59th year. Her funeral will be from the First Baptist Church, 10th st, on Sat afternoon at 3 o'clock. [Mar 28th newspaper: Grand Jury Room, Mar 27, 1857. Mr P F Bacon announced the death of Mrs Peter Force, & moved that a cmte be appointed to draft resolutions sympathizing & condoling with the bereaved family. Hamilton Loughborough & Robt Beall were appointed such cmte. Peter Force was the Foreman of the Grand Jury. –Chas L Coltman, Chairman; Robt White, Sec.]

The whaling barque *H Crapo*, of Dartsmouth, Mass, was capsized Jan 19, & 20 seamen were lost. The capt & 1 seaman was saved on a raft, & subsequently rescued & carried to St Helena by the British steamer **England**.

In Equity-Circuit Court of Wash Co, D C. J B H Smith, vs Jas K Marshall, Edw C Marshall, John Marshall, B A G Taliaferro, F Lewis Marshall, M M Archer, Jas F Jones, John S Smith, John Marshall, of Oak Hill, Thos M Marshall, Ashton A Marshall, Mary M Marshall, heirs at law of the late John Marshall. This bill states that the late John Marshall died seized in fee of the undivided third part of lots 7, 8, & 9, in square 219, in Wash City, D C; that the above named dfndnts are his heirs at law; that the said dfndnts, through their agent & atty, the said Jas K Marshall, on Apr 28, 1852, agreed in writing [which writing is filed as compt exhibit] to sell & convey to said cmplnt all their title & estate in & to said lots; that said cmplnt has fully complied with the said agreement on his part, & is willing & ready & has frequently tendered to pay the balance of the purchase money due by him on account of his purchase of said lots; that the said dfndnts have at various times, through their atty, promised to procure & deliver to said cmplnt a deed conveying their estate in said lots but they have heretofore altogether failed & neglected so to do, giving always as their reason for such failure the difficulty of obtaining the execution of said deed, owing to the dispersion of said dfndnts in various rural districts of the country, & the almost impossibility on this account of executing such deed before the necessary authorities; that the said dfndnts all reside out of D C & beyond the jurisdiction of this honorable Court. The absent dfndnts are to appear at the ofc of the clerk of this Court on the first Monday of Aug next. –Jno A Smith, clerk

Orphans Court of Wash Co, D C. In the case of Randolph Eickhon, exc of Michl Keller, deceased: the executor & Court have appointed Apr 21 next, for the final settlement of the personal estate of said deceased, with the assets in hand.
-Ed N Roach, Reg/o wills

Superior rosewood & other furniture at auction: on Apr 2, at the house lately occupied by Senators Mason, Hunter, & Butler, at 434 G st, between 7th & 8th sts. -A Green auct

Selma [Ala] Reporter of Mar 18: we announce the death of Maj W B King. This sad event occurred at his residence in this city on Wed night last. He had been suffering for some time with a slight attack of pneumonia, but was thought to be recovering until Wed, when he was attacked with a chill, which terminated in his death. He was a model gentleman, & highly respected by all who knew him.

Household & kitchen furniture at auction on: Apr 2, at the residence of Dr Wallace, on Indiana ave, between 1st & 2nd sts. -Jas C McGuire, auct

Three men drowned on the Susquehanna river on Monday, near McCall's Ferry, York Co, Pa, by which Wm Patten, Henry Shultz, & Abner Reese were drowned. They were out in a boat, with Horatio Dunkle, gathering iron from the remains of an old bridge which had been carried down by the recent freshet. The boat sunk, & only one, Dunkle, escaped by swimming ashore.

Two Farms for sale in Buckingham Co, Va, One contains 230 acres, is known as *Owen's Mills*, with a small dwlg house & necessary out-houses. Adjoins the Mosely & Garrett Gold Mines. The other tract lies within ¼th miles of the first one, & contains 216 acres. The undersigned wishes to close his farming operations in & offers it for sale or exchange for city property. Address E Owen, [now upon the premises,] at Buckingham court-house, Va, or E Owen & Co, 212 Pa ave, Wash.

SAT MAR 28, 1857
Appointments by the Pres:
Wm Medill, from May 1, 1857, to be First Comptroller of the Treasury, vice Elisha Whittlesey, resigned.
Ofcrs of Custom:
S B Phinny, Collector for Barnstable, reappointed.
Myer Jacobs, Surveyor for Charleston, reappointed.
Hamilton Stewart, Collector for Galveston, reappointed.
John Boston, Collector for Savannah, reappointed.
Wm N Peden, Naval Ofcr, Wilmington, N C, reappointed.
Wm B Flanner, Surveyor, Wilmington, N C, reappointed.
Wm C Barker, Surveyor, Providence, R I, reappointed.
Asa Gray, Surveyor, Tiverton, R I, reappointed.
Gordon Forbes, Surveyor, Yeocomico, Va, reappointed.
Isaac Hutchinson, Surveyor, Evansville, Ind, reappointed.
Danl Wann, Surveyor, Galena, Ill, reappointed.
Jas W Simmons, surveyor, Copano, Texas, vice H D Norton, resigned.

On Mar 7, as Thos Phair, of Johnsville, Bucks Co, was returning home from John K Spencer's, of Warminster, his clothes took fire from a spark from his pipe, & the wind being high at the time he was unable to put it out. Mr Spencer heard his cries for help & ran out & threw water on him, but his vest & under clothes were burnt off down to his waist. Dr Wm M Mann, of Hartsville found him to be badly burnt, & dressed his wounds. He was taken to his home at his son-in-law's, Chas Trimmer, at Johnsville, where he died on Mar 16, after much suffering. He was about 68 years of age. –Doylestown [Pa] Democrat

John N Wagonseller, the Cashier of the Bank of New Castle, who recently absconded with $50,000, was arrested yesterday in this city. –Phil North American, Thu. [Apr 11th newspaper: John M Wagonseller, the absconding cashier of the Newcastle [Pa] Bank, has been finally committed to answer a charge of embezzling $27,000 belonging to that instutution, on the oath of Dr Chas T Whippe, Pres, & Mr Jos Kissick, a director.]

A mill belonging to Christian Stouffer, & rented to John Hoover, on the Antietam creek, between Leitersburg & Waynesboro, Md, was destroyed by fire on Sat last, with 6,000 bushels of wheat & 100 barrels of flour. There was no insurance.

Wm C Wright, a young married man, was killed on Thu at Vincentown, N J, by being caught in a belt at a grist mill. He was nearly torn to pieces before the machinery could be stopped. A daughter of D W Bills was also dangerously injured in the same way in a grist mill near Tom's river, Ocean Co.

MON MAY 30, 1857
Leonora, the eldest daughter of Baron Lionel Rothschild, has recently been married to Baron Alphonse, the eldest son of Baron Jas Rothschild, of Paris. The bride was attended by 16 bridesmaids, all attired alike in white dresses. She was met at the door by her mother. She was completely enveloped, her whole figure & person, in a veil which reached to the ground, & which is worn in compliance with the Scriptural verse in Genesis relating to Rebecca. –Boston Post

Danl Petigru & Henry King, of Charleston, S C, who were recently sojourning in Wash City, left Friday in charge of the remains of the late Capt Petigru, U S Navy.

Trustee sale of valuable real estate on Pa ave: by 2 deeds of trust executed by Eliz Braiden, deceased, to the undersigned, recorded in the land records of Wash Co, D C, in Liber J A S 113, pages 196 etc; sale on May 1 next, all the right, title, & interest of said Eliz in lot 9 in square 226, in Wash City, with two 3 story brick houses thereon, at the corner of Pa ave & 15th st. The said right, title, & interest consist of three-fourths of two leases for different portions of said lot, but covering the whole of it for 99 years, renewable forever, with a reservation of a ground rent. –Saml Chilton, trustee -C W Boteler, auct

A letter from **Fort Myers** dated Mar 8: this morning an express arrived from Capt Stevenson, commanding in the **Big Cypress**, stating that Lt Freeman, with G Co, 5th infty, who were in advance reconnoitering **Garden Hammock**, near Bowlegstown, were fired on by the Indians. Lt Freeman was wounded severely in the arm, & 3 privates wounded. The loss of the 5th infty is 4 killed, 6 wounded, & 1 missing.

From Calif: 1-Gov Johnson has offered a reward of $2,500 for the murderers of Sheriff Barton, of Los Angeles. 2-Anastacio Garcia, a notorious desperado, was hung in the jail at Monterey, where he was confined on a charge of murder, on Feb 16, by a band of men, who broke open the doors in the night time. 3-Juan Flores, the captain of the band that killed Sheriff Barton, was taken from the jail on Feb 14 by the people & executed.

Yesterday morning Mrs Mary Reed, the wife of Jas Reed, the bookbinder, living in the First Ward, was found lying dead at the foot of a flight of stair-steps in their house. No evidence of foul play could be adduced. The verdict of the jury simply recorded her death was caused by her own imprudence.

Mrd: on Mar 20, in Portsmouth, Va, by Rev Mr Wingfield, Theodore A Walters, of Norfolk, to Miss Georgiana Read, of Portsmouth, Va.

Appointments by the Pres:
Land Ofcrs Reappointed:
Jas H Ware, Register at Huntsville, Ala.
John S Nance, Receiver at Huntsville, Ala.
Wm J Owen, Register at Champagnole, Ark.
Wm T Sargeant, Receiver at Champagnole, Ark.
Henry P Johnson, Register at Wash, Ark, vice Jett.
Chas B Mitchell, Receiver at Wash, Ark.
Thos O Glascock, Register, at Montg, Ala.
Oliver Basham, Register at Clarksville, Ark.
Monroe Donoho, Register at Tuscaloosa, Ala.
Jas W Warren, Receiver at Tuscaloosa, Ala.
Leroy B Cunningham, Register at Fayetteville, Ark, vice Blakemore.
Jos L Dickson, Receiver at Fayetteville, Ark, vice Yell.
Postmasters:
Jacob Carter, at Concord, N H, reappointed.
Reuben S Cheney, at Jackson, Mich, reappointed.
John Morris, at Balt, vice Jacob G Davies.
Nathl A Balch, at Kalamazoo, vice Deyoe.
John E Hunt, at Toledo, Ohio, reappointed.
Danl Stephens, at Elmira, N Y, reappointed.
Cornelius O'Flinn, at Detroit, vice Brodhead.

Criminal Court-Wash-Sat. In the case of Doddridge C Lee, on trial for the murder of David Hume, the jury returned with a verdict of not guilty. The prisoner was then released & retired.

TUE MAR 31, 1857
William, James, & John Morrissy, confined on a charge of murder, & Jas W Barker, in durance for larceny, escaped from the Peoria, Ill, jail on Fri week, by filing off the gratings of a window. One hundred dollars each is the reward offered for the arrest of the fugitives.

The ***White Sulphur Springs*** of ***Greenbrier*** have been sold for $750,000. The prominent stockholders are Messrs Caperton & Berne, of Monroe, Macfarland, of Richmond, & Wm Calwell, of Greenbrier. Mr Calwell is to be continued as the active manager. –Charlottesville, Adv

Handsome & nearly new household & kitchen furniture at auction on: Apr 3, at the residence of Kingman F Page, on 4½ st, south of Ind ave. -Jas C McGuire, auct

I desire to sell my Farm, ***Bleak Half***, containing 1,000 acres of land; together with 50 negroes, of average value. The Farm is situated at the mouth of Mattox Creek. For further particulars address the subscriber, at ***Oak Grove***, Westmoreland Co, Va. -Wm Wirt

Dr Champney died at his residence in Brooklyn, N Y, on Mar 13th, from poison received while making a post mortem examination.

The owners of the ***Blooms' Grove*** tract of Land & Brown Stone Quarries, in Va, offer the same for sale. This valuable property is in Prince Wm Co, Va; contains 500 acres; with an excellent frame dwlg house, stone ofc, overseer's house, blacksmiths' shop, & other necessary out-bldgs, on the property. Apply to I Louis Kinzer, Alexandria, Va.

Died: on Mar 26, at the family mansion in PG Co, Md, Mrs Eliz Calvert, in her 77th year, relict of Edw Henry Calvert, who was the eldest son of Benedict Calvert, of ***Mount Airy***, & grandson of Chas Calvert, the 6th Lord Baltimore.

Died: on Feb 11, at San Juan, of dysentery, Dr Wm H Saunders, surgeon of the Nicaraguan schnr ***Granada***, aged 37 years. Dr Saunders formerly resided in Wash City, where he has left relatives & numerous friends to lament his loss.

Died: yesterday, in Wash City, Mr Geo P Maxwell, in his 69th year. His funeral is this afternoon at 3 o'clock, from his late residence, 123 south D st, between 9th & 10th sts.

Circuit Court for Montg Co, sitting as a Court of Equity. Geo Taylor vs Theodore Mosher, Eliz Brent, widow, & al, heirs at law of the late Brent, deceased. The object of this bill is to procure a valid title in fee to certain lands sold by the dfndnt, Mosher, to the cmplnt, & which were conveyed to Mosher by Eliz Brent, widow, for herself, & acting for her 4 minor children, viz: Francis N, Virginia, [or Mary Virginia,] Clementina D, & Emily C Brent; John Carroll Brent for himself, & as trustee, a cmte of Geo Brent, Chas E Brent, all of the District of Columbia; Thos W Brent & Mercer G Brent, his wife, of Fla; Henry J Brent & Welths A Brent, his wife, of N Y. The bill alleges that the dfndnts, widow & heirs of Wm Brent, deceased, conveyed certain lands, lying in Montg Co, Md, by deed to the dfndnt, Mosher, for a valuable consideration, & covenanted to make such further assurances as might by said Mosher or his assigns, or their counsel, be found necessary to complete the title; that the said Mosher conveyed said lands with like covenants to the cmplnt; that the deed from the first named dfndnts to Mosher is defective & insufficient in law, & prays a sufficient deed may be made the dfndnts or a trustee, & that until such deed is made the dfndnt, Mosher, be enjoined from enforcing his judgment for the balance of the purchase money against cmplnt & his sureties; & whereas it is alleged that the said several dfndnts are non-residenct of the State of Md, it is order that the absent dfndnts appear in the Court, in person or by solicitor, on or before the 2nd Mon of Nov next. –Jas G Henning, Clerk Circuit Court for Montgomery Co.

WED APR 1, 1857
Appointments by the Pres:
John Thomson Mason, Collector for Balt, vice Thomas.
T D Winner, Collector for Great Egg Harbor, reappointed.
Edw T Hillyer, Collector for Newark, reappointed.
R B Willis, Collector for Oxford, reappointed.
G Dell, Collector for St Johns, Fla, reappointed.
Jos Sierra, Collector for Pensacola, reappointed.
Michl Shoemaker, Collector for Detroit, vice Harman.
Levi K Bowen, Naval Ofcr for Balt, vice Kettlewell.
Isaac W Mickle, Surveyor for Camden, N J, reappointed.
Geo W Finley, Surveyor for Balt, vice Wharton.
Chas Parker, Surveyor for Snow Hill, Md, reappointed.
T Rush Spencer, Register at Hudson, Wisc, vice Henning.
Robt J Walker, Govn'r of Kansas, vice Geary.
Fred'k P Stanton, Sec of Kansas, vice Woodson.
John W Watkins, Marshal for Md.
Wm M Addison, Atty for Md.
Geo N Sanders, to be Navy Agent at N Y.
David Small, Postmaster at York, Penn, reappointed.
T Brashears, Postmaster at Steubenville, O, reappointed.

Hon Kensey Johns, Chancellor of the State of Delaware, died at his residence in Newcastle on May 28, in his 66th year. His death leaves a void not easily filled.

Trustee's sale of valuable bldg lots at auction: on May 15 next, by virtue of 2 deeds of trust from Estwick Evans, dated Jun 20th & Aug 15th, 1854, & duly recorded in the land records of Wash Co, D C: sale of part of lot 15 in square 368, on N st, between 9th & 10th sts, & part of lot 13 in square 494, on the Island, fronting on Va ave.
-H B Sweeny, Trustee -A Green auct

Col H O McEnery, for many years a resident of Petersburg, Va, died in New Orleans on Mar 14th. He had been appointed register of the U S land ofc at Monroe, La, but died before hearing of his appointment.

Wash-Circuit Court met yesterday: the jurymen in attendance:

Edw H Edelin	Wm Bond	Chas Skippon
John Ball	Saml Grubb	Amos Davis
David A Gardiner	Thos Sylvester	Jas Lynch
Robt H Martin	Geo W Sothoron	Saml Hanson
Saml McKnight	Martin P King	Leonides Bowen
Patrick McKenna	Benj F Clark	Jas Fullalove
Edw Krouse	Thos A Tolson	Saml Phillips
Wm Martin	Brook Edmonston	Edgar H Bates
Peter Hepburn	John W Ott	Thos Gallagher

Orphans Court of Wash Co, D C. Letters testamentary on the personal estate of Noah Fletcher, late of Wash Co, deceased. –Jos A Clay, B P Fletcher, excs

Criminal Court-Wash-yesterday: 1-Laura Turner was convicted on each of 3 indictments for larceny, & sentenced to a years' imprisonment & hard labor in the penitentiary in each case. 2-Jos E Birch, police ofcr, was tried for an assault on Mr Jonah Levy. [Apr 3rd newspaper: 1-Jos E Birch fined $10 & costs.]

Orphans Court of Wash Co, D C. Letters of administration on the personal estate of John Couney, late of Wash Co, deceased. –Wm A Griffin, adm

St Louis, Mar 31. Santa Fe dates of Feb 28th received here today. There had been several skirmishes between the Mexicans & Indians, & numbers on both sides were killed. It is reported that Judge Hoppen, Jas Lucas, & 2 other Americans had been killed by the Indians near El Paso; also, that Jas Hubble, who had gone to Sonora to bring mules, had been killed by a Gov't party.

THU APR 2, 1857
Died: on Apr 1, Wm Dalton, aged 21 years. His funeral will take place from the residence of Mr J Pilling, on 15th st, on Thu, at 3 o'clock.

Hon Samson W Harris, a Rep from the State of Alabama, died yesterday, at his late lodgings in Wash City, after an illness of several weeks' duration. He was a member of the late House of Reps; 48 years of age; & a victim of laryngitis, complicated with pneumonia, following in such quick succession that of the late Mr Brooks & of the late Mr Disney.

N Y: A long pending suit, in which Dr M Price Moore sought to recover property valued at near $50,000 which he transferred many years ago to put it beyond the reach of creditors, has at length been decided in his favor; & it is said his counsel will receive the handsome fee of $10,000 for his services, which, had an adverse decision been rendered, would have gone unrewarded.

Jos Horner, who was emigrating to the West with his family, was robbed in the cars between Harrisburg & Greensburg, Pa, on Fri last, of $800. This constituted all the money the man had in the world. His pocket was picked while he was dozing, & the thief was unknown, & of course escaped.

Very valuable property for sale: at public auction, on Jun 18 next, at the *Aldie Mills*, in Loudoun Co, Va, all my Real Estate, to wit: the *Aldie Mill* property, embracing 5 acres of land adjoining. The Merchant Mill on Little River Turnpike, 34 miles from Alexandria. The Store House & Lot, in Aldie, occupied by J P H Green as a store house. Also, 50 acres of Wood Land, adjoining the lands of John J Canel, Saml Simpson's heirs, J E Douglass, & others. Also, about 150 acres of land, adjoining Dr Lacey's heirs, W N Berkeley, & others. Also, 75 acres on the Little River turnpike. I am anxious to sell all this property, & invite the attention of the public to it. The terms of payment will be reasonable. –John Moore

For sale: a farm of about 194 acres, in Va, with a dwlg house of 6 rooms & good out bldgs, all new & in fine order. Also, several farms in Md. Apply at 564 M st; or through the post ofc to H N Lansdale, Real Estate Agent.

Mrd: on Mar 31, in Wash City, by Rev W Krebs, Henry F Bibb to Martha A Harper, both of Va.

FRI APR 3, 1857
The body of the wife of P W Thompkins, former member of Congress from Mississippi, after being buried 17 years, was lately taken up & found to be in a perfect state of preservation, the features natural & the hair as flexible as in life. She was buried in a zinc coffin filled with alcohol, & the coffin packed in charcoal.

The last thing heard of John Smith was his elopement from Lansingburg, N Y, with Mgt Pollock. John left a wife & 5 small children, & Mgt deserted an infirm & helpless husband.

Appointments by the Pres:
Chas E Mix, Chief Clerk Indian Ofc, Com'r of Indian Affairs ad interim.
Geo F Shepley, of Portland, Atty for the U S for the district of Maine, reappointed.
Wm K Kimball, Marshall of the U S for the district of Maine, vice the present incumbent.
Land Ofcrs:
John W Whitfield, Register, & Danl Woodson, Receiver for the Delaware district, in Kansas.
Fred'k Emory, Register, & Jas P Downer, Receiver for the western district of Kansas.
Wm H Doak, Register, & Epaphroditus Ranson, Receiver for the Osage district, in Kansas.
Ofcrs of Customs: -Collector:
Moses Macdonald, at Portland, Maine, vice Ezra Carter, jr, whose term has expired.
Robt Burns, at Passamaquoddy, Maine, vice the present incumbent.
Dudley F Leavitt, at Bangor, Maine, vice the present incumbent.
John H Kennedy, at Waldoboro, Maine, vice the present incumbent.
Thos Cunningham, at Wiscasset, Maine, vice the present incumbent.
Jos Berry, at Bath, Maine, vice the present incumbent.
A F Parlin, at Machias, Maine, vice the present incumbent.
Enoch Cousins, at Kennebunk, Maine, reappointed.
Luther Jenkins, at York, Maine, reappointed.
Thos D Jones, at Ellsworth, Maine, reappointed.
Saml J Anderson, Surveyor at Portland, Maine, vice the present incumbent.
Jas Nicholas, Surveyor at Eastport, Maine, vice the present incumbent.
Postmasters:
Saml Jordan, at Portland, Maine, vice Nathan L Woodbury, whose commission has expired.
Leonard Jones, Bangor, Maine, vice Isaac C Haynes, whose commission will expire Apr 5, 1857.
Jos C Snow, Bath, Maine, in place of the present incumbent, whose term has expired.
Jos Mayo has been re-elected Mayor of the city of Richmond, Va, & Raleigh T Daniel, Commonwealth's Atty.

Monument to Mr Legare. The remains of the late Hugh S Legare, of S C, now repose at *Mount Auburn Cemetery*, near Boston, without a tablet to mark the spot. The editor of the Charleston Courier, after interesting himself to discover their resting place, has opened a list at his ofc for the subscriptions from all who desire to contribute to the erection of a suitable monument over the grave of the deceased.

Criminal Court-Wash-Wed. 1-Geo W Mahoney, colored, convicted of stealing $60, but recommended to the mercy of the Court: sentenced to 1 year in the penitentiary. 2-Chas Hurdle was acquitted of a charge of assault & battery. 3-Jas Hagan was acquitted of a charge of burglary on the premises of Basil White.

Circuit Court of D C-sitting in Chancery, Mar Term, 1857. John H Gassaway, Jane A Gassaway, & others, cmplnts, vs Chas B Ott, Maria Ott, Philip Mauro & Eliz Mauro his wife, Catherine Riley, & John W Ott, only surviving devisees & heirs at law of David Ott, deceased, & others. The bill states that David Ott, deceased, on Mar 27, 1818, in consideration of the sum of $3,300, to be paid in 3 equal payments on May 1 in the years 1819, 1820, & 1821, sold, &, by his contracts in writing, bound himself & his heirs to convey to Hanson & John Gassaway the west half of part of lot 4 in square 408, in Wash City, free of all encumbrances; that the said H & J Gassaway passed to the said D Ott their 3 promissory notes for said purchase money, each for $1,100, payable at the times so appointed; that they paid the first note to said David Ott; that said premises by sundry assignments became the separtate property of Hanson Gassaway; that David Ott died about the time the second note became due, & the same was not paid; that the third note was endorsed by said David Ott in his lifetime, & passed to one Edw Dikraff, & was paid at maturity by said Hanson Gassaway; that letters of administration on the personsl estate of said David Ott was granted to Phineas Bradley & Andrew Way, who possess themselves of the said second note, which fell due on May 1, 1820, & Hanson Gassaway shortly after tendered payment of the principal & interest owing thereon to the said administrators, & requested them to receive such payment & to procure for & furnish him a deed for the said lot, executed by the widows & devisees of the said David Ott; that the administrators refused to comply with the said request; that they afterwards died, leaving the personal estate of the said David Ott unadministered, & letters of administration de bonis non thereon were granted to Wm A Bradley; that David Ott, by his last will, devised his real estate to his wife, Mary Ott, his mother, Catherine Ott, his sisters, Julianna Ott, Maria Ott, Eliz Mauro, wife of Philip Mauro, & Catherine Riley, wife of Wm Riley, & his brothers, Jacob Ott & Chas B Ott; that by the death of Catherine Ott, the mother, intestate, & of Julianna, the sister, & Jacob, the brother of said David, intester & without issue, & of Wm Riley, the husband of said Catherine, the parties named dfndnts in the preceding caption & titling have become & are the only heirs & devisees of the real estate of the said David Ott. The bill states that the said Mary Ott, the widow of David Ott, renounced all benefit of the devisees in her favor contained in the said bill, & sued for & recovered her dower in the said premises, & that the said Hanson Gassaway purchased a relinquishment thereof at a cost of $600.50. The bill further states that the title of the said David Ott to the said premises was, at the time of the sale thereof to the said H & J Gassaway, altogether defective, & that the cmplnts were obliged to employ counsel to perfect the same at an expense to them of $150. The bill further states that the said premises have been sold by John Marbury, who was appointed for that purpose a trustee under a decree of the said court, to pay sundry debts of the said H Gassaway charged thereon by mortgage & deeds of trust. The object of the bill is to have an adjustment, under the supervision of the said court, of the claim by the administrator de bonis non of David Ott against the estate of Hanson Gassaway for the unpaid purchase money of the said premises, & that the amount thereof, when ascertained, may be paid by the trustee by whom said sale was made out of the proceeds of such sale, & that the said parties named dfndnts in the preceding caption & titling may be decreed, by a day certain, after the payment of the said purchase money, to convey the said premises & all the estate therein of David Ott, at the time of his death, to the said John Marbury, trustee, for the purpose of the decree under which he has made sale thereof, or in such other manner, for the like purpose, as the Court may order. The bill states that the dfndnts, except John W Ott, Wm A Bradley, & John Marbury, are non-residents. Absent dfndnts to appear in person or by solicitor, on the first Mon of Oct next. -Jno A Smith, clerk

Circuit Court of Wash Co, D C-in Chancery, Mar Term, 1857. Evan Lyons, John Davidson, Saml McKenney, & Thos Brown, survivors of John Kurtz & others, cmplnts, vs Wm B Scott, Philip B Key, Chas Jenkins, Walter D Davidge, John D Kurtz, Walter S Cox, & Clement Cox, dfndnts. The bill states that Wm B Scott, Thos Smith, & Saml Stott, as sureties of the said Wm, being indebted unto the cmplnt & others whom they have survived, on their bond dated Jan 18, 1847, in the sum of $14,000, with a condition thereunder written that the same shall be void of the said Scott should pay to the cmplnts & heir deceased co-obligees the sum of $7,212 in 4 equal successive yearly payments from the said date, with interest thereon; in order to secure the payment of the said debt & interest, the said Wm B Scott & his wife, by their deed, conveyed to John Kurtz & Clement Cox a certain parcel of land in Wash Co, & in Montg Co, Md, called **Dalecarlia**; that the said deed contains a provision that if the said Wm B Scott & his reps & assign should fail to pay any part of the principal debt or interest when due, that the said John Kurtz & Clement Cox,or the survivors of them, or the heirs of such survivor, should have power to sell the said parcel of land or any part thereof at public auction, on such terms & conditions, & after such public notice of the manner, time, place & term of sale, as the person making such sale should approve, &, after paying the expenses of executing said trust, apply the proceeds of such sale to the payment of the said debt & interest. The bill states that the said Wm B Scott paid part of the said principal debt & interest on the whole sum up to Jan 1, 1856; & that there is still owing on the said bond & due to the cmplnts the full sum of $4,250.62, with interest thereon from the day last aforesaid; that the time fixed for the payment of said debt in & by the said bond has long since elapsed; that the said cmplnts have applied to the obligors in the said bond for payment of the unpaid portion of said debt, but neither the said Wm B Scott or the said Smith or Stott have paid the same or any part thereof; that the said Clement Cox & John Kurtz are both dead, leaving the trusts of the said deed unexecuted; that Walter S Cox & Clement Cox are the only surviving heirs at law of said Clement Cox, deceased, & John D Kurtz the only heir at law of said John Kurtz. The bill states that after the date of the deed aforesaid the said Wm B Scott, being indebted to the U S A in some amount of money to the cmplnts unknown, did by his deed, dated Jul 20, 1850, & since recorded among the land records for the said county, in Liber J A S No 15, at folio 343 etc, convey the same parcel of land to Philip B Key & his heirs, in order to secure the payment of the last mentioned debt. That afterwards the said Wm B Scott sold the same parcel of land to one Chas Jenkins, & by his deed conveyed the same to the said Jenkins in fee; that the said Chas Jenkins by his deed, dated Aug 4, 1855, after reciting that he was indebted to said Scott in the sum of $26,300, by his deed of that date conveyed the same parcel of land to Walter D Davidge & his heirs to secure the payment of the said last mentioned sum of money, with power to sell if there should be a default on the part of the said Chas Jenkins to pay the same; that said Jenkins is by himself or his agents in possession of the said premises, & his cutting the wood & quarrying the stone on the said land & selling the same for his own benefit; that the said named heirs at law of Clement Cox & John Kurtz either decline to act, or are, from their position, unable to act as trustees in the premises; the said Wm B Scott, Philip B Key, Chas Jenkins, Walter D Davidge, John D Kurtz, Walter S Cox, & Clement Cox are made dfndnts to the said bill. The object of the bill is to have a decree passed by the said Court for the appointment of some proper person to act as trustee in the premises in the place of the said deceased, John Kurtz & Clement Cox, & for a sale by such trustee of the premises in the said bill mentioned for the payment of the debt & interest thereon due to the cmplnts, & such other relief as to the Court may seem right in the premises; & for as much as it appears to the Court that the said Chas Jenkins, Clement Cox, & John D Kurtz do not reside in D C, cannot be found therein. Absent dfndnts to appear in person or by atty on the first Monday of Oct next. -Jno A Smith, clerk

Died: on Apr 2, Wm B Draper, aged 27 years. His funeral will take place from the residence of Mr J Pilling, on 15th st, on Thu at 3 o'clock.

Circuit Court of D C –Mar Term, 1857. John A Gassaway & others, heirs at law of Hanson Gassaway, vs Nathl Jewell. The trustee sold the west part of lot 4, & part of lot 5, in square 408, in Wash City, to Wm B Kibbey, for $21,600, & the purchaser has complied with the terms of sale. –Jno A Smith, clerk

Circuit Court of Wash Co, D C-in Chancery, Mar Term, 1857. John A Gassaway & others, heirs at law of Hanson Gassaway, deceased, cmplnts, vs Richd B Dorsey, Robt E Dorsey, Jas W Dorsey, Anna M Johnson, Julianna Johnson, Franklin Knight, & Lavinis Knight, heirs at law & descendants of Wm H Dorsey, deceased, dfndnts. The bill of cmplnt states that Wm H Dorsey, late of Balt Co, Md, deceased, by his deed dated Jul 1, 1808, in consideration of the sum of $320 to him paid by one Ignatius Edelin, did convey, or design to convey, to the said Edelin & his heirs & assigns lot No 5 in square 408, in Wash City aforesaid; that the said deed contains the usual covenants of warranty; that Hanson Gassaway, deceased, was in his lifetime & at the time of his death entitled to an equitable estate in fee simple to that part of said lot No 5 adjoining lot 4 in the same square, with certain alley privileges in said bill mentioned; that said Hanson Gassaway devised his title to the said part of lot 5 through the said deed from Wm H Dorsey, by a purchase from Jos Forrest, a trustee appointed by decree of the said Court in the case of Combe's & Meade's heirs; that Forrest died without having conveyed the said premises to said Hanson

Gassaway; that said Hanson Gassaway mortgaged the same & other real estate in connexion therewith to secure the payments of sundry debts; that the said premises have been sold by John Marbury, trustee, under the decree of the said Court, to pay said debts, but he is unable to give the purchasers a satisfactory title to the same because the deed aforesaid from the said Wm H Dorsey is supposed to be defective in this, that it was executed in Balt Co aforesaid by said Wm H Dorsey, & contained a letter of atty authorizing one Thos Herty to go before some persons authorized to take the acknowledgment of deeds in D C & asknowledge the said deed to be the act & deed of the said Wm H Dorsey; that one of the subscribing witnesses to the said deed & letter of atty appeared before the said Thos Herty, who was a notary public residing in Wash Co, D C, & proved before him the execution of the said letter of atty by the said Dorsey; & thereupon the same Thos Herty, without further proof of the execution of the said letter of atty, went before the Com'r of Public Bldgs in Wash City & acknowledged the said deed to be the act & deed of the said Wm H Dorsey. The bill states that the said Hanson Gassaway died intestate & without issue, & that the cmplnts are his heirs at law, & as such filed this petition in the said cause of Combe & Meade's heirs, praying for the appointment of a trustee in the place of the said Forrest, & that the legal title in the said premises should be conveyed by such trustee to the said John Marbury & his heirs, to enable him to execute the trusts confided to him as trustee aforesaid; that said decree was passed by the said Court. The bill further states that the said Wm H Dorsey died intestate, leaving several children, his heirs at law; that the dfndnts named in the preceeding caption & titling are his heirs at law, & that the title to the said premises, through such defect in the acknowledgment of the deed aforesaid, is now vested in them; but, as trustees for the persons claiming & showing titles thereto as assignees of the said premises from the said Ignatius Edelin, the object of the said bill is to have a decree directing the said named dfndnts to convey unto John Marbury, of D C, all the legal estate & title in that part of said lot No 5, in square 408, herein before described, with the alley privileges in the bill of cmplnt mentioned, in trust, to enable him to effect & fulfill the objects & purposes for which he was appointed trustee by a decree of the said Court passed on Nov 22, 1856, in a certain cause in the said Court depending, in which the said cmplnts were plntfs & one Nathl Jewett was dfndnt, being No 462 on the Equity Docket of the said Court, & for other relief. And for as much as the Court is satisfied that the said named dfndnts are not inhabitants of D C & cannot be found therein, it is by the Court ordered that the said absent dfndnts appear in person or by solicitor on the first Monday in Oct next. –Jno A Smith

Orphans Court of Wash Co, D C. Letters of administration with the will annexed on the personal estate of Alex'r H Lawrence, late of Wash Co, deceased.
–Jane Lawrence, admx w a

SAT APR 4, 1857
Dr A H Saunders, a clerk in the 6th Auditor's ofc, died suddenly at his residence in Alexandria yesterday morning.

Hon Saml Brenton, of Indiana, died at his residence at **Fort Wayne** on Mar 29. He was a Member of the last House of Reps. [Apr 16th newspaper: Mr Brenton was born in Gallatin Co, Ky, Nov 22, 1810, & was therefore in his 48th year. He entered the ministry when he was 20 years old, but when struck with paralysis, in 1848, he resigned his pastoral ofc, & was appointed by Gen Taylor the next year as Register of the **Fort Wayne** Land Ofc. He was elected to Congress in 1851, &, with the exception of 2 years, when he acted as Pres of the **Fort Wayne** College, has been continued in that position ever since. His funeral was a very large one.]

Circuit Court of Wash Co, D C-in Chancery, No 1,255. John Bayne vs Chas H Venable, John Milstead, & Eliza Milstead. The object of this suit is to procure a decree annulling & vacating a certain deed of indenture dated Sep 24, 1856, duly executed by the said dfndnt, Chas H Venable, conveying certain real estate, which is particularly described in the bill, to the said dfndnt, Eliza Milstead, & to procure a sale of said real estate for the purpose of satisfying a certain judgment recovered by the cmplnt against the said dfndnt Venable. The bill states that the said Chas H Venable, being indebted unto the cmplnt in the sum of $876, with interest from Nov 27, 1855, the cmplnt brought suit against the said dfndnt Venable at the Mar term, 1856, of the Circuit Court of D C, sitting as a Court of common law, & that at the Oct term following recovered a judgment; that the cmplnt caused a writ of fieri facias to be issued on said judgment, & that said writ was returned nulla bona by the marshal; that whilst indebted as aforesaid the said Venable was seized & possessed of the real estate described in the bill, but that after said suit was brought, & before said judgment was obtained, the said dfndnt Venable conveyed the said real estate to the said dfndnt, Elza Milstead, the mother of the said Venable & wife of the said John Milstead, in consideration, as recited in said deed, of the sum of $2,000, purporting to have been paid by the said Eliza Milstead to the said Chas H Venable; that the said sum of $2,000 was not in fact so paid, & that said conveyance was not made bona fide & for a valuable consideration, but was made without any valuable consideration whatever, & that said Venable was largely indebted at the time of the execution thereof to the cmplnt & to other persons, & that he had little or no property besides that conveyed by said deed, & no means of discharging his liabilities, & that said conveyance was therefore fraudulent & void as against said cmplnt & the other creditors of said dfndnt Venable; & that said John Milstead resides out of D C. Absent dfndnt to appear in person or by solicitor, on or before the first Monday of Sept next. –Jno A Smith, clerk

For rent: the residence lately occupied by Hon Jas Thorington, 483 11th st, between E & F sts. –Francis Miller, Grocer, 301 F st, corner of 12th st.

Criminal Court-Wash-Thu. 1-Thos F May was found guilty for an assault at the President's House on Mar 6, with a recommendation to the mercy of the Court. The Court fined him $5. 2-Ham Degges, charged with an assault & battery at the same time & place: fined $5.

Appointments by the Pres:
Geo R Berrell, Appraiser for the port of Phil.
Moses Bates, jr, Collector for Plymouth, Mass, vice Little.
Amos Robins, Collector for Perth Amboy, vice Brinley.
W S Jackson, Collector for the district of Vienna, Md, vice Smith.
Lyndon Taylor, Surveyor for Pawcatuck, T I, reappointed.
Warren Hathaway, Postmaster at Eastport, Maine, reappointed.
Edgar Whidden, Postmaster at Calais, reappointed.
Saml Edwards, Postmaster at Belfast, vice Noyes.
R H Glass, Postmaster at Lynchburg, reappointed.
J R Sharpstein, Postmaster at Milwaukee, vice Noonan.
Danl C Brown, Postmaster at Janesville, Wisc, vice E H Strong.

Mr E C Glasgow, a young man of unexceptionable character, met his death on Friday night by falling from the suspension bridge, & striking upon the rocks below the bluff, on this side of the river. Glasgow had walked on the bridge with a friend & while his friend had gone midway on the bridge to see a steamboat coming up, Glasgow sat on the railing awaiting his return. When the friend returned he became alarmed when Glasgow was gone, fearing that he had fallen in the river. The light of day confirmed his fears. Glasgow laid dead 140 feet from the flooring of the bridge. –Nashville Gaz, 29th.

Mrd: on May 29, near the **Old Fields**, Md, by Rev J Scrivener, Burton Smith to Martha M Randall, both of PG Co, Md.

Mrd: on Apr 2, in Wash City, by Rev W Krebs, John H Robey to Georgia Emma Bede, both of Wash City.

Mrd: on Apr 2, in Wash City, by Rev Wm H Chapman, Mr Francis Lockey to Miss Clarissa A Mitchell, all of Wash City.

Mrd: on Apr 2, in Wash City, by Rev S A H Marks, Mr Jno T Burgess to Miss Ellen Jones.

Died: on Apr 2, at his residence, 4th & East Capitol sts, Mr Jonas Middleton, stonecutter, aged 51 years & 13 days. He was born near Lancaster, England, & came to this country in 1850.

MON APR 6, 1857
Household & kitchen furniture at auction on: Apr 8, at the residence of the late Ann Marten, on 9th st, between L & M sts. -Jas C McGuire, auct

Household & kitchen furniture at auction on: Apr 7, at the residence of Mrs J A Curran, on north A st, No 18. -A Green auct

Death of an African explorer. Intelligence received this week at the Foreign Ofc, from the British Consul at Tripoli, of the assassination of Dr Vogel, whose arrival at Kuka, on the borders of lake Tsad, in the best health & spirits, we announced Jun, 1854. The letter received at Tripoli is from Cpl Maguire, one of the Sappers sent out with Dr Vogel, & is written from Kika. Dr Vogel had departed from that place, comparatively alone, on a most perilous journey eastward, with the view of reaching the Nile. He is said to have advanced through Brigirmi into Waddy, & to have been there murdered. –London paper

Administrator's sale of stock of groceries, household & kitchen furniture at auction on: Apr 10, by order of the administrator, the personal effects of the late C G Rozenthall, at his late residence & store, on Pa ave, near 19th st.
–Wall, Barnard & Co, auct. –Barnard & Buckey, aucts

J Alfred Halsey, formerly of Petersburg, Va, & lately of N Y, committed suicide by taking strychnine, at the Girard House in Phil, on Wed night. He is supposed to have been about 25 years of age.

Comr's sale: by order of the Circuit Court of Wash Co, D C, passed on Apr 1, 1857, in the matter of the petition of the heirs of Wm Phillips, late of Wash Co, deceased, we will, on May 1 next, sell the real estate of which the said Wm Phillips died seized & possessed in the said county: lot with 3 dwlg houses in Tenallytown, containing 1¼ acres of ground; another lot in the same town containing 1 acre with a stone bldg on it; a parcel of land on River road, containing 19¾ acres of ground, highly improved; also, one undivided seventh part of the real estate of the late Theophilus Robey, consisting of about ¼ acre of ground in Tenallytown; & 60 acres, parts of 2 tracts of land known as *Dry Meadow* & the *Vale*, about a mile n e of Tenallytown.
-Joshua Peirce, Notley Moreland, John E Chappell, David Shoemaker, Peirce Shoemaker, Commissioners. Any further information will be given by calling on Jas Phillips, Tenallytown, D C. –Barnard & Buckey, aucts
+
Administrator's sale of the personal property of the late Wm Phillips, deceased, in Tenallytown, D C: one horse, one mule, one cow, one two-horse wagon, one one-horse wagon, 5 fine beds & bedding, stoves, & a great many articles not mentioned
-Jas Phillips, adm

The Independence [Mo] Messenger of Mar 21 records the death by drowning, at Maxwell's Landing, of Messrs Jas Talbot, Thos Smith, & ___ Harris. The boat they were in capsized, when they were crossing the river to go geese hunting.

Obit–died: on Mar 28, at his residence in Newcastle, Dela, Hon Kensy Johns, in his 66th year. He was for 4 years a Rep in the U S Congress, for 25 years Chancellor & Pres Judge of the Court of Errors & Appeals of the State of Delaware, & for 42 years a Ruling Elder in the Presbyterian Church. He was called away suddenly, but the messenger found him ready to go, for he found him praying. He had spent the evening with his family, retired to his chamber, & while rising from his knees, at the conclusion of his secret devotion, the hand of death was laid on him, & in a few moments his spirit passed away. –J B S -Newcastle, Del, Apr 3.

Dred Scott. Democratic canvassers in the town of Gloucester, R I, struck the names of the colored voters in that town from the lists before the election on Wed, alleging that they were justified in this action by the decision in the case of Dred Scott. The Providence Journal intimates that legal proceedings will be commenced against them.

Orphans Court of Wash Co, D C. Letters of administration on the personal estate of Saml W Handy, late of Wash Co, deceased. –Mgt W Handy, admx

Appointments by the Pres:
John Appleton, of Maine, Assist Sec of State, vice J A Thomas, resigned.
Custom-house Ofcrs:
Jacob Fry, Collector, Chicago, vice Conley.
Edmund Wright, Collector, Edenton, N C, reappointed.
Robt Parks, Collector, Cuyahoga, Ohio, reappointed.
John P Baldwin, Collector, Key West, reappointed.
Augustus Jenkins, Collector, Portsmouth, N H, vice Zenas Clement.
Josiah G Hadley, Surveyor, Portsmouth, N H, vice Sheldon.
Geo R Berrell, Appraiser, Phil.
Timothy Rives, Collector, Petersburg, Va, vice Banks.
Land Ofcrs:
Chas G Wagner, Register at Stillwater, Minn, vice Fullerton.
Milton H Abbott, Receiver at Stillwater, Minn, vice Holcombe.
Saml Plumer, Register at Faribault, Minn, vice Lowell.
Geo B Clitherall, Register at Ojibway, Minn, vice Plumer.

Dr Jean Baptiste Theopile Dorion, a wealthy physician of the vicinity of Montreal, was convicted a few days ago of robbing his brother, also a physician, when at the point of death, & sentenced to 2 years in the penitentiary. He was terribly affected upon hearing the sentence.

As the freight train which left Charleston for Columbia on Thu was passing near *Four Holes Swamp*, one of the rails broke, & 5 of the cars were precipitated from the track. The conductor, Mr John Gilbert, was fatally crushed between 2 boxes, & one of his assistants was killed by the car falling on him. [No name given.]

Moses Harrelson, who escaped from jail at Marion Court-house, in S C, in 1855, while under sentence of death for the murder of E A Rogers, was lately retaken, & has again been sentenced to be hung on Jun 5 next.

Alfred Countryman was executed, according to legal sentence, at Rockford, Ill, on Mar 27, for the murder of the sheriff of that county, John F Taylor, on Nov 11 last.

Mrd: on Mar 24, at Key West, Fla, by Rev Mr Herrick, Lt M Carrington Watkins, U S Navy, to Miss Hortense Tatine, of Key West.

Died: on Apr 2, in Wash City, Mr Henry White, of Mobile, Alabama.

Died: on Apr 1, after a long & painful illness, in her 33rd year, Eliz Graves, wife of Wm Graves, of St Mary's Co, Md, & daughter of Thos & Eliz Howell, of Wash City. She was a dutiful daughter, a kind sister, an affectionate wife, & a fond mother.

Application will be made to the Com'r of the Gen Land Ofc of the U S for the issue of land scrip on duplicate Warrants of Nos 4,373 & 4,374, each for 1,333 $1/3^{rd}$ acres, issued by the Register of the Land Ofc of the State of Va on Oct 29, 1789, in the name of Jas Carroll, a midshipman in the Va State navy in the war of the Revolution, which warrants have been lost or mislaid & cannot be found. –R B Bagby, atty

Orphans Court of Wash Co, D C. In the case of Isabella Mothershead, admx of John Mothershead, deceased: the Court & administratrix have appointed Apr 28 next, for the final settlement of the personal estate of said deceased, with the assets in hand. -Ed N Roach, Reg/o Wills

TUE APR 7, 1857
Valuable & beautiful farm or country seat, about 3 miles from the Capitol, at auction: on Apr 23, the *Vineyard*, the residence of the late John Agg, handsomely situated on the Heights, north of Wash, adjoining the farm attached to the Military Asylum, & within a half a mile of Rock Creek Church. Apply to E J Middleton, at the City Hall. -A Green auct

The last arrival from Europe brings the intelligence of the death of a divine whose name is well known to some of our older citizens, Hon & Rev [formerly Capt,] Chas R Pakenham, a priest of the <u>Passionist order</u>. He was born in 1821, was formerly one of the aids-de-camp to her Majesty the Queen, holding the commission of captain in the Guards. Having resigned the profession of arms & joining the religious order of the Passionists, he was ordained a priest in the Roman Catholic Church. He was son of the late brother to the present Earl of Longford, & was a nephew of the late Duchess of Wellington, wife of the Iron Duke, & first cousin to the present Duke of Wellington. His surviving brother is Hon & Very Rev Henry Pakenham, Dean of St Patrick's, Dublin.

I O O F. Members of the Grand Lodge of D C, are to meet this afternoon at 2 o'clock, to attend the funeral of our late Brother, P G John Tyssowski.
–J T Bangs, Grand Sec

Louisville Journal of Mar 30. Our intelligent young friend, Chas W Kleisendorf, has just returned to his home in this city from Nicaragua. He left Walker's headquarters at Rivas on Mar 6 & San Juan del Sud on Mar 7. He left here last Aug, & upon arriving in Nicaragua was made a lt. He contracted malaria & was in the hospital for some time. The following are all of the "boys" who went out from this city now with Walker: Capt J W Gaskell, Lt John Hooe, Wm J Gray, Sam Downing, Geo Daniels, Pat Rooney, Emmets Scales, John Parker, & Ed Parker. None of these are fit for service excepting Sam Downing. Capt J B Green has recovered from wounds received in battle, & is not dead, as was reported. Mr McKay, of Nelson, also reported dead, was well. It is with the greatest difficulty that any one can leave Walker's service. Mr Kleisendorf was only permitted to resign his commission through the instrumentality of powerful letters from the Administration at Washington, obtained by Mr Henry J Lyons, who dispatched Mr S McKaig to Nicaragua with them.

Appointments by the Pres: 1-Jas D Reymert, Receiver at Hudson, Wisc, vice Otis Hoyt, resigned, to take effect May 1, 1857. 2-Wm T Galloway, Register at Eau Claire, Wisc. 3-Noel Byron Boyden, Receiver at Eau Claire, Wisc.

Mrd: on Apr 5, by Rev F S Evans, Mr Gustavus Cozens to Miss Marian Lucas.

Died: on Apr 1, J C Henry, of Hambrook, near Cambria, Md. He was a gentleman of great worth & usefulness, & is much lamented by the community in which he lived.

Died: on Apr 4, in Clarksburg, Montg Co, Md, of pneumonia, Jane C Stuck, aged 53 years, wife of F F Stuck, & daughter of the late Isaac Cooper, of Wash City.

Meeting of the Law Ass'n on Apr 7, at Temperance Hall, at 7½ o'clock. Members of the profession & students of law are invited to attend. –G F Gouley, sec

I O O F. Members of the Oriental Lodge, No 19, of D C, are to meet this afternoon at 2 o'clock, to attend the funeral of our late Brother, P G John Tyssowski. –Wm H Dietz, Noble Grand

Mrs M A Speir, will introduce her new styles of Spring Millinery, on Apr 9, at 356 D st, Wash, D C.

Teacher wanted: a tutor in my family [for 4 or 6 pupils] well qualified to teach in Latin, Greek, Mathematics, & the usual branches of an English education. Good references required. Direct to Pearson Chapman, Pomonky P O, Chas Co, Md.

WED APR 8, 1857
Orphans Court of Wash Co, D C. Letters testamentary on the personal estate of Murry Barker, jr, late of Wash Co, deceased. –Matilda Barker, excx

Orphans Court of Wash Co, D C. In the case of Jeanna Hughes, [late Ryon,] admx of Thos Ryon, deceased, the administratrix & Court have appointed May 4 next, for the final settlement of the personal estate of said deceased, of the assets in hand.
-Ed N Roach, Reg/o wills

Orphans Court of Wash Co, D C. In the case of John S Finch, adm of David Finch, deceased, the administrator & Court have appointed Apr 28 next, for the final settlement of the personal estate of said deceased, of the assets in hand.
–Ed N Roach, Reg/o wills

Appointments by the Pres: Thaddeus Sanford, Collector, Mobile, reappointed.
Wm S Bowen, Collector, Bridgetown, N J, reappointed.
Moritz Schoeffler, Collector, Milwaukee, vice White.
Stephen Willits, Collector, Little Egg Harbor, N J, reappointed.
W W W Wood, Collector, Vicksburg, vice Walker.
A T Walling, Postmaster at Keokuk, vice Patterson.
C R Rudd, Postmaster at Evansville, Indiana, vice Stinson.
John Moore, Postmaster at Vincennes, vice Dick.
John M Talbott, Postmaster at Indianapolis, vice Wick.
T F Young, Postmaster at Saratoga, vice Close.
John Fraser, Postmaster at New Bedford, vice Kent.

The new iron steamer **General Rusk**, in honor of the distinguished Senator from Texas, has lately been built at Wilmington, Dela, for the Southern Steamship Co of New Orleans. She is to run between New Orleans & Texas, connecting with the railroad at Berwick's Bay. Her length is 200 feet keel, 25½ feet beam, & 9½ feet hold. She has 4 water-tight compartments.

A terrible affair occurred in Bullitt Co, 2 or 3 miles from Shephersville, on Thu last. Eliz Buchey was forbidden by her father, Mr Julius Buchey, in seeing a young man he found objectionable. Thinking she was secretly going to meet him, instead of spending the day at Mr Elias Hall, a neighbor, the young lady protested that she had no thought of meeting him, & rebuked him for his lack of confidence. Mr Buchey became excited & drew his revolver & fired a shot at her & she began to run, when he fired another, killing her instantly. He then discharged the contents of a third barrel into his own head, & expired as he fell. The father had been highly esteemed by his neighbors. He was well to do in the world, & apparently happy.

Harrisburg, Apr 6. 1-Senator Penrose, of Phil, died here today, & both Houses have adjourned in consequence. 2-The Govn'r has appointed Jas M Armstrong, of Lycoming Co, Supreme Judge, in place of Judge Black.

Watertown, N Y, Apr 6. The dwlg of Mr Grimshaw, near Cape Vincent, was burnt on Sat, & Mr Grimshaw, with his wife & children, perished in the flames.

The Mount Sterling [Ky] Whig tells of the murder in Estill Co last week. A young man, Edw Hawkins, stole a horse in Estill, when constable Jas Land & Mr J Irwin gave him pursuit & caught him before he was out of the county. He gave himself up to the ofcrs without resistance, & was placed on behind Mr Land on his horse to be taken to the county jail. They had not proceeded far when Hawkins, having espied a revolver in the breast pocket of the ofcr, thrust his hand in, drew it forth, & discharged the contents of a barrel in the head of Mr Land, killing him instantly; then leveled the revolver at the head of Mr Irwin, discharging another barrel, & killing him also. The audacious murderer then took to the fields & woods & escaped. [May 12th newspaper: Hawkins was arrested in Estill Co, Ky, some weeks ago, & placed on a horse behind the Sheriff, with a man along as guard, & managed to draw a revolver from the pocket of the Sheriff & killed both of them. He was tried, found guilty of murder, & will be hung on May 29. He is said to have married 5 wives, & is barely 21 years old.] [May 28th newspaper: Hawkins is a grandson of Tom Harper, a notorious brigand, who was prominent in the bloody scenes of early Ky history.–Louisville Democrat]

John A Calhoun is announced in the Abbeville paper as a candidate for Congress, in place of the late Preston S Brooks. C P Sullivan is also a candidate.

Mrd: on Mar 30, at St Louis, by Rev Dr Rice, W M Corcoran, of St Paul, Minn, to Annie H, daughter of Maj H C Denny, U S Army.

Died: on Mar 31, at Staten Island, N Y, Chas Rhind, in his 79th year.

Died: on Apr 8, in Gtwn, George Thomson Derby, son of David L & Estelle E Shoemaker, aged 3 years, 2 months & 27 days.

The Jamestown Society will meet at Masonic Hall, this evening, at 7½ o'clock.
-C W C Dunnington, sec

THU APR 9, 1857
Excellent household & kitchen furniture at auction on: Apr 15, at the residence of Hon Caleb Cushing, the west house in *Franklin row*, between 12th & 13th sts.
-C W Boteler, auct

This is to give notice that I intend applying to the Com'r of Pensions for the renewal of Bounty Land Warrant No 49,366, for 120 acres of land, issued to the subscriber on Feb 8, 1856, under the act of Congress approved Mar 3, 1855, & sent to my agent, Jno Johnson, who mailed said warrant to me Feb 11, 1856, but which has never come to hand. A caveat has been duly filed to prevent an improper location of said warrant. –Chas Jenkins, of Chas Co, Md.

The iron & ship chandlery store of Mr John Bushnell, at New Albany, Ia, together with several adjoining bldgs, were burnt on Sunday last. The loss amounted to $49,000, on which there is but little insurance.

Wash Corp: Mayor's nominations confirmed: W H Berry, M D, as physician to the Wash Asylum; Geo Mattingly, as Com'r of the Wash Asylum; Thompson Van Reswick, as Com'r of Improvements for the 5th & 6th Wards; J B Gardner, as apothecary to supply the poor of the 5th Ward with medicines; Theodore Mosher, as wood & coal measurer, & as measurer of grain & bran for the 2nd district; Jas H Suit, as police constable for the 3rd district; & Wm Bird, as police constable for the 7th district.

Detroit Advertiser of Apr 4. Breach of promise. Eunice C Hall vs Geo W Carne, trial at the Circuit Court on Thu, concluded yesterday, the jury finding for the plaintiff, & assessing the damages at $5,000. The parties had some slight acquaintance in 1852, but at that time no great intimacy existed between them. About Aug 18, 1856, Miss Hall came from her residence at the East to this city, on a visit to her sister, the wife of Vincent J Scott. At Suspension Bridge she was met in the cars by Mr Carne, who introduced himself, & accompanied her to Detroit. He was invited by the family of Mr Scott to call at their house while the lady remained, which he did almost every other day; attended church with her, & escorted her on other occasions. His last call was about Nov 2. Mr Duffield, of counsel for plntf, offered 4 letters in evidence, addressed by the dfndnt to Miss Hall & one to her father. The first, dated Sep 25, 1856, was simply an excuse for not calling; the second, dated Sep 28, 1856, was addressed to her father, asking his consent to their marriage, setting forth that he was engaged in a lucrative business, & he had a high esteem for the daughter. The third letter, of Oct 6, accompanied a present of a portfolio to the lady. The fourth, of Nov 1, enclosed a check for $100, for shopping purposes. The fifth letter, dated Nov 3, he stated that he had met with many unpleasant remarks, & had received some letters in regard to the union about to take place, & for that reason, & for fear that unhappiness might preside at their fireside, he must break off an engagement which he felt he had entered upon hastily. In a postscript, written several days after, he said he had been unwilling to send the letter to her, but, though he was sorry to be compelled to do so, he felt that he must, for the sake of their mutual happiness. On coming home that day, Mr Scott found the family in distress, & he thereupon called upon the dfndnt at the brewery. *Crane said that he had found out that the family was not respectable, & for that reason he must break off the match. This was the last the family had to do with him until the trial. Mr Carne is a brewer in the 10th Ward, an Englishman, of some pretension to fashion, & a wealthy man. [*Crane copied as written.]

Mrd: on Sunday last, by Rev Mr Finckel, Mr Jas Lavender, jr, to Miss Charlotte Berry, all of Wash City.

Died: on Apr 7, Mrs Sarah Butt, aged 92 years. Her funeral will be from the residence of Richd Butt, Wash Co, D C, this morning at 11 o'clock.

Died: on Apr 8, in Wash City, in her 21st year, Josephine E Stone, the beloved wife of Thos Stone & daughter of Wm Jos Smith.

Orphans Court of Wash Co, D C. Letters of administration on the personal estate of David Ridgely, late of Wash Co, deceased. –Maria Ridgely, admx

Orphans Court of Wash Co, D C. Letters of administration on the personal estate of Alfred G Ridgely, late of Wash Co, deceased. –Maria Ridgely, admx de bonis non

The Philonomosian Society of Gtwn College, Apr 8, had a meeting to pay a tribute of respect. We sincerely mourn the loss in death of John E McCluskey, of Maine. -Rev Jos O'Callaghan, S J, pres. –Jas L O'Byrne, sec. Fancis X Ward, Robt F Lovelace, Cornelius E O'Sullivan, cmte.

FRI APR 10, 1857
Trustee's sale of valuable bldg lots near the Railroad Depot at public auction, by deed of trust from Elias Yulee & wife to the subscriber, recorded in Liber J A S No 56, folios 262 thru 264,of the land records for Wash Co, D C: sale on May 11, of lots 23 thru 25, according to Crutchet's subdivision of part of square 630; title said to be unquestionable. –Henry Naylor, trustee -A Green auct

Prof Tuomey died on Monday last at his residence at the State University, of disease of the heart. He was the Professor of Geology & Agricultural Chemistry. A large number of people followed the remains of the lamented disease to his last resting place. –Tuscaloosa [Ala] Monitor [Apr 13th newspaper: Prof Tuomey was a native of Ireland, & emigrated to Va at an early age. He married an accomplished lady of Md.]

Extensive sale of gilt-frame mirrors, oil paintings, engravings, at auction. Mr John Wagner, intending to change his business, will sell, on Apr 20, his entire stock at his establishment, 255 Pa ave, between 12th & 13th sts. –C W Boteler, auct

On Mar 17, while M Otto, a Roman Catholic member of the Prussian Chamber of Reps, was beginning a speech on the budget of the Ministry of Public Worship, he sank to the floor & expired almost immediately.

Senator Finisch, of Hamburgh, died on Mar 7 at Vevay. He left a fortune of twenty-five-million francs, a large part of which he bequeathed to his nephew, Dr Riecker, Envoy of Hamburgh at the English Court.

Manuel Quintana, the celebrated Spanish poet, died at Madrid on Mar 11. He was formerly preceptor to Queen Isabella.

Winona Argus of Mar 19. Mr Polhemus was shot & killed near Tepotah, on Dr Enright's claim, last Friday. He had been employed by Dr Enright in his absence to take charge of his house & claim. He was shot by some person unknown.

Gen Sir Chas J Napier is added to the long list of England's departed heroes. Sir Wm Napier has done both himself & his brother justice. Chas Napier was born at Whitehall on Aug 18, 1782; his father-Hon Geo Napier, was distinguished by high virtues of character as well as by extraordinary physical powers; his mother was Lady Sarah Lennox, whom the passion of George III so nearly raised to a throne. At 12 he received his commission & accompanied his father to the camp. His regt was quartered in Ireland. Chas Napier obtained his majority in 1806, & at the end of 1808 was ordered to the Penisula & took part in the battle of Corunna, heading his regt, the 50th, into action, & being taken a prisoner. His life was saved by a French drummer named Guibert, but not until he was wounded. When Ney heard he had a blind & widowed mother, he released him, on condition of his not serving until he should have been exchanged. In May, 1810, he got leave of absence. Married in 1827,he lost his wife in 1833, & in 1834, having a prospect of being entrusted with the gov't of a new Australian colony, he married again. His second wife was a widow with a family of her own, & soon after his remarriage he lost a great portion of his savings in an American investment. Thus, in sorrow, poverty, & obscurity, he lived on till 1839, & then, in his 57th year, he was appointed to the command of the northern district at a time when a Chartist insurrecion was daily expected. He assumed command of the Northern district in the spring of 1839, which he held for 2 years. In 1841 he went to India, & was sent to Seinde in 1842. There are two more volumes of a work still to come.

Miss Jaquet, of Chester Co, Pa, & Mr Batchell, of Ohio, were married in sport about a year ago, on the impulse of a banter. She now is applying for a divorce.

An inquest was held yesterday by the Coroner on the body of a free colored man named Fletcher, who it appears was pursued & beaten on Tue by his employer, Henry Kendrick, the keeper of a restaurant between 3rd & 4½ sts, so severely that he died the next morning. Kendrick has decamped.

$100 reward for runaway, Caroline Commodore, [or Caldwell,] a slave, brown complexion, about 22 years of age. –Eliza Peyton, No 5 Indiana ave.

Died: on Apr 9, in Gtwn, D C, after a painful illness, Mary Ann, in her 17th year, daughter of the late Patrick & Alice Moran. Her funeral is on Apr 12 at 2 o'clock, from the residence of her mother, 24 Water st.

Died: on Apr 5, at Grassland, Fauquier Co, Va, Mary E Tebbs, wife of Willoughby W Tebbs, & eldest daughter of Col Saml J Tebbs. A rapid pulmonary effection has removed from our midst the youthful mother of 2 infant children. She was exemplary in her duties of daughter, wife, & mother.

U S Patent Ofc, Wash, Apr 8, 1857. Ptn of Harriet V Terry, admx of Wm D Terry, deceased, of Boston, Mass, praying for the extension of a patent granted to the said Wm D Terry, on Jul 12, 1843, for an improvement in cast iron pavements, for 7 years from the expiration of said patent, which takes place on Jul 12, 1857.
-Chas Mason, Com'r of Patents

SAT APR 11, 1857
Information has been received at the Dept of the Interior confirmatory of the painful rumors that have circulated respecting the fate of Henry L Dodge, U S agent for the Navajo Indians, who has been missing for some time past. Kendrick, commanding at *Fort Defiance*, sent a command to search for Mr Dodge, & his corpse was discovered about 30 miles south towards the headwaters of the Gila river. Dodge was a favorite among the Navajos. A victim of this cruel act is the son of Hon Henry Dodge, the venerable ex-Senator from Wisconsin.

Among the articles recently contributed to the Tennessee Historical Society by Mrs Sarah Polk was a beautiful pitcher, presented to her by Lee-Sic, a native Cherokee, wife of Geo W Gunter, also a native & citizen of the Cherokee Nation, accompanied by a letter dated: Shin-Bayou District, Cherokee Nation, Apr 27, 1847. The pitcher was used in the council convened at Hopewell in 1785, which concluded the long bloody war between the U S & the Cherokee tribe. It was called the Pitcher of the Chiefs, & descended to them from Oken-stan-tah, the great King of all the Cherokees. Oken-stan-tah, the last great king, terminated his reign in 1765.

Col Jacob Carter died on Mar 24 in Covington Co, Miss, in his 99th year. He was born in Morris Co, N J. He was in many a battle, was shot in the head & taken prisoner by the enemy. He was long a citizen of Mississippi, & for many years an honored & exemplary member of the Baptist Church.

Capt Chapman, of the steamer **Dardanelles**, which arrived at New Orleans on Apr 3 from Arkansas river, we learn that on the Tue preceding the steamer **Forest Rose**, Capt Allen, when a mile & a half from Napoleon, exploded, by which the following were killed: Ben Hodge, of Hot Springs, passenger; D Thompson, engineer; son of Capt Allen. Melvin, the pilot, was badly scalded & burnt.

St Louis, Apr 8. A collision occurred yesterday between the Ohio & Miss & Terre Haute & Alton trains at the crossing near Illinoistown. Danl Jackson, a runner, was killed, & a brakeman had a leg broken.

Appointments by the Pres:
Chas G Greene, naval ofcr, Boston, reappointed.
John T Hammond, Collector, Annapolis, vice Sands.
Geo S Patterson, Collector, Sandusky, vice Jones.
Henry B Smith, Collector, Champlain, reappointed.
Saml Ridenour, Postmaster at Hagerstown, reappointed.
A W McCormick, Postmaster at Marietta, vice Bishop.
Pliny M Bromley, Collector, Genesee, N Y, vice Jas C Campbell, resigned.
Dennis Cochlin, Collector, Miami, Ohio.
Theophilus Peugnet, Collector, Cape Vincent, N Y.
Wm J Morton, Postmaster at Mount Vernon, Ohio.

The Earl of Fife recently died at his residence, Duff House, Scotland. He was 81 years old, & descended from Macduff.

Sales of lots in Wash City have been lately made; about 100,000 feet of land west of & adjacent to the residence of Hon S A Douglas have been purchased by that gentleman, Hon H M Rice & Hon Jacob Thompson, Sec of the Interior. The total amount of sales exceeds $50,000. Hon Senator Bright & W W Corcoran have purchased the square between First & Second & D & E sts near the railroad depot for $35,000. Hon Mr Douglas has bought of Alex Ray, the vacant lot at the corner of 16th st & Pa ave, consisting of 14,000 square feet, at $1.25 a foot.

Mrd: on Apr 9, in Wash City, by Rev Dadney Ball, Mr Thos F Curtain to Miss Eliz C Harris, both of Wash City.

MON APR 13, 1857
Handsome household, & kitchen furniture at auction on: on Apr 16, at the residence of Chas G Wagner, on north H, between 6th & 7th sts. -Jas C McGuire, auct

Trustee's sale of frame house & lot on 7th st: by 2 deeds of trust from Saml Curson, dated Jun 8, 1852, recorded in Liber J A S No 39, folio 324, & one dated Feb 13, 1855, recorded in Liber J A S No 91, folios 383: public auction on May 18, on the premises, parts of lot 7 & 8 in square 419, fronting 25 feet on 7th st, with a 2 story frame dwlg house & back bldg. –J W McKim, R H Clark, W H Ward, trustees -J C McGuire, auct

Appointments by the Pres:
Postmasters:
Geo W Porter, of Harrisburg, Pa, vice John H Brant, resigned.
Wm N Friend, at Petersburg, Va, reappointed.
Cornelius Courtney, at Coloma, Calif, vice Robt F Davis, removed.
Jesse Elder, at Sacramento City, Calif, vice Ferris Forman.
Geo L Patrick, at Sonora, Calif, vice Wm G Hoslep, removed.

Land Ofcrs:
Jesse B McClenden, Receiver at Greensburg, La, vice John M Vernon.
Henry W Palfrey, reappointed Receiver at New Orleans.
Louis Palms, reappointed Register at New Orleans.
Henry B Welsh, Receiver at **Fort des Moines**, Iowa, vice Phineas M Casady, resigned.

Indian Agents:
Christopher Carson, reappointed, for the Indians in the Territory of New Mexico.
Saml M Yost, for the Indians in the Territory of New Mexico, vice Abraham G Mayers, resigned.

At a meeting of the Nat'l Institute on Apr 6, resolutions were passed expressive of the sorrow of the members at the recent death of two of their friends & fellow-members, Alex'r Hamilton Lawrence & Dr John Tyssowski, & of condolence with the families of the deceased. Dr Tyssowski died on Apr 4th; was the Librarian of this Institution; as an assist Examiner of Patents he was second to none; a master of Latin, Greek, Polish, German, French, Italian, & in English was sufficiently well versed for all the purposes of his profession. He was born at Tarnow, in the province of Galicia, Polish Austria, in 1811.

Mrd: on Apr 8, in Wash City, by Rev Andrew G Carothers, Mr J H Turpin to Miss Helen Stanley, both of Wash City.

Mrd: on Mar 25, in St Paul's Church, Alexandria, Va, by Rev Jas T Johnson, D D, Mr Geo T Whittington to Miss Jane Luckett.

Died: on Apr 12, in Wash City, of pneumonia, Judge E Smith Lee, late of Michigan, in his 63rd year. His funeral will take place at his residence, 309 F st, between 11th & 12th sts, on Apr 14, at 3:30 P M. The friends & acquaintances of the family, & members of the Masonic Fraternity, are respectfully invited to attend.

Died: on Apr 10, in Wash City, Mrs Jane Edwards, at the advanced age of 93 years, a hunble & devout Christian. She was a native of St Mary's Co, Md, but for 40 years past a resident of Wash City.

Died: on Apr 11, in Gtwn, D C, of consumption, Mrs Mary A Leishear, in her 69th year. Her funeral is this evening, at 2 o'clock, from her late residence, 17 3rd st.

Died: on Apr 11, in Wash City, Jas C Young, a native of Scotland, in his 37th year. His funeral will take place today at 2 o'clock, from his late residence, B st south, between 9th & 10th sts.

Orphans Court of Wash Co, D C. Letters testamentary on the personal estate of Wm Bidly, late of Wash Co, deceased. –Thos C Donn, Thos J Fisher, excs

TUE APR 14, 1857

Household & kitchen furniture at auction on Apr 16, by order of distrain for house rent due & in arrears by Wm M Brown to Edw Owen, at the residence of said Brown, 447 Mass ave, between 6th & 7th sts. —A E L Keese, bailiff —Bontz & Coombs, aucts

Household & kitchen furniture at auction on Apr 20, by order of the Orphans Court of Wash Co, D C, at 227 Pa ave, the personal effects of the late Saml W Handy, deceased. —A Green auct

The contents of a Cigar & Tobacco Store to be sold at auction, on Apr 17, at 398 Pa ave, recently occupied by John Sessford, jr. —A Green auct

Mr & Mrs Barney Williams have met with unprecedented success in Europe. They have played over 200 nights to large audiences at the Theatre Royal Adelphi in London. The Queen, Prince Albert, & the royal family have been frequently present.

Chas L Carter & Jas Magee, convicted of the murder of warden Tenney & deputy warden Walker, of the Mass State prison, were sentenced to death at Boston on Sat last. They will be confined separately in the jail of Suffolk Co for one year.

At Dover, N H, last week, Mr Saml D Smith attempted to jump upon the cars after they were started, but fell between the cars & the platform. His legs & feet were shockingly mangled & broken. He died the next morning.

For sale: a very desirable private residence near Staunton, Va. My engagements as acting partner at the Rockbridge Alum Springs having compelled a change of residence. I offer for sale my property lying just outside the corporate limits of Staunton. It consists of about 30 acres of land, with a new brick mansion house, & out-houses & stables. Apply to Mr Wm M Tate of John D Imboden, who will show the property, or by letter addressed to me at the Springs. —Wm Frazier

Died: on Apr 13, in Wash City, after a brief illness, George Frederick, only son of Hugh Bernard & Eliza D Sweny, aged 11 years. His funeral is this evening at 4 o'clock, from the residence of his father, on H st, between 6th & 7th sts.

Phil, Apr 13. Ex-Pres Pierce left here today for N H, & will return on Sat. Mrs Pierce remains at the La Pierre House, under charge of Sidney Webster. Her health is improving.

WED APR 15, 1857

Old Trinity Church on 5th st, is to be revived in all respects. A minister, Rev Geo W Bassett, of Ill, but formerly of Phil, has accepted the call. We need hardly remark that the church is now in the hands of Congregationalists.

From Calif to Mar 20. 1-Henry Bates, the late State treasurer, has been tried & convicted. The amount of his defalcation was $124,000. He has been declared incompetent hereafter to hold any ofc of public trust or honor in the State. He has also been indicted, & is to be proceeded against criminally. Mr Rowe remains in prison. Comptroller Wheatman has been impeached for malfeasance, but has not been tried. 2-Calif has fewer idiots & many more lunatics, in proportion to her population, than any other State in the Union. Number of lunatics in the lunatic asylum 172, & constantly on the increase.

In Phil on Fri, a young lady, Sarah Caldwell, about 21, was on a visit to the house of her brother-in-law, Rev Wm Cathcart, of the Baptist Church, & in the act of removing an article from a mantel shelf, a loaded pistol wrapped in a woolen cloth fell to the floor & exploded. The ball entered her jaw. Dr Chas Taylor immediately succeeded in extracting the ball; but the sufferer died in a few hours. She was a native of England, but had recently arrived in Phil a few days ago, on a visit to her sister, Mrs Cathcart.

Circuit Court: 1-On Monday Messrs Henri Herrisse & Robt K Scott were admitted as attys & counselors of this court. 2-The Court discharged from the control & custody of Platt H Skinner the mute children, John Quinn, Ann S Szymanoske, Isaac Winn, Wm Blood, & Jas Henry, & the Marshal was ordered to bring them before the Judge of the Orphans' Court to be bound out as apprentices, or otherwise dealt with according to law. They continue in the charge of Mr G A Clark until thus disposed of by the Orphans' Court. The Court yesterday reduced the amount of bail in the case of said Skinner, charged with perjury & now in jail, from $2,500 to $1,000. 3-Jury trials have agains commenced, & the case of Ed M Linthicum vs Wm Robinson was tried, & an inquisition returned for the plaintiff.

Washington: the Canal deepening conducted by the Corp, under the general charge of Mr Geo Wise, is proceeding diligently & with great advantage to the navigation. The removal of the mud has been actually made to the hard bottom, which is 11 feet below the water surface.

Our neighbors in the good old town, Gtwn, had the pleasure on Sunday evening of seeing most of their streets lighted up with a good quality & supply of gas. Only the side & back streets were lighted, the principal thoroughfare, Bridge st, having to wait, till the arrangements of the Com'r of Public Bldgs shall have been matured.

The Balt papers report the arrest, by Balt ofcrs, of J W Barnaclo, on the charge of swindling numerous merchants of Balt by purchasing goods under false pretences. He represented himself to be worth $5,000 in property in this city, whereas it appears that he had made an assignment of all his goods to a relative here to whom he was largely indebted. The trial will take place in May.

An inquest was held on Monday, on Pa av, on the body of Thos Edwards, aged 55 years, who was found dead in his bed from the effects of laudanum, which he took the day before, with suicidal design. He left 3 letters written to as many different persons, describing his depressed state of mind & distaste of life, which, as he said, had no longer any thing to offer him. $22 was found in his pocket. He requested, in these letters, to be buried decently. He was a soldier in the Florida war, & was a perfectly sober man.

Died: on Apr 13, in Wash City, G Rexford Smith, in his 21st year. His funeral will take place at the Foundry M E Church, on Apr 15 at 3 o'clock.

Died: on Apr 13, Harry Day, aged 3 months & 18 days, youngest child of Noble D & A Margaret Larner. His funeral will be from the residence of his father, 432 I st, between 9th & 10th sts, this afternoon, at 3:30 o'clock.

Furniture Warerooms: sale of cabinet furniture, made of walnut, rosewood, & mahogany. –W McL Cripps, 499 11th st.

THU APR 16, 1857

Auction sale of fancy goods, perfumery, combs & brushes, French mirrors, showcases, counters, & store fixtures, on Apr 28, by deed of trust from Selby Parker, recorded in the land records of Wash Co, in Liber J A S No 129, folios 1 to 10; at the store of the said Parker, under the Nat'l Hotel, in square 491, Wash City. By order of the trustees: Jas M McRae & Wm H Parker. -A Green auct

The Gainsboro [England] News announces the sudden death of Rev Dr H J Symons in a railway carriage. It was Dr Symons who read the burial service over the body of Sir John Moore at Corunna.

The slave Jim Breckinridge, who was so fortunate as to draw half of the capital prize of $30,000 lately at Louisiville, has purchased himself & entire family at a reasonable price. Mr Isaac R Greene, his owner, referred the matter of value to Judge Piertle, by whom the valuation was fixed. The remaining money has been placed in the case of Mr Jas Speed, who will act as trustee for the man.

Fires in Gtwn this week: Fire in the interior of Mr Jos Libbey's residence on First st, destroyed some hundreds of dollars worth of property before it was put out. The stable & arbor in the rear of Mr Vincent Taylor's dwlg were burnt; careless use of matches in the hands of some boys. The most serious fire broke out in the roof of the 3 story brick residence of Mrs Magruder, near the chimney-stack, & communicated thence to the adjoining house of Mrs Abbott, & to that owned & occupied by Com Stephen Cassin. All these were burnt out leaving nothing but bare walls. Scarcely any furniture was saved. The fire companies found water to be very scarce.

Mr Carimill was walking out with his wife in Hartford, Conn, on Tue, when she suddenly burst a blood vessel, & the blood gushed from her mouth. She died in her husband's arms.

Mr Stoddard, a prominent missionary from N Y in Persia during the past 15 years, died at Oroomiah of typhus fever on Jan 22 last.

Trustee's sale: by deed of trust executed by Geo Thomas on Dec 4, 1854, recorded among the land records of St Mary's Co, Md: safe on Apr 30, of a tract of land in said county on the Wycomico river, near Chaptico, known as **Bashford**, containing 280 acres, more or less. The improvements are a brick dwlg, containing 7 rooms, kitchen, work house, quarters, granaries, stables, carriage-house, ice-house, now filled with ice, overseer's house, & 3 tobacco-houses. Immediately after the sale of the land the subscriber will proceed to sell the personal property, consistingof 12 valuable negroes, stock, & farming utensils. –W H Thomas, trustee

Mrd: on Apr 7, at Norwood, Powhatan Co, Va, by Rev E M Rodman, Capt Henry Heth, U S A, to Harriet, eldest daughter of Miles C Selden.

Died: on Apr 14, in Wash City, Mrs Jane Emery, wife of John W Rogers, aged 21 years. Her funeral will take place at the Rev A G Carother's Church, corner of I & 5th sts, this afternoon, at 3 o'clock.

Died: on Apr 12, in her 79th year, Mrs Anne Henderson, widow of the late Alex Henderson, of Alexandria.

For rent, the delightful cottage residence of Rev J W French, situated 3/4th of a mile n w of Columbia College, near Rock Creek. Inquire at 266 F st.

FRI APR 17, 1857
The subscribers, excs of the late Gen Jas Thompson, at the request of his heirs & devisees, will sell at public sale, on May 4 next, all his real estate in Wash City, to wit: his spacious brick dwlg house on square 25, & the following:
Lots 19 thru 27 in square 25.   Lot 6 in square 80.
Lots 12 thru 14 in square 28.   Lot 24 in square 88.
Lots 2, 5, & 7 in square 37.   Lot 23 in square 100.
Lot 1 in square 51.   Lot 16 in square 126.
Lot 13 in square 55.   Lot 8 in square 196.
Lot 21 in square 77.
-W H T Taylor, J B H Smith -A Green auct

Orphans Court of Wash Co, D C. Letters testamentary on the personal estate of Mary A Nally, late of Wash Co, deceased. –Chas Keenan, A L Newton, excs

Trustee's sale of valuable brick house & lot at auction: by deed of trust from Chas Wierman, dated Oct 28, 1852, recorded in Liber J A S No 47, folios 68 thru 70, of the land records for Wash Co, D C: sale on May 8 next, of all ground known as lot 11 in square 222, with a fine large brick house & other improvements: located on 15th st west, between N Y ave & H sts. –Saml Fowler, trustee -A Green auct

Mr Stephen P Hardenbrook, a police officer of N Y, was murdered in that city on Wed morning whilst patrolling his beat. He discovered 2 burglars coming out of a clothing store, each with a load of plunder. He seized one of the thieves, but the other thief stabbed him in the back inflicting a mortal wound. The murderers have thus far escaped discovery.

Circuit Court of Wash Co, D C. A P West & al vs Bowie & al. Trustee reported that he has sold the interest of cmplnts in part of lots 261 & 262, of Beatty & Hawkin's addition to Gtwn, to Conrad Schwartz for $450, & part of lot 262 to Eben G Brown for $100, & they have complied with the terms of the sale. –J A Smith, clerk

Mrd: on Apr 12, in Wash City, by Rev John C Smith, Mr Geo W Nokes to Miss Margaret E Castel.

Died: on Apr 15, in Wash City, in the second year of her age, Mary Llewellyn, daughter of Dr Johnson & Mary J L Eliot.

Obit-died: on Apr 1, at **Hambrooks**, his beautiful residence, near Cambridge, Md, in his 70th year, John Campbell Henry. The partner of his life, his children, 4 sons & 4 daughters, all grown, two of his sons-in law, a nephew, & his physician, who was also his relative, being still about him on the night of his decease, with a number of his servants, at their request, were admitted into his chamber, he said: "I know you all; God bless you." He soon after tranquilly died.

The Sunday School of the First Baptist Church, 10th st, between E & F sts, will give it first exhibition on Apr 21st at the church. –Wm J Rhees, superintendent

Emory Chapel, a neat & commodious house of worship, on the Plank Road, 4 miles from the city, will be dedicated on next Sabbath. Sermon by Rev Dr Doggett.

Defalcation of John Oxnard, of New Orleans. The Charleston Courier says he was a well known stock & exchange broker, & is not only a defaulter to the extent of $80,000, but has disappeared in the steamer **Havana** with a large amount-estimated as high as $50,000, of exchange & promissory notes obtained from various parties, under the plea that he could dispose of them forthwith.

SAT APR 18, 1857
The Naval Medical Examining Board recently in session in New Orleans have reported the following candidates for Assist Surgeons in the Navy as having passed a satisfactory examination: Fred'k Van Bibber, Va; Jno W Sandford, jr, N C; H B Trist, D C; Thos J Charlten, Ga; Chas Lowndes, jr, Md; Chas E Lining, S C.

The newly appointed Com'r of Indian Affairs, Hon Jas W Denver, late Rep from Calif, yesterday assumed the duties of his office.

The names of the persons who lost their lives by the falling of the walls of a burnt bldg during a recent conflagration at Balt, Md, are as follows:

Jos R Bruce, 19   Herman Bollman, 20
John Wagner   Jas Hussey, 21
Jos Ward, 21   Thos Buckley, 38
Geo Boyle, 17   Theodore A Brun, 18
Jacob Marshek, 17   Alex'r Brown, 16
Wm E Abell, 20   Saml B Hargrove, 18
Jas Payne, 18   Jos Letzinger, 23

Badly burnt & recovery is hopeless: Frank Welch, Geo B Wietzell, & John Shaney.

Appointments by the Pres-the following appointments of Land Ofcrs in Nebraska Territory are officially announced:
Geo H Nixon, of Tenn, Register for the Nemaha land district.
Chas B Smith, of Minn, Receiver for the Nemaha land district.
Andrew Hopkins, of Pa, Register for the South Platte River Land district.
Edw Desloude, of Ala, Receiver for the South Platte River land district.
John N H Patrick, of Nebraska, Register for the Dakota land district.
John C Turk, of Nebraska, Receiver for the Dakota land district.

Saml W Brady died in Winchester, Va, last week. He was one of the 3 survivors of the Dade massacre in the Florida war, & was a soldier in the whole of the Scott campaign in Mexico. At Chepultepec he was foremost among those who scaled the walls, & was so severely wounded as to be at first reported in the list of killed.

$100 reward for runaway, from the *Arlington Estate*, a young mulatto man, Levi Burke. Reward will be paid by application at Arlington.

Mrd: on Apr 16, in Gtwn, D C, by Rev Thos Sewall, of Balt, Mr Chas H Cragin to Henrietta F, youngest daughter of Saml McKenney.

Mrd: on Apr 15, in Wash City, at St John's Church, by Rev Dr Pyne, Capt Roger Perry, of the U S Navy, to Estelle F, daughter of B Ogle Tayloe.

Rose Cottage for sale: a frame house, 32 x 42 feet, nearly new, with 2 acres of ground. Located 1½ miles from the Post Ofc. Apply to Wm Stickney.

MON APR 20, 1857
Appointments by the Pres: 1-Jas W Denver, of Calif, Com'r of Indian Affairs, vice Manypenny, resigned. 2-Thos J D Fuller, of Maine, Second Auditor of the Treasury, vice Philip Clayton, resigned. 3-Wm M Gillaspie, reappointed Receiver of Public Moneys at Jackson, Miss.

Excellent household & kitchen furniture at auction on: Apr 28, at the residence of John W Forney, on 8th st, between E & F sts. –C W Boteler, auct

The resignations of the following ofcrs of the army have been accepted by the Pres: Capt Francis E Patterson, 9th Infty, & 1st Lt Robt E Patterson, 6th Infty, from May 1, 1857; Assist Surgeon John Byrne, the medical dept, from Oct 11, 1857.

Died: on Apr 18, Mrs Anne Maria, wife of Wm H Upperman, aged 51 years. Her funeral will take place from the residence of her husband, 482 Pa ave, between 4½ & 3rd sts, on Tue next, at 10 o'clock.

Heirs of Ann C Taggart, or Catherine Ann Taggart, formerly of Phil, who died about 1838, will please give their names & residences. Address P O Box 2,107, Phil, Pa.

Walter D Wyvill, successor to Francis Y Naylor, Manufacturer of Stoves, Copper, Tin, & Sheet Iron Ware, Roofing, Guttering, & Spouting, is now prepared to fill orders, on reasonable terms, at 453 Pa ave, near 3rd st. –W D Wyvill

TUE APR 21, 1857
A Map of the World by Bartholomew Columbus, 1488. Bartholomew Columbus was, like his brother, the celebrated Christopher Columbus, a man of experience & skilfull in sea-causes, & could very well make sea-cards & globes, & other instruments belonging to that profession, as he was instructed by his brother. Like his brother, his is said, under unfavorable circumstances, to have gained his livelihood by making & selling sea-charts. Bartholomew Columbus was sent out to England by his brother to King Henry VII, to lay before him his scheme about a navigation to the west. After many difficulties he at length began to deal with Henry VII, & drew for him a map of the world, which was presented to the King to show to him which way & how the Columbus' intended to sail. We have no special description of this map. Fernando Columbus gives us nothing of the contents of the map of his uncle but a few Latin verses.

Ann Eliza Tyler died suddenly on Thu last in Richmond, Va, from the bite of a spider. She was bitten on the right cheek the night before & died the following evening from the effects.

Naval: Capt Saml F Dupont has been ordered to the command of the steam frig-**Minnesota**, about to sail to China. Capt John B Montgomery has been ordered to the command of the steam-frig **Roanoke**, about to make a trial trip cruise of 6 months from Norfolk navy yard. All the ofcrs of the frig **Merrimac**, except her captain & purser, have been transferred to the **Roanoke**.

A man named Michl McLeod, employed in the Brooklyn White Lead Factory, was on Friday accidentally caught in the machinery & killed. He leaves a family.

Apr term of the Superior Court of Taylor Co, Ga: case of the liability of railroads for damages in negligently killing a passenger. In Dec, 1855, Uriah Paulk, a worthy citizen of Alabama, was killed by a collision between 2 passenger trains upon the Sourthwestern railroad near Flint river, in said county. An action for damages under the act of 1850 as brought against the company by the legal reps of Mr Paulk, & the trial at common law came off this week: verdict for the plntf of $20,000. The dfndnt has taken an appeal to a special jury. –Mobile Register

Amos Butler, for many years one of the proprietors & editors of the N Y Mercantile Advertiser, died on Apr 13, at the residence of his son, at Natchez, Miss, at the advanced age of 78 years.

On Sat last Mr Henry C Matthews received the appointment of Collector of the port of Gtwn, vice Mr Robt White.

Yesterday Mr Andrew Hoover, a well known citizen of Wash, was suddenly stricken by apoplexy whilst in his shoe store on Pa ave. He was bled, & then taken to his son's, Mr Peter Hoover, on F st, between 6th & 7th sts, where, at the time of writing this, he lies in a critical state.

The Hagerstown Mail states that the removal of St James' College from that county is now a fixed fact. The location chosen is in Balt Co, near **Glencoe**, on the line of the Northern Central railroad. The time for removal has not been definitely fixed.

Mrd: on Apr 16, by Rev Stephen P Hill, John Richey to Eliz Harrover, all of Wash City.

Died: on Apr 20, in Wash City, Michl McDermott, aged 65 years, born in Armagh Co, Ireland, & for the last 36 years a resident of Wash City. His funeral will take place from his late residence, 69 Missouri ave, near 3rd st, Apr 22 at 3 o'clock.

Died: on Apr 20, in Wash City, Mrs Johannah C Griffin, relict of the late Peter Griffin, & last surviving child of the late J C P Baron De Krafft, aged 69 years, leaving several children & a large circle of friends to mourn her irreparable loss. Her funeral will take place today at 4 o'clock, from her late residence, 389 I st south.

Chickering & Sons' Pianos for sale. Just received a supply of Parlor Grand & Louis XIV Pianos. Second-hand pianos taken in part payment. –Richd Davis, Pa ave.

Llangollen at auction: on Jun 4 next: the subscriber offers his fine estate, lying in Loudoun Co, Va, containing 788 acres. The dwlg house is of brick, built in modern style, stuccoed & roofed with tin. –J G Gray, M D, Upperville, Fauquier Co, Va.

Valuable property in Nelson Co, Va, for sale: about 900 acres, about 350 acres are cleared. Apply to Goddin & Apperson, Richmond, or to Wm Gordon, Lovingston, Nelson Co, Va.

WED APR 22, 1857
Household & kitchen furniture at auction on: Apr 23, at the residence of Mr Henry Wingate, on the corner of Montg & Beall sts, Gtwn. –Barnard & Buckey, aucts

Henry J Adams, the free-State candidate for Mayor of Leavenworth, Kansas, has been elected by 180 majority.

Orphans Court of Wash Co, D C. Letters of administration on the personal estate of Dennis Hardy, late of Wash Co, deceased. –Dennis Burns, adm

U S Patent Ofc, Wash, Apr 20, 1857. Ptn of Pliny Robinson, of Leonardsville, N Y, praying for the extension of a patent granted to him Jul 20, 1843, for an improvement in machines for cleaning streets for 7 years from the expiration of said patent, which take places on Jul 20, 1857.

For rent: the large house & premises on C st, recently vacated by Judge Campbell, late Postmaster General. Inquire of J H Reily, 519 12th st.

Mrd: on Apr 1, in Wash City, by Rev Morsell, Mr John H Dobbs, of N Y C, to Miss Eliza Jane McGreery, of Wash City.

Mrd: on Apr 16, in Wash City, by Rev Wm H Chapman, Mr Bernard M Bryan to Miss Sarah V Howe, all of Wash City.

Mrd: on Apr 14, in Wash City, by Rev S A H Marks, Mr Christopher McKenney to Miss Marion E Kirby, all of Wash City.

Died: on Mon, in Gtwn, in her 63rd year, Mrs Mary B Smoot, relict of the late Walter Smoot. Her funeral will be from her late residence, corner of Prospect & Market st, this afternoon at 4 o'clock.

Died: on Apr 20, in Alexandria Co, Va, Mrs Christiana Stuart, in her 67th year.

Died: on Apr 21, in Wash City, George Allen, aged 19 years, son of Mrs Adeline & the late John Sergeant. His funeral will be from the residence of his mother, E st north, between 9th & 10th sts, on Thu afternoon, at half-past 2 o'clock.

Chicago, Apr 18. Eli Griffore, a half-breed, accused of killing John Ingalls, in Jackson Co, was hung by a mob on Apr 11.

Sale of Phillips' Mill, in PG Co, Md, on May 2, containing about 15¾ acres of land. Mr Carrol, the miller, will show the premises, & for other information address the subscriber near the Navy Yard, Wash. –John D Boteler

THU APR 23, 1857
The following ofcrs have been ordered to join the steamer **Minnesota**, about to sail to China: Capt-Saml F Dupont; Lts: Wm B Remshaw, Miles K Warington, Chas C Sims, Colville Terrett, & Robt R Carter; Acting master-J C Chaplin; Surgeon-R T Barry; Passed assist surgeon-Chas Martin; Assist surgeon-R L Sheldon; Purser-Robt Pettit.

Appointments by the Pres:
Richd Roman, appraiser general at San Francisco, Calif, vice Saml J Bridge, removed.
Henry C Matthews, Collector, Gtwn, D C, vice Robt White, whose commission has expired.
Michl Kane, appaiser, San Francisco, Calif, vice O P Sutton, removed.
Henry E Stoughton, district atty for Vt, vice Peck, whose commission has expired.
R Biddle Roberts, district atty for West Pa, vice Thaler, resigned.
Jas Conner, district atty for S C, vice Evans, commission expired.
Wm Morrow, marshal for Delaware, reappointed.
F J Moreno, marshal for North Fla, reappointed.
E E Blackburn, marshal for South Fla, reappointed.
G S Walden, district atty for North Alabama, reappointed.
W H H Tison, marshal or North Mississippi, vice Jordan, commission has expired.
Richd Griffith, marshal for South Mississippi, reappointed.
Jaas C Pennie, marshal for South Calif.
Wm H Welch, chief justice of Minn, reappointed.
John Pettit, assist justice of Minn, vice Chatfield, commission expired.
R R Nelson, assist justice of Minn, vice Sherburne, commission expired.
Saml W Black, of Pa, assist justice of Nebaska, vice Underwood, resigned.
Edw Lander, chief justice of Wash Territory, reappointed.
Geo H Williams, chief justice of OregonTerritory, reappointed.
Matthew P Deary, assist justice of Oregon Territory, reappointed.
Cyrus Olney, assist justice of Oregon Territory, reappointed.
Appointment by the Sec of the Treasury: Jas Mills, deputy collector & inspector of customs, St Paul, Minn, vice L B Wait, removed.

Hon Benj Tappan, of Ohio, died on Sunday, at Steubenville, in his 85th year. He was a decided anti-slavery man, & on that account lost caste with the Southern Senators. He was in the U S Senate from 1839 to 1845. –Cin Gaz

Wm Jackson & Saml Gilmore, convicted of murder in the Circuit Court at Chicago, have been sentenced to be hung on May 14.

Mrd: on Apr 21, in Wash City, at the Methodist Episcopal Church South, by Rev Dr Doggett, Mr Geo K Fitch, of San Francisco, Calif, to Miss Clara V Duvall, of Wash City.

Died: on Apr 21, in Wash City, after a very brief illness, Andrew Hoover, in his 57th year. His funeral is this afternoon at 3 o'clock, from his late residence on Pa ave, opposite the Seven Bldgs.

The Wytheville [Va] Times says: on Apr 4, Drs Robt & Jos Grockett, of this place, & Dr Kincannon, of Smyth, were performing a surgical operation upon the 5 year old son of Mr Bonham, of Smyth Co, when almost immediately after he was administered a mixture of chloroform & ether, he died. The operation was to remove a fungus tumor from his back, which was accomplished just as he died.

Trustee's sale: pursuant to a decree of the Circuit Court of Wash Co, D C, as court of chancery, in the case of Jos E Law vs Jas Adams' exc & others, the subscriber, as trustee, will sell, at public auction, on May 8, the remaining lots belonging to the estate of Thos Law, deceased. –Jas Adams, trustee -J C McGuire, auct

FRI APR 24, 1857
Circuit Court-Wash-Thu. 1-Mr Szymanoski, father of a mute child, Ann Szymanoski, appeared in Court, & by his counsel Maj G Toshman, prayed the restoration of his child, recently apprenticed by the Orphans Court of Wash Co, D C to the institution of which Amos Kendall is Pres. The Court decided that under all the circumstances appearing the child should remain in her present condition. 2-A case of Chas Koones against Wm D Acken was tried. This was for the amount of a bill for funeral expenses of Mrs Acken, deceased, who, by mutual agreement, had separated from her husband, the dfndnt. Plntf's counsel claimed that the article of separation for separate maintenance only held good during her life, & that the funeral expenses fell legally upon the husband. The dfndnt pleaded that he had never incurred or assumed the debt, & that the bill of expenses was actually drawn by Koones against the estate of Mrs Acken herself, & that Mrs Acken had received a large sum of money very shortly before her death. The Court held that it mattered nothing as to how much money had fallen into Mrs Acken's hands, the legal liability of her husband was not removed thereby. Verdict for plntf the whole bill.

Lt Gardner, of the navy, died suddenly in his carriage on Wed, at Augusta, Geo.

On Fri night, Mrs Mgt McFarland, of Balt, died from a dose of arsenic taken by mistake for magnesia.

Law of the U S: 1-Payment of the sum due Lt John Guest, U S Navy, $617, for services rendered in the survey of the coast from Apalachicola bay to the mouth of the Miss river, for the practicability of establishing a navy yard & naval station which should best serve the commerce of the Gulf of Mexico, & for other lawful claims of ofcrs who were employed in that survey.

Pres Buchanan was 66 years old yesterday. –Star

Washington Monument meeting on Sunday: 1st Vice Pres, Mr Vespasian Ellis, called to the chair. Mr Jos H Bradley spoke. Other members of the Board present: Messrs Mayor Magruder, 2nd Vice Pres, Mr Jno M McCalla, Treasurer, Mr S Y Atlee, Sec, & Messrs Jos H Bradley, Josiah F Polk, T W Craig, & R J Knight, Managers.

Bottle paper received at Observatory: No 1-steamer **Geo Law**, Capt J P McKinstry, bound from Aspinwall to Havana, Jan 19, 1855, lat 22 degrees 33 north; long 85 degrees 00 west. The finder will please send this, with date & position, to the U S Observatory, Wash. –Wm L Maury, Lt U S Navy [Picked up Mar 27, 1857, lat 25 degrees 53 north, long 80 degrees 10 west, by Lt S H Weed, 4th artl, & forwarded to the Observator by Capt Jos Roberts, U S Army.]

Meeting of the Jamestown Society of Wash, on Apr 22, resolved to celebrate the anniversary of the settlement of Jamestown on May 13 next. Subscription lists in the hands of the Pres of the Society, P R Fendall, Hon W F Phillips, C W C Dunnington, Geo W Hinton, Wm Towers, & Col Lumpkin. –C W C Dunnington, Sec

Jos Horton, formerly of Bromsgrove, Worcestershire, Eng, will immediately communicate {confidentially, if desired} with Mr Scott, of Bromsgrove, he will hear of something greatly to his advantage, arising through an unexpected event which has lately occurred in the family.

Jno McIlveen, cashier of the firm of J Beck & Co, dry goods dealers, 355 Broadway, has been arrested charged with having embezzled moneys of his employers for a series of years past. The amount is believed to exceed $130,000. The firm failed some months since & were totally unable to account for the enormous deficit. An investigation of the books discovered the deficit. McIlveen has always stood well in the community. –N Y Mirror

Mrd: on Apr 15, in Christ Church, Raleigh, N C, by Rev Dr Mason, Kenelm H Lewis, of Edgecombe, to Miss Bettie, daughter of Hon John H Bryan.

Obit-died: on Mar 11, 1857, at his residence in the city of Selma, Ala, Maj Wm B King. He was born on Nov 25, 1798, in Bertie Co, N C; removed from the State of N C to Alabama in 1841, & has since resided in Dallas Co, which he represented in the State Legislature during the session of 1845-46; since then he has declined to accept any public station. To his neighbors & the community his loss will not be easily repaired, but his departure to his only sister is irreparable.

Health report: Ofc of the Com'r of Health, Wash, Apr 23, 1857. Monthly report of deaths from all causes: 69. –Chas F Force, Com'r of Health

Orphans Court of Wash Co, D C. In the case of Jas F Haliday, adm of Christopher R Byrne, deceased, the administrator & Court have appointed May 12 next, for the settlement of the personal estate of said deceased, of the assets in hand.
–Ed N Roach, Reg/o wills.

SAT APR 25, 1857

In 1817 Paul Spofford, now one of the most prominent merchants in N Y, entered into a copartnership with Amos M Hatch in the boot & shoe business at Haverhill, Mass. In 1823 they separated, but there was no formal dissolution of partnership. Mr Spofford grew richer, while Mr Hatch grew poorer, & in 1816 he was declared a bankrupt. In 1847 he filed a bill in the late Court of Chancery against the present plaintiff for an account under the partnership, founded upon an instrument under seal dated 1829. An answer was put in, but the suit was discontinued in Nov, 1856. Mr Hatch commenced a suit in a Connecticut court, the basis of which is the copartnership agreement. Damages are laid at the modest sum of $600,000. The cmplnt in the Supreme Courrt is filed by Mr Spofford, asking an injunction restraining the prosecution of any suit based on the copartnership in question. A preliminary injunction has been granted & a motion is now pending to dissolve it.

Four persons were found frozen at Petersburg, Rensselaer Co, on Apr 20, on Williamstown mountain, about half a mile from the Mass line: Amaza Blew & his wife Hannah Blew, apparently 40 years of age; Taut Curtiss, colored, & her son, Henry Curtiss; the woman 35 ot 40 & the son 10 years old. They were basket-makers by trade. It appears they all got drunk together & froze to death. A faithful dog was lying between 2 dead bodies and fought with desperation the persons who came to take the bodies away, &, when he could do not more, he followed the corpses to Petersburg, & insisted on being near them.

For sale: a splendid mansion in Phil, one of the most pricely & gorgeously furnished in the U S; located on the highest elevation on Broad st; the bldgs are 160 feet in depth; the house was commenced Jun, 1850, & with furniture, statuary, paintings, cost over $150,000. The grounds are finely laid out, with a brown stone & iron fountain in the centre that cost alone $3,500. For further particulars apply to E A Brigham, 101 Walnut st, Phil, Pa.

Mrd: on Apr 23, in Gtwn, at the residence of John Marbury, sr, by Rev C K Nelson, E Poinsett Tayloe, of King Geo Co, Va, to Louisa C, daughter of the late Caldwell Carr, of Upperville, Va.

Portion of *Portland Manor* at private sale: the subscriber will sell four-sevenths of the valuable estate. Apply to me at Govnr's Bridge post ofc, Anne Arundel Co, Md, Jas W Kent.

Paper-hangings: John Markriter, 500 7th st, next door to Odd Fellows' Hall.

MON APR 27, 1857

We understand that the governorship of Utah Territory has been tendered to Maj Benj McCullough, of Texas, & that there is every reason to believe that he will accept the office.

We are requested to state that Mr Donald Mcleod, of the St Louis Leader, is not our fellow townsman of that name, now of Cincinnati.

Mormon Immigration: the 850 Mormon immigrants who arrived at Boston from the packet ship **Geo Washington** on Wed left that city over the Worcester railroad on Thu; they will proceed immediately to Utah. Charlotte Steede, one of the Mormon emigrants from Marlborough, Worchestershire, England, died on the wharf on Thus, soon after landing from the ship. –Boston Post

John G Montgomery, Democratic member of the 35th Congress from the district composed of the counties of Luzerne, Columbia, Montour, & Wyoming, died on Fri at his residence in Danville. He was a lawyer of standing & had served with credit in the State Legislature.

Chas Entrée has been arrested at Toledo, Ohio, charged with robbing the U S mail.

John Mitchell Kemble, a son of the late Chas Kemble & brother of Mrs Fanny Kemble, died at Dublin on Mar 26 of inflammation of the chest. He was distinguished as an Anglo-Saxon scholar, & was the author of work on the English Saxons.

The relatives of Capt Smith P Bankhead in Balt have received a despatch contradicting the rumor of his death at Jackson, Tenn. Capt Bankhead [who is a son of the late Gen Bankhead, U S Army,] had been ill of pneumonia, which gave rise to rumor of his death.

Circuit Court-Wash-Fri. The Court ordered the delivery of Wm Ridgeway, the insane man heretofore consigned to the Insane Hospital, by their direction, to be given into the custody of his father, Hanson Ridgeway.

The Spirit Lake [Minnesota] Massacre by the Sioux, 42 settlers killed. Capt Bee, who commanded the detachment set out from *Fort Ridgeley* to ascertain the facts connected with that massacre, & to chastise the perpetrators, if found, has returned, having left his command at Spirit Lake. He reports that the news is too true. 42 settlers were killed, 5 women taken prisoners, & 33 horses stolen. A merchant, who was killed, had all his goods carried off. The Indians were said to number five or six hundred. Col Smith, the commandant of *Fort Snelling*, responded to the call of the people of St Peter, & yesterday had 3 companies & 12 wagons laden with supplies & ammunition on the march to the southwestern border.

+

Fort Dodge, Iowa, Apr 10, 1857. On Mar 24 we started from this place, divided into 3 companies, under the command of Maj Wm Williams, of the firm of Williams, Hann & Co, bankers, in this place. After a tedious march of 6 days we arrived at a place called the Colony, in Palo Alto Co, about 70 miles to the northwest, settled by Irish immigrants. On the 27th the Indians first robbed the store of Geo & Wm Wood. Wm Wood was killed & Geo Wood is missing, supposed to have been burnt with the store. The Indians went to the house of Mr Thomas. His 10 year old son was killed; Mr Thomas was wounded in the arm, rendering amputation necessary; David Carver was shot through the arm, the wound is not considered dangerous; Miss Drusella Swiver received a ball in her shoulder which passed out the other side. John Bradshaw & a man named Markham fired upon the Indians. It was reported by an Indian to a man named Shigley that 9 were killed & 5 wounded. Towards night the Indians withdrew. Why the pursuit was thus given up I do not known. The men sent to Spirit Lake returned. They visited the house of Mr Thatcher & found the bodies of A Noble, & Mr Ryan. They visited the residence of Jonathan House; here 9 bodies were found dreadfully mangled-men, women, & children; the body of Jonathan House is reported missing. The next house was Granger's. A man named Snyder was found dreadfully mangled with a broad-axe. The Granger's have one missing, probably both killed. They next went to Mattock's house, where 11 were found. The men & women shot & children tomahawked were some 12 persons, one missing. About 70 persons have been killed & taken prisoners.

+

From the Chicago Press of Apr 22. Massacre at Springfield, in Blue Earth Co: killed-Wm Wood, Geo M Wood, Mr Church, & Josiah Stewart. Mr Wm Wood, a trader, & an old settler of Manhato, had been proceeding to have a talk with the Indians on the bank of the river, when he was shot dead & his body burnt. Mrs Church loaded guns for the men in the house. Mrs Maruel & Miss Gardner were taken prisoners by the Indians. 38 volunteers left Mankato, under Capt Lewis. The N Y Times of Sat last said the payment of the moneys due the Indians will settle all the troubles, & that the force detailed for the protection of life & property is not needed.

Orphans Court of Wash Co, D C. Letters testamentary on the personal estate of Benj Taylor, late of Wash Co, deceased. –John Taylor, exc

Orphans Court of Wash Co, D C. Letters of administration on the personal estate of John Tyssowsky, late of Wash Co, deceased. −P Hannay, adm

Died: on Sat last, in Wash City, Mrs Ann Evens, the beloved wife of Saml Evens, a native of Paington, Devonshire, England, in her 41st year. Her funeral will take place this afternoon at 3 o'clock, from her late residence, 411 E st, between 9th & 10th sts.

TUE APR 28, 1857
Sale by order of the Orphans Court of Wash Co, D C of groceries, liquors & furniture: on May 1, at the store & late residence of Dennis Hardy, deceased, corner of north K & 27th sts. −Dennis Burns, adm -A Green auct

Public sale of desirable real property in Gtwn D C: the subscribers, excs of the late Gen Jas Thompson, of Wash City, at the request of his heirs & devisees will sell at public auction, on May 7, all of his real estate in Gtwn, D C:
Lot 61, old Gtwn, on the south side of Bridge st, & 90 feet on the east side of Jefferson st, having thereon 3 tenements under rent.
Parts of lots 60 & 61, Old Gtwn, 65 feet on Jefferson st, 107 feet deep, with 3 frame dwlgs thereon under rent.
Part of lot 20, old Gtwn, 20 feet on north side of Bridge st, & 123 feet & 4 inches deep.
One-third part of lot 223, Beatty & Hawkins' addition, 23 feet 4 inches on the north side of 6th st, 150 feet deep.
South part of lot 137, Beatty & Hawkins' addition, 60 feet front on the west side of Greene st, & 60 feet deep.
Southeast part of lot 151, Beatty & Hawkins' addition, 30 feet on the north side of Gay st, & 30 feet on the west side of Montg st.
The sale will commence at the house on the corner of Bridge & Jefferson st, now occupied by Mr Jos F Burch. −W H S Taylor, J B H, Smith, excs

Trustee's sale of the entire furniture & effects of Dexter's Hotel, at the corner of La ave & 7th st. −Chas S Wallach, trustee -Jas C McGuire, auct

Superior rosewood & 7 octave piano-forte, household & kitchen furniture at auction on Apr 30, at the residence of Dr C H Van Patten, corner of 26th & Pa ave. Also, a milch cow, wheelbarrows, iron railing & garden tools. -Jas C McGuire, auct

Mr W M Magraw, one of the superintendents of the nat'l wagon road to Calif, late of Md, will start from Independence, Mo, about May 20. Mr Lander, of Mass, a well known explorer, & a brother of Chief Justice Lander, of Wash Territory, is the engineer of this expedition, & Dr Cooper, of N Y, the surgeon. The first named gentleman is a daring pioneer of the South & West, & the two last were in Gov Stevens' celebrated northern expedition. −Sun

Nathl P Banks, sen, father of the Speaker of the Nat'l House of Reps, died at his residence, at Waltham, Mass, on Apr 23, at the age of 64 years.

Capt S Barron, U S Navy, has been assigned to duty as a member of the Light-House Board, vice Capt S F Du Pont, ordered to the command of the steam frig **Minnesota**.

Art matters. 1-Turner, the great painter, left, by will, 1,000 pounds sterling for a monument to his memory in St Paul's. It is to be a statue, & the sculptor chosen to execute it is Mr McDowall, R A. All the sculptors resident in London who are Royal Academicians sent in competing designs for the structure. 2-The statue of the Virgin of the Immaculate Conception has been successfully cast in bronze at Rome. 3-Jerome Thompson, the well-know painter, has recently completed a beautiful piece, called "Recreation"-a picnic scene in Vt. 4-The friends & pupils of M Paul Delaroche, at Paris, have resolved to make a public exhibition of his works as at once the truest homage to his memory & a real service to art. 5-Baron Marochetti's monument to Princess Elizabeth, daughter of Charles the First, a commission from Queen Victoria, is finished, & set up in St Thomas' Church, Newport. The monument represents the figure of a youthful female reclining in a recess resembling the cell of a prison. The pillow on which the head of the figure rests is an open Bible, in which can be seen the following words: "Come unto me all ye that are heavy laden and I will give you rest."

The Va papers announce the death of Chas Yancey, of Buckingham Co, at the advanced age of 88 years. He was the artisan of his own fortune, mainly by agricultural pursuits.

Rev Antoinette Brown appears to have made a failure in her first pastoral. The church at South Butler, N Y, over which she was settled, is now dissolved & the meeting-house closed.

Ocean encroachments: N J geological report show that the Atlantic is steadily & rather rapidly encroaching upon the land on its coast. Along the bay shore, at Cape Island the surf has eaten inward full a mile since the Revolution. Along the bay shore, at Cape May, the marsh wears away at the rate of a rod in 2 years. One of the beaches upon it is mentioned as having shoved inward 100 yards in the last 20 years.

Joshua A Spencer, a distinguished lawyer of N Y, died at his residence in Utica on Sat last. [May 2nd newspaper: Joshua A Spencer was born in 1790, at Great Barrington, Mass, & was remotely connected with the family of the late Chief Justice Ambrose Spencer & the late Hon John C Spencer. He commenced the practice of law in a small town in Madison Co; served as a subordinate militia ofcr on the northern frontier in the war of 1812; resumed his profession; removed to Utica in 1829; served at one time in the State Senate, has been a member of Congress, & Mayor of Utica. –Buffalo Commercial Advertiser]

Died: on Apr 27, in Wash City, after much suffering, John Augustus, youngest son of Chas & Sophia Werner, aged 1 year & 4 months.

Lt Wm Ross Gardner, U S Navy, who died suddenly while riding in his carriage with his wife at Augusta, Ga, on Apr 23, was in his 40th year. His disease was neuralgia of the heart. H had been in the navy for 26 years, of which nearly 12 were spent at sea. He was last at sea in June, 1855. After that he was stationed for awhile at the Naval Observatory, Wash, & for several months previous to his death had been residing in Augusta waiting orders.

Maj Jas Jackson, for many years a Professor of Franklin College, died at Gainesville, Ala, on Mar 26, in his 70th year. He was the 2nd son of Gov Jas Jackson, & was a native of the city of Savannah, where he commenced his education.

Conway Robinson, of Richmond, Va, bought the beautiful county seat, The *Vineyard*, the residence of the late John Agg, for $8,500, subject to a claim of $3,453: total $11,953. It adjoins the Military Asylum.

Mrd: on Apr 23, in Wash City, by Rev Wm H Chapman, Richd Brooks to Miss Harriet E Smallwood, all of Wash City.

Mrd: on Apr 22, in St James' Church, Wilmington, N C, by Rev Dr Drane, Wm H C Whiting, U S Army, to Kate D Walker, 2nd daughter of John Walker.

Valuable farm & pleasant residence in Fairfax Co, Va, for sale: by decree of the Circuit Court for Fairfax Co, Va: sale of the tract called ***Collingwood***, the residence of the late H Allen Taylor; about 4½ miles below the city of Alexandria; contains 244¼ acres of land; improvements consist of a new & commodious frame dwlg, kitchen, & other out-houses, built of the best materials, situated on a beautiful eminence, in full view of the Potomac river. –W Arthur Taylor, John A Washington, Com'rs of sale.

WED APR 29, 1857
Sale by trustees in Chancery of valuable real estate, by virtue of a decree of the Circuit Court of D C: in cause, No 1,066, wherein Agnes M Easby is cmplnt, & Horatio N Easby, John W Easby, Wm R Smith & Wilhelmina his wife, Henry King & Marian E his wife, & Cecilia J Hyde are dfndnts: public auction May 20th next of:

Lot 7 in square 61
Lot 3 in square 88
Lot 3 in square 89
Lots 6 & 13 in square 1028
Lot 7 in square 1031
Lot 5 in square 1034
Lot 10 in square 1111
Lots 5 & 6 in square 1121
Lot 8 in square 1122

On May 21 next: Lot 8 in square 631. Lots 1 thru 7 & 12 in square 925.
-Wm B Webb, Richd H Clarke, Jos H Bradley, jr, trustees -Jas C McGuire, auct

+
Executor's sale of improved & un-improved real estate: the undersigned, excs of the last will & testament of Wm Easby deceased, in conformity with the directions contained in said will, & under & by virtue of a decree of the Circuit Court of D C, in Chancery, supplemental to the decree heretofore passed in a cause, No 1,066, wherein Agnes M Easby is cmplnt, seeking an admearurement of dower & other relief in equity, & Horatio N Easby, & John W Easby, Henry King & Marian his wife, Cecilia J Hyde, Wm R Smith & Wilhelmina his wife, are dfndnts, will proceed to sell at auction, on May 20 next, in Wash City, the following parts of parcels of real estate, to wit:
Lot 1 in square 705
Lot 13 in square 708
Lots 1 thru 3 in square east of 708

On May 21:
Lot 14 in square 559
Part of square 907, on 7th st east, with two 2 story brick houses
Part of lot 1 in square 907, on 8th st

On May 22 next:
Lot 2 in square 10, improved by a substantial stone wharf, now rented by the Cumberland Coal & Iron Co & used for a coal depot.
Part of lot 2 in square 11, part of same wharf
Lot 3 in square 12, improved by three 2 story brick houses
Lots 5 & 6 in square 12
Lot 8 in square 19, improved with four small 2 story brick houses
Lot 12 in square 12
Lots 2, 4, 5, & 6, & part of 3 in square south of square 12. Lot 2 fronts on Water st, between 26th & 27th sts; improved by a frame workshop; 4 fronts on 27th st, improved by 2 frame workshops, & by a wharf, which is now, & has been for 26 years, occupied as a ship yard, & known as *Easby's ship yard*. Lot 6 fronts on 26th st 114 feet 8 inches, & is improved by a brick ice-house.
Lot 9 in square 20   Lot 2 in square 59
Lot 3 in square 22   Lot 2 in square 44
Lots 2, 3, 4, & 5 in square 63, lying between Water st & the C & O Canal
Lots 6 thru 8 in square 63, improved by 3 small frame houses
Lots 9 thru 11 in square 63, fronting on Water st 66 feet, with valuable lime kilns, known as the *Hamburg lime kilns*
Lots 1, 4, 5, & 14 in square 88   Lot 1 in square 129
Lots 4 thru 7 in square 89
-Horatio N Easby, John W Easby, Agnes M Easby, excs -J C McGuire, auct

J W Wilkins & Edw Montgomery, who recently, while standing on the deck of the steamer **John Simonds**, at New Orleans, were severely wounded by a cannon fired from the steamer **Falls City**, have entered suits against her owners, Mr Wilkins claiming $25,000, & Mr Montgomery $10,000 damages.

The telegraph announces the death of Thos B Carroll, Mayor of Memphis, Tenn. He was the son of the late Gov Wm Carroll, of Tenn.

Contradicting the rumors. Mrs Polk has no intention to reside in Washington. She has never been out of the U S, nor has she been out of the State of Tenn since the death of Pres Polk. Nashville is her home for life.

The Warrenton [Va] Flag chronicles the death of Mrs Judith Keith, at the advanced age of 98 years. She was a mother before the Revolution. She was the mother of 5 generations & her living descendants number more than 100.

Trustee's sale of *Potomac Iron Furnace & Furnace Tract*; by deed of trust recorded in the ofc of the County Court of Loudoun Co, [Va] in Liber 5 H, folio 116: sale on Jul 1 next, on the premises, the *Furnace Tract* contains 626 acres; upon it, as a part of the property to be sold, the well known *Potomac Furnace* with all its bldgs & a large dwlg house & out bldgs, besides a number of smaller dwlgs on different parts of the tract. The property to be sold is the same which was formerly owned by Dr B E McMurtrie. Terms of sale: $48,000 cash, & the residue in 4 equal annual instalments. –J M Orr, trustee

Some time on Tue 2 prisoners, Kane & Slattery, managed to escape from the prison of this county. They sawed off a bar of their cell & of the window. The Marshal has offered a reward for their recovery.

Farm for sale containing 160 acres of land, more or less, on the Wash & Brookville turnpike, about 12 miles fromWash, together with stock; good frame dwlg-house, & out houses necessary to farming purposes. Inquire of Benj Bohrer, Beall & Montg sts, Geo W Bohrer, High & Gay sts, Gtwn, or of Mr Harp, on the premises.

St Louis, Apr 27. A file of the Santa Fe Gaz of March has been received. The remains of Indian Agent Dodge had been found & were interred at *Fort Defiance*. Maj Fry had arrived at Albuquerque with $150,000 for the Gov't.

THU APR 30, 1857
Exec's sale of valuable farm & town lots at auction: on May 13, a tract of 70 acres in Alexandria Co, Va, adjoining the farm of Robt Cruit. Also, a 5 acre lot on Ridge road, adjoining the farm of Capt Maddox. Also, the south part of lot 280 in Beatty & Hawkins' addition to Gtwn, fronting 100 feet on Fayette st, running back 120 feet; will be divided into 3 lots. Also, the middle part of lot 280, 77 feet, running back 120 feet. Also, parts of lots 69 & 70 in Beatty & Hawkins' addition to Gtwn, fronting 63 feet on First st & 87 feet on Fred'k st; will be divided into 2 lots of 31½ feet on First st. The above property, being the real estate in part of the late Wm Jewell, deceased, will be sold to the highest bidders, without reserve. –Thos Jewell, for the excs -Barnard & Buckey, aucts

Superior rosewood 7 octave piano forte, furniture & household effects, at auction, on May 4, at the residence of W P Mangum, jr, on F st, between 10th & 11th sts. –J C McGuire, auct

Excellent rosewood piano-forte, furniture & household effects at public auction: on May 7, at the residence of Mr E H King, on 11th st, between E & F sts. –Jas C McGuire, auct

Valuable bldg lots at public sale: under direction of Hon David Stewart, of Balt, as atty in fact of the devisee of Miss Eleanor Davidson, late of Balt: sale on May 6 of: lot 7 in square 211, fronting on 15th st west, between L & M sts. Lot 14 in same square on 15th st. Lots 27 thru 30, & 33 in Davidson's subdivision of square 340, fronting on 9th st. For title, which is indisputable, reference may be made to W S Cox, of Gtwn. –Jas C McGuire, auct

The Columbus [Ga] Times announces the death of Saml W Flournoy, who died in that neighborhood on Apr 22, after a long & painful illness. He had been connected with the press of Ga for many years, & in his prime was the foremost Whig editor of the State. He often represented Muscogee Co in both branches of the Ga Legislature.

Jas Johnson was yesterday brought before Justice Goddard on a charge of shooting 2 persons, Sibley & Gladmon, near the Park, on 7th st. The two young men, with others, were drinking freely, & were throwing stones at the dwlgs on the road side. Mr Johnson's house was amongst those assailed, & he came out & discharged a single barreled gun containing buckshot at the party, wounding Gladmon in the side severely, & Sibley in the arm. Johnson was held to bail in the sum of $400 in each case, to appear at the next term of the Criminal Court.

A gentleman, Saml Turner, died in Yorkville, S C, a short time since, at the age of 98 years. During his long life a maiden daughter had lived with him, nursed him in old age, & resigned all other society & associations for the pleasure of loving & being loved by her venerable parent. In two days after his decease, she died also, at the age of 72 years. –Natchez Courier

For sale: a pair of Morgan Bay Horses, well matched in style & speed, 6 years old, & perfectly sound & gentle. Apply to E Cowling, 299 G st, between 13th & 14th sts.

A young man named Walter Shivers, son of Mr John Shivers, of Isle of Wight Co, Va, a cadet in the Chuckatuck Military Institute, 17 years of age, was killed by the accidental discharge of a pistol in his overcoat pocket on Sat week. He lived about 12 hours in excruciating pain & expired. He was with his sister at the time.

Mrd: on Apr 28, by Rev W Krebs, Wm Pierce Venable to Clarissa Milcah Griffin, both of Wash City.

John Van Lear, for many years the cashier of the Wash Co Bank, Wmsport, Md, died suddenly on Fri last, in his 70th year. He resided a short distance from Wmsport, & was seized with illness on the road, but managed to reach his house, where he expired in a few moments.

Mr Fred'k J Watts, a schoolmaster on South river, Anne Arundel Co, Md, who had been indicted for the chastisement of Wm H Purdy, one of his scholars, & son of Mr Saml Purdy, was honorably acquitted by a jury in the circuit court of Annapolis last week.

Mrd: on Apr 23, at Christ Church, Cincinnati, by Rev Dr Brooke, Hunter Brooke to Miss Fannie Butler, daughter of Rev C M Butler, all of said city.

Mrd: on Apr 28, in Wash City, in the First Presbyterian Church, by Rev Dr Sunderland, L Johnston Rothrock, of Fredericksburg, Va, to Sarah Halsey, daughter of J S Miller, of Wash City.

FRI MAY 1, 1857

The steamer **Scott** explosion: by the late arrival at N Y from Panama we have the following list of the persons killed & wounded on the **Scott** on the San Juan river: Killed: Maj Wm Morris, Capt Schlicht, Lts Volgen & Coghlin, Thos Alexander, M M Beidleman, John Buffington, Chas York, J L Fewell, Joe Murray, Wm Edmonson, C S Thomas, Jas Wilson, Robt Higgins, J A Sistere, Chas Lansing, Jas Rooney, & Jas McCree. Severely injured: Col Frank Anderson, Lt Col Chas Doubleday, Capt Marcellus French, Capt W W Berrington, Lt Mulholland, Chas Kennedy, Frank Crawford, Alex'r Bailey, & E Baker. There were 16 others slightly injured. [No date-current news item.]

Richmond Enquirer: *Vaucluse*, the beautiful former residence of the late Judge Upshur, Sec of State under the administration of Pres Tyler, has now passed into stranger hands. Other forms now darken the doorway in which its gifted owner so lately stood. The *Vaucluse* of Abel P Upshur has become a classic name.

The princely residence of Howard Tilden, of Phil, is on Broad st, a few minutes drive from the noise & bustle of that great city. It is superior to any thing ever seen in this country. So says a Phil journal. It appears by an advertisement that this desirable property is offered for sale.

John A Chisholm, charged with abstracting a $100 bill from a letter in the Columbus, Ga post ofc, was found guilty in Savannah on the 21st ult. Judge Nichol pronounced the sentence of law on him, a term of 10 years' imprisonment in the penitentiary. His father, brother & relations were present at the sentencing.

The Cathedral at Cincinnati was, on Sunday, the scene of the consecration of 2 bishops, Rt Rev Jas Fred'k Wood, D D, & Rt Rev Henry Damien Juncker, D D. The former was consecrated as Coadjutator Bishop of Phil, the latter as Bishop of Alton, in Illinois. Archbishop Purcell was the consecrator, assisted by the following bishops: Carrell of Covington, Henrie of Milwaukee, Lefevre of Detroit, Miles of Nashville, Newman of Phil, Reppe of Cleveland, Spalding of Louisville, St Palais of Vincennes, Whelan of Wheeling, & Young of Erie.

Sale of valuable lots under decree of the Circuit Court of D C, in a cause wherein Thos Sewell & others are cmplnts, & the adms, widow & heirs of John Brereton are dfndnts, being No 1,152 in equity: auction on May 25, on the premises: lots 4, 5, & 11, in square 218, in Wash City. –W Redin, trustee -A Green auct

Yesterday as the steamer **Baltimore**, from Alton, was nearing St Louis, Capt Hawley was collecting fare from the deck passengers, when a respectably dressed German working-man handed him a letter, addressed to Mrs Mathias Hugle, St Louis, Mo, & a pocket-book containing a variety of memoranda, & then, without a word, jumped overboard & disappeared beneath the waters of the Mississippi. He could not be saved. The letter as translated from German; Alton, Ill, Apr 18, 1857. My Dear Wife: I have to tell you to come over here, as I intend remaining here, having a good place. Come as soon as possible & bring every thing along. Your faithful husband, Mathias Hugle. Postscript, written in pencil. Don't come. I ended my existence on Apr 21, because you always had such a foul mouth & always tried to wear the breeches, which you can do now. Adieu, & shift for yourself. –M Hugle [The deceased was a stone-cutter by trade. –St Louis Leader of 24th ult.]

Maniac in a Stage. Strange affair on the 10th ult, about 2 miles from Eddyville, Iowa, as the Western stage coach reached that point a passenger, Jos Patterson, jr, from Joliet, Ill, exclaimed, "Why did you kill my cousin?" With a pistol & dirk-knife he then commenced a most terrible onslaught upon the passengers, mortally wounding Dr Timmons, of Knoxville, Marion Co, Ohio, & severely injuring Mr Hylawder, of Jasper Co, Iowa. He was an entire stranger to all the parties injured, & insanity can only be assigned for the commission of the act.

Grave apprehensions are felt for the safety of the screw steamship **Tempest**, which left N Y for Glasgow on Feb 13 last, as she had not arrived at her destination up to Apr 3, having been 49 days out. There was only one passenger on board. The **Tempest** was to have been the first of the Anchor line of steamers from Glasgow to Montreal. –Montreal Transcript

Mrd: on Apr 21, by Rev Mr Krebbs, Mr Abraham Paynter to Miss Mary G Hendley, all of Wash City.

Died: on Apr 29, in Wash City, Mrs Mary Lawton, wife of Jos Lawton, in her 47th year, a native of Lincoln, England, but for the last 17 years a resident of Wash City.

Died: on Apr 28, in Wash City, Edw Lancaster, aged 75 years.

N Y, Apr 30. The brig **Ellen**, which had cleared for Loando, was seized this afternoon by the revenue cutter **Washington** as a slaver.

SAT MAY 2, 1857
Household & kitchen furniture at auction on: May 7, at the residence of Chas Munroe, corner of 2nd st & Indiana ave. –C W Boteler, auct

Frightful massacre upon the French settlements in New Caledonia by the natives. The township of Marori was the scene of the attack. Eleven Frenchmen & a number of Sandwich Islanders were there to obtain sandal wood. About Jan 20th the natives attacked the settlement & murdered every one of the inhabitants. Among the victims is Mr Berard, attached to the firm of Vial, D'Aram & Co, of Australia, & who has for some time been Commissary-General for the French settlements in the Pacific.

Saml Nicholson, one of the partners of the banking-house of Brown, Brothers & Co, died at his residence in N Y Wed. He was about 60 years of age, & widely known & esteemed.

Joshua A Spencer, the distinguished lawyer, whose decease at his residence in Utica has been announced, was born in 1790

Romulus S Chipman was convicted in Greensboro, N C, on Tue of last week, for the murder of Miss Penix, & May 15 was fixed upon for his execution, but he has appealed to the Supreme Court. He is a young man, only 20 years of age, of very good appearance, good education, & appeared in the court-room well dressed. His parents are both living, are of the highest respectability, & are wealthy. His mother has written several religious volumes of interest. The evidence on which he was convicted was entirely circumstantial, but overwhelming.

The Balt Patriot of Thu records the death of Francis J Dallam, one amongst its oldest & most esteemed citizens. He died at his residence in Balt, after a lingering illness, in his 70th year. The deceased was at one time the cashier of the old Citizens' Bank. He served several years as a member of the City Council, & was Pres of the Balt Equitable Society, having resigned the latter only a few days since in consequence of his declining health.

Middleton's Ice for sale: 10,000 tons of best quality ice constantly on hand.
-L J Middleton, Ofc & Depot s w corner of F & 12th sts.

Indian war in New Mexico: from the Santa Fe Gaz of Mar 28. On Mar 8 Capt Gibbs' rifles left *Fort Fillmore* in pursuit of the Indians who had run some animals belonging to the surveying party, in charge of Mr Gerretson, Deputy-Surveyor of the Territory; & on Mar 9 the trail was struck about 5 miles from Roblero, the robbers, 7 in number, were overtaken, with 6 Indians killed & 1 mortally wounded. The stolen animals were recovered. In this affair Capt Gibbs was severely wounded by a lance in the hand of the chief, whom he shot. Cpl Collins fell in charge of the party after Capt Gibbs was wounded & compelled to dismount, having become very faint from loss of blood. Lt Baker [Rifles] left *Fort Thorne* on Mar 10 for Mr Tigil's camp, & found the Indians had driven off all his animals. Their trail was followed for over 70 miles, & on the 11th the Indians were found in camp a few hundred yards off. The camp was attacked, [Shawano's band,] completely surprising it. In the action pvt Patrick Sullivan was killed. Sgt Dugan, Cpl Brady, bugler Reid, & pvt Dougherty were wounded. Five horses were also wounded.

Copartnership existing under the name of Guy & Briggs is this day dissolved by mutual consent. Either of the partners is to settle any business of the concern.
-Wm Guy, J G Briggs, Wash, May 1, 1857

N Y, May 1. One week later from Europe. Queen Victoria has given birth to another daughter, & the English journals are filled with rejoicings over her safe accouchment. Mother & child are doing well.

MON MAY 4, 1857
W H Buchanan, of Marshall Co, Va, a well-known Va poet & author, died suddenly in Wheeling, on Apr 30, of disease of the heart. Mr Buchanan was 63 years of age, & had long been a correspondent of the Nat'l Intelligencer & Home Journal. [May 5th newspaper: Mr Buchanan died at the McLure House, having been attacked with neuralgia of the heart, while coming up Monroe st. He sunk down upon the pavement, & was carried into the store of Saml Neel, & thence brought to the McLure house. He has long been a resident of this county.]

A detachment of about 310 U S troops left Carlisle barracks on Thu last for Kansas. A majority of them will be stationed at *Fort Leavenworth*, & 40 recruits, intended for light company B, 3rd artl, at *Fort Snelling*. Lts Griffin, Starr, Tyler, Stanley, Wheaton, & Taylor accompanied the 1st detachment, & Maj Sherman the 2nd. These young robust men were enlisted principally in Phil, N Y, & Boston, & thoroughly drilled under the immediate supervision of Col Chas A May.

Lewis W Washington, of Beall-Air, in this county, has been appointed by Gov Wise, Cmder-in-Chief of Va, as his Aid-de-Camp, with the Brevet rank of Colonel of Cavalry. He is an estimable gentleman & will fill the appointment with credit to himself & honor to the State. –Va Free Press, Apr 23.

Excellent furniture & bar fixtures at auction at Flint's Hotel, on the premises, by deed of trust dated Jan 3, 1857, recorded in Liber J A S No 126, folios 99 et seq: north E st, between 13th & 14th sts. –Thos J Fisher, trustee -Jas C McGuire, auct
+
Trustee's sale of the valuable premises known as Flint's Hotel, being part of lot 6 in square 254, in Wash City, fronting 37 feet 3 inches on north E st, between 13th & 14th sts west, running back 159 feet to a 30 foot alley. –Wm P Williams, trustee -Jas C McGuire, auct

Household & kitchen furniture at auction on: May 11, all the effects of Mrs Eliza Anderson, on Pa ave, between 11th & 12th sts. –Thos J Fisher, trustee -Jas C McGuire, auct

The ship **Cathedral**, lost at Cape Horn, was owned by Enoch Train, of Boston. The vessel cost $125,000, on which there is an insurance of $75,000.

Mrd: on Apr 15, in Trinity Church, Buffalo, by Rev Edw Ingersoll, D D, Chas Seaforth Stewart, U S Corps of Engineers, to Cicilia Sophia De Louville, daughter of J A Tardy, & grand-daughter of M _____, Russian _____. [Paper is creased.]

Died: on Apr 24, at Sabula, Iowa, of pneumonia, Dr Martin H Johnson, of Wash City, in his 30th year.

Balt, May 3. Rev Dr Elder, of Mount St Mary's College, was consecrated at the Cathedral today Bishop of Charleston. A huge gathering witnessed the ceremonies.

Celebration of the first-settlement of Va: the Jamestown Society of Wash, in conjunction with citizens & military companies of Va, will celebrate the 5th semi-centennial anniversary on May 13, 1857. The anniversary address will be pronounced by ex-Pres Tyler, & an ode suited to the occasion will be delivered by Jas Banon Hope. Cmte of Arrangements:

P R Fendall, Pres	Thos Lumpkin	Jas M McRea
Jno T Towers, Treas	Gen A Henderson-	A H Cook
C W C Dunnington-	V Pres	Thos J Massie
Cor Sec	Beverly Tucker-	Thos J Galt
Wm Towers	Cor Sec	

TUE MAY 5, 1857
Farm for sale in Montg Co, Md: containing 233¼ acres, about 10 miles north of Wash City, in the neighborhood of the 7th st road; adjoins the lands of Dr Macall & Mrs Lee, & is in the vicinity of the *Burnt Mills* & the lands of Mr Porter, Dr Duvall, & Mr Beal. Improvements consist of 2 small frame tenements & a small barn or stable. Terms: $25 per acre; one half cash; remainder in 6, 12, & 18 months. Apply immediately to S H Young, Wood & Coal dealer, 9th st, between D & E sts, Wash

Died: on Apr 22, at Augusta, Ga, very suddenly, of an affection of the heart, Lt Wm Ross Gardner, of the U S Navy, aged 39 years.

St Louis has established the so-called Washington University, just inaugurated by an address from Edw Everett, & which is intended to be equal to the best in the U S. Among the gifts for the practical dept is land worth $60,000 by Col John O'Fallon & $20,000 in money by other friends. John Horn, of St Louis, also has offered $30,000 additional to purchase land & Mr O'Fallon $27,000 towards completing the institution.

For sale, in *Oak Hill Cemetery*, Gtwn, a fine Brown Stone Family Vault, substantially built of the best materials, containing 22 separate divisions, in a sublime situation, overlooking Rock Creek. Apply to Henry Parry, Marble Works, Pa ave, between 18th & 19th sts. The attention of persons about building family vaults is respectfully called. It will be sold low; which can be ascertained by the price vaults heretofore built in the cemetery have cost.

Orphans Court of Wash Co, D C. Letters of administration on the personal estate of Michl McDermott, late of Wash Co, deceased. –John McDermott, adm
+
The business heretofore carried on by the late Michl McDermott will be continued in his name, under an agreement between the undersigned, his widow & distributees. Persons indebted to the deceased will make payment to his administrator.
-Letitia McDermott   Jas McDermott   Jos Arthur McDermott
John McDermott   H Francis McDermott

WED MAY 6, 1857
Miss Myrtilla Miner, a young lady from Western N Y, has established & maintained for the past 4 years in Wash City a school for the education of free colored youth, & the nation is responsible for the well being of its population; because there are there 11,000 of this suffering people excluded by law from schools & destitute of instruction; & because there are in the adjoining State of Md & Va 180,000 equally destitute, who can be reached in no other way. This school is placed under the care of an association, consisting of the following trustees:

Benj Tatham, N Y   G Bailey, Wash
Saml M Janney, Loudoun Co, Va   L D Gale, Wash
Johns Hopkins, Balt   H W Bellows, N Y
Saml Rhoads, Phil   C E Stowe, Andover
Thos Williamson, Phil   H W Beecher, Brooklyn

Exec Cmte:
S J Bowen, of Wash   M Miner, Principal,
J M Wilson, of Wash   Wm H Beecher, of Reading, Sec
L D Gale, of Wash

Capt C K Stribbling, U S Navy, has been ordered to relieve Cmdor Rousseau, on Jun 1, in command of the navy yard at Warrenton near Pensacola, Fla.

The Pacific squadron will be reinforced by a large detachment of marines, which left N Y yesterday in the steamship **Illinois**, under the command of Lt Broome.

According to the Courrier Franco-Italien M Caruana, historical painter of Valetta, in the Island of Malta, has discovered that slate is superior to wood for engravings.

N Y, May 6. The trial of Mrs Cunningham, indicted, with J J Eckel, for the murder of Dr Burdell, was commenced on Monday before Judge Davies, in the Court of Oyer & Terminer. The opinion prevails that the testimony, mostly circumstantial, will be insufficient to convict. [May 12th newspaper: The acquittal of Mrs Cunningham for the alleged murder of Dr Burdell was the work of but little more than half an hour. Eckel was discharged upon his own recognizance, & it is said the authorities are upon the track of the real murderer.]

Rev John B Byrne, pastor of St Matthew's Church, [Catholic,] of Wash City, having been duly elected to the ofc here by the Council, & the action being confirmed at Rome, will be consecrated Bishop of the See of Pittsburg at the Cathedral of this city. -Balt American

The St Paul Pioneer states that the new Govn'r, Sam Medary, arrived in that city on Apr 22 & entered upon his ofc. No inaugural address was given.

The Montreal Pilot records the death of Mr Frank Wills, the architect, who died in Montreal on Apr 23. He was employed to furnish plans for the parish church & cathedral there. During a residence of 10 years in the U S he was the architect of upwards of 50 churches. He was an Englishman by birth, & about 35 years of age.

Mr Jas Brigham, of this city, came to his death on Apr 30 by an attempt to jump on the cars while the train was under headway near Dover, Ala. He lost his balance, fell under the wheels, & a portion of the train passed over him, mutilating his limbs in a horrible manner.

Circuit Court of D C: Mar Term, 1857. John A Gassaway & others, heirs at law of Hanson Gassaway, vs Nathl Jewett. The trustee sold the west part of lot 4, & part of lot 5 in square 408, in Wash City, to Wm B Kibbey, for $21,600, & the purchaser has complied with the terms of sale. –Jno A Smith, clerk

Judge Ebenezer Alexander died at his residence in Knoxville, Tenn, on Apr 29.

Mrd: on May 5, in Alexandria, Edgar Snowden, jr, of Alexandria Gaz, to Mrs Clarence Powell, of that city.

In Chancery-No 1,232. John Costigan, cmplnt, against Mary A Perkins, admx, & Mary Lewellener, Geo W, Sarah C, Ann Eliza, & Thos V Perkins, heirs of Thos Perkins. The parties above named & Mary A Perkins, guardian ad litem of the infant heirs, are notified that on May 18, at my ofc, in Wash City, I shall state an account of the personal estate of the deceased, of the debts due from him, & inquire whether it is necessary to sell his real estate for payment of his debts. –W Redin, auditor

Obit-died: The Boston Transcript of Sat announces the sudden death of Jos K Angell, of Providence, R I, & says: Mr Angell came to Boston yesterday to superintend the publication of a new work now in press by Little, Brown & Co, on the Law of Highways. He was taken ill & carried to the Massachussetts Genr'l Hospital, where he died of apoplexy. He was 60 years of age & was unmarried. We believe he has no near relatives, but connected with several influential families in R I.

Died: on May 4, in Wash City, Bessie, the infant daughter of Wm H & Nannie L Hull, aged 1 year & 3 months. Her funeral will take place from her grandfather's, Jas J Randolph, on 7th st, near I st, at 3 o'clock this evening.

Died: on May 2, at Martinsburgh, Berkeley Co, Va, in her 14th year, Florence Forrest Boarman, daughter of Capt Chas Boarman, of the U S Navy.

Died: on Apr 29, in Wash City, after a few days' illness, Mrs Mary Bishop, a native of Somersetshire, England, aged 67 years.

Died: on May 4, in Wash City, in his 67th year, Rev Wm McKenney, Chaplain of the U S Navy. Faith, Hope, & Charity were the leading virtues of his life, but the greatest of these was Charity.

St Louis, May 4. The Democrat contains advices from **Fort Des Moines**, Iowa, to Apr 21, stating that from five to six hundred Indians crossed the Des Moines river, in the neighborhood of **Fort Dodge**, on Sat. Fears were entertained that it had been attacked, as the force of the fort was insufficient to repel such a body of Indians. Companies were organizing to to the assistance of the fort. Several families had sought refuge at **Fort Des Moines**, & the greatest consternation prevailed in the neighborhood.

THU MAY 7, 1857
Orphans Court of Wash Co, D C. Letters of administration on the personal estate of Andrew Hoover, late of Wash Co, deceased. –A P Hoover, adm

Trustee sale of improved property & household furniture: by deed of trust from the late Lynde Eliot & Jane B Eliot, his wife, dated Apr 9, 1856, recorded in Liber J A S No 115, folios 223, of the land records of Wash Co, D C: public sale on May 14 of lots 1, 2, & 20, in square 4, with the improvements on Lot 2, being a 2 story brick house, with a 2 story back bldg in good repair. –L J Middleton, trustee
-Jas C McGuire, auct

Harman Folk, a son of Mr Wesley Folk, of Lexington district, S C, was accidentally shot & killed a few days ago. He was in company with a lad named Dickard, found a pistol, which they supposed to be unloaded. Dickard took the weapon & playfully told his companion he was going to shoot him, when it exploded & the ball went through Folk. He died the next day.

From the **Fort Dodge** Sentinel: massacre at **Spirit Lake** by the Indians. Recently we conversed with 8 of the 10 families comprising the settlements in Buena Vista & Clay Counties, of their women being abused, their cattle, horses, & provisions destroyed, & other acts of violence. The families were Ambrose S Mead, Leroy F Frinch, Geo M & Wheeler S Gillett, Jas Bicknell, Abner Bell, Jas W Williams, & John A Kirchner. The Indians passed last spring from Minnesota, indicating no acts of violence in their march. On Feb 21st they returned by the same route, & attacked the first settlement. This being sudden, & the nearest house, occupied by the Gilletts, 12 miles from Abner Bee, the occupant of the first, & his family were compelled to submit, from inability to defend themselves or procure assistance. On the 24th the house occupied by the Gilletts was suddenly entered by 10 armed warriors; the 2 families, temporarily under one roof, consisted of 5 small children & the heads of each family. After enduring outrages too horrible to relate, they managed to escape at midnight on the 24th, & the next day reached the residence of Mr Bell. The whole setttlement was destroyed & finally abandoned. On Mar 26th, suddenly the residence of Mr Stewart was attacked, killing him, his wife, & 2 daughters. One only of the Stewart family escaped, a boy about 8 years of age, who safely got out of the house & concealed himself. The Indians attacked the storehouse of Wm Wood, killing him & burning the bldg; his brother is missing & supposed to be killed also. A son of Mr Thomas, aged 12 years was killed. On Friday some 50 dragoons, dispatched from **Fort Ridgely** under the command of Capt Bee, reached Springfield. The Indians fled towards the Missouri. Nothing remained for our relief party except the burying of the dead. Those buried were: A Noble, wife, & child; E Rian; Mrs Joel Howe & 5 children; child of J M Thatcher; man possibley named Granger; W W Mattock, wife & 4 children, eldest 14 years old; Robt Clark, of Waterloo, in this State; J H Harriet, Jos Harsham, ___ Cropper; Rowland Gardner, wife, & child 12 years old; Mrs Mary, wife of Harvey Luce, Albert & Amanda Luce. There calmly let them rest. Among the missing were Mrs Thatcher, Jos Howes, Sardis Howes, daughter of T Howes, aged 14, 3 children of Mattock's, Harvey Luce, & Abigail Gardner, 4 of whom are known to have been taken captive by the Indians.

Mrd: on May 6, in Wash City, at Trinity Church, by Rev Dr Cummins, Dr Delavan Bloodgood, U S Navy, to Jinnie E Ruger, daughter of the late Hon John Ruger, of Syracuse, N Y.

Mrd: on May 5, in Wash City, by Rev B Sunderland, D D, Dr Wm H Mussey, of Cincinnati, to Caroline Webster, 2nd daughter of Dr Lindsly.

Died: on May 5, in Gtwn, D C, Emily, wife of Edmund H Brooke. Her funeral will take place this afternoon, at 3 o'clock, from the residence of her mother, Mrs Getty, on Dunbarton st.

Died: yesterday, of typhoid fever, Mrs Viginia Gallaher, widow of the late Marcellus Gallaher, & daughter of Mr Lewis Brooks, of Gtwn, D C, in her 27th year, leaving an infant son in his 3rd year. Her funeral will take place this afternoon at 4 o'clock, from the residence of her father, Mr Lewis Brooks, High st, Gtwn.

FRI MAY 8, 1857
Foreign Items: 1-The death of the Duchess of Gloucester was almost daily anticipated in England. 2-The Bishop of Exeter, who is now 80 years of age, is also very ill, & there is little hope of his recovery.

The Balt papers announce the death, in that city, yesterday, of Rev John A Collins, a well known popular preacher of the Methodist Episcopal Church, & a native, we believe, of this city.

The following letter from Sir John Franklin is said to be the last received from his pen: Whale Fish Island, Bay of Disco, July 11th, 1845. My Dear Sister: The appearance, dress, & manners of the Esquimaux bespeak that care is taken of them by the Government. Several of them can read the Bible with ease, and I am told that when the families are all collected the children are obliged to attend school daily. I looked into one of the huts arranged with seats for this purpose. When the minister comes over from Disco he superintends the schools; at other times the children are taught by a half caste Esquimaux. How delightful it is to known that the Gospel is spreading far and wide, and will so do until its blessed truths are disseminated through the globe! Every ship in these days ought to go forth to strange lands bearing among its officers a missionary spirit; and may God grant such a spirit on board this ship! It is my desire to cultivate this feeling, and I am encouraged to hope that we have some among us who will aid me in this duty. We have divine service twice on each Sunday, and I never witnessed a more attentive congregation than we have. May the seed sown fall upon good ground and bring forth fruit abundantly to God's honor and glory! Ever your affectionate brother, John Franklin

The march of civilization is onward! A clergyman in a Springfield, Massachusetts' church, last Sunday, married a couple, substituting the words "gentleman & lady" for "man & woman."

Thos Kerr, a stranger visiting in Gtwn, D C, who was born in the north of Ireland more than 70 years ago, tells of his life. Death robbed me of my friends, & poverty drove me from my native land. The ship in which I sailed brought me to Phil in 1812. The war between England & America had already commenced; men were wanted to join Hull in his invasion of Canada; I volunteered my services, & became an assistant in the quartermaster's dept. After the declaration of peace I was honorably discharged. For weeks I floated on the beautiful Ohio & the turbid Mississippi, obtaining my food by hunting & fishing. I had some narrow escapes from the tomahawk. In Louisiana I was employed as an overseer on a large plantation, became acquainted with the negro character, killing coons & oppossums with them at one time & at another directing them in their labors. I emigrated to Illinois & taught school for awhile, farmed for a living about 2 years, & remember to have killed a deer at the mouth of the Chicago river. I joined a party of Indians & spent a year hunting buffaloes on the prairies of Missouri. I was thrown from a horse which seriously injured my spine, & for a few months I anticipated the hand of death. I went to Tenn and heard Andrew Jackson speak. I later came to the Greenbrier country. Before leaving Ireland I had become a member of the Masonic fraternity; I carry my papers with me always. I tried the efficacy of my papers in Wash, but without success; I could not find a friend. In Gtwn I have been more successful. I shall now go all the way home on foot; & if the prayers of a poor old sinful man like me can avail anything, the Masons of Gtwn shall be gratified in all temporal & eternal wishes.

The following are the names of Gen Walker's men, most of them having been under command of Col Lockridge, who arrived at New Orleans last week on the steamer **Empire City**: Officers: <u>Majors</u> Ellis, Baldwin, Kelly, Moon, Capers; <u>Capts</u>: Williams, West, Walker, Conklin, Harris, Scott, Barrington, Dr Welch, Dr Anderson; <u>Lts</u>: Mulholland, Allen, Clever, Sandford, Colmen, Reed, Muzzy.
<u>Privates:</u>

R H Randolph	E Maud	John Wells
R H Hays	J M Brooks	H M Lyon
T Wydick	A Rogy	Wm Batchellor
Jas Noble	John Macann	J R Williamson
W Stupp	Thos Ashmore	J H Herbert
J M Kilts	Wm M Harvey	B J Reed
S T Logan	Wm McCulley	E Winniford
W A Limbecker	Wm Brochim	A Hays
J M Wheelock	Jas Brown	R W Cubies
J R Coleman	G W Wemly	B S Brom
A Temple	P A Peoples	J Dellavaine

R M Chester	S Serf	G M Cuddy
J R Owen	J Flynn	Jno H Flowen
Jerry Regger	S Wilmer	E A Window
Edw Hunter	A C Allen	A McDonough
J Chace	A F Roddy	Robt Broyinton
P O'Brien	John Lamki	R A Harris
R H Mears	Chas Martis	L Y Jennings
Jas Galwin	Wm Callahan	John T Nolan
L McGregor	S M Woodmorton	R McGriff
Sam Jenks	J D McDonough	J Stoball
Walter Cross	J H Wilson	J M Baldwin
John Robertson	Chas Reinhart	J N Williams
J M Cury	W W Ellinder	J E Foster
Wm Moore	Thos P Thackaray	E P Crook
Wm Smith	F Nolan	L H Culbert
Wm Hamilton	Fred'k Marts	N P Parson
J S Spear	Ben Brady	
Z Landman	T F Conway	
Miles Lester	Wm F Johnson	

Richard Langhorne, a lawyer, was unjustly condemned & put to death as a traitor in the reign of Charles II. Just before his execution he wrote a poem: [A few lines of the poem:]
It is told me I must die:
O, what happiness!
I am going
To the place of my rest;
To the land of the living;
To the haven of security;
To the kingdom of peace;
To the palace of my God;
To the nuptials of the Lamb;
To sit at the table of my King;
To feed on the bread of angels;
To see what no eye hath seen;
To hear what no ear hath heard;
To enjoy what the heart of man cannot comprehend.

A Armstrong, of Delaware, has purchased 209 acres of land in Spottsylvania Co, Va, for about $15 per acre. Dr Heston, of the same place, purchased 127 acres in the same county for $2,400.

Mrd: on May 7, at Derbyshire Vale, Balt Co, by Rev Edw L Lycett, Geo Lycett & Eliza A, daughter of Rev Thos Flint.

On the morning of Apr 10, in Putnam Co, Indiana, Mrs Martha Ann Mullinix, wife of Greenbury O Mullinix, was found at her own house, in the last agonies of death, her skull being broken in 3 places. She was a lovely young woman, & had been married only 3 or 4 weeks. Her husband is charged with the murder, & is now in the Putnam Co jail awaiting his trial in the circuit court.

The sale at the Printing Ofc square yesterday by Mr McGuire resulted in the disposal of 58 out of 60 lots; prices ranged from 15 to 44½ cents per foot. The residence & landed property of the late Gen Jas Thompson, in the 1st Ward, was put up at auction yesterday. The residence sold for $8,000, & was purchased by Mr Reeside, of Gtwn.

Died: on May 3, at the Univ of Va, of scarlet fever, Anna, daughter of W H McGuffey & Laura Howard McGuffey, in her 4th year.

SAT MAY 9, 1857
Trustee's sale: by deed of trust from the late Jas Coyle & wife, & by direction of Geo Thomas, the party interested iin the debt secure thereby, I shall, on Jun 1, on the premises, sell at auction, that part of lot 180 in Beall's first addition to Gtwn, adjoining the ground leased by D Reintzel to H Kingsbury, with house & improvements thereon. –W Redin, trustee -E S Wright, auct, Gtwn

N Y: John F A Sanford, an emiment merchant of the city, died on Tue, in his 51st year. He began life as a trapper & ended it in the possession of wealth, but this was beyond his enjoyment, as he died insane. He deserved commisseration even in the midst of his great wealth.

Mr Chas Mason, the Com'r of Patents, returned to Wash City yesterday from a visit of some 4 or 5 weeks to his home in Iowa.

The U S sloop of war **Dale** sailed from Hampton Roads on May 5, bound to Madeira. List of her ofcrs: Wm M Blair, Capt; Joel S Kennard, T Lee Walker, Hunter Davidson, A Boyd Cummings, & Thos P Pelot, Lts. Passed assist surgeon, Wash. Sherman; Richd C Dean, assist surgeon. John S Cunningham, purser; Chas H Hasker, boatswain; John Gaskins, gunner; John A Dixon, carpenter; Stephen C King, sailmaker.

Death of the oldest person in N H. The Manchester [N H] American says that Widow Rebecca Carleton recently died in Bartlett, N H, at the advanced age of 103 years. She was born in 1753, & was 22 years of age when the Revolutionary war began. Her 8 children are all living, the youngest being over 60.

Died: on May 2, at Rochester, N Y, Charlotte Hunter, youngest daughter of Maj E S Sibley, U S Army, aged 8 months.

Died: on May 7, at Balt, of pneumonia, Rev John A Collins, in his 56th year, & in the 26th year of his ministry in the Methodist Episcopal Church. At the time of his death he was Presiding Elder of the Cumberland district, from whence he had a few days previously returned to Balt to attend the quarterly conference.

Metropolitan Railroad Ofc, Gtwn, D C: May 7, 1857. –Jas W Deeble, Sec & Treas.

For sale: my residence on the corner of N J ave & C st south, Capitol Hill, fronting on the avenue 162 feet & 9 inches, & on C st south 206 inches, containing nearly 34,000 square feet. –Wm F Phillips

MON MAY 11,1857
English Royalty: Queen Victoria is the mother of 5 girls & 4 boys, all healthy & robust children, & yet she & her husband are less than 38 years old. The immediate royal family of Great Britain consists as follows: Alexandrina Victoria, born May 24, 1819, married Feb 10, 1840, to Francis Albert Augustus Charles Emanuel, born Aug 26, 1819.
Children: Victoria Adelaide Mary Louisa, Princess Royal, born Nov 21, 1840
Albert Edward, Prince of Wales, born Nov 9, 1841
Alice Maud Mary, born Apr 25, 1843
Alfred Ernst Albert, born Aug 6, 1844
Helena Augusta Victoria, born May 25, 1846
Louisa Carolina Alberta, born Mar 18, 1848
Arthur Wm Patrick Albert, born May 1, 1850
Leopold Geo Duncan Albert, born Apr 7, 1853
Princess _____, born Apr 14, 1857.

Superior cabinet furniture, Chickering piano forte, elegant curtains, carpets & mirrors, carriage & harness, & milch cows, at auction on May 15, at the residence of Capt H L Shields, U S A, on I st, between 13th & 14th sts. -Jas C McGuire, auct

Excellent household & kitchen furniture at auction on: May 14, at the residence of John Calvert, on G st, between 11th & 12th sts. [The house is for rent-inquire on the premises.] -J C McGuire, auct

Henry Willard, a portrait painter, formerly of Boston, but lately residing in N Y, while walking upon the track of the Boston & Maine railroad in Madden, on Tue last, was run over by the Portland express train, & instantly killed. Mr Willard spent several months in Wash during the last year, & many condemn his sudden death.

Wm P Irvin, of Pike Co, Ga, was killed at a steam saw-mill in that county on Wed last. In attempting to arrange some of the machinery he was caught by one of the bands, drawn into the machinery, & his brains crushed out, causing his instant death.

Orphans Court of Wash Co, D C. Letters testamentary on the personal estate of Rebecca Ford, late of the city of Phil, Pa, deceased. —Stephen C Ford, exc

Orphans Court of Wash Co, D C. Letters testamentary on the personal estate of Mary A King, late of Wash Co, deceased. —Jno D Barclay, exc

Strayed or stolen, a blue cow with white spots. The return of said cow will be thankfully received by the owner. —Thos Sullivan, H st, between 2nd & 3rd sts, **English Hill**.

N Y: The demolition of the old **Columbia College** bldgs & the transfer of this renowned seat of learning to another locality, have awakened feelings of regret amongst those who have received education there. The exercises are to be resumed on May 12th st in the bldgs in 49th st, & continued until the new & larger edifices shall be erected on or near the 5th ave, in the neighborhood of 50th st. The cornerstone of the old bldg was disinterred, & is to be used as a tablet in the new one, to show the origin of the institution. The inscription on it is in Latin & translated reads: "The most excellent Charles Hardy, Knight Vanneret and most worthy Governor of this Province, on 3d August, 1756, placed this foundation-stone of this college called Kings established by Royal diploma in honor of Almighty God and for the advantage of the Church and the Commonwealth."

TUE MAY 12, 1857
Mr Benj S Dey, of Currituck Co, N C, while ploughing in his field, a few days ago, dug up a pile of old Spanish gold & silver coin to the amount of about $6,000. It rather gives credence to the tradition that there was money deposited on that part of the coast by Blackbeard the pirate. —Norfolk Herald of May 7.

The manufacture of hoop skirts is shortly to be entered upon on a large scale at *Sing-Sing prison* under State contract.

Obit-The funeral of Prosper M Wetmore, jr, took place at Ascension Church, yesterday, at 6 o'clock, Rev Dr Bedell officiating. The beautiful Episcopalian service was never more touchingly performed or more impressive. The deceased spent the last fall & winter at Cuba, where he received the friendly hospitalities of the Capt-Genr'l & of many American friends there. He returned only in time to have the last offices of affection paid him by his sorrowing family, & to breathe his last sigh in his mother's arms. We sympathise with Gen Wetmore at this last stroke of misfortune. Thrice flew the shaft, & thrice his peace was slain. We have felt for him in his loss of property; in the assault upon his fame; in the desertion of sunshine friends, too happy once to bask in his favor; & in his manly & persistant struggle against adversity, now rudely assailing him. A large number of persons were present at the funeral, men of the highest standing in this city, & among them Govn'r Marcy, Mr Schell, & some of our oldest merchants. -N Y Mirror of May 9

Mrd: on May 5, at the Methodist Protestant Church, Gtwn, by Rev Dr Murray, Parker Hall Sweet, of the Genr'l Land Ofc, to Georgeanna, 2nd daughter of Thos B Griffin, of Wash City.

There appears to be a strong prospect that the proposition to erect a new structure to supersede the dilapidated bldg where the congregation of St Patrick's Church has for so many years assembled will speedily be carried into effect. [May 16th newspaper: Cmte formed: Francis Mohun called to the chair; Messrs H B Sweeny & Wm W Ward appointed secs. Louis L Long to be the architect. Auditing cmte: Messrs H B Sweeny, John Maron, & W E Stubbs.

Collecting cmte:

Edw Simms	Dr A J Semmes	Richd H Clarke
Col J G Berrett	A L Newton	Richd Lay
Francis Mohun	C S Jones	Thos Stephens
John F Coyle	Val Harbaugh	P Gallant
E C Dyer	P O'Donnoghue	W H Ward
Geo Savage	John F Ellis	H Donohoe
Gregory Ennis	John McDermot	Thos Holden
John H Goddard	John F Ennis	
Philip Talty		

The Ky papers announce the death of Hon B Mills Crenshaw, of the Court of Appeals, & Chief Justice of that State. He died at his residence in Glasgow on Tue of pneumonia. The term for which he was elected will not expire till Aug, 1859. There will be a special election next Aug to supply the vacancy.

Departed this life, on Apr 22, at the residence of her brother, Col Wm L Calhoun, in Abbevile district, Martha Cornelia Calhoun, in her 31st year. Miss Calhoun was the youngest daughter of the late John C Calhoun. She was a communicant of the Episcopal Church. Her death was sudden & unexpected by her friends. –Charleston Courier

Salem, Mass lost 2 highly respected citizens last week. Wm Pickman, a retired & wealthy merchant, died on Fri, at the age of 82. Capt Jas W Cheever died on Sat very suddenly of an apoplectic attack, aged 67. He was at his accustomed places of resort on Fri evening as well as ever & unusually cheerful.

The Wash City Councils last evening elected the following for Com'rs of Election:

D Serrin	J P Dickinson	W B Downing
J Germon	W H Degges	R A Hyde
T Drury	C L Coltman	I W Clark
J B Hines	W P Shedd	Jos W Davis
H R Wright	G H Plant	Thos Rich
R W Denham	Edw Dyer	M W Galt

Jas W Boss	Wm F Price	J W Thompson
Robt Israel	John H Wise	Lawrence Tuell
Fred Iddins	Isaac C Bartlett	T H Barron
Alex McD Davis	Thos Hutchinson	B S Kinney
Warren C Choate	Geo Brown	Jas E Johnson
Thos H Havenner	Edw Evans, jr	J P Murphy
John T Killmon	Chas H Grodon	Woodville Latham
Stephen C Wailes	Caleb Stewart	J L Henshaw

Rev Benj N McPhail, pastor of the Presbyterian churches at Snow Hill, Newton, & Pitts' Landing, in Worcester Co, Md, committed suicide, about 9 o'clock on Sat night, by jumping into the bay from the hurricane deck of the steamer **Wilson Small**. For several months before he had been in delicate health, & it was observed nearly 2 weeks ago that his mind wandered. He was called to Snow Hill about a year ago. He leaves a wife & 5 children to mourn their said bereavement.

WED MAY 13, 1857
Kidnapping case: The Beames' case in Arkansas is ended. A family of free negroes named Beames, residing among the Choctaws & Creeks, were kidnapped & run into Arkansas, where they were sold, one of them passing through several hands. Through the perseverance of Col Cooper, agent for the Choctaws & Chickasaws, with the consent of the Indian Bureau, suits were commenced for their recovery & freedom in the Arkansas court, which were resisted by the parties who had purchased them. These suits have all been decided in favor of the negroes, who have regained freedom under the decrees of the courts. –Louisville paper

Chicago Journal of May 7. Dreadful accident on the Southern Michigan Railroad on Tue night, when the express train ran over a cow between Toledo & Adrian, throwing the tender off the track & causing the first passenger car to be thrown crosswise over the track. The second passenger car then ran against the hind end of the first, staving it clear into the baggage car in advance, instantly killing 5 persons in the first car. A gentleman & wife from Mercer Co, Pa on their way to settle in Wisconsin, together with one of their children, some 18 months old, were among the killed, leaving another child some 3 years old unharmed. A man, name unknown, from Wayne Co, N Y, bound to Wisc, was killed. He was about 30 years old & well dressed in black. Lastly, a child some 18 months' old, of Mrs Ellen Brown, was killed in her mother's arms. Mrs Brown, together with her mother, Mrs Palmiter, were quite seriously injured. Mr P, his wife, & 2 boys, with Mrs Brown, were emigrating from New Lyme, Ashtabula Co, Ohio, to Sheboygan Co, Wisc. The father & younger son were somewhat injured. The bodies of the killed were taken to Adrian for inquest.

Chas K Graham, Civil Engineer, of N Y, has been appointed Civil Engineer at the Brooklyn Navy Yard, vice Mr J McLeod Murphy, removed.

Chancery sale of valuable lot in the west end of Wash City: by decree of the Circuit Court of D C, in Chancery, made in a cause, No 106, depending in said court, wherein Jas W Strange et al are cmplnts, & Mgt Strange et al are dfndnts: auction, on the premises, on Jun 4 next, of lot 7 in square 127, located on H st, between 17th & 18th sts, in a rapidly improving neighborhood, & is nearly opposite to the late residence of Gov Fish. –W B Webb, trustee -Jas C McGuire, auct

We notice the demise, at her residence in Picadilly, of Hesther Maria Viscountess Keith, in her 95th year. She was the eldest daughter of Henry Thrale, & the husband of Hesther Salusbury, afterwards known to the world by the name of her second husband, Mrs Piozzi. From her mother she learned to cultivate intellectual pursuits, & from her father she derived those sterling qualities which belong especially to the high-toned English character. On the death of her father & the marriage of her mother to Signor Piozzi, [with whom she spent many years in foreign travel,] Miss Thrale was deprived of her home. When the time arrived appointed by her father for her majority, she established herself in a handsome house in London with her younger sisters, who were many years her junior. In 1808 Miss Thrale became the wife of Geo Keith Elphinstone, Viscount Keith, one of the most distinguished of those cmders by whom the naval honors of Great Britain were so greatly exalted. Viscountess Keith resided for many years on her husband's property of Tulliallan, in Clackmannanshire, where she was the generous bencfactress of the poor. In 1823 she became a widow; & in 1831 her only child, Georgiana, was married to John Augustus Villiers, 2nd son of the Earl of Jersey. By a former wife Viscount Keith had a daughter, Margaret, now the wife of the distinguished diplomatist Count de Flahault. Besides her daughter already mentioned, [the Hon Mrs Villiers,] Viscountess Keith is survived by 2 sisters, Miss Thrale, of Ashgrove, near Seven Oaks; & Mrs Mostyn, resident at Brighton. –English paper

A fatal casualty happened on Monday to a worthy man, John Connor, who was engaged in unloading from a wagon he had driven from the railroad depot a barrel of potash, which rolled upon him & so crushed him that he did not survive an hour. Medical assistance was punctually at hand, but the injury was too severe. He leaves a wife & family of 3 children. He was an employee at the depot.

Obit-died: Judge Wm Wilson died at his residence in White Co, Ill, on Apr 29, about in his 69th year. He was one of the early pioneers of Ill, & was Chief Justice of the Supreme Court from 1819 to 1849. –Chicago Tribune

Chief Justice Oakley, of the Superior Court of N Y died on Monday at the age of 73 years; & John Turner, formerly publisher of the N Y Gaz, died the same day at the advanced age of 85 years.

Orphans Court of Wash Co, D C. In the case of Chas Walter, adm of Danl Roemle, deceased: the administrator & Court have appointed Jun 2 next, for the final settlement of the personal estate of the deceased. –Ed N Roach, Reg/o wills

Valuable red-stone land for sale: on Jun 4, a farm in Prince Wm Co, Va, called *Deseret*, containing about 1,100 acres; adjoining the farm of S J Tebbs, known as *Tecumseh*, & the lands of Latham, Lynn, & others, near the Loudoun line. Mr Mathews, who resides thereon, will show the farm, or Mr Hutchison, the manager of the adjoining farm. Possession given immediately. –Col S J Tebbs, near Middleburg, Loudoun Co, Va, or to Fowle, Snowden & Co, 57 & 59 King st, Alexandria, Va.

Geo Wilson & his sister, Mrs McMasters, were murdered at Elizabeth township, Pa, last week on Thu evening, & their house was robbed of $800. Three persons, one of them a woman, have been arrested as the murderers.

THU MAY 14, 1857

The telegraph yesterday brought us tidings of the death of Hon Stephen Adams, late a Senator from the State of Mississippi. He removed to Memphis, Tenn, at the close of his official term, with a view to the resumption of his profession as a lawyer.

A bounty land warrant of 160 acres was issued from the Pension Ofc on Fri to Hon John P Kennedy, of Balt, for his services as a private soldier in Capt Warfield's company of volunteers which took part in the defence of Balt in 1814.

Obit-died: on Monday, Hon Thos J Oakley, Chief Justice of the Superior Court of N Y C, after a brief illness. He was born in 1783, & was in his 74th year; a Yale College graduate in 1801; in 1813 attained a high position at the bar; was elected to Congress, making his entry into public life simultaneously with Webster & Calhoun; in 1817 he returned to the bar; in Jul, 1819, was appointed Atty Gen of the State, succeeding Martin Van Buren; elected to Congress again in 1827, but resigned before the expiration of the first session to accept that judicial position on the bench of the Superior Court of N Y C. –Commercial Advertiser

Mrd: on May 13, at St Matthew's Church, in Wash City, by Rev J B Donelan, B Frank Gallaher, Purser U S Navy, to Miss Eliza A Buckner, 2nd daughter of the late Richd Bernard Buckner, of Fauquier Co, Va.

Mrd: on May 12, at St Paul's Church, Balt, Md, by Rev O Hutton, John W Boteler, of Wash, to Fannie M, daughter of T C Miller, of Enfield, Balt Co, Md.

Died: on May 9, at the residence of her mother, Mrs F T Fitzhugh, Mrs C M Balestier, aged 45 years. Blessed are the pure in heart, for they shall see God.

Died: on May 12, at Balt, John Beard, in his 67th year. He was one of the defenders of Balt in 1814, having been a sgt in one of the companies of the 27th regt, which mustered at the battle of North Point 82 men, of whom only 4 are yet living. In later years he became by a series of promotions lt colonel of the regt.

Died: on Apr 30, at her residence in Calvert Co, Md, Mrs Mary Williams, in her 78th year.

Died: on May 13, Francis Ward, in his 60th year, a native of the county Monoghan, Ireland, but for the last 35 years a resident of Wash City. His funeral will take place from his late residence, corner of 12th & C sts, on May 15, at 9 o'clock.

Richmond, May 18. J Randolph Tucker [brother of Beverley Tucker, late of the Sentinel] was nominated today by the Democratic Convention for Atty Genr'l.

I have stopped the Pawnbroker's business, & all persons having goods pledged with me must see to the payment at maturity, as I shall not renew any tickets, but sell the goods as soon as forfeited. –John Robinson, 349, opposite Brown's Hotel.

FRI MAY 15, 1857

The Jackson [Michigan] Citizen announces the sudden death of Mr Allen Hiscock, of Princeton, Ill, formerly of Jackson, while proceeding in the cars to Ann Arbor, where his wife was visiting, & where he was to stop. He was attacked with a violent toothache, & a physician on the train administered chloroform to ease the pain. On arriving at Ann Arbor he complained of fainting, soon swooned away, & died.

Household & kitchen furniture at auction on: May 16, at the late residence of Mr R B Nally, deceased, 416 G st, between 7th & 8th sts. –C W Boteler, auct

Administrator's sale in Gtwn: wagons, carts, blacksmith tool, iron & lumber, at auction, on May 18, at the Wagon & Blacksmith shops of Thos Tucker, deceased, near the Bridge st bridge. –C F English, adm -Bernard & Buckey, aucts

Mrd: on May 13, in Wash City, by Rev W H Chapman, T Edw Clark to Jane Maria, eldest daughter of Wm Bland, all of Wash City.

Mrd: on May 14, in Wash City, by Rev Mr Krebbs, Mr Arthur J McGuiggan, of Va, to Miss Adeline T Hobbs, of Wash City.

Mrd: on May 14, in Wash City, in the Fourth Presbyterian Church, by Rev John C Smith, Henry D Morgan to Miss Eliza Jane, daughter of Sidney DeCamp, all of Wash City.

Mrd: on May 12, at the residence of G B Hatcher, Fauquier Co, Va, by Rev Dr J J Murray, John Eliason, of Gtwn, D C, to Miss Mary C Chunn, of the former place.

Mrd: on Apr 28, in Richmond, Indiana, by Rev J F Smith, Mr Wm H Bennett to Miss Martha B Compton, of Wash City.

Mrd: on May 5, by Rev Mr Knight, Dionysius Sheriff to Mary A, daughter of Philip Hill, all of PG Co, Md.

SAT MAY 16, 1857
Household & kitchen furniture at auction on: May 19, at the late residence of Miss King, deceased, on G st, next to the corner of 18th st west. –A Green auct

Jacob Neuislein, who was to have been hung at St Louis on Fri last for the murder of his wife, has received a respite until Jun 19. Saml Ingram, of Pa, was to have been executed on May 5 at Rock Island, Ill, also for the murder of his wife, but received a respite for 30 days. Saml Gilmore, under sentence of death at Chicago, has had his sentence commuted to imprisonment for life.

At Brentsville, Prince Wm Co, Va, on Wed, the jury in the case of the Commonwealth vs Sinclair, for the murder of Hewett, in that county, about 2 years since, found the prisoner guilty of murder in the 1st degree. The counsel for the prisoner moved the Court for a new trial.

Constable's sale: by virtue of 16 writs of fieri facias, at the suits of J B Wilson, T J Galt, & W M Galt, trading under the firm of Galt & Co, & Michl Fowler, against the goods & chattels, lands, & tenements of Edw Willson & Wm H Haywood, trading under the firm of Willson & Haywood, to me directed, I have seized numerous articles, too many to mention: auction on May 19, on the premises, Union Hall, on La ave, near 7th st. –A E L Keese, constable

Mrd: on May 14, in Wash City, at the Foundry Church, by Rev S Register, Mr D Chapman Ourand to Miss Julia F Taylor, both of Wash City.

Mrd: on May 14, in Wash City, by Rev Bernard Maguire, Pres of Gtwn College, Stephen A Cromwell, of St Louis, Mo, to Miss Mary E Cluskey, daughter of Chas B Cluskey, of Wash.

Died: on May 13, in Wash City, Geo B McKnight, Surgeon U S Navy, in his 65th year. His funeral will be from his late residence on 3rd st, this evening at 4 o'clock.

Died: on May 12, in Wash City, Mrs Sarah E Coale, consort of the late Wm Coale, of Md, & daughter of Edmund & Eliz W Bradford, of Fauquier Co, Va.

MON MAY 18, 1857
European Intelligence: 1-The anticipated decease of the Duchess of Gloucester, the last surviving child of George III & aunt to Queen Victoria, occurred on Apr 30th. She had entered upon her 82nd year. 2-Mr F Peel, Sec of War, had resigned, & would probably be succeeded by Mr Massey, a new member of Parliament from the borough of Salford. 3-Sir Jas Brooke, Rajah of Sarawak, in the island of Borneo, has narrowly escaped destruction at the hands of the Chinese residents in the settlement.

Valuable improved property near the Steamboat Wharf at public auction: on May 22, on the premises, I shall sell lots 10 thru 16 in square 355, fronting on 11th st, between F & G sts, with an excellent 2 story brick dwlg house, being the property formerly occupied by Capt Mitchell. -Jas C McGuire, auct

Died: on May 16, at Jordan's Springs, Va, Eliza Ann, wife of Col Chas Thomas, U S Army. Her funeral will be from the residence of her husband, 342 N Y ave, at 4 o'clock, this afternoon.

Louisville, Ky, May 16. A riot took place here yesterday on the acquittal of 4 negroes charged with having murdered the Joyce family. The mob was led by young Joyce, son of one of the parties murdered. On a second try, the mob went to the jail with a cannon to get to the negroes. Mr Thomas, the jailor, & his deputies, & Mayor Pilcher, found further resistance would have been utterly futile. The keepers immediately capitulated, when 3 of the negroes were seized & hung to a tree. The other negro cut his throat in jail, preferring to die thus than by the hands of the mob. Young Joyce, who headed the rioters & who is supposed to be insane, has been put in close confinement.

Orphans Court of Wash Co, D C. Letters testamentary on the personal estate of John Peake, late of Wash Co, deceased. –Chas Wilson, exc

TUE MAY 19, 1857
Died: on Apr 17, in San Francisco, Charles P, son of Capt C P & Maria L Stone, aged 4 months & 17 days.

The Wash correspondent of the N Y Times states that the War Dept has assigned Maj Deas & Lts Carr & Walker as Gov Walker's military aids. Also, that Judge Drummond, now in Wash, will be offered the Governorship of Utah, if Maj McCulloch declines.

The ship **Mary Caroline Stevens** sailed yesterday from Balt with full freight & 185 emigrants for Liberia. Rev Mr Wilson, white teacher, of the Alexandria High School, at Monrovia, & Mr De Lyon, colored, of Monrovia, are the only cabin passengers. The vessel will take out the machinery for a large sugar mill, 3 frame houses, ready for erection on arrival, 100 bedsteads, & 200 chairs.

Robt Webb & H K Eaton arrived in St Louis on Wed night last, from Pittsburg, &, being strangers, lost their way in the street. They encountered two villains who demanded their money; a fracas ensued, & the strangers were thrown over a precipice 30 feet deep, causing the death of Mr Webb on Fri & dangerously injuring Mr Eaton. The former was from Lewistown, Pa, & was going to Kansas to establish a newspaper.

Mrd: on May 17, in Wash City, by Rev G D Cummins, Dr Wm C Foster, jr, of Bloomington, Ind, to Indiana Miller, 2nd daughter of the late Richd M Beall, of Wash City.

Mrd: on May 12, in Brooklyn, by Rev T B Sawyer, Mr Arnold B Johnson, of Rochester, Mass, to Miss Harriet M Barrows, of Brooklyn, N Y.

Mrd: on May 4, at New Orleans, at the residence of her sister, Mrs Col T F Hunt, by Rev Fr Flanigan, Capt W S Walker, 1st cavalry U S Army, to Miss Dora Hernandez, daughter of Gen Jos M Hernandez, of Florida.

WED MAY 20, 1857
Salt Lake City to Apr 1. A man named Parrish, a seceding Mormon, had determined upon leaving the Territory & coming to the States, & sold his property & purchased some horses & a wagon. These were stolen the night before he was to leave. He found them in Prova, but the Mayor of Provo refused all relief. Parrish, with his 2 sons, & 2 other men named Potter & Darger set out on foot. They had left the place more than a few hundred yards behind when they were attacked by a number of men armed & disguised. Potter was shot dead. Parrish was killed, & one of his sons was struck down, his throat cut, & his abdomen ripped open. The other young Parrish & Darger escaped. A similar tragedy occurred about 70 miles from Parowan, when Tobin & Peltro, seceding Mormons emigrating to Calif, were shot & killed as they sat encamped at the foot of some rocky hills.

Died: on May 7, in Balt, Mrs Mary E Hance, wife of Dr Thos Hance, of Calvert Co, Md, & daughter of the late Capt Garner, U S Army.

Died: on May 15, in Gtwn, in his 73rd year, Mr Jos Mountz, of Gtwn, & formerly for many years a clerk in the Treasury Dept.

"Rev" Mr Kinney, who was arrested in Fred'k, Md, several months ago on the charge of having robbed the Roman Catholic Church at Martinsburg, [of which he was formerly the pastor,] of a silver vase & other valuables, was convicted in the court of Berkeley Co, Va, during the past week & sentenced to the penitentiary for the term of one year.

Westmoreland Co, Va, May 1, 1857. Col John Washington, who came with his brother to America in 1657, settled on the bank of Bridge's creek, a small inlet of the Potomac, where he lived & was buried. He had 2 sons & a daughter, & it was to the second of these sons, Lawrence Washington, that the proprietors of the Northern Neck of Va granted a tract of land at the mouth of Pope's creek, on Jun 24, 1696. Lawrence Washington was thus an original proprietor, & in his will, dated Mar 11, 1698, he says: "I give the tract of land where I now live" to John Washington. Other bequests are made to his 2nd son Augustine, & to his daughter, who was named Mildred, after her mother. But John removed to Gloucester Co, & sold the *Popes creek estate* to Augustine, the father of George. This is shown by the will of Lawrence Washington, & by the deed from John T Augustine, which after diligent research I have found in the archives of this county, duly recorded. Nothing now remains at the Bridge's creek but the burial ground & vault in which are interred the remains of the father, grandfather, & great-grandfather of the Pater Patriae, with those of their respective families. The birth-place is nearly a mile distant, upon a somewhat elevated plateau, around which sweeps, in a semi-circular curve, *Pope's creek*. The house in which George Washington was born was destroyed by fire soon after the family left to reside on their *Staffordshire estate* near Fredericksburg. A subsequent proprietor either repaired one of the outhouses or a wing of the old one, or built a small house for his overseer out of the old materials. I am inclined to think the latter. A small monumental slab, sadly mutilated, lies upon the ground in a clump of fig trees, where it was removed from the site of the birth-mansion. It originally bore this inscription: "Here, the 11th February, 1732, Washington was born," and was placed there by his ward, G W P Custis, in June, 1815. It is due to the Washington family to say that when Col Geo C Washington [who resided in Gtwn, & owned the *Mount Vernon* books now in the Boston Athenaeum] sold *Wakefield*, which comprises the Bridge's Creek, & the *Pope's Creek estates*, on Oct 13, 1813, to John Gray, of *Traveller's Rest*, near Fredericksburg, he reserved 60 feet square of ground around the vault. In Feb, 1856, Col Lewis W Washington, [son & heir-at-law of Geo C Washington] presented these reservations to the mother State of Va in perpetuity, on condition solely that the State require the said places to be permanently enclosed with an iron fence, based on stone foundations, together with suitable & modest tablets, to commemorate to the rising generation these notable spots. Gov Wise accepted the donation & asked an appropriation of $2,000 to comply with the conditions. Different bills were passed, but a cmte of conference was not chosen, & the hallowed shrines are neglected. The estate now belongs to John E Wilson, [who is connected by marriage with the Washington family,] a gentleman whose courtesy & hospitality I acknowledge with gratitude. -Perley

Appointments by the Pres:
John W Baughman as Appraiser Genr'l, Balt, vice Pouder, removed.
David C Springer as Appraiser, Balt, vice Gosnell, removed.
Beale H Richardson, as Appraiser, Balt, vice Poultney, removed.

Dr F W B Perkins, of Burke Co, committed suicide on May 13th by taking morphine. He expired in 9 hours after having taken the dose.

The post mortem examination of Mr Petriken, from Harrisburg, Pa, who died from the effects of the malady contracted at the Nat'l Hotel in Wash City, did not show the slightest evidence of mineral poison in his stomach. -Union

The Levy Court on Monday elected the following supervisors of roads in this county: Selby B Scaggs, John Lighter, Wm Sanderson, Jesse Harshman, Rezen Arnold, Thos R Brightwell, Enos Ray, Mark Hewling, Thos Brown, Jas McGee, E M Middleton, Jas Anderson, & John B Kibbey.

The new St Patrick's Catholic Church is to be built on 10th st, between F & G sts: architect-Mr Louis C Long, of Balt, Md.

THU MAY 21, 1857
Longevity: obituary notices of the past month:
Eliz Goldizen, Hardy Co, Va, 118
Christiana Phillips, colored, New Haven, Conn, 109
John Keley, Steuben, Maine, 101
Jos Letendre, St David Canada, 100
Jacob Carter, Covington Co, Miss, 99
Mary Bennett, Burlington, Mass, 99
Jos Thompson, Coleraine, Mass, 98
Judith Keith, Warrenton, Va, 98
Hannah Babcock, Northborough, N Y, 96
Thos Majors, Richmond, Ky, 95
Eleazer Butler, Yarmouth, N S, 95
David Chambers, Brooklyn, N Y, 95
Lemuel Reed, N Dartmouth, Mass, 93
John S Edwards, Springfield, Mass, 93
Sarah Butt, Washington, 92
Zipperah Howell, Bridgehampton, L I, 92
Mary Brown, N Y, 92
Jacob F Burkhardt, N Y, 91
David Geer, N Y, 91
Dinah Williams, colored, N Y, 90
Chas Yancey, Buckingham, Va, 90
-Journal of Commerce

T H Wright, a lt of the U S dragoons, committed suicide a few days ago at Chicago, Ill. His body was found near Gibson's Station, about 26 miles south of Chicago, with a bullet through his heart. No pistol, however, could be found on him or near the body.

Passed-The following is the list of the candidates for admission into the naval service of the Gov't who passed satisfactory examinations for Third Assist Engineer places before the Board recently in session at Phil. They passed in order as number here:

1-Wm P De Sanno, of Phil
2-Francis J Lovering, of Balt
3-C A C Duplaine, of Phil
4-Chas B Kid, of N Y
5-Wm L Walters, of Wash, D C
6-Thos Cronin, of Phil
7-Benj C Bampton, of Brooklyn, N Y
8-N Littig, of Balt
9-J B Houston, of Wash, D C
10-Eben Hoyt, of Chelsea, Mass
11-Wm H King, of Portsmouth, Va
12-Wm R Schley, Fred'k, Md
13-Geo S Bright, of Wash, D C
14-Saml Savage, of Phil
15-Geo J Houston, Wash, D C
16-Jos H Warrington, of Phil
17-John Johnson, of Wilmington, Del

The 3 story frame dwlgs on St Asaph st, Alexandria, belonging to Mr Saml Beach, were destroyed by fire on Sunday night. The houses were not insured.

Govn'r Pollock, of Pa, has appointed Aug 21, for the execution of David Stringer McKim, convicted of the murder of Saml T Norcross, near Altoona, Pa, on Jan 16 last. Norcross was found with his throat cut & his skull fractured.

The York Pennsylvanian states that Rev B Hutchins, formerly pastor of the Episcopal church in that borough, but now residing at Albion, Ill, recently lost 7 out of 9 children in 10 consecutive days from scarlet fever, & at last accounts the other two were ill.

Mrd: on May 20, in Wash City, by Rev Wentworth L Childs, Jos Hart to Lucy H Studs, both of Fairfax Co, Va.

Mrd: on May 20, in Wash City, by Rev Smith Pyne, D D, Dr Geo K Wood, U S Army, to Louisa M, only daughter of Hon John W Allen, of Ohio.

Orphans Court of Wash Co, D C, May 16, 1857. In the case of Juliet V Howison, admx of Henry Howison, deceased, the administratrix & Court have appointed Jun 9 next, for the settlement of the personal estate of said deceased, of the assets in hand.
-Ed N Roach, Reg/o wills

Circuit Court of D C-in Equity, No 1,269. Wm W Hough, cmplnt, against, Eleanor, Christian M, Enoch G, Abraham F, Eliza J, John B, Christiana E K, & Philip H Hines, widow, administrator, & heirs of Abraham Hines. –W Redin, auditor

FRI MAY 22, 1857
Extensive sale of superior wines, liquors & cigars, at auction: on May 28, at the warehouse of Robt O Brooke, who is about declining business, No 558 7th st. –C W Boteler, auct

On Jun 10, I shall sell, on the premises, the tract of land known as *Anacosta*, adjoining the farms of Col Wm Hickey & W W Corcoran, about 2 miles from Wash: tract divided into 5 lots, varying from 11 to 55 acres. On lot 2 there is a dwlg house & the usual outbldgs for farm purposes. –C W Boteler, auct

Trade sale of glass & crockery ware: on Tue, at our Wareroom. Haslup & Weeden's Bldg. –Wall & Barnard, aucts

Excellent household & kitchen furniture at auction on: May 29, at the residence of Hon F P Stanton, in Corcoran's bldgs, on I st, between Vt ave & 16th st. -Jas C McGuire, auct

Valuable bldg lot at public auction, by deed of trust from Chas Dyson & wife, recorded in Liber J A S No 117, one of the land records of Wash Co, D C: sale on the premises of lot 7 in square 513, fronting 60 feet 6 inches on M st north, between 4th & 5th sts. –Jno C C Hamilton, Saml Hamilton, trustees -Jas C McGuire, auct

Five children of Saml Cannon, of Caseumpee, Prince Edward's Island, were burnt to death on Apr 9th, during the absence of their parents from home. The oldest child, a girl of 12 years, escaped, but was so severely burnt it is feared she will not recover.

On Apr 26 Alex'r Eudy, who lived about 6 miles from Greensboro, Miss, went out turkey hunting. On proceeding to secure his game he was horrified to find that he had shot his near neighbor, Mr John Herron. Mr Herron died in a few moments.

The Judge of this Court yesterday affirmed judgment in the case of E D Worrell, for the murder of Mr Gordon, once assistant engineer on the North Missouri railroad; & likewise in the case of Shultz, for the murder of one Inkamp, which transpired in St Louis Co. Both are ordered to be executed on Jun 19. –St Louis Republican of 16th.

At N Y, on Tue, Ellen Kelly, aged about 20, was accidentally burnt when a bottle of cologne fell upon a grate fire, & the fluid ignited her clothes. She died soon after.

Dr Algernon S Garnett, of Va, has been appointed an Assist-Surgeon & the Rev Chas A Davis, of Wash City, a Chaplain in the Navy.

Circuit Court of D C-in Equity. Selden, Withers & Co, vs Edmund Roberts & Helen his wife, Danl J Sutherland & Anne his wife, Mary C Nicholson, Henry W B Nicholson, & Leonard L Nicholson & others, heirs of Augustus A Nicholson. The bill in the above cause states that the cmplnts are creditors of the late Augustus A Nicholson in the sum of $2,700, by his note, dated Jan 27, 1854, at 90 days; that he hath departed this life intestate, leaving the said debt unpaid, & the above named dfndnts & others his heirs at law; that his personal estate is entirely insufficient for the payment of his debts, & that he left a considerable real estate in this District, which is liable therefore in aid of his personal estate; that the object of the bill is to obtain a sale of so much of his real estate as will pay the debts of the cmplnts & such other of his creditors as may come in & claim. The dfndnts above named do not reside in this District. They are to appear on the first Monday of Oct next, to answer the said bill. –Jno A Smith, clerk

Circuit Court of D C-in Equity. John Hooper & Jas Hooper, vs Abel Bird, Mgt Bird, & Robt Henry, & Chas Bird, & others, heirs of Wm Bird. The bill states that the cmplnts obtained a judgment against the late Wm Bird, to be released on the payment of $145.83, with interest from Nov 24, 1852, & costs, which is unpaid; that said Bird, before his death, conveyed divers lots & premises in this county to Wm H Ward, in trust, to sell for payment of his debts; that the said trust hath been partly executed, but that portions of the property so conveyed remain to be disposed of, & the cmplnts' & other debts to be satisfied; that there is no personal estate out of which they can be paid; & the object of the bill is to obtain a sale of the residue of the real estate of said late Wm Bird in aid of his personal for payment of said judgment & his other debts. Abel Bird, Mgt Bird, & Chas Bird do not reside in this District; they are to appear in this Court on the first Monday of Oct next.
-Jno A Smith, clerk

The city of Charlestown is greatly disturbed by the sudden disappearance of Alderman Edw Ward. He left on last Wed & it is thought he has taken from $15,000 to $20,000 with him of money belonging to the firm of Thos Greenleaf & Co, [lumber business.] Ward has had the principal care of the business. His family is still residing in Charlestown. –Boston Traveller

Despatch from Sandusky, Ohio, dated on Tue: this morning while a vessel was being built by Capt Dibble, the mast broke & fell, severely injuring Chas McKinney, John Potter, Capt Dibble, John Hill, & Geo Littlejohn. Potter died this afternoon, & McKinney will not probably live till morning. The others are not dangerously injured.

At Cape Sable on May 5, 2 privates of Co H, 4th artl, were capsized while sailing in the bay, & one of them named Dunn, while swimming ashore, was seized by a shark & eaten up. His companion got safely ashore.

U S Patent Ofc, Wash, May 20, 1857. Ptn of Norbert Rillieux, of N Y, praying for the extension of a patent granted to him on Aug 26, 1843, for an improvement in sugar, for 7 years from the expiration of said patent, which takes place on Aug 26, 1857. –Chas Mason, Com'r of Patents

SAT MAY 23, 1857
Tradition rather than a matter of record that the remains of a British nobleman, buried under the chancel of the old English Church when it stood in the middle of State st, were taken up & re-interred under the present church when it was built in 1804. His name was Lord Howe & he was killed at the time of Burgoyne's surrender at Saratoga. There is no monument, mural tablet, gravestone, or even a pavement inscription to mark the spot or attest to the fact. We are indebted to an antiquarian friend for the following more authentice version of the story, by which it appears that Lord Howe fell, not at Saratoga, but at Ticonderoga, & not during the Revolution, but in the French war. George, Lord Viscount Howe, eldest son of Sir E Scrope, second Lord Viscount Howe, in the peerage of Ireland, was born in 1725, & succeeded to the title on the death of his father in 1735. In the forepart of 1757 he was ordered to America, being then colonel commanding the 60th or Royal Americans, & arrived at Halifax in July following. On Sep 28, 1757, he was appointed colonel of the 55th Foot, & on Dec 29th brig genr'l in America. The next year, when Abercrombie was chosen to proceed against Ticonderoga, Pitt selected Lord Howe to be the soul of the enterprise. On Jul 8 he landed with the army at Howe's Point, & the outlet of Lake George, & marched for Ticonderoga. They came upon a party of Frenchmen near Frontbrook, who were lost, & a skirmish ensued, in which his lordship foremost fighting fell, & expired immediately. In him, says Mante, the soul of the army seemed to expire. Howe's corpse was escorted to Albany for interment by Philip Schuyler, a young hero of native growth, afterwards general in the Revolution, & was buried in St Peter's Church, Mass erected a monument to his memory in Westmnster Abbey, at an expense of L250. Lord Howe was a member of Parliament for Nottingham at the time of his decease.

Public auction on May 27, on the premises, of part of lot 20 in square 539, being the part on the public alley between E & F sts south & 3rd & 4½ sts west, with improvements, consisting of 2 nearly new frame houses, being a portion of the estate of Jos T Evans. -Jas C McGuire, auct

Judge Eustace Conway, of Fredericksburg, Va, is dead. He was but recently elected a judge of one of the ciruits in place of Judge Lomax. His disease was cancer in the face, which proved fatal in but a few weks from its appearance. [No death date given-current item.]

N Sperry & Co, N Y, have recently completed the largest church clock ever built in the U S. It is designed for St George's Church, & will indicate the time by 8 dials on 2 towers, 4 of them being regulated at a distance of 70 feet.

The Democrats of Calvert Co, Md, have the following nominations: Nathl Duke for State Senator; John Bond & F Lewis Griffin for Delegates; Danl Kent, for Clerk of the Circuit Court; Jas G Allnutt for Register of Wills; O C Bowen for Sheriff. The meeting approved unqualifiedly the course of Hon T F Bowie in the last Congress.

Horticultural meeting on Wed: Mr Joshua Pierce presented some fine specimens of Victoria rhubarb that he raised; exceedingly large asparagus shoots by Mr Cammack; & Mr John Howlett reported having strawberries of the largest size.

Mrd: on Apr 30, at Huntsville, Mo, by Rev S T McMasters, Frank C Edwards, of Pana, Ill, to Miss Sarah Josepha Cleveland, of the former place.

MON MAY 25, 1857

The correct parentage of Mr J R Clay, our Minister to Peru. He is the son of Jos Clay, of Phil, a Rep in Congress in 1803-08, from Pa. Mathew Clay was a Rep from Va, & no relative of Joseph. Further, Mr John Randolph was not Minister at Bogata but St Petersburg.

The house of Arthur G Burley, at Chicago, on May 1, was blown up with gas. They had no gas in the house for several days, & the gas company had 2 men at work searching out the cause. We were annoyed with the odor of gas. Examination afterwards showed that the pipe which connected with the house was broken.

The oldest veteran in the Prussian service, named Karnasch, was buried on Apr 28 at Pilitz, a small village near Breslau. He entered the army in the reign of Fred'k the Great. When Fred'k, near 80 years ago, wrote a letter to Washington, he called himself the oldest soldier in Europe; here is a soldier who served under him, yet had outlived him 70 years.

Great sale of lots in Gtwn: on Jun 1, at public auction 28 bldg lots, being the subdivision of the upper part of that property known as **Cunningham's Garden**, fronting on the south side of West st. These lots have a depth of about 100 feet, with an average front of about 26 feet. The sale will begin with lot 1, which adjoins the property of Mr Kessler. –Barnard & Buckey, aucts

Near Troy, Ill, a German pedlar, Fred'k Graftenich, came to this city & was returning home when he was robbed and shot by 3 men. He was taken to Troy, where he died on Sat. –St Louis Intelligencer

The Pittsburg papers learn from private letters received in that city that Jos & Thos McMasters, 2 brothers, were drowned a short time since at Landing, near Lake Pepin, Minn, by the upsetting of a sail-boat. They were both printers, & were highly esteemed in Pittsburg. They had established a new paper, the Wimodee Herald.

Fire on May 20 at No 8 Stillman st, Boston, house owned by Joshua Bennett, & occupied by Mrs Fitzpatrick as a boarding house. The bodies of Mr David Fisher, by trade a cork cutter, & Mrs Fitzpatrick, the lessee & keeper of the house, were discovered afterwards. -Boston Journal of May 21.

Orphans Court of Wash Co, D C. Letters of administration on the personal estate of Mathew Digges, late of Wash Co, deceased. –Jane Digges, admx

Lady Ashburton died at Paris on May 3. She was the eldest daughter of the sixth Earl of Sandwich, & was married to the present Lord Ashburton, then Mr Bingham Baring, in 1823.

Public sale of valuable limestone land, on Jun 15, in Charlestown, Jefferson Co, Va, my two farms: **Burnley** contains 262¼ acres, with a good frame house & out-houses; & **Grassmere**, contains 294¾ acres, & adjoins **Burnley**; with a frame house. Apply to me personally or by letter to Richd B Washington, living near the premises, or to the proprietor. –John A Washington, Mr Vernon, near Alexandria, Va.

Mrd: on May 20, at Balt, by Rev Dr Wyatt, Andrew Sterrett Ridgely, a member of the bar of that city, to Camilla, daughter of the Hon Reverdy Johnson.

Mrd: on May 19, by Rev Dr Backus, Wm F Turner, of Va, to Sidney, daughter of Edw Patterson, of Balt, Md.

Died: on May 5, at his residence at the Virginia University, Fauquier Co, Wm M Coy, in his 65th year. In politics he was a Whig & in religion a Presbyterian.

Died: May 20, in N Y, Mrs Susan M Varnum, wife of Jos B Varnum, jr, in her 38th year.

Died: on May 24, in Wash City, at his residence, Dr Chas S Frailey, aged about 53 years. His funeral will be from his late residence, N Y ave, between 13th & 14th sts, on May 26, at 4 o'clock P M.
+
I O O F: Members of Oriental Lodge No 19 are notified to attend the funeral of our late brother, P G Charles Frailey. –Wm H Deitz, N G
+
Masonic notice: Members to attend the funeral of our late brother, M W Past Grand Master Chas S Frailey. –G A Schwarzman, Grand Sec

TUE MAY 26, 1857
Piano forte, household & kitchen furniture at auction on: May 28, at the residence of Mr S S Briggs, on K st, between 8th & 9th sts. -A Green auct

On May 29, after the sale of the Machen property, I shall sell the n w corner of square 296, fronting 90 feet on B st, running back on 13th st west 125 feet.
-A Green auct

Elopement: Mr Wm R Owens ran away with his wife's siter, Miss Julia Tungate, both of Macomb, Ill. He borrowed all the money he could, as well as a horse & buggy. They were pursued, caught, & Mr Owens lodged in jail for stealing the horse & buggy.

Richmond Dispatch: from Buckingham, May 20. Murder in this county last Sunday: Geo Winfrey was at the bar of P J Garrett, with Robt P May, & both were in a short time intoxicated; upon some trifling misunderstanding May struck Winfrey 2 blows, the last one on the head, fracturing the skull & causing his death on Tue. The murder is considered a very outrageous one, Winfrey being a man advanced in years, & very inoffensive. May is quite a young man.

Telegraphic dispatch from Worcester, dated May 21, states that 4 murder cases were brought before the Supreme Court of that city since Thu, with the following result: John Glynn, for the murder of Peter Naughton & his wife last Nov, was found not guilty; Saml Gleason, for the murder of his infant child in Jan, was discharged on his own recognizance; Godfried Rediman, for the murder of Saml Fleehiman last Dec, plead guilty on a charge of manslaughter, & was sentenced to 2 years' imprisonment in the house of correction; & Lucina Ransom, colored, tried on a charge of killing a colored girl, was dismissed by nol pros.

On Mar 9 last before the Historical Society of Pa, was presented the Belt of **Wampum** delivered by the Indians to Wm Penn at the great treaty under the elm tree in 1682. The Executive Cmte have made a report thereon, from which we gather that Granville J Penn, a great grandson of Wm Penn, brought with him from England, for the purpose of presentation to the Society, the Belt referred to, & desired its deposite in their archives. [Wampum is an Iroquois word, meaning a muscle.]

An arrest was yesterday made by Ofcr Kimbel of Mr Johnathan S Jenkins, present U S Consul at Navigator Islands, in the Pacific, founded on an affidavit by Mr Aaron Van Camp, late U S Commercial Agent at the port of Apia, in the same islands, setting forth that said Jenkins had committed an act of piracy in seizing the cargo of the schnr **Eudorus** at the port. The cargo was owned partly by the proprietors of the ship **Rambler**, of Nantucket, & partly by Mr Van Camp, who was acting at the time as agent for said owners. The crime with which Mr Jenkins is charged not being bailable, he is now in our county jail awaiting a requisition from the Exec of the State of N Y for his removal thither. The property illegally seized was worth $70,000.

Died: on May 24, in Wash City, of pneumonia, Saml Champion, in his 48th year. His funeral is this afternoon at 4 o'clock, from his late residence, Va ave & 3rd st east.

The steamer **Atherton**, a fairy little high pressure steamer, belonging to John B Henry, the nephew of the President, arrived here on Sunday from Balt, & was yesterday displayed on the bosom of our noble river.

Trustee's sale: by deed of trust from David Jones & wife: public sale on Jun 25; on the premises, all that part or parcel of land whereon the said David Jones now resides, containing 92 acres, & which property formerly belonged to the late Douglas Voss. Improvements consist of a large & commodious frame dwlg, & every necessary out-bldg. –N C Stephen, trustee, Bladensburg, Md.

For sale: desirable property in Kanawha Co, Va. The undersigned offers at private sale the property on which he now resides, on the banks of Kanawa river, about 1½ miles above Charleston, & is the same which his father Danl Ruffner, improved & upon which he so long lived. The property consists of 90 acres, & the dwlg house is of brick, large & well arranged. Apply by letter or otherwise to my agent SA Miller, or the undersigned, at Kanawha Court-house, Va. –Jas Ruffner

WED MAY 27, 1857
Household & kitchen furniture at auction on: May 29, at the residence of Thos Watson, 76 K st, near the Circle. -Jas C McGuire, auct

Hon Jas Bell, of N H, died yesterday at his residence in Concord. His health had been delicate for some time past. He was the son of a former eminent Senator from that State, the Hon Saml Bell, who represented his State some 20 years ago.
[Dec 18th newspaper: Jas Bell was born in Francestown, Hillsborough, on Nov 13, 1804; finished his studies, preparatory to entering college, at Phillips' Academy, in Andover, Mass; in Sep 1819, before he had completed his 15th year, he entered the sophomore class in Bowdoin College; graduated in 1822, & commenced the study of the law with his brother, Hon Saml D Bell, who is at this time a justice of our supreme court. He finished his course of study to qualify him for admission to the bar at the celebrated law school at Litchfield, Conn; in 1825, before he was quite 21 years of age, he was admitted to the bar, & commenced the practice in Gilmanton, then in Strafford Co, in his native State. He remained at Gilmanton about 6 years, when he married a daughter of the late Hon Nathl Uphan, of New Hampshire, & removed to Exeter, Rockingham Co, where he remained till 1846, when he removed to Gilford, & resided there until his death.]

The new Catholic church, St Patrick's, is to be built on the land on 10th, between F & G sts, bequeathed for the purpose by the late Rev Wm Matthews. The parsonage, which is separate, will cover a space of about 3,000 feet. There are 3 towers, with spires whose loftiness rear heavenward, & taper with exactness & harmony.

Hon Andrew P Butler, a Senator from the State of S C, died at Edgefield on May 25, in the presence of his family & sympathizing friends. His disease was dropsy. [Jun 3rd newspaper: Andrew Pickens Butler is no more; he expired at **Stonelands**, his residence, about 5 miles from the village of Edgefield, on May 25, in his 62nd year. He was born in Edgefield district in 1796, a son of the late Gen Wm Butler, of Va, & his mother Behethland Moore, of Edgefield, the former having migrated from Va to this State. He had 6 brothers, among them George, a gallant ofcr in the war with Great Britain, who died young; Hon Wm Butler, M D, formerly a surgeon in the U S navy, & member of Congress from Greenville & its associated districts; Pierce M Butler, formerly Govn'r of the State, & afterwards the gallant Colonel of the Palmetto Regt, & winner of a glorious death & deathless renown in the hour of victory, at the head of that peerless corps, in the memorable field of Churubusce. They were of patriot stock, their father having done Revolutioanry & warrior service in the war of independence. Their mother, too, did patriotic service in the same hallowed cause, & was at one time a prisoner to the enemy. His sister was the first wife of Hon Waddy Thompson, & all his brothers having preceded him to the grave he now completes the obituary roll. He was a pupil of Dr Jas Waddell, at Willington Academy, that school of illustrious men. He graduated at the College of S C in 1817, with the distinction of having been awarded a third honor in a class of which the first & second honors were awarded to Chas Fishburn & Archibald C Baynard, & of which Chancellor Caldwell, Judge Glover, & Hon Wm McWillie were members & graduates.]

Geo McCaffrey, a native of Ireland, 23 years of age, died at N Y on Sat from the effects of laudanum, taken by mistake for other medicine. He had been confined to his bed by paralysis, & his physician had left some medicine for him. Late on Friday night he screamed out with pain, & his wife, in her haste, handed him a vial of laudanum, which he drank, & death ensued a few hours after.

Alpheus Poindexter, a son of Mr Wm Poindexter, a respected citizen of Lexington, drowned himself last week in the Ohio river by jumping from the hurricane deck of the steamer **Statesman**, [Capt Sullivan,] on which he was a passenger. He left a note: Farewell, father and mother, brother and sister. I am tired of my life. Benj Franklin Weigert, the penitentiary thief from Lexington, Ky, is the cause of this. Good-bye, my friends. A N Poindexter,Lexington, Ky. [My youngest brother, beware of your company and the bottle.] -Ky Observer

Election Notice. Office Oak Hill Cemetery Co, Gtwn, D C, May 26, 1857. The Holders of Lots in the **Oak Hill Cemetery** Co containing 300 feet & upwards are hereby notified to attend a meeting to be held at the Cemetery, on Jun 1, 1857, at 5 o'clock P M, to elect 4 Trustees to manage the affairs of the company for the ensuing year. As an exhibit of the financial condition of the company will be made, all the lot-holders are invited to attend. –Henry King, Sec

Orson Pratt, the Mormon elder, was killed on May 14, near Van Buren, Ark, by Hector Mann. [May 29th newspaper: Mr Hector H McLean, with his wife & family, a few years since, emigrated from New Orleans to Calif. Whilst living there, in perfect accord with her husband, Mrs McLean was drawn by curiosity to hear the Mormon preaching. She formed an acquaintance with Parley P Pratt, one of the Mormon Twelve Apostles, & the Pres of the "Stake" in Calif. She became a Mormon & left her husband & 3 children; not, however, before making endeavors to get possession of the children, & take them to Utah, to reside. For better security of the children their father had sent them back to his parents in New Orleans, whither Mrs McLean also returned, but she could not get the children & went alone to Utah. At Great Salt Lake City she was sealed to Parley P Pratt, becoming his 9th wife. She kept school, the pupils chiefly children of Pratt by his numerous spirituals. Impelled in part by maternal instincts, but probably more by Mormon policy & the counsels of Pratt, she accompanied him in the fall of last year to New Orleans once more to strive for the possession of her children. She simulated to her husband's family complete conversion from Mormonism, saying she had found out all its errors & succeeded in lulling all suspicions as to her sincerity. She one day absconded taking the coveted children with her. Their son in Calif was apprised of what had happened; he followed their trail, & overtook them on their route northward towards Utah, under the personal direction of Pratt. LETTER: **Fort Gibson**, Cherokee Nation, May 7, 1857. Dear Friends: I have just returned from a sore tramp, on which I succeeded in coming up with Eleanor & the children, & have taken the children from her by force. I have placed Eleanor in charge of the U S Marshal, I have succeeded also in arresting Pratt, who is now in the guard-house of the fort. The U S Marshal will start with his prisoners for Van Buren tomorrow, & I will, by a different route, in company of Capt Cahil & lady, leave with the children for the same place. I arrested Pratt & E J on a charge of larceny, in stealing the clothing on the children when kidnapped, in value $8 or $10. This is the only way I could reach them in these Territories. When I fail before the U S Com'r at Van Buren, I mean to have Pratt arrested for having fled from justice from St Louis, Missouri, & get a requisition from the Govn'r of Missouri for him. They were brought up for trial before the Com'r, & were discharged. Pratt, as soon as released, mounted his horse & left Van Buren. McLean soon after started in pursuit, & overtook Pratt & shot him. Pratt died in about 2 hours. You will thus learn that it is not Orson Pratt who is killed, but Parley P Pratt, & that H H McLean, & not Hector Mann, was his slayer. Orson Pratt is a brother of Parley. He is now in England, of which country he & Parley are natives. Yours, respectfully, Michaux -Wash, May 27.]

THU MAY 28, 1857
Wash Corp: 1-Board of Alderman granted Mrs Mary A Lewis permission to erect a frame dwlg house: passed.

On Monday on an excursion train from Memphis to Charleston ran off the track & Mr Wendell of Memphis was fatally injured.

Punishment of crime in Wilmington, Del: 1-Jos Newman, tried for purchasing property from boys who had purloined or stolen it, was convicted. The court sentenced him to pay a fine of $20, & to stand in the pillory one hour on May 23, to be imprisoned 6 months, & wear the convict's jacket, 6 months following his liberation. 2-Sarah Bostick, who was convicted of stealing from the store of Saml Ritchie, was sentenced to pay $36.78 as restitution money, to be whipped on May 23 with 12 lashes, & to be sold for a period not exceeding 7 years.

Mr Julius G Heileman committed suicide on Tue, in his room at the Marshall House, Alexandria, by shooting himself with a pistol through the heart. He formerly resided near Wash City, & was a midshipman in the Navy, which position he resigned some time since. He was in this city on business, & had been unwell for the past 2 or 3 days, & was laboring under a temporary aberration of mind at the time. -Gazette

Valuable farm & pleasant residence in Fairfax Co, Va, for sale: by decree of the Circuit Court of said county, I offer for sale *Collingwood*, the residence of the late H Allen Taylor; about 4½ miles below the city of Alexandria, & contains about 244¼ acres; with a new & commodious frame dwlg, kitchen, & other out-houses, built of the best materials. -W Arthur Taylor, John A Washington, Comr's of sale.

Phil Bulletin of Tue. The wharf at the Navy Yard presented the steam-frig **Minnesoto**, Capt Dupont, & the dock was crowded with persons anxious to go on board & inspect this splendid work of marine architecture. Lt Simms was at the head of the gangway passing those on board who had the proper credentials. Some of the guns are of a peculiar construction, invented by Capt John A Dahlgren, head of the ordnance dept at the Wash navy yard. She will touch at the Gosport navy yard, prior to sailing for China with Minister Reed on board. On board when she leaves our shores will be nearly 700, commanded by the following. Capt, Saml F Dupont; 1st Lt, Wm B Renshaw; 2nd Lt, A G Clay; 3rd Lt, Jas M Duncan, C C Simms, Colville Territt; Purser, Robt Pettet; Surgeon, Robt T Barry; Passed Assist Surgeon, Chas Martin; Assist Surgeon, H L Sheldon; Acting Master, J O Chaplin; Chief Engineer, Michl Quinn; 1st Assist Engineer, Jas H Warner; 2nd Assist Engineer, F B C Stump; 3rd Assist Engineer, Wm Frick, jr, Chas Shroeder, A J Kursted, Wm H Hunt; Boatswain, Geo Smith; Gunner, Jonathan M Ballard; Carpenter, John Southwick; Sailmaker, Geo T Lozier; Marine Ofcrs, Brvt Major G H Terrett, Lt Edw Jones. There is still another lt & also a chaplain necessary to complete the list of officers. Who they are is not yet known on board. There are 3 surgeons on board, in consequence of the insalubrity of the country to which she is to be sent.

Geo Rohdenberg, a German, 18 years of age, died at N Y on Tue from the effects of a large dose of oxalic acid which he had taken by mistake for Epsom salts. He had purchased the poison from a druggist, who gave it to him instead of the salts.

N Y, May 26. A trial of 3 prisoners is going on for the murder of Olisias Lawson, capt of the brig **General Pierce**, on the high seas, on Feb 10 last. It appears that the vessel was about to be used as a slaver, & the conflict, which ended in the death of the capt, was the result of a refusal on the part of these men to serve in that business.

A bride fell dead at midnight, amid the rejoicings of the bridal party that had a few hours before witnessed the marriage ceremony, at Cleveland, Miss, on May 6. She was Miss Mary Roberts, & had just been married to Mr W McKree, Principal of the Gtwn Academy.

A son of Mr Colin Unseld, residing in Wash Co, Md, was drowned in the Chesapeake & Ohio canal on Friday last. He was riding along the tow-path when the horse took fright & plunged into the canal, drowning both the son of Mr Unseld & a negro boy who was riding with him.

A correspondent of the Little Rock Democrat, writing from camp, near **Fort Thorn**, in New Mexico, on Apr 4, gave an account of a fight with the Indians, in which Capt Alfred Gibbs, of the mounted rifles, was wounded severely in the abdomen, but was recovering.

A large framed muscular man, 30 years of age, named Hartshorn, of Newton, Upper Falls, was awakened last Sat by a stinging pain above his elbow, radiating from a small red spot. A black spider was discovered where his arm had rested. The swelling rapidly extended down the arm; on Sunday he was sick all day; on Monday he was seized with pain in his bowels, until he died at 5 o'clock.
-Walton [Mass] Sentinel

Anthony Hyde was admitted to the bar of the Circuit Court-Wash, on Tue.

Mrd: on May 26, in Wash City, at Trinity Church, by Rev Geo D Cummins, Rev Thos Duncan, of Fauquier Co, Va, to Maria L, daughter of the late Cmdor Morris, of Wash City.

Mrd: on May 21, in Harrisonburg, Rockingham Co, Va, by Rev Thos D Bell, Mr John Ott, of Wash City, to Miss Annie Augusta, only child of Jos G Effinger, of Harrisonburg.

Died: on May 26, at **Seven Oaks**, in PG Co, Md, Wm Tolson. His funeral is on May 28 at 11 o'clock, from his late residence.

Orphans Court of Wash Co, D C. In the case of Francis Ballinger, adm of Susan Ballinger, deceased: the administrator & Court have appointed May 20th next, for the settlement of the personal estate of the deceased, with the assets in hand.
–Ed N Roach, Reg/o wills [The date of May 20th-copied as written.]

FRI MAY 29, 1857

Trustee's sale of valuable real estate: by decree of the Circuit Court of D C, in a cuase in which Sarah B French & others are cmplnts, & Junius French & Rose French are dfndnts: public auction, on Jun 22, 1857, [the purchaser of the above property failed to comply with the terms of the sale,] of part of lot 16 in square 457, on E st north, between 6th & 7th sts; with a large & commodious dwlg house.
–Saml Chilton, Christopher Ingle, trustees –C W Boteler, auct

Trustee sale of valuable property: by deed of trust from K H Lambell, to secure Ben Pollard, recorded in Liber J A S No 37, folios 453, of Wash Co, D C: sale at public auction on Jun 22, of part of square 742, on N J ave, with a 3 story brick house & other improvements thereon. –Thos Carbery, trustee –Jas C McGuire, auct

The subscriber will sell the valuable farm on which he now resides, in D C, containing about 110 acres, with a new frame dwlg containing 8 rooms, with all the necessary out-houses. The property lies about 2 miles from the Navy Yard bridge. Apply to Mr T M Hanson, 512 7th st, Mr Jas E Thompson, Pa ave, or to the subscriber on the premises. –Anthony Addison

For sale: 1,700 acres of land on the Blackwater river, Dorchester Co, Md. This estate has been in the hands of the undersigned & his ancestors for 70 to 190 years. Call on the proprietor at Bridge Farm, near Cambridge, Dorchester Co, Md.
–Thos J H Eccleston

Public sale on Jun 11th, of valuable real estate, by decree of the Circuit Court of PG Co, sitting as a Court of Equity: sale at R H Locher's store, at **Long Old Fields**, of that portion of the real estate of Elisha Berry, deceased, heretofore assigned by com'rs to the heirs-at-law of Wm E Berry, deceased. The land contains 141 acres, & is part of the estate known as **Springfield estate**, & adjoins the dower of Mrs Deborrah Berry, & is about 5 miles from Washington. The land will be sold clear of the widow's dower she having agreed to take her share thereof in money.
–D C Digges, C C Magruder, trustees

Hon Fayette McMullin, of Va, has accepted the position of Govn'r of Wash Territory, not long since tendered to him by Pres Buchanan.

Trustee's sale of valuable square of ground at auction: on Jun 5 next, on the premises, by deed of trust from Walter A True to the subscriber, dated Feb 10, 1855, recorded in Liber J A S No 93, folios 135 thru 137, of the land records for Wash Co, D C: all of square east of square 590, bounded by Dela ave, 1st st, I st, & Public Space. Terms cash. –H B Sweeny, trustee –A Green auct

Valuable farm & quarry land for sale: on Jun 4, at the Little Falls Bridge, that portion of *Rich Point farm* north of *Primmett's Run*, containing 100 acres, more or less. This property is situated on the Leesburg turnpike road 4 miles from Wash City. -Jas C McGuire, auct

Summer residence for the Pres. The Pres of the U S has accepted the invitation of the Directors of the Military Asylum, on the north of the city, to spend as much of his time as may suit his convenience, during the coming hot season, on their pleasant domain. The dwlg he is to occupy is the same in which Dr King has resided.

Lt Strain, who failed in the attempt to explore a route for an isthmus ship-canal, died at Aspinwall on May 15. [May 30th newspaper: Lt Strain was leader in the Darien exploring Expedition sent out by a Gov't a few years ago. He died at Aspinwall on the night of May 13 & the next day was buried in the *Mount Hope Cemetery*, attended by most of the ofcrs of the ship **Cyane** & a few from the ship **Wabash**, 14 of whom acted as pall-bearers & 12 as substitutes for marines. The Episcopal burial service was read & 3 volleys were fired over the grave.]

Washington actress. Miss Avonia Jones promises to wear & improve the histrionic honors of her mother & preceptor, Mrs Malinda Jones. She is a beautiful young lady, who has scarcely numbered 18 summers, & made her first appearance at the Boston Theatre on Monday, in the character of Parthenia, in Mr Lovell's translation of the German play of Ingomar.

New Orleans, May 27. The steamship **Empire City**, from N Y on May 18, via Havana, has arrived. She brings the Calif mails & passengers of May 5. Among them are Gen Wm Walker & staff, who have abandoned the field of operations in Central America. Gen Walker capitulated on May 1 to Capt Davis, of the U S sloop-of-war **St Mary's**, & with his staff & 260 men, [the remains of the army] were brought to Panama by the St Mary's. Gen Walker surrendered because Capt Davis signified his intention of seizing the schnr **Granada**, which held his [Walker's] reserve. Gen Walker was kept a close prisoner by the U S Cmdor at Panama, notwithstanding the terms of capitulation, which allowed him & his ofcrs their liberty, & giving them the privilege of retaining their side arms. The **Empire City** reached her wharf this evening. 10,000 people were present to receive Gen Walker, who was accompanied by Col Jacques, Mr Pilcher, & Mr Turner in a carriage to the St Charles Hotel, where he spoke twice before the crowd was satisfied. .

SAT MAY 30, 1857
Appointment by the Pres: Wm B Reed, of Pa, to be Envoy Extraordinary & Minister Plenipotentiary of the U S A to China. -Union

Died: on May 28, in Wash City, Marmaduke Dillian Hodgson, aged 75 years, formerly of Delaware, but for the last 40 years a resident of Wash City.

Chancery sale of valuable house & lot on 20th st west, between Pa ave & H st north: by decree of the Circuit Court of Wash Co, D C, made in the cause wherein Wm W Hough is cmplnt & Eleanor Hines, widow, Christian N Hines, adm, Enoch G Hines & others heirs at law of Abraham Hines, deceased, are dfndnts: the subscriber will sell at public auction, on Jun 25 next, part of lot 27 in square 101; with a well built 2 story brick dwlg house. –Chas S Wallach, trustee -Jas C McGuire, auct

The English papers record, as a truly tragic episode of the Persian war, the death, each by his own hand, of Gen Forster Stalker, cmder of the forces, & Cmdor Etheridge, of the navy. Gen Stalker came by his death from a pistol shot inflicted by his own hand in a fit of temporary insanity. No paper was left, & he was merely heard to complain that the 3rd cavalry was not given him; & was uneasy about the responsibility of sheltering the European troops during the approaching hot weather. Cmdor Etheridge destroyed himself with his own hand while suffering under mental aberration, brought about by long continued anxiety connected with the duties of his command.

The suit of Mrs Castle to recover damages of Col Duryee, of the Nat'l Guard, for the injuries she received at their encampment in Kingston in 1855, terminated before the circuit court in a verdict of $1,500. The unfortunate shot which wounded the mother & killed the child was fired at the time the regt was drawn up for parade on the day the encampment was to close. It is a great stretch of liability to make him responsible, when he was the only one of the troops present whose innocence of the fatal shot is self-evident. –Albany Argus

Mrd: on May 28, in Wash City, by Rev Mr Boyle, Chas E Stanford to Louisa, daughter of Geo Webster, of PG Co, Md.

Mrd: on May 28, by Rev Dr Hall, Geo W Hopkins to Miss Mary Anna, [only child of Chas Borremans,] both of Wash City.

Newark May 28. Destructive fire this morning in one of the large 4 story factories of the Newark India Rubber Co: Jacob Allen, foreman of Engine Co No 4, & one of the firm of J & L Allen, fire-engine manufacturers, was instantly killed by a falling wall, & John B Thom, 4th assist engineer, was seriously injured: recovery is doubtful.

MON JUN 1, 1857
Army Medical Board recently in session in N Y C adjourned on the 27th ult. The following candidates were found qualified for appointment in the medical staff of the army:
1-Roberts Bartholow, of Md
2-Jos C Baily, of Pa
3-J Cooper McKee, of N Y
4-Kirtly Ryland, of Mo
5-Wm A Carswell, of S C

The prosecution instituted some years ago against Otho Hinton, in the Circuit Court of the U S for the district of Ohio, for alleged depredations on the mails, was, this month at Cincinnati, finally dismissed by order of the court.

Ellen Murray died in N Y C by taking a dose of oxalic acid in mistake for epsom salts. The poison was kept in the house for cleaning iron & resembled salts in appearance, the mistake was easily made.

Chancery sale: by decree of the Circuit Court of Wash Co, D C, made in the cause of Armand Jardin & Honorine his wife vs Albertine Favier et al, No 1,253, equity, dated May 27, 1857: public auction on Jun 23, on the premises, the whole of square 160, heretofore used & occupied by A Favier, deceased, as a mineral water manufactory. On Jul 24 , by virtue of a decree of the same court, in the cause of Jardin et al vs Favier et al, No 1,063, I will offer at public auction, the western part of lot 2 in square 119, in Wash, fronting 25 feet on H st, running back 96 feet, more or less.
–Walter S Cox, trustee -Jas C McGuire, auct

Desirable dwlg house & lot near the navy yard at public auction, on Jun 9, by order of the Orphans Court of Wash Co, D C. Sale of the north half of lot 8 in square 904, [save & excepting the most northern 3 feet & 4 inches of said lot in said square, which was sold & conveyed by said Mary Kelly to one Thos Bayne.] -Zebedee Kirwan, Guardian -J C McGuire, auct

Trustee's sale of farm near Bladensburg, Md: on Jul 6, by deed of trust from Robt Strong, dated Jul 25, 1856, recorded in Liber J A S No 117, folios 6, of the land records for Wash Co, D C: & in Liber C S M, No __, folios 321, of the land records for PG Co, Md, all that parcel of land being partly in D C & partly in PG Co, called ***Chillon Castle Manor.*** And also as appurtenant to the land herein before granted a perpetual right of way through, over, & along the adjoining land of Wm Scott from the land hereby granted to the public road, as the said right of way was granted by said Scott to said Strong, & his heirs & assigns & their household, family, servants, carriages, horses, wagons, carts, cattle, flocks & herds, & to & for all persons going to & returning from said land. –Thos J Fisher, trustee -Jas C McGuire, auct
[Aug 24th newspaper: the above property, ***Chillon Castle Manor***, is advertised for sale on Sep 26th at the auction rooms of J C McGuire, Wash.]

On the 24th ult at Auburn, N Y, Miss Laura Green, age 18 years, a domestic in the family of Thos M How, was burnt when her clothes accidentally took fire from a spirit-gas lamp. When help reached her she was dead.

The Texas papers state that in the party of Capt Edw Beal, of the Pacific wagon road, will be employed 25 camels & dromedaries. The object is to test their endurance & adaptability to the climate.

Rev Valentine Felder, a German Catholic priest, who resided at Newark, N J, was run over at N Y on Thu night by a railroad car, & instantly killed.

On Fri a party of 11 French people, workmen & wives in the employ of Messrs Gigon & Seydel, watch-case makers, embarked on the sailing yacht **Rambler** for a sail on the Delaware. The boat was suddenly capsized by a sudden squall. Miss Cecilia Humbert was in the cabin of the vessel at the time. Mr Willemin & his daughter were washed off & disappeared. The remainder were rescued by a steamer & taken to Phil.

For rent, The U S Hotel, Wash, D C. This hotel, having just been closed, is now offered for rent; thoroughly furnished. Inquire of P W Browning.

Orphans Court of Wash Co, D C. May 30, 1857. In the case of Wm T Borughs & Jane E Borughs, adms of Benj Lucas, deceased: the administrator & Court have appointed Jun 23 next, for the final settlement of the estate of the deceased, with the assets in hand. –Ed N Roach, Reg/o wills

TUE JUN 2, 1857
The good barque **William & Anne** arrived at this port from Barcelona yesterday, where her long & successful career brought her into immediate notice. She was built in 1757, & in 1759 carried Gen Wolfe to Quebec. She is commanded by Capt Magull, & looks staunch & strong. –Savannah Republican, May 29.

A man named Peters died a few days ago at Arnheim, Netherlands, at the age of 112. He was born at Leuwarden in 1746, & served in the Swiss army for some time; subsequently he entered the French service, & made the campaign in Egypt under Napoleon. He possessed all his faculties up to his last hour.

On Thu two men were run over by the cars beyond Harrisburg & killed. One of them was recognized as Geo R Vickroy, who had on his person a large quantity of counterfeit paper, & a few dollars of good money.

On May 16, at Watertown, Ohio, the wife of Mr G J Woodruff accidentally killed herself. She was sweeping the room occupied by Elias Woodruff, her father-in-law, & she no doubt took the gun, near his bed, by the muzzle, & it discharged.

WED JUN 3, 1857
Household & kitchen furniture at auction on: Jun 4, at auction, at the residence of Mr L Lepreux, on 7th st, between M & N sts. –Wall & Barnard, aucts

N Y, Jun 1. Died: Theodore Banks, Pres of the N Y Corn Exchange, in his 48th year.

Lt Albert Allmand, of the U S Navy, died suddenly of apoplexy on board the frig **Cumberland**, lying at Boston, on Sun. He was about 39 years old; a native of Va. [Jun 4th newspaper: It appears he was present at divine service on board the U S frig **Cumberland**, & on its conclusion was standing on deck conversing with his brother ofcrs, when he fell prostrate from a fit of apoplexy, & died in less than an hour. He was a native of Va, resident at Norfolk, about 30 years of age, & had been in the service since 1841. For nearly 13 of 15 years he had been constantly at sea.]

Valuable farm & country residence near Wash for sale: the estate of the late Andrew Hoover, in Alexandria Co, Va; contains about 160 acres; the dwlg house is about 42 foot square. Inquire of A P Hoover, 331 Pa ave, Wash.

Mrd: on Jun 2, in Wash City, at Browns' Hotel, by Rev G W Samson, Mr Gustavus G Carter to Miss Edmonia B Redd, both of Henrico Co, Va.

Mrd: on Jun 2, in Wash City, in the Wesley Chapel, by Rev W Krebs, John W P Myers, of Gtwn, to Anna C McNeir, of Wash City.

Obit-died: on May 15, Lt Isaac G Strain, U S N, at Aspinwall, whither he went to report himself for duty on board the ship **Cyane**. He was a native of Pa. [See May 29th newspaper.]

N Y, Jun 2. Accident to an express on the Erie railroad today near Addison; Dr Wm Peck, of Cincinnati, was instantly killed.

On Monday, election day, by the earliest train, bands of ill-looking men, mostly a year or two under age, with the generic & suggestive name of Plug-Uglies, arrived from Balt, crowding our side-walks, when a sudden attack was made upon a naturalized citizen in the rank of voters, & an effort made to drive all such from the polls. In this onslaught, Mr Richd Owens, Com'r of the Ward, was badly shot in the arm as well as wounded in the head; Mr F A Klopfer struck in the forehead by a spent shot; Mr Geo D Spencer severely bruised on the left cheek by a stone thrown by a man not 4 feet distant; Justice Goddard stricken in 3 places with brickbats; Justice Donn stoned; Ofcr H Degges bruised on the chin; Capt Baggot, Chief of Police, Policeman Birckhead, & other policemen were wounded & driven from the field. A young German, Christian Lendig, died late Mon night; McElfresh, age about 18, also dead; young Fenton, about 16, died yesterday; Chas Pestelle was shot in the shoulder-blade, a bad wound; Robt Slattery, shot slightly in the leg; Danl Biddleman, very bad wound in the arm, got in a contest with a Marine; F F Bell, living on the Island, shot by a ball through the knee; Thos Wills, a young man, from Anne Arundel, shot by a revolver; Chas Wood, wound in the neck; Mr Ebenezer Hughes severely wounded; Morgan Fanell, wounded in the head, badly; John Fouche, wounded in the head; Somers, a saddler, severely wounded; & John Cabell, wounded in the calf of the leg. Yesterday Coroner Woodeard commenced taking a round of inquests on the bodies of the killed. He began with that of Mr Allston, whose residence was at 9th & N sts. He came to his death from a bullet or bullets shot from one or more of the muskets of a body of soldiers under the control of the Mayor of Wash. The Coroner then proceeded to the case of young Lendig, on F, between 10th & 11th sts. [Jun 6th newspaper: the cause of the death of Cornelius H Alsten was from a gunshot wound received while standing peaceable & quietly at the corner of 7th st, from a detachment of U S Marines, acting under the control of the Mayor of Washington; that from the testimony of all the witnesses, the firing by the Marines was all subsequent to the obtaining possession of the swivel.]

THU JUN 4, 1857
Trustee's sale under decree of the Circuit Court of Wash Co, D C, in a cause, No 1,179 on the equity docket, wherein Pairo & Nourse are cmplnts & R S Chew & others are dfndnts. Auction on Jun 26 of lots 10 thru 16 in square 144, in Wash City.
-W Redin, trustee -J C McGuire, auct

Appointments by the Pres:
Wm A Richardson, of Ill, Govn'r of the Territory of Nebraska, vice Mark W Izard, the present incumbent.
Jos A Wright, of Indiana, Envoy Extra & Minister Pleni of the U S at the Court of his Majesty the King of Prussia, vice Peter D Vroom, of N J, recalled at his own request.
Henry C Murphy, of N Y, Minister Resident of the U S at the Court of his Majesty the King of the Netherlands, vice Auguste Belmont, of N Y, recalled at his own request.
Isaac R Diller, of Ill, Consul of the U S at Bremen, vice Wm Hildebrand, the present incumbent.
Wm Thomson, of N Y, Consul of the U S at Southampton, England, vice Jos R Croskey, resigned.
Gabriel G Fleurot, of N Y, Consul of the U S at Bordeaux, France, to fill an existing vacancy. -Union

Mrd: on Jun 3, at *Evergreen Cottage*, Fairfax Co, Va, by Rev F E Boyle, Gibson A Terrett to T Victoria Young, daughter of the late Henry A Young, of PG Co, Md, all of said county.

Died: on May 31, at Charleston, S C, Mrs Harriott Post, consort of Rev Reuben Post, D D, Pastor of the Independent or Congregational Church in that city. She was in her 53rd year of her age, & died of congestion of the liver, after an illness of about 2 weeks. She was a Virginian by birth, & a grand-daughter of Richd Henry Lee, of the Revolution.

____ersburg, Jun 3. Wm Maghee, a well known delegate & respectable citizen was killed while getting on the ____ & Tenn railroad. [Paper creased.]

New Orleans, Jun 1. The steamship **Louisiana** was burnt in Galveston Bay on Sunday. Eleven persons were certainly lost in her, & Col Bainbridge, of the army, & 31 others are missing. Twenty-five persons were saved by the steamer **Galveston**.

Grafton, Jun 2. The excursionists arrived here last night; this morning the company set forth again over the Parkersburg branch of the Balt & Ohio railroad, & Dr G D Lewis, a professor in the Eclectic Medical Institute at Cincinnati, had his skull fractured yesterday on the road from Wheeling, by imprudently thrusting his head from a car window while passing through the Broad Tree tunnel, 40 miles from this place. He is still living, but his recovery is hopeless.

The Mountain House, Capon Springs, Va, will be opened for the reception of visitors on Jun 22. –J N Buck, proprietor

Congress Hall, Cape Island, Cape May, N J. The undersigned, having leased from W B Miller the above first class Hotel, & it will be open on Jun 15. –Jno West, late of Jones' Hotel, Phil. –R R Thompson

Highly valuable property for sale in Gtwn, D C: the desirable brick dwlg on the south side of Gay, between Green & Montgomery sts, well known as the residence of the late Col Saml Humphreys. The house is large & commodious; the lot fronts 60 feet on Gay st, & runs back about 210 feet to Olive st. Apply to M Adler.

Carlisle **White Sulphur Springs**, Cumberland Co, Pa, will be open on Jun 20. For further information address the proprietors, Owen & Chandler, Carlisle Springs, Pa.

The undersigned Dry Good Merchants inform the public that they have determined to close their respective place of business at 7 o'clock P M from Jun 1 to Sep 1.
Harper & Mitchell
Clagett, Newton, May & Co
Clagett, Dodson & Co
Wm R Riley
Wm M Shuster & Co
R W Carter
Coley & Sears
Geo F Allen
J C Gibson
Frank A McGee
Perry & Brother
-Star

Circuit Court of Wash Co, D C, in equity, No 83. Law vs Law. Jas Adams, the trustee, reported that he has sold the particular lots & premises described & specified in his report of May 29, & the several purchasers have complied with the terms of said sales.
John C Fitzpatrick, part of lots 4 thru 7 in square 741: $82.68.
H A Mathieson, lot 7 in square 770: $90.00
M Pettibone, 1/6th lot in square 228: $50.72.
John Grinder, 1/6th square 699: $158.75
Mrs Joise, part lot in square 732: $12.50.

Geo Collard, 1/6th lots 1, 2, & 3 in square 741: $64.48.
John Purdy, 1/6th lot 3 in square 575: $486.35.
J M Carlisle, lot 5 in square 633: $3,213.00
Richd Patton, 1/6th lot B, sub 1.30, square 693: $128.04.
C Buckingham, 1/6th west half of lot 8, square 350: $198.71.
Edw Stell, 1/6th part of lot C, sub 5, square 690: $77.05.
N C Towle, part of east ½ lot A, sub 5, square 690: $95.37.
N C Towle, part of lot B, sub 5, square 690: $54.37.
Mary E Broom, 1/6th lot west ½ A, sub 5, square 690: $94.00
Chas Lyons, part of lots 4, thru 6, 9 thru 15, 18 thru 22, sub square 695: $170.49.
John Purdy, 1/6th part of lot 9 square 575: $151.51.
B F Dyer, part of lot C, sub lot 1 & 30, square 693: $23.50.
John Grinder, 1/6th lots 7 thru 9, sub 743: $49.04.
Ann Bean, 1/6th lot 14 & part 15, square 770: $69.00
J W Jones, 1/6th part lot 15, square 770: $20.00.
Thos Blagden, 1/6th lots 7 & 8, square 742: $50.87.
Wm Marshall, lot 2, square 324: $1,796.76.
J M Broadhead, part 2, square 689: $193.91.
D W Middleton, part 3, square 690, & house: $4,000.00
Jos Saxton, lot 5, square 692: $1,133.00.
Richd Barry, 1/6th lot 16 sub square 695: $28.00.
Richd Barry, 1/6th lot 3, sub square 695: $12.00
By order of the Court, John A Smith, clerk

FRI JUN 5, 1857
Appointments by the Pres: 1-Jos Williams, of Iowa, Associate Justice of the Supreme Court of Kansas, vice Thos Cunningham, resigned. 2-Calvin F Burns, U S Atty for the Eastern District of Missouri, vice Thos C Reynolds, resigned.

The new painting for the Capitol of Md. The cmte of the Legislature of Md, of which Senator Hoffman, of Balt, is chairman, have recently contracted with Mr Edwin White, of N Y C, for the painting of the great historical picture of <u>Washington Resigning</u> his Commission, for which the Legislature of 1856, on the anniversary of his birth, appropriated $3,000.

The Richmond, Va, papers announce, on Jun 3, the death of Robt C Stanard, an emiment lawyer of that city, & but recently & for several years a member of both Houses of the Genr'l Assembly, & of the last Convention to revise the Constitution of the State. [Jun 29th newspaper: Obit-died: Robt C Stanard, son of the distinguished Robt Stanard, of the Court of Appeals. He was the tenderest of husbands, & the kindest of fathers. –Richmond, Jun 6]

Mrd: on Jun 3, in Gtwn, D C, by Rev B F Brooke, Jas L Towner, of Va, to Jennie, daughter of David English, of Gtwn.

Mrd: on Jun 3, at *Evergreen Cottage*, Fairfax Co, Va, by Rev F E Boyle, Oscar W B Bailey to Mollie L Young, [daughter of the late Henry N Young, of PG Co, Md,] all of PG Co, Md.

Thos Biddle, of Phil, died on Wed, at his country residence, near Paoli, Chester Co, after an illness of several weeks, at the ripe age of 80 years. He was long & favorably known in Phil, especially in financial circles, in which for a number of years he took a leading part. He was a cousin of the late Nicholas Biddle.
–Phil Bulletin

Ex-Gov Bebb, of Ohio, who recently fired upon a party of serenaders at his residence in Winebago Co, Ill, & killed one of them & wounded others, has been honorably discharged, after a full investigation of the matter. The serenaders, it appears, were a gang of insolent rowdies, who surrounded his house & insulted his family, until he was compelled to fire upon them, after begging them to leave.

Rome, May 8, 1857. After mouldering undisturbed for 262 years under the simple slab placed over them by the pious monks at St Onotrio, whose kindly ministrations soothed his last hours, the remains of the poet Tasso have at length been transferred to the long projected tomb provided for them in a new chapel of the same sanctuary. Archbishop Bedini conducted the religious rites. The old leaden coffin containing the remains was so much decayed that it was raised with difficulty; but the poetic ashes were carefully transferred to the appointed urn, which also holds a certified memorandum of the ceremonial in a glass tube, & deposited in the monument. This memorial of Italy's most charming poet was conceived some 30 years ago by the sculptor Fabris, whose unflagging zeal has finally achieved it, with the tardy aid of the present Pope & some other sovereigns. The monument symbolizes both his faith & his vocation.

The Detroit Free Press announces the death of Geo R Griswold, a purser in the navy, aged about 45 years. He died on board the brig **Dolphin**, at sea, off the west coast of Africa, on Apr 5.

Two Ewe Sheep were taken up on May 29, supposed to be strayed from Wash or Gtwn; both are marked with tar on the forehead. Owner is to come forward & take them away. –John O Harry, Tennellytown

Last week the dead body of a man, about 60 years of age, was found near the Blue Mountain Dam, 2 miles from Hamburg. The night was very dark & it is supposed that he fell over the bank into the stone quarry & was instantly killed. Papers on his person show he was a German by birth & named Jacob Rothweiler; also that he had a son of the same name, who was a Methodist preacher in Cleveland, Ohio.
-Reading [Pa] Gaz

A few nights ago 3 villains, Harrison, Cundiff, & Hull, went to a house occupied by Mrs Shirley, on Mike's Run, in this county, beat the old woman badly, violated her daughter, &, after breaking up the furniture & tearing down the house, left. Cundiff has been lodged in jail, & Harrison was arrested at Grafton on Tue last. Hull is still at large. —Piedmont [Va] Independent

Mary Baird, wife of Peter Baird, was found dead in her bed, at her residence 55 Milberry st this morning. Marks & bruises were found upon her body, & the husband was arrested upon suspicion, to await the result of the coroner's investigation. The woman was grossly intoxicated yesterday, & it is probably that she received her bruises by falling.

New Orleans, Jun 4. The steamer **Texas** has arrived with the Mexican mails & papers. The latter contain no positive information regarding the fate of Capt Crabbe & his party. It is probably that the fears of their execution will be realized.

St Louis, Jun 4. David H Burr, late Surveyor Genr'l of Utah, has arrived in safety, having avoided the spies & assassins of Brigham Young.

To the public: We the subscribers, Merchants in the Dry-Good trade, on 7th st, in order to give our clerks recreation during the summer season, do hereby agree to close our respective stores at 7½ o'clock, commencing from Jun 5 & continuing until Oct 1. -C F Perrie, R Brice Hall, R G Hyatt, & A Goddard.

SAT JUN 6, 1857
Valuable market farm [belonging to, & for the past 14 years occupied by, the late Ninian Beall,] for sale at auction, lying in Wash & Montg Counties, about 3 miles from Gtwn: contains 54 acres; improvements are a good, nearly new commodious 2 story frame dwlg with back bldg, cottage for gardener, & necessary out-houses. Apply at the place, or to 120 Bridge st, Gtwn. -Geo W Beall, for the heirs.
-Wall, Barnard, aucts

Large stock of fancy goods, perfumery, jewelry, & cigars, at auction: on Jun 11, at the store of Messrs Samstag & Bro, 339 Pa ave, between 6th & 7th sts, their entire stock. —Wall, Barnard, aucts

Appropriations made during the 3rd session of the 34th Congress:
1-Act for the relief of Geo K McGunnegle, surviving partner of the late firm of Hill & McGunnegle, of St Louis, Mo: for the balance due by the U S for commissary & other suppies furnished for the use of the Illinois militia, in 1832: $2,282.67.
2-Act for the relief of Jas Harrington: for loss of time & expense incurred during sickness caused by melting lead while in the employment of the U S: $500.00.
3-Act for the relief of Peter Grover: for injuries received while in the employment of the U S in a dangerous service, & for medical & other expenses incurred: $800.00

4-Act for the relief of A S Bender: for his services as superintendent of the U S lead mines of the upper Miss, from Aug 2, 1844 to Oct 16, 1847, it being the difference between his pay as such superintendent to which he is entitled, & the pay of acting superintendent, which he did not receive for the same period: $1,281.92

5-Act for the relief of J Randolph Clay: envoy extraordinary & minister plenipotentiary of the U S to the Gov't of Peru, the difference between the salary allowed him as charge d'affaires from Mar 16, 1853, [the date of his appointment as minister,] to Jun 30th following, after which he was allowed a compensation according to his rank: $1,312.00

6-Act for the relief of Hannah F Niles: to pay her, or to her legal reps, in consideration of the meritorious services of her father, Capt Robt Niles, during the war of the Revolution: $3,000.00.

7-Act for the relief of the surviving children of Sarah Crandall, deceased: to pay to her surviving children the sum of $96 per annum, from Jan 1, 1848, to the date of her death, being the amount she would have received, under a special act for her relief approved Jul 24, 1854, had she survived: indefinite.

8-Act for the relief of Chas L Denman: to pay him $200, the same to be in full consideration of a like sum by him advanced to the Pacific mail company, for the passage of 2 American citizens from Acapulco, Mexico, to San Francisco, Calif: $200.00

9-Act fot the relief of Jos White: for the amount of money by mistake omitted to be credited to him as navy agent in settling his accounts at the Treasury: $661.02.

10-Act for the relief of Amos B Corwine: for moneys expended by him in forwarding destitute citizens of the U S from Panama to San Francisco: $27,804.33.

11-Act for the relief of the heirs of Maj Gen Arthur St Clair: for services & sacrifices in the war of the Revolution & in the Indian wars, the Sec of the Treasury is directed to pay to his heirs, one-sixth to each of his 6 children: $30,000.00

12-Act for the relief of Jas P Fleming, of Augusta, Ga: for extra services in transporting the mails on route 33,313, in 1854: $1,450.00.

13-Act for the relief of John H Horne, of Miss: to pay him $650.50.

14-Act making a reappropriation from the surplus fund for the relief of Lt John Guest, U S navy, & others: to Guest: $617.000, & for other lawful claims of ofcrs who were employed in said survey of the coast from Apalochicola bay to the mouth of the Miss river, 1841 & 41: $1,760. 49.

15-Act for the relief of Sally T Mathews: for the services of her late husband, Wm P Mathews, as an extra clerk in the Treas Dept between Sep 1, 1842, & May 14, 1843: $351.00

16-Act for the relief of Ransdell Pegg: for the amount of difference of pay received by him as a watchman at the east wing of the Patent Ofc & that received by the other watchmen of said bldg, from Jul 23, 1849, to Oct 1, 1850: $108.50.

17-Act for the relief of Mary Reeside: excx of the will of Jas Reeside, the sum of $188, 496.06, with interest thereon from Dec 6, 1841, being in full for the amount due upon a verdict & judgment thereon rendered by the circuit court of the U S for the eastern district of Pa, in a suit in which the U S were plntfs & Jas Reeside aforesaid was dfndnt: indefinite.

18-Act for the relief of Jos D Beers, of N Y C: for interest & damages on a bill of exchange drawn by Thos B Nalle, a purser in the U S navy, on Wm Ballard Preston, late Sec of the Navy, for $20,000 payable to the order of Thos Ap C Jones, cmder-in-chief of the Pacific squadron, 3 days after sight, dated Jan 21, 1850, & endorsed by Thos Ap C Jones, to Moffall & Co, or order, & by them to the order of said Jos D Beers: indefinite.

19-Act for the relief of the heirs of the late Col John Hardin: for balance due them under the agreement between Gen Wilkinson & Col Hardin, & to be in full satisfaction of all claims on their part against the U S Gov't: $5,600.00.

20-Act for the relief of John C McConnell: for fresh beef furnished by him to Gen Quitman's brig of volunteers in the Mexican war in Apr, 1847: $993.42.

21-Act for the relief of Whitemarsh B Seabrook & others: to examine & settle, upon the principles of equity & justice, the claim of:

Whitemarsh B Seabrook
Wm C Meggett
Benj Bailey
W E Wood
Edw Mitchell
Jos J Murray
Chas Townsend
John Patterson
Wm R Hart
Jos Jenkins
Edw Bailey
Henry Seabrook
Cato A Beckett
Benj S Whaley
Isaac Auld
John Ailcock
Jas B Adams
Wm Beckett
Edw Beckett
Jas Beckett
Wm G Baynard
Chas Bailey
Henry Bailey
Francis Bowler
Henry Calder
Jas Clark, sr
Robt Chisholm
Gabriel Crawford
Wm Clement

Jas Dignan
Thos Dunmire
Wm Edings
Geo W Freeman
Barney Gilbert
Wm Hannahan, jr
Henry J Jones
Christopher Jenkins
Benj W Jenkins
Robt S Jenkins
Danl Lowrey
Robt Mason
Ephraim Mikell
Jno C Mikell
Josiah Mikell
Jno Mikell, sr
John Raven Matthews
Isaac C Moses
Mungo Mackay
John McDougall
Robt McLeod
John C Pillans
Robt Pillans
John Pattieson
Wm Seabrook
Gabriel Seabrook
Jos A Seabrook
Andrew Seabrook
Lewis Strobel

Jas Swinton
Christian Staley
Danl Shandley
Andrew E Thayer
Danl Townsend
Thos Tompson
Geo M Towers
Edw Whaley
Jos Whaley

Wm Wilkinson
Christopher Wilkinson
Morton Wilkinson
Thos Wescoat
Wm J Wescoat
Randall Wescoat
Walley Meggett
Mingoe Crawford,
Jos Beamer

they being the ofcrs, musicians, & privates composing the Edisto Island company of militia, in the State of S C, in the war of 1812; that he allow to those named, who are living, & the heirs of the deceased, the amount of pay & allowance to which each of them would have been entitled, according to their respective positions, under the regulations of the service at that time, for such length of time as they shall each of them be proved to have served in defence of said island during the said war; & that he allow them just & reasonable compensation for the material & labor which shall be proved to have been expended by them in the erection of 2 fortifications on the island, for the purposes of defence in said war: indefinite.

22-Act for the relief of C B R Kennerly: for medical services rendered the military escort of the U S boundary commission in the years 1854 & 1855: $536.66.

23-Act for the relief of Jesse Morrison, of Ill: for damage in being dispossessed of his storehouse at **Fort Jackson**, Mich Territory, for the use of the U S military force, & for rent of the same by the Gov't during the Black Hawk war: $500.00.

24-Act for the relief of John Shaw, a soldier in the war of 1812: for his extraordinary services as a scout & spy on the upper Mississippi frontier in the war of 1812: $2,000.00

25-Act for the relief of Thos B Steele, passed assist surgeon of the U S navy: for the difference of compensation to an assist surgeon & passend assist surgeon from Apr 24, 1853, to Apr 21, 1855: 717.66.

26-Act for the relief of John Huff, of Texas: for damages done to his property whilst his house & premises were in possession of a btln of U S infty in Dec, 1848: $1,556.00.

27-Act for the relief of Geo Schellinger: for damages sustained by him by reason of destruction of property by the U S army during the Black Hawk war: $284.25.

28-Act for the relief of Lyman N Cook: for an annual pension of $22.50 per month during his natural life: indefinite.

29-Act for the relief of Wm Kendall: for all articles furnished by him to soldiers there recruited or stationed during the late Mexican war; & in all cases where the several amounts claimed were regularly entered on the original muster or descriptive rolls which accompanied the detachments from said fort, & were thus charged against the respective soldiers, but were not transferred to the company rolls, nor retained out of the soldiers' pay & allowed to the said Kendall: indefinite.

30-Act for the relief of the heirs of Saml R Thruston, late Delegate from Oregon: for the difference between the pay he has already received for mileage & that now allowed to & received by the present delegate: indefinite.

31-Act for the relief of Collins Boomer: for the sloop & provisions captured from him in 1813 by the British, in consequence of his employment of the sloop in the conveyance of American troops upon the St Lawrence river: $1,000.00

32-Act to reimburse the estate of Jos McClure, a paymaster in the war of 1812: for the amount of a judgment paid by said McClure to the U S for moneys paid out by him for which the vouchers were burnt, but which was paid by him to his regt: $551.36.

33-Act for the relief of Don Piatt: the amount of the difference between the salary received by him as sec of legation at Paris & that of charge d'affaires, for the term of 14 days in Oct 1854, & from Dec 26, 1854, until May 1, 1855, & also from Sep 3 to the 11th, 1855: $2,114.00.

34-Act for the relief of Wm L Davidson: to allow for himself & the other children of Lt Col Wm Davidson, of N C line, in the continental army of the U S, who was killed in battle on Feb 1, 1781, at Cowan's ford, on the Catawba river, the amount of the half pay for 7 years of the said Col Davidson as a lt col of infty: indefinite.

35-Act for the relief of Cmder John L Saunders: for entertaining on board the ship **St Mary's,** Colonel John C Eldridge whilst a bearer of dispatches from Pensacola to Aransas in Sept, 1845: $80.00.

36-Act for the relief of Adam D Stewart: the difference between the sum contracted to be paid to him & that which he received: $7,297.50.

37-Act for the relief of Jos Graham: for his services as acting charge d'affaires at Buenos Ayres from Aug 3 to Sep 11, 1852; from Nov 25, 1852, to Mar 26, 1853; & from Mar 31, 1854, to Oct 20, 1854: $4,479.60.

38-Act for the relief of Robt S Wimberly: to pay to him, from Dec 1, 1855, $8 per month, from thence during his natural life: indefinite.

39-Act for the relief of Thos Crown: for the sum to which he is entitled under a contract made by him on Mar 16, 1826, for the delivery of bricks to be used in the fortifications at Oak Island, at the mouth of Cape Fear river, in N C: $3,500.00.

40-Act for the relief of Matthew G Emery: for hauling marble for the Gov't from Sep 7, 1852, to Apr 7, 1853, which account is set out in the ptn filed by the claimant in this cause; $3,375.00.

41-Act for the relief of Mrs Mary Gay: the widow of the late Wm Gay, Indian agent for the Shawnees of Kansas Territory, who was killed while in the discharge of his official duties, as indemnity to cover his salary, the amount of money of which he was robbed, & the expenses of the widow & family in returning to their home, in the State of Michigan: $2,000.00.

42-Act for the relief of Jefferson Wilson, adm, with the will annexed, of John F Wray, deceased: to pay the sum which was paid by John F Wray, deceased, for three-quarters of secion 16, in township 9 of range 5, east of the meridian line, of the Chickasaw lands in the State of Miss, the title to which tract of land had been adjudged by the competent tribunals not to have been in the U S at the time of the sale: $602,19.

43-Act for the benefit of John W Cox, of the State of Ky: to place his name upon the roll of invalid pensions, & pay to him from Jan 1, 1856, $8 per month during his natural life: indefinite.

44-Act for the relief of the surviving children of John Gilbert, a Revolutionary soldier: to pay the surviving children of Gilbert, late a soldier in Col W B Whiting's regt, the full pay of a private, under the act of Congress of Jun 7, 1832, to the time of his death, on Apr 12, 1852: indefinite.

45-Act for the relief of Catharine V R Cochrane, sole surviving child of the late Gen Philip Schuyler: to pay to her, or her legal rep, in full payment & discharge of all claims on account of services rendered or losses sustained by Gen Philip Schuyler in the war of the Revolution: $9,960.00.

46-Act for the relief of Wm W Belden, adm of Ebenezer Belden: for the amount of loss sustained by Ebenezer Belden by the destruction of his stock of goods by the British on Dec 19, 1813, at Buffalo, N Y, in consequence of his store being used in part as a military depot by order of the Quarter-master Gen of the U S army: $8,624.84.

47-Act for the relief of the surviving children of Sarah Van Pelt, widow of John Van Pelt, a Revolutionary soldier: to pay to the surviving children of John Van Pelt & Sarah Van Pelt the pension due to her, from Jul 4, 1838, to her death, which occurred on May 29, 1854, at the rate of $31.75 per annum: indefinite.

48-Act for the relief of the heirs of Wm Easby, deceased, partner of Easby & Henly: for the value of 306 barrels of lime shipped on board the schnr **Elizabeth** on Mar 4, 1842, by order of Col R C De Russey, for & on account of *Fort Monroe*, Va, & lost by the vessel getting aground at Old Point Comfort: $413.10.

49-Act for the relief of Geo Chorpenning, jr: to enable the Postmaster Gen to adjust & settle the claim of said Chorpenning, as surviving partner of Woodward & Chorpenning, & in his own right, for carrying the mails by San Pedro, & for supplying the post ofc in Carson's Valley, & also for carrying part of the Independence mail by Calif, etc; & for damages on account of the annulment of Woodward & Chorpenning's contract for carrying the U S mail from Sacramento, Calif, to Salt Lake, Utah Territory, as shown in the affidavits & proofs on file in the House of Reps: indefinite.

50-Act for the relief of Thos Rhodes & Jeremiah Austill: to pay them for their expenses in constructing a road from Mobile, Ala, to Pascagoula bay, for the transportation of the mail, in 1828: $4,000.00.

51-Act for the benefit of Wm L Oliver, of Davis Co, Iowa: to place his name upon the roll of invalid pensions, & pay him from Jan 1, 1856, the sum of $10 per month during his natural life: indefinite.

52-Act for the relief of Benj W Smithson: for the pay & emoluments of a capt, from the date of his resignation until he was informed by his commanding ofcr of the acceptance of the same, & discharged from the service of the U S, deducting therefrom such amount as may have been paid him for services during the same time: indefinite.

53-Act for the relief of Mark & Richd H Bean, of the State of Arkansas: to adjust upon principles & justice their claim, to pay whatever may be found due, deducting what they have heretofore received: $15,000.00.

54-Act for the relief of Isaac Swain: for freight on stores for the U S army, from Benicia, Calif, to the Gov't hulk or post-landing near that place, & for injuries received by his ship **Ellen Brooks**, whilst lying at said post-landing: $4,800.00.

55-Act for the relief of Robt Davis: for the value of a horse lost by him in battle: $140.00.

56-Resolution to authorize the Sec of the State & the Sec of the Interior to settle the claim of Wm Carey Jones, for services performed by him in 1849 & 1850, as special agent of the U S to Mexico & Calif; & that the amount which shall be allowed by them shall be paid to said Jones, on his givng a receipt therefore, & in full compensation for said services: indefninte.

57-Joint resolution in favor of J W Nye: for improvements made upon public grounds, for which he has received no compensation: $3,200.00.

Appointments by the Pres: 1-Nahum Capen, postmaster at Boston, vice Bailey, resigned, to take effect from Oct 1. 2-Benj F Tillotson, receiver of public moneys, at Faribault, Minn, vice Smith, resigned. 3-Volney Hascall, register at Kalamazoo, Mich, vice Kidder, who declines the ofc.

The devoted wife of Sir John Franklin, in whose bosom the hope of her distinguished husband's safety has never expired, has fitted out another expedition to the Arctic seas out of the wreck of her fortune, aided by the good will, advice, & assistance of a few experienced voyagers & geographers, who believe that traces of Sir John Franklin can yet be found.

Christopher Noble clung on the rear portion of a car on the Great Western railroad last Tue, & while the train was going at full speed, let go his hold & got off. He was thrown a distance of no less than 41 feet and was picked up dead. –Cincinnati Gaz

Weston, Mo, May 28, 1857. Mr Saml Gilbert arrived in this city last night from Great Salt Lake City. He left on the road, about 200 miles from here, Gen Burr, U S Surveyor Gen of Utah; Judge Stiles, of the U S district court of Utah; Peter Dodson, U S Marshal; Mr Murrell, U S Postmaster of Salt Lake; Thos Williams, & a large number of gentiles coming into the State. They will arrive in about 2 days, when the particulars of the news from Salt Lake by this arrival will be given to the public.

Died: on May 30, at his residence, in Gtwn, Hamilton Jackson Smith, in his 44th year, a gentleman much esteemed for many virtues.

Locust-Grove Academy, near Greenwood Depot, Albemarle Co, Va, will be opened on Sep 1 next. Its object is to prepare boys to enter the Univ of Va or any college. -Ed B Smith, A M, principal

Metropolitan Female Institute, a Boarding & Day School for Young Ladies, 436 G st, between 7th & 8th sts, Wash: will be opened on the first Monday in Sept next. -Mr & Mrs T H Havener, Principals, 336 G st, Wash.

MON JUN 8, 1857
Trustee's sale of valuable real estate, by deed of trust, recorded in Liber J A S No 114, of the land records for Wash Co, D C, at public auction, on Jun 10, 1857, the eastern half of lot 6 in square 518, commencing for the same 22 feet west from the east line of lot 6, on H st north, & running south 100 feet; thence west 22 feet to the line of property conveyed by Stabler & Hallowell to Thos C Donn; north along said line to H se, with improvements, consisting of a large & desirable dwlg house, being the same as conveyed by Wm Douglas to Martha E Dixon by deed duly recorded, of the land records of Wash Co. –Jos H Bradley, jr, trustee -Jas C McGuire, auct

Henry Hubbard, the aged ex-Senator in Congress, died suddenly on ____ morning at his residence in Charlestown; his residence has been in the pleasant village of Charlestown on the bank of the Connecticut river. –Boston Post [Death date blurred. Current item.]

From Utah. Mr David H Burr, Surveyor Genr'l of the Territory of Utah, & long a resident of this city, arrived here yesterday accompanied by his son, Mr David Burr, who left Washington in March to join his father in Salt Lake City. They met on May 13th at Ash Hallow, about midway between **Fort Kearny** & **Fort Laramie**. Mr Burr left Salt Lake on Apr 15, in company with a large number of Gentiles, who found the Mormon country had become too hot to hold them any longer. Only 3 Gentiles, Kerr, Bell, & Mendenhall, & the Indian Agent, Dr Hurt, remain behind.

Local Item: the dedication of the Western Presbyterian Church took place yesterday; opening services by Rev Dr Burney, Pres of Columbia College, & the dedication sermon by the pastor of the church, Rev Mr Haskell. The sermon in the evening was by Rev Dr Sunderland.

Hon Wm Haile was inaugurated Gov'r of N H on Thu last. He condemns the Dred Scott decision of the Supreme Court & advises a legislative protest against it.

Mrd: on Jun 3, in Wash City, by Rev W H Chapman, Mr John J Smith to Miss Anna Dammond, all of Wash City.

Mrd: on Jun 2, in Wash City, by Rev Fr Young, Lt Wm C West, U S Navy, to Mary Josephine Jameson, daughter of the late Dr Chas Jameson, of Chas Co, Md.

Died: on Jun 2, at the residence of Ex-Pres Tyler, his sister, Mrs M O Beekmann.

Serious accident on Fri last on section six of the Wash Water Works' line, by the sudden caving in of a bank which the men were excavating. The bodies of the killed, Jno McCarty, of Wash, & a man from Phil, were brought down in coffins by the packet on Sat.

The body of a worthy woman, Mrs Harriet Wells, wife of Mr Danl Wells, now residing on Mason's or Analostan island, was on Fri last caught up in a seine which was being used in the shad fishery along the shores of the island. It is supposed that she threw herself into the water in a fit of temporary alienation of mind, caused by depression of spirits; to which she was at times subject. She was about 45 years of age, & leaves an interesting family of children.

New Orleans, Jun 4. Late papers from Mexico confirm the execution of Col Crabbe & 58 of his followers. It is rumored in the city of Mexico that a terrible revenge is being taken in Calif, by murdering all the Mexicans to be found.

Orphans Court of Wash Co, D C. Letters of administration on the personal estate of Saml Arnold, late of Wash Co, deceased. –Mary Ann Arnold, admx

TUE JUN 9, 1857
Household & kitchen furniture at auction on: Jun 16, at the residence of C Laurie, 314 Delaware ave, north of the north Capitol gate. –C W Boteler, auct

Public sale of valuable bldg lots, on Jun 15, on the premises, lot 3, in subdivision made between Nicholas Young's heirs of square 414, fronting 91 feet 6 2/3rd inches on 8th st west, by 99 feet on H st south: on the Island. –Chas S Wallach, atty -Jas C McGuire, auct

The steamship **Louisiana**, Capt Sheppard, which was recently burnt in Galveston Bay, & in which Col Bainbridge, of the 1st Infty, U S Army, perished, is a total wreck. Much property was lost, together with the mail, a considerable amount of specie, & many lives. The steamship **Galveston** brought Mr Chas H Hughes, the purser of the **Louisiana**. He confirms Mr Grover's statement that the fire broke out about 1 o'clock, when most were asleep.
+
News Ofc, Sunday: The revenue cutter is just in, & she brings Capt Sheppard alive. He was picked up clinging to some life preserving chairs, nearly exhausted. Jas Brown, watchman of the **Lousiana**, was brought in alive; & Saml Wells, passenger, Wisconsin. The pilot boat brings in 3 persons alive & 6 dead bodies. The rescued persons, are passengers S W Fichlin, of Va; John Sanford, of Texana; & John Howley, fireman. The dead are 3 German women, & a 2 year old boy, names unknown; & Col Bainbridge, U S Army; also, a young American lady, name

unknown. The passengers give the highest praise to Capt Dennison, of the **Galveston**, for the noble exertions he made; also to Capt Cornell, of the revenue cutter, & to Capt Walters, of the pilot boat. Mr John E Wheeler was saved. The following are the names of some of the persons lost & supposed to be lost: Col Bainbridge, U S army; Jos Hamilton; Mr Mills, of Lavaca, Texas; Mr Millhouse, of Dallas, Ala; F A Nance, of Powderhorn; Lacey Jones & lady; Mrs Mitchell; Mrs E Hart; Mr Frickland; Mr Aaron Clark; S D Clark, mate; John Thompson, engineer; Jas Brown, watchman; Ed McManus, steward; Lydia Travers, chambermaid; 12 seamen & 6 firemen, 6 boys in cabin & 3 cooks. The following is a list of those who are known to have been saved: Mr Cleveland, wife, child, & servant, of Lavaca; Dr Arnold, of Mo; Mrs Eliz Hart, of Corpus Christi; W R Friend & servant; Rich Smith, 2nd mate; Miss A E Frisbee, of N Y; Mr Kennedy, Chas H Hughes, G W Grover; Danl Sullivan, St Louis, Mo; John Ezell, St Louis; John E Wheeler, Powderhorn; M W Garrison; P S Miller, of N Y; Dr Early & his brother, of Greene Co, Va.
[Jun 11th newspaper: the Galveston Civilian furnishes a revised & corrected list of those saved & lost by the burning of the steamship **Louisiana**. Dead & bodies recovered: Philip Milhouse, Ala, old man; Joel Hamilton, Gonzales; M G Mills, Clinton, La; Col Henry Bainbridge, U S Army; Eliz Travers, chamber maid; Mrs Tschaeke, New Branufels; German lady & supposed grandchild, 2 years old; another German lady, unknown; Henry ___, porter. Missing & certainly lost:
E J Brown, bar-keeper; negro man of Cleveland, of Lavaca; Franz Tschaeke & 3 children, New Branunfels; Young Millhouse, Ala; W P Dixon, Alexandria, Va; Mrs Mitchell, Cibolo, Texas or New Orleans; Benny S D Etter, 10 years old, Indianola; R C Brenham, Columbia, Mo; ___ Temps, discharged soldier, with Col Bainbridge; Lacy Jones & lady; Aaron Clarke; 9 seamen, 6 of negro crew, one belonging to Oscar Farish. Saved: A D Cleaveland, lady, child, servant girl, Lavaca; John E Wheeler, Indianola; Danl Sullivan, Lavaca; P S Miller, N Y; Moses W Garrison, N Y; Geo W Grover, Galveston; W R Friend, Clinton, DeWitt Co; negro woman & man of Mr Friend; Ross Kennedy, Texas; Mrs Eliz Hart, Corpus Christi; Miss A E Frisbie, Phelps, Ontario Co, N Y; Dr John F Early, Charlottesville, Va; Miss Tschaeke, 11 years old, [her father, mother, & 3 children lost;] Wm Smyth, Alexandria, Va; Young Early, Va; Slaughter W Ficklin, Charlottesville, Va; Dr Arnold, Columbia, Mo; John Sanford, Texana, Texas; Saml Wills, Wisc; M Weil, Goliad; Frank V D Stucken, Fredericksburg, Texas; Capt Henry Shepard, cmder of the lost steamer; Chas H Hughes, clerk; S D Clark, 1st mate; Andrew Smith, 2nd mate; John Driscoll, cabin boy; Richd Finn, 1st engineer; Michl Howley, fireman; Bryan Cowley, fireman; Saml Walker, pantry-man; Christian Scharpff, pastryman; Jas Brown, watchman; John Howley, fireman.]

A celebrated historical personage has just died in Paris, the famous Vidocq, who, from one of the most expert thieves in Europe, was promoted to the Prefectship of Police. He retired from his ofc with a competenee, & died at his residence in Paris, age 78. [No death date given-current item.]

Application will be made to the Com'r of the Land Ofc of the U S for the issue of scrip on duplicate or triplicate Warrant numbered 4,399, for 2,666 2/3 acres of land, which issued from the Land Ofc of the State of Va on May 1, 1788, to Lot Harcum, a midshipman in the Va State Navy in the war of the Revolution, which warrant has been lost, mislaid, or destroyed, & cannot be found. –R B Bagby, Atty for Robt Moon & others, heirs of Lot Harcum.

Cow strayed or stolen, on May 30th, with a collar on her neck with the name of the undersigned, & with the number of his house & street. Liberal reward for the return of the Cow. –Dr Cornelius Boyle, 4½ st, near Pa ave.

Montpelier, the residence of the late Pres Madison, for sale; situated in Orange Co, Va, equal distant about 80 miles from Richmond & Alexandria; contains 1,165 acres, is offered for sale, in whole or in part. It has been divided, by a recent survey, into 2 tracts; one of 765, & one of 400 acres. On the larger tract is the Mansion. The premises will be shown by the subscriber, & any additional information given by him at Orange Court-house, Va. –Alfred V Scott

WED JUN 10, 1857
Com'rs sale of valuable real estate: by order & decree of the Circuit Court of Wash Co, D C, in the matter of the heirs of Fred'k Mohler, deceased, made on Apr 13, 1857: public auction on Jun 18, of all of square 234, with small frame house; & all of square 271. –Saml E Douglass, E C Carrington, Thos E Lloyd, Chas Walter, Theodore McGlue, Com'rs. -A Green auct

West Point Academy: Jun 2 the Board of Visiters for the annual examination of the Military Academy was organized. Following members of the Board were present:

Edw H Bryan, M D, Miss
Col Benj F Butler, Mass
Maj Wm H Chase, Fla
Hon Henry C Deming, Conn
Gen Noble S Elderkin, N Y
Geo W Houk, Ohio
Robt B Lindsay, Ala
Prof Campbell Morfitt, M D, of Md
Rev J Phelps, D D, Iowa
Prof Danl Read, L L D, Wisc
Gen Conrad Shimer, Pa

Orphans Court of Wash Co, D C. Letters of administration, with the will annexed, on the personal estate of Hamilton J Smith, late of Wash Co, deceased.
–John Chandler Smith, adm

Died: on Jun 8, in Wash City, in her 78th year, Mrs Milcah Donn, relict of the late John Donn, formerly of Havre-de-Grace, Harford, Co, Md, & for the past 27 years a resident of Wash City. Her funeral will take place from the residence of her son-in-law, Wm Thompson, on Md ave, between 4½ & 6th sts, this morning at 10 o'clock.

Mrd: on Jun 9, at *Cool Spring Farm*, near Wash, by Rev W J Purrington, Dr J C R Clark, of Missouri, to Miss Julia R Dawes, adopted daughter of Mrs Martha Isherwood.

On Sunday morning last Rev W H Chapman, pastor of the Ebenezer Methodist Episcopal Church, announced to the congregation that the church had been made the recipient of a handsome gift by Mr C W Boteler, sr, of a very handsome silver communion set & baptismal bowl. On the motion of Mr John Clapham, seconded by Mr G P Page, the thanks of the congregation were unanimously tendered, & it was made the duty of the Recording Steward, Rev Mr Marks, to communicate to Mr Boteler their appreciative action.

THU JUN 11, 1857
Harness, saddles, bridles, & store fixtures at public auction: by deed of trust or assignment from Josiah F Bailey, dated Jun 9, 1857, recorded on the same day: public auction on Jun 18, at his late place of business, 373 Pa ave, between 4½ & 6th sts, all his stock in trade. –Edw Swann, trustee -Jas C McGuire, auct

Peremptory sale of brick house & lot: on Jun 15, the east half of lot 4 in square 140, fronting 27 feet on L st north, between 18th & 19th sts, running back 110 feet to a 30 foot alley, with a 2 story brick house. By order of heirs. Wall, Barnard, aucts

The annual examination of the *West Point Military Academy* commenced on Jun 2 & has not yet concluded. The following is a list of the first-class. All its members have been in the Academy since July, 1853.

John C Palfrey, Mass
Richd K Meade, jr, Va
Geo C Strong, Mass
E Porter Alexander, Ga
Henry M Robert, Ohio
Thos G Baylor, Va
H S Putnam, N H
J L Kirby Smith, at large
Wm P Smith, Va
Geo A Kensel, Ky
Thos J Berry, Ga
Chas H Morgan, N Y
Abram C Wildrick, N J
Oliver H Fish, Ky
Wm Sinclair, Ohio
Francis Beach, Conn
A G Robinson, Me
Chas J Walker, Ky
Edw R Warner, Pa

Manning M Kimmel, Mo
Geo H Weeks, Me
Sam W Ferguson, S C
J T Magruder, at large
P J Quattlebaum, S C
Amelius F Cone, Ga
Geo A Cunningham, Ala
Harry C McNeill, Texas
Ira W Claflin, Iowa
Edw J Conner, N H
Jos S Conrad, N Y
Lafayette Peck, Tenn
John S Marmaduke, Mo
Geo W Holt, Ala
Robt H Anderson, Ga
Thos J Lee, Iowa
Geo Ryan, Conn
Chas E Farrand, N Y

The delegation from the State of Va in the next Congress will consist of the following gentlemen, all Democrats:

M R H Garnett	Paulus Powell	A G Jenkins
J S Millson	Wm Smith	H A Edmundston
J S Caskie	C J Faulkner	G W Hopkins
Wm O Goode	John Letcher	
T S Bocock	Sherrard Clemens	

Hon Geo W Hopkins is elected to Congress by a majority of 9 votes.

N Y: Jos S Taylor, the Com'r of Streets, died this afternoon, Jun 9.

A fire at Chelsea, Mass, on Monday, midnight, destroyed 19 dwlg-houses, valued at $8,200 each, & nearly all owned by Geo W Gerrish.

Fauquier White Sulphur Springs, Va, now open for public reception.
–Thos B P Ingram, Alex'r Baker

Theoph Herrmann, Teacher in mathematics, surveying, French & German languages, wishes to give lessons to private pupils or in a school. References given. Application made to Mr A Gross, near the Union Bldg.

For sale: a young negro man, competent to wait on table, do house-work in general, or drive a carriage. The subscriber wishes to sell him to a resident of Va, Md, or D C, his object being a good home for him near his family. Address C S Picton, Wash, D C.

A pleasure boat was capsized in Buffalo harbor on Sunday last & the following were drowned: Richd Smithwick, a clerk with Sidney Shephard, hardware merchant, Abraham Smith, clerk with Cone, Levin & Co, & Garret Hays, a clerk.

$200 reward for runaway negro man Jacob Shorter, age 21 years. He has relatives in PG & Anne Arundel counties, Md. –Wm C Fowler, Dunkirk, Calvert Co, Md.

Orphans Court of Wash Co, D C. In the case of Mary A Paine, adm of Orris S Paine, deceased: the administratrix & Court have appointed Jul 7 next for the final settlement of the personal estate of the deceased, with the assets in hand.
–Ed N Roach, Reg/o wills

FRI JUN 12, 1857
Rev Isaac Braman, of Gtwn, Mass, in the course of a few remarks to his society on Sunday last, stated it was 60 years that day since he had been ordained. Mr Braman is now 88 years of age, & is still hale & vigourous.

Promotions & appointments in the Army: since the publication of Gen Orders No 10 of Sep last: Promotions:
Lt Col Danl D Tompkins, Deputy Quartermaster Gen, to be Assist Quartermaster Gen, with the rank of Col, vice Hunt, deceased. Maj H Crossman, Quartermaster, to be Deputy Quartermater Gen, with the rank of Lt Col, vice Tompkins, promoted. Capt Ebenezer S Sibley, Assist Quartermaster, to be Quartermaster, with the rank of Major, vice Crossman, promoted.

Assist Surgeons: Thos C Madison & Jos K Barnes, to be Surgeons.

Corps of Engineers: Capt Geo Dutton, to be Major, vice Chase, deceased; Capt Alex'r H Bowman, to be Major, vice Dutton, promoted; 1st Lt John Adams, to be Capt, vice Radford, resigned, Co F; 1st Lt Jas McIntosh, to be Capt, vice McClellan, resigned, Co D.

2nd Regt of Cavalry: 1st Lt Richd W Johnson, to be Capt, vice O'Hara, resigned, Co F.

Regt of Mounted Riflemen: Lt Col Wm W Loring, to be Col, vice Smith, appointed Brig Gen; Maj Geo B Crittenden, to be Lt Col, vice Loring, promoted; Capt Chas F Ruff, to be Major, vice Crittenden, promoted; 1st Lt Geo McLane, to be Capt, Dec *38, 1856, vice Ruff, promoted, Co I. [*Copied as written.]

2nd Regt of Artl: Lt Col Matthew M Paine, of the 4th Artl, to be Col, vice Bankhead, deceased; Capt Martin Burke, of the 3rd Artl, to be Major, vice Monroe, promoted to 4th Artl.

3rd Regt of Artl: 1st Lt Lucian Loeser, to be Capt, vice Burke, promoted to 2nd Artl, Co I.

4th Regt of Artl: Maj John Munroe, of the 2nd Artl, to be Lt Col, vice Payne, promoted to 2nd Artl; 1st Lt John A Brown, to be Capt, vice Rains, resigned, Co M.

1st Regt of Infty: 1st Lt Theophilus D'Oremieux, to be Capt, vice Eastman, promoted, resigned. 1st Lt Danl Huston, jr, to be Capt, vice D'Oremieux, resigned, Co D.

3rd Regt of Infty: 1st Lt John Trevitt, to be Capt, vice Eaton, resigned, Co F. 2nd Lt John W Alley, to be 1st Lt, vice McFerran, who vacates his regimental commission, Co C.

5th Regt of Infty: Capt Seth Eastman, of the 1st Infty, to be Major, vice La Motte, resigned.

6th Regt of Infty: 1st Lt Franklin F Flint, to be Capt, vice Todd, resigned, Co A. 1st Lt Geo W Lay, to be Capt, vice Woods, appointed Paymaster, Co E.

9th Regt of Infty: 1st Lt Henry M Black, to be Capt, Sep 10, 1856, vice Bowman, deceased, Co G.

Appointments:
Brvt Maj Gen Persifer F Smith, Col of the Regt of Mounted Riflemen, to be Brig Gen, to fill an original vacancy.

Quartermaster's Dept: 1st Lt Geo H Paige, of the 2nd Infty, to be Assist Quartermaster, with the rank of Capt, vice Sibley, promoted. Saml H Montgomery, of Arkansas, Wm R Gibson, of Oregon Territory, Jas A McNutt, of Tenn, & Lawrence Taliaferro, of Pa, to be Military Storekeepers.

Subsistence Dept: Brvt Capt Henry F Clarke, 1st Lt in the 2nd Regt of Artl, to be Commissary of Subsistence, with the rank of Capt, vice Casey, deceased.

Medical Dept: Chas F Alexander, of Arkansas, Bennet A Clements, of N Y, & Lewis Taylor, of Pa, to be Assist Surgeons.

Pay Dept: Brvt Maj Saml Woods, Capt in the 6th Regt of Infty, & Abraham B Ragan, of Ga, to be Paymasters.

Military Academy: Brvt Maj Henry L Kendrick, in the 2nd Regt of Artl, to be Professor of Chemistry, Mineralogy, & Geology, vice Bailey, deceased.

The following promotions & appointments in the army have been made by the Pres since the adjournment of the Senate:

Promotions:

2nd Regt of Artl: 1st Lt Josiah H Carlisle to be Capt, vice Kendrick, appointed Prof of Chemistry, etc, at the Military Academy, Co B.

5th Regt of Infty: 1st Lt Thos H Neill, to be Capt, vice Fowler, resigned, Co C.

9th Regt of Infty: 1st Lt John W Frazer, to be Capt, vice Patterson, resigned, Co C.

Appointments:

Quartermaster's Dept: Chester B White, of Missouri, to be Military Storekeeper.

2nd Regt of Artl-7: Presley O Craig, of Pa, to be 2nd Lt, Co D, Thos E Turner, of Calif, to be 2nd Lt, Co K.

4th Regt of Artl-1: Junius B Roane, of Va, to be 2nd Lt, Co H.

1st Regt of Infty-6: Robt H Offley, of N Y, to be 2nd Lt, Co D.

5th Regt of Infty-2: John Elwood, of Ky, to be 2nd Lt, Co C. Henry D Bristol, of Mich, to be 2nd Lt, Co D.

6th Regt of Infty-3: John Heth, of Kansas, to be 2nd Lt, Co D.

7th Regt of Infty-4: Elias K Potts, of D C, to be 2nd Lt, Co C.

9th Regt of Infty-5: Elisha E Camp, of Illinois, to be 2nd Lt, Co I.

Gen John DeBarth Walbach, the oldest ofcr in the U S army, died at his residence in Balt on Wed night, in his 93rd year. He was born at Alsace, on the Rhine, in Oct, 1764, & entered the military service at an early age. In Dec, 1782, he was ensign in the Royal Alsace regt, [French service,] which belonged to Prince Maximilian, its colonel, who was afterwards the King of Bavaria. In Jan, 1786, he was 2nd lt in the Lauzun Hussars, [French service,] & in May, 1789, was promoted to the post of 1st lt. Returning then to his native country, he entered the German service in Oct, 1793, as a capt in the Rohan Hussars, & in Nov, 1795, received a commission as major in the same corps. In 1796 he came to America, landing in Phil, where in Apr, 1798, be became the volunteer aid-de-camp of Brig Gen McPherson, [subsequently in the U S service.] His father, having a large estate in this country, located at Phil & in Va. Young Walbach determined upon studying law, & for that purpose went to the ofc of Alex'r Hamilton, at N Y. But, having a fondness for the life of a soldier, he applied for & obtained on Jan 10, 1799, a commission as lt of cavalry in the army of the U S. Gen Walbach's first active service in the army of the U S was as an aid to Gen Wilkinson on the frontier; in the war of 1812-14 he bore a conspicuous part, & was twice breveted for gallant conduct. In 1807 he married a lady of Phil, from which marriage there is one son & 3 daughters living. In his earlier life he commanded at Portsmouth, N H; at Frankford arsenal, at Old Point Comfort, & at Annapolis. He resided in Balt a number of years, & was generally esteemed & respected. On Sunday evening last he was attacked with hernia of the abdomen, & sunk rapidly until he died.

N Y, Jun 10. John C Stevens, well-known as an enterprising ship-builder, died today at Hoboken. He was at the head of the N Y Yacht Club.

A scene of violence yesterday at the lager-beer saloon of Jos Gerhard, on Md ave, when 3 men from Alexandria, Rudd, Smith, & Hall, called for & obtained drink at Gerhard's, for which they refused to pay. An altercation ensued, in which Mrs Gerhard participated; Henry Shulte, the barkeeper, assisted his employers. Outside the parties freely used sticks & stones; Gerhard advanced with a pistol, & as Gerhard prepared to fire Shulte turned himself around in front of Gerhard and received the shot in the breast. Poor Shulte fell & almost instantly expired. Gerhard was arrested, & after hearing 21 witnesses, Gerhard was held to bail in the sum of $3,000. John Robinson, one of the navy yard men, was arrested as a participant in the riot, & held to $300 bail for futher examination. The ofcrs have been dispatched to Alexandria to secure the arrest of the others involved in the violence. [Jun 13th newspaper: Investigation yesterday ended with the Magistrate's holding Hall & Ellet to bail each in the sum of $266 for appearance at Court, & the discharge of Robinson.]

On Sat last Col Jas Price, an old citizen of Clark Co, Ky, & his son, were found lying on a public road in that county, weltering in their blood; the son was shot by a bullet from a revolver, & the father received the contents of a double-barrel gun. Both were breathing when found, the father may recover, but the son is not expected to survive. The Cincinnati Commercial states that Mrs Price was the author of an article in the Ohio Farmer, to which a man named Gay took exception as personal to himself. Meeting Col Price riding along the road, he fired upon him, & upon young Price interfering, shot him down also, & then escaped.

SAT JUN 13, 1857
Appointments by the Pres: 1-Wm B Gere Marshal for the Territory of Minnesota, vice Irwin, resigned. 2-B F Cheatham, of Tenn, Consul at Aspinwall.

Spiritualism claims 2 more suicides. Geo Stiles, of Milford, Wisc, shot himself through the heart last week, & a day or two afterwards, his uncle, Wm [letters missing,] stabbed himself with the shank of a hay fork. –Balt American

Dr Thos Y Simons died suddenly in Charleston, S C, of an attack of apoplexy. He was in a few days of completing the 60th year of his age.

The N Y papers announce the death, on Wed last, of John C Stevens, extensively known for his connexion with American yachting. He was intimately concerned with his brothers, Edwin & the late Robt L, in organizing & controlling the Camden & Amboy railroad. He leaves a large estate at Camden, together with handsome possessions in different other localitles.

The Rt Rev Dr Phelan, Bishop of the Roman Catholic diocese of Kingston, Canada, died on Jun 6. Bishop Phelan was born in Ireland, in the diocese of Ossary, Feb 1, 1795, & was in his 63rd year at the time of his death. He emigrated to Canada at a very early age, & was educated at the college of Montreal, being called to the priesthood in 1825. He was appointed coadjutor Bishop of Carsha in 1843; became administrator of the diocese of Kingston in 1852; on the death of Bishop Gaulin he was appointed in May last to the titular bishopric of that diocese, but had only held the ofc one month & 2 days when he died. He caught a severe cold when attending to the grave the remains of his friend & predecessor the late Bishop of Kingston. This finally settled upon his lungs, & resulted in death.

Lt Col Henry Bainbridge, who was recently lost by the burning of the steamer **Louisiana**, near Galveston, was attached to the 1st regt U S Infty. He graduated from West Point in 1821, & was brevetted during the Mexican war for gallant conduct. [Jun 15th newspaper: Col Henry Bainbridge was the son of John Taylor Bainbridge, a distinguished lawyer of N Y, & a nephew of the late Com Bainbridge, of the U S Navy. Col Bainbridge was on his return home on leave of absence to visit his now desolate wife. His age was about 54. –Springfield [Mass] Republican]

Christopher C Sharp, the murderer of Dr Stout, escaped from the State prison at *Fort Madison*, Iowa, some months ago, by the stratagen of making a dummy. He then went to Tenn & married a young girl of 16, the daughter of a wealthy & respectable citizen of that State. His wife discovered his whereabouts visited him, & had him arrested for bigamy. He has just been returned to his old quarters in prison in Iowa.

Col H W Hunt, editor of the Corrector, published at Sag Harbor, died at his residence there on May 31. He was in his 83rd year, & had been editor for the last 36 years.

Jefferson Randall, who had been sent from Rockingham Co, Va, by a vigilance cmte for numerous alleged lawless acts, was held in custody to see if he could not be surrendered into the hands of the law on legal proof. Not being able to accomplish that object, the cmte on Tue took him out & hung him on a tree until he was dead. Jones, a son-in-law of Randall, was also in the custody of the cmte, & was to have been hung on Wed.

Mrd: on Jun 11, at Balt, Md, by Rev Mr Seeley, John L Smith, of Wash, to Virginia C Smith, daughter of Jas Lownds, of the former place.

Mr Russell Hubbard, of Norwich, Conn, feeling unwell on Sunday, took some brandy mixing with it, as he supposed, some laudanum, to increase its efficacy. He became worse & found he had taken by mistake a solution of corrosive sublimate. He died that evening.

N Y, Jun 11. 1-The city has experienced a serious loss in the death of Dr Alex'r F Veche, a prominent physician, who, in the cholera season of 1832, was very active & useful. He was the author of several treatises on the subject of cholera. 2-Wm Browning & Chas B Minor, of New London, Conn, have been arrested, per direction of the Com'r of Pensions, for the perpetration of frauds on his bureau in order to obtain bounty land warrants. They are now in prison, awaiting examination. -Star

There no longer remains a doubt as to the fate of young Mr Dixon, late of Alexandria, who was lost at the destruction of the steamer **Louisiana**, on May 31, in Galveston Bay. He was the only & cherished son of fond parents, a youth of high promise & fine talents. We share with them the grief they experience.
--Alexandria Gaz

Died: yesterday, Geo McNeir, in his 64th year. His funeral will be on Sunday at 3 o'clock, from Wesley Chapel.
+
Members of the Levy Court are invited to attend the funeral of the late Geo McNeir, a member of the Court, from his residence on F st, between 6th & 7th sts, on Sunday, at 3 o'clock. –Nich Callan, Sec
+
Soldiers of the War of 1812 are invited to attend the funeral of their deceased brother, Maj Geo McNeir, at his late dwlg on F st, one door west of 6th st, on Sunday next, at 2 o'clock.

The news from Calif gives details of the massacre of Capt H A Crabbe & his party. Crabbe himself was led out alone, his arms tied above his head to a post, & his body riddled by a hundred bullets. It is feared that some general plan of revenge against the Mexicans will be adopted.

Piney Point Pavilion wil be opened on Jun 20 for a limited number of guests. Since the destruction of 73 rooms last winter, the properitor regrets he will be unable to accommodate excursions bringing the masses for the present. –W W Dix

Orphans Court of Wash Co, D C. Letters testamentary on the personal estate of John Ousley, late of Wash Co, deceased. –N Callan, exc

MON JUN 15, 1857
Public auction, on Jun 25, that valuable property at the west end of G st, known as the *Fry Property*, containing about 26,550 feet of ground, with a large brick bldg. Terms at sale. -Jas C McGuire, auct

N Y, Jun 13. 1-John Newton, son of Cmdor Newton, U S navy, was found on Friday night lying in an insensible condition at Front & Fulton sts. There was a deep gash over his left eye & a contused wound on the back of his head. Foul play is suspected, & a post mortem examination was ordered. 2-The Rockville Republican contains an account of the death of Miss Sarah J Colburne, of Chaplin, from the bite of a common black spider.

Mrd: on Apr 21, at Pass Christian, Miss, at the residence of Wm B Lightfoot, by Rev Dr Savage, Dr Philip L Lightfoot, of Green Co, Ala, to Miss Isabella Drummond.

Died: on Jun 14, Mr Thos Davidson Brooks, son of Mr Lewis Brooks, of Gtwn, in his 25th year. In the death of this exemplary young man, the 6th member of the family in less than 4 years, the bereaved relatives have the assurance that he was cheered to the last by the Christian's well-founded hope. His funeral will take place, from the residence of his father, on Tue morning, at 10 o'clock.

The Board of Managers of the Wash City Protestant Orphans' Asylum gratefully acknowledge the receipt of the following donations & collections taken in churches since their annual meeting in Jan last; from Mrs Susan Ireland, $500; Col Larned, $100; Miss Coleman, $50; Mrs Wm T Carroll, $25; Mrs Col Freeman, $25; Mrs Ann W Smith, $20; Mr B V Read, $10; Miss Virginia Tayloe, $10; Mr Vaughn, $10; Mrs Holt, $5; Mrs S H Hill, $5; Mrs Thornton, $5; White & Co, $5; Rev Mr Cummins, of Trinity Church, $351; Rev Mr Hall, Church of the Epiphany, $187; Rev Mr Sunderland, of Frist Presbyterian Church, $150; St John's Church, Rev Dr Pyne, $128; Rev Mr Samson, Baptist Church, $84; Rev Mr Carothers, Presbyterian Church, $64; Rev Mr Finkle, German Reformed Church, $40; Rev Mr Morsell, Christ Church, $32. Donations: from Mr Gideon, printing 150 reports, also re-binding & adding to the book of minutes; Maj Bacon & his regt a barrel of bread, a basket of meat, & 20 yards of cotton; Messrs Farnham & Clubb, 4½ dozen books & 6 atlases. By order of the Board, Susan R Coxe, Sec -Wash, Jun 11, 1857

Toledo, Jun 12. Return J M Ward, who was convicted of the murder of his wife at Sylvania, Ohio, in Feb last, was hung in this city today. He confessed to the murder of 2 men & his wife.

Valuable farm for sale: desirous to move to the West: farm in Montg Co, Md, 295 acres of land; with a brick dwlg with 16 rooms & out bldgs of every description. Address or inquire of the subscriber, living on the premises, near Forest Oak post ofc, Montg Co, Md, or of Hutchinson Munro, Pa ave, Wash. —Jos Thompson

TUE JUN 16, 1857
Valley View Farm at auction: on Jun 30, the late residence of the late John H King, containing about 50 acres, well known to be one of the most beautiful & desirable pieces of property on the picturesque heights of Gtwn, D C: the bldgs are a large family residence, a small cottage for a gardener's family, & necessary out-bldgs. -Ellen J King, admx -E S Wright, auct [Jul 3rd newspaper: *Valley View Farm* at auction on Jul 9th.]

T H Barron, House Carpenter & Builder: Shop one door from 7th st, on Louisiana ave; residence 169 South G st, between 4½ & 6th sts.

Criminal Court-Wash: present his Hon T Hartley Crawford, Judge. Grand Jury:

Geo W Riggs	Jos C G Kennedy
Geo McCeney	Buckner Bayliss
Wm A Bradley	Geo C Ames
Jas E Morgan	Lewis Carbery
Geo S Gideon	Darius Clagett
Joshua Peirce	Alex Hamilton Dode
Robt S Patterson	Isaac Clark
Geo A Bohrer	Thos J Galt
Wm J Stone, sr	Saml Bacon
Wm T Dove	Wm B Todd
John P Ingle	Jonathan Prout
Z W McKnew	Lawrence A Gobright

Petit Jury:

Danl Lightfoot	A Lewis Newton
Wm T Jones	Benj E Gittings
Seraphim Masi	John E Kendall
John W Ott	Saml Stott
Robt H Harrison	John E Neale
Geo M Sothoron	Z K Offutt
Jas B Holmead	Abraham Butler
John T Bradley	Thos J Davis
Robt H Watkins	Wm Van Reswick
Jas Barnes	Southey S Parker
Thos J Williams	Jas Fullalove
Jas M Taylor	N Boyd Brooks
Saml McKnight	Alfred Ray
Francis B Lord	Peter Hepburn
Thos D Larner	Aaron Divine

For sale: bldg lot fronting Conn ave, on 17th st, between north I &K sts, on the same square of Mrs Gen Macomb's residence, being lot No 31, in square 126. -A Green auct

Trustee's sale of Dry Goods, furniture, china glass, crockery, cigars, & looking glass, at auction, by deed of trust from Jos F Crown: all the Merchandise at the store of said Crown, 335 Pa ave, between 6th & 7th sts. -A Green auct

Executor's sale of 30 bldgs lots in Wash City, belonging to the estate of the late Col Saml Miller, deceased, at auction, on Jun 29, by order of the executor, at my auction room, 526 7th st, Wash. –Francis Peters, exc -A Green auct

Obit-died: on Jun 7, 1857, at his residence in Wash City, Maj Wm Bushrod Scott, who was born in the State of Md on Jul 28, 1792. Maj Scott was one of the children of Gust Scott & Mary Hall Caile, who resided on the Eastern Shore of Md, & who removed to Washington at the earnest solicitation of Gen Washington, whose friendship the family ever retained. In early life their son Wm was placed in the marine corps, &, if he had continued in the navy, would have been next in rank to the present gallant Gen Henderson. After retiring from the navy, Maj Scott was for some years in the Legislature of Md. After his removal to this city he held several positions in the city councils, until he was appointed by Pres Van Buren navy agent at Washington, which position he occupied for about 8 years, until his removal by Pres Taylor.

Valuable real estate at private sale: with a view of closing the trust estate of the late Mrs Margaretta Nicols, under the deed of trust of Nov 19, 1855, recorded among the land record books of Anne Arundel & PG Co, Md: at the request of R Nicols Snowden, residing on said estate, offers for private sale on Jul 1 next: contains 1,200 acres of land adjoining the Depot at Laurel Factory. The dwlg house is of brick, large, nearly new, & all suitable out-houses on the estate. –Frank H Stockett, trustee

Died: on May 12, 1857, at Norfolk, Va, in her 26th year, Emily C, wife of Brev Maj Henry J Hunt, Capt 2nd Artl, & daughter of Lt Col B E De Russey, Corps of Engineers, U S Army.

The ***Bonaparte Estate*** at public sale: on Jun 24, at the Merchants' Exchange, N Y, the extensive park & grounds of Henry Beckett, at Bordentown, N J, formerly the property of Jos Bonaparte, containing 234 acres of land; a large & very handsome modern mansion, about 60 feet square; handsomely furnished throughout. Apply to Albert N Nicolay, auct, N Y. [Jun 29th newspaper: there were no bidders last Wed, although the auctioneer offered to commence with a bid of $60,000 for property which it is said cost $200,000.]

Cincinnati, Jun 13. This forenoon, as 4 of the U S deputy marshals were arresting a fugitive slave & his wife, the slave stabbed one of them, Mr J C Elliott, with a long sword knife, upon which another of the marshals shot the slave in the abdomen 4 times. The marshal's wound is dangerous, & the negro's is considered to be mortal.

Columbus, Jun 15. W H Gibson, the State Treasurer, has resigned. A deficit of over half a million having been discovered in the treasury, Mr Gibson says the deficit existed when he took office, & that it was caused by the defalcation of John G Breslin, the former State Treasurer. The Govn'r has appointed a cmte to investigate the affair.

Land Warrant No 89,597, for 120 acres, issued on Jan 7, 1857, in the name of Alfred Johnson, as reported by the Pension Ofc & sent to me, not having been received, this notice is given to enable the claimant to obtain a duplicate land warrant in lieu of said lost warrant. –J P Neely

WED JUN 17, 1857
Ex-Govn'r P F Thomas, of Md, has declined the Pres' tender to him of the Govnership of Utah, made some time since.

The graduates of the Naval Academy, who graduated last week at Annapolis, Md, & who have been warranted as passed midshipmen in the navy:

1-F B Blake
2-J W Alexander
3-H D Todd
4-C J Graves
5-J M Prichett
6-E Terry
7-B Wilson
8-T M Mills
9-M Bunce
10-J W Kelly
11-H B Seely
12-F V McNair
13-A B Yates
14-H W Miller
15-C Merchant

The following passed midshipmen have been detailed for service on the U S steam frig **Minnesota**: F B Blake, H D Todd, C Y Graves, E Terry, H B Seely, F V McNair, & H W Miller. The following midshipmen have been ordered to join the U S steamship **Mississippi**: J M Pritchett, T B Wilson, T B Mills, & A R Yates.

We learn at the instance of Gen Jas L Maguire, special agent of the Post Ofc Dept, Mr Hughes, deputy U S marshal for Western Va, on Fri last, arrested Thos E Day, postmaster of Green Spring Run, Hampshire Co, Va, charged with opening a registered letter containing an article of value after the ofc had been discontinued by the Dept. -Sun

Trustee's sale of unimproved property: on Jun 24, by deed of trust from Edmund Briscoe, dated Oct 8, 1856, recorded in Liber J A S No 122, folios 193, of the land records of Wash Co: lots 2 & 3 in square 593; lots 4 thru 7, 13 thru 17, in square 1,009; lots 1 thru 5 in square 1,031. –Jno R Ashby, trustee -Jas C McGuire, auct

Land Warrant No 46, 507, for 160 acres, issued Oct 21, 1856, in the name of John Rutledge, as reported by the Pension Ofc & sent to me, not having been received, this notice is to obtain a duplicate land warrant. -John F Webb

Crabbe's expedition: the following are the names of the unfortunate persons who fell in the late filibuster expedition to Sonora, in Mexico:
San Joaquin: Henry A Crabbe
Contra Costra: R N Wood, H McCoun, M Porter, F Perkins, E Tucker, Geo Gill
Tuolumne: John D Oxley, D S McDowell, H L Watts, Benj E Gillion, Geo E Hoyt, Wm Wilson, Thos Coates, Dr Thos J Oxley, Chas E Parker, Jas McGraw, T R Taylor, John Edmondson, Dr Evans, Chas A Lewis, Wm Anderson, J M McFaul, Jas W Woods, Saml Kemmel, W N Miller, J G Carrison, Wm Randolph, Wm A Allen, Thos Crain, A Allen, E Chaplin, S Bunker, B Quarles, W J Vandorne.
Solano: Robt M Holladay, Thos M Maupin, B C Hendricks, Wm Stephenson, Hugh Seaton.
Marin: Geo T King, John Lamarue.
San Francisco: J W Evans, John H Cortelyou, F B Wilder, Richd Perry.
Yreka: Chas W Tozer, Robt C Wood
Unknown: F Hohenhausen, A Hine, Robt Rutton, Edw Kaufman, R W Madison, E O Wilcox

Land Warrant No 46, 507, for 160 acres, issued on Oct 21, 1856, in the name of John Rutledge, as reported by the Pension Ofc & sent to me, not having been received, this notice is given to enable the claimant to obtain a duplicate land warrant.
-John F Webb

The Richmond [Ky] Messenger of Jun 5 states that Edw Hawkins, who was hung on May 29, at Irvine, Ky, met death boldly & fearlessly. He denied being related to little Harpe, of notorious memory; had only committed 4 murders; had 6 wives, 5 living, & the 7th in progress of courtship, & he was not 21 years old when he forfeited his life to the law.

Mrd: on Jun 16, in Wash City, by Rev Fr Young, Dr John C Riley to Rebecca, daughter of Maj Park G Howle, U S Marine Corps, all of Washington.

Obit-died: on Jun 12, Geo McNeir, of a disease supposed to have been contracted at the Nat'l Hotel. He was in his 64th year. It is stated by one who knew him well that during the invasion of his native State of Md by the British forces in 1814 he was promptly at the post of duty; for many years he filled the ofc of postmaster at Annapolis; was appointed an ofcr in the House of Reps, in which capacity he had charge of the funeral cortege which accompanied the remains of ex-Pres John Quincy Adams to Mass; recently was appointed by Pres Buchanan one of the Judges of the Levy Cout for Wash Co. During the space of 45 years Maj McNeir has been an exemplary member, filling many important official stations, in the Methodist Episcopal Church. The veterans of the war of 1812 & a large body of sympathizing friends attended his remains to **Greenwood Cemetery** on Sunday, Rev Mr Kres having previously preached, at Wesley Chapel, a most eloquent sermon, founded on the theme of a Christian soldier who had fought the good fight.

THU JUN 18, 1857
Household & kitchen furniture at auction on: Jun 25, at the residence of J Madison Cutts, on 15th st, between G & H sts. -J C McGuire, auct

Household & kitchen furniture at auction on: Jun 22, at the residence of Lt Balch, of the U S navy, in the navy yard. -A Green auct

The Examination at West Point: the following named gentlemen, who had been, as usual, invited by the Sec of War to attend the examination of Cadets, constituted the Board of Visiters for the present year:
1-Saml H Blake, Maine
2-Col Benj F Butler, Mass
3-Henry C Deming, Conn
4-Gen Noble P Elderkin, N Y
5-Gen Conrad Schiemer, Pa
6-Prof Campbell Morfitt, Md
7-Col Galloway, N C
8-Gen Paul Simmes, Ga
9-Robt B Lindsay, Ala
10-Dr Edw H Bryan, Miss
11-Col L G DeRussy, absent, La
12-Geo W Houk, Ohio
13-Maj Wm H Chase, Fla
14-Rev J Phelps, Iowa
15-Prof Reed, Wisc

For promotion in Engineers, Topographical Engineers, Ordnance, Artl, Infty, Dragoon, Mounted Riflemen or Cavalry.
1-John C Palfrey
2-Richd K Meade, jr
3-E Porter Alexander
4-Henry M Robert

Topographical Engineers, Ordnance, Artl, Infty, Dragoon, Mounted Riflemen or Cavalry:
5-Geo C Strong
6-J L Kirby Smith
7-Thos G Baylor
8-Haldemann S Putnam
9-Wm S Smith

Ordnance, Artl, Infty, Dragoon, Mounted Riflemen or Cavalry
10-Geo A Kensel
11-Thos J Berry
12-Chas H Morgan
13-Oliver H Fish
14-Abraham C Wilderick
15-Chas J Walker
16-Francis Beach
17-Wm Sinclair
18-Augustus G Robinson
19-Saml W Ferguson
20-Marcus A Read
21-Edw R Warner
22-Manning M Kimmel
23-Geo A Weeks
24-John T Magruder
25-Geo A Cunningham
26-Henry C McNeil
27-Ira W Claflin

Infty, Dragoon, Mounted Riflemen or Cavalry:
28-Aurelius F Cone
29-Paul J Quattlebaum
30-John S Marmaduke
31-Geo W Holt
32-Jos S Conrad
33-Edw J Conner
34-Geo Ryan
35-Robt H Anderson
36-Chas E Farrand
37-Thos J Lee
38-Lafayette Peck

Mrd: on Jun 16, in Frederick, by Rev Fr Villiger, Dr Florence O'Donnoghue, of PG Co, Md, to Nellie M, daughter of the late Lt Jos Stallings, U S N.

Mrd: on Jun 17, at Wesley Chapel, by Rev Wm Krebs, Milton C Dove, of Montg Co, Md, to Mary F, daughter of Jas Lawrenson, of Wash City.

Orphans Court of Wash Co, D C. In the case of Jas H Durham, adm of Robt A Carter, deceased: the administrator & Court have appointed Jul 7th next, for the final settlement of the personal estate of the deceased, with the assets in hand.
–Ed N Roach, Reg/o wills

Orphans Court of Wash Co, D C. In the case of Christiana Railey, admx of Benedict J L Railey, deceased: the administratrix & Court have appointed Jul 11th next, for the final settlement of the personal estate of the deceased, with the assets in hand.
–Ed N Roach, Reg/o wills

Orphans Court of Wash Co, D C. In the case of Wm A Rich, adm de bonis non of Com Chas W Morgan, deceased: the administrator & Court have appointed Jul 11th next, for the final settlement of the personal estate of the deceased, with the assets in hand.
–Ed N Roach, Reg/o wills

On Thu Mr Jerome Edgar was shot twice by Mr John M Clay, in this city. Edgar had been in the merchant tailor's store room of Geo A Bowyer, on Main st, in conversation, when Clay came in with his pistol in his hand, & shot Edgar. Edgar is in a fair way of recovery. The ofcrs have not yet found Clay.
–Lexington [Ky] Observer

Trustee's sale of large brick house & lot on 6th st, between C & Louisiana ave: by deed of trust from John E Clokey, dated Nov 26, 1855, recorded in Liber J A S No 108, folios 425 thru 429, of the land records in Wash Co, D C: sale of part of lot 6 in square 459, fronting 25 feet on 6th st, with a good brick house containing 10 good rooms & other necessary out-bldgs. –Wm H Ward, trustee -A Green auct

Trustee's sale under decree of the Circuit Court of Wash Co, D C, in a cause wherein Francis Wheatley & others are cmplnts, & Chas H Winder & Wm H Winder are dfndnts, being No 1037 in equity: auction on Jul 10, on the premises, lots 1 thru 6 in square 170, Wash City. –W Redin, trustee -A Green auct

Administrator's sale of 2 handsome bldg lots on Mass, between 13th & 14th sts, at auction, on Jun 24, on the corner lot at Vt ave & N st, lots G & H, in subdivision of original lot 17 in square 247. –P Hannay, adm -A Green auct

Died: on Sunday last, at the Infirmary, in Wash City, aged about 28 years, Mr John H Kaibel, a German, who was shot just below the knee, at the first precinct of the 4th Ward, on Jun 1, by the fire of the marines.

On Wed last Mr Chas P Prather, the engineer at Grove, Griswold & Co's foundry, was instantly killed when the strap on an emory-wheel broke, catching the iron in its revolution, throwing it with such force against the head of Mr Prather as to completely smash in the skull producing instant death. –Terre Haute Journal

FRI JUN 19, 1857
Hostilities of the plains: correspondence of the St Louis Republican, near *Fort Riley*, Jun 9, 1857. One of the survivors, Mr A P Weaver, has reached this place, & makes the following statement: on Jun 6th, about 150 Indians, mounted, charged on our train & surrounded it. They commenced firing & killed S D Weaver, M Lewis, & Saml Smith. The wounded are J Houston, J Smith, & a woman, name unknown. Capt Hendrickson, with 2 companies of the 6th infty, who had just arrived here from *Fort Leavenworth*, has gone out to bring in the survivors. This may be looked upon as the commencement of the Cheyenne war. Col Sumer has gone out after this tribe.

Surviving soldiers of the War of 1812 met yesterday, in Wash City. Members of the association answered to their names:

W W Seaton	F R Dorsett	Wm Miles
Jno S Williams	John Varden	Jas Lawrenson
St John B Skinner	Peter Bergman	John S Anderson
Richd Burgess	Wm Clark	Paul Stevens
Dr Wm Jones	Chas Fletcher	Michl Caton
W P Young	David Kuntz	Thos Quantrill
Jas Andrew Kennedy	Saml B Beach	Edw Semmes
Isaac Holland	Thos Donoho	Theodore Mead
John Sessford	Almon Baldwin	
John Allen	Edw Lacy	

Mr John Jones, of Delaware, also came to attend the meeting.

Orphans Court of Wash Co, D C. Letters testamentary on the personal estate of Saml Champion, late of Wash Co, deceased. –Richd A Boarman, Wm Little, excs

Died: on Jun 18, in Wash City, in her 88th year, Mrs Eliz Dove, consort of the late Thos Dove, formerly of Anne Arundel Co, Md. The deceased has been a resident of Wash City for more than 57 years. Her funeral will take place on Jun 19, at 8 o'clock P M, from the residence of her son-in-law, Saml Harkness, 7 K st, between 8th & 9th sts.

Died: on Jun 11, at the residence of his son, in the county of Morrow, State of Ohio, Thos Levering, a native of Phil & long a resident of Wash City.

Died: May 18, after a severe illness of seven weeks, Mary Frances, aged 2 years, 7 months & 2 days, youngest daughter of Wm & Catharine Bagnam. Her funeral will take place on Jun 19, at 5 o'clock, from her father's residence, on 18th st, between E & F sts.

Died: on Jun 17, Saml Vivans, 3rd son of S B & Marie C Waite, aged 8 years, 2 months & 16 days.

It is now pretty certain that Theodore Maria Ganz, who was killed on the railroad on Tue, committed suicide. He doubtless walked deliberately to the railroad, when he saw the train approaching drew his hat over his head & laid upon the track. It seems that it was disappointment in love which led to the suicide. –Rochester Union

San Antonio, May 29, 1857. News received of the murder of a Mexican woman, named Garsa. Warrant was issued for Bill Hart & 2 confederates of his, Wood & Miller. Ofcr Fieldstop with a warrant went to arrest Hart. Fieldstop shot Wood dead, & Miller attempted to interfere, & he was shot down. Fieldstop was shot just above the left eye. Three men dead, & the daring desperado Hart still lived, determined to resist to the last. Matters remained in this position for awhile, when Capt Jas Taylor, from Attacosa, with several others, made a rush for the door, which, being locked, broke it open, when Bill Hart, who was standing behind it, shot Taylor in the breast; but before he fell he drew his revolver & shot Hart, who fell mortally wounded. Taylor is likely to recover.

SAT JUN 20, 1857
Trustee's sale of valuable improved property: by deed of trust from Jas H Boss & wife, & Geo W Donn, trustee, dated Aug 11, 1855, recorded in Liber J A S No 102, of the land records of Wash Co, D C: public auction of part of lot 1 in square 517, with bldgs, consisting of a large 3 story frame bldg in complete repair.
-Chas S Wallach, J C C Hamilton, trustees -J C McGuire, auct

Proposals will be received until Jun 27, for grading 5th st, between Pa ave & B st. –Stephen Coster, Com'r Wards 5 & 6. -John W Meade, E G Handy, Assist Com'rs.

Closing out sale of fancy goods jewelry, on Jun 22, at the store of Messrs Samstag & Bro, on Pa ave. -Wall, Barnard, aucts

Tornado on Sat passed over Utica; at Deerfield, & Mr Warren saw it approaching his dwlg, & rushed in seized 2 of his children & rushed for the cellar, urging his wife to follow him with another. Before his wife had done so the tornado struck the bldg, leaving it a perfect wreck, killing her & dangerously injuring the child. A barn belonging to M Budlong, & another owned by John M Budlong, were crushed to pieces.

Hon Augustus Young, State Naturalist & formerly a member of Congress from Vt, died at his residence in St Albans on Jun 17.

List of candidates for Congress in the different districts in Tenn:

American:	Democrat:
Hon N G Taylor	W H Maxwell
Horace Maynard	A C Graham
Col Wm Heiskell	W W Wallace
Gen J G Pickett	Hon S A Smith
Hon C Ready	Col J H Savage
No opposition	Col J C Guild
No opposition	Hon G W Jones
F K Zollicoffer	Hon J V Wright
Hon E Etheridge	No opposition
W H Stephens	Gen J C D Atkins
	W T Avery

St Mary's School, Raleigh, N C: the 31st term of this school will begin on Jul 8. Punctual attendance of the pupils is desired. –Rev Albert Smedes, D D, Rector

On Jun 15 Ruth Gove & Mary & Abby Foss, operatives in the Whitehouse Mill, Gonic, N H, visited Plains village in a chaise for shopping purposes; returning at night, they extended their ride onto the Bridge, where the carriage struck a passing wheelbarrow & threw them all out. Ruth Gove & Mary Foss fell off the bridge into the river & both drowned. Abby Foss, a young woman, received severe injuries.

A lady, Mrs Sarah Henderson, residing in Cincinnati, being indisposed a few days ago, took a dose, as she thought, of Epsom salts, but it proved to be oxalic acid, which resulted in her death in 20 minutes. She leaves & husband & 6 children.

Mrd: on May 20, near Livingston, Miss, by Rev Dr T C Thornton, Col Wm C Love to Mary Louisa, eldest daughter of Rev D S Goodloe, all of Madison Co, Miss.

Mrd: on Jun 18, in Wash City, at McKendree Chapel, by Rev John Lanahan, Rev L D Walter, of Phil Conference, to Miss Mary A Suter, of Wash City.

Died: on Jun 18, in Wash City, Mary, wife of Jas Miller, [formerly of Scotland, but for the last 12 years a resident of Wash City,] in her 38th year. Her funeral is tomorrow at 4 o'clock, from her late residence, 13 13½ st, between C & D sts.

Died: on Jun 16, at the residence of Mrs Major Walker, near Rock Creek Church, Harry Parker, infant son of Lt Jno H & Kate A Upshur, aged 4 months.

New Ice-cream Saloon, [up Stairs.] The subscriber has fitted up a saloon over his store for the accommodation of ladies & gentlemen, where they can be supplied with the very best of Ice-cream & Confectionary, on reasonable terms. Give me a call. –U H Ridenour, 307 Pa ave, Wash.

MON JUN 22, 1857
The examination at the Naval Academy at Annapolis terminated last Wed. None of the graduating class failed. Francis B Blake, son of Capt Blake, U S Navy, took the first honors. Prayers were by Rev Theo B Barton, & the class of graduates was addressed by Cmder Thos Jefferson Page, who was deputed to perform the duty of Capt Goldsborough & the Board of Visiters.

Valuable farm & beautiful country residence at public sale: on Jun 39, the late country residence of A Hoover, deceased, lying in Alexandria Co, Va, 1 mile from Gtwn; contains about 160 acres; the dwlg is nearly new, is 42 feet square, surrounded with a 10 foot wide portico, large parlors, roomy hall, 5 large chambers, kitchen, bath-room, water-closet, & every modern convenience; also new barns sheds, stables, & styes. –A P Hoover -Wall, Barnard, aucts

Trustee's sale of valuable bldg lots, fronting on Mass ave, between 13th & 14th sts: by deed of trust, dated Jul 3, 1854, recorded in Liber J A S No 80, folios 51 to 54, of the land records of Wash Co, D C: sale of lot 17 in square 247, on Mass ave, next to the corner of 13th st. –J T Stevens, trustee -A Green auct

We have already recorded the death of 7 children of Rev B Hutchins, of Albion, Ill, formerly of York, Pa. The Grayville Herald contains an obituary of the 8th, a daughter 7 years old. Within a few weeks the parents have buried 8 out of 9, all from scarlet fever.

Boarding: Mrs S Crooks, 286 N Y ave, between 6th & 7th sts, can accommodate several gentlemen with good rooms & excellent board on reasonable terms.

Prof D Barton Ross, author of the Southern Speaker & other class books, attempted to commit suicide in Petersburg, Va, on Thu, by taking chloroform & stabbing himself in the region of the heart with a clasp knife. On Friday little hope was entertained of his recovery. The wound was inflicted while shut up in his room at Powell's Hotel. On the bed were letters addressed to his friends & wife, indicating disappointment & depression of spirits

Aunt Till, a slave belonging to Capt Lewis Bissell, of this neighborhood, died on Jun 8, at the advanced age of 130 years. Such an instance of longevity has not come under our observation for many years. –St Louis Democrat

In Hamilton Co, Ohio, Wat Eckman, said to be a wealthy man, was taken violently ill on Jun 15 & died. The next morning the body was coffined & taken to the church, where a funeral sermon was preached. The choir was singing, when interrupted by kicks on the inside of the coffin. The coffin was opened & Mr Eckman was alive & kicking. At last accounts he was able to walk about his room.

Jackson, who murdered Morris, in Lake Co, Ill last fall, suffered capital punishment on Friday in the presence of 25,000 spectators. The place of execution was about 3 miles from Chicago. He confessed his crime 3 days previous.

Criminal Court-Wash-Sat: 1-John McLaughlin was tried for petty larceny, & the jury found him guilty. He was sentenced to one year's imprisonment in jail. 2-Thos Fletcher, colored, was found guilty of assault & battery on Ellen Bruce, also colored, with felonious intent. He was sentenced to 3 years in the penitentiary. 3-Adolphus Barker, a colored man, indicted for malicious mischief, was sentenced to pay a fine of $5 & costs. 4-Jos Penny, colored, was found guilty for larceny in stealing boots & shoes. He was sentenced to the penitentiary for 18 months.

Mrd: on Jun 9, by Rev J Peterkin, of St James' Church, Richmond, E H Skinker, of the city of Richmond, to Roberta R, daughter of Col Henry T Garnett, of Ingleside, Westmoreland Co, Va.

Died: on Jun 18, in Loudoun Co, Va, Mrs Jane Wells, in her 39th year, consort of Thos C Wells, of Wash City.

Died: on Jun 19, at the residence of Mrs L Allen, of bilious & nervous fever, Miss Juliet H P Grimes, only daughter of Warren Grimes, of PG Co, Md. This estimable young lady leaves a large circle of friends to mourn their irreparable loss. Her remains will be taken to her native place.

TUE JUN 23, 1857
Household & kitchen furniture at auction on: Jun 26, at the residence of Mr S Good, corner of 24th & M sts. Nearly new & well kept. Wall, Barnard, aucts

In pursuance of the provisions of a deed of trust from Wm H Faulkner to the undersigned trustee, dated May 26, 1853, recorded in Liber J A S No 56, folio 293, I shall sell on Jul 6 next, lot 25, Reservation A, on the south side of Pa ave, between 3rd & 4th sts, on which is erected a new first class brick bldg, now occupied by said Faulkner. Title indisputable. –Andrew Wylie, trustee -Jas C McGuire, auct

Mr Louis Byer, of John, a young man from Hagerstown, Md, who was returning from the West, on Sunday fell from the car near Hancock, & the whole train passing over him, he was instantly killed.

Mrs Eliz Grumby committed suicide by taking arsenic in St Louis on Monday night last. She was 61 years of age, & her husband had a few months ago left her & gone to Europe, as it appears, because of domestic troubles. There he had enlisted in the army, from which he announced in a letter he would not be released for 3 years, after which he promised to return home. Capt Grumby, her husband, had a large circle of friends in St Louis, & his wife was living in a very comfortable style, as they were well to do in this world's goods.

Valuable land for sale: I will sell at private sale the farm on which I reside, containing 765 acres, in PG Co, Md, a mile of the village of Piscataway; improvements good, & in tolerable repair. My advanced age & long continued ill-health prevent my giving the necessary attention to farming operations, which is the sole cause of my desire to sell this fine estate. –B I Semmes, Piscataway Post Ofc, Piscataway Co, Md.

Mrd: on Jun 14, by Rev Wm H Chapman, Wm H Lindsay to Miss Mgt A Mockabee, all of Wash City.

Died: on Jun 22, after an illness of one day, Mary Elizabeth Stelle, infant daughter of H M B & Edith McPherson, aged 4 months & 21 days. Her funeral will be from the residence of her grandfather, 366 7th st, near I st, this morning at 10 o'clock.

The subscriber wishes to engage for the ensuing year a Teacher to take charge of a school in a private family. One educated at the Va Univ would be preferred. Address Edw C Turner, **The Plains**, Fauquier Co, Va.

Portsmouth, Va, Jun 22. Chas Cowlain, a clerk in the post ofc of this city, was arrested today upon a charge of having embezzled over $5,000 from the mails. After his arrest Cowlain acknowledged his guilt.

WED JUN 24, 1857
Household & kitchen furniture at auction on: Jun 29, at the residence of H Pardon, on 563 4½ st east. -A Green auct

Fine business stand & lot on which it stands, corner of north I & 10th sts, & vacant lot fronting N Y ave, at auction on Jun 30, it is now & has been for many years occupied as a drug store by Dr S E Tyson. The house contains 9 rooms besides the store room. Also, vacant lot fronting 19 feet on N Y ave, adjoining the frame house, which is part of lot 7 in square 1,682. -A Green auct

Examination before U S Com'r Mather of Wm Browning & Chas B Minor, charged with obtaining warrants for bounty lands by means of forged documents, was resumed yesterday. Browning was held to bail in the sum of $4,000; failing to give bail, he was committed. Minor's case was postponed. –New London Chronicle, Sat

Six of them. John Lapoint, for the murder of Robt Wheaton; Israel Shoultz, for shooting John Inham; & Jacob Woeslin, for killing his wife, were executed in the jail yard in St Louis on Fri; & at Edwardsville, Ill, Geo W Sharpe & John Johnson were hung for the murder of Barth. On the same day, Jackson, who murdered Morris in Lake Co, Ill, last fall, suffered capital punishment in the presence of 25,000 spectators, about 3 miles from Chicago. He confessed his crime 3 days previous.

Ky: The rival parties have nominated candidates for Congress as follows:

Amer
Owen Grimes
Jas L Johnson
Warner L Underwood
Wm C Anderson
*Humphrey Marshal
Roger W Hanson
*Leander M Cox
Wm S Rankin
Dem
*Members of the late House.

*Henry C Burnett
Saml O Peyton
Jos H Lewis
*Albert G Talbott
*Joshua H Jewett
*Jos M Elliott
Thos H Holt
Jas B Clay
J C Mason
J W Stevenson

Naval Intelligence: 1-Lt Wm H Wilcox, of the U S Navy, has resigned his commission. 2-We understand that the Navy Dept has determined not to send the steamer **Arctic** on the surveying expedition on the Isthmus of Darien, for which Lt Craven has been designated. This vessel has been temporarily transferred to the coast survey, to be employed under Lt Berryman in taking deep-sea soundings connected with that branch of the service. 3-The steamer **Water Witch** has been ordered to proceed to Phil to convey the stores & effects of the Minister to China to the steamer **Minnesota**, now lying in the harbor of Norfolk, & expected to sail on Jun 25, or soon thereafter, for her destination in the East. 4-The sloop-of-war **Cumberland** sailed from Boston yesterday for the coast of Africa.

A *Fort Dodge* paper wants information of any friends of a little boy now in that town, a single survivor of a whole family butchered by the Indians at Springfield, Minn, in March. He gives his name as John Sidman Stewart, son of Josiah Stewart, formerly of Indiana Co, Pa. His mother's maiden name was probably Fleming. Also of the friends of a young lady, about 16 years old, named Eliz Gardner, who alone of her family escaped death. Her father was formerly of Steuben Co, N Y. She too is at *Fort Dodge*, but knows none of her relatives.

Desirable summer property for sale: the summer residence of Geo M Bibb, about 2 hours' ride from D C: contains about 400 acres, with a fine new house nearly finished, besides the family residence. Inquire at his residence, Fayette & 2nd sts, Gtwn, D C, or through the post ofc of the same place. –Geo M Bibb

The Charleston, S C, paper announces the death of Col Matthew Irvine Keith, a prominent citizen of that city. He was born in Gtwn, S C, in 1786, & removed quite young to Charleston; studied law & was admitted to the bar, but soon exchanged the toga for the sword. The war of 1812 called him into the military service of his county; after the war he was repeatedly elected to the State Legislature; about 1825 was elected Master or Com'r of Equity, & subsequently Register of Mesne Conveyances for Charleston District, which ofc he resigned in 1854. His death has mingled surprise with sorrow.

Jordan's *White Sulphur Springs*, Fred'k Co, Va, now open. Hot & cold Sulphur Baths. -Doct R M Jordan & Bros.

U S Patent Ofc, Wash, Jun 22, 1857. Ptn of Jos Battin, of Phil, Pa, praying for the extension of a patent granted to him on Oct 6, 1843, for an improvement in machine for breaking coal, for 7 years from the expiration of said patent, which takes place on Oct 6, 1857. –Chas Mason, Com'r of Patents

Criminal Court-Wash-Monday. Wm Talbert was found not guilty of receiving from a negro 8 bushels of wheat, the property of Washington Beall. He did not know it was stolen.

Died: yesterday, after a lingering illness, Mary Ann, wife of Henry Polkinhorn, of Wash City, in her 37th year. Her funeral will take place this afternoon, at 4 o'clock, from her late residence, on B st, near 10th st.

Masonic-the members of Wash R A Chapter 16 are to attend at Masonic Hall this morning, for the purpose of joining in the procession to celebrate the anniversary of St John the Baptist. –Chas L Schwarzman, Gr Sec

One week later from Europe. 1-The news by Persia is generally unimportant. Douglas *Jerold is dead. [Jul 1st newspaper: the funeral of Douglas *Jerold took place on Jun 15, & was attended by a large number of the most eminent men in literature & art, including Messrs Dickens, Thackeray, Landseer, Sir Chas Eastlake, & others. The remains were interred at *Norwood Cemetery*.] *Copied as written.

THU JUN 25, 1857
Indian Murders: a party consisting of C B Weaver & wife, A P Weaver, R Weaver, M Lewis, Saml Smith, E Garrison, J Smith, Wm Smith, & J Huesten, from Carroll Co, Ark, & Barry Co, Missouri, were attacked by 100 Cheyenne Indians on their way to Calif. The Indians robbed the wagons; killed 4 men & wounded 2 men & 1 woman. Two of the men escaped to the Younkin settlement, where a company of 12 men was raised to proceed to the relief of the defeated party. –St Louis Republican

Geo Baker, age about 10 years old, son of Fred'k Baker, residing in Balt, was instantly killed on Monday by the train for Phil. He had got upon the cars at the depot, & when he attempted to get off he was thrown beneath the car. His head was mashed.

Annual Commencement of Columbian College took place yesterday in the E st Baptist Church: the Pres of the U S was present; prayer was offered by Rev Dr Tyland, of Richmond College, Va. The first oration, announced by Pres Binney, was by Mr R A Christian, jr, of Middlesex Co, Va; Mr Giles T Eubank, of Lancaster Co, Va, followed; the third was by Mr L J Barnes, of Hertford Co, N C. Mr Chastain C Meador, of Bedford Co, Va; Mr G W H Morgan, of Marion Co, Va; Mr Alex D Moore, of Wash, D C; & Mr Wm F Mattingly, of Wash, D C; each spoke. List of the graduating classs: for the Degree of Bachelor of Philosophy: John W Kennedy, D C, & Wm F Mattingly, D C. For the Degree of Bachelor of Arts: Travis Bagby, of Va; Luther J Barnes, of N C; Richad A Christian, jr, of Va; Giles T Eubank, of Va; Chastain C Meador, of Va; Alex D Moore, of D C, & G W H Morgan, of Va. For the Degree of Master of Arts: Richd H Rawlings, of Va.

Died: on Jun 23, in Lynchburg, Va, Annie Harding, infant daughter of Dr S K & Augusta M Cox, aged 6 months.

Orphans Court of Wash Co, D C. In the cae of Catharine E Beall, excx of Beverley W Beall, deceased: the executrix & Court have appointed Jul 18 next, for the final settlement of the personal estate of the deceased, with the assets in hand.
-Ed N Roach, Reg/o wills

FRI JUN 26, 1857
Household & kitchen furniture at auction on: Jul 1, at the residence of A Moise, 340 9th st, [*Doughty's Row*,] next to L st north. -A Green auct

John Steiner, of Phil, is the aeronaut who was dipped in Lake Erie on Thu. When over the lake he counted 38 vessels in sight, & at the height of 3 miles he could hear the shouts of the crews who caught sight of his flying ship. Mr Steiner was picked up while swimming by men in one of the propeller's boats. The balloon was swept off by the gale.

The Atty Genr'l of Ohio has brought suit against John G Breslin, & another against Wm H Gibson, the 2 late State treasurers, for the recovery of the money lost by them to the State.

Tyre Maupin, editor of the Martinsburg [Va] Gaz, died at that place on Jun 21. He was the founder & editor of the Harrisonburg Republican, & conducted it for several years. He has since been connected with papers in Staunton & Richmond. He was also a fluent & able public speaker.

Portraits of Washington. The first portrait of Washington, at age 41, was painted at Mount Vernon, in 1772, by Chas Willson Peale, who also executed others in '78, '81, '83, '86, & ' 95. Various likenesses have been made by Houdon, Trumbull, Pine, Cerachi, Wertmuller, Stuart; & again by C W Peale & his son, Rembrandt Peale, to whom, jointly, Washington gave sittings in the autumn of 1795. A portrait, in senatorial costume, intended to combine the merits of theses studies from life, [chiefly his own & his fathers,] was executed by Rembrandt Peale, under peculiar excitement, entirely for his own gratification, & without any view to emolument. It, however, received the unexpected approbation of his father, who had so often painted the venerated form he had known so long & so well, & elicited the spontaneous applause of Washington's relatives & most intimate friends; &, after having been an object of interest in his painting rooms in England, France, & Italy, was bought in 1832, by a unanimous resolution of the Senate of the U S, for $2,000. A portrait, in military costume-the study for an equestrian picture to commemorate the siege of Yorktown-was simultaneiously painted, & remains in Mr Peale's possession. Chas Willson Peale states that his first acquaintance with Washington, who was then a colonel of the Alexandria militia, in 1772, was at **Mount Vernon**, where he painted his portrait, & those of several members of his family, conversing daily with him during several weeks. After he received the appointment of Cmder-in-Chief of the armies of the 13 Colonies, I painted his portrait for Mr John Hancock, the first Pres of Congress, & several others for some of the States for different individuals. While sitting for one of them [a miniature for Mrs Washington,] he received despatches communicating the surrender of Burgoyne.

Mr Slade, a printer, & his wife, attempted to put an end to their lives at Memphis, Tenn, a few daysa go by swallowing laudanum. Pecuniary embarrassment & a diseased intellect, produced by intemperance, are supposed to have been the cause of this rash move. Medical aid was procured in time to save their lives.

The New Orleans Courier of Jun 11th says a man named Vanderlin went to the residence of Mrs Estelle Wezell, & discharged one barrel at her without effect, & knocked her down with the butt of the pistol. He then blew his brains out. The parties were formerly husband & wife, she having obtained a divorce from him about 5 years ago.

On Jun 17, at Harper's Ferry, a young man alighted from the Balt cars, laboring under the effects of liquor. He introduced himself to Dr Clagett, whom he had just met, as Geo W Hamar, the son of the late Gen Hamar, of Ohio. During the evening he fell from the wall at the Winchester depot, & died the following morning. His remains were decently interred in the cemetery of Harper's Ferry.

Mrd: on Jun 24, at Wesley Chapel, by Rev Wm Krebs, John W Smith to Louisa M Duvall, all of Wash.

Mrd: on Jun 23, by Rev Wm H Chapman, Benj F Fowler to Mary A Henn, all of Wash City.

Mrd: on Jun 6, by Rev J L Gilbert, Wm Chas Murdoch, of New Haven, Conn, to Miss Sarah Catharine Forrest, of Wash City.

Mrd: on Jun 23, at the Union Hotel, by Rev W Krebs, Richd F Jones to Mary Ella Ford, both of Va.

Mrd: on Jun 25, in the Wesley Chapel, by Rev W Krebs, Jos Hamacker to Eliza A Davis, both of Wash City.

Died: on Jun 25, in Wash City, Edward Ulysses, eldest son of John B & Louisa P Ward, aged 5 years, 2 months & 16 days. His funeral is this morning at 10 o'clock. Carriages will be in readiness at 9 o'clock at the residence of U Ward, Missouri ave, to convey them to his father's residence.

Country hams to arrive on Sat morning, cured by Mr Wm Z Beall, PG Co, Md. For sale by Jas H Shekell, 279 F st, corner of 13th st.

SAT JUN 27, 1857

Commencement at Princeton. The annual Commencement of the College of N J being the 110th anniversary of that venerable institution. Oration by Hon Wm C Alexander, of N J. Among the honoray degress conferred by the Board of Trustees, was that of Dr of Divinity upon Rev Geo D Cummins, of Wash City.

Movement of the troops. The steamship **America**, Capt Nelson, arrived at New Orleans on Jun 19, from Fla, bringing from **Fort Meyers**, Puenta Rosa, Pavillion, Key & Cape Sable, companies D, C, E, F, & K, 5th infty-480 men in number, & the following ofcrs: Capt C C Sibley, commanding; Capt & Brvt Major N B Russell, Capt J C Robinson, Capt H R Selden, 1st Lt B Wingate, 1st Lt W H Lewis, 2nd Lt L L Rich, 2nd Lt Hill, 2nd Lt J F Ritter, Acting Adj, & Assist Surgeon A C Ridgeley. They are on their way to Jefferson Barracks.

The Hartford Press of Tue says that great surprise has been excited in business circles there by the discovery that Dan W King, of Suffield, cigar-maker, has been for some time past, probably more than a year, engaged in quite a complicated series of forgeries. He is about 45 years old, & has a wife & children. He forged endorsements of Lucius Hathaway, Sheriff S B Kendall, & most largely of Dan King, [his father,] D W Norton, & others.

The Democratic Convention of Chas Co, Md, recently in session, nominated Mr John F Gardiner to represent the county in the State Senate, & F B F Burgess & Nicholas Stonestreet for the House of Delegates.

Circuit Court of D C, sitting in Chancery. Mary Ann Queen, cmplnt, vs Henry P Queen, Jos C Queen, & Ellen R Queen, & others, dfndnts. Saml Queen, late of D C, was her lawful husband. That before & during the time of their marriage he was seized in fee & possessed of a part of a tract of land called *In* or *Enclosure*, & part of *Haddock's Hills*, containing 30 acres, 3 roods & 13 perches, & marked lot No 1, in the division of the real estate of Richd Queen, & died leaving cmplnt, his widow, who as such was, & now is, entitled to dower in the said premises, & to one-third of the rents, issues, & profits which have accrued thereon, from the death of her said husband, which happened in Jan, 1831. That at the death of her said husband the said Henry P Queen & others, who are named dfndnts in the said bill, & against whom subpoenas & the said Jos C Queen & Ellen R Queen at a subsequent date, were in possession of the said premises, & they or some of them have continued & now are in the possession thereof, claiming title thereto under & through the said Saml Queen, & have taken the rents, issues, & profits of the said premises to their own use, & have failed & refused to account with the cmplnt therfore, & pay her any part thereof. The object of the bill is to have an account taken of the rents, issues, & profits of the land of which the said Saml Queen was so seized before & during his marriage with the cmplnt, & which have been received by the dfndnts or any of them since the death of said Saml, or which without their gross neglect they could have received, & to have one-third thereof paid to her in respect of her dower-right in the said premises, & that one-third of the said land of which her said husband was so seized as aforesaid may be set apart & delivered to her for her life, & as for her dower therein. The dfndnts named do not reside in D C, & cannot be found therein. They are to appear within 4 months from Jun 26, 1857, to answer the said bill.
-Wm M Merrick, A J -Jno A Smith, Clerk -Marbury, Solicitor

U S Patent Ofc, Wash, Jun 25, 1857. Ptn of Henry Burt, of Newark, N J, praying for the extension of a patent granted to him on Sep 23, 1843, for an improvement in knitting machines, for 7 years from the expiration of said patent, which takes place on Sep 23, 1857. –Chas Mason, Com'r of Patents

Cmdor Kearny, U S Navy, has entered upon his duties as Commandant of the Brooklyn Navy Yard; & Cmder Thos R Roots has reported for duty upon this station.

For rent, that desirable residence at 417 13th st, having in it a bathroom, abundance of water, furnace, gas, & every modern improvement, in complete order. Apply at 10th & Pa ave, over the Savings Bank, to Grafton D Hanson.

Valuable real estate for sale: the subscriber offers *Largo*, situated in the *Forest of PG Co*, Md, containing 360 acres of land; adjoins the estates of Dr David Craufurd, Geo T Craufurd, Zachariah Berry, sen, Dr Benj Lee, & others, & lies on the road leading from Bladensburg to Upper Marlborough. –Z B Beall

Public sale of valuable real estate: by decree of the Circuit Court for PG Co, in Court of Equity, the undersigned will expose to public sale at Richd H Locker's Store, at the ***Long Old Fields***, on Jul 10 next, all that portion of the real estate of Elisha Berry, deceased, heretofore assigned by com'rs to the heirs-at-law of Wm E Berry, deceased. This land contains 141 acres, & is a part of the estate known as ***Springfield estate***, & adjoins the dower of Mrs Deborah Berry.
–Danl C Digges, C C Magruder, trustees

Equity, No 157. In the matter of the Writ De Lunatic Inquirendo on Rozier T Daingerfield. In the Circuit Court of PG Co, as Court of Equity. In pursuance of an order passed in the above cause on Jun 11, 1857, the creditors of Rozier T Daingerfield are notified to file their claims against him, duly authenticated, with the Clerk of the Circuit Court, on or before Oct 1 next. -Wm H Daingerfield, cmte

I will sell lot 2 in square 573, fronting 60 feet on Indiana ave, & the same on D st, in the most improving part of Wash City. Room for 6 houses of 20 feet each. Title indisputable or no pay required. –John H Houston, ***Green's Row***, Capitol Hill

The last accounts from Mr Crawford are of an encouraging kind. His disease is a cancerous tumor behind the eye; & he has been for some time in London under the charge of Dr Fell, an American physician residing there, who has acquired a high reputation by his treatment of diseases of this class. Dr Fell's treatment consists mainly in the application of some eating substance which gradually consumes the body of the tumor. –Boston Courier

Criminal Court-Wash-Fri. 1-Rory O'More, found guilty of assault & battery, & sentenced to 6 months; imprisonment in jail. 2-John Nugent found not guilty of assault & battery with intent to kill. 3-Emily Bryant found guilty of larceny in 2 cases, in stealing silver plate; sentenced to a week in jail & 18 months in the penitentiary. 4-Albert Stewart found guilty of assault, & sentenced to 3 months; imprisonment. 5-Mary Brown found guilty of petit larceny, & sentenced to 9 months' imprisonment.

Mrd: on Jun 26, in Wash City, by Rev G W Samson, Mr Geo L Baker, of Lexington, Va, to Miss Ellen Virginia Bryan, of Rockbridge Co, Va.

Three parties, Williams, Cropsey, & a woman named Hayzell, charged with having stolen a quantity of articles, found at the house of a woman on 6th st, near the Canal. Many of the articles are fully indentified. Williams & Cropsey have been committed for trial at court; the woman at the time of this writing was seeking security for $500 for her appearance at court.

Died: on Jun 19, at Carlisle, Pa, Margaret, daughter of Julia G & Lt Geo B Balch, U S Navy, aged 4 months & 24 days.

Died: yesterday, in his 69th year. John Smith, for the last 22 years an efficient clerk in the Gen Post Ofc Dept. He was born in Montg Co, Md; during the war with Great Britain he occupied a responsible position under the late Gen John Mason, in Gtwn; in 1825 he was appointed a Clerk in the Post Ofc at Balt, from which, at the period first referred to, he removed & entered upon duty in the Dept in Wash City. The Heads of Bureaus & Clerks of the Gen Post Ofc, also of the Ofc of Auditor of the Treasury for the Postal Dept, Ofcrs of the Genr'l Gov't in Wash City, & friends generally, are invited to attend his funeral from the dwlg of Mr J R Wore, on 12th, between H & N Y ave, this afternoon, at 4 o'clock.

Trustee's sale of valuable real estate in Surry Co, Va: by deed of trust from P B Wills, for purposes therein specified, we will sell on Jul 9, 3,600 acres of excellent Farming, Timbered, & Wood Land; in said county, within 5 miles of *Chip Oaks*, a tide-water inlet from James river. The plat of the property may be seen at the ofc of Thos Branch & Sons. –R D McIlwaine, J P Branch, trustees, Petersburg.

MON JUN 29, 1857
Yesterday Capt Manning, of the Independent Detective Police, of this city, arrested Nelson Driggs, who had in his possession $5,465 in counterfeit money. Driggs had also in his possession four plates for the manufacture of bogus money. Driggs was taken before Justice Herckenrath, who committed him for future examination.
–St Louis Republican, Jun 24

Calif: the trial of Edw McGowan, charged with being accessory to the murder of Jas King, of Wm, terminated. The jury returned a verdict of not guilty.

Calif: a rumor prevailed that Col Hararzthy, melter & refiner of the branch mint of the U S, is a defaulter to a large amount, variously estimated at $100,000 to $500,000. He had, however, made over all his property to the Gov't as security for a deficiency charged against him.

Hon Zeno Scudder died at his residence in ___nstable, Mass, on Friday. He has had failing health about 3 years. He was respected by all who knew him.

Breach of promise: recently in the court of Carroll Co, Ohio, Rev Jos Barclay was found guilty of seduction of & breach of promise of marriage to Eliz Sharp, & mulcted in damages to the value of $5,000. The dfndnt was a preacher of the Covenanter or Seceder faith.

Gov Wise has appointed John Taylor, of Chatterton, King Geo Co, an aid-de-camp to the cmder-in-chief of the State forces, with brevet rank of colonel of cavalry.
–Fred'g Recorder

Saml Clay, jr, of Bourbon Co, Ky, has just returned from Mexico, where he has been purchasing mules & horses. He succeeded in purchasing about 300 mules & 40 horses, which he drove to Illinois, through Texas, the Indian Territory, & Missouri, a distance of 2,000 miles.

Lightning in Balt Co, on Jun 16, struck Mr Jos H Gorsuch, of **Charlsby Farm**. His horse was killed instantly & Mr G only showed signs of life after a long while. The usual remedy of water was applied, or no doubt it would have proved fatal.

During the storm on Sunday last, 3 men were riding in an open wagon from Bass river to Harrisville, Burlington Co, & were struck by lightning & instantly killed. Two of them were Richd Adams, hotel keeper at the former place, & Mr Tyler. The name of the other man was not known. -Trenton American of Sat

A farmer named Hays, residing in Knoxville, Fred'k Co, Md, was about to hive a swarm of bees, when he was stung in a terrible manner. He died the next day.

On Thu Mr Jas Pryor was working in his pyrotechnic laboratory on Main st, when a tremendous explosion occurred. He was horribly burnt & could not possibly survive. Jas Richards was injured by falling bricks. -Cin Gaz

A son of Mr F Wilson, residing near Limestone Hill, Orange Co, N Y, came to his death on Tue last, when a gun in the barn accidentally discharged. His youngest brother, who was with him, was unhurt.

On Monday, in South Danvers, Mass, Mrs Mary Prescott was burned in a serious manner, when a fluid lamp exploded.

Criminal Court-Wash-Sat. 1-Saml Anderson, colored, was found guilty of assault, & fined $8. 2-Jas Holland was found guilty of assault, & sentenced to 2 months' imprisonment. 3-John Shekells, tried for malicious mischief, was found not guilty. 4-J W Wilsey was fined $25 & costs for assault.

Mrd: on Jun 25, by Rev Wm H Chapman, John F Taylor to Miss Sophia Caddington, all of Wash.

Mrd: on Jun 25, by Rev Jas Donelan, Chas F P Cummin to Thora, eldest daughter of Selmar Seibert, all of Wash City.

A farm wanted: improved city property for sale. The subscriber wishes to exchange improved city property for a small farm not more than 5 miles from the Capitol. Refer to H N Gilbert, 548 Pa ave, or A G Pendleton, 463 2nd st east.

Montreal, Jun 27. The loss of the steamer **Montreal** [on Jun 26,] has been reported here. The steamer contained no less than 500 passengers, generally emigrants from Scotland. The boat was off Cape Rouge at the time of the disaster. We learn that only 175 persons were saved. It is certain that over 200 passengers were drowned, & that very many others were burnt to death.

Four days from Europe: 1-The funeral of Douglas Jerold took place on Jun 15, & was attended by a large number of the most eminent men of literature & art. 2-The baptism of the infant Princess of England took place in the chapel in Buckingham Palace on Jun 16. She was named Beatrice Mary Victoria. [Jul 1st newspaper: The infant princess received the names of Beatrice Mary Victoria Feodore. The sponsors were the Princess Royal, the Duchess of Kent, & Prince Fred'k William of Prussia.]

Select Family School for Young Ladies, English & French, 309 F st, Wash. Principal, Donald Macleod, A M, Univ of Glasgow, formerly head master of Ravenscroft College & Ashwood School, & Prof of Rhetoric & Belles-Lettres in the Columbia Institute. This school will be opened on the 2nd Mon of Sep next.

TUE JUN 30, 1857
Household & kitchen furniture at auction on: Jun 29, at the residence of H Pardon, 563 4th st east. -A Green auct

For sale at auction: in pursuance of a power of sale contained in the last will & testament of the late Gottlieb C Grammer, duly proved & recorded in the Orphans Court of Wash Co, D C, sale on Jul 7, of lot 15 in square 200; fronts on Vt ave, between H & I sts north; with a convenient 2 story brick dwlg, occupied by Mr A E Le Merle. Title indisputable. –Christopher Grammer, J E Grammer, trustees for the heirs of the late Gottlieb C Grammer. -A Green auct

Extensive sale of lumber at auction: on Jul 6, at the lumber yard of John Purdy, near the Capitol. -A Green auct

Capt Drayton, of the schnr **Pearl**, convicted of stealing 70 slaves in 1848, sentenced to 20 years' imprisonment & pardoned after 4 years' incarceration, committed suicide at New Bedford, Mass, on Jun 24. He leaves a widow & several children.
+
[Aug 14th, 1848 newspaper: Criminal Court-Wash: Edw Sears charged with slave stealing: not guilty. [Chester English testified: he was one of the parties arrested & found on board the schnr **Pearl** at the time of her capture & imprisoned with Drayton & Sears ever since, being introduced against Sears.] [Aug 22nd 1848, newspaper: Chester English has been discharged, as there is no evidence to prove his participation in the design of abducting the slaves.]

Charleston News of Jun 26. Hon Langdon Cheves died last night at Columbia. He was born in Sept, 1776, on a branch of Calhouns' creek, Abbeville District; he was in his 81st year. He was admitted to the bar about 1800, & formed one of the firm of Peace & Cheves, in large & successful practice. He was twice elected to Congress.

Mr G W Edwards, a machinist in the sugar-house in Boston, on Fri afternoon fell a distance of ten stories to the sidewalk, injuring him so severely that he died shortly after. At the time he was ascending to the upper story on an elevator run by steam, & the person attending at the time did not understand the working of the machinery.

The agent of the Post Ofc Dept has caused the arrest of Lewis Lane, assist postmaster at Starkeville, G, for secreting a valuable letter. Lane is bound over in a bond of $2,000 for his appearance.

Later advices from Mexico confirmed the destruction of Crabb & his party at Cavorca. We also learn the safety of Mr Rasey Biven, brother-in-law of Mr Crabb, who had been thrown in prison, & was detained about 3 weeks.
–San Francisco Bulletin

Four men drowned at St John's, N B, who were in the employ of Mr Lingley, of Indiantown. They were passing the falls in a boat on Mon when the boat capsized: drowned were Henry McHugh, Albert Belyea, Robt Collins, & John Kelley. The deceased were all good & industrious workmen, & leave families to mourn their loss.

Mountain View for sale: having determined to move West, I offer the farm on which I now reside, containing 1,040 acres [it is susceptible of division,] on the Rappahannock river, in Culpeper Co, Va, about 4 miles from the **Fauquier White Sulphur Springs**; with comfortable dwlgs on each of two tracks, one of which is a large stone dwlg, with all necessary out-bldgs. Apply at the post ofc at Milleview, Fauquier Co, Va, or to Rice W Payne, atty, at Warrenton, Va. –Thos A Keith

I shall offer a farm for sale publicly on Jul 25, in Orange Co: contains 241 acres of land; improvements consist only of a few out-houses. Apply in person on the adjoining farm, or by letter at Rapid Ann station, Culpeper Co, Va. -Henry Maple

Died: on Jun 28, in Wash City, Wallace, infant son of Wallace & Eugenia E Eliot.

WED JUL 1, 1857
Orphans Court of Wash Co, D C. In the case of Catharine Mohun, excx of Philip Mohun, deceased: the executrix & Court have appointed Jul 18 next, for the final settlement of the personal estate of said deceased, with the assets in hand.
–Ed N Roach, Reg/o wills

Speech of a veteran of 117 years; from the Chicago Tribune; at the Pioneer Festival in Madison, Wisc, on Thu last. What events have been crowded into this man's life! Jos Crelie, is probably the oldest man in the U S. A native of Detroit, he was partly raised at Kaskaskia & Prairie du Roche, in Ill, & subsequently became an inhabitant of St Louis, under Spanish rule. In 1814 a participant with the Americans in the conflict at Prairie du Chien, he served as express-carrier in the Black Hawk war. 41 years ago he located at the Wisc Portage, & nearly a third of a century since was a mail carrier between Mineral Point & Green Bay. He was married 3 times, & of 9 children but a single one survives-the seventh by my first marriage, & she has nearly reached the age of three score & ten. He has grandchildren almost without number.

Hon Jas D Green, in introducing Mr Everett at the Bunker Hill celebration, stated that the house was still standing in Cambridge in which Gen Ward had his headquarters, & where the Cmte of Safety wielded the whole executive power of the province. The mansion is at the n e corner of the common, in good preservation. The house of Elbridge Gerry, at Cambridge, used as a hospital for the sick & wounded of the American army after the battles of 1776, is now the residence of venerable Rev Chas Lowell, D D; Washington's headquarter's, near by, is now the noble mansion of Longfellow; at no great distance the majestic elm under whose grateful shade, Jul 3, 1776, Washington took command of the Continental army.

The steam-frig **Wabash** arrived at N Y on Sunday last, bearing the broad pennant of Cmdor H Paulding, bringing 121 ofcrs & men, 13 women, & 5 children, who served under Gen Walker in Nicaragua. Seventy of those who have returned are sick & wounded, some very severely. Philip R Thompson died Jun 24, & was buried at sea. Chas Winner & Wm Bagley died on board the ship **Cyane**, on her passage from Greytown to Aspinwall. Names of the returned filibusters:

Ofcrs:

Edw J Sanders	Benj F Whittier	Jas C Schermerhorn
P R Thompson [dead]	Wm Northbridge	John G P Hooe
E H McDonald	Jerome Johnson	Goodwin Brown
Henry L Potter	Jas H Hearsey	Arthur Callahan
Geo W M Leonard	Jas Small	John Brinkerhoof
John M Griffin	Wm F Harmell	Wm Dolman
Jas Dunnican	Robt C Tyler	

Privates:

Nicholas Trapp	D J Donovan	Wm Keiley
Geo H Tompkins	A J Harrison	M P Stewart
Wm H Holmes	D C Williams	Thos Kelly
Henry Miller	Wm Carson	E M Williams
John D Fontaine	Jas Tryon	M H Blake
A N B Sharpe	Wm McGilvroy	Alex Owens
Henry Ames	J W Hart	John White
Jack Williams	John Kayser	Wm Miles

Walter J Scott	John Roars	Jas Brenan
Patrick Ward	Geo McMillan	Oscar Carson
A O Lindsuy	Frank Martin	Jas H Neill
Jas Allen	L P Heath	Geo Lown
A J Lincoln	W J Andrews	Edw F Mullen
John C Clarke	N Trowbridge	Alex Leggett
John Dacey	W J Jemell	Wm H Coe
Wm Rhea	Nathan Parmer	Geo Canfield
Stephen Brinckley	Jos R Reneau	Wm H Lester
Jacob McKinney	Hiram Marshall	A J Hanway
Levi Price	Jas A Adams	John Jickerson
Thos Doyle	Wm Kerr	Frank Bennett
S M Cansby	John Williams	John Rodgers
R W Seinney	Robt R Craig	John M West
John Bartlett	M McNeill Rainey	Henry Bartow
Jas Thompson	Chas W Graves	John Blanderman
J Karnbacher	Robt Bruce	P S Granes
Michl Lamb	Carlos Allen	Benj Weed
John Anderson	Jos Clumph	Thos Clarke
Alex Barr	Geo Whittemore	Jas E Teel
Jos Avent	Henry C Wells	Wm Porter
D Livingston	Henry D Loomis	Hugh McKay
Wm H Carson	M P Hunnycut	
Jas M Norman	Michl Hertz	

Citizens:

Robt Luke	Jas L Cole	Wm Butts
Woolsey Teller	Jacob Calmos	Flavel Belcher

Women & Children:

Mrs Sanders	Mrs Thompson	Juliana Cole
Octave Potter	Chas A Seiler	Mrs Gardner
Henry Potter	Jose Arbaca	Mrs Swingle
Mrs Fulton	Mrs Hearsey	
Mrs Harwell	Mrs Potter	

Among the sick are Levi Pryor, of Balt, with an ulcer & loss of the right arm; Wm J Jewell, of Va, ulcer; D C Williams & E W Miller, of Ohio, the latter with a ulcer & the former with a gunshot wound; John Adams, of Md, gunshot wound; Nathl Trapp, of Md, gunshot wound; Wm H Coe, of Md, gunshot wound through the right thigh; Capt J C Schermerhorn, of Va, wounded in the leg; Col Wm Butts, De Witt C Williams, & Wm H Holmes, of Ohio, gunshot wounds; Lt John Hooe, of Va, wounded in the foot; Col John Faber & Jas Brennan, of S C, gunshot wounds; Wm Porter, of Pa, gunshot wound; Jack Williams, heel shot off by a cannon ball; N Parma, probably mortally wounded; J B Renau, of Tenn, fell upon his bowie-knife & was badly injured. All the sick & wounded will probably be sent to the N Y hospital.

We left in Rivas about 18 sick & wounded, who were unable to be removed. Among these were Maj Dolan, of New Orleans; Lt Rayburn, of Va; Capt C S West, of New Orleans; & private Rainsford, a printer, of N Y. Capt N Taft, of Texas, came down the river with us to Greytown, but was left behind by the **Cyane**. The sick in Rivas were left in charge of Dr Robt T Royston & Dr J H Coleman, who were engaged for that service by Gen Canas.

Rev John C Young, Pres of Centre College, Ky, with which institution he was connected for about 30 years, died suddenly at Danville, Ky, on Tue. He was an eminent Presbyterian clergyman, & married a sister of Vice Pres Breckinridge.

Criminal Court-Wash-yesterday. The parties charged with rioting & illegal interference with the exercise of the right of suffrage in the late election were: Wm Warnock, John Webster, Wm Wilson, Isaac Stoddard, & Wm Williams: all guilty as indicted; & Jesse Williams, not guilty.

Young Austin, who shot Jas Henry Birch on Sunday last at the door of Mount Carmel Church, near Ball's Cross-roads, will be brought before the preliminary examining court on Monday next, to sit at Alexandria. The quarrel out of which the deadly feud sprung originated at a picnic held on Jun 20th, at Hall's Spring, in the same county. It seems to have been the purpose of Austin's assailants to prevent him from exercising the ofc of teacher at Mount Carmel. Young Birch's remains were yesterday committed to the grave. Austin had been in the habit of acting in the capacity of teacher for members in their casual absence from the Sunday school at Mount Carmel. [Jul 9th newspaper: Manville Austin has been released by the Court of Inquiry for Alexandria Co from legal redress, thereby holding him acquitted of the charge of willfully murdering Jas H Birch at Mount Carmel, in said county, on Sunday, Jun 28. The evidence showed that his assailants had combined to maltreat him, & were carrying out their purpose when he shot Birch in self-defence.]

Dissolution of the partnership existing under the name of Fitzhugh Coyle & Co, is this day dissolved by mutual consent. –Fitzhugh Coyle, Edw F Simpson
+
To the public: Having this day sold to Mr Edw F Simpson my entire stock of Agricultural Implements, Field & Garden Seeds, I most cheerfully commend him to the patronage of my friends & customers. –Fitzhugh Coyle

Valuable real estate for sale in PG Co, Md. Intending a change of residence, offer at private sale his present residence, **The Lodge**, containing 100 acres; within 2 miles of Alexandria; dwlg is very commodious & roomy, suitable for a private residence as well as for a public academy; with other farm bldgs. Also at private sale another fine farm called **Beach Hill**, of 130 acres; new bldgs on this farm. The premises will be shown by the subscriber, or by Thos Grimes. Address Gustavus Finotti, care of Thos Grimes, Wash City P O.

Valuable lot for sale: part of lot 16 in square 454, on H st, near 7th, adjoining the 3 handsome dwlgs erected by Henry I Davis. Inquire of Dr Hill, 6th & F sts.

Obit-died: Hon Stephen C Phillips, of Salem, perished by the burning of the steamboat **Montreal**, on the passage from Quebec for Montreal. He had been to Three Rivers, where one of his sons resides, & was on his way to Montreal to take the railroad home. Mr Phillips has been for many years a prominent citizen in the political as well as the mercantile community. He was the only child of Capt Stephen Phillips, a wealthy merchant of Salem, where he was born on Nov 4, 1802; graduated with high honors at Harvard College in 1819; adopted his fathers' profession & was a successful merchant of Salem. –Boston Daily Advertiser

THU JUL 2, 1857
Handsome & spacious brick house & lot fronting on Pa ave, between 3rd & 4½ sts, at auction. It has 14 inch walls, contains 16 conveniently arranged rooms with wide passages, & all other necessary out-bldgs. It is occupied by Mr Wm H Faulknew. Title indisputable. -A Green auct

On the 15th ult Mr Casper Hibler, residing near Dallastown, York Co, Pa, went to his well, in the yard, to draw water, when the walls caved in, precipitating him down the well some 17 feet, [the well is about 40 feet deep.] He was alone at the time, his wife visiting his ill mother. On her return she found that he was in the well, & the alarm was given to the neighbors to rescue him. As fast as they removed the earth, more fell in upon him. He spoke with his wife for the last time. It was on Apr 14 last, he led her to the altar as a bride. On Tue he ceased to exist, & his lifeless body was found much bruised with one hand off.

Elegant Paris-made cabinet furniture, French-plate mirrors, superior household effects, pair of carriage horses, buggy, & harness, at auction, on Jul 15, at the residence of Mr de Cramer, Sec of Russian Legation, on 15th st, between N Y ave & H st north. -Jas C McGuire, auct

Trustee's sale of nearly new furniture & housekeeping effects, on Jul 7, by 2 deeds of trust, duly recorded, sale at the Burnett House, corner of 4½ st & Pa ave.
–B Milburn, trustee -Jas C McGuire, auct

The Jackson [Tenn] Whig of the 19th ult chronicles the death, in Henderson, Co, Tenn, of Mr Miles Darden, beyond all question, the largest man in the world. His height was 7 feet 6 inches, higher than Porter, the celebrated Ky giant. His weight was a fraction over 1,000 pounds. He measured round the waist 6 feet 9 inches.

The oldest book in the U S, it is said, is a manuscript Bible, in the possession of Dr Witherspoon, of Alabama, written over 1,000 years ago.

Commencement of the Univ of Va took place on Monday. Among the graduates were Osborne Ingle & Woodville Lathan, of Wash; W R Abbott, of Gtwn; Wm T Morrill, of Alexandria; Wm N McDonald & Henry Brannen, of Winchester.

The York Pennsylvanian states that of 4 members of the family of Mr Henry Shiding, of that borough, who partook of apple butter made in a copper kettle, 2 of the children, aged 6 & 9 years, are dead, & the surviving 2, the mother & a child 4 years old, are out of danger. The surviving child is in a pitiable condition. He is running around, is fat & looks well, but is deranged from the effects of the poison.

The sentence of death passed upon young Worrel, formerly of Md, was duly executed on Fri last at Union, Missouri.

Criminal Court-Wash-Wed. 1-Geo Johnson found guilty of assault: fined $10 & costs. 2-Robt Cross, one of the most prominent rioters on election day, was arrested by Ofcr Harper, assisted by Ofcr Robinson. Cross is now confined in jail.

In Equity, N C, Rutherford Co, Spring term 1857. Moses Simmons, et al, vs Joshua Simmons et al, heirs at law of Chas Simmons, deceased. Ptn for sale of real estate in Rutherford Court of Equity. In this case it appearing to the court that publication has been duly made as to the non-residents to appear & claim their distributive share of said estate, & it further appearing to the court that Frances Wade, one of the heirs entitled to partition, has failed to appear & claim her part of said estate, it is thereupon ordered by the court that publication be made in the Nat'l Intell, published in Wash City, for 4 weeks, notifying the said Frances Wade or her heirs, if she be dead, to appear at the next term of this court to be held in Rutherford Co, at the court house, in Rutherfordton, on the 9th Monday after the 4th Monday in Sept next. –L B Bryan, Clerk & Master of said Court of Equity, at ofc the *9th Monday after the 4th Monday, in Mar A D, 1857. *Copied as written.

In Equity, N C, Rutherford Co, Spring term, 1857. John Baxter, adm, vs, Moses Simmons et al, heirs at law of Chas Simmons, deceased. Bill to settle estate filed in Rutherford Court of Equity. In this case it appearing to the court that publication has been duly made as to the non-residents to appear & claim their distributive share of the personal estate of Chas Simmons, deceased; & it further appearing to the court that Frances Wade, one of the heirs entitled to partition, has failed to appear & claim her part of said estate, it is thereupon ordered by the court that publication be made in the Nat'l Intell, published in Wash City, for 4 weeks, notifying the said Frances Wade or her heirs, if she be dead, to appear at the next term of this court to be held in Rutherford Co, at the court house, in Rutherfordton, on the *9th Monday after the 4th Monday in Sept next, & make claim to her share of said estate or be forever thereafter barred. Witness: L B Bryan, Clerk & Master of said Court of Equity, at ofc the *9th Monday after the 4th Monday, in Mar A D, 1857. *Copied as written.

Nat'l Hotel, Main st, Staunton, Va. Wm D Gilkeson, Proprietor. [Ad]

Died: on Jul 1, in Wash City, of cholera infantum, Edward Duval, infant son of Chas F & Mary B Perrie, aged 6 months & 12 days. His funeral will be from the residence of his grandfather, H H McPherson, 366 7th st, on Thu at 4 o'clock P M.

Died: on Jun 30, in Wash City, after a few days' illness, dear little Rose, aged 18 months & 21 days, beloved child of Wm C & Harriet A Zantzinger. This lovely bud now blooms in Heaven. Her funeral will be this morning at 11 o'clock, from the residence of her grandparent, Mrs Fischer, on C st.

FRI JUL 3, 1857
Appointments by the Pres: 1-John Hunter, Collector of the Customs, Natchez, Miss, vice Jas W McDonald, removed. 2-Andrew J Decatur, Surveyor of the Customs, Bayport, Fla, vice John E Johnson, resigned. 3-Thos W Sutherland, Collector of the Customs, Sacramento, Calif, vice Chas C Sackett, removed.

Mr T B Mattingly, of Ky, went out to Nicaragua in Apr last to endeavor to find & persuade to return home certain youths who left their parents & friends last year for Central America to join Gen Walker. He found Hines, Hardin, Mckay, & Daniels, all of whom are to come home in the ship **Roanoke**. Wickliffe & Gray he could hear nothing of, but thinks they are in Costa Rica with the American prisoners & deserters.

The French papers: Guillaume Hyde de Neuville, recently died, in his 82nd year. He was born in Jan, 1776; a thorough royalist, a legitimist, from boyhood to the hour of his death. In 1816 he was sent Minister to the U S, & held the ofc 5 years.
-Boston Traveller

Henry Winter, an American, is at the head of the ship-bldg establishment of the Danube Navigation Co, one of the largest & most successful in the world.

A biography of Geo Stephenson, "the father of the locomotive," is in press in England. In 1825 people laughed when he said he could run his engine at the rate of 10 miles per hour. In 1845 he saw hundreds run at a speed of 50 miles an hour. He died in 1848, aged 67.

Miss Ann B Herron, who fell a victim to the epidemic of 1855, in Norfolk, bequeathed to her near relative, Jas H Behan, of that city, a splendid mansion. Having heard Miss Herron express the intention or desire to appropriate this valuable property to the purpose of founding an infirmary, Mr Behan, though under no legal obligation to do so, has relinquished his claim to it, & given it up to be converted into an infirmary, as contemplated by his kinswoman. The property is estimated to be worth from $25,000 to $30,000.

The Archduchess Sophia, of Austria, who died recently, was only 2 years, 2 months & 24 days old. She was the oldest child of the present Emperor, & she & her little sister were both attacked with an infantile disease soon after the imperial family went to Buda. The younger one by last accounts was convalescent. –Phil Bulletin

N Y, Jul 1. Mayor Wood has appointed John McLeod Murphy, formerly constructing engineer of the navy yard, head of the Bureau of Surveyors of N Y C. The ofc is worth $5,000 per annum.

Mr Francis Brooks, son of the late Peter Brooks, of this city, was drowned yesterday while bathing with some friends in the Mississippi river, near the dike on the Illinois shore. He was a young man much respected & beloved. –St Louis Rplcn, Jun 26.

The fourth of July will be celebrated by the Everett Literary Society of St John's College, by the reading of the Declaration of Independence by Mr John W Dorsey, of Howard Co, Md, to be followed by an oration from Mr Andrew Chapman, of Chas Co, Md.

Criminal Court-Wash-Thu. Richd T Jones, a prisoner in jail, charged with an assault with intent to kill Rebecca Martin, whilst she was visiting him [Jones] in the jail of this county. The aim of the defence, conducted by Mr Ratcliffe, to show that Jones was insane at the time of committing the deed. The jury brought in Jones "guilty" as indicted, & the Court sentenced him to 4 years in the penitentiary, to take effect from & after the termination of the period of 9 months' imprisonment in jail he is now undergoing.

Fire broke out yesterday in the gunsmith shop of Mr C H Munck, 6th & Pa ave, & extended to the other tenements of the bldg occupied by Mr Reese, plumber, Mrs King, milliner, & Mr D'Unger, proprietor of the Capitol City printing ofc. The whole was reduced to a complete ruin. The bldg was owned by Messrs Middleton & Beall, & was fully insured. No doubt about the incendiary origin of the fire.

Orphans Court of Wash Co, D C. In the case of Ellen McFadden, admx of Wm McFadden, deceased: the administratrix & Court have appointed Jul 21 next, for the final settlement of the personal estate of the deceased, of the assets in hand.
-Ed N Roach, Reg/o wills

Died: on Jun 2, in Wash City, Mr Benj F Bell, aged 22 years. His funeral will take place from the residence of Mr Jno Larcombe, sr, at 612 south 7th st, this afternoon at 2 o'clock, where his relatives & friends are respectfully invited to attend.

Died: on Jul 1, after a brief illness, Saml W Bradley, in his 22nd year. His funeral will be on Fri at 3 o'clock, from his late residence, 410 G st, near 7th, Navy Yard.

Richmond, Jul 2. Last night the northern train from this city, when near Fredericksburg, ran into a culvert, which had been undermined by the storm. David Crowder, the engineer, & Edw Southard, baggage master, were badly hurt.

In Chancery-No 1,224. Edwin C Morgan, adm of Lewis J Kennedy, vs Jos C Lewis, Richd Felton, John Gregory, et al. The object of this suit is to procure the sale of lot 10 in square 288, in Wash City, for the payment of a debt due the cmplnt as administrator of Lewis J Kennedy, deceased, which is a lien thereon. The bill states that administration of the personal estate of L J Kennedy, a free colored man, then deceased, was duly granted by the Orphans Court of D C to cmplnt on Nov 2,1 855; that on Sep 26, 1854, cmplnt, intestate, loaned Jos C Lewis, John Gregory, Thos B Griffen, & Enoch Burnett [acting as trustees of the 13th st Baptist Church] the sum of $1,000, to be used in the erection of a church on said lot 10, in square 288, which was then vested in said trustees in fee simple; that said trustees, for the purpose of furnishing said Kennedy with evidence of said debt, & securing the return of said sum of $1,000, with interest, at the expiration of 2 years, on Sep 26, 1854, executed an instrument of writing acknowledging said debt, that it was to be paid as before stated, & pledging said lot for its punctual payment; that said trustees subsequently, viz, on May 3, 1855, conveyed said premises to one John McKenny in trust to secure the return to one Richd Felton, of N C, the sum of $5,000, alleged to have been loaned him; that said Felton loaned said money to said trustees [if it was really loaned.] with a full knowledge of the prior lien of said Kennedy on said premises; that said McKenny & said Felton had full notice at the time of taking said deed of trust of the prior claim of said Kennedy. The bill further states that, subsequently, viz on May 16, 1855, one Thos C Teasdale prepared an assignment, to be executed by said Kennedy, of his said claim to one Mgt Waggoner, & on the same day caused said Kennedy to attempt to affix his signature thereto, & obtained from him the certificate given to him by said trustees; that said Mgt, at the instance of said Teasdale, subsequently executed a release of said debt to said trustees, in consideration of their paying to her $60 a year during her life; that on May 16th, & for some time prior thereto, & thenceforth until his death, the said Kennedy was not of sane mind, & was utterly imcompetent to transact any business, & that, said trustees did not authorize said acts of said Teasdale. It appears that Richd Felton & John Gregory, two of said dfndnts, reside without said District. They are to appear at said Court on the first Monday of Nov next. By order of Wm M Merrick, A J. Test: Jno A Smith, clerk -Stone, for cmplnt.

SAT JUL 4, 1857
Sale of brandies, wines, liquors & cigars: on Jul 8, at the store of R D Tweedy, on Pa ave, between 9th & 10th sts, his entire stock. -Jas C McGuire, auct

Mrd: on Jul 1, at Balt, by Rev Dr J C Backus, Lt Geo H Bier, U S Navy, to Josephine V, daughter of Dr John P R Stone, of Ibervlle, La.

Revolutionary Reliques. "The reliques of the Revolution, like the leaves of the Sybil, they increase in value as they diminish in number." John Quincy Adams Our venerable friend of Arlington, Mr G W P Custis, now the only surviving member of Washington's domestic circle has an ancient trunk, covered with black leather, bound with brass clasps, & having on its lid G W, wrought in brass nails. This old trunk contains documents, papers, & accounts relating to the estates of the father & grandfather of its present possessor, upon which estates Washington administered. Some of these papers date back so far as 1760, or almost a 100 years ago, such date being one year after the marriage of the Provincial Colonel, in 1759.

More lynching in Iowa. 1-A man named Page, living in Clinton Co, was shot & killed, when the cmte proceeded to his house, on suspicion of his being a horse-thief. They were received with shots fired from the house. 2-On Thu, the cmte proceeded to arrest an old man, Benj Warren, who lives in Cedar Co, long been suspected of horse thieving. The decision was made to hang him; a rope was fixed across a tall limb & fastened around his neck. He was raised 10 feet & hung a corpse.

Marshal's sale: by writ of fieri facias, issued from the ofc of the Circuit Court of Wash Co, D C: public sale on Jul 30th, of lot 12 in square 729, in Wash City. Seized & levied upon as the property of Benj E Green, & will be sold to satisfy Judicials No 56, to Oct, 1857, in favor of Nathl Carusi. –J D Hoover, Marshal for D C.

Miss Coutts, a wealthy English lady, who has rendered herself so notorious by her love for the singer Mario, died recently in Paris from injuries received by the burning of her clothes. It is said the origin of her passion was a dream, that they have never spoken together; but she followed him in this travels throught the world, attending all his performances. –Newark Daily Advertiser

Mr Martin Howley, a contractor on the Pittsburg & Steubenville railroad, got into a quarrel with some of his workmen on Monday, when one Peter Saledine shot him in the shoulder with a pistol ball. A riot commenced, ending in bloody heads.

Mr Wm R Black, a toll collector on the Nobleston plank road, near Temperanceville, Pa, was very severely stabbed while asleep in bed beside his wife early on Tue. The unknown assassin hoisted a window & did the deed.

Mr Thos T Cropper, of Norfolk, was shot by a infuriate man named Bartholomew in the streets of the city on Tue. The inciting cause supposed to be jealousy. Mr Cropper is dangerously, but not believed to be mortally wounded.

Died: on Jul 2, in Wash City, Mrs Ellen *M__de, late of Alexandria city, in her 60th year. Her funeral is on Sunday at 3 o'clock, from the Wesley Chapel, 5th & F sts. [*Could be Meade.]

Died: on May 8 last, at Westport, Oldham Co, Ky, John Hines, sr, an old soldier of 1812, aged about 83 years, a native of Fred'k Co, Md, but for many years a citizen of Gtwn, D C. He was the oldest of 12 children, 2 daughters & 10 sons, 4 of whom are yet living in Wash, D C.

Wash City Ordinance: Act granting Mrs Mary A Lewis permission to erect a frame dwlg house within 24 feet of her brick dwlg house, in square 172; provided the consent of the Pres of the U S be first obtained. –Saml Yorke Atlee, Pres of the Board of Common Council. –Robt Clarke, Pres of the Board of Alderman. Approved, May 27, 1857, Wm B Magruder, Mayor. Approved, Jas Buchanan.

Railroad accident: Marietta, Ohio, Jul 2. Accident between Marietta & Cincinnati yesterday- wounded: Wm Williams, of Harper's Ferry, Va; Jacob Rosner, of Wheeling, & B Iverson, of Balt. Killed: Mrs Wm Bigham, of Marietta, Mr Richardson, of Boston, & a man whose name is unknown. [Jul 6th newspaper: Killed were Mrs Brigham, of Indianapolis; W G Richardson, of Boston. Two sons of Dr Bullard, of Indianapolis, were badly wounded; also Wm Brigham, of Marietta, K G McCuffey, of Columbus, & E M Stansberry, of Morgan Co. –Cincinnati Gaz]

Handsome cottage for sale: in square 847, on 6th st east, near G st south, now occupied by Dr Aaron W Miller, for sale on reasonable terms. Apply next door to Jas H Jones, house-painter, or to John G Adams, grocer, corner of 8th & L sts, Northern Liberties.

Teacher wanted: I wish to engage a young man to take charge of a small School the first of Sept, in a private family. Address Thos B Gibbons, Lower Marlborough, Calvert Co, Md.

MON JUL 6, 1857
Died: on Jul 5, Mrs Susan, wife of Chas Weirman, of Wash City, formerly of Easton, Pa. A worthy member of St Paul's English Lutheran Church, after a lingering & painful illness which she bore with Christian resignation. Her funeral will be from the residence of her husband on 15th st, between N Y ave & H st, this day at 5 P M.

Masonic Notice: members of the New Jerusalem Lodge, No 9, will meet for the purpose of attending the funeral of their late brother P A De Saules. –Jno Geo Smith, sec

Telegraphic dispatch of yesterday; scrap of paper dated Ballston Springs on Sat, Jul 4th read: Mr Wm L Marcy was found dead in his bed about noon today. He appeared to be in his usual health this morning.

Seventeen Sisters of Mercy sailed from England in the Brazilian steamer **Avon**, to attend the Yellow Fever Hospital at Rio de Janeiro.

Mr Geo W Norwood, deputy sheriff of this county, was accidentally shot on Sunday last, while traveling in the railroad cars somewhere in S C. It seems that he was asleep, & it is supposed that a pistol in his breast pocket was discharged by the jolting of the cars. After arriving here, Dr Hill extracted the ball. We congratulate Mr Norwood on his escape. –Raleigh Register

On Wed at Atlanta, Ga, Col D H Witcher, one of the proprietors of the Fulton House in that place, undertook to reprimand his son, Wm, aged 18 or 20 years, for drinking, when the youngster drew a pistol & fired at his father, causing his father's death on the following day. The parricide immediately made his escape.

Balt, Jul 5. The Fourth passed here very quietly. A man named Robt Frazier killed a German in a tavern row. Two children were accidentally shot by the careless use of fire-arms, one of whom is dead & the other fatally injured. [No names.]

TUE JUL 7, 1857
Household & kitchen furniture at auction on: Jul 9, at the residence of Mrs Blunt, 8th & E sts. -Jas C McGuire, auct

Mr John Plumbe, the Daguerreotypist, & well known to many of our citizens, recently committed suicide at Dubuque, Iowa. He was the first to introduce the art in this country.

Letter from Leavenworth City, dated Jun 29. On that day, at the election polls, a man named Mitchell shot at Jas H Lyle twice, & another man by the name of Haller stabbed him in the back & killed him. Lyle was unarmed. It was a cold blooded murder. Haller was arrested. –St Louis Republican

The song of <u>Hail Columbia</u>, by Judge John Hopkinson, was written in the summer of 1798, when a war with France was thought to be inevitable-Congress being then in session in Phil, deliberating upon that important subject, & acts of hostility having actually occurred. Chorus: Firm, united, let us be, Rallying round our liberty; As a band of brothers joined, Peace and safety we shall find.

Criminal Court-Wash-Friday. 1-Edw P Walsh guilty of an assault & battery on John Shaw, a colored patient at the Insane Asylum: fined him $5 & costs. 2-John Mullony, Mary Mullony, Mary Collins, John Collins, & Mgt Nugent were put on their trial for a general riot & row among themelves, disturbing the neighborhood, known as *Swampoodle*. The Jury found them not guilty. 3-John Thomas, a free colored man, was found guilty of assault & battery, & fined $8 & costs. 4-John Waggner, indicted for keeping a disorderly house at Uniontown: found not guilty.

Died: on Jul 5, in Wash City, P A Desaules, aged 56 years.

Died: on Jul 5, Mrs Mary A Jordon, wife of Richd L Jordon, of Wash City, a member of the Methodist Episcopal Church, after a lingering & painful illness. Her funeral will be from her late residence, on 7th st, between I & G sts, this day at 3 o'clock P M.

Boston, Jul 5. The Nat'l holyday was celebated with the usual patriotic demonstrations. As the public display of fireworks was progressing upon the Common a shell rocket mortar burst, killing Geo Tewksbury, formerly harbor master of this port; Asa L Lebby, Patrick Cook, & John McMahony, & badly injured Mr Wiseman Marshall, the tragedian, & John C Robinson. [Jul 8th newspaper: Cook was 20 years of age. Tewksbury was 49 years of age, & leaves a widow & 7 children, 4 daughters & 3 sons. Mr Libbey was a cabinet-maker, about 44 years of age, & leaves a family, who are absent in the vicinity of Elliot, Me. John McMahan, about 15 years of age, whose parents reside in Hartford place, was sitting on the fence & was struck by a piece of the mortar & almost instantly killed. Wyseman Marshall was struck on the shoulder & neck by a piece of mortar & conveyed to his residence 36 South Russell st, & thought not to be in any particular danger. Mr John W Robinson, who resides at 59 Hull st, had his head injured by a blow from a piece of the mortar. He is recovering quite favorably. –Boston Journal]

U S Patent Ofc, Wash, Jul 4, 1857. Ptn of Henry Burden, of Troy, N Y, praying for the extension of a patent granted to him on Sep 14, 1843, for an improvement in machinery for making horse shoes, for 7 years from the expiration of said patent, which takes place on Sep 14, 1857. –Chas Mason, Com'r of Patents

WED JUL 8, 1857
Hon Elias Brown died at his residence in Carroll Co, Md, on Friday last. He had been in Congress, served several terms in the State Legislature, & was a member of the Convention that adopted the present State Constitution.

The late Wm L Marcy was in his 71st year, being born in 1786; his native place was Sturbridge, Worcester Co, Mass; graduated at Brown Univ in 1808; commenced business as a lawyer in Troy & was appointed Recorder of that city in 1816; State Comptroller in 1823; removed from Troy to Albany; appointed a Justice of the Supreme Court in 1829; chosen U S Senator in 1831; in 1832 elected Govn'r, & re-elected in 1834; in 1845 he was appointed Sec of War by Pres Polk, & in 1852 Pres Pierce tendered him the Secretaryship of State, which he accepted. Govn'r Marcy was spending a few weeks at Balston, previous to his departure with his family for Europe. On Friday he visited Albany, calling on Mr Corning & other friends, & stopping at Troy to see his daughter. Mrs Marcy was visiting some friends in the West previous to her departure, & other members of his family were absent with the like motive; & he was comparatively alone at the time of his decease. The remains of Mr Marcy have been conveyed to Albany for interment.

Col Thos Hite, aided by other citizens of Jefferson Co, Va, set free 80 of their slaves on Thu last. The Colonel, as the agent of the owners, accompanied them to Middleburg, Pa, when, handing each individual $40 in money & equipping them all with sufficient clothing, they were set at liberty, with the chance of starving.

Annual Commencement at Gtwn College yesterday: addresses were delivered by Wm Choice-Valedictory, Jas A Wise, Eugene Digges, Alphonse Rost; Henry Bowling; Wm D Clare; W Jas Blakely; Emile Rost; Jas F McLaughlin; Francis A Lancaster; John F Marion; Chas A Hoyt; & Chas B Kenny. Annual Address of the Philodemic Society by Hon Wm M Merrick. The diplomas, medals, & premiums, were passed by the Pres of the U S. Degree of A M was conferred on: Peter J McGary, M D, Va; F Mathews Lancaster, M D, Md; Wm M Smith, Pa; Benj L Wheelan, Ala; & Wm H Gwynn, M D, Md. The degree of A B was conferred on: Emile Rost, La; Henry A Bowling, Md; Chas A Hoyt, Vt; Eugene Digges, Md; Jas M McLeod, D C; Wm Choice, S C; Wm J Hill, Md; Francis A Lancaster, Pa; Jas D Doughty, Pa; & Wm Sanders, Md. The medal in the class of philosophy was awarded to Mr Emile Rost, of Louisiana. Medals were presented to Jas D Dougherty, of Pa; Cornelius J O'Flinn, of Mich; Chas B Kenny, of Pa; & Jas P Neale, of Md.

Criminal Court-Wash-Tuesday. 1-Chas Schusssler was on trial on 2 charges of keeping a disorderly house & selling liquors without a license. On the first he was found not guilty, & having submitted the latter, was fined $16 & costs. 2-Antoine Ruppel's case was similarly disposed of. 3-Cordelia Hazel was put to trial & found guilty of stealing counterpanes & other property of Capt Lullay. She was removed to jail.

Died: Jul 3, at residence of her mother-in-law, Newtown, L I, of congestion of the brain, Susan W, wife of Mr Edw N Strong, & daughter of Mr John Warren, of N Y.

THU JUL 9, 1857
Lexington, Ky, Jul 4, 1857. The corner-stone for the monument of Henry Clay was erected today in the cemetery where his mother is entombed. He wished to be interred by the side of his mother, Eliz Watkins Clay, where he had inscribed on her tomb, "This monument, a tribute to her many domestic virtues, has been prompted by the filial affection and veneration of one of her grateful sons-H Clay." The remains of Henry Clay arrived in Lexington in the summer of 1852. The ceremonies of the day commenced at early dawn by the firing of a nat'l salute of 31 guns; procession followed; in it was the old family carriage of Henry Clay; next were the surviving members of the family of Mr Clay; Mr Henry T Duncan, Pres of the Henry Clay Monument Association, spoke; Mr Theodore N Wise, Grand Master of the Masonic Fraternity, laid the corner stone; oration of the day was delivered by Rev Robt J Breckinridge, D D; a Ky barbecue followed; dinner being ended, the military were reviewed by his Excellency Gov C S Morehead.

Montpelier, the magnificent estate of the late Pres Madison, was sold on Monday last to our former townsman, Thos J Carson, for $30,250, or $32 per acre. The mansion house is large & elegant, with a front of 150 feet, & the tract had on it all the improvements & bldgs necessary to the operations of a large farm.
–Balt American

Suit decided in the Circuit Court of Chicago some days ago, involving the right of property to a 3 year old colt, in which there were 60 or 70 witnesses & the costs amount to no less then $2,000. In 1855 a yearling colt, bay, white snip on the nose, white star in forehead, & white hind foot, strayed from the farm of Mr Jos S Eby, of Edgington, in this county, & in the fall of the same year was taken up by Mr Alex'r Thompson, of Perryton, Mercer Co. Mr Thompson had a colt the same age & as near like it as one pea is like another. These colts lived together till Feb, 1856, when Mr Thompson sold one of the them to Mr Lorenzo Elliot, of Edgington. The other colt had been bitten by a mad dog, & in the spring, showing signs of hydrophobia, was shot by Mr Thompson. In the fall of 1856 Mr Eby saw at Elliot's the colt he [Elliot] bought. Elliot replied that he purchased it of Thompson, & refused to give it up. Eby then replevined the colt, & it was then taken possession of by the Sheriff. The suit was in regard to the right of property. After Eby had replevined the colt, it is reported that the neighbors of Eby & Elliot advised a settlement of the suit, & that Eby offered to submit it to arbitration at any time, but a settlement could not be effected for the reason that Thompson had authorized Elliot to defend the suit. One portion of the witnesses positively indentified the colt as the one raised & owned by Thompson, & the balance being equally certain that the colt was Eby's lost colt. The controversy has been carried on in good nature. The verdict of the jury was for the plntf Eby, & a motion was made by the dfndnt's counsel for a new trial.

Dr Jas R Smith, Professor of Physiology & General Pathology in the Oglethorpe Medical College of this city, died yesterday. He had been complaining of slight indisposition for a week spast. While reclining on a lounge in the ofc of Dr Le Hardy, he was attacked suddenly with congestion of the lungs & expired in a few minutes. –Savannah Republican, Jul 4th.

There recently died in Snowshoe township, Centre Co, Pa, a pioneer of that county named Saml Askey, aged 81 years. He was born in Path valley, Franklin [then Northumberland] Co, Pa; for some time in the service of his country under Gen Harrison; after his services were no longer required he returned to the place of his nativity; he later settled about a mile from the Little or Black Moshannon; he was one of the two first settlers that followed in the trial of the Indians. His life would compare with that of Danl Boon or Col Crocket. He spent much time in hunting, which proved to be a most lucrative business.

Late accounts from the West discredit the reports that 150 soldiers & teamsters of Col Sumner's command had been massacred by Indians west of **Fort Kearny**. Gen Harney, at Leavenworth, places no confidence in it.

Franklin Co: on Monday last Mr Patrick Gallaher, a highly esteemed citizen of the county was shot, & probably killed by a man named Blackwell. Gallaher was the owner of a mill in Franklin Co, & some words had passed between them. Blackwell went to Wangler's store & procured 2 pistols & a shot-gun-the last loaded with buckshot. He returned to the mill with his son, & found Gallaher & a young man named Kearny. Gallaher was shot with the gun, & as he fell Kearny ran up to support him, & he was wounded by a shot fired by a son of Blackwell; after which the latter fired at & killed him also. The murderers escaped, & the male population turned out in pursuit of them. –St Louis Republican

On Monday a pleasure party, consisting of Mr J W Leslie, of the firm of G P Putnam & Co, booksellers, his niece, Miss Palmer, Mr Porter, of the firm of Lane & Porter, dry-good dealers in N Y, & 5 other persons, a family of brothers & sisters, whose names we have not heard, were sailing in a small boat on the Ronconkow lake, on Long Island, when the boat capsized, & Mr Leslie, Miss Palmer, & Mr Porter were drowned. All the rest were rescued. –N Y Com Adv

The Columbia Institution for the Deaf & Dumb & the Blind: incorporated by Congress during its last session. The Directors are: Hon Amos Kendall, Pres; Wm Stickney, Sec; G W Riggs, Treasurer; Wm H Edes, Judson Mitchell, J C McGuire, Davis A Hall, & Byron Sunderland. Mr Edw M Gallaudet, recently an instructor in the American Asylum at Hartford, Coon, & a son of the late Rev Thos H Gallaudet, L L D, has been appointed Superintendent, & will be assisted by his mother, who is herself a mute, & was among the first educated in America. The institution is located about a mile north of the Capitol.

New Hardware Store, 34 Centre Market Space, between 6th & 7th sts: John W Baden.

Orphans Court of Wash Co, D C. In the case of Caroline Cox, excx of Geo Cox, deceased: the executrix & Court have appointed Aug 1st next, for the final settlement of the personal estate of the deceased, of the assets in hand.
–Ed N Roach, Reg/o wills

Died: in Brooklyn, Mrs Rebecca M, wife of O M Bradford, [of the Associated Press, & recently of this city,] aged about 20 years. [No death date given-current item.]

Died: on Wed, in Wash City, after a short illness of about 36 hours, Kate Ellar, infant daughter of C M & M A Keys, aged 4 months & 12 days. Her funeral is today at 3 o'clock, from her parents' residence, 540 13th st, Island.

FRI JUL 10, 1857

Household & kitchen furniture at auction on: Jul 14, at the residence of J W Nairn, N Y ave & 15th sts. -Jas C McGuire, auct

A young man named J H Keplinger, aged 17 years, while on a excursion to the Relay House on Tue with the Westminster Presbyterian Sabbath School of Balt, to which he was attached, was drowned in the Patapsco Falls while bathing. He was from Shepherdstown, Va, where his parents reside, & was employed at Enoch Bennett's fancy dry-goods house.

The Distribution of Premiums at the Academy of the Visitation in Gtwn was held on Wed in the pretty, but far too diminutive Odeon of the Academy. In the musical exercises Miss Carrie Hickey, the Misses Pizzini, Miss LeCompte, Miss Poe, Miss Schwartze, & Misses Gilliam & Dougherty took prominent parts. The fine display of needlework & art were by Hannah Mabee; Carrie Hickey, Elve Moore, Miss E Pizzini, Lavinia Clements, Miss Plowden, Misses Mabee, of Indiana, & M Pizzini, of Richmond, Va. The Convent of which the Academy is a part is making a very extensive addition to its capacity in the erection of a bldg on 3rd st that will contain approaching 100 rooms, & will cost in the neighborhood of $25,000. The plan is an old one, given in 1839 by the late Robt Mills, & the construction is under the charge of Mr Richd Pettit.

Superior Statuary, constructed both from native & Italian marble, may be seen at the marble-yard of Mr Wm Rutherford, on E st, between 12th & 13th sts, Wash.

Criminal Court-Wash-Wed. 1-Jos Gerhard was arraigned for manslaughter in shooting his barkeeper, Schulte, on Jun 11. The Court gave instructions that if Gerhard had reason to believe & did believe that his wife's life was put to imminent peril, or that she was in danger of great bodily harm, the accused was justified in his purpose of shooting the assailants, & if by mischance he shot another party, he is not guilty. Mr Key replied, taking the ground that Gerhard did not fire in order to protect his wife, but to gratify a vindictive passion against the party who had come to his house to drink. The Jury retired & had not concluded on a verdict. 2-Robt King, for an assault on Wm Mastin, submitted, & was fined $5 & costs. Not being able to pay or give security, King was put into the custody of the Marshal.

Obit-died: yesterday, at Phil, Wm Ogden Niles, well known throughout the political circles of the country, after a severe illness of a day or two. He was a son of the late Hezekiah Niles, the founder of Niles' Register, & succeeded his father in the publication of that national work, which he edited with marked ability. –Balt American

John S Hollingshead, Justice of the Peace & Notary Public, 8th & E sts, Wash. [Ad]

Runaway was committed to the Wash Co jail, Md, on Jul 3, negro David Johnson; says he is from Bedford, Pa, & is free. The owner is to come forward & prove property, otherwise he will be discharged agreeably to law. −B A Garlinger, Sheriff

Mrd: on Jul 7, by Rev Mr Linthicum, Mason E McNew to Margaret A Godman, all of PG Co, Md.

Died: on Jul 2, at St Louis, after a severe & protracted illness, Tubman Jones, late of Wash, D C, in his 61st year. He had for many years been a Gov't ofcr of the U S at Wash, D C. Six weeks ago, accompanied by his wife, he made a visit to St Louis, when he was taken dangerously ill. He languished on a bed of sickness until Jul 2nd, when the messenger of death relieved him. He was a native of Somerset, Md.

Died: on Jul 9, at the residence of her son-in-law, B S Kinsey, s e corner of Md ave & 6th st, Ruth Drinker, relict of the late Geo Drinker, of Alexandria, Va, in her 86th year. Her funeral will take place today at 1 o'clock.

Died: on Jul 8, Andrew Foote, in his 57th year.

Died: on Jul 8, John B Jillard, in his 9th year, eldest son of Geo E & Cordelia M Jillard.

SAT JUL 11, 1857

Trustee's sale, by deed of trust from Robt Cochran to Andrew Wylie, dated Mar 15, 1854, duly recorded, public auction on Jul 17, all the household & kitchen furniture of said Cochran at his dwlg house on B st, between 13th & 13½ sts. -A Green auct

House & lot on E st at auction: by deed of trust from Mrs Mary E Barney & others, dated Nov 29, 1856, recorded in the Land Records in Wash Co, D C, in Liber J A S No 136, folio 5 to 19, adjoins with that portion of said lot 6 which was conveyed by David Saunders & wife to Roger C Weightman, to the use of Mary S Scott: public auction on the premises on Aug 4, all that part of the lot of ground numbered 6 in square 456, in Wash City, with a good 3 story brick dwlg, with a large 2 story back bldg, arranged for a residence & ofc. −Henry M Morfit, trustee -C W Boteler, auct

Orphans Court of Wash Co, D C. In the case of Ulysses Ward, adm of Richd H Rawlings, deceased: the administrator & Court have appointed Aug 1 next, for the final settlement of the personal estate of said deceased, with the assets in hand.
−Ed N Roach, Reg/o wills

A letter in the San Antonio Texan, dated Loredo, Texas, May 25, states that "Wild Cat," the celebrated Seminole chief, who gave the U S so much trouble during the Seminole war, is dead. He, with 40 of his followers, having fallen victims to the smallpox.

Hon Franklin W Bowdon, formerly a member of Congress from Alabama, died lately in Texas, of which State he had become a resident.

Distribution of premiums on Jul 8-Visitation Academy-Gtwn. Premiums distributed by his Excellency the Pres of the U S, assisted by Very Rev C H Stonestreet, S J, & Rev B A Maguire, S J, Pres of Gtwn College. Premiums distributed to:

Priscilla Neale, Chas Co, Md
Anne Lecompte, Wash City, D C
Hibernia Farrall, Halifax, N C
Mary Dougherty, Harrisburg, Pa
Jane Poe, Gtwn, D C
Mary Maguire, St Louis, Mo
Adelaide Frederic, Augusta, Ga
Kate Smith, Reading, Pa
Florence Poe, Gtwn, D C
Vandalia Lancaster, Wash City, D C
Susie Plowden, St Mary's Co, Md
Annie Horne, Milledgeville, Ga
Louisa Keegan, New Orleans, La
Emma Keenan, Balt, Md
Celestia Semmes, PG Co, Md
Elviana Moore, Bayou Fordouche, La
Maggie Freeman, Wash City, D C
Libbie Pizzini, Richmond, Va
Helena Ward, Balt, Md
Jane Springer, Cincinnati, Ohio
Hannah Maybee, Ill
Sallie Davis, Wash, D C
Francillia Alexander, Wash City, D C
Camilie Malacher, New Orleans, La
Louise Malacher, New Orleans, La
Marietta Culloni, Carthage, Tenn
Eugenia Moore, Columbus, Ga
Clara Crouse, Lyunchburg, Va
Maggie Keenan, Balt, Md
Virginia Coolidge, Gtwn, D C
Emma Malbon, Gtwn, D C
Georgie Gray, Gtwn, D C
Ida Ryon, Barnwell, S C
Mary Gormley, Gtwn, D C
Mary Peters, Gtwn, D C
Eliza Sweeny, Wash City, D C
Ellen Foley, New Orleans, La
Susan Mathews, Phil, Pa
Mary Waring, Montg Co, Md
Mary Callan, Gtwn, D C
Mary Moxley, Gtwn, D C
Alice Knight, Gtwn, D C
Mary Ann Kelly, Albemarle Co, Va
Kate Irving, Sunny Side, N Y
Lucinda Clements, PG Co, Md
Mary Ivy, Berwick City, La
Clio Bignon, Augusta Ga
Bettie Hurdle, Gtwn, D C
Cecelia O'Donnoghue, Gtwn, D C
Clementina McWilliams, Chas Co, Md
Annie Pickrell, Gtwn, D C
Helen Clements, Gtwn, D C
Fannie Petit, Gtwn, D C
Lilla Risque, Gtwn, D C
Eliz Boucher, Gtwn, D C
Mary Jane Canson, Wash, D C
Ellen Kelly, Albemarle Co, Va
Helen Brooks, Gtwn, D C
Alice Seymour, Gtwn, D C
Mary Mann, Gtwn, D C
Clara Kidwell, Gtwn, D C
Mary Ellen Smith, St Mary's Co, Md
Mary Cleary, Wash City
Josephine Clarke, Gtwn, D C
Mary Scott, Campbell Co, Va
Eliza Newman, Gtwn, D C
Mary Cleary, Gtwn, D C
Mary Ellen Smith, Gtwn, D C
Mary Delaigle, Augusta, Ga
Jane Barbour, Gtwn, D C
Mary Rainy, Gtwn, D C
Amelia Ross, Gtwn, D C
Teresa Keegan, New Orleans, La
Maris Jane Briscoe, Wash City, D C
Mary Semmes, Canton, Miss

Eliz Harty, Charlotte, N C
Josephine Heron, Gtwn, D C
Agatha O'Neil, Gtwn, D C
Augusta Goodwin, San Jose, Calif
Amanda Payne, Gtwn, D C
Albina Gilliam, Dinwiddie Co, Va
Amanda Irvy, Berwick City, La
Bettie Kirkman, Madison Co, Va
Pauline Seymour, Gtwn, D C
Sybilla Frederic, Augusta, Ga
Caroline Hickey, Wash City, D C
Mary Chadwick, Newark, N J
Octavia Prudhomme
Josephine Morse, Natchitoches, La
Mary McLeod, Gtwn, D C
Sarah Jane Cunningham, Gtwn, D C
Isabella Schwartze, Wash City, D C
S Dankworth, Wash City, D C
Virginia Payne, Gtwn, D C
Alice Waddell, Natchitoches, La
Harriet Essex, Gtwn, D C
L Crawford, Gtwn, D C
Lizzie Dahlgreen, Wash, D C
Melany Duveyrier
Mary Pizzini, Richmond, Va
Ellen Thecker, Gtwn, D C

Criminal Court-Wash-Thu. 1-The Jury in the case of Jos Gerhard, tried for manslaughter, could not agree, & were dismissed. 2-Patrick Cahill guilty of assault & battery on a woman: sentenced to 2 weeks in prison & fined $10. 3-Cordelia A Hazel found not guilty of receiving a breastpin, knowing it to be stolen. 4-Jas M Minor charged with assault on Eli Lake submitted his case.

Fine Confectionery: bake house on my own premises. All I ask is to give me a fair trial. -U H Ridenour, 304 Pa ave, between 9th & 10th sts.

$5 reward for return of a small black & tan English Terrier Dog, that strayed on Jul 9. W Marquis, 400 Pa ave, between 4½ & 6th sts.

The advertiser offers his services to parents & guardians as a Private Teacher, in which capacity he has had a successful experience. Address Adam P Johnson.

Circumstances beyond my control lead me to resign the Rectorship of Ascension Parish, Wash. –Henry Stanly
+
Letter to Rev Henry Stanly: with every assurance of respect & esteem, we remain, reverend & dear sir, your friends & parishioners, Gustavus Waters, Chas F Perrie, Church Wardens. C W Bennett, D McCarty, J T Stevens, Ezra Williams, Gustavus Waters, Chas F Hurlbut, J C Bowyer, & Jona Guest, Vestrymen.

MON JUL 13, 1857
1-Purser Edw D Reynolds, of the U S Navy, who was recently ordered to the U S frig **Mississippi**, bound to the East Indies, has resigned his commission. He has been some 11 years in the service, 7 of which have been spent at sea. 2-Purser Thos B Nalle has been detached from the Wash Navy Yard, & ordered to the U S steam frig **Mississippi**, bound to the East Indies, vice Purser Reynolds, resigned; & Purser Andrew J Watson has been ordered, vice Mr Nalle, to the Wash Navy Yard.

The partnership existing under the firm of Boyne & Wood was dissolved by mutual consent on Jul 1. –Thos J Boyne, W W Wood

A boy named Narcisse Lamontague, aged 13 years, saved 8 children from the wreck of the steamer **Montreal** by seizing the door of a state-room, placing the children upon it, & pushing it before him while he swam, that, at different trips, he landed on a dry rock, or on the beach. They would have otherwise met a watery grave.

A report of the death of Robt Holmes, the celebrated Irish barrister who defended Emmet in 1803 & John Mitchell in 1848, has been going round the papers. He is alive & well & resides at present with his son-in-law in London.

Mr Saml Y Pace, deputy postmaster of Purdy, Tenn, & the son of the postmaster, was arrested last week for robbing the mail, & is now in jail. He is quite young. A $50 bill he had in his possession, was recognized by Mr Leroy M Huggins, a merchant of McNairy Co, as one which he had placed in a registered letter sent to New Orleans. The letter was received but there was no money found therein.

N Y: The funeral of Messrs Leslie & Porter, & Miss Palmer, who were drowned in Roukoma lake on Monday last, took place on Friday in St Peter's Episcopal Church, in State st, in the presence of about 1,500 persons.

Accidents on the Fourth. 1-At Mefield, Mass, Mr Edw Sewall & Joel Morse were severely wounded by the premature explosion of a cannon they were firing. Mr Sewall had 3 fingers blown off & badly injured his face. Mr Morse had his arm very badly broken, & his face filled with the powder. Thaddeus Morse, of the same place, was badly burnt in the face & it is feared that he will lose his eye-sight. 2-At Plantsville, Ct, Logee Taber, aged 20, had his whole foot, except the heel, blown off by the premature discharge of a small cannon, before the muzzle of which he was standing. 3-The wife of Mr N G Smith, was instantly killed, as she stood with her husband at a window when a rocket came through the window striking her in the forehead.

The Boston Journal, from Hanover, N H, Jul 9, states that H E B Stowe, a son of Mrs Harriet Beecher Stowe, a member of the freshman class in Dartmouth College, was drowned in the Connecticut river that afternoon. [Jul 14th newspaper: H E B Stowe, son or Prof Stowe, was drowned in the Conn river on Thu while bathing. He had just returned from Europe, where he had spent the last year traveling with his mother. They arrived in Persia on Tue & the young man reached home Wed. He was 19 years of age.]

Died: on Jul 11, at the residence of his parents, West st, Gtwn, Chas H Browne, in his 28th year. His funeral is this day at 2 o'clock.

Died: on Sat last, after a brief illness, Frederico Casali, a native of Rome, Italy, in his 34th year. His funeral will take place this afternoon at 3:30 o'clock, from the residence of his friend C Brumidi, 308 Dela ave, Capitol Hill, between B & C sts.

Died: on Jul 11, in Wash City, Mary Ann, wife of W Thompson, proprietor of the Washington News.

U S Patent Ofc, Wash, Jul 10, 1857. Ptn of Jas Sanford, of Redding, Conn, praying for the extension of a patent granted to him on Oct 12, 1843, for an improvement in straw cutters, for 7 years from the expiration of said patent, which takes place on Oct 12, 1857. –Chas Mason, Com'r of Patents

Orphans Court of Wash Co, D C. Letters of administration, with the will annexed, on the personal estate of John Smith, late of Wash Co, deceased. –Wm T Duvall, Walter H Adamson, adm w a

Orphans Court of Wash Co, D C. Letters of administration on the personal estate of John Robert, late of Wash Co, deceased. –W B Magruder, adm

TUE, JUL 14, 1857
Rev Mr Tracy passed through Detroit on Thu with a troop of 60 boys picked up in the streets of N Y C for distribution to new homes in the West. The Press says that they were a good looking lot of little fellows & seemed to enjoy themselves hugely.

Fanny Johnson, age 6 years, fell from the second story window of her parents' residence, at Balt, on Sat last, & was almost instantly killed. Her mother had gone out, leaving her daughter in the room.

Judge Mathew Dunbar, the oldest lawyer of the Kanawha, [Va,] bar, & the last Judge of that Circuit under the old constitution, died suddenly on Jul 5. He filled the post of Commonwealth's Atty for Kanawha at the time of his death.

Col Ethan Allen's grand-daughter resides at Mill Point, Ottowa Co, Midh. She has in her possession the identical sword with which the Colonel backed up his demand for the surrender of Ticonderoga-"in the name of the Great Jehovah & the Continental Congress." The sword is 27 inches in length; handle is 7 inches in length, of bone or horn; & the mounting is silver, but was washed with gold while worn by Capt Allen to match his uniform. The gold is partially worn off. A dog's head of silver forms the end of the handle. On one of the silver bands of the scabbard the name Ethan Allen is engraved in large letters; on another E Brasher, maker, N Y, & on still another, in script, Martin Vosburg, 1755.

On Jul 4th, in Belmont Co, Ohio, Dr Drake, a young physician, was killed by exploding fragments; John Scott, jr, was wounded & not expected to recover.

Font Hill, the Farm & residence of the late Gen Ridgely, containing about 400 acres, on Elkridge, Howard Co, Md, is for sale. There is a large 2 story brick & frame double dwlg house, with a connecting hall of 25 feet width, out houses for negroes, dairy, & stabling. Apply to John S Ridgely, on the premises, post ofc Ellicott's Mills, Howard Co, or to Andrew Sterrett Ridgely, Atty at Law, 23 St Paul st, Balt.

The train for Louisville on the New Albany railroad met with a serious accident on Tue at the Wea bridge, 3 miles distant from Lafayette, when the wheels of the tender flew off the track. The following persons were severely injured: John T Baccus, Alex'r Flack, Albert Knapper, Mrs Samantha Tucker, & Conductor Drought.

Jos P Mahony, from Fred'k Co, Va, in entering the Jersey City Railroad depot, on Wed, to take the train for Phil, was robbed by some dexterous pickpocket of his pocket-book containing $1,235 in money & 2 notes of $617 each.

Orphans Court of Wash Co, D C. In the case of Benj F Larned, exc of Eliz R Larned, deceased: the executor & Court have appointed Aug 4 next, for the final settlement of the personal estate of the deceased, of the assets in hand.
–Ed N Roach, Reg/o wills

Criminal Court-Wash: 1-Jos Gerhard was acquitted. 2-John Kelley was acquitted of an assault on Thos Thorn. 3-Thos Harper acquitted of petty larceny. 4-Eliz Ellington, colored, acquitted of assault on Adeline Smith.

Died: on Jul 13, in Wash City, suddenly in his 43rd year, Mr Theodore Foster, of N Y, late a clerk in the U S Capitol. His funeral will be from his late residence, [Mrs Cudlipps',] 427 Pa ave, this afternoon, at 4 o'clock.

Died: on Jul 13, at his residence in Montg Co, Md, near Beltsville, of scarlet fever, in his 43rd year, Wm Burford, son-in-law of Wm Thompson, magistrate of Wash City. His funeral will be from the residence of the deceased this afternoon at 4 o'clock.

Died: on Jul 5, at Norfolk, Va, after an illness of 2 days, in his 63rd year, Harrison Allmand, jr, a merchant of proverbial integrity.

Died: on Jul 13, in Wash City, Judge Thos Jefferson Smith, formerly of N Y. Due notice will be given of the time of his funeral.

WED JUL 15, 1857
Executor's sale of 30 valuable bldg lots in Wash City, belonging to the estate of the late Col Saml Miller, deceased, at auction, on Jul 27th. –Francis Peters, exc
-A Green auct

Household & kitchen furniture, liquors, wines, & contents of a restaurant, at auction, on Jul 21, at the restaurant of J DeSaules, 225 Pa ave, between 14th & 15th sts, opposite Willard's. –A Green auct at auction

The Eastern Shore of Md. The ancient town of Berlin is not without its historical relic or reminiscence. About a half mile from its centre stands the house in which Cmdor Decatur is said to have been born. It is now used as a barn, & is in dilapidated condition. There has been much dispute, in time past, as to his birthplace, but there cannot be any reasonable doubt that this is the spot, although his parents did not long remain here after his birth. Another relic are the ruins of the Buckingham Presbyterian Church, built in 1784, about three quarters of a mile from the town. The graveyard will be kept up, & considerable pains be taken to adorn it.
–Sylvanus

American Nat'l Executive Cmte: the following appointed the Executive Cmte:
Anthony Kennedy, Md
Jacob Broom, Pa
A B Ely, Mass
Wm R Smith, Ala
Vespasian Ellis, Wash
J Scott Harrison, Ohio
Jas W Barker, N Y
Jas Bishop, N J
Kenneth Raynor, N C
F K Zollicoffer, Tenn
E Brooks, N Y
Henry W Davis, Md
A H H Stuart, Va

Gen Jos M Hernandez, the first delegate from Florida to Congress, died at Cuba on Jun 8. He was a Spanish citizen of Florida before its transfer to the U S, & was a brig general in the U S army during the Indian war in that Territory.

Since the first of Jan last there have arrived in this country, by 4 different vessels, upwards of 2,100 emigrants who had espoused the Mormon faith in the old country, & were on their way to Utah Territory, in the Great Salt Lake basin. These Mormons were composed mostly of Welsh & English, with a sprinkling of Danes & Norwegians, & a few Germans.

Kent Co News of Sat: Wm R Boyer & Thos Anderson were arrested for passing counterfeit notes. Boyer held to bail for a further hearing. Anderson is in prison.

Fatal encounter in Ky, from a correspondent writing from Summerville, Green Co, Ky, under date of Jun 16: difficulty occurred between Robt J Peace & Wm M Sknaggs, when Beauchamp, who was the brother-in-law of Sknaggs, interposed & begged the parties to desist. Peace ordered Beauchamp to get out of the way or he would kill him. Beauchamp drew a revolver, fired, missed, & retreated, & was followed up by Peace, who placed his rifle against his antagonist, fire, & literally tore his heart out. The fatal encounter was witnessed by the wife & children of the deceased. –Louisville Democrat

Wash City Ordinance: Act for the relief of Nicholas Vedder: to pay him the sum of $1.94, for taxes erroneously paid by him. Approved: Jul 9, 1857.

Letter in the official journal of the late Sec Marcy. Wash, Mar 3, 1857. The undersigned, clerks in the Dept of State, cannot allow the official relation, which they have held towards Hon Wm L Marcy, Sec of State, terminate without expressing their wishes for the prolongation of your useful life.

W Hunter	H D J Pratt	W C Reddall
Edw Stubbs	Geo Bartle	R S Chilton
Js Mackie	Thos C Cox	Wm E Stubbs
Edmund Flagg	W P Faherty	Wm Hogan
R W Young	Francis Markoe	H C Mclaughlin
A H Derrick	R S Chew	Jno C Nevins
J P Polk	Geo J Abbot	Ferd Jefferson
Geo Chipman	H D Johnson	
Wm J Bromwell	Aled'r Dimitry	

Indian affairs in Minnesota. St Paul [Min] Pioneer of Jul 7. On Jun 29, Mr Flandrau, the agent for the Sioux, received intelligence that 3 Indians, members of Ink-pa-du-ta's band, were lurking in the neighborhood of the Yellow Medicine agency. He dispatched a trusty Indian to the band, & upon his report that a son of Ind-pa-du-ta was certainly in the neighborhood, & probably 2 others of the band, Mr Flandrau promptly formed his plans to arrest the murderers. He procured from **Fort Ridgely** a detachment of Co D, 10th infty, under command of Lt Murray. They were accompanied by several Indian guides, among them was Ho-ton-wash-te, or Beautiful Voice, one of the Indians who risked his life to secure the release of Miss Gardiner. The soldiers surrounded the lodge in which the Indians were staying, but one of the Indians ran out & took refuge in a ravine. They soldiers fired inflicting several wounds. The Indian retired fire & a soldier rushed forward & bayoneted the savage. He was the son of Ink-pa-du-ta, who, having married with the Annuity Indians, at the time he was killed was on a visit to his father-in-law. He is the identical savage who dragged Mrs Noble from the lodge of the Yankton chief who purchased her, & beat her to death with clubs.

E A Rowe, Deputy Treasurer, who has been confined 6 months on board the prison brig at Sacramento, has finally consented to purge himself of contempt, by answering such questions as may be propounded touching the mysterious disappearance of the Treasury moneys. The Court of Sessions not being in session, the Judge refused his application.

Criminal Court-Wash-Tue. 1-Wm Taylor, John Hale, & Frank Etlet put on trial for rioting at Gerhard's tavern, on Md ave, at the time of the accidental shooting of Henry Schultze by said Gerhard. They Jury found them guilty, & the Court sentenced each of them to 3 months in jail & a fine of $10.

Asheville [N C] Spectator of Jul 9. Rev Dr Elisha Mitchell, of Chapel Hill, about 2 weeks ago arrived here on his way to the Black Mountains, for further explorations of that region. His body was found yesterday in the Cat-Tail fork of Caney river. Is seems that he was walking on the edge of a precipice when his feet slipped & he fell 40 feet. He died a martyr to science & scientific knowledge. [Jul 25, 1857: Dr Mitchell was a native of Connecticut; graduated at Yale College in 1815. He had been with his son, but separated from him to visit the Caney River Settlement.]

San Jose [Calif] Tribune. Maj R C Wood & Maj Tozer, who, with the exception of the boy Chas Evans, detained by the Mexicans in Sonora, are the only survivors of the ill-fated expedition under Gen Crabb, arrived in San Jose from Los Angeles on Wed, & proceeded to San Francisco yesterday.

Explosion of a locomotive on Wed, between Montezuma & May's Point, a few miles from this city, killed Mr Ostrander, contractor, & the engineer Clements. Ambrose Christian, the fireman, was hurled through the air & killed instantly.
–Auburn [N Y] American of Fri.

Died: on Jul 13, in Wash City, Mrs Eliz Talbot, aged 80 years. Her funeral will take place on Wed afternoon from Grace Church, on the Island, at 4 o'clock.

Utica, Jul 14. The State Lunatic Asylum, located here, took fire this morning; Dr L F Rose, a prominent citizen, is feared to be fatally injured. Inmates were not injured.

THU JUL 16, 1857
The Pres has appointed D R Eckles, of Indiana, to be Chief Justice of the U S Court for the Territory of Utah.

Valuable farm at auction: on Jul 27, on the premises, the highly improved farm, the property of Mrs Dyer, 2½ miles from Gtwn, & adjoining Tenallytown, containing 68 acres; the bldgs are good & nearly new, & consist of a frame dwlg, with back bldg, servants' house, stable, carriage-house, barn & corn-house. Apply to Barnard & Buckey, aucts

On Jul 7 a terrible affray occurred in Americus, with Harvey W Shaw & Wm Shaw on one side, & sundry persons on the other side, which resulted in the death of Henry W Shaw, & the shooting of Wm Shaw, though not fatally. An assault was made the previous day by H W Shaw on Chas W Hancock, who was bruised. Shaw was arraigned before the Mayor & fined $20 & costs for the offence committed, which was paid, when leaving the court-house Hancock met Shaw & a verbal assault continued. Mrs H W Shaw fired 3 discharges with a revolver at Mr McBain, without doing any damage. When her husband fell, saying he was a dead man & asking for his children, Mrs Shaw fainted, & was in a very critical condition yesterday.
-Macon Citizen of Jul 8.

Peremptory sale of pair of superior matched carriage horses: on Jul 16, the span of beautiful black Horses belonging to Mr De Cramer, who is about to leave for Europe. –Jas C McGuire, auct

Mrs Catherine Ferries, a widow lady 70 years old, was struck by a train of cars while walking on the track of the Boston & Worcester railroad on Sat last, & was killed.

Andrew Tillner was on Fri last, in St Louis, fined $50 for using obscene language on the street while ladies were passing. The magistrate who administered that sentence should have a monument. –Balt American

Henry Fife, Monroe Stewart, & Charlotte Jones, indicted for the murder of Geo Wilson & Mrs McMasters, have been convicted at Pittsburg.

Obit announcement in the Montreal Gaz of Wed last: "Perished, on the steamer **Montreal**, Jun 26th, Bryce Hall, Brydekirk Village, Dumfriesshire, Scotland, aged 43; also, Jane, his wife, aged 47; Wm, their son, aged 23; Simon, 14; Robt, 10; Peter, 7; Catherine, their daughter, 18; Mary Ann, 12."

Notice is given that Land Warrant No 11,842, for 160 acres, issued to Allen McFales, & by him assigned in blank & bought by one Wm Norris for Geo Crittenden, has been lost, & the location of said warrant is duly caveated, & in proper time application will be made to the Pension Oc for a duplicate issue of said warrant. –C W Downson, Agent for Geo Crittenden

Notice: Whereas by virtue of a decree entered in a suit pending in the Circuit Court of Rappahannock Co, Va, in which J Richd Nicklin & Delia Calvert are plntfs, & Cecilius Calvert, Hannah Jett, Jas Jett, & John Jett, adms of Ann Coxe, deceased, & others are dfndnts, among other things it was adjudged, entered, & decreed that the com'r, who was directed to take the accounts directed in said cause, should inquire & state to the court whether the said Sarah Henrietta Birch, a sister of the half-blood to the said Ann Coxe, was living at the time of her death; & if she was dead whether her said husband survived her & the said Ann Coxe; & whether she left a child or children, descendant or descendants; & for that purpose the said com'r is to cause advertisements to be inserted in the Nat'l Intelligencer & Union weekly for 4 weeks, for the said Sarah Henreitta Birch, her child or children, descendant or descendants, or other person or persons entitled to her interest in the said estate, to come in before said com'r & make out his, her, or their claim to partake in the distribution of the said estate. Same to appear in my ofc on Aug 15, 1857. –J Y Menefee, Com'r, Wash, Rappannock Co, Va.

Mrd: on Wed, in Wash City, by Rev John C Smith, Mr Priestly H McBride, of Missouri, to Mrs Adaline R L Dyson, of Wash City.

Died: on Jul 6, at Fairfield, Fauquier Co, Va, C Lewis Marshall, in his 18th year.

Died: on Jul 15, in his 30th year, Louis Lehmann, a native of Germany. His funeral will be from the Washington Infirmary this evening, at 4 o'clock.

FRI JUL 17, 1857
At Cape Elizabeth, Maine, last Sat, Helen McFarland, residing in the family of Clement Jordan, went into the Spurmick river with 3 little girls to bathe. Awhile later she drowned. The girls hastened to the shore for assistance. After some time the body of the young woman was found in water not over 2½ feet deep.

Shocking incident occurred on Sunday in this borough. The family of Mr Burke, who resides near the Catholic Church, consists of himself, wife, & a sprightly lad of 18 months. The father often amused the child by firing gun caps. On Sunday he put a cap on the lock of the empty barrel, as he wrongly supposed, & firing it off, the whole charge entered the lad's mouth killing him instantly. The report of the gun brought in the neighbors, who found the 3 weltering in blood on the floor, one dead & 2 frightened to unconsciousness. –Conneautville Cour

Promotions & appointments in the U S Army made by the Pres since the publication of Genr'l Orders of Jun 1, 1857, as follows:
Promotions:
Corps of Topographical Engineers
1st Lt Wm B Franklin, to be capt.
1st Lt Wm F Raynolds, to be capt.
2nd Lt Jos C Ives, to be 1st lt
2nd Lt Henry L Abbot, to be 1st lt.
Ordnance Dept:
1st Lt Thos J Brereton, to be capt.
2nd Lt Oliver O Howard, to be 1st lt.
1st Regt of Dragoons:
2nd Lt Milton T Carr, to be 1st lt.
2nd Regt of Dragoons:
2nd Lt John B Villepigue, to be 1st lt.
Brvt 2nd lt Wm P Sanders, to be 2nd lt.
3rd Regt of Artl:
Maj Chas S Merchant, to be lt col.
Capt John B Scott, to be major.
4th Regt of Artl:
Lt Col Francis S Belton, to be col
1st Lt Albert L Magilton, to be capt.
2nd Lt John T Goode, to be 1st lt.
1st Regt of Infty: Maj Gouverneur Morris, to the lt col.

3rd Regt of Infty:
Capt Nathl C Macrae, to be major.
1st Lt Henry B Schroeder, to be capt.
2nd Lt Junius Daniel, to be 1st lt.
Quartermaster's Sgt Alex N Shipley, to be brevetted 2nd lt.
Appointments:
Medical Dept:
Calvin G Hollenbush to be assist surgeon.
Robt Bartholow to be assist surgeon.
3rd Regt of Artl: Alex'r B Montgomery, to be 2nd lt.
4th Regt of Artl: Lawrence Kip to be 2nd lt.
6th Regt of Infty: Wm H F Lee, to be 2nd lt; Edw Dillon, to be 2nd lt.
Military Academy:
Patrice de Janon, instructor of the sword exercise, to be Professor of Spanish.
The following-named Cadets, graduated of the Military Academy, are attached to the army with the brevet of 2nd lt, in conformity with the 4th section of the act approved Apr 29, 1812, to take rank from Jul 1, 1857.

Corps of Engineers:
John C Palfrey	Edw P Alexander	
Richd K Meade, jr	Henry M Robert	

Corps of Topographical Engineers:
Jos L K Smith	Haldemand S Putnam	Wm P Smith

Ordnance Dept:
Geo C Strong	Thos G Baylor	

Dragoon Arm:
Thos J Berry	Saml W Ferguson	
Chas J Walker	Marcus A Reno	

Cavalry Arm:
Oliver H Fish	John T Magruder	
Manning M Kimmel	Geo A Cunningham	

Regt of Mounted Riflemen:
Henry C Mcneill	Ira W Claflin	

Artl Arm:
Geo A Kensel	Francis Beach	Edw R Warner
Chas H Morgan	Wm Sinclair	Geo H Weeks
Abram C Wildrick	Augustus G Robinson	

Infty Arm:
Aurelius F Cone	Jos S Conrad	Chas E Farrand
Paul J Quattlebaum	Edw J Conner	Thos J Lee
John S Marmaduke	Geo Ryan	Lafayette Peck
Geo W Holt	Robt H Anderson	

Transferred:
2nd Lt Richd S C Lord, 3rd artl, to the 1st dragoon, to take place on the Army Register next below 2nd Lt Wm Gaston.

Casualties
Resigned: 1st Lt Benj Allston, 1st dragoons
Declined: John Heth, the appointment of 2nd lt 6th infty.

We, the undersigned, known as deserters from the forces of Walker, after having become convinced that his cause was an infamous one, & that the basest deception had been practiced upon us in the U S to entrap us into his service, do hereby desire to make known to the world, & especially to the Gov't & people of Costa Rica, our sentiments with regard to the manner in which we have been treated by them since we abandoned the robber who deceived us & threw ourselves upon their generosity. There are now in the country around San Jose more than 60 of our friends & comrades employed by the people & paid much higher wages than they pay their own people.

Geo H Steel	Jas Attarnelli	Thos Butterfield
Thos Harris	P Nolan	J D Gilpatrick
C R Brown	W Speirs	S Moore
J E Milsop	J L Langley	Wm Wall
Alfred Newton	Jas Spanks	Chas Campbell
E Sliney	John Furlough	Jas Cumingham
Chas G Moran	John Wilson	J Sweney
John O Malley	Geo Cross	H Mitchell
H Hiller	R Merrill	J Winton
Michl Scannell	L McDonald	John Sheriden
John McKinney	G S Lore	Geo Blair
David Watt	John Warren	John Wetherspoon
Martin Dolan	Chas Macon	Thos Robinson
Geo Williams	J McAllister	Geo Elliot
N Bailey	Hugh McNabb	Saml Watts
Robt McGanity	C Cadwell	J W Oaks
Patrick Dodd	Saml Leggett	B Fangamon
J P Reams	Julus Brown	Jas White
P Brangan	R J Donner	P Ryan
Geo R G Wolff	C P Hynes	C W Boggs
J F Bridgman	P Friry	Ed O'Brien
John Dempsey	W Hill	John Sheriden
Denis Byrnes	Jas Jogan	A Cooper
H Price	John Moran	Oscar Burt
S Norton	Wm George	Patrick Brenan
Peter Gallagher	Wm Rohon	Frank Caranagh
A King	John Webber	Thos U Ball
Saml Dueincker	Theo Klingshor	H Quincy
A Sperry	Christian Kros	Wm Walker, [Capt]
Benj Downes	Robt Jackson	A Thomas
Mn G Simes	John McGuire	John A Smyth

G R Rivels	Jas Dobbins	L Libaher
Wm M Presley	Wm S Lucas	Wm Maicke
Henry Tallmadge	D Maguire	J Khingsohr
John Lee	Chas Wilson	M O Abenel
Jas Hynes	Thos Hardy	F W Innmen
Thos Egan	John Corcorn	C N Sams
John Curren	Saml Walker	Jas Masloor

On Sunday a daughter of Mr Coleman Barteau, aged 3 years old, residing in Brooklyn, was burnt to death by her clothes taking fire. She had found some matches lying about the house, which she ignited & placed among some shavings on the floor.

Criminal Court-Wash-Thu: In the case of Robt Cross, indicted for an assault on ofcr Thos H Robinson, with intent to kill him: Jury returned a verdict of "Guilty as indicted." Cross was sentenced to 8 years' hard labor in the Pententiary, the longest time the law allows. [Dec 14th newspaper: The Court disallowed the appeal: the sentence of 8 years imprisonment & hard labor in the penitentiary will take effect.]

Died: on Jul 16, in Wash City, in his 56th year, Z K Offutt. His funeral will take place from his late residence, 419 Mass ave, between 5th & 6th sts, this day, the 17th, at 5 o'clock P M.

Died: on Jul 16, in Wash City, Maj Parke G Howle, of the Marine Corps, in his 69th year. His funeral will take place at St Patrick's Church, on Jul 18, at 10 o'clock. The friends of the family are invited to attend from his late residence on 14th st, [Island,] at 9½ o'clock.

SAT JUL 18, 1857
Anniversary of the Association of the Alumni of Harvard College was celebrated at Cambridge on Thu. The following honorary degrees were conferred: <u>Dr of Laws</u>: Jacob Bragelow, M D, of Boston; Hon Franklin Dexer, of Beverly; Thos Natick, of Wash, D C; John Fries Frazer, Prof of Natural Philosophy in the Univ of Pa.
<u>Dr of Divinity</u>: Rev Ralph Sanger, of Dover
Rev Wm Seymour, Prof of Green Literature in Amherst College
Rev Rollin Heber Neale, of Boston
Rev Oliver Stearns, Pres of the Theological School at Meadville, Pa
Rev Geo Edw Ellis, of Charlestown
<u>Master of Arts:</u>
Horatio Adams, M D, of Waltham
Jos Gibbons Harlan, Prof of Mathematics in Haverford College, Pa
Rev Martin Wyman Willis, of Nashua, N H
Luigi Monti, Instructor in Harvard College
Philip Sidney Coolidge, of Boston

Appointments by the Pres:
Richd Kidder Meade, of Va, Envoy Extra & Minister Pleni to the Empire of Brazil, vice Wm Trousdale, of Tenn, the present incumbent.
Benj F Angel, of N Y, Minister Resident to Sweden, vice Francis Schroeder, recalled at his own request.
Mirabeau B Lamar, of Texas, Minister Resident to the Argentine Confederation, vice Jas A Peden, the present incumbent.
Wyman B S Moor, of Maine, Consul Gen for the British North American Provinces, from Sep 1 next, vice Israel D Andrews, of Maine, resigned.
Wm Previtt, of Ohio, Consul at Valparaiso.
Henry Owner, of Calif, Consul at Tahiti, [Society Islands,] vice Wm H Kelley, of Mass.
John F Porteous, of S C, Consul at Oporto, vice Nicholas Pike.
Chas Glantz, of Pa, Consul at Stettin, vice Frederic Schillird.
Saml E Fabens, Consul at Cayenne.
Francis M Weems, of Fla, Consul at Santa Martha, New Granada.
Jas C Dirickson, of Md, Commercial Agent at Apia, Navigator's Islands.
Moses Jeserun, of N Y, Consul at Caracao.
Chas E Flandreau, Associate Justice of the U S Court for the Territory of Minnesota.

The Richmond Dispatch states that Rt Rev John Johns, Bishop of the Diocese of Va, was married in Norfolk on Tue evening to Mrs Angelina E Southgate, of that city.

Hanover Academy: the school will commence on Oct 1, 1857, & close on Jul 31st following. Lewis M Coleman, M A, Principal; Hilary P Jones, M A; & Walter Wren, M A. For a catalogue address L M Coleman, Taylorsville, Hanover Co, Va.

Episcopal High School of Va, at Howard, 3 miles west of Alexandria: the 17th session of this institution will commence on Sep 9 next. Rev John P Maguire, Rector, Theological Seminary Post Ofc, Fairfax Co, Va.

Criminal Court-Wash-Thu. The Marshal's posse arrested the following, indicted by the Grand Jury for participation in the riots of Jul 1: Danl Stewart, Isaiah Stewart, Washington Browning, Van Ogle Johnson, Wm Dobbins, Chas Sanderson, Chas Hurdle, Wm B Wilson, Geo C Wilson, Wm Garner, Robt Slatford, Chas Spencer, & Wm alias Bud Jones. Their trials will take place early in the coming week.

Public sale of valuable land on Aug 24, in Abingdon, Wash Co, Va, our farm known as **Hall's Bottom**: contains between 700 & 800 acres; with 2 frame & weatherboarded dwlgs, & out-bldgs. Apply in person or letter to either of the undersigned, at Abingdon, Va: John A Campbell, Edw M Campbell, Jos T Campbell, Jas C Campbell.

Mrd: on Jul 9, in Alexandria, Va, in the Methodist Episcopal Church, by Rev L F Morgan, Milton Y Partlow to Mary Eleanor, eldest daughter of Benj H Lambert, all of Alexandria, Va.

Mrd: on Jul 14, in the Christian Church, by Edler Jas Chalien, J Augustus Johnson, of Rhode Island, to Miss Sarah M Barclay, of Staunton, Va.

N Y, Jul 17. Simeon Draper, Chairman of the Police Com'rs, has resigned his office.

Storehouse for rent on 7th st, near Pa ave. –Henry Thorn, 8th st, between D & E sts.

MON JUL 20, 1857
The honorary degree of LL D, reported as conferred on Thos Ustrick, or Natick, of Wash City, by the old & honored Univ of Cambridge, has been bestowed on Thos Ustick Walter, U S Architect. Architects are knighted by the Crown in England, the highest civil honors being conferred on them.

Criminal Court-Wash-Sat. 1-Wm Lucas was sentenced for an aggravated assault & battery on Jas H McKenny, because he had remonstrated with said Lucas for beating a negro to excess: fined $10 & costs. 2-John Butler, alias Williams, negro, convicted of the robbery of Mr R W Carter's store on Jul 12th: sentenced to 3 years' labor in the penitentiary, to commence today.

Fire yesterday on the property of Mr Edw Fuller, whereby the ice-house was destroyed.

Mrd: on Jul 14, by Rev John N Coombs, Mr Jos R Keene to Miss Sarah E Conrad, both of Tennellytown, Md.

Mrd: on Jul 16, in the Dunbarton St M E Church, by Rev John N Coombs, Mr Jos Koons to Miss Josephine Donaldson, all of Gtwn, D C.

TUE JUL 21, 1857
The imposing ceremony of laying the corner-stone of a monument in honor of Gen Wayne took place at Stony Point, N Y, on Jul 16, a large number of the citizens of Rockland Co being present, with guest from N Y C, Westchester, West Point, & from other parts of the State. It was laid according to Masonic forms & ceremonies. The orations were by Hon B F Butler & Erastus Brooks.

Sale of horses, cows, wagons, hay, farming utensils, furniture: at public auction on Jul 29, at the farm of the late Andrew Hoover, deceased, in Alexandria Co, Va, the entire personal estate. We will sell a servant woman, with her 5 children, slaves for life. They will be sold as a family, without separation. –Wall & Barnard, aucts.

Obit from the Jacksonville [Florida] News: Died, at the plantation of his son, Senor Martin Hernandez, near Matanzas, Cuba, on Jun 8, 1857, Gen Jos M Hernandez, of Florida. Gen Hernandez has been associated with the history of Florida ever since its transfer to the American Confederacy. Upon the breaking out of the Indian hostilities he was made a Brig Gen in the service of the U S, & participated in the most important events of the war.

Orphans Court of Wash Co, D C. In the case of Saml & Peter F Bacon, excs of Henry Hoffman, deceased: the executors & Court have appointed Aug 11 next, for the final settlement of the personal estate of the deceased, of the assets in hand.
-Ed N Roach, Reg/o wills

Teacher wanted: the Trustees of Alleghany Co Academy, Cumberland, Md, desire to procure the services of a gentleman to take charge of their institution as Principal.
-Thos J McKaig, Pres of the Board of Trustees

Died: on Monday, in Wash City, after a long & painful illness, Eliza, relict of the late Richd M Beall. Her funeral will be from her late residence, 448 D st, between 2nd & 3rd sts, on Wed at 4 o'clock.

Died: on Jul 16, in Preston Co, Va, Geo W Clutter, First Auditor of the State of Va. During the Mexican war he held a commission as captain.

Died: recently, in Montg Co, Pa, Mrs Ann Tyson, in her 81st year. A woman of cultivated mind; the venerable & highly respectable mother of Hon J R Tyson, late Rep in Congress from Phil.

The family & friends of the late Robt Farnham are invited to attend his funeral on Wed at 4 o'clock, from his late residence on M st, west corner of 11th.
+
Sad intelligence arrived yesterday about the death of Mr Robt Farnham, bookseller & stationer, for a long series of years a resident of Wash City, & one of our best citizens & leading men in business. He left Wash yesterday by train for a tour of pleasure at the North, taking with him his son & 2 daughters. He was not less than 60 years of age. Wilmington, Del, Jul 20. While the train from Balt was waiting at Stanton for the Phil train, Mr Robt Farnham, of Wash, got out, & was standing on the track. The Phil train approached & struck him, killing him almost instantly. The remains of Mr Farnham will be forwarded to Wash by the midnight train. The impression among those who witnessed the scene was that he became spell-bound & momentarily lost the sense of danger. Inquest will show that Mr Farham was looking towards & saw the approach of the train, the engineer gave the usual signal of danger, but no attempt was made to escape the train.

A school-teacher, A L Morrison, who was married at Tipton, Ind, on Jul 7, was arrested the same evening at Konomo on a charge of bigamy. He is said to have 8 wives.

WED JUL 22, 1857

Trustee's sale of frame house & lot 11 in square 450, on north L, between 6th & 7th sts: by 2 deeds of trust from Wm Ross, one dated Feb 8, 1851, & the other Feb 5, 1853, duly recorded. –John W McKim, Richd H Clarke, trustees
-Jas C McGuire, auct

Calvin C Jackson, of Mich, & Robt H Clark, of Dela, have been commissioned as Pursers in the Navy by the Pres of the U S.

We understand that the Columbus "Statesman" has been purchased by Mr Geo W Manypenny, ex-Com'r of Indian Affairs, & will be conducted under his direction.

Mr C S Hall, of this city, with some youthful companions, went yesterday to the canal for the purpose of bathing. Being unable to swim, when he lost his hold on a plank floating about, he drowned. For some time he was a student of the Theological Seminarty, after which he came to this city as a professor of music. –Alexandria Gaz

Mrs Zollicoffer, the wife of our rep in Congress, Gen F K Zollicoffer, died yesterday. Her illness was very brief. –Nashville Banner, of Jul 14.

U S Patent Ofc, Wash, Jul 20, 1857. Ptn of Jas Millholland, of Reading, Pa, praying for the extension of a patent granted to him on Sep 23, 1843, for an improvement in railroad car springs, for 7 years from the expiration of said patent, which takes place on Sep 23, 1857. –Chas Mason, Com'r of Patents

The Navy Dept has just received intelligence of the death of Lt John P Decatur, who died at the Naval Hospital, N Y, on Jul 17; & of the death of Lt Geo M Totten, son of Gen Totten, U S Army. Lt Totten died at Brooklyn, N Y.
+
Died: on Jul 18, at Mendham, N J, Lt Geo M Totten, of the U S Navy. His funeral will be from the house of his father, 203 G st, between 18th & 19th sts, this morning at 10 o'clock.

Died: on Monday last, in Wash City, John R McLeod, aged 27 years.

Died: on Jul 21, in Wash City, after a short but painful illness, Josephine E, only child of Thos & Josephine E Stone, aged 3 months & 14 days.

Died: on Jul 11, at Clarksdale, near Newcastle, Dela, Mrs Eliz B Clark, wife of Cantwell Clark, & youngest daughter of the late Saml Bootes, of Gtwn.

THU JUL 23, 1857
Richd Boylston, editor of the Farmers' Cabinet, Amherst, N H, died on Sunday at that place of paralysis, after a lingering illness of several months. He was the oldest editor in New England. His age was 75 years.

Meeting of the Soldiers of the War of 1812 was held at Phil on Sat: Hon Joel B Sutherland, Pres, & Gen Adam Diller, Sec. The following were elected ofcrs: Pres, Joel B Sutherland; Vice Presidents, Col Wm Bozarth, Wm T Elder John Ke_er, B H Springer, John K Warner; Sec, Hiram Ayres; Treasurer, Jas Benners; Exec Cmte, Adam Diller, Geo Emerick, T Blackstone, J L Leclerc, & Peter Hay.

Private John Mc_ann, of Co I, 1st Infty, having been tried by a court-martial at Camp Cooper, Texas, for the shooting of Sgt Lively, & found guilty, was sentenced to be shot. The Pres of the U S has mitigated the sentence to forfeiture of all pay & allowances, & hard labor with ball & chain, & confinement under guard when not at labor, during the period of his enlistment.

Florence McCarthy, a respectable mechanic, aged about 40 years, & his step-son, were drowned in the Erie canal, in Syracuse, last evening. His wife was on the bank.

N Y, Tue: Policeman Eugene Anderson was shot dead by a burglar, an Italian, about 40 years of age, named Frank Pelfesser. [Jul 28th newspaper: the funeral of Eugene Anderson took place today. There was a very large attendance, the deceased having been very popular.]

A little daughter of Jacob Barton, near Harrisburg, Pa, was killed last Sunday by the breaking of a swing-rope. Her father was swinging her at the time.

Died: on Jul 21, in Wash City, Richmond, infant son of A W & E M Johnson. His funeral will take place from the residence of Dr R Johnson, 175 Pa ave, between 17th & 18th sts, this morning at 9 o'clock.

Died: on Jul 21, in Wash City, Lurena Wood, aged 64 years. Her funeral is this day, at 4 o'clock, from the residence of her son, 6th & N sts west.

Health Dept monthly report of deaths in Wash City for Jun, 1857: 71. –Chas F Force, Com'r of Health

FRI JUL 24, 1857
The body of Wm Cessford was found in the ruins at the Utica Asylum last Tue night. He was burnt to death by the falling of the walls of a large cistern & burning timbers, while in the discharge of his duties as a fireman.

Appointment by the Pres: Capt Henry B Tyler, adjutant & inspector of the Marine Corps with the rank of major, vice Maj Parke G Howle, deceased.

Clarence Derrick has been appointed by the Pres to fill a vacancy at large in the Military Academy at West Point. Young Derrick is a son of the late Mr Derrick, who filled the ofc of Chief Clerk of the State Dept during a portion of the time when Pres Buchanan was at the head of that Dept.

The Cincinnati papers of Jul 22nd has details of the dreadful tragedy which took place in that city yesterday morning: Mr Nicholas T Horton, an old, well-known, & influential citizen, of the firm of N T Horton & Co, manufacturers of enameled grates & marbleized iron, has been brutally murdered at his private residence in the suburbs of the city. He was struck in the abdomen with a butcher-knife by a German servant, for some time in his employ, named Jos Loefner. Loefner was found near the green-house with his throat cut & nearly dead. He confessed to having committed the murder, & further stated that he had killed his own wife. Jealousy is supposed to have been the cause of this tragedy.

Orphans Court of Wash Co, D C. Letters testamentary on the personal estate of Dabney Ball, late of Wash Co, deceased. –Penelope Ball, excx

Orphans Court of Wash Co, D C. Letters of administration on the personal estate of Fred'k Casali, late of Wash Co, deceased. –T Bastianelli, adm

Caution: I warn the public against trusting any person or persons on my account without a written order from me, as I will pay no debt incurred without such order. -Zadock Williams, Blagden's Wharf

Lightning at White Mountains, at the *Flume House* on Sat, struck Mr W H Smith, of Cambridge, killing him, & stunning Rev Theodore B Romeyn, of N J, who was conversing with him. Mr Blandon, the clerk of the house, was struck & killed instantly. Mr Tyler, the keeper of the house, was struck, one eye remaining blind, he was otherwise uninjured. The body of Mr Smith was brought to this city by his widow, accompanied by Mr Brackett, yesterday noon. She is an invalid, & was taken to the mountains by her husband for the benefit of her health.

The wife of Rev Jonas Colburn, a retired clergyman, residing at Amherst, was found dead in her chamber Thu. She was attacked by heart disease, with which she had for some time been troubled. Her age was 70 years. –Springfield Republican

Death of a Revolutionary Hero. Mr Stephen Meeker, aged 89 years, who participated in the Fourth of July celebration at Elizabeth, N J, & carried the American standard, died on Fri last in that city.

Mr Saml Basnett, of Basnettville, Marion Co, Va, received a kick from a horse last week, from the effects of which he died in a few hours.

Mr Robt Breckinridge was shot in the head & instantly killed in Jackson, Tenn, on Sat last, by Mr Saml W Elrod.

Mount Hope Cemetery, near Boston, has been purchased by the authorities of that city for $35,000. It contains 85 acres.

Mrd: on Jul 21, by Rev D Ball, of the McKendree Church, Mr Almanzer W Layton to Miss Julia W Lacey, both of Wash, D C.

Mrd: on Jul 19, by Rev Dabney Ball, Mr Jas B Elliott to Miss Hannah M Moulton, all of Fairfax Co, Va.

Died: on Jul 23, in Wash City, Mrs Caroline Balk, aged 57 years.

Petersburg, Jul 23. A desperate shooting affair occurred today at Goldsborough, N C. Dr John W Davis, a prominent citizen, was shot down by two German Jews, father & son, named Odenhammer, both of whom shot at the same time. Dr Davis is not expected to live. There is great excitement here in regard to the assault.

SAT JUL 25, 1857

Kansas: on Jul 13th, the candidates named below were elected almost without opposition: For Mayor: Jas Blood; for Aldermen: Wm Hutchinson, Wm A Phillips, Geo Ford; P R Brooks, B W Woodward, Gains Jenkins, Geo W Hutchinson; for Marshal: S W Eldridge; for Assessors: J Boyer, R Morrow, J Wilder; for Justice: Edw Clark; for Treasurer: Columbus Hornsby. John H Lane was appointed to organize the people in the several districts to protect the ballot-boxes at the approaching election in Kansas. Nominations for State ofcrs & for Congress as follows: Sec of State: P C Schuyler; State Auditor: Dr G A Cutler; Judges of the Supreme Court: M F Conway & S N Latta; for Congress: Marcus J Parrot.

A personal rencontre occurred in Louisville, Ky, on Tue, between Geo D Prentice, editor of the Louisville Journal, & R T Durrett, editor of the Courier, in which pistols were used on both sides. Prentice was slightly wounded.

Good & well kept household & kitchen furniture at auction on: Jul 28, at the house known as Mrs Gunnel's Cottage, on 6th st, Gtwn, near High st, the entire effects. Barnard & Buckey, aucts

The Regulators of Iowa hung 2 horse thieves, Soper & Gleason, on Jul 11. Gleason confessed, wrote a letter to his mother, & before the horses were driven off, jumped from the wagon & became a corpse. Soper confessed but struggled for life.

N Y: We find the deceased, found floating in the bay near Clifton, came to his death from pistol-shot wounds received at the hands of Jane Wilcox, while committing a burglary on the premises of Mr Phillip Fingler, on York ave, Staten Island, on Jul 21. We also commend the noble conduct of Miss Wilcox in defending the property of her friend at the hazard of her own life. Miss Wilcox slept in the rear of the store. Mr Fingler slept overhead. [No name given for the burglar.]

Lost Child. Mary Emrich, 3 years old, dark curly hair, dark eyes, light dress, dark apron, & white bonnet, strayed from the residence of her parents yesterday. She speaks the German language only, but understands English when spoken to. Geo Emrich, corner 4th & E sts.

Having been induced to leave the city at a short notice, I have left the settlement of my business with my brother, Jos W Nairn, who is authorized to act for me without restriction. –John W Nairn

Washington College, Va: commencement exercises came off Jul 2; addresses were by W Y Chester, of Ark; J M Boyd, of Lynchburg; A S Pendleton, of Lexington; valedictory by A H Jackson, of Lewis. Dr Jenkins awarded diplomas to the following young gentlemen: A S Pendleton, Lexington; J M Boyd, Lynchburg; W Y Chester, Ark; J L Massie, Augusta; W T Poague, J W Poague, Rockbridge; John Campbell, Monroe; A E Arnold, Rockbridge; & A H Jackson, Lewis. At the dinner, Bolivar Christian, of Staunton, was Master of Ceremonies, who was witty, grave, & eloquent, as the occasion required.

Blenheim is for sale: by decree pronounced by the Circuit Court of Albemarle: public auction on Sep 22, on the premises, the beautiful estate & late residence of Hon Andrew Stevenson, deceased, in said county: contains about 900 acres; lies in the section of country known as the **Red Land District of Albemarle**; the bldgs are all new & commodious. –N H Massie, Com'r & adm of A Stevenson, deceased, Charlottesville, Albemarle Co, Va.

Mr Root, 75, celebrated the 4th at Exeter, Green Co, Wisc, by shooting dead his son-in-law, Mr Foster. The old gentleman had deeded his property to Foster on the condition that he & Mrs Root were to be taken care of as long as they lived by his daughter & her husband. The old couple were subsequently taken very sick, with symptoms of poisoning, & Mrs Root died; but Mr Root drank plently of milk, which he thinks neutralized the poison. Some time thereafter he wished to have the body of his wife dug up & examined, but Foster opposed it violently, & the parties came to blows. Then followed the deliberate killing of Foster, in the presence of his wife. Old people who have property, & wish to be well treated by their heirs, had better keep it in their own hands as long as they live.

Mrd: on Jul 13, at St Peter's Cathedral, by Rt Rev John McGill, Bishop of Richmond, Jos P Kavenaugh to Maria Teresa Vincent Hely, of Richmond, Va.

MON JUL 27, 1857

Excellent household & kitchen furniture at auction on: Jul 30, at the residence of J H Drury, corner of North L st & Vt ave. -Jas C McGuire, auct

We announce the death of the wife of Hon W P Fessenden, one of our Senators in Congress. She died at Glen House yesterday morning. Mr Fessenden was awakened by his wife telling him that she felt fatigued; in a few minutes she was dead. She had been in feeble health for some time past, but her death came unexpectedly. She was an affectionate wife & mother, & a kind friend. –Portland Argus

Died: on Jul 25, in Wash City, in his 68th year, Mr Geo M Grouard, a veteran printer, who came to Wash City about 43 years ago, & was well known to & esteemed by the fraternity. During the greater part of that time & up to the day of his death he had been employed at the Nat'l Intelligencer ofc, & for about 20 years its active manager. The last 8 or 10 years he had been much afflicted, though still capable of useful effort. He was of a genial & kind disposition. His funeral will take place at 10 o'clock this morning, from his late residence on 6th st.

Died: on Jul 25, in Wash City, Hardee, infant daughter of Robt & Jane E Kellen, of San Francisco, Calif. Her funeral will take place this afternoon at 4 o'clock, from the residence of her grand-father, A H Young, on I st, between 9th & 10th sts.

Died: on Jul 17, in Phil, Charles Carroll, son of J Stoll & Marianna Chronise, aged 1 year.

Died: on Jul 26, Paulus Edward, son of Paulus & Mary Parthenia Thyson, aged 11 months & 5 days. His funeral will be this evening at half-past 4 o'clock, from his parents' residence, 393 7th st.

TUE JUL 28, 1857

The Claviaccord is a new musical instrument invented by M Gavioli. It has bellows that are actuated by a part of the hand or hands, whilst the same are playing on the key-board. It is portable & a great extent of notes obtained within a very small volume.

The Duchess Regent of Parma has just conferred a gold medal upon Luigina Spazzina, a girl of 15, as a reward for the spirit which she exhibited in defending herself & the household against a robber who broke in while Luigina was left alone there. She attacked him with a knife, wounded him, & put him to flight. When her father returned home she went with him & a man named Gobbi in pursuit of the robber, who was arrested.

Richd Southgate, one of the oldest settlers of Newport, Ky, died at his residence there on Fri last, after a lingering illness; age 83 years. He read law at Albany, N Y, & went to Newport about 60 years ago. He was several times elected the Legislature of Ky, both to the Senate & House. He amassed property estimated at about a million of dollars, most of which is in real estate, lying in Cincinnati, Covington, & Newport, & in the vicinity of the two latter.

The undersigned, formerly of Va, having leased this well known House, is now called <u>Smith's Virginia House</u>, formerly the U S Hotel, & will open on Aug 15. –Logan O Smith, proprietor

Orphans Court of Wash Co, D C. Letters testamentary on the personal estate of Thos J Smith, late of Wash Co, deceased. –S E Smith, excx

Orphans Court of Wash Co, D C. Letters of administration on the personal estate of Andrew Foote, late of Wash Co, deceased. –Henrietta Foote, admx

My valuable farm in Montg Co, Md, at private sale: contains 300 acres, 2½ miles above Tennallytown. Apply to me on the premises, or to Dr S C Busey, Wash. My post ofc if Tennallytown, D C: Peter D Posey.

Valuable farm for sale near Warrenton, Va: the farm of Mrs Mgt G Lee, within a half mile of Warrenton, Fauquier Co, Va; contains 853 acres. –Rice W Payne

Excellent household & kitchen furniture at auction on: Jul 31, at the residence of Dr J E Clawson, 484 I st, between 7th & 8th sts. -A Green auct

Executor's sale of frame house & lot: on Aug 3, in front of the premises, a good 2 story attic & cellar frame-house & lot, belonging to the estate of the late Christian H Weber, deceased, being the west half of lot 4 in square 874, fronting 25 feet on south G st, next to the residence of Rev S A H Marks. –Antonia Ponts, Phillip Arth, trustee -A Green auct

<u>Redemption of Va 5% stock: holders are required on Oct 31, 1857, to surrender the certificates at the Ofc of the 2nd Auditor. Whether surrendered or not, the interest will cease on that day.</u>
1835: Baring, brothers & Co, of London: $5,000.
1834: Rev Robt Tritton, of Morden, Surry Co, England: $13,000.
1840: Jas Hutchinson, of the Stock Exchange, London, Gentleman, & Wm Robson, of Darlington, Durham, London, Gentleman, with benefit of survivorship: $10,000.
1844: Richd Thornton, of Old Swan Wharf, upper Thames St, London, Merchant: $15,000.

1846: Francis N Watkins, Clement C Read, Jacob W Morton, John Dupuy, Henry E Watkins, Thos T Treadway, & Chas S Carrington, & their survivors in trust, for the benefit of the Union Theological Seminary: $4,100.
1846: Thos Cotterill, a citizen of the U S, at present residing at Birmingham, England: $8,000
1849: Thos Cotterill, do: $5,000.
1850: Thos Cotterill, do: $1,666.67
1849: Wm Death, of Harlow, Essex, Gentleman: $1,666.66.
1849: Woodham Death, of Nettleswell, Essex, Gentleman: $1,666.67.
1850: Benj Moses, of London: $6,000.
1855: Geo Peabody & Co, of London: $25,000.
1856: Hugh Brown, of Broadstone, Parish of Birth, Ayrshire, Scotland: $34,000. -Stafford H Parker, Register. Geo W Munford, Sec'y of the Com'th of Va, Com'rs of the Sinking Fund.

Died: on Jul 26, in Wash City, of congestion of the lungs, Edwin Ruthven, 2nd son of John P & Emily C Bentley, aged 8 years & 10 months. His funeral will be from the residence of his father, 518 L st, between 9th & 10th, this morning at 9:30 o'clock.

Phil: Lt Edmund W Henry died at York, Pa, Jul 26. He was on the retired list.

WED JUL 29, 1857
Circuit Court of Wash Co, D C-in Chancery. Jacob Bigelow vs Gilbert L Thompson, Wm H G Dorsey, Josiah R Sturgess, Elisha Averill, & Chas Stearns. The bill of cmplnt states that one Alva B Taylor recovered on the law side of the Circuit Court of D C, on Apr 13, 1855, a judgment against the said Gilbert L Thompson for $8,000 damages, & all reasonable costs of suit; that, by its terms, the said judgment was to be released upon the payment of of $3,255.50, with interest as follows, that is to say, on $1,000 thereof from Feb 4, 1848, on $1,000 thereof from May 4, 1848, on $255.50 from Aug 2, 1848, till paid, & the said reasonable costs; that the said judgment was duly & formally assigned for a valuable consideration to the cmplnt, Jacob Bigelow, & entered to his use upon the docket of said Court; that, upon said judgment, a writ of fieri facias was issued, directed to the Marshal of the Dist of Col, commanding him of the goods & chattels, lands & tenements of the said Thompson to make the aforesaid judgment, & that the said Marshal returned the said writ of fieri facias nulla bone; that in fact at the time of the recovery of the said judgment, & of the issuing & return of the said writ of fieri facias, the said Gilbert L Thompson was possessed of a very valuable tract of land, called **Meridian Hill**, situated in Wash Co; that the said Gilbert L Thompson purchased the said tract of land about Nov 8, 1851, & that at his instance & request the deeds thereto were made to one Wm H G Dorsey, so that in form the said tract of land was conveyed to the said Dorsey; that the said Gilbert L Thompson retained the said deeds in his own possession & did not place them upon the record of deed for the said Wash Co until Jun 30, 1857; tha the said Dorsey was not informed that the said deeds were so made

as aforesaid, or that the said tract of land had been conveyed to him as aforesaid, until 4 years after the date thereof; that they were not delivered to the said Dorsey, & that he never accepted the same nor admitted the validity thereof; that, in fact, the said tract of land was purchased by the said Thompson for his own use, & altogether paid for out of his, the said Thompson's means; that the said Gilbert L Thompson, some time in the fall of 1855, pretended to make a sale of the said tract of land to one Chas Stearns, & applied to the said Dorsey to make a deed thereof to the said Stearns, that the said Dorsey refused, & that said Thompson conveyed the said tract of land to the said Stearns by a deed which is recorded among the aforesaid land records; that the pretended consideration having failed, the said Stearns made a reconveyance of the said tract of land to the said Thompson, & that the said Thompson kept the said deed of reconveyance in his own possession & off of the land records of said Wash Co, & that the same had never been recorded; that the said Gilbert L Thompson afterwards, that is to say, in the fall of 1856, made another pretended sale of the said tract of land to one Sturgess & made a deed therefore to the said Sturgess, that the said Sturgess immediately thereupon executed 3 deeds of mortgage to one Elisha Averill, by means of which he pretended to convey said tract of land to said Averill to secure certain bonds therein specified, that afterwards the said Sturgess filed a bill on the Equity side of the Superior Court of Balt City against the said Dorsey & the said Thompson, for the purpose of obtaining a sufficient deed for the said tract of land, & that the said Court did order such a deed to be made; that on Jun 30 & on Jul 1, 1857, the said Thompson did place or cause to be placed upon the land records of Wash City the several deeds mentioned & a certified copy of the decree passed by the said Superior Court; that the said Thompson retained the said deeds to said Dorsey in his possession without recording them, for the purpose of defrauding the cmplnt, & that the several deeds of the said tract of land from said Thompson to said Sturgess, from said Stearns to said Sturgess, & from said Sturgess by way of mortgage ot the said Averill, are fraudulent, & are all for the purpose of defrauding, hindering, & delaying the said cmplnt in the recovery of the said judgment. The bill further states that the said Gilbert L Thompson, Wm H G Dorsey, Josiah R Sturgess, Elisha Averill, & Chas Stearns dod not reside within the Dist of Col. The object of the bill is to obtain a full & true disclosure & discovery of the several matters & things within the knowledge of the several parties touching the aforesaid conveyance, a decree setting aside the said deeds for fraud, & for the sale, under the directions of the Court, of the said tract of land called **Meridian Hill**, for the purpose of paying the said judgment. Absent dfndnts are to appear in person or by solicitor on or before the 1st Monday of Dec next. –Jas Dunlop. John A Smith, clerk W B Webb, Solicitor

Mrd: on Sat, at **Way Side**, Fairfax Co, Va, by Rev Mr Brown, Col Wm McNair, of Wash, D C, to Laura V, youngest daughter of the late Gen Jno C Hunter, of that county.

Capt Henry Henry, of the U S Navy, expired on Sunday night at York, Pa. He entered the navy in 1812, & served during the war with Great Britain, when our infant navy won its brightest laurels. His last service was performed as captain of the sloop-of-war **Plymouth**, about 10 year ago. He was placed upon the retired list, among many others, when Congress determined to attempt the reform of the navy. Capt Henry was about 65 year of age at the time of his decease.

In the Board of Alderman, on Monday, the subjoined Report & accompanying evidence, in reference to the case of contested election from the 4th Ward, was submitted from the Cmte on Elections & ordered to be printed. Mr Moore, from the Cmte on Elections, to which was referred the case of contested election from the 4th Ward, submitted the following report; the ptn of John H Goddard, protesting against the right of Matthew G Emery to a seat in this Board as an alderman from the 4th Ward, that at the election held Jun 1st last, he received 193 votes, & Mr Emery received 295; & at the 2nd precinct he received 220 [should be 221] votes, & Mr Emery 128 votes. Mr Emery had a majority of 10 votes. Mr Goddard protested against Mr Emery's right to the seat & claims it for his own. Mr Goddard's reason is that many of his friends were prevented from voting by an armed mob. Depositions were taken of: Jos Williamson; Police Ofcr B T Watson; J W Baggott, Chief of Police; Police Ofcr T H Robinson; Police Ofcr Wm L Ross; Aquila R Allen-opened his restaurant & saw a crowd of men coming in; Cyrus Martin; Wm J Donohoo; Justice R C Donn; Thos C Donn; Wm W Moore; Theodore Sheckels; E F Queen; Edwin J Klopper; & Major H B Tyler. Alderman Evans appeared & said he was not at the polls on the day of the riot; his son was invited to be present, can you account for his absence? My son is confined to bed with illness, & the physician states that it would be hazardous to his life if he were to attempt to answer the summons. [Rumors implicated him with the disorders.] He made an affidavit before his father-in-law, which I endeavored to obtain for the use of the cmte, but could not find it. Evidence was given by: Jas H Boss; Fred'k Iddins; Wm Douglass; Robt Israel; & Richd B Owens;

The Dept, with pain, announces to the Navy & Marine Corps the sudden death, from apoplexy, of Cmdor John T Newton, who expired in Wash City on Jul 28. He entered the Navy on Jan 16, 1809, having been in the service nearly half a century. His funeral will take place from the Meade House, on F st, Jul 30, at 10 A M. -I Toucey, Sec of the Navy, Navy Dept, Jul 28, 1857. [Jul 31st newspaper: The remains of Cmdor Newton were conveyed to the *Congressional Burying Ground* yesterday. Religious services were performed at the Meade House whence the corpse was taken by Rev Dr Hall, of the Church of the Epiphany. The Marine Corps attended under Maj Zeilen, accompanied by the band of the same.]

Died: on Jul 27, in Wash City, Estelle Chapman, infant daughter of Rev S A H & Ann Marks. Her funeral will be from her father's residence, 398 G st south, Navy Yard, this afternoon at 4 o'clock.

Died: on Jul 17, in Phil, Mr Geo D Klinehanse, aged 49 years.

Died: on Jul 28, at her residence near Beltsville, PG Co, Md, after a brief illness of 40 hours, Mrs Maria McKnew, aged 57 years, relict of the late Thos McKnew. Her funeral will take place this afternoon at 3½ o'clock, from her late residence.

Died: on Jul 28, in Wash City, Mrs Mary Starbuck, wife of N H Starbuck. Her funeral is this afternoon at 5 o'clock, from the residence, 437 Mass ave.

Died: on Jul 24, at Warrenton, Fauquier Co, Va, Charles B, youngest & infant son of Charles B & Sally F Maury, of Wash City.

THU JUL 30, 1857
Govn'r Wise has appointed Jonathan M Bennett, to be Auditor of Public Accounts of Va, to supply the vacancy occasioned by the death of Geo W Clutter.

Judge McKierman, of Memphis, on Jul 16, passed sentence of death upon Levi Storer, convicted at the present term of the Criminal Court of the murder of Aaron B Stares. The deed was committed during late winter. The sentence will be executed on Aug 14.

Affidavits, forming a part of the evidence which was submitted to the Board of Alderman on Mon last with the Report of the Cmte on Elections, which with other portions of evidence was published in yesterday's Intelligencer.
1-Frederick Schaeffer, a legal voter, was challenged as being a foreigner, although it as known he had voted for 6 years without being challenged: he was born in Phil.
2-John M Flynn, his vote was refused because the seal of Circuit Court of D C was faint on his school tax, he was insulted by one of the com'rs, & left without any satisfaction.
3-Simeon Smith, judges refused his vote on the ground that his name was not on the poll list for said precinct; that he had for 2 years previous voted at the same precinct, paid all required taxes, for 3 years past, been assessed for real estate on the books of the Corp & paid the same.
4-Dennis O'Connor, he was refused his vote on account of the seal of his naturalization papers being faint; he procured an additional seal; was refused admission to the poll by the mob.
5-John O'Connor, intended to vote but found the polls were lined up with rowdies, & informed it was dangerous to endeavor to vote, he then desisted.
6-Thos Noonan, his vote was refused by the com'rs on the ground that the seal on his naturalization papers was not sufficiently plain.
7-Edw Sheesy, his vote was refused by the com'rs on the ground that the seal on his naturalization papers was not sufficiently plain.
8-Thos Hogan, he was in line to vote when he was assaulted by the mob, & left to save his life.

9-John Conner, was in line to vote & was shot in the leg, & struck with a stone, & was deterred in voting.
10-Peter Conlan, was there early to vote, when the line was broken up by the mob, & the polls were closed.
11-John Cusick, he was assailed by persons with stones, & compelled to flee for his life.
12-Thos Duffy, he was in line when rowdies assailed them & he & others had to flee.
13-John Herlihy, he was in the line to the window & was driven away.
14-Michl Kelly, driven from the polls by the mob & prevented from voting.
15-Patrick Scanlon, driven away by the mob.
16-John Conner, 2nd, the line was assailed by the mob & he had to flee for his life.
17-John Sexton, beaten off by the mob & prevented from voting.
18-Timothy O'Brien, beaten off by an armed mob & prevented from voting.
19-Timothy Green; John Melson; Michl Ragan; John F Ellis; Michl Enright; Philip Cronin; Dennis O'Connor; Mathew Butler; David Fitzgerald; Cornelius Brosnahan; & Jas Sullivan; driven away by the mob & prevented from voting.
[Aug 5th newspaper: witnesses examined: Jackson Edmonston; Mr Wm Douglas; Mr Jas H Boss; Mr C M Alexander; Mr Jas Bowen; Mr Jno T Merrill; & Henry Burns, who was one of the marines, wounded in the face by a ball.] [Aug 6th newspaper: witnesses examined: Mr Nimrod Garretson; Mr Robt T Larner; Mr Jas Randolph; Mr Wm Lord; Mr Richd Wallach; Mr Ashton White; Mr Alex'r Aldrich; Mr T G Clayton; Mr Wm B Sothoron; & Mr Jas Nokes.]

Died: on Jul 28, in Balt, Nathan E Worthington, of Wash City, aged 24 years. His funeral will take place this evening at 4 o'clock, from the residence of his parents, 387 9th st.

For sale, the farm on which I reside, 3 miles from Staunton, of about 320 acres; the bldgs are handsome & spacious & well watered by Lewis' Creek. Address Wm B Johnson, Staunton, Va.

Valuable plantation for sale; in Red River, 35 miles below Natchitoches, in the parish of Natchitoches, Louisiana, known as the plantation of Gen Francis Gaiennie; consists of 4,400 acres; with dwlg house, steam gin house, corn cribs, stables, negro quarters, & other necessary bldgs. Address the undersigned, at Cloutierville, parish of Narchitcoches, La, or to B Toledano & Taylor, Commission Merchants, New Orleans. -Valery Gaiennie

Orphans Court of Wash Co, D C. Letters of administration on the personal estate of Wm Payne, late of Wash Co, deceased. –Wm Wise, adm

The firm of Ager & McLean [Jas B Ager & Wm McLean] was dissolved on Jul 23 by mutual consent. Either partner has authority to receive & receipt for debts due to the late firm. –Jas B Ager, Wm McLean

FRI JUL 31, 1857
Wash Corp, Jul 27, 1857. Nominations from the Mayor:
For Com'rs of the Asylum: Geo W Emerson, Geo Mattingly, & Jacob Gideon.
For Com'rs of the Markets:
Stephen P Franklin, Wm Orme, & Hudson Taylor for the Centre Market.
Francis Jenkins & Geo Johnson for the Eastern Market.
Wm H Walker & Solomon Stover for the Western Market.
Geo H Jones & Jas F Devine for the Northern Market.
Com'rs of West Burial Ground: Jos Borrows & Wm Wilson. August Miller, Secton.
Com'rs of East Burial Ground: John D Brandt & Geo W Oyster. John O'Neale, Sexton.
For Police Magistrates: Saml Drury; Danl Smith' John H Goddard; Patrick McKenna; Jas Cull; & Danl Rawland.
F A Klopfer, Chief of Police, in the place of Jas W Baggott, who declines a re-appointment.
For Police Constables:

Wm Daw	Wm L Ross	R Collins
John T May	Edw McHenry	Thos H Robinson
Wm H Fanning	Henry Yeatman	Francis S Edelin
Jos Williamson	B F Watson	Jno M Lloyd
Jas H Suit	Geo T Barrett	Jos H Gill

For Inspectors & Measurers of Lumber: Peter Gallant, Wm Douglass, Saml R Beyer, & Wm Dunnawin.
For Members of the Board of Health:

Philip C Davis, M D	Jos Bryan	F S Walsh, M C
J B H Smith	Wm P Johnston, M D	John D Brandt
Robt K Stone, M D	Jas Lawrenson	Jas F Morgan, M D
Chas L Coltman	J B Gardiner, M D	Geo Mattingly
Wm H Berry, M D	J P Ingle	

The beautiful & eligibly situated Farm of the late Wm Voss for sale, or exchanged for improved city property. This Farm is in Alexandria Co, Va, adjoining the country residence of the late Andrew Hoover. On the farm is a cottage-built house, a new barn, & out bldgs. Inquire of Mrs L J Voss, of H H Voss.

Died: on Jul 16, at his residence, West River, Anne Arundel Co, Md, Benj Welch, in his 78th year.

Died: on Jul 9, in Wash City, Henry H, the beloved son of John H & Mary Ballman, aged 15 months & 22 days.

Large & pleasant rooms for rent: Mrs Jane Taylor, 411 3rd st, 2 doors north of Pa av.

Two young ladies & a young man were drowned by the upsetting of a skiff at the lower wharf last evening. As they were pleasure-riding the steamer **Dr Kane** passed & the skiff was overturned. Miss Kate Meade & Miss Ann Meagher, & ___ Tuley, were drowned. Jas Dorsey, who was in the skiff at the time, narrowly escaped with his life. –Louisville Democrat, 25th.

Mrs Delaney, who weighs 550 pounds, was married at Pittsburg on Sunday last, to Mr O'Neil, the agent for the exhibition. They started on Monday for Memphis, & on the same day Wm Delaney telegraphed from N Y that he would arrive in 24 hours at Pittsburg to travel with his wife. It will be difficult for her to hide from him.

The undersigned have entered into Partnership, under the name of McLean & Munro, will continue the Sawing & Plaining business heretofore carried on by Ager & McLean, corner of 13th st & the canal. –Wm McLean, G A Munro

Foreign News: Gen Asnon, the Cmder-in-Chief in the East Indies, died of cholera at Kurnaud on May 27. Sir Patrick Grant has been appointed to succeed him temporarily.

SAT AUG 1, 1857
Democratic nominations in Md: the Democratic State Convention of Md met at Balt on Jul 30th, nominated Hon John C Groome, of Cecil Co, for the ofc of Govn'r of Md. Bradley T Johnson, of Fred'k Co, for Comptroller of the Treasury; Dr Joshua R Nelson, of Harford Co, for Lottery Com'r, & Jas Murray, of Anne Arundel, for Com'r of the Land Ofc.

A dispatch from Phil announces the death in that city, yesterday, of Mrs Campbell, wife of Ex-Postmaster General Campbell. [Aug 3rd newspaper: Mrs Campbell died at **Chestnut Hill**, after an illness of several months' duration. –Phil Inquirer]

Copartnership formed in the Grocery trade: Herman H Voss, Otis W Marsh, 285 s w corner of 10th & Pa ave, Wash.

The Clarksville Tobacco Plant says: the estate of Alex'r Moore, of Halifax Co, was appraised, immediately after his death in 1850, at between $12,000 & $22,000. The executor, Woodson Hughes, kept the estate together until Oct 1856, when he sold this property at public auction for cash or its equivalent for the immense sum of $70,000. –Richmond South

Orphans Court of Wash Co, D C. In the case of Eliz Jewell, Thos Jewell, & Ann Jewell, excs of Wm Jewell, deceased: the executors & Court have appointed Aug 22 for the final settlement of the personal estate of the deceased, with the assets in hand. -Ed N Roach, Reg/o wills

Criminal Court-Wash-Fri. Witnesses in regard to the riot of Jun 1st last: Mr Hanson Ridgway did not recognize Chas Hurdle as among the rioters. Mr Edw F Queen saw Michl Hoover; cannot say he was encouraging the crowd or not. Mr John D Frere, a member of the Auxiliary Guard heard Vanloman Johnson say at the polls: "go in boys, go in." Saw Eggleston squaring off to ofcr Digges, & put his hand to a pistol then in his pocket. Mr Richd Queens assisted as one of the challengers. Mr Richd Owens was shot in the chin & in the arm. Danl Stewart had a gun. His brother, Isaiah, told him to shoot, you are near enough. Mr Peter Bacon came to deponent & proposed something about bringing out the volunteers. Mr Philip S Piles saw Robt Slatford, running an Irishman away from the polls.

Elmwood, an elegant estate near Lexington, for sale at public auction: it is my purpose to remove to Chicago, & will sell at public auction, on Sep 2, this beautiful estate; lies on the north bank of the North River; contains 500 acres with a dwlg house, barns & other necessary houses. It was originally 2 farms, which I shall sell that way. The upper, or ***Hall Farm***, contains 200 acres with a dwlg house. The other division, ***Elmwood***, my place of residence, contains 300 acres; with a handsome dwlg house in the modern cottage style. The mill property adjoining these farms is separate & distinct. The mills, now in course of erection, will be completed under the superintendence of my son Edward, who is half owner of that property, & business will be conduted by Edw J Leyburn & Co. -Alfred Leyburn

Com'rs sale of Crab Bottom Lands in Highland Co, Va. By decree of the Circuit Court of Highland Co, rendered on Jul 16, 1857, in the suit of Scott, Baker & Co, vs G N Kinney & others, we will proceed, in the town of Monterey, on Sep 8, to sell a tract of land containing about 400 acres, being the same conveyed in trust by Geo N Kinney to Wm C Jones. Also, the following personal property: a slave named George, about 20 years old; 1 slave named Jenny, about 10 years old; 1 grey horse; 6 cows & calves; & all the household & kitchen furniture of said G N Kinney. On Sep 9 we shall sell, on the premises, in Crab Botton, Highland Co, the tract conveyed in trust by A K Sitlington & A K Sitlington & wife to Robt Sitlington & David Fultz, to wit: a tract containing about 305 acres; one tract of 40 acres; another tract of about 35 acres. Also, on the same day, the following real & personal property, conveyed [in trust] by John Sitlington & wife to Thos O & John W Sitlington, to wit: a tract of land of about 600 acres; also, 5 slaves, Jane & her child Mary, John, Duffey, [an old woman] & Lewis; also, 5 head of horses, 6 cows & calves, 1 yoke of oxen, 15 hogs, 14 young cattle, & all the farming implements & household & kitchen furniture of said John Sitlington. -Adam Stephenson, Felix H Hull, Com'rs

F B Ogden, U S Consul at Bristol, England, died on the 4th ult. He was appointed by Gen Jackson as Consul at Liverpool, where he served 11 years, & was then transferred to Bristol.

Farm for sale: about 144 acres in Montg Co, Md, about 3/4ths of a mile from Colesville, Md. Mr A Bassler, residing on the place, will show it.

Valuable land for sale: under a decree of the Circuit Court for Chas Co, Md, as a court of equity, of the real estate of Jno Beale Fergosson, late of said county, deceased, at Port Tobacco, Md, on Aug 25: some 1,000 acres of land in said county, lying on the Potomac, with a dwlg & various out-houses. –Jno W Mitchell

$100 reward for runaway servant woman Ellen Davis: dark complexion; she has been living with Mr Lindsley, on 7th st, Plank Road, & has been absent since Jul 27th. -Chas I Stuart, E & 10th sts.

Died: on Jul 30, Joseph Fenimore, son of Leonard & Winifred S Harbaugh, aged 3 years & 1 month. His funeral will take place from his parents' residence, on F st, between 6th & 7th sts, this evening, at 4 o'clock.

Mr & Mrs Chas L Powell's Female Seminary, at Winchester, Va, will begin on the first Monday in Sep next, & end on the last Fri in Jun, 1858.

MON AUG 3, 1857

A cane & spy-glass that belonged to Gen Washington were sold in Balt, on Thu, with a certificate of their genuineness from the venerable Geo W P Custis, for $205.00. The purchaser was Col John S Gittings, acting for the Ladies of the **Mount Vernon Association** of Va & Md, who purchased the relics to present them to Hon Edw Everett as a mark of their gratitude & regard for his noble & successful exertions in behalf of their patriotic cause. The Balt Patriot says the sum received was much less than was generally expected, the owner having refused offers of much larger sums in former years. He was offered $100 for them only a few days since for public exhibition in N Y for 3 days.

At Springfield, Ill, on Jul 23, the mail agent, Mr W C Gillespie, was arrested by Marshal Dixon, at the instance of Finley D Preston, general mail agent for the West. He was lodged in jail charged with purloining money from letters passing through the mail, & with other offences against the post ofc laws. Mr Gillespie is lately from Christian Co, & was House journalist of the last session of the Illinois Legislature.

Union Hotel, Fairfax C H, Va: prepared to accommodate a limited number of boarders. Prices moderate & fare unequalled. –Jas W Jackson, proprietor

Transfer of Instruments. On Thu last Mr David A Burr, son of Mr David H Burr, late Surveyor Gen of the Territory of Utah, left Washington for Salt Lake City, to deliver into the hands of the newly-appointed Surveyor of the Territory all the archives, books, documents, & instruments belonging to that branch of the public service.

Mayor's Ofc, Gtwn, D C, Aug 1, 1857. To the Board of Aldermen & Common Councilmen: It is with pain that I announce to you the decease of our venerable Clerk John Mountz. He expired at his residence, on Bridge st, in this place, this morning, in the bosom of his family, after a brief illness, in his 87th year. Exempt from most of the infirmities of age, to the day of his recent & fatal sickness he was still capable of valuable effort. Gtwn was incorporated in 1789, & by the journal of the proceedings of the Corp, kept in his own characteristic handwriting, it appears that "on Monday, the 28th day of Nov, 1791, John Mountz, jr, is appointed Clerk, in the room of Thos Turner, who hath resigned;" & from that time, when scarcely 21 years of age, he entered upon his duties. He was present & assisted the Father of his Country in the ceremonies at the laying of the corner-stone of the Capitol of the U S at Washington, & he was an eye-witness of the encampment of the French troops in our suburbs when on their march to the battles at Yorktown, which closed the military operations of the Revolutionary war. A portrait of his familiar countenence should grace the walls of the Town Hall. I suggest an appropriation to secure from a competent artist a copy of his likeness. –Richd R Crawford, Mayor

The corner-stone of the new Ebenezer Church, east Wash, near the Navy Yard, was laid on Fri last, with ceremonies performed by the Masionic fraternity. Religious services were performed by Rev Wm H Chapman, pastor of the Church. The articles depositied with the corner-stone were: a copy of the Sacred Scriptures, Hynm Book of the Methodist Episcopal Church, Discipline of the same; a copy of the Christian advocate, the Wesleyan Advocate, the Nat'l Intelligencer, the Constitution of the U S, the Consitutition of the Grand Lodge of Free & Accepted Masons of D C, & of proceedings of the Grand Lodge for 1856; seal of the Grand Lodge; parchment containing the names of the bishops of the Methodist Episcopal Church, the pastors of Ebenezer Church, presiding elders of the Potomac District, pastors of the Methodist Episcopal Church in D C, official board of station, trustees of the station, oldest members of the Ebenezer station, bldg cmte, finance cmte, pres & Vice Pres of the U S, & Cabinet ofcrs.

Died: on Aug 2, Chas Frankenberger, aged 32 years. His funeral will be from his late residence, 7th & G sts, this evening at 6 o'clock.

Died: on Jul 23, at her residence in Alexandria, Va, Mrs Lucinda M Fletcher, widow of the late Capt Geo Fletcher. Her numerous friends in this city lament her loss.

Died; on Jul 25, at the Univ of Va, Mrs Martha M, wife of Prof John B Minor.

Died: on Jul 16, at Charlottesville, Va, Mrs Patsy J Taylor, eldest daughter of Col Thos J Randolph, & wife of John C R Taylor.

Died: on Jul 28, at **Edgehill**, Albemarle Co, Va, Mrs Cary Ann N Ruffin, 2nd daughter of Col Thos J Randolph, & wife of Frank G Ruffin.

St Paul, Jul 29. Col Noble, the superintendent of the wagon road, via the South Pass, has arrived here. The expedition, for the present, susupended, & the encampment west of the Big Sioux river broken up, in consequence of further progress being violently opposed by the Yancton Indians. Crossing the country frighten away the buffalo, the sole means of the Indians subsistence. Col Noble will held a council with the Indians on Aug 20. If it should fail his intention is to proceed in despite of their hostilies.

Young Ladies Institute, English & French, 490 E st, Wash, D C -Chas H Norton, A M. S H Mirick takes great pleasure in recommending his successor Mr Chas H Norton, as a gentleman amply qualified to take charge of the Institute.

Boarding, the rooms at present occupied by Hon Chas Mason, Com'r of Patents, will be vacated in a few days. Apply to Mrs M A Stettinius, 8 Louisiana ave.

For rent: 2 large 3 story brick houses, lately occupied by Mr King as a boarding-house. Possession given immediately. –J P Pepper, for the heirs

The firm of Gray & Ballantyne is this day dissolved by mutual consent. The business hereafter will be conducted by Wm Ballantyne at 498 7th st.
-Austin Gray, Wm Ballantyne, Aug 1, 1857.

TUE AUG 4, 1857

Judicial elections: 1-12th judicial district of Va, to fill the vacancy occasioned by the resignation of Hon G W Hopkins, took place on Thu last. Contest between Mr Stras, of Tazewell, & Mr Fulkerson, of Wash, resulting in the favor of Mr Stras, by a few votes. 2-Election for a judge of the 8th judicial circuit, to supply the vacancy occasioned by the death of Judge Eustice Conway, resulted in the choice of Richd H Colemen, of Caroline Co, by a majority of 105 votes over John L Marye, of Fredericksburg. Mr Coleman received 1,572 votes, Mr Marye 1,467 votes, & there were 1,884 votes cast for 4 other candidates. There are 11 counties in the district.

The Charleston [S C] Courier notices the death of a venerable citizen of that city, Henry Muckenfuss, at the great age of 91 years, being born in 1766. He had been in the volunteer service in the war of 1812, & was the oldest surviving member of 2 somewhat celebrated companies, the Ancient Btln & the Lafayette Artl. The late anniversary of Jun 28 & Jul 4 were the first instances of his absence for many years. He was 10 years old when he witnessed the cannonading of *Fort Sullivan*.

New fortifications in N Y Harbor: a tract of land, embracing about 130 acres, has been purchased for the fortification at *Wilkin's Point*, L I, by Lt Q A Gillmore, Engineer Agent U S Army, on behalf of the Gov't. The property was owned by Mr Geo Irving, & the sum paid is $200,000.00 -N Y Com

Lord Lyndhurst, of England, from the Boston Traveller. Lord Lyndhurst was born in this place on May 21, 1772, & is little more than 85 years old. He was the son of John Singleton Copley, the eminent American painter. Mr Copley was a loyalist & of good family, being descended, on his mother's side, from the Winslows, 2 members of which family were Govn'rs of the Old Colony, namely Edw Winslow in 1633 & 1644, & Josias Winslow, his son, from 1673 to 1680. Both were men of eminent talents. Edw Winslow was one of the signers of the first instrument of gov't ever adopted by the English race in America. His son distinguished himself as a soldier in the war with Philip. He commanded the army which the United Colonies sent against the Narragansetts, & which won a victory of the first magnitude over that valiant tribe. Govn'r Winslow lived at *Careswell*, where he exercised a liberal hospitality. His wife, a member of the Pelham family, was a woman of great beauty & accomplishments. The most distinguished member of the family in the last centery was Gen John Winslow, perhaps the ablest soldier our country every produced while it belonged to England. Since then the name has been little known here, & Mr Sabine is right in saying that the Winslows of British America are probably, at the present time, the nearest direct descendants of Edw Winslow, the **Mayflower** Pilgrim. He might have added that Edw Winslow was one of the founders of the first American Union. The United Colonies of New England, was formed in 1643. Descended from such a family, Mr Copley was naturally a loyalist. He married to a daughter of Richd Clarke, a Boston merchant, & prominent on the same side. He & his sons were among the consignees of the teas sent here in 1773, & it was at his warehouse in King [now State] st that the famous interview took place between the Whig Cmte, of which Warren was a member, & the consignees. I shall have nothing to do with you, was Clarke's rough & peremtory answer to the requirement that the teas should be sent back in the same bottoms in which they were shipped. Mr Copley left America forever, when the future Chancellor of England was but a little child. He died in 1815, at the age of 77, before his son had attained to high honores, but not before his talents had been recognized. The Clarke family were harshly treated. Richd was proscribed & banished, & went to England in 1775, where he died 20 years later. His son Isaac was mobbed at Plymouth, when there on business. Lord Lyndhurst, then Mr John Singleton Copley, was here more than 60 years since. He was born in Boston, & was carried to England when about 2 years old, before the Revolution.

Massacre of Missionaries. Letter from Rev A Medland, of Meerut, dated May 16, says: "The missionaries & native Christians at Delhiare, I believe, are killed. A letter in the London Times from Rev T C Smith, chaplain of Meerut, India, says: The Rev Mr Jennings, chaplain of Delhi, & his grown-up daughter were murdered in the palace, where they were living with Capt Douglas, [also killed,] commandant of the guards. The Delhi Bank was plundered & burnt, as were all cantonments, together with the premises of the Delhi Gaz, the treasury sacked, & the church burnt. Not a single European or native Christian is left alive in Delhi or in the neighborhood.

The steamer **Europa** brings intelligence of the death of the great lyric poet of France, Pierre Jean Beranger, who was of very humble extraction, & owed his first introduction to the literary world to Lucian Bonaparte, brother of the great Napoleon, who aided him both by purse & encouragement. He has been ailing for a long time. Beranger died at Paris, on Jul 14, in his 77th year. [Aug 12th newspaper: Paris, Jul 20, 1857. The son of a poor tailor; the boy long a vagrant in the capital, a gamin de Paris, then a printer's apprentice; a simple, unpolished person, received a tribute in his coffin such as has been reserved for the kindred & the most exalted functionaries of royalty. His only 2 remaining relatives in the capital are 2 cousins-one a journeyman printer, the other a musician of the band of an artillery regiment. These plebian worthies led the grand procession, side by side with Prefects. Beranger expired on the 16th, & his funeral took place the next day.]

Among the passengers by the steamer **Europa**, at Boston, are 2 young English noblemen, who have probably come over to make the tour of the States. They are Lord Althrop & Lord Hervey. The first is the son & heir of Earl Spencer, a descendant of the great Duke of Marlborough, & nephew of Viscount Althorp, the distinguished statesman who was Chancellor of the Exchequer in the Melbourne Administration. Lord Hervey is the 2nd son of the Marquis of Bristol. They are both under 25 years of age & unmarried. –N Y Times

Lynching, mob murders in Iowa. The hanging of Wm B Thomas in Montezuma was as foul a murder as was ever perpetrated by a midnight assassin. The mob took him from the jail as he pleaded his innocence. The mob hung him, then let him down, demanding his confession. He pleaded his innocence. A second time they did the same thing, threatening to set a fire at his feet and burn him to death. He again pleaded his innocence. Again they hung him until he was dead.

Charlottesville [Va] Advocate: the negro woman who murdred her mistress, Mrs Hall, near Gordonsville, a few weeks since, was sentenced on Monday last by the Louisa Co Court to be hung on the 21st of next month.

On Jul 24 Mr Wm Gant, residing about 6 miles from Shelbyville, Tenn, was murdered in his bed, & his wife & son were so badly injured that it was believed they would die. The murderers carried off about $1,300, mostly in specie.

Orphans Court of Wash Co, D C. Case of Wm B B Cross, exc of Thos Ritchie, dec'd, the executor & Court appointed Aug 25 next, for the final settlement of the personal estate of said deceased, of the assets in hand. –Ed N Roach, Reg/o wills

Died: on Aug 3, in his 67th year, William Dunawin, a native of Fred'k city, Md, but for the last 30 years a resident of Wash City. He was one of the defenders of Balt in the last war with England. His funeral will be from his late residence, 15th & Mass ave, today at 3 o'clock.

Murder at Nevasink, N J, on Sat, in the Seaview House: Albert S Moses, temporary bar-keeper, was killed when his throat was cut by J P Donnelly, the book-keeper of the house. The deceased had won some $50 from Donnelly, & the assassination was the result of a desperate resolution on the part of Donnelly to recover the money. Donnelly hails from Wash City.

WED AUG 5, 1857
In the list of pensions just granted by the British Gov't, we find the following names of persons known on this side of the Atlantic.
Philip Jas Bailey, author of Festus, L100, in consideration of his literary merits.
Chas Swain, the poet, L50, in consideration os his literary merits.
Dr Wm Pulteney Alison, L100, [late professor of the practice of physic in the Univ of Edinburgh,] in consideration of his scientific attainments.
Mrs MaryAnne A'Beckett, L100, in consideration of the literary merits of her husband, the late Mr Gilbert A'Beckett; also of the eminent services rendered by him in his capacity of a police magistrate in the metropolis, & of the destitute circumstances in which she, his widow, & their children are now placed.
Mrs Mary Philadelphia Merrifield, L100, in consideration of the valuable services she has rendered to literature & art, & the reduced circumstances in which she is placed.
Mrs Lycia Falconer Miller, L70, in consideration of the eminent services rendered to literature & science by the works of her late husband, Mr Hugh Miller, & the straightened circumstances in which she is placed by his decease.
Mrs Mary Hayden, L115, an additional pension of L25 a year, in consideration of the eminent servies rendered to literature by her late husband,Mr Jo Hayden, & the straitened circumstances in which she is placed by his decease.

The oldest man. St Louis Republican, writing from Elwood, K T: living on his claim near the edge of this city is Mr Jas O'Toole, born in the County of Donegal, in Ireland, about 1730. He was an old man in the Irish rebellion of 1798, when, becoming implicated with Lord Edw Fitzgerald, he fled his county to seek freedom in our then new Republic. His life has been checkered with many changes. He moved to St Louis 30 years ago, & established the first brewery there. He moved to the Platte Puchase in 1838, & lived in Buchanan Co, near Bloomington, until 2 years ago, when he came to Kansas & made a pre-emption, & can now walk 8 or 10 miles with ease to visit his friends or attend to business affairs. He says his age is about 125 years.

The colors chosen by Mr Ten Broeck for the jockeys of his horses in England are the crimson & white satin stripes of the American flag, with blue cap & white stars.
-Spirit of the Times

On Sat, the two sons of Mr Rodinski, a farmer living in Marbletown, Ulster Co, N Y, were drowned in Esopus Creek, where they had gone to bathe.

Senator Thos J Rusk, one of the Senators from Texas, in his 3rd Senatorial term, unexpectedly died.
+
Phil, Aug 4. New Orleans advices from Texas state that Senator Rusk committed suicide, at his late residence, [*Nacogdoches*,] on Jul 29th, by shooting himself through the head with a rifle. There is no cause assigned. [Aug 14th newspaper: Gen Rusk has, ever since the death of his lady, suffered under a mental depression which at times bore him down beneath its weight. He had, to a great extent, secluded himself from society. A severe illness, from which he was just recovering, had prostrated him for weeks, & he was suffering greatly from a rising on the back of his neck. He was buried with Masonic honors. An obituary address was delivered by Hon W B Ochiltree.]

Archibald Campbell, aged 101 years, & an active participant in the Revolutionary war, died in Greenbrier Co, Va, Jul 20. The Lewisburg Chronicle says:"We believe that we have now in Greenbrier no witness of those eventful times that tried men's souls to relate the many hardships of that memorable period. With Archibald Campbell, the last of the noble Romans of '76, residents of Greenbrier Co, have passed away. Let us kindly cherish their memory.

Geo Lake, who escaped from the N Y Lunatic Asylum during the late fire, was arrested on Sat last. It appears that after his escape Lake made his way to Newburg, where he proceeded to Lagrange, Dutchess Co. Upon arriving at the house where he murdered his wife & 2 children he applied for lodging. A woman who resided in the house recognized Lake & called in some neighbors, by whom he was detained until Ofcr Robinson arrested him. He was brought back to the Poughkeepsie jail.

Orphans Court of Wash Co, D C. Letters testamentary on the personal estate of Geo M Grouard, late of Wash Co, deceased. –Ellen B Grouard, excx

U S Patent Ofc, Wash, Aug 4, 1857. Ptn of Moses S Woodward, of Chester Co, Pa, praying for the extension of a patent granted to him on Dec 4, 1843, for an improvement in carriage brakes, for 7 years from the expiration of said patent, which takes place on Dec 4, 1857. –S T Shugert, Acting Com'r of Patents

Died: in Wash City, Sidney, only son of Sidney & Mary J DeCamp, aged 4 months & 14 days. His funeral is today at 4 o'clock. [No death date given.]

U S Patent Ofc, Wash, Aug 4, 1857. Ptn of H M Smith, of Richmond, Va, praying for the extension of a patent granted to him on Feb 20, 1844, for an improvement in straw cutters, for 7 years from the expiration of said patent, which takes place on Feb 20, 1858. –S T Shugert, Acting Com'r of Patents

Obit-died: Mr Chas Stuart Hall was born in the State of N Y of most worthy & pious parents. Several of his early years were passed there, but for the last 8 or 10 years he has resided in Va. He was a student at Yale College, & more recently a graduate in several of the schools of the Univ of Va. His pecuniary means were but limited. His devotion to his widowed mother shone brightly amongst the brightest of his virtues. Mr Hall, whose death is yet recent, lost his life by drowning whilst bathing in the Potomac. [No death date given.]

Died: on Jul 24, at the residence of his father, Dr Robt Hare, of Phil, Lt Geo Harrison Hare, U S Navy. The final illness of this gallant ofcr was painful & protracted. As a son, brother, & friend he was devotedly affectionate. He died with prayers on his lips, confessing the Christian faith, his sure support & trust. He rests in peace!

Died: on Aug 2, at Richmond, Va, Mr Thos Bailie, printer, in his 41st year. He has been connected with some of the prominent papers of Richmond for the last 25 years. His illness was quite brief.

Buffalo, Aug 3. About 100 tons of rock fell from the precipice at Goat Island, Niagara Falls, about 300 feet below the British Falls, yesterday. Four persons were beneath it at the time & 3 of them were hurt. G W Parsons, of Cleveland, it is feared is fatally injured; F G Williams, of New Haven, has an arm broken, & a boy named Henry, a leg broken.

THU AUG 6, 1857
Capt Geo S Blake has received preparatory orders to relieve Capt Goldborough on Sep 15 as Superintendent of the Naval academy at Annapolis, Md. Capt W J Cluney has received preparatory orders to succeed Capt Blake in the superintendency of the construction of Stevens' war steamer at N Y. Cmder Edw R Thompson has been ordered to report at the Phil navy yard on Aug 7 as ordnance ofcr, vice Cmder Thos Turner.

The U S steam frig **Roanoke**, Capt J B Montgomery, arrived at N Y on Mondy, in 14 days from Aspinwall, bringing home 204 of Gen Walker's late Nicaraguan army. 27 of the unfortunates are sick, & will be sent to the hospital. Geo W Turner died on passage. None of the men from the frig **Independence** came in the Roanoke. Names of the returned filibusters:

A W Marsh	W K Williams	Henry Grey
T J Binns	C Syple	Geo Saunders
J J Goff	B Somers	Chas Webster
G W Holden	L Felix	John Callahan
J C Green	W H Burroughs	L D Smith
B H Withers	M C Cavana	John Rutter
Chas Camper	G R Gaston	W McCullough
W Boman	John Boswell	Jas Adams

E G Vanover	M L Truesdell	M D Steel
M R Warmick	T B Moore	H McKay
W B Thompson	P Coleman	Wm Parish
Chas Jones	G W Jordan	J Griffin
J Baker	Fred'k Machen	R N Payne
John Cooper	A P Deshield	D W C Gallup
J C Graham	Louis Deshield	O C Keith
Nat Mills	Jas H Levey	T C Bell
Robt Lynn	A C Hewes	F W Jones
J H Wingo	Edw McCabe	J A McClure
H C Sillis	John Duckwood	G W Hamilton
J J Reese	D McKesson	Geo Howard
Thos Howard	Orlando Ellis	Mark Smith
Wm Russell	Jas B Seely	John Grover
Geo Leinhart	B Ludlan	Milton Rogers
Jas W Conklin	John Hoffman	H Samain
John Jacob	T Micon	Caspar Slasinger
Wm Stone	Victor Simon	John Carson
Danl Lathrop	L P Morris	C C Higgins
N J Parsons	M K Lyons	Henry F James
D E Cooper	J R Crambo	John Denmann
Webster Higgins	Jas Dougherty	S J Clarke
Henry Badey	Alfred Cantrell	Thos Winters
Geo Sullivan	Danl Strausbuug	J M Steptoe
Edw Pennell	G L Wilson	Jas Moore
Richd H Kearney	John Hayes McLees	J M Wallington
Wm Allen	Alex'r Gillen	Robt Marsh
Henry Adams	W L Randall	Hampton Miller
Edw R Ryan	Wm Stephens	A C Wagstaff
Thos Fitzpatrick	Saml Moore	Louis Whiting
P Smith	John Karn	Henry Whiting
Chas Gerrald	Chas Hagan	L W Dake
P Margioli	Jas Edgar	Wm Lewell
A Bosket	J C Drinkhouse	P D Nellis
M J Colbert	Jas R Fagan	J H Earthman
D J Moulgomer	E C Hart	J A Cooper
Wm Schaffer	Wm Coul	T Woelfer
Wm Hendricks	Thos Stewart	M J Castle
Danl Shea	J B Green	Chas La Blas
Wm H Tola	J F McKneeh	Jas Craig
Wm Anderson	M Pitts	G Titus
Jas Mullen	A Flehatfield	John Harkin
Jas Johnson	B Bancroft	J Burt
Esinhart	T B Waller	Maurice Scully

W C Page	J C Campbell	W B Woodson
D R Bailey	L T Poland	Jas McGee
F F Archibald	Jas Fitzpatrick	Jos Miller
N Brown	Fred'k Levouse	Julius Slinker
Wm Jones	Jas A Campbell	F Hecht
Henry C Ball	Geo Western	P Hasey
R T Leckel	John R Giles	I H Olmstead
John Lago	Robt McGill	Wm Hall
Lysander Johnson	H Tricon	T J Bartelson
F W Peters	M Chene	Robt Richardson
John Ryan	Wm Higgins	Wm Roberts
Eysell Hamilton	D C Forrest	Michl Dowd
G W Parks	Henry Pollard	Richd Hill
J F Musgrove	F E Satone	W E Parks
W C Grant	J Nicholl	Wm Kobbe

[We tender to Capt Montgomery, his ofcrs & crew, our heartfelt gratitude for their timely assistance rendered to us upon our arrival in Aspinwall, in a destitute condition, & that their untiring efforts to render our situation as comfortable as circumstances would permit shall ever be held by us in grateful remembrance. To Dr David Harlan, surgeon of the ship, we are particularly indebted for the untiring efforts on his part to ameliorate the condition of the sick.]

It was announced some time ago that a French frig was lost on the Banks of Newfoundland. It appears now that it was the boat **Newton**, a steam dispatch boat of 220 tons, under the command of Mr Sagot Devauroux. The **Newton** has belonged for a few months past to the French squadron stationed off Newfoundland, & went ashore at the entrance of Port-au-Choix. No lives were lost. It was found impossible to raise her.

The prize fight between Dominick Bradley & Saml S Rankin, of Phil, for $1,000, took place at Point Abino, Canada, on Sat last; about 4,000 persons were present. Both parties were severely punished. Some 150 rounds were fought, occupying nearly 3 hours, the advantage being all the time on the side of Bradley. For the last few rounds Rankin actually stood up to be knocked down, being too weak from the loss of blood to return a blow. He still continues in that city in a very critical condition. It is humiliating to think that such brutality should be not only sanctioned, but applauded.

For sale or rent: my house on 5th st, opposite City Hall. –W H Gunnell

Peter Boyle was killed almost instantly at the little Railroad bridge. As the train was passing Laury's station he stuck his head out of the window, which coming in contact with the timbers of the bridge took his scalp entirely off.
–Allentown [Pa] Democrat

An infant som of Dr F C Bailey, or Rockville, Conn, during the doctor's absence from home, crept into a room where morphine had been spilt & carelessly left on the carpet, & ate enough of the powder to produce death, in spite of an emetic which the mother gave him.

Shirley Female Seminary, Urbana, Fred'k Co, Md. Geo G Butler, A M, Principal; Prof Otto Fox, Dept of Music. The 3rd session will commence on Sept 2.

The subscriber offers at private sale the Farm on which he resides, near Wash, containing 220 acres; with a fine frame house of 8 rooms, with large water-tank & bathing room. Also, the Farm belonging to my son, adjoining the above lands on the west side of Rockville Pike, containing 185 acres of improved land. The improvements are good. Refer to Bradley & Son, Wash, & O Z Muncaster, Gtwn.
-G M Watkins

Died: on Aug 4, Owen Murray, in his 47th year; a native of the county Down, Ireland, but for the last 24 years a resident of Wash City. His funeral is on Aug 6, at 4 o'clock, from his late residence, K & 20th st west.

Died: on Aug 5, of cholera infantum, Mary Ann, infant daughter of Sgt Robt Hamilton, of the Marine Corps. Her funeral is today at 2 o'clock.

FRI AUG 7, 1857
Hon Jas C Dobbin, late Sec of the Navy, died at Fayetteville, N C, on Aug 4, though by no means unexpected, is not the less a subject of deep sorrow. He was born in 1814, & was in his 44th year. He was graduated at the Univ of N C in 1832; read law in the ofc of the late Judge Strange; elected to Congress in 1845, & declined re-election; was elected to the Legislature from this county in 1848 & 1850; was Speaker of the House of Commons at the latter session; & finally entered the Cabinet as Sec of the Navy in 1853, serving through the entire Administration of Pres Pierce. His devotion to the aruduous duties of that station cost him his life.

Public sale of Potomac lands & fisheries: by decree of the Circuit Court of PG Co, as a court of equity, the subscriber, acting as the trustee, will expose to public sale, on Sep 3, at the residence of Arthur Adams, on Broad Creek, PG Co, Md, near the premises, all the right, title, & interest of Rozier T Daingerfield, of, in, & to a certain portion of the **Bellmonte Estate**, containing 600 acres of land, more or less. The property is divided into 2 tracts of about equal size.
–Wm Henry Daingerfield, trustee

J D Lakeman, Merchant Tailor & Gentlemen's Furnishing Goods, 281 Pa ave, between 10th & 11th sts, has commenced the business on his own account.

Danl Scully, of the New Orleans Picayune, who shot Mr Kennedy, of the New Orleans Delta, at Leavenworth, Kansas, on Jul 20, inflicting a serious wound, wrote to Mr Kennedy, in which he says he was led to make the unfortunate assault through a misapprehension of facts & circumstances, & hopes this confession will remove from his breast any sense of wounded honor.

Boston Courier: Rev Laban Ainsworth, of Jaffrey, N H, is the oldest living graduate on the catalogue of Dartmouth College, being in the class of 1778, which is the 9th in the history of the institution. He has been 75 years pastor of the church in Jaffrey, & completed his century of years Jul 27, 1857. On that day, which was Sunday, he walked from his dwlg to the church & listened to a discourse from his colleague. Among the honorary degrees conferred at the recent Commencement at Dartmouth that of Dr of divinity on Rev John Sawyer, of Maine, 103 years old next Oct, was most judicious & grateful; grateful to his friends, if indifferent to him, as very likely it is. He graduated in 1785, & is the oldest man among the graduates, though not the oldest graduate.

Criminal Court-trial of Election Rioters: witnesses examined: 1-Franklin Birkhead-testified that Isaiah Stewart advised him to have nothing to do with the party from Balt, they were murderers, & were armed with pistols & knives. 2-John G Frere was recalled & said he had known Stewart for 10 years. 3-Israel Cross testified that he lives in the 6th Ward, Navy Yard. 4-Testified: Wm Mills; Jas Forrest; Dr Chas Everett; Mr Robt Israel; Mr Robt M Baird; Mr Henry Lyles; Mr Chas Lemon; Mr Jas R Riley; Mr Ketterman; Mr Hiram Ritchie; Jas Handy; Dr Chas Everett; Mr Walter Lenox; & Elijah Edmondson. Mr Ashton White was recalled. [Aug 8th newspaper: Testified: Mr Alex'r Patterson-was one of the Marines at the riot on Jun 1. Mr John Rainbow is a ship carpenter in the U S navy & well acquainted with guns. Mr Josh M Downing testified to seeing Michl Hoover on the day of the election, & that he took no part in the affray whilst deponent was there. Jas A Gordon testified to being on the platform in front of the City Hall. Mr Saml E Douglass, ex-Register, testified to having known Hughes, who was shot on Jun 1. As a fireman, & one of the Union Fire Company, he was a peaceful man. Patrick Kearney, also a Marine, never pointed a gun at Mr Nokes. Said he never saw him until it was all over. Maj Jacob Zeilin was called, commanded the 1st company. Ofct Wm Ross examined-knows Jas R Riley since Jan 1st last.]

Died: on Aug 5, at the residence of his aunt, near Rockville, Md, Hugh Tyler, infant son of Thos R & Mary C Suter, aged 10 months.

St Louis, Aug 6. Advices from Leavenworth on Monday that Woods & Knowlton, companions of those who were hung on Friday, wee being tried by judges of a vigilance cmte. The people were intensely excited, & had expressed a determination to lynch the prisoners at all hazards. Judge Lecompte & Gov Walker had addressed the populace & failed to pacify them.

SAT AUG 8, 1857

Memphis paper of Aug 2. Yesterday, Knox, the second son of our friend, J Knox Walker, was thrown from his horse, &, his foot catching in the stirrup, he was dragged for some distance, his head on the ground, as to cause his immediate death. He was about 10 or 12 years of age.

The bodies of 50 of those Swedish emigrants who were lost off Newfoundland, in the wrecking of the barque **Monasco**, have been recovered & buried. Five bodies are still missing.

The U S sloop-of-war **Portsmouth**, Capt Foote, left Singapore for Siam on May 21, conveying W C Bradley, LL D, with the ratification of the treaty between the U S & Siam.

Kansas City Enterprise of Aug 1. Letters received at Lecompton on Jul 25 which state that the Cheyenne or Sioux Indians, or both, had attacked several of the U S surveying parties in the s w portion of Nebraska & murdered a number of men. The report is that 5 of Capt Caldwell's, 4 of Capt Berry's, & all of Col Manner's party, including the latter, had been murdered. We have been unable to learn particulars.

Died: on Jul 27, at **Hazlewood**, St Louis Co, Mo, Maj Richd Graham, in his 78th year; last surviving son of Richd Graham, of Dumfries, Prince Wm Co, Va; brother of Geo Graham, acting Sec of War during the administration of Pres Monroe; Com'r of the Gen Land Ofc; of John Graham, 1st U S District Atty for Louisiana, Sec of Legation to Spain, Com'r to the South American Republics, & Minister Plenipotentiary to Brazil; & of Mrs Catherine Ramsay, of Wash City, all now deceased. Maj Graham entered the military service during the last war with Great Britain, & served with distinction as Aid-de-Camp on the staff of Maj Gen Harrison. He participated in all the perils of the northwestern army, & was promoted to Major for his gallantry & good conduct. The war over, Maj Graham was appointed Indian agent for the extended Territory of Missouri, in which ofc he continued until 1829. He was also appointed by the Pres one of the Com'rs to establish the boundary lines of Illinois. With ample fortune, Major Graham has for many years been surrounded by his devoted family, & led the happy life of a country gentleman. He was a consistent, pure, & humble Christian. The study of the Holy Scriptures was his daily ofc. -St Louis Republican

N Y: the cmte on the subject have awarded Gen Jackson's gold box to Lt Col Garrett W Dykeman, as the bravest of the N Y volunteers in Mexico.

Farm for sale: tract called **Valley Forge**, containing 17 acres, about 4 miles north of Wash City, on the Plank Road, with a good frame dwlg house containing 4 rooms, with kitchen, carriage-house, & stabling for 3 horses. Apply on the premises to Danl V Colclazer.

The Home School. Day & Boarding School for Young Ladies, 52 Sharp st, Balt, Md. Principals: Mrs Robt W Cliffe & Miss Dunnington. The Institution will resume its duties on the 1st Monday of Sept. References:
Rt Rev W R Whittingham, Balt, Md
Rt Rev Thos Atkinson, Wilmington, N C
Rev Aristides Smith, Norfolk Institute, Va
Dr A B Carter, Yonkers, N Y
Dr J R Keech, Herford Co, Md
Dr A Cleaveland Coxe, Balt
Dr John Buckler, Balt
Robt H Archer, Patapsco Institute, Md
A W Robins, Gloucester Co, Va
Saml R Fowle, Washington, N C
Thos J Hall, Anne Arundel Co, Md

Phil College of Medicine, 5th st, below Walnut-Session 1857-58.
–B Howard Rand, M D, Dean

Central Academy, corner of E & 10th sts, will be open on Sep 1.
-Silas Merchant, A M, Principal

Aston Ridge Seminary for Young Ladies, re-opens Sep 10. Address: Rev B S Huntington, near Chester, Delaware Co, Pa.

Valuable land in Iowa for sale: 1,400 acres in Wisconsin, which I will exchange for Va lands. Also, a small house on 9th st, above I st, for sale on easy terms-monthly payments. –A W Fletcher, 430 F st, between 6th & 7th sts.

Mrd: on Aug 6, at Wesley Chapel, by Rev W Krebs, Thos E Shoemaker to Sarah J Herbert, both of Wash City.

Mrd: on Aug 5, at Fredericksburg, Va, by Rev Mr Hodge, Lt G U Morris, U S Navy, to Miss Mattie Thorburn, of Fredericksburg.

Died: on Thu, in Wash City, after a brief illness, Helen Augusta Upton, of Fairfax Co, Va, who had just reached her 60th year.

Died: on Aug 7, in Wash City, at the residence of his grandfather, Cmdor Lavalette, at the Navy Yard, George Frederick, son of G W & M L Duval. His funeral will take place this evening at 5 o'clock.

Augusta, Aug 7. Mr Maguire, special agent of the Post Ofc Dept, has arrested Saml C Scott, postmaster at Colliers, Edgefield district, S C, for robbing the mail. Scott is now in jail at Augusta. He was caught by a decoy letter.

Circuit Court of Wash Co, D C-as Court of Chancery, to Oct term, 1857. Archibald McDaniel vs John M Springman, Fred'k Whyte, & Jas Whiteman, & Jos Whiteman, Executors of the last will & testament of Jos Morrisen. The cmplnt at the Oct term of said court in 1856, obtained a judgment against the dfndnt Springman, for $188.25, with interest thereon & cost of suit, a copy of which said judgment is exhibited with his bill; that a short time before the rendition of the said judgment, the said Springman being seized in fee, or otherwise entitled to an absolute estate in equity, in lot 13, in reservation D, in Wash City, D C, convey the same to one Fred'k Whyte & his heirs in trust, to secure the payment of a certain debt of $1,000, with interest thereon, alleged to be owing by the said Springman to one Jos Morrisen, of Loudoun Co, Va, & payable several years after the date of the said deed; that the said Morrisen is since dead, having in his lifetime made a last will & testament, in which he appointed the said Jas & Jos Whitman his executors, who have qualified as such, in said county; that there is no estate, real or personal, of the said Springman, known to the cmplnt, out of which he can enforce the payment of the debt due to him on the said judgment; that he is advised that said judgment is an equitable lien on the right of redemption of the said Springman in the said lot of ground. The object of the said bill is to obtain a decree by said court for the sale of the said lot, & the application of the proceeds thereof, under the direction of the court, to the payment of the liens thereon as to the court shall appear consistent with law & equity. Jas & Jos Whiteman are not citizens of D C, & do not reside therein. They are to appear on the first Mon in Jan next, & answer the said bill. –Jas Dunlop, Ch J -J A Smith, clerk

MON AUG 10, 1857
Died: on Aug 9, after a lingering illness of 2 years, Catharine W Garner, in her 56th year. Her funeral will take place at Rev Mr Hill's Church on 10th st, this morning at 10 o'clock.

Died: on Aug 7, in Wash City, after a severe illness of 2 weeks, of typhoid fever, Clara A Mills, daughter of Capt John & Mary Ann Mills, in her 11th year.

Died: on Aug 6, at Alexandria, Robert W, son of Francis L & Sarah G Smith, aged 9 months & 4 days.

Died: on Jul 17, at Platten Rock, Mo, in her 29th year, Margaret Frances Lee, youngest daughter of the late Edw W Clark, of Wash City, & consort of Dr J W Lee, of the former place.

+
Died: on Jul 30, at Herculaneum, Mo, the residence of her uncle, Dr Wm E Clark, Eliz Bacon, infant daughter of Margaret Frances & Dr J W Lee, aged 22 days.

S S Cunningham, of Washington Co, Md, declines the Democratic nomination for Com'r of Public Works.

Mr John Janeway, an Englishman, & a very reputable citizen, employed as miller at Marrs' flouring mill, about 8 miles s w of the city, came to his death Aug 3. He was entering the city in a buggy when his horse took fright & backed onto the track in front of the Terre Haute train. The locomotive, running slow, was brought to a stand still, but Mr Janeway was frightened to death. —Indianapolis Sentinel, Aug 4.

The largest man in the world, Miles Darden, died in Tenn some weeks ago. He weighed in 1845 871 pounds. His height was 7 feet 6 inches. His weight when he died, as nearly as could be ascertained was a fraction over 1,000 pounds.

Three men, Miley Peterman, Jas Lehman, & Jas Berry, were taken before Ald Field, at Phil, on Thu, on the charge of shooting a boy. The men were shooting at a mark in the yard of a hotel & the ball passed through the fence & entered the body of a lad named Jas McConnell. The wounded boy was conveyed to St Joseph's Hospital & expired yesterday morning. The three men were committed to prison.

Miss Brooke's English & French Boarding & Day School for Young Ladies, Seven Bldgs, 138 Pa ave, Wash. This Institution will resume on Sep 14.

TUE AUG 11, 1857
Judge Chas Mason has retired from the ofc of Com'r of Patents & Mr Shugert has become the Acting Com'r. Judge Mason is a little more than 40 years of age; graduated at West Point; became a Professor there; studied & practiced law; became a judge, & at one period conducted a newspaper. He has made himself wealthy. He is rather slender, dark, wears a full black beard, affects nothing & expresses himself in the simplest language. He is about to return to Iowa, where the whole Democratic party & his own energetic spirit will impel him to again assume position as a prudent, courageous, & effective leader in politics. Mr S T Shugert is about 50 years old; is from the interior of Pa; long time in connexion with other pursuits; conducted a weekly newspaper; & is a quiet, modest man.

Yesterday a little boy about 8 years old, son of Mr Jas L McDonough, fell from the 3rd story window of his father's residence, 30 feet, on to Main, near 12th st. His skull was fractured by the fall. —Richmond Whig

The St Joseph Gaz announces the death of Madame Cecille Roy, the widow of John Baptiste Roy, of St Joseph. She was 70 years of age. Her history is intimately connected with that of Missouri. During the war of 1812 her husband & herself made a noble resistance to the attack of the Indians against a blockhouse occupied by them at Cote sans Dessein, in Callaway Co. A large number of Indians attacked them; 3 times they were repulsed, Roy & his wife keeping up an incessant fire upon them. Madame Roy not only loaded the guns, but she used the rifle herself, & the Indians, when they did retreat, left 13 of their warriors dead within the stockade of the fort.

Indianapolis Sentinel of Aug 3: arrests of counterfeiters. Dr Patterson, of Carthage, Rush Co, was arrested; Dr Rogers, of Knightstown, a man with a large family, arrested; Perry Bennett, of St Omar, who has been a terror of the country, arrested; Dr Lewis Francis was arrested in Jonesville, Bartholomew Co; Dr Allen Robinson was arrested at Mandistown. Mr Reany says the new counterfeit bills were put in circulation in Rush, Henry, Decatur, & Bartholomew Counties, that they were in Ky & Indiana.

The <u>oldest engine</u> in the country. We find in a N Y paper that the first Phil fire engine is to appear & perform at the great Firemen's Convention at Elmira, N Y. It was built as an experiment in London, in 1689, & was the first ever made on the air-tight chamber principle. It was brought by some of the descendants of Penn, & brought to Phil, where it was kept for a long while. It was eventually sold to the borough of Bethlehem, where a company was formed calling themselves the Perserverance Fire Co, which company is still in existence, & retains possession of the old relic.

Three men who registered their names as Wm Hughes, T J Arbuckle, & A J Dearth, were arrested at Louisville, Ky, on Thu, on the charge of being counterfeiters. They were examined on Fri & committed in default of $1,500 bail each.

The arrest at Cameron, Pa, last week of Joe Miller, the king of counterfeiters, has been followed by the arrest of 2 more of his gang at Moundsville & Wheeling. One named Jones was arrested at Moundsville. Geo Johnson was arrested at Wheeling. He is from Ohio, & his real name is supposed to be Middleton; a wagon driver.

Situation as a Teacher wanted. Address Stromer L Edgeworth, Charlottesville, Va.

Orphans Court of Wash Co, D C. Letters of administration on the personal estate of Parke G Howle, late of Wash Co, deceased. –P C Howle, adm

Mrd: on Aug 10, at the Kirkwood House, in Wash City, by Rev W Krebs, W L B Hale to Miss L L B Neill, both of Fauquier Co, Va.

Died: on Aug 9, in Wash City, Mary Eliz, wife of Wm E Stewart, & eldest daughter of Joshua Banks, aged 22 years. Her funeral will take place from the residence of her father, 5th & H sts, this morning at 10 o'clock.

Died: on Aug 4, in Amherst, N H, Mrs Abby A, widow of the late Robt Means, of Lowell, Mass.

Warrenton Male Academy, Va: will be resumed on Sep 1 & continued until Jul 15. Apply to S C Lindsay, Principal.

Wash City Ordnance: Act for the relief of John Patch, agent for Mrs John Brereton: the sum of $6.68 be paid, that amount erroneously paid for lighting the streets. Approved: Aug 4, 1857.

WED AUG 12, 1857
Household & kitchen furniture at auction on: Aug 15, in front of the Auction Rooms, belonging to the estate of the late Wm Bigly. –T C Donn, Thos J Fisher, trustees -Jas C McGuire, auct

Mr Crawford's case-Dr Gibson's exploration. In looking over the N Y Evening Post, I was astonished to find a letter of May 2, 1857 from my son, Prof Chas Bell Gibson, of Richmond, Va, in reply to one of Mrs Louisa W Crawford, wife of Thos Crawford, the celebrated American sculptor of Rome, dated Paris, Apr 7, 1857, charging me with having seriously injured her husband by an explorative operation. I deem it necessary, in my own justification, to disabuse the American people on the subject; &, in order to make my statement perfectly clear & intelligible to non-professional readers-professional ones requiring no elucidation whatever-I shall give a short history of Mr Crawford' case. Whilst in Rome last winter I received from Mr Crawford the following note: Vila Negroni, Tue, Dec 2, 1856. Will you call at my house & give Dr Smyth, who is attending me, the benefit of your advice regarding my eye: Thos Crawford. I used an exploratory needle. A solid tumor was found, which not only filled up the posterior part of the orbit, but might possible have its origin in the brain. I wrote to Dr John W Francis, of N Y, an old acquaintance, an eminent physician, & the uncle of Mrs Crawford. I received a reply from Dr Francis, & a postscript from Mrs Crawford, thanking me for the warm interest I had taken in Mr Crawford's case. I also wrote to Dr Wm Lawrence, one of the oldest & most eminent of London surgeons, but he could give me no opinion because of the complicated symptoms. I refused to extirpate the tumor, stating that Mr Crawford would not live, if performed, an hour; that he might live, if let alone, several months. Mr Crawford repaired to Paris to see Dr Wm Gibson, M D-near Geneva, Switzerland, Jun 7, 1857. Dr Wm Gibson, Velpeau, Nalation, Desmarres, E Beylard, & Sichel, D M, all agree that the exploratory needle operation did not cause the slightest injury.

Hon H L Turney died of congestion on Aug 1. He had spent the day in town attending to his business in the circuit court. His son, Peter Turney, walked with him about a half a mile when he left him in fine spirits. He was found by one of his neighbor's negro boys sitting by a tree. He told the boy he was sick; to take one of his mules from his wagon & take him home. He went about a half a mile & told the boy to take him down; he thought he should die. The boy took him down, galloped to his house to give the alarm. A gentleman walking on the farm ran to him in time to see him breath his last, but too late for him to speak. He was a U S Senator from Tenn from 1845 to 1851.

N Y, Aug 10. The French brig **L Gillis** has arrived, bringing several of the crew & passengers of the barque **Monasco**, which, with 50 of her passengers, was lost at Buren, N F, a little while past.

A female sculptor, Miss Harriet G Hosmer, who has executed some beautiful pieces of statuary in Italy, is about returning home. She is the daughter of Dr Hosmer, of Watertown, Mass.

Obit-died: Mr John T Towers, after a painful illness of several weeks' duration; a native of Alexandria, but for the last 30 years a resident of Wash, & one of our most popular & useful public men. He was in his 47th year.
+
Died: on Aug 11, John T Towers, in his 47th year. His funeral will take place this afternoon, at 4 o'clock, moving from his late residence, on K st, between 8th & 9th sts, to Trinity Church, on 3rd st, where the funeral services will be performed.
+
Masonic: Members of Nat'l Lodge No 12 to attend the funeral of our late Brother John T Towers. –W M
+
I O O F. Ofcrs of the Central Lodge No 1 are to attend the funeral of P G M John T Towers. -E White Middleton, sec
+
I O O F. Members of the R W Grand Lodge of D C, are requested to attend the funeral of the late P G M Jno T Towers. –Jno T Bangs, Grand Sec

Musical. Wanted, a situation at the South as a Teacher of Music, by a young lady who has had some years experience as teacher of the piano. Would instruct in the usual English branches if required, but prefers Music alone. Address, until Sep, Annie R B Snow, Wash, D C.

THU AUG 13, 1857
Curious mistake occurred on Sat at York Assizes, in connexion with the trial of Ann Edmondson, indicted for the murder of her child at Caverly. The prisoner engaged no counsel, but Mr Price, at the request of the judge, defended her. The prisoner overwhelmed with grief, sobbed the word Guilty. She was indistinctly heard, & in a confused state, & her plea was taken as one of Not Guilty. She was instead of being condemned on her own confession, she was placed on her trial, & the jury rendered a verdict of not guilty. She received the full benefit of the error, & a self-confessed murderess has escaped the legal penalty of her crime. –Lancaster [Eng] Chronicle

On Jul 27 the marriage of the Archduke Maximillian, of Austria, & the Princess Charlotte, of Belgium, took place in the palace of Brussels. The civil ceremony took place in a room in the palace; the religious part of the ceremony was performed in the chapel.

Naval: 1-Capt John Pope has been ordered to the command of the navy yard at Portsmouth, N H, vice Cmdor Newton, deceased. 2-Capt Wm W McKean has been appointed Govn'r of the Naval Asylum at Phil, to relieve Cmdor Storer.

The New **Gaslights** which have been placed on Bridge st, in Gtwn, & lighted up since Monday last, lend a much-improved appearance to the streets. They are set at the expense of the General Gov't, & we trust constitute but an item in the catalogue of good things yet to come to our neighbors from the same guardian source.

Four young ladies, residing in Waterville, drowned in Crummett's stream on Thu. Two were the daughters of Mr D G Soule, & the other 2 were daughters of Mr Grant, a pianoforte manufacturer. Their ages varied from 11 to 14. –Bangor [Me] Whig

Mr Lyon, warden of the almshouse in Marlborough, feeling a little unwell, drank what he thought was peppermint, & proved to be bed-bug poison. He lingered several days, but death came at length to his relief. –Boston Traveller

Mrd: on Aug 11, at Laurel, Md, by Rev Mr Chapman, Jos T W Ourand, of Wash, D C, to Miss Maggie Arthur, 2nd daughter of Jas Arthur, sr, of the former place.

Mrd: on Aug 5, at the residence of Maj Symington, [Allegheny Arsenal,] Rev S R Bertron, of Port Gibson, Miss, to Ottilia M A , daughter of the late Hofrath Franz Mueller, of Freibourg, Grand Duchy of Baden.

Died: on Aug 12, in Wash City, aged 50 years, Jos L Peabody, a native of Newburyport, Mass, for many years a resident of Wash City.

FRI AUG 14, 1857
The Board to make trial of breech-loading rifles. A board of ofcrs to be composed of Lt Col B L Beall, 1st dragoons; Maj Henry Hill, paymaster; Capt Thos Duncan, mounted rifles; Capt Henry Heath, 10th infty; Capt Thos J Brereton, ordnance dept; & 1st Lt John Gibson, 4th artl-ordered to assemble at West Point, N Y, on Aug 17, to make trial of breech-loading rifles, with a view to ascertain which is best suited for military service.

Died: on Aug 13, in Wash City, after a severe illness of 5 days, George W, son of John W & Martha A Fitzhugh, aged 5 years, 5 months & 23 days. His funeral will be on Friday at 4 o'clock, from the residence of his parents, 12th st, between I & K sts.

Died: on Aug 13, in Gtwn, at the residence of A H Pickrell, Alice Graham, aged 3 months, only child of Robt H & Sarah E Watkins.

Obit-the funeral of the late & lamented Jos L Peabody will take place this morning, at 10 o'clock, from the residence of his brother-in-law, Wm H Ward, 40 Missouri ave. The deceased was a native of Newburyport, Mass, but for many years past he has resided in Wash City. To the intelligence of an educated gentleman & the matured virtues of manhood he united the innocence & modesty of a child. He was a sincere Christian. May he rest in peace!

SAT AUG 15, 1857
Mrs Leslie Combs, wife of Gen Leslie Combs, of Lexington, Ky, died on Monday, after a long & painful illness. She was a native of Rhode Island. She was a woman in every sense of the word-beautiful, talented, lovely, & agreeable.
–Louisville Journal

Circuit Court for Montg Co, sitting as a Court of Equity, Jul term, 1857. Isaac Young & Henry Young, excs, & Isaac Young & Mgt Young his wife, & Henry Young, Benj E Hughes, & Catherine S Hughes, vs Geo Young, John Young, Eliz Young, Sarah E Young, & Mgt Young. This suit is to procure a decree for a sale of certain real estate of which Henry Young, late of said county, deceased, died seized & possessed of. The bill states that the said Henry Young, deceased, previous to his death signed, sealed, published, & declared in writing his last will & testament to convey real & personal property, which said last will & testament has been properly admitted to probate in the Orphans' Court of Montg Co, & among other items, the said Henry Young, deceased, constituted Isaac Young & Henry Young his excs of said will & testament, & also devised as follows, that is to say 4th; I devise that my real estate be valued by good judges, & that it be sold to the highest bidder as soon as it can advantageously be done consistent with the situation of my family. I further desire that a majority of my heirs shall rule in the disposition of my real estate, & recommend their advising with their older relatives. If a majority of my heirs will permit my son George to put his farm in Missouri into my estate by selling the same & returning into my estate as much money as I have given him, & he, George, takes in lieu thereof his regular part of my estate, I do so desire, but do not urge that or wish it unless a majority of my heirs so agree. I hereby empower my excs to divide my estate as though I had but 6 children, as my son John has not been heard from for a long time. Thus empowering them to do, I require that they take from each of my heirs an obligation to pay their proportional part of what he would be entitled to when he may be found. And the said bill further states that it would be impossible for the execs to sell & divide the real estate of the said Henry Young, deceased, equitably, & justly among the heirs at law of the said Henry Young, deceased, according to the provisions of said will, there being several of the heirs minors & under the age of 21 years, as also a widow, who refuses to sell her dower in said lands, & demands that the dower in said real estate should be laid off to her, & that the said execs could not take the obligation of the minor heirs until they arrive at the age of 21, to secure to John Young his proportion in the event he should be found. And that the said Henry Young, deceased, in his lifetime, with a view to advance his son, Geo Young, laid out a large sum of money in land in the State of Missouri, which said sum of money is properly a charge against the said Geo Young in the division of the real estate of the said Henry Young, deceased, among his heirs at law, which the said excs cannot settle without the intervention of this court; & that the said Henry Young, deceased, left a considerable real estate in Montg Co, Md, in which his widow Margaret Young, is entitled to dower, & that it will be for the interest & advantage of the heirs at law to sell the said real estate, & the proceeds thereof be divided among them in their just proportions; & that the said Geo Young & John Young reside in the State of Md. Absent dfndnts are to appear in this court, in person or by solicitor, on or before Mar 1 next. –Nicholas Brewer, Circuit Judge –Jas G Hening, clerk

Mrd: on Aug 13, in Wash City, at the Assembly's Church, by Rev Andrew G Carothers, Mr Eli Duvall, jr, to Miss Alice Carey Ball, both of Wash City.

Mrd: on Aug 12, in Wash City, by Rev Dr Gurley, L J Brown to Julia, youngest daughter of Nathl Carusi, all of Wash City.

Died: last evening, Wm J Fitzpatrick, in his 29th year. His funeral will take place from the residence of his father, Jno C Fitzpatrick, 294 south B st, on Sunday, at 5 o'clock P M.

Died: on Aug 14, Robt Thurston Barry, M D, surgeon U S Navy, in his 48th year. His funeral will be this afternoon at 4:30 o'clock, from the residence of J M Carlisle.

Died: on Aug 10, in Charlestown, Va, at the residence of Mrs E M Griggs, Eliza Frame, daughter of Rev R T Berry, of Martinsburg, Berkeley Co, Va, in her 7th year.

The subscriber, Principal of the Columbia Institute for Young Ladies, proposing to discontinue his school for an indefinite period, would respectfully recommend to his patrons the Boarding & Day School of Miss M Harrover, on F st. –Prof Geo Henry Steuckrath

Gtwn Female Seminary for sale or rent. This institution, being vacant, is offered for sale or rent-sale preferred. Miss English, by whose efforts it was built up & for many years so prosperously & usefully conducted, in consequence of impaired health, desires to relieve herself of all responsibility in connexion with it. Address Richd Henderson, agent, Care of Miss L S English, Gtwn, D C.

MON AUG 17, 1857
Died: on Aug 16, in Wash City, Mark McNeill, in his 35th year. His funeral will take place today from his late residence on 4½ st, below Pa ave, at 4 o'clock.

Trustee's sale: by deed of trust, executed by Benj E Green, dated Mar 27, 1845, recorded among the land records of Wash Co, D C, in Liber W B 115, folios 327 thru 330: public auction on Oct 17, of part of lot 13 in square 729. Also, lot 14 in square 729. This property fronts on First st east, between East Capitol & a streets south. –Johnson Hellen, Jas Adams, trustees -Jas C McGuire, auct

Steamboat collision in Long Island Sound on Sat morning. The steamer **Metropolis**, bound from Fall River to N Y, encountered the propeller **J N Harris** under full headway, cutting her in twain amidships causing her to sink immediately. The following are among the lost: Stephen Prentice, mate of the propeller; Clara Williams, cook; Eliz, aged 7 years, Mary aged 5 years, children of Capt Leonard Smith; Wm Bunce; Miss Gordon, daughter of Mr S Gordon, of police dept, N Y; wife of Alfred W Smith; daughter of A W Smith, aged 11 years; a gentleman, wife, & babe, names unknown; other passengers, names unknown. The **Metropolis** was commanded by Capt Brown, & the propeller by Capt Leonard Smith. The latter has sustained a severe loss. Six of his children had died previously. He has a wife & one child now living at New London. The three now lost were returning from an excursion they had been making during their school vacation. He says the blow to his wife will be overpowering. An additional circumstance in his affliction is the loss of Miss Gordon, who was placed under his care by her father, a friend of Capt Smith. He owned a portion of the propeller, which was protected by a fire but not by a marine policy. About half an hour after the collision Geo Tappan, of New Bedford, who was a passenger on the **Metropolis**, & eagerly discussing with several persons the possibility of danger to that steamer, fell down in an apopletic fit & expired.

Hon Franklin Dexter died at Beverly, Mass, on Thu. He was a son of the great orator, Saml Dexter. He was born in Charlestown, graduated at Harvard College n 1812, & studied law, in which profession he became eminent at the Boston bar. His age was about 60 years. Of late he had retired to the elegant enjoyments of leisure & fortune.

Died: on Aug 15, in Wash City, Hon Jas B Hunt, of Pontiac, Mich, in his 59th year. He was a native of the State of N Y, & for several years the law-partner of Michl Hoffman. He removed to Michigan about the period of its admission into the Union; & elected from the 3rd district to the 28th & 29th Congress. His funeral will take place from the house of Mrs Gilbert, head of Delaware ave, at 10 o'clock this morning.

Died: on Aug 15, of lock-jaw, Gen Danl Smith Lee, U S Consul to Basle, in his 35th year. His remains will be carried to Strasburg, Va, this morning.

Died: on Aug 15, in Wash City, Mary, wife of Michl Joyce, in her 49th year. Her funeral will take place from her late residence on N st, between 12th & 13th sts, this afternoon at 3 o'clock.

Died: on Aug 15, in Wash City, Eliza A M Owens, wife of Mr R B Owens.

Died: on Aug 16, Alice, infant daughter of Thos J & Charlotte M Fisher. Her funeral will be this morning at 10 o'clock, from the residence of its parents, 383 N Y ave.

TUE AUG 18, 1857
The public are notified not to take a note given by Conrad Sohl to Wm D Bell, or any one for him, on account of the purchase of a stall, dated on or about Jul 31st last, for $200, as an attachment has been laid upon the same in the hands of said Sohl.
--Geo Rhodes, jr

The Liverpool Times of Jul 24 says: Notice has been given at Lloyd's that her Majesty's Gov't requires a ship immediately to carry 400 male convicts from England to Freemanlie, Western Australia. Perhaps a more remarkable set of convicts never left the county at one time than will go out in this ship. Among them will be found Sir John Dean Paul Strahn & Bates, the fraudulent bankers; Robson, the Crystal Palace forger; Redpath, who committed the forgeries on the Great Northern Railway Co; & Agar, who committed the great gold robbery on the Southwestern Railway. The notorious bank forger, Barrister Saward, alias Jem the Penman, the putter up of all the great robberies in the metropolis for the last 20 years, also goes out in this ship, which will leave England about Sep 25, embarking the convicts at Depford, the little Nora, Portsmouth, Portland, & Plymouth.

Storehouse for rent, 7th st, near Pa ave. Apply to Henry Thorn, 8th, between D & E.

Distribution of premiums at St Mary's Institute, Bryantown, Chas Co, Md, Jul 30, 1857.

Maria Conlan, Wash, D C
Kate Lloyd, Chas Co, Md
Jane McGarr, Wash City, D C
Eliza Matthews, Chas Co, Md
Rose Mudd, Chas Co, Md
Mary Keating, Wash City, D C
Mary C Sanders, Chas Co, Md
Louis Keating, Wash City, D C
Lizzie McGarr, Wash City, D C
Sarah Woodward, Wash, D C
Mgt Kehler, Wash, D C
Louisa McLean, Wash, D C
Nellie Neale, Cahs Co, Md
Anna Surratt, PG Co, Md
Mgt Bagnam, Wash, D C
Alice Berry, PG Co, Md
Mary M Dyer, Wash, D C
Bettie Diggs, Chas Co, Md
Pamelia Edelen, PG Co, Md
Olivia Gwynn, PG Co, Md
Mgt McGarr, Wash, D C
Mary Wills, Chas Co, Md
Louisa Wilson, PG Co, Md
Celestia Warren, Chas Co, Md
Nannie Jones, Eastern Shore, Md
Clodine Miles, Chas Co, Md
Bettie Tyler, Wash City, D C
Virginia Schaefer, Balt, Md
Mary Dobbyn, Wash City, D C
Josephine Lord, Chas Co, Md
Regina Gardiner, Chas Co, Md
Isabel Bonling, Chas Co, Md
Eliza Hatton, PG Co, Md
Nellie Brent Digges, Chas Co, Md

Mgt Bowling, Chas Co, Md
Mollie Neale, St Mary's Co
Honoria Fitzpatrick, Wash, D C
Annie Jameson, Chas Co
Ellen Keleher, Wash City
Sarah Keleher, Wash City
Maria Conlan, Wash, D C
Martha Sasscer, PG Co, Md

Jane Ratcliffe, Chas Co, Md
Josephine Jenkins, Chas Co, Md
Mary Holmes, Chas Co, Md
Estelle Gardiner, Chas Co, Md
L Higdon, Chas Co, Md
N Jones, Talbot Co, Eastern Shore, Md

On Monday last Mr Brown, editor of the Oskaloosa Herald, shot & killed Mr Bowen, a citizen of that place. The difficulty originated in an article in the Herald reflecting upon the personal character of Mr Bowen. Brown was arrested. –Iowa State Journal

Died: on Aug 17, Joshua Clay, son of Jos S & Susan A Boss, aged 4 months & 5 days. His funeral will be on 7th st, near O st, this afternoon, at 5 o'clock.

Died: on Aug 16, Sarah Waters, aged 41 years, of Newcastle, England, but for the part year a resident of Wash City.

Died: on Aug 17, at his residence, **Mount Hope**, Gtwn Heights, Col Wm Robinson, in his 76th year. His funeral will take place this evening, at 6 o'clock, from his late residence.

Died: at the residence of Walter Henderson, near ___burg, Va, Walter, infant son of Dr Geo Henry & Mary E Capert__, aged 5 months.

WED AUG 19, 1857
Trustee's sale of very desirable property on K st: under & by virtue of a deed of trust from John R McLeod, dated Oct 25, 1855, recorded in Liber J A S 104, folios 224, of the land records of Wash Co, D C: public auction on Sep 23, of part of lot 3 in square 515, in Wash City: improved by a fine & well-built brick residence.
-Wm H Ward, trustee -A Green auct

Fayetteville Observer furnishes us with the following: Henry Potter, U S Judge for the District of N C, an office which he has filled with dignity for 55 years, & which, at the great age of 91, he still survives to fill at the universal satisfaction & respect of the community in which he resides. He is now, perhaps, the oldest surviving subscriber to the Nat'l Intelligencer, for which he remitted payment not long since for his 55th year. The venerable Judge was born in Granville Co, in this State, in 1765; he was present & heard Gen Washington deliver his first message to the U S Congress of the U S that convened in Phil after his election. His residence is called **Chelsea**.

Capon Springs, Aug 15, 1857. This afternoon stage coach from Strausburg was turned over in the road leading down the mountain. Mr Jarrett, of Petersburg, & Chas G Kerr, of Balt, were riding outside at the time & neither sustained any hurt. Mr Wm A Bradley, of Wash, had his arm broken; Miss Bradley, his daughter, had her hand severely bruised, the weight of the loaded coach resting upon it until the gentlemen were able to lift it off; Mrs Bradley escaped with a few slight contusions; Mrs Fitzhugh, of Fairfax Co, had her collar-bone broken; & Miss Worthington, of Washington, was injured about the head, but is doing well. A servant of Mrs Fitzhugh was jarred & bruised.

Correspondence of the London Times. Experiments in laying the **Atlantic Telegraph**: Queenstown, Jul 30. The entire squadron, 5 magnificent ships-of-war, now about to proceed to the consummation of this great enterprise, are at this time anchored in the harbor of Queenstown. They consist of the **Niagara**, Capt Hudson; the **Susquehanna**, Capt Joshua Sands; the **Agamemon**, Mast Comder Noddall; the **Cyclops**, Capt Dayman; & the **Leopard**, Capt Wainwright. To Mr C T Bright is committed the entire control & responsibility of depositing in its ocean bed this wondrous example of the united power of science & industry. Queenstown, Aug 3, 6:30 P M. All the ships are now steaming out of the harbor of Valencia.

Four days from Europe. 1-Eugene Sue, the great French novelist, died in Paris on Aug 3. 2-W F A Delane, for many years manager of the London Times, is dead.

Home School for Boys: between the ages of 10 & 14 will be received. Address Rev E R Lippitt, Alexandria, Va.

Mrd: on Aug 18, in Wash City, at the Assembly's Church, by Rev Andrew G Carothers, Mr Francis A Reed to Miss Marinda Eldridge, both of Alexandria, Va.

Died: on Aug 14, at Eldridge, Md, Richard Stuart, aged 11 months, son of Lt F K Murray, U S N, & Anna M Murray.

THU AUG 20, 1857

The N Y Times contains a letter dated Jun 9th on board the U S frig **San Jacinto**, at Hong Kong, China: Some 3 months since Capt J D Simms, of the U S Marine Corps, attached to the **San Jacinto**, was mysteriously missing, gone nobody but our executives knew where. It is understood that he was to proceed to Formosa, in the city of Fungshang, hoist the Amercian flag & take formal possession of the island. We regard this statement as highly improbable. No such intelligence has been received in any other quarter.

Hon John Long died at his residence in Randolph Co, N C, on Tue.
–Greensboro Patriot

The Dundee [Scotland] Advertiser records the demise of Thos Dick, the well known author of the Christian Philosopher & other kindred works. Dr Dick, who was in his 83rd year, expired at Broughty Ferry, near Dundee, on Wed last. He was born in the Hilltown, Dundee, on Nov 24, 1774, his father being Mungo Dick, a small linen manufacturer. About 8 years ago he was prostrated by a severe illness, from the effects of which he never wholly recovered.

Prince Chas Bonaparte, Prince of Canino, eldest son of Prince Lucien, brother of the first Napoleon, died on Jul 29 at his residence in the Rue de Lille, in Paris, at the age of 54, having been born in 1803. He had married the Princess Zenaide, only daughter of Jos Bonaparte, King of Spain. The deceased has been a widower since 1854. He leaves 8 children, of whom the eldest, Prince Jos Lucien Chas Bonaparte, serves in the army, & the 2nd, Prince Lucien Louis Joseph, has embraced the clerical profession. He is one of the Pope's Chamberlains, & is expected to be soon promoted to the purple. The deceased Prince Charles was a distinguished savant. –Paris letter, Jul 30.

Leesburg Academy will be resumed on Sep 1. –Chas H Nourse

Penn Life Ins Co of Phil. J Riggles, agent for Wash, Pa ave & 17th st. –Danl L Miller, Pres; Saml F Stokes, Vice-Pres; John W Hornor, Sec. Thank you letters from: 1-Balt, Aug 5, 1857, from Doris Degenhard, 53 Thames St, for receipt of $1,000 on the life of her husband, Chas Degenhard, now deceased. 2-Balt, Aug 7, 1857, from Margaret Little, 2 McHenry st, for receipt of $1,000 on the life of her late husband, Danl Little, for the benefit of herself & children. Both letters were addressed to A A Kennard, 59 Second st, Balt, Md.

Bleakwood for sale. The subscriber, as executrix of the late Washington Adams, will offer that beautiful farm upon which the deceased resided, at public auction, on Sep 2 next. This farm is located in Howard Co; contains 254 acres & 36 perches, more or less; with a new frame 2½ story dwlg, with back bldg, & other necessary out bldgs. -E Cuyler Adams, excx

Died: on Aug 19, in Wash City, Theodore, aged 8 years & 11 months, only son of Chas & Mary Ann Scrivner. His funeral will take place this afternoon at 4:30 P M.

3 days from Europe: Dr Bloomfield, Bishop of London, is dead, in his 71st year.

FRI AUG 21, 1857
Capt Jas Davis, one of our oldest citizens, died at the Hot Springs on Aug 7. He formerly resided in Norfolk, but has lived in Richmond for the past 20 years. He held a commission in the navy during the war of 1812, & his conduct in that trying period was unexceptionable. He was 81 years of age at the time of his death.
-Richmond Enquirer

Household & kitchen furniture at auction on: Aug 24, at the residence of Michl Joyce, 457 N st, between 12th & 13th sts. –Jas C McGuire, auct

The brig **King Brothers**, from Madina Jun 24, landed at N Y on Wed morning with about 60 Portuguese, who have been compelled to leave their native island by religious persecution.

Breach of promise case: in 1853, the plntf, a young gentleman of N Y, Moses Inglee, became acquainted, during a tour in Italy, with the beautiful widow of the late Amos Binney, of this city, & the two pledged themselves to a matrimonial alliance on their return home. The lady postponed the fulfillment of the agreement, deserted him & became the wife of Dr Geo Hayward, of this city. The damages are laid at $25,000. Dr Hayward & his wife are now abroad in Europe. –Boston Journal

Kanawha Star: on Aug 3, two young ladies, in attempting to cross Coal river at Peytons, Boone Co, Va, were precipitated into deep water & drowned. One was a daughter of Mr Wm Meadows, & was to have been married in a few days; the other was Miss Douglas, daughter of Thos Douglas, deceased. The mother of the latter, an invalid, was so overcome that her life is despaired of. –Richmond Dispatch

Montgomery Co. The American party of this county have nominated the following ticket: for the Senate: Elisha John Hall; House of Delegates, Dr Washington Waters & H Franklin Viers; Clerk, Jas G Henning; Register, Silas Browning; Com'rs, Thos English, Wm Cook, Dr Chas Willett, Thos Rollins, Jos White; Surveyor, Wm Musser; Sheriff, Jas G House.

Obit-died: on Aug 9, at his residence, near Jefferson, Fred'k Co, Md, Wm Lynch, in his 70th year. He was called 3 times to represent his fellow-citizens in the Md Legislature. He was an active & faithful member of the Protestant Episcopal Church.

SAT AUG 22, 1857
The widow of Rouston, the well-known Mameluke of Napoleon I, has just died at Versailles, at a very advanced age.

The first European settlement in the Island of *Formosa* was made by the Dutch about 1620, & they continued to occupy a portion of the west coast up to 1661, when a body of Chinese, headed by Coxuiga, having vainly contended against the Tartar invasion, left the province of Fokien & sought refuge in Formosa, & after a short struggle conquered the Dutch, & remained in quiet possession up to 1683, when they were brought under the Tartar rule by the Emperor Kanghi.

Mrd: on Aug 18, in Wash City, by Rev W McLain, Mr Jas V Dishman to Miss Martha J Ashton.

Died: on Aug 21, at his residence, *Locust Grove*, near Washington, Edw Fenwick, in his 53rd year. His funeral will take place on Sunday afternoon, at 3 o'clock, from St Peter's Church, Capitol Hill.

Died: on Thu, in Wash City, Mr Richd Furtner, aged 54 years, after an illness of 2 years. His funeral will take place from his late residence, on 6th st, near N Y ave, tomorrow afternoon at 3 o'clock.

Died: yesterday, Mrs Charlotte Davis, wife of Rev Chas A Davis, Chaplain U S Navy. Her funeral will be on Sunday afternoon at 4 o'clock, from the residence of Chas E Davis, on 18th st, between H & I sts.

Died: yesterday, Laura Virginia, youngest child of J D & Eliza J Townley, aged 2 years & 1 month.

Phil, Aug 21. Mr Brayman, editor of the Democrat, was arrested this morning for robbing the post office drawers of money & letters; they were found in his possession. He waives an examination, & is held to bail for $9,000.

Hollidaysburg, Pa, Aug 21. McKine, the murderer of Norcross, was executed today. He died protesting his innocence, & spoke 2 hours from the scaffold. He attempted suicide before being taken from his cell this morning.

Letter from the Plains. St Louis, Aug 21. A letter to the Republicans, from *Fort Kearny*, dated Aug 5, says that the 10th Infty & Philips' battery had arrived there. Capt Van Vliet had gone in advance on important business. He had lost nearly 500 by desertion.

Brookeville Academy, Mongt Co, Md: next session will commence Sep 7. The Principal wishes to engage a competent Housekeeper immediately.
-E B Prettyman, A M, Principal

1,700 acres of land for sale: most desirable farm for sale on Jackson's River, at the terminus of the Central Railroad: land is in Alleghany Co. On it a large brick dwlg house, & the ordinary outhouses. Col Saml Carpenter, who resides near Covington, is authorized to sell & will show the land. The title is believed to be good, being derived from Gen Douglas B Layne. –E Fontaine, Agent

For sale at public auction: on Sep 7 next, I shall offer for sale, before the Courthouse door, in Alexandria Co, a desirable tract of land containing about 160 acres, within 7 miles of Wash, & about 4 miles of Alexandria. On the premises are 2 large brick tenements, with the necessary out-bldgs, [the last named, however, in part somewhat injured by the late storm.] -Christopher Neale, Agent

Was committed to the jail of Carroll Co, on Aug 12, runaway negro boy Fred'k Thomas. He says he is free & his mother resides in Balt Co, near Chas Painter. The owner is requested to come forward, prove property, pay charges, & take him away. -Jos Shaeffer, Sheriff Carroll Co, Md.

MON AUG 24, 1857
Chancery sale of valuable house & lot on 20th st west, between Pa ave & H st north. By decree of the Circuit Court of Wash Co, D C, made in the cause wherein Wm W Hough is cmplnt & Eleanor Hines, widow, Christian M Hines, adm, Enoch G Hines & others, heirs at law of Abraham Hines, deceased, are dfndnts: public auction on Sep 17, 1857, part of lot 27 in square 101, with a well built 2 story brick dwlg house. -Chas S Wallach, trustee -Jas C McGuire, auct

Trustee's sale of farm near Bladensburg, Md: on Sep 26, by deed of trust from Robt Strong, dated Jul 25, 1856, & recorded in Liber J A S No 117, folios 6, of the land records for Wash Co, D C, & in Liber C S M, No __, folios 321, of the land records for PG Co, Md, the piece of land being partly in D C, & in PG Co, Md: being part of a tract called ***Chillon Castle Manor***. And also, as appurtenant to the land herein before granted, a perpetual right of way through, over, & along the adjoining land of Wm Scott from the land hereby granted to the public road, as the right of way was granted by said Scott to said Strong & his heirs & assigns & his & their household, etc. –Thos J Fisher, trustee -Jas C McGuire, auct

In the city of Lexington, on Aug 5, Mr John Blount, bridegroom, a deaf mute, who was brought up in Alabama, but received his education at the Ky Institution for the Deaf & Dumb at Danville, where he is at present an accomplished & highly esteemed instructor, was married to Miss Lucretia Ann Hoagland. [He is a tall & fine-looking specimen of a man.] His bride is also a deaf mute educated in the institution at Danville. Mr & Mrs Wm Hoagland, the parents of the bride, at whose house the marriage took place, are also both of them deaf mutes. They received their education some 25 or 30 years since at the same institution. They have 3 other children, two of whom hear & talk; their youngest, a little boy of 9 years, is like the bride, a mute. The attendant of the bride was Miss Mary Boyd, from Harrison Co; formerly a class-mate of the bride. The officiating clergyman was Rev S B Sheek, Vice-Principal of our State Institution at Danville. –Lou Jour

The Worcester [Mass] Spy of Friday contains the particulars of the robbery in that city of an elderly man, Jesse Rollins, of Haverhill, N H, who had just sold his place in the country. The money, about $1,940, was in a carpet bag, & part of it was the possession of an elder son. Yesterday they went to Auburn to look at a farm he intended to purchase. While absent the younger son & graceless scamp seized the money & made off with it, & has not been seen since.

Orphans Court of Wash Co, D C. Letters of administration on the personal estate of John T Towers, late of Wash Co, deceased. –W Gray Palmer, Will Towers, admx

Died: on Jul 22 last, at *Olive Hill*, near Petersburg, Va, Geo Whitlocke, in his 83rd year.

Died: on Jul 17, in Valejo, Calif, James A Kelly, son of Wm Kelly, of Wash City, aged 43 years. May he rest in peace!

Quebec, Aug 23. Three hundred miles of the cable of the Atlantic Telegraph had been laid on Aug 10th, & every thing was working well.

Wilmington, Dela, Aug 23. Yesterday a terrible explosion took place at Dupont's powder mills. Mr Alexis J Dupont died of his wounds. Edw Hunt, foreman, & Anthony Doughtery are also dead. Louis Vache is mortally hurt, & John McClafferty & Geo Fisher are injured.

Chicago, Aug 22. A terrible hurricane passed over the town of Woodland, Wisc, last night. Mr Fox, the railroad station agent, was run over & instantly killed while endeavoring to stop a train of freight cars which the wind had set in motion.

TUE AUG 25, 1857
The Whigs of Chas Co, Md, held a meeting at Allen's Fresh on Aug 15, to appoint delegates to a Whig Convention of the 6th Congressional district, to be held at Bladensburg on Aug 29. John Ware, presided, & J G Chapman, was sec. Delegates appointed: John Ware, J Grant Harris, J G Chapman, Thos O Bean, & Saml Cox.

Meeting of the Delegates from the district of Anne Arundel Co, convened at Annapolis on Aug 22, to elect 4 delegates to represent the county in the Whig Congressional Convention to meet at Bladensburg, on Aug 29; John T Hodges, in the chair; Dr John Ridout, jr, appointed secretary. Delegates chosen: Frank H Stockett, Chas F Worthington, Dr Wm Q Clayton, & Edwin Gott.

Notorious character Jerry Cowden has been arrested in Cincinnati, having in his possession $1,500 in spurious bills, mostly on the Commercial Bank of Millington, Md, which bank does not exist. -Sun

N Y: On Wed last Mr Alanson Weed, a resident of Brooklyn, started to go to his place of business & has not been heard of since.

Hon Henry W Hoffman, a Rep in the last Congress from the Alleghany, Wash, & Fred'k district of Md, has been nominated for re-election by the American party.

Valuable farm for sale: the subscriber will sell his farm, *Sudley View*, in Prince Wm Co, half a mile from the *Sudley Springs*: contains 150 aces. The land is at present in the occupancy of Mr John Surghnor, who will show the premises. There is a comfortable dwlg-house, with necessary out-houses, on the farm. Address B F Gill, Richmond, Va.

Laying the Atlantic Telegraph. Valentia, Aug 10th. The work of laying down the Atlantic cable is going on as satisfactory as the best friends of the great enterprise could desire. Up to the present about 300 miles of the cable have been laid. The depth of the water is nearly 2 miles; the signals on board the steamer **Niagara** are every thing that an electrician could desire. The steamers are heading west, with a moderately fair breeze, & the cable is being run out from on board the **Niagara** at the rate of about 5 miles per hour, & messages are being constantly received on shore. The propeller **Edinburgh**, Capt Cummings, which arrived at N Y on Sunday, is supposed to bring later, &, if her Capt did not mistake as to the vessels, still more encouraging intelligence then the above of the progress of the Telegraph expedition. [The expedition sailed from Valentia, Ireland, on Aug 7, owing to an accident on shore, connected with the landing of the cable.]

Family School for Young Ladies, Kalorama, Staunton, Va: next session commences on Oct 1. Mrs Sheffey & Daughters, having for 12 years past conducted this school, have an intimate knowledge of it. Letters address to: Mrs M Sheffey, Kalorama, Staunton, Va.

Assistant teacher is wanted for Charlotte Hall School, St Mary's Co, Md. He should be a gentleman of character & experience. Salary $500. Apply to the Register. -Wm T Briscoe

A respectable lady, who lost her baby 4 months old, wants a situation as wet nurse. Inquire of Mr John Reidy, 6th & G sts.

Trustee's sale of land: by decree of the Circuit Court for Chas Co, Md, the undersigned, as Trustee, will offer at public sale, on Sep 1, at the *Trappe*, in said county, all that real estate of which Dr Bennett Dyson, late of said county, died seized & possessed, consisting of 300 acres of land, more or less, parts of 2 tracts, called *Burditt's Rest* & *Meek's Adventure*, lying on Nanjemoy creek, in said county, adjoining Dr Dyson's late residence. The land is without improvements, except a dwlg out of repair. –Jno W Mitchell, trustee

Mrd: on Aug 20, at Covington, Ky, Beverly W Tull, of Williamson Co, East Tennessee, to Miss Catherine Reed Michell, daughter of Rev Dr Michell, chaplain U S Army, *Fort Chadbourne*, Texas.

Died: on Aug 24, in Wash City, Mrs Eliz O Beck, wife of the late Jos W Beck, in her 64th year. Her funeral is today at 3 o'clock, from her late residence, corner of 3rd & A sts, Capitol Hill.

Died: on Aug 14, in Winchester, Va, after a brief illness, Mrs Sarah Thruston, widow of the late Thos L Thruston, of Wash City.

N Y, Aug 24. The Surrogate today decided against Mrs Cunningham's claim to the Burdell estate. He gives it to the blood relations of the deceased.

Missing: Geo Johnson, slave, left Kalorama last night, & has not since been heard of. Any information respecting him will be thankfully received at Kalorama.

WED AUG 26, 1857

A fine marble monument, 26 feet in height, is now nearly completed, & will soon be placed over the remains of Abbott Lawrence, at *Mount Auburn*, near Boston.

Geo E Humphries, of the Coast Survey, attached this season to the schnr **Hassler**, left Bath, Me, on Thu in a sloop boat to join his vessel, then lying in the Sheepscot river. He was accompanied by a young man named Nichols. The boat capsized; Nichols clung to the boat, but Mr Humphries leaped from her & sunk. Mr Humphries resided in Cambridge, Mass, & was about 21 years old. –Boston Traveller

Battle with the Indians in New Mexico. Col Roberts, U S Army, from Albuquerque, New Mexico, arrived in St Louis on Aug 21, after a journey of a little over 4 weeks. At Santa Fe he received a despatch by the commanding ofcr, stating that Col Miles, in command of the southern column of the army in New Mexico, had met the Gila Apache Indians, on the Gila river, & in the battle which ensued 25 of the Indians were killed & more than 30 wounded. Lt Steen, of the 1st Infty, Lt Davis, 1st Dragoons, & 9 privates were wounded; but how severely was not stated in the despatch. –St Louis Republican

In N Y last week a coroner's inquest was held on the body of a child nearly 3 years old, Jane Eliza Davis, whose death was caused by a needle having been thrust into her heart. On Tue she played with the needle & stuck it into her dress, a few moments later she fell & the needle entered the right oracle of the heart. At every pulsation of the heart the needle has caused laceration & the wound was found to be about the size of a half dollar.

Yesterday a German lad, Pistole, aged 7 years, was run over & instantly killed by the railroad cars. –Balt Sun

For rent: ***Tudor Place***, one of the most desirable residences of the Heights of Gtwn. For particulars inquire on the premises.

I will sell at private sale my Farm on which I now reside, containing 60 acres, in Fairfax Co, 7 miles to Gtwn; improvements consists of a frame dwlg house, 2 stories high, 25 x 35 feet, good kitchen, barn & stable. Terms made known on application.
–Chas G Eskridge

Mrd: on Aug 22, by Rev Wm H Chapman, Thos Sweeney to Miss Amanda E Osborne, all of Wash City.

Mrd: on Aug 24, by Rev Wm H Chapman, Geo Spates to Miss Clara Maddox, all of Wash City.

Mrd: on Jul 11, by Rev Wm H Chapman, Thos A Buckley to Miss Sarah H Gardner, all of Wash City.

Died: on Aug 25, in Wash City, Maria Frances, aged 9 months & 25 days, daughter of Thos F & Maria Maher. Her funeral will be this afternoon at 4 o'clock, from the residence of her parents, 598 7th st.

Died: on Aug 24, in Wash City, Florence A, infant daughter of Edwin J & Jane F Klopfer.

THU AUG 27, 1857
The steamer **America**, which arrived at Halifax yesterday, brings the unwelcome intelligence of the failure of the first attempt to lay the cable of the Atlantic Telegraph. At a distance of 330 miles from the Irish coast the cable broke, &, further operations being thereby suspended, the squadron returned to England, where it was a matter of consultation with the Directors of the Telegraph Co whether the attempt should be renewed without unnecessary delay or postponed until the ensuing season.

A new life & surf boat has been invented by Richd C Holmes, of Cape May, N J. A crew of 6 or 8 persons found it impossible to capsize this boat until they had drawn a plug from the bottom & let her fill.

Mrs Eliz Kimball, a well known lady of Waltham, Mass, the oldest person in the town, died on Aug 18, at the advanced age of 94 years. She retained her mental & physical powers in an eminent degree to the last. She saw the battle of Bunker Hill from a house-top in Charlestown, & witnessed the battle of Lexington. She gave birth to 11 children, from whom spring 51 grandchildren & 56 great grandchildren.

$600 reward for runaway negro men, Ben-38; Warren-33; & George, 19 years old.
-Chas Brown, living in Montg Co, Md.

Orphans Court of Wash Co, D C. Letters of administration on the personal estate of Wm J Fitzpatrick, late of Wash Co, deceased. –Catherine M E Fitzpatrick, admx

Boston Traveller. Prince Metternich completed his 84th year on May 15. He was born in 1773, when Maria Theresa was Empress-Queen of Germany & Hungary, Louis XV, King of France, & George III in the 13th year of his reign, & Catharine II was Czarina of Russia.

Died: on Aug 25, in Wash City, after a long & painful illness, Mrs E Stewart, in her 70th year. Her funeral will be this afternoon at 3 o'clock, from the residence of her daughter, Mrs Brereton, 216 N Y ave, between 4th & 5th sts.

Died: on Aug 10, in Alexandria, H Allen, youngest son of the late H Allen Taylor.

FRI AUG 28, 1857
Queen Victoria has selected Montreal as the permanent capital of Canada, the question having been referred to her for final decision by the Legislature of the Province.

The venerable Chief Justice Taney, who some 6 weeks ago went to the Fauqier White Sulphur Springs, at Warrenton, Va, in a debilitated condition, is said to be now in the enjoyment of excellent health & spirits. He has reached his 80th year. -Union

The steamer **St Nicholas**, Capt Guy, which left Balt on Wed, with some 200 ladies & gentlemen aboard, on an excursion to Annapolis, ran into a brig in tow of the steamer **Belvidere**. The bow was injured & Capt Guy found it necessary to run her ashore. She is now lying off *Sandy Point* in 12 feet of water. No lives were lost. The people were conveyed to the shore & many remained in Annapolis during the night. The brig run into was not seriously injured. --Patriot

N Y, Aug 26. Mrs Eliz Drinkwater, sister-in-law of Mr Henry Elkins, was filling some lamps with burning fluid, when the liquid took fire & exploded, covering her clothes & setting them in a blaze. In her fright she ran up stairs & fell down, when her sister, Mrs Elkins, came after her with a child in her arms. The sight was so shocking to Mrs Elkins that she also fell to the floor. The sufferer bore her agony with great fortitude for 8 hours previous to her death.

San Antonio, Aug 5, 1857. The San Antonio & San Diego mail train, which left on Jul 25, under charge of Capt Wallace, was attacked by a party of about 100 Indians, Apaches, near Devil's river. The party consisted of Capt Wallace & 5 men, one six-mule coach, & 21 head of mules. Wallace was wounded; & W Clifford, of New Orleans, was killed. The first mail, which went out in charge of Capt Henry Skillman, is supposed to have gone through safely.

Fatal railroad accident on Wed on the Hudson River railroad, by which Thos Sewell, a retired merchant of Balt, was killed. It appears that in attempting to get into the cars at Peekskill, while they were in motion, he made a false step & fell upon the track, & before the train could be stopped 3 cars had passed over his body. He was about 68 years of age, & was traveling for his health, having recently had an attack of palsy.

On Sunday Mrs Mary Parker, residing in Staten Island, was burnt to death by the explosion of a fluid lamp which she was imprudently filling while lighted. She was in her 98th year. Mrs Lynch, residing in the same house, was also very severely burnt.

Case of drowning. The steamer **Georgia**, Capt Pierson, was returning from Cambridge & a young man, John Langley, was on board. After being induced to partake freely of liquor by his companions, at the bar, he was seen to fall from the hurricane deck into the Patapsco river. A search was made for him, but they could not see him. He was aged about 25 years, married, & resided in South Balt.

Runaway was committed to Wash Co jail on Aug 21, a negro man, Thos Jordan; says he belongs to Geo Runnell, of Berkeley Co, Va. Owner is to come forward & prove property, otherwise he will be discharged agreeably to law.

Mrd: on Aug 20, at Enfield, Conn, by Rev Mr Birchard, Mr A Geo Wilkinson, of Wash, D C, to Miss Julia A Dorman, of Enfield.

Died: on Aug 27, in her 18th year, Josephine, youngest daughter of J W & Mary Ann Ross. Her funeral is this afternoon, from the residence of her parents, at 3 o'clock.

Died: on Aug 25, Mrs Mary Gibbs, widow of the late Thos Gibbs, of Anne Arundel Co, Md, aged 78 years.

Died: on Aug 5, at his residence in Rockingham Co, N C, Hon Thos Settle, in his 66th year. He was a distinguished citizen of the State.

SAT AUG 29, 1857
Appointments by the Pres:
Beverley Tucker, of Va, Consul at Liverpool, vice Nathl Hawthorne, resigned.
Henry W Spencer, of N Y, Consul at Paris, vice Duncan K McRae, resigned.
John Endlich, of Pa, Consul at Basle, vice Danl S Lee, deceased.
Chas J Fox, of Mich, Consul at Aspinwall, vice Francis A Thornton, resigned.
Ernest Volger, of Va, Consul at Barcelona, vice Pablo Anguera, present incumbent.
Jacob Forney, of Pa, Superintendent of Indian Affairs for Utah.
J B Danforth, jr, Purser in the Navy, vice John V Dobbin, resigned.
Chas E Sinclair, Associate Justice for the Territory of Utah, vice Stiles, removed.

The U S sloop-of-war **Falmouth**, E W Farrard, cmder, arrived yesterday from Rio Janeiro, which port she left on Jul 11th. List of the ofcrs: Cmder, E W Farrard; Lts, Geo W Rodgers, W W Pollock, J R Franklin, W R McGunnigle; Master, F M Ramsay; Surgeon, J J Aberthney; Assist Surgeon, Wm M Page; Purser, C Wabbott; Passed Midshipmen, M C Campbell, W A Kirkland, W S Bradford; Capt's Clerk, Thos H Lee; Boatswain, E B Bell; Gunner, F A Cunningham; Carpenter, J W Stinson, Sailmaker, T W Rurth; Purser's Clerk, M R Moore.

A fortune of an immense amount has lately been discovered to belong to somebody besides the present holders, by the turning up of some old papers in Camden. It appears that Judge Thos Leonard, a resident of Princeton, N J, before the Revolution, became the owner of immense estates, as appears by his will, which is said to be on record in due form at the ofc in Trenton, N J, & left those estates to his male descendants as long as the name of Leonard existed; & after the name of Leonard ceased to be to the female descendants, preferring the males to the females, thereby entailing the property to a time indefinite. This may be a happy windfall to the heirs, if they are able to gain possession of the estates, of which they have the most sanguine hopes. –N J State Gaz

The Florida War: from the Tampa Peninsula of Aug 15. Capt J F P Johnston's company of mounted volunteers commenced a scout; he reports the country submerged to such an extent as to render it impracticable to prosecute the scout. Capt S L Sparkman has accepted an order to raise another company of mounted volunteers, to succeed his present company. He has now finished his third term of service. Capt McNeill has returned from his recent scout. He made no discovery of Indians or fresh signs. Lt Warren S Lothrop, one sgt, 2 cpls, & 12 privates have been detailed as a guard, & are now stationed on the Key.
Mounted Regt Florida Volunteers: list of her ofcrs:
Field: S St Geo Rogers, Col; A J T Wright, Lt Col; J L Dozier, Major; Wm S Harris, adj; ___, Quartermaster. Staff: W J C Rogers & W H Pope, Surgeons.
Capt N P Willard, Madison Co; Capt N A McLeod, Marion Co; Capt W Stephens, Marion Cp; Capt L A Hardee, Duval Co; Capt W H Cone, Columbia Co; Capt H Harrington, Columbia Co, Capt A A Stewart, Columbia Co; Capt S Whitehead, Aluchua Co; Capt John Parkhill, Leon Co; Capt John Brady, St John's Co.
Capt Brady's company was mustered into the U S service, at Ocala, on Aug 8, by Lt Lee, mustering ofcr. Col Rogers & staff were mustered at Ocala, on Aug 10, by Lt Lee, mustering ofcr. Capt Parkhill's company arrived at this place on Tue last. Col Rogers & staff arrived at this place on Thu last. The headquarters of the regt & 5 companies at or in the vicinity of **Fort Denaud**, & 5 companies at or in the vicinity of **Fort Myers**. Capts Hardee's & McLeod's companies left this place on the U S steamer **Gray Cloud**, Aug 14. The other companies will start in a few days.

Orphans Court of Wash Co, D C. Letters of administration on the personal estate of Robt T Barry, late of the U S Navy, deceased. –Susanna E Barry, admx

Keysville, Aug 26. Hon G A Simmons, M C, while conversing with some friends on the steps of the Ausable House, was struck with paralysis, & now lies in an insensible condition.

$100 reward. Information wanted relative to the whereabouts of Wm Barker, a brother of Moses Barker, of Va, if living, or a copy of his will if dead. Any person who sends the first copy of his will to me shall receive a reward of $100 for his trouble & expense in obtaining the same; & if an atty at law, he will be employed, if legal advice is necessary. It is supposed he died in the South or Southwest.
–R A Hyde, 407 I st. Wash, D C.

Died: on Aug 28, in Wash City, Mrs Eliz Gill, wife of Christopher Gill, in her 56th year. Her funeral will take place from the residence of her husband, 13½ & C sts, [Island,] on Sunday at 3 o'clock.

Died: on Aug 27, after a short & painful illness, Chas Schussler, in his 54th year. His funeral will take place today, at 3 o'clock P M, from his late residence, [Park House,]

Hartford, Aug 27. Judge Ingersoll, of the U S District Court, yesterday sentenced Minor, the pension forger, of New London, to 5 years imprisment in the State prison. The prisoner plead guilty.

Public sale of valuable real estate, in PG Co, Md. By written authority from Mrs Eliz Herbert, the undersigned, as her Atty, will expose to public sale, on Oct 7, at Grimes' Tavern, at the Cross Roads, in Spalding's District, PG Co, Md, the real estate which was devised to the said Mrs Eliz Herbert by the last will & testament of her late uncle, John B Kerby, which real estate in lying in PG Co, Md, adjoining the lands of Thos E Berry, **Oxen Hill**, Thos Berry, of Wash, & others. Lot 1 contains 211 acres, 3 roods, & 24 perches; with one small tenement thereon. Lot 2 contains 79¼ acres; with one small tenement thereon. Lot 3 contains 69 5/8 acres; with a fine barn. The same will be shown by Mr Francis A Kerby, residing near the premises, on the public road leading from Grimes' Cross Roads to the Alexandria Ferry.
–J Contee Mullikin, Atty for Mrs Eliz Herbert. –John R Walker, auct

MON AUG 31, 1857
Sale of valuable property: by deed of trust, dated Aug 1, 1853, recorded in Liber J A S No 61, folios 95, 96, of the land records of Wash Co, D C: public sale on Sep 15, 1857, of lot 1 in square 253, in Wash City, running west along F st 35 feet 4 inches, & running to lot 26; also, part of lot 26 in same square, with improvements; & part of lot 2 in the same square. The above parts of lots 1 & 26 will be sold subject to the tenant's interest therein. –B Johnson Hellen, trustee -A Green auct

Mr Wm G Dix is to deliver before literary associations his instructive Lectures on the Andes, which he has recently delivered in Boston.

Father Wheeler, a Catholic priest of N Y, was shot while at the Islands yesterday in company with the Bishop & Priest & some other Catholics of this city, & was sitting upon a fence talking. He received a pistol ball through his shoulder, injuring him seriously, if not fatally. It is supposed to have been done accidentally.
–Portland Argus, Aug 17

Mrs Catherine Van Rensselaer Cochran, one of the old Knickerbocker stock, is dead, aged 76. She was the daughter of Maj Gen Schuyler, of Revolutionary memory. She was twice married-first to the son of Gen Malcolm, & then to the son of Dr Cochran, the Surgeon-General of the Revolutionary army. They cleared the present ground where Albany now stands for a habitation. She was a sister-in-law of Gen Alex'r Hamilton. She was born in Albany Feb 20, 1781, & was baptized on Mar 4, 1781, by Rev Ellaedus Westerlo, of the Dutch Reformed Church, Gen & Mrs Washington, Jas Van Rensselaer, & Margarita Schuyler being her sponsors in baptism.

The English papers announce the death, in London, on Aug 11, of Rt Hon John Wilson Croker, the well known reviewer, at the age of 77. Mr Croker, though of English descent, was born in Galway, educated at Trinity College, Dublin, practiced there at the bar, & for many years represented the borough of Downpatrick & afterwards the Univ of Dublin, in the House of Commons. He also held several important public offices. He was one of the founders of the Quarterly Review, which was started in 1809, his associates having been Scott & Canning.
–Phil Evening Journal

The funeral of the late Cmdor Stephen Cassin took place yesterday from the family residence on Gay st, Gtwn. Numerous ofcrs of the navy assisted in these last rites, among whom we mention Cmdors Smith, Aulick, Tilton, Capts Ramsay, Delarouche, & Lts Morris, Johnston, & Hunter. The place of sepulture was the *Catholic Burying ground* on the heights of Gtwn. Divine services were performed by Rev B Maguire, in Trinity Church.

Mules, from Ky, for sale, on accommodating terms by Jas H Shreve, 7th st.

Dr C H Van Patten, Dentist, expects to reach his home by Sep 8th, when, with renewed vigor, he will resume his professional duties. He has practiced in Wash during the last 18 years. Ofc [as heretofore] at his residence, *Cedar Hill Villa*, Pa ave, near Gtwn.

French & English Academy, Boarding & Day School for Young Ladies: 103 Monument st, between Park & Howard, Balt, Md. Mr & Madame Desponniers & Miss Blades, Principals. The institution will be resumed on Sep 14.

Mrd: on Jul 3 last, Passed Midshipman W A Kirkland, attached to the U S sloop **Falmouth**, to Senhora Isadora Carvalhina De Ferieira, widow of a Brazilian officer.

Died: on Aug 29, at his residence in Gtwn, D C, Cmdor Stephen Cassin, U S Navy, in his 76th year.
+
Meeting of the ofcrs of the U S frig **St Lawrence**, held in the wardroom of that ship on Jul 14, 1857, in the harbor of Rio de Janeiro, on motion of Lt Murphy, Cmdor French Forrest called to the chair & Assist Surgeon Francis L Galt appointed Sec. Tribute to the memory of Lt Ch Cheever: proceedings to be forwarded to the relatives of our departed friend. –French Forrest, Com'dg in Chief U S naval forces, coast of Brazil, Chairman.

Metropolitan Collegiate Institute, for Young Ladies: 436 G st, between 7th & 8th sts: will open on Sep 7. Mrs J H Havenner, Belles Lettres & Moral Philosophy. Rev J Newman Hawk, A M, Ancient Languages & Math. Miss Barbara Ross, English Branches. Prof G Staubly, Modern Languages. Wm McLeod, Painting & Drawing. Md'lle De Boyd, Music-Piano.

French Instruction: Mr Chas Roux: address Mr R through the post-office.

$150 reward for runaway, my servant man, Eli Brown, about 38 years of age.
-John B Boone

TUE SEP 1, 1857
On the 28th ult, Govn'r Wise, of Va, received the first message by the Richmond, Charlottesville, & Staunton telegraph line, which is now finished & in full operation throughout its entire length.

Household & kitchen furniture at auction on: Sep 17, at the residence of Frank S Shulze, 404 north I, near 12th st west. -Jas C McGuire, auct

Paris, Aug 4, 1857. 1-Eugene Sue, the celebrated novelist, died day before yesterday at Annecy, in Savoy, where he had resided since his depature from Paris in 1852. He was never married. He leaves a sister, the wife of Mr Caillard, formerly manager of the menageries. 2-The body of the late Prince Canino, a member of the Bonaparte family, has been sent for interment to the family vault in Corsica by his own request. He was the son of the first Emperor's brother Lucien, & father of Prince Napoleon, who accompanied the body to Marseilles.

Died: on Aug 31, in Wash City, Mr Saml Wardell, aged 64 years. His funeral will take place from his late residence, near the Circle, this evening at 4 o'clock.

Died: on Aug 28, at his residence in Wash City, after a painful illness, Danl Campbell, in his 48th year.

Chronological history of the **electric telegraph**.
1726-An Englishman named Wood discovered that the electric fluid could be conducted long distances by wires.
1746-Herr Winkler, of Leipsic, discharged a Leyden jar by a friction machine through a wire of considerable length; the river Pleis forming part of his circuit.
1747-Dr Watson made a successful experiment of a similar character, over a space of 4 miles, at Shooter's Hill, near London, embracing his circuit of 2 miles of wire & an equal distance of ground.
1748-Dr Franklin set fire to spirits by an electric current sent across the Schuylkill on a wire, & allowed it to return by the river & earth.
1774-M Lesage, of Geneva, constructed an electric telegraph, consisting of 24 wires, each properly insulated, & terminating at one end in a pith ball-electrometer.
1784-M Lomond, of France, communicated telegraph signals to a neighboring room by means of a potato ball electrometer, acted upon by electricity.
Mr Reiser illuminated letters upon plate glass; formed of tin foil, by means of electricity.
1785-M Cavalo preposed to from an electric telegraph by fireing a gas pistol at the distant end of a wire, & thus to give signals.
M Sav_ry attributes the first idea of an electric telegraph to Dr Franklin.
1798-Betaneourt established a telegraph between Madrid & Aronjuez, 26 miles, through which a current of electricity was passed & gave signals for letters.
1809-Schmering constructed the first galvanic telegraph at Munich, which operated by the decomposition of water, & which he also caused to ring a bell at the opposite end of the wires.
1816-Dr John Redman Cox, of Phil, proposed to establish an electric telegraph, & to make signals at a distance, by the decompostion of water & metallic salts, causing a change in color to ensure.
1819-Prof Versted, of Copenhagen, discovered electro-magnetism or electro-magnetic motion.
1820-M Ampere, of France, discovered the electro-magnetic telegraph. This he constructed of as many wires as there were letters, & used the deflection of the needle as a signal. He broke & removed the circuits by finger keys; something similar to those of the keys of a piano-forte.
1823-Francis Ronalds, of England, proposed a telegraphy by the use of frictional electricity.
1825-Mr Barlow, of Greenwich, England, made an attempt to put a galvanic telegraph in operation, but was baffled by the diminution of the fluid; when he endeavored to transmit it for a great distance, so as to produce mechanical effects. This difficulty the discoveries of Henry, however, afterwards overcame. In the same year Mr Sturgeon, of England, constructed the first electro-magnet, by coiling a copper wire round a piece of iron of a horse-shoe form, the bent turns of the wire

being so far apart as to prevent contact. The wires were afterwards coated with non-conducting substances & wrapped around the iron in close contact, as we now see them.

1826-Mr Harrison Gray Dyer erected a telegraph on Long Island, N Y. He used frictional electricity, & dyed marks on chemically prepared paper by the passage of sparks.

1831-Prof Jos Henry, of Princeton College, discovered a method of forming magnets of intensity & of quantity produced from correspondent batteries, & by the use of which, with relay magnets, prepared by him, he made known the practicability of producing mechanical effects at a distance say from 1,000 to 2,000 miles.

1832-Baron Schilling, of St Petersburg, contrived a deflective magnetic telegraph, which had an alarm bell connected with it.

1833-Gauss & Weber first constructed the simplified electro-magnetic telegraph.

1837-Stienhiel constructed & put in use, between Munich & Bogenhausen, in July of this year, his registering electro-magnetic telegraph. On Jun 12th of this same year the deflective electro-magnetic telegraph of Cook & Wheatstone was patented in England. They first employed receiving & relaying magnets.

In Oct following, Saml F B Morse, of N Y, entered his first caveat for an American electro-magnetic telegraph, in which he chiefly relied on a kind of type & port-rule for making signals by the mechanical force of electro-magnetic motion. Morse claimed that he first thought of magnetic telegraph in his passage to the U S in the brig **Sully**, in 1832.

1838-Edw Davy, of London, had his patent sealed for a chemical telegraph, which was engrolled Jan 4, 1839.

1846-Alex'r Bain obtain his English patent for his improved electro-chemical telegraph, & got his American patent in 1849.

1848-49-Royal E House, of N Y, obtained, in conjunction with Mr Brett, a patent for their ingenious & valuable printing electric telegraph.

1849-50-Mr Hern, of N Y, invented his igniting telegraph, which made dots & lines by burning them on slips of revolving paper by the heat of the electric fluid while passing. About the same time Mr Johnson, of N Y, contrived a machine worked by electro-magnetism to let that drop on to slips of paper, which, being prepared at the same moment, left visible marks which stood as signs for letters. Also, about the same time, Mr Danl Davis, of Boston, prepared an Axial telegraoh, which, with that of Horn & Johnston, does not seem to have met with much attention.

1855-Mr Hughes obtained his patent for his ingenious & admirable combined printing telegraph, which is destined to effect a revolution in all the existing systems. Not only does it transmit messages with greater rapidity, but it has the advantage of receiving & transmitting simultaneously on a circuit of at least 600 miles, performing the work of 2 ordinary wires on one; it is also less liable to interruption from atmospheric electricity.

WED SEP 2, 1857
Handsome Wharf property at auction, by deed of trust from Walter Lenox to me, dated Mar 10, 1855, recorded in Liber J A S No 109, folio 13 et seq, of the land records of Wash Co, D C: public auction on the premises on Sep 15, of square 270, containing about 19,554 square feet of ground, known as *Lenox's Wharf*, with the brick warehouse thereon. –Edwin Ludlow, trustee -A Green auct

Railroad collision on Aug 27, on the Galena & Chicago Union railroad, killed Mr Sargent, the baggage master of the train, instantly, near the Wheaton station.
–Chicago Press, Aug 28

The only son of Mrs Panson, of Montreal, age 13, was drowned at Brockville, C W, on Friday. His mother, on hearing of his death, immediately died of a broken heart.

On Friday of last week, the 3 children of Mr Reidhead went into the barn to play among the hay, & while there set fire to it. The two children, aged 4 & 5 years perished in the flames. The youngest child, an infant, crawled out of the door.
–Minneapolis Democrat of Aug 22.

Supreme Court of the U S, No 193, Dec Term, 1856. Isaac M Fisher, appellant, against Jacob M Halderman. Mr Fisher, of counsel for the appellant, having suggested the death of Jacob M Haldeman, the appellee in this cause, moved the court for an order, to make th proper reps parties. It is now ordered by the Court that unless the proper reps of the said Jacob M Halderman, deceased, shall voluntarily become parties within the first 10 days of the ensuing term, the appellant shall be entitled to open the record, & have the same reversed if it be erroneous. Attest: Wm Thos Carroll, Clerk Supreme Court U S.

Mrd: on Sep 1, by Rev B A Maguire, W H Clagett to Adele, 2nd daughter of the late Wm Clark, of Wash City.

Mrd: on Sep 1, at the Assembly's Church, by Rev Andrew G Carothers, Mr Thos J Albright, of Lancaster, Pa, to Miss Ann Maria Beedle, of Wash City.

Mrd: on Sep 1, at *Ingleside*, by Rev Dr Gurley, Hiram Walbridge, of N Y C, to Jenny M Blake, daughter-in-law of the late Dr Chas Blake, of Massachusetts.

Died: on Aug 24 last, at his residence in Lagrange, Mo, Dr Wm E Ellery, in his 44th year, formerly of Balt, Md.

THU SEP 3, 1857
Household & kitchen furniture at auction on: Sep 7, at the residence of Mrs S A Reed, A st, between Delaware ave & 1st st. -Jas C McGuire, auct

Capt John H Greeland, 4th Artl, a native of Pa, died at *Fort Myers*, Fla, on Aug 17.

By the capsizing of a boat just below Staten Island, on Mon, Mr Henry Longhurst, of Brooklyn, was drowned.

Creedo is the name of the town that is to be built in Wayne Co, Va, on the Ohio river, 2 miles above the mouth of Big Sandy river, by the Homestead Aid Society, of which Eli Thayer, of Worcester, Mass, is President. –Alexandria Gaz

Administrators sale of carpenter's tools, lumber & wagon, at auction, on Sep 7, by order of the Orphans Court of Wash Co, D C; at the carpenter's shop on 10th, between F & H sts, the personal effects of John R McLeod, deceased.
–Selby Parker adm -C W Boteler, auct

Brandies & whiskeys at auction on Sep 5, being the stock in part of R C Brook, who is declining business. –Wall & Barnard, aucts

Washington Seminary has secured the services of Prof Sestini for the Math Dept, & also Prof Danl Lynch, the former vice-Pres of Gtwn College. The schools will be resumed on Sep 7. –B Villiger, Pres

Orphans Court of Wash Co, D C. Letters of administration on the personal estate of Chas Schussler, late of Wash Co, deceased. –A E L Keese, adm

U S Patent Ofc, Wash, Sep 1, 1857. Ptn of Jas Phelps, of Sutton, Mass, praying for the extension of a patent granted to him on Nov 24, 1843, for an improvement in a washing machine for washing rags, for 7 years from the expiration of said patent, which takes place on Nov 24, 1857. –S T Shugert, Acting Com'r of Patents

Wash Corp: 1-Bill for the relief of Stephen P Franklin, assignee of Corbin Baker. 2-Bill for the relief of Danl Barry: passed.

Mrd: on Aug 22, by Rev John C Smith, Mr Silas Johnson to Miss Ellen Abbegil, both of PG Co, Md.

Mrd: on Aug 27, by Rev John C Smith, Gabriel Knapp to Mrs Eliz Ort, all of Wash City.

Mrd: on Sep 1, by Rev John C Smith, Mr Andrew J McAuley to Miss Mary Woods, all of Wash City.

Mrd: on Sep 1, by Rev Chas H Hall, P C Johnson to Mrs M W James.

Died: on Sep 1, after a lingering illness of 20 months, which he bore with Christian resignation, Jos Chapman Peck, in his 26th year. His funeral will take place this evening, at 3½ o'clock, from the residence of his father, Capt Jos Peck, on E st, between 9th & 10th sts.

Three days from Europe: 1-Gen Barnard & Sir Henry Lawrence are dead.

Cincinnati, Sep 2. The mail train from Dayton to Sandusky ran off the track near Castalta & Henry Ross, the baggage master, David Cassel, train-boy, & Mr Kunkle, editor of a Sandusky paper, were instantly killed.

Orphans Court of Wash Co, D C. Mary A Holmead, guardian, reported she sold 5 acres, 3 roods, & 14 poles of land, at the junction of the road leading to Pierce's Mill & the Old Piney Branch road, at public auction, to J P Klingle, for $1,013.94, being at the rate of $324 per acre; & that said Klingle has complied with the terms of sale. -Wm F Purcell -Ed N Roach, Reg/o wills

FRI SEP 4, 1857
N Y, Sep 3. Letters received here stating that Prof Francis was killed in a duel at Napo river, Ecuador, by Prof Moore. Both parties belonged to the exploring expedition which left Iowa last Autumn for South America. Other accounts state that the death of Dr Francis was the result of an accident, by the premature discharge of a gun which Prof Moore was cleaning. [Sep 7th newspaper: Letter from Geo C Edwards, a member of the expedtion, states that it was a duel between Francis & Moore, their weapons were double-barreled fowling pieces heavily loaded with buckshot, & the distance agreed upon was 5 rods. Francis was shot just below the region of the heart. Thus ended one of the most savage duels ever known in this country.] [Sep 8th newspaper: the N Y Times confirms that the shooting of Prof Francis, in Ecuador, was accidental. Prof Moore accidentally shot his friend. While clearing his gun it went off, & the contents of buckshot entered the breast & neck of Prof Francis, which caused his death in a few days.] [Sep 10th newspaper: Mr Francis was accidentally wounded on Apr 19. Despatch received on the 4th instant from the Minister of the U S in Ecuador, dated Jul 17, appears to preclude the idea that the death of Mr Francis was the result of a duel: "I now learn, by letters from Messrs Moore & Geo Corbin Edwards, that, after suffering intensely for some 2 months, Dr Francis died of his wound on Jun 15. Mr Moore pursues the object of the exploration alone, & has proceeded down the Maranon & Amazon rivers."]

Saml Carusi will resume his scientific instructions in Vocal & Instrumental Music on the first Monday in Sep. Communications left at Carusi's Saloon, will receive due attention. -Saml Carusi

Musical Notice: J P Caulfield, Prof of Music at Gtwn College & Organist at St Matthew's Church, will resume his business on Sep 7. Apply at the music stores of J F Ellis & Richd Davis, or through the post ofc.

Mr Hurlburt, Register of Ascension Parish, informs us that Rev Wm Pinkney, D D, of Bladensburg, Md, has accepted the call of the Vestry of Ascension Parish, in Wash City, & will assume the Rectorship on Oct 11.

SAT SEP 5, 1857
Mr Justice Curtis has resigned his seat upon the bench of the Supreme Court of the U S-for reasons growing out of his private affairs. He was appointed by Pres Fillmore in 1851.

N Y, Sep 3: The boiler attached to a pile-driving machine in Brooklyn exploded yesterday, & killed Thos Gaveny, who was sitting by the boiler eating his dinner. Thos Henry was seriously injured.

Calif, San Francisco Bulletin of Aug 5. The American party candidates: for Govn'r, G W Bowie, of Sacramento; Lt-Govn'r, J A Raymond, of Shasta; Comptroller, G W Whitman, of Tuolumne; Atty-Gen, J B McFarland, of Nevada; Surveyor-Gen, L B Healy, of Santa Clara; State Printer, B H Monson, of San Francisco; Treasurer, J C Crandall, of Placer; Judge of the Supreme Court, H Ralston, of Sacramento.

Ofcrs of the Nat'l Emancipation Society: Pres: Prof Benj Silliman, sen, LL D, Conn. Vice Presidents: Rev Mark Hopkins, D D, Mass; Hon J B Williams, N Y; Hon Erastus Fairbanks, Vt; Rev F M Post, D D, Mo; John W Tatum, Dela; Corr Sec: Elihu Burritt, Conn; Rec Sec: Robt Sears, N Y; Treas: Robt Lindley Murray, N Y.

Univ of Va will commence on Oct 1 & end on Jun 29. –S Maupin, Chairman of the Faulty.

East Washington Seminary, Masonic Hall, Va ave & 5th st east, Navy Yard: is now open. Apply to J Wm P Bates, Principal, successor to Dr J E Clawson.

$5 reward for return of strayed of stolen dun-colored Horse. –Geo Carll; Centre & Northern Markets.

Notice: The public are cautioned against receiving any note or notes purporting to be drawn or endorsed by the undersigned, as such notes, being unauthorized, will not be paid by me. –Mary Larner

John Wagner, 255 Pa ave, continues the manufacture of Looking Glasses, Portrait & Picture frames of all kinds.

Orphans Court of Wash Co, D C. Letters of administration on the personal estate of Owen Murray, late of Wash Co, deceased. –Mary Murray, admx

Orphans Court of Wash Co, D C. Letters testamentary on the personal estate of Danl Campbell, late of Wash Co, deceased. –Jane Campbell, excx

Mrd: on Sep 3, by Rev Andrew G Carothers, Mr Benj F Morris to Miss Hannah V Dawson, both of Wash City.

Mrd: on Sep 2, by Rev Chas Hall, Wm Stump, of Davenport, Iowa, to Mary B, daughter of J Bartram North, of Wash City.

Mrd: on Sep 3, in Balt City, by Rev Mr Abbott, Mr Henry Reeves Pollard to Miss Julia E Williams, of Wash, D C.

Wash City Ordinance: 1-Act for the relief of the estate of Wm T Wheat: to pay said estate $1.95 for taxes erroneously paid for the year 1856. Approved, Aug 11, 1857.

MON SEP 7, 1857

Liquore, Liquors, at auction on Sep 8, at the store of Messrs Dorothy & Kirkpatrick, 388 7th st east, between H & I sts. –A Green auct

Handsome farm property within 3 miles of Wash at auction, on Sep 17, about 90 acres, on the back Bladensburg road, being a part of the farm on which Col Brooks resides, adjoining the farms of Messrs E Tucker, McCaeny, & N L Queen. Title indisputable. –A Green auct

Among the promotions in the Legion of Honor announced in the Moniteur of Aug 14 is that of M Camile Dollfus, second Sec of the French Legation at Wash.

Hon Joel K Mann, formerly for many years a rep in Congress from the Montgomery district, Pa, died at his residence in Cheltemham Valley, Montg Co, on Fri last, at the good old age of 77.

St Paul Pioneer, Aug 25. Fight with the Indians. In the neighborhood of Washington, on Friday, an Indian fired & killed one of the cavalry, a young man, Mr Donnell. The cavalry fired & killed the Indian.

Fire at Alexandria on Sat last consumed the n e corner of King & Royal sts. The property was owned by Messrs John Jones, of Alexandria, & Geo Keating, of Wash, & occupied as follows: H Blondhaem, clothing store; John Jones & Saml Harper, tobacconists; J T Taylor & Son & Geo L Deeton, shoe-finding establishments; & John Fornshil, gun-smith. –Alexandria Gaz

The death of Dr Vogel was confirmed & will be received with sad interest by the scientific world. He was the worthy rival of Drs Livingstone & Barth in opening up the interior of Africa to the knowledge of the civilized world.

English papers record the decease of Fred'k S Archer, the inventor of the collodian process in photography. [No other information-current item.]

Valuable farm for sale: the subscriber offers at private sale the farm on which he resides, near the Wash & Rockville Turnpike: contains 220 acres. Also, his farm lying on the east side of the above road, containing 130 acres with a fine frame house of 8 rooms, with large water-tank & bathing room. Also, the farm belonging to my son, adjoining the above lands on the west side of the Pike, containing 185 acres. Refer to Bradley & Son, Wash, & O Z Muncaster, Gtwn. –G M Watkins

Orphans Court of Wash Co, D C. Letters of administration on the personal estate of Chas H Brown, late of Wash Co, deceased. –Stephen T Brown, adm

Died: on Sep 5, at his residence in the county, after a long & painful illness, Zachariah Walker, one of the oldest & most respected of our citizens. He filled various public positions in the county, & the country is indebted to him for the removal & safe-keeping of its records during the capture of the city of Washington in 1814. He was one of the few who witnessed the laying of the corner-stone of the Capitol & that of its extension. He was a native of this District.

Died: after a short sickness, John S Devlin, of Wash City, for many years an ofcr in the marine corps, in his 59th year. His funeral is this evening, Sep 7, from his residence on Capitol Hill, 629 Pa ave, at 4 o'clock. [No death date given.]

Albany, Sep 4. Willard P Daniels, Pres of the Niagara Co Bank, at Lockport, was robbed last night on the Central railroad cars of a pocket-book containing drafts to the amount of $30,000. Payment has been stopped.

TUE SEP 8, 1857
Trustee's sale of valuable property by deed in trust from Wm D Bell & wife to the undersigned, dated Aug 12, 1856, recorded in Liber J A S No 126, folios 328, 329, & 336, of the land records of Wash Co: sale on Sep 25, of a parcel of land containing about 1 acre, on 7th st, adjoining the land occupied by W D Bell, bordering on the Plank road, a short distance north of the Park. The improvements consist of a 2 story frame dwlg with out bldgs. –W P Brooke, trustee -C W Boteler, trustee

The Camden & Atlantic railroad was on Sat the scene of a collision, which caused the death of W A Siner, of Phil; Wm Donnely, of Cooper's Point, conductor of the express train; & John B Edwards, fireman of the express train.

The Ohio papers bring news of the decease of an able & virtuous citizen, Benj Ruggles, of St Clairsville, Ohio, at the mature age of 74 years. He served his State in the U S Senate during 3 successive terms, from 1815 to 1833. In personal qualities he resembled much the late estimable Saml Prentiss, of Vt, for some time his contemporary in the Senate, alike modest, single-minded, clear-headed, & faithful.

Hon John Jay has recently purchased the house in Lewisborough, Westchester Co, in which Maj Andre, the spy, was confined subsequent to his interception at Tarrytown by Paulding, Williams, & Van Wert. The bldg is a one story plain structure, with a basement or high cellar underneath, & is in a good state of preservation. Mr Jay has stepped in in good time to secure & perpetuate this object of Revolutionary interest, which, in common with too many others of a similar character all over the country, have thus far been suffered to go unreclaimed.

Wash City Ordinance: 1-Act for the relief of Stephen P Franklin, assignee of Corbin Baker: to refund to Franklin $58.33, being part of the amount paid for a tavern license which said Baker took out in Nov, 1855, for the sale of spirituous liquors, which business he relinquished in Mar, 1856. 2-Act for the relief of John W Rozier: to pay him $6.95 for taxes erroneously paid on part of lot 5 in square 525. 3-Act for the relief of the heirs of Edw & Mary Murphy, deceased: the sum of $30 be paid to John Murphy, for that amount of an unexpired tavern license for the year 1857.

Recollections of the Private Life of Lafayette, by Dr Jules Cloquet. Lafayette was tall & well proportioned; inclined to embonpoint, though not obese; his eyes were grayish-blue; his nose was aquiline; his complexion was clear; &, at age 77, not a single wrinkle furrowed his countenance. Lafayette died at Paris on May 20, 1834, aged 77 years.

John B Robertson, cashier of the Eagle Bank at Rochester, N Y, charged with an attempt to poison his wife, has given bail to answer at the next oyer & terminer. Mr Robertson has heretofore occupied a high position in society, & his arrest has caused the most intense excitement.

Riot at Balt after midnight on Sat: Emanuel Beninger, ball through the thigh; John P Hennick, shot with 2 balls in the back & wounded in the leg, his wounds are severe; Philip Cratz, wounded in the leg & thigh with buckshot; John J Plant, shot through the calf of fleshy part of the left leg; Lewis Burns wounded in the leg; & Jos Gilbert shot in the neck & ear. More shooting on Sat night, while 2 men, Wm Reynold & Henry Jenkins, were sitting in front of the 17th Ward House, on Light st, some person fired a gun from an alley, & wounded both of them. Geo Roten & Wm Clements were standing at Wm & Warren sts, & were shot by Augustus Ford, against whom charges were made, & he was sent to prison.

Fire in Brattleboro, Vt, on Friday. Completely burnt to the ground: Jos Clark's drug & hardware store, Estey & Green's large melodeon manufactory; Willard Frost's shoe-store, a large dwlg-house owned by Nathan Woodcock, Woodcock & Vinton's paper mill, Crane & Vinton's machine shop, Chas L Mead's rule factory, a dwlg-house occupied by 4 familes & owned by Luther Weld, Dr E C Cross's dwlg-house, John Pellet's dwlg-house, Fred'k C Edwards' dwlg-house, Emory Farnsworth's dwlg- house, occupied by 3 families, & an unoccupied store owned by Saml Root. –Brattleboro Phenix

By the last will & testament of Mrs H H Coalter, [relict of Judge John Coalter,] of Stafford Co, who died last week, some 92 negroes have been freed. This provision of the will is to take effect on Jan 1 next. Charles, her favorite man servant, received his freedom at once, & an annuity of $100 for life, & sufficient money to take him to such State or country as he may elect to live in. For the remainder the execs are to ascertain what fund will be sufficient to provide the usual outfit for removing them to Liberia or any other free State or country in which they may elect to live. The will further provides that if any of the servants prefer to remain in Va, they are permitted to select a master from among the relatives of the deceased. –Richmond South

The 3 Naval Courts of Inquiry of yesterday: in Court No 1, the case in the hands is that of Lt Geo R Gray; in Court No 2, Lt Abbott's case; & Court No 3 is engaged on that of Cmder Lockwood.

Orphans Court of Wash Co, D C. Letters of administration on the personal estate of Benj O West, late of Wash Co, deceased. –Helen M West, admx

Mrd: on Sep 3, at the residence of Mrs McTavish, in Balt, by Rev T Foley, of the Cathedral, Randolph Rogers, artist, of Rome, Italy, to Rosa Ignatia, youngest daughter of late Henry Gibson, of Richmond, Va.

WED SEP 9, 1857
Mr John H McLeod, residing near Dayton, in this county, has presented us with a bottle of molasses which he has made from the Chinese sugar-cane. The molasses was expressed by means of an ordinary cider press, the cane being ground in the cider mill. –Valley Democrat

Naval: 1-The U S sloop-of-war **Plymouth** was at Lisbon Aug 19. 2-The following ofcrs have been ordered to the U S steamer **Fulton**, now fitting at the Washington navy yard for the home squadron: Lt Commanding John J Almy; 1st Lt M K Warrington; 2nd Lt, J B Stewart; 3rd Lt, Robt Selden; Purser, R H Clark; Master, M C Campbell; Passed Assist Surgeon, John L Bartt; 1st Assist Engineer, H Newell; 2nd do, R V McCleery; 3rd do, J S Albert; 4th do, W P Barron; 5th do, J B Houston.

Assassination of African travellers: official confirmation of the murder of Dr Vogel at Wara, the capital of Wadi, has been received. He was beheaded by order of the Sultan. Cpl Maguire, R E, was murdered by a party of Tuaricks, some 6 marches to the north of Kuks. —Boston Courier

The body of a man named Spradlin, a tobacco peddler, was found in a hollow tree, near Roanoke Red Sulphur Springs, about 20 miles from Fincastle, Va, on Sep 2. He had about $800 on his person & doubtless he was murdered for his money. No money was found on him.

Mr W F Ferguson, formerly of Lynchburg, Va, but latterly a resident of Nashville, Tenn, while the subject of delirium, induced by brain fever, with which he had been ill for several days, committed suicide in the latter city, Fri, by shooting himself with a pistol.

From a Manuscript of family record in **Nantucket**. Tristam Coffin, [believed to be one of the original grantees of the island of Nantucket,] the common ancestor of all in this country who bear the name, settled in Salisbury, Mass, in 1642, & removed in 1662 to Nantucket, where he died in 1681, aged 160 years. In 1719 his descendants were estimated at 749; in 1722, at 1,580; & in 1827, at 25,000, a fourth part of whom at least were inhabitants of Nantucket.

Mrd: on Sep 7, at Germantown, Pa, by Rev Wm Suddards, Henry Morton, of Mo, to Mary A R, only daughter of the late Jonathan Sowers, of Phil.

Died: on Sep 1, at St Catharine's Mills, near Charlotte, N C, Isabella, aged 11 months, only daughter of John & Jeanie R Wilkes.

Augusta, Sep 8. A destructive fire occurred on Sunday in the town of Americus, Sumter Co, Ga, destroying the houses of H W Shaw, John C Holmes, S S Kendrick, F Vogelsang, J P Griffin, B Greenwold, Wm S Johnson, & Johnson & Evans.

Evansville, Indiana, Sep 8. Hon Jas Lockhart, member of Congress elected from this district, died yesterday morning.

THU SEP 10, 1857
At Gloucester, Mass, on Sunday, Mrs Davis, her 2 sisters, & Mrs Douglas left home to go berrying. While there Saml Davis, the husband of Mrs Davis, came up to where she was standing with her sister, & shot her in the breast. She almost immediately died. Mr Davis then aimed the pistol at his breast & fired. He died immediately. Jealousy is said to have been the cause.

Accident on Monday on the Hudson river railroad when the train came upon 2 women with 3 or 4 children walking between the tracks. Mrs Thos Smith & her daughter were killed as they rushed across the tracks.

The pilot boat **Dragonet** sailed from Newport on Thu, under the command of Henry Tisdale, on a pleasure excursion, with a party of well-known citizens of Newport. Mr Tisdale was seized with a fit, rendering him speechless. The yacht put in at *Holme's Hole* on Fri, but the doctor cound render no assistance; so they bore away for Newport. Mr Tisdale died on board the yacht, off Seaconnet, on Sat morning. The **Dragonet** arrived at Newport on Sat, with the dead body on board.

Sales at auction: by decree of the Circuit Court of Wash Co, D C, pronounced in a cause wherein Francis Wheatley, survivor of Nathl Walker, is cmplnt, & Henry Holt & others are dfndnts, being No 1,085, in Equity, the subscriber, as Trustee, will expose to sale at auction, on Oct 9 next, the property in Wash Co, known as *Jackson Hill*, being part of *Pretty Prospect*, containing 13 acres of land & upwards; adjoining the tract of land conveyed to John Q Adams, being part of the same tract; to intersect the 20th line of the conveyance from Jonathan Shoemaker to Roger Johnson; to land conveyed to Henry Holt by Ashton Alexander Dec 21, 1844. Also, part of a tract called *Mount Pleasant*, which, in the division of the real estate of Robt Peter, deceased, fell to the share of David Peter, being also the beginning of a tract called *Plain Dealing*, which stone is marked No 309; containing 13 acres & 23 perches of land, being the same piece of land as was conveyed to Henry Holt by Robt S Wharton in Sep, 1848, with improvements. –Wm R Woodward, trustee
-A Green auct

Miss Mary C Valentine, 2nd daughter of Dr Jas T Valentine, dentist, in N Y, was burnt to a crisp when fluid she used for filling lamps spilt upon the stove. She died 10 hours later in great agony. Her mother, Mrs Valentine, was severely burnt in endeavoring to extinguish the flames, & her brother-in-law, Mr Robt Morrison, was also burnt about the arms & face.

Judge Bailhache, one of the oldest citizens of Alton, Ill, died on Sep 2 from the effects of being thrown from a carriage down an embankment 40 feet high. Mr B was many years an editor in Ohio & Illinois.

Auburn Advertiser: two children of Mr John R Hopkins, a girl of 7 & a little boy, fell into the water and would have drowned, if a gentleman had not rescued them both.

Mr Alex'r Addington Cabury & Miss Gertrude Rose Leggett, both of N Y, were married at Falls of Minnehaha last Wed. Several ofcrs & ladies from *Fort Snelling* were present. Maj Patten, the ofcr & poet, who was present, wrote a pretty little poem upon the event. –St Paul's Advertiser of Aug 29.

Notice to the heirs of Eliz Spencer, deceased. Jacob S Swann & als, vs Hector McNeill & al. Com'r Ofc, Petersburg, Va, Aug 14, 1857. The objects of this suit are to ascertain the validity & construction of certain portions of the will of Mrs Eliz Spencer, formerly of Petersburg, who died there in 1799 or 1800, & to distribute her estate among the parties entitled. Wm T Joynes, of Petersburg, the counsel conducting the case in behalf of the heirs, has collected a great deal of information in relation to the heirs of Mrs Spencer. All persons claiming under any transfer by deed, or will, or otherwise, must furnish an authenticated copy of the transfer. The only transfers now in the case are the following:
1-From John Swann, son of Thos Swann, the brother of Mrs Spencer, to Martin Baugh, by deed of Jun 15, 1814, conveying his interest in the estate of Mrs Spencer, & also his interest in the estate of his sister, Mrs Eliz Stratton.
2-From Saml Swann, also a son of Thos Swann, to Thos T Swann, by deed of Jan 29, 1815, conveying his interest in the same estates. It does not appear to which Thos T Swann this assigment was made.
These papers were found on the records of the Hustings Court of Petersburg. Hector McNeill, in his answer, claims to have received assignments from Thos Swann, Martin Baugh, & Thos Stratton, but no such papers have been found.
The cause will remain open before me until Oct 15 next. Communications may be addressed to me or to Wm T Joynes, at Petersburg, Va. –D M Bernard, Com'r

Elizabeth Spencer:
Was a widow, & died without issue in the latter part of 1799 or the beginning of 1800. Her heirs at law were 4 brothers & a sister, or their descendants. It is known that some of the brothers survived Mrs Spencer, & the division must therefore by per stirpes, or by families, giving one-fifth part to each family.
The brothers & sister were as follows:
I-Saml Swann
II-Thos Swann
III-John Swann
IV-Thompson Swann
V-Mary, the wife of Josiah Thompson
I-Saml Swann: died leaving as only child, John Thompson Swann, his heir at law, who died, leaving the following children his heirs at law:
1-Jacob S Swann
2-Geo W Swann
3-Mary Swann
4-Ann Jefferson Swann
5-Tabitha Swann
The 1st, 2nd, & 3rd of them are living. The 4th [Ann Jefferson Swann,] married Alex'r Graves, & died leaving as her heir at law her daughter Georgiana Graves, now the wife of John Pryor.
The 5th, [Tabitha Swann] married Theodorick Robertson, & died leaving the following children her heirs at law:
    1-Mary Ann, now the wife of T S Kilby, living in Richmond.

2-Harriett, now the wife of Wm S Royston, living in Richmond.
3-Jas Robertson, living in N Y.
II-Thos Swann: was twice married. By his first marriage he had the following children, who, with the child of the second marriage, were his heirs at law:
    1-Harriett, who married Martin Baugh. Baugh & his wife are both dead, & their children & heirs at law are the following:
        1-Wm M Baugh
        2-Mary Brooks
        3-Thos C Baugh-these 3 living in Giles Co, Tenn.
        4-Eliz Anderson, living in Lincoln Co, Tenn.
        5-Harriet Baugh
        6-Rebecca Williamson-these 2 living in Tuscaloosa Co, Ala
        7-Richd Baugh
        8-John V Baugh
        9-Archibald B Baugh-these 3 living in Selby Co, Tenn
        10-Edwin H Baugh, living in Caddo parish, La.
        11-Martha Tarpley, who died leaving as her heir at law her daughter, Mary Tarpley, living in Giles Co, Tenn.
    2-Eliz, who married Thos Stratton, who is now living in Sumner Co, Tenn. Mrs Stratton died Mar 16, 1808, having had only one child, who died the day before. This person is mentioned in the will of Mrs Spencer by the name of Betsey Swann, daughter of my brother Thos Swann.
    3-Nancy, who married Wm McLaurine, both now living in Giles Co, Tenn.
    4-Mary, who married Thos Eastland, both now living in White Co, Tenn.
    5-Saml Swann, living in Texas.
    6-John Swann, living in Powhatan, Va.
    By his second marriage, [with the widow of Thos Thompson Swann, son of Thompson, formerly Judith Ligon] Thos Swann had one son, whose name was Thos Thompson Swann, born about 1803, & who died in Mississippi in 1852, leaving the following children his heirs at law:
1-Newton Swann
2-Othela, wife of Thos J Wiggin
3-Clementine, wife of Geo Oswalt.
4-Thos T Swann
5-Harriett Swann
6-John Swann
All of whom live in Chocktaw Co, Miss.
III-John Swann: left the following children his heirs at law:
1-Thos Swann, who died many years ago without issue.
2-Dr John T Swann, who died about 1844. He had one daughter, who married Wm Selden, & died leaving an only child, Wm A Selden, living in Wash City.
3-Saml Swann, who died without issue.
4-Edw Swann, living in Powhatan Co, Va.

5-Richd Swann, who died leaving the following children his heirs at law:
   1-John S Swann, living in Powhatan Co, Va.
   2-Thos B Swann, living in Kanawha Co, Va.
   3-Saml R Swann, living in Powhatan Co, Va.
   4-Geo A Swann, living in Missouri.
   5-Eliza M Swann, living in Pittsylvania Co, Va.
   6-Sally T Swann, who married Walter Coles, of Albemarle Co, Va, & died leaving the following children her heirs at law:
      1-Edw Coles
      2-Isaac Coles
      3-Thos Coles-these 3 living in Albemarle Co, Va
      4-Jane T, wife of Dr John Fisher, living in South Carolina.
   7-Caroline M Leake, died without issue.
   8-Jane, wife of Geo Deguid, living in Powhatan Co, Va.
   9-Eliz Swann, who died unmarried & without issue.
   10-Meliosa Swann, who died unmarried & without issue.
   11-Geo Swann, who died without issue.

IV-**Thompson Swann**: who left the following children his heirs at law:
1-**Thos Thompson Swann**. He was twice married, & died in Cumberland Co, Va, Mar 1, 1800. By the first marriage he had 2 children, Thompson & Sally, both of whom died unmarried & without issue. By the second marriage he had the following children his heirs at law:
   1-John T Swann, living in Dacatur Co, Ga.
   2-Wm Swann, living in Jackson Co, Fla.
   3-Elizabeth, who married Obadiah Michaux, & died leaving the following children her heirs at law:
      1-Jos T Michaux
      2-Harriet Michaux
      3-Josephine Michaux
      4-John T Michaux
      5-Wm O Michaux
      6-Eppanina, wife of Wesley Kyle
      7-Narcissa, wife of Macon Michaux-the above 7 all living in Decatur Co, Ga.
      8-Judith, who married ___ Sweet, & died leaving the following children, her heirs at law:
         1-J L Sweet
         2-Evander Sweet-both living in Randolph Co, Ga.

2-**John Swann**. He died in 1814, leaving the following children his heirs at law:
   1-Jefferson Swann, living in Powhatan Co, Va.
   2-Fred'k Swann, who has been absent from Va many years & is supposed to have died without issue.
   3-Henry Swann, living in Powhatan Co, Va.
   4-Alex'r Swann, died without issue.

  5-Geo Swann, living in Powhatan Co, Va.
  6-John Swann, living in Powhatan Co, Va.
  7-John R Swann, died without issue.
  8-Mary L, wife of Miller W Michaux, living in Powhatan Co, Va.
3-Saml Swann. He died leaving the following children his heirs at law:
  1-Thos Thompson Swann, who died in 1845, in Cumberland Co, Va, leaving the following children his heirs at law:
    1-Geo T Swann, living in Jackson, Miss.
    2-Wm S Swann, a lt in the U S Navy, who was lost in the ship **Grampus** in 1843, & left 2 children his heirs at law, namely, Wm M Swann & Julia A T Swann, both living in Portsmouth, Va.
    3-Sallie P, wife of Dr Hiram C Hubbard, living in Cumberland Co, Va.
    4-Jane E, wife of Peter B Stratton, living in Bates Co, Mo.
    5-Fleming L Swann
    6-Thos T Swann
    7-Jas S Swann-these 3 living in Jackson, Miss.
    8-John T Swann
    9-Mary A Swann-these 2 living in Cumberland Co, Va.
  2-Saml G Swann, who died leaving the following children his heirs at law:
    1-Geo Eugene Swann, who died, leaving his only child, Heth Swann, living in Richmond, his heir at law.
    2-An Adelaide Swann
    3-Mary Eglantine Swann-the above 2 living in Gloucester Co, Va.
  3-Geo Swann, who died without issue
  4-Ann, who married Dr Dabney M Wharton, now of Mississippi, & died leaving the following children her heirs at law:
    1-Geo S Wharton, living at Port Gibson, Miss.
    2-Mary, now wife of Alfred Johns, living in Clinton, Miss.
  5-Jane, who married Nelson Robinson, of Alabama, & died leaving the following children her heirs at law:
    1-Chas A Robinson, living in Fayetteville, Tenn.
    2-Mary J Walker,
    3-Nelson Robinson, jr
    4-Wm H Robinson-these 4 living in Bellefonte, Ala.
4-Willie Swann, who died in Nashville, Tenn, leaving the following children his heirs at law:
  1-Ann B Morgan
  2-Jos Swann-both living in Nashville, Tenn.
  3-Wm Swann, who died without issue.
  4-Catharine, who married Vincent Hubbard, & died many years ago without issue.
  5-Judith Swann, who died unmarried without issue.
  6-Willis Swann, who died unmarried without issue.

7-Eliz, who married Thos Stratton, of Sumner Co, Tenn, the same who married Eliz Swann, daughter of Thos Swann, who was the brother of Mrs Spencer. She died many years ago, leaving the following children her heirs at law:
    1-Madison Stratton
    2-Thos Stratton
    3-Catharine, wife of A J Snow
    4-Jane, wife of K J Morris
    5-Willis S Stratton
    E-Eliz, wife of Geo Bolling-6 above all living in Nashville, Tenn.

5-Catharine, who married Col Wm Mayo, of Powhatan Co, & died leaving the following children her heirs at law:
  1-Danl Mayo, who died leaving the following children his heirs at law:
    1-Henry Mayo
    2-Goodrich Mayo
    3-Geo Mayo
    4-Mgt Mayo
    5-Judith Mayo
    6-John Mayo
    7-Martha Mayo-these 7 all living in Powhatan Co, Va
  2-Eliz Railey, living in Albemarle Co, Va.
  3-Janet Ligon, living in Powhatan.
  4-Polly, who married Chas Railey, of Ky, & died, leaving children whose names are not known.
  5-Catharine, who married Wm Mayo, of Cumberland Co, Va, & died leaving the following children her heirs at law:
    1-Wm H Mayo
    2-Catharine, wife of Wm E Spears
    3-Jas Mayo
    4-Jos Mayo
    5-Maria Mayo
    6-Lewis Mayo
  6-Mary, wife of Jos Railey, living in Ky.
  7-Frances, who married ____ Rodman, & died without issue.
  8-Arethusa, wife of ____ Steel, living in Ky.
  9-Wm Mayor, living in Missouri.

6-Mary, who married Maj Thos Hubbard, & died leaving the following children her heirs at law:
    1-Green K Hubbard
    2-Thos Hubbard
    3-Vincent Hubbard
    4-David Hubbard

      5-Eliz Hubbard, who married John Wilson, & died , leaving children whose names are not known.
      6-Margaret Hewlett
      7-Stephen Hubbard, who died leaving children whose names are not known.
      8-Jas Hubbard
      9-Catharine Morris-the survivors are supposed to be living in Alabama.

7-Eliz, who married Wm McLaurine, & died leaving the following children heirs at law:
      1-Willis McLaurine, living in Giles Co, Tenn.
      2-Robt McLaurine, who died leaving the following children his heirs at law:
          1-Mary, wife of Wm Naples, living in Giles Co, Tenn.
          2-Edw McLaurine
          3-Elizabeth, wife of Reese W Porter, living in Giles Co, Tenn.
          4-Robt McLaurine, who died without issue.
      3-Geo McLaurine, who died without issue.
      4-Madison McLaurine, who died leaving children whose names are unknown.
      5-Wm McLaurine, who died leaving children whose names are unknown. They are supposed to live in Tenn.
      6-_____, who married ___ Owen, & died without issue.

V-Mary, who married Josiah Thompson, & died leaving the following children her heirs at law:

1-Josiah Thompson, who died, leaving the following children his heirs at law:
      1-John Thompson
      2-Sam Thompson-both living in Arkansas
      3-Mary, wife of Hugh Stokes
      4-Maria, who married ___ Woody, from whom she is divorced.
      3 & 4 supposed to be living in So Carolina.
      5-Christinan, wife of Wm Latimer

2-Wm Thompson, who died leaving the following children his heirs at law:
      1-Josiah Thompson
      2-Davl Thompson
      3-John Thompson
      4-Martha Thompson
      5-Mary Thompson-these 5 above are supposed to be living in So Carolina.

3-Swann Thompson, who died, leaving the following children his heirs at law:
      1-John Thompson, died leaving the following children his heirs at law:
          1-Mary Emily, who married Harding Davis, & died leaving as her heir as her only child, Jas W Davis, living in Richmond, Va.
          2-Eliza J, wife of Jas L Davis, living in Richmond, Va.
          3-Martha C, who married Andrew Green, & died leaving the following her heirs at law: 1-John Green 2-Mary Green; both living in Richmond.
      4-John Swann Thompson, living in Richmond.
      2-Eliz R Hughes, living in Missouri

  3-Anderson H Thompson, living in Missouri
  4-Waddy Thompson, living in Missouri
  5-Jane L Eanes, living in Amelia Co, Va
4-Mary, who married Thos Watkins, of Powhatan, died, leaving the following children her heirs at law:
  1-Josiah Watkins, living in Mississippi
  2-Richd Watkins, who died, leaving the following children his heirs at law:
   1-Lucy Watkins
   2-Eliz Watkins
   3-Melissa Watkins
   4-Erasmus Watkins
   5-Josephine Watkins
   6-Benj Watkins-These 6 all living in Cumberland Co, Va.
  3-Edw Watkins, who died leaving the following children his heir at law:
   1-Laconia Watkins
   2-Waddy Watkins
   3-Edw Watkins
   4-Hymenia Watkins
   5-Boyd Watkins-These 5 all living in Powhatan Co, Va.
  4-Geo Watkins, died without issue.
5-Waddy Thompson, who died, leaving the following children his heirs at law:
  1-Eliza Earle
  2-Maria Harrison
  3-Sarah Cleveland
  4-Emily, wife of Thos Jones
  5-Caroline, wife of Robt A Means-These 5 all living in So Carolina.
  6-Cornelia, who married ____ Armstrong, & died leaving the following children her hiers at law: 1-Waddy T Armstrong; 2-Ralphine Armstrong, both living in So Carolina
  7-Waddy Thompson
  8-Henry Tazewell Thompson
  9-Theodore Thompson
  10-Thos W Thompson
  11-Wm Thompson, who died leaving the following children his heirs at law:
   1-Waddy Thompson
   2-Wm Thompson
   3-Sally Thompson
6-Elizabeth, who married Thompson Swann, & died without issue.
7-John Thompson; & 8-Saml Thompson: These died young & probably before their mother. The above statement has been made out with great labor & care, from a large number of letters, memoranda, & other materials in my possession, & is believed to be, for the most part, correct. —Wm T Joynes

Dwlg houses & lots for sale: the one on E st, near 3rd st west, is a large 3 story brick house. —Grafton D Hanson

Mrd: on Sep 2, by Rev Mr Boyle, at St Patrick's Church, G B Cantatore to Sarah M Waggaman.

Mrd: on Sep 8, by Rev Wm H Chapman, Hezekiah Payne to Miss Sarah E Ridgaway, both of PG Co, Md.

Died: on Sep 9, in Wash City, Tabitha, wife of Raphael Jones, in her 80th year. Her funeral will be from her late residence on 8th st, this day, at 3 o'clock.

FRI SEP 11, 1857
Chancery sale of valuable property in the First Ward; by decree of the Circuit Court of Wash Co, D C, made in the cause of Arman Jardin, et al, against A Favier's heirs & adms: public auction on Oct 6, square 119, fronting 24 feet 1 inch on 19th st west, between north H st & Pa ave, with a 2 story dwlg-house. —W S Coxe -Jas C McGuire, auct

Yesterday was the anniversary of the victory on Lake Erie by Com Perry, on Sep 10, 1813; & this day is the anniversary of the victory on Lake Champlain of Com MacDonough, on Sep 11, 1814.

Appointments by the Pres: 1-Jos Holy, of Ky, Com'r of Patents. 2-John M Stockdale, Register of the Land Ofc at **Fort Dodge**, Iowa, vice Merritt, resigned.

The death of Hon Geo G Dunn, of Indiana, was announced by the Louisville Democrat. The sad event occurred at his residence on Sep 4. He had labored for 18 months under an affection of the spleen, & his death was not unexpected. He died at age 44 years, admired by all who knew him.

We announce the success of that experienced ofcr, Capt W H Kendrick, of the Independent Volunteers, who is scouting the vicinity of Istapoga Lake. On Aug 20th he struck the trail of 6 warriors. The Indians halted & snapped their rifles; Capt K charged, killing one warrior & capturing a child 4 years of age.

The jury agreed that the accident on the Camden & Atlantic railroad caused the death by a collision of the express train, leaving Cooper's Point, on Sep 5, & the freight train, of John B Edwards & Wm Donnelly. Evidence of neglect & disregard of duty by Robt M Tuttle, conductor of the freight train, & that Geo T Brooks, engineer of the same train, is likewise censurable. The company, through their agent, Wm Marshall, is highly censurable for not being particular in enforcing the time rules of said company.

At Phil, a few days since, Henry Myers, an illiterate, hard-working man, filed an affidavit before Alderman Eneu, setting forth that one John Hester had defrauded him out of 3,000 acres of land in Ritchie Co, Va, by falsely representing that he wanted the land for Hom John M Botts, giving as an equivalent therefore a bond for $1,000 purporting to be the issue of the Western Va & Ky Coal Co, & a certificate for 85 shares in the stock of that company. Hester was arrested & on Sat examined before Alderman Eneu. Hon John M Botts, of Va, being put upon the stand, testified to having never authorized Hester to purchase lands for him, & indeed he had never seen him before. Hester was held in $3,000 to answer to the charge.

Chas Crowell, an ordinary seaman, lately sentenced by the naval court martial convened at N Y was found guilty of striking, disobeying, & treating with contempt his superior ofcrs; & was sentenced to 3 years' confinement at hard labor in the penitentiary of the District of Columbia, to be deprived of his pay, & to be marked with a D on his right hip. The Atty Gen holds there is nothing illegal in the sentence. -Union

Mr Oliver March, of Lowell, for the last 15 or 20 years prominent in the book-trade of that place, lost his life on Sunday last by falling from the window of his room at the Merrimack House while in the act of closing the blinds. He was a native of Portsmouth, N H, & about 50 years of age.

By 3 executions issued by Thos C Donn, J P in Wash Co, D C, at the suit of Johnson Elliott against the goods & chattels of Philip Mackey, to me directed, I have seized & taken in execution all the right, title, & interest of said Mackey in & to one negro girl named Lurean, a slave of the said Mackay; on Sep 18, I will offer for sale the negro girl Lurean, to the highest bidder for cash. –H R Maryman, Constable

Mrd: on Thu, in the Seventh St Presbyterian Church, by Rev B F Bettinger, Mr Phillip H Linton to Miss Martha A Burch.

Died: on Sep 9, Wm L Voss, in his 22nd year. His funeral will be today at 4 o'clock.
+
I O O F-The members of Excelsior Lodge No 7 will meet to attend the funeral of our late brother Wm L Voss. –Wm Cooper, N G

SAT SEP 12, 1857
Mr Caleb Cushing proposes to engage in the practice of law in Boston, in conjunction with Sidney Webster, formerly private Sec to Pres Pierce. Mr Webster is a graduate of Yale College, & also of the Law School at Cambridge. –Boston Courier

Mrd: on Sep 10, by Rev Geo D Cummins, Rev Chas H Hall, Rector of the Church of the Epiphany, to Lizzie M, daughter of Geo C Ames, of Wash City.

John Stubbs, age 14 years, son of John Stubbs, of Wyanet, was smothered to death in a wheat bin at the freight-house in that place on Sat last. He was playing with other boys, when he sunk down into the cavity formed by running out of grain, & covered from above. Every effort possible was made by Mr Nicholas & others, but they were unable to get him out until some 15 minutes had elapsed. Life was extinct.
-Princeton [Ill] Democrat of Sep 3.

Col Chas A May, U S Army, recently in command of Carlisle Barracks, has been relieved by Col Crittenden, & left the place. A public dinner was tendered to him by the citizens of Carlisle, which he was compelled to decline by other engagements.

Mrs Catherine Donnelly, whose death at Woodstock, McHenry Co, on Tue last was announced in this paper, was 111 years of age, & was probably the oldest person in the State. She was a native of the county Tyrone, Ireland. She was the mother of 12 children. She retained the full use of her faculties to the last, & until a very recent date was able to move about the house. For the last 50 years she has restricted herself to one meal a day, & that was always partaken of after 12 o'clock in the day.
-Chicago Journal, Sep 5

N Y, Sep 10. 1-A telegraphic dispatch from Washington announces that the Pres has determined to commute the punishment of John Smith, alias Francisco Soares, [the Portuguese sailor who was convicted of the murder of the cook of the brig **General Pierce**,] from death to imprisonment for 7 years in the State prison of the southern district of N Y. Smith was originally sentenced to be hanged on Aug 13, but was reprieved until Sep 11. 2-Danl S Page, one of the 300 liquor dealers charged with violating the Sunday ordinance, has been discharged, on the ground that the commitment was illegal, as it required $200 bail, whilst the statute fixes it at only $100.

Book notice: The Chief of the Pilgrims; or, the Life & Time of Wm Brewster, Ruling Elder of the Pilgrim company that founded New Plymouth, the parent colony of New England, in 1620. By Rev Ashbel Steele, A M. Phil, J B Lippincott & Co: 1857.

The valuable property known as the ***Old Gas Works*** lot, being all of lot 7 in square 382, fronting 108 feet 6 inches on Louisiana ave, 120 feet on Canal st, & 69 feet on west 10th st, with an average depth from north to south of 90 feet, containing more than 10,000 square feet of ground, with the large bldg thereon, is offered for sale. Inquire of the undersigned, at the ofc of the Wash Gas-Light Co, 514 11th st.
-J F Brown, Sec in charge.

Died: on Sep 11, in Wash City, Mr John S Gatewood, formerly of Richmond, Va, in his 83rd year. His funeral will be at the residence of his daughter, Mrs Franklin Edmondson, 439 6th st, between E & F sts, this evening at 4 o'clock.

Died: on Sep 11, Sarah, infant daughter of John & Sarah Flaherty. Her funeral will take place from the residence of its parents this afternoon, at 5 o'clock, 579 C st north, Capitol Hill.

Died: on Sep 9, Samuel Smoot, aged 1 year, 11 months & 20 days, youngest son of the late Jas M Dorsett.

Died: on Sep 11, Emma Augustin, only daughter of Jacob F & Josephine King, aged 3 months & 3 days. Her funeral will take place from the residence of her parents, 509 L st, tomorrow at 10 o'clock.

Obit-died: on Sep 2, Benj Ruggles, in his 75th year; born in Windham Co, Conn; his father dying when he was some 12 years old. By teaching school he got the means to read law with Judge Peters; admitted to the bar in Conn, he emigrated to Marietta, Ohio. He took the ofc as Judge in 1810. He returned to Conn for a wife. He lost his first wife in 1816. Eight years afterwards he married a widow. She is now the worthy widow that survives him. He was a patron & frequent attendant of the Presbyterian Church, in which his wife was a communicant. He died of cholera morbus, after an illness of 48 hours, apparently without pain. On Wed morning he gently passed away. -G

MON SEP 14, 1857

Circuit Court of Wash Co, D C-in Chancery. Saml A Peugh vs Enoch Ridgeway, Thos Lewis, Geo W Donn, Edw C Eckloff, Jos A Ridgeway, Selby Parker, Thos N Brashears, Jas Johnson, Richd N Loker, Henry Barrow, Wm Glover, Geo S Donn, Henrietta F Ridgeway, [wife of Enoch Ridgeway,] Wm McL Cripps, Thos Foster, & Thos C Donn. The bill: Robt Cruit, in 1847, obtained against Enoch Ridgeway 2 judgments, which amounted, in 1857, to about $3,900, upon which the Marshal of D C returned nulla bona, which judgments, for a valuable consideration, were transferred to Saml A Peugh. That in fact at the time of said return the said Enoch Ridgeway had an equitable interest in several pieces of property in Wash Co, D C, to wit, lot 7 in square 372; south half of lot 22 in square 296; south half of lot 18 in square 293. That in 1845 said Enoch Ridgeway bought of Thos Lewis lot 7, as stated above, which was conveyed to him by deed of Thos Lewis, & which the said Enoch Ridgeway immediately encumbered by a deed in trust to Geo W Donn to secure to Thos Lewis the payment of the note of said Enoch Ridgeway for $500, payable in 5 years, which said note remains yet unpaid in part or in whole, & the deed of trust remains unexecuted. And on Oct 5, 1855, said Enoch Ridgeway conveyed lot 7 in square 372 to Edw C Eckloff; &, on Jul 8, 1856, said Eckloff conveyed the west half of lot 7 in square 372 to Jos A Ridgeway; & subsequently the said Jos A Ridgeway conveyed the west half of lot 7 in square 372 to Enoch Ridgeway & Thos C Donn to secure a debt of $1,000 said to be due to Wm Glover. That Enoch Ridgeway contracted with Wm McL Cripps, in 1845, for the purchase of lot 22 in square 296, upon which lot said Enoch Ridgeway erected 2 brick houses.

That in 1846 Enoch Ridgeway conveyed his title thereto to Thos N Brashears; in 1849 said Brashears conveyed it to Jas Johnson; in Nov, 1850, said Johnson conveyed it to Edw C Eckloff; & in Sep, 1853, said Cripps conveyed the title in fee to Edw C Eckloff; & in Feb, 1856, said Eckloff conveyed the south half of lot 22 in square 296, to Thos Foster-the north half having been meanwhile sold in bona fide. That about 1845 Enoch Ridgeway bought of Selby Parker the south half of lot 18 in square 293, which at the request of said Enoch Ridgeway-who erected a valuable house thereupon-was conveyed Jun 1, 1846, to Thos N Brashears; & by said Brashears to Jas Johnson on Jan 31, 1848; & by said Johnson on Nov 3, 1850, to Edw C Eckloff; & by said Eckloff to Richd N Loker on Feb 27, 1851; & by said Loker it was attempted to be conveyed on May 1, 1855, to Henry Barron; & said Barron, by his deed of Nov 12, 1855, conveyed in trust to Wm Glover & Geo S Donn, for the use of Henrietta F Ridgeway, [wife of Enoch Ridgeway,] for & in consideration of her many acts of kindness, personal care & attention for several years past, & being deeply grateful & desirous to make some suitable return to her, & for the further sum of $10. The bill further charges that these several conveyances of these 3 pices of property are fraudulent & defective, & are all for the purpose of defrauding & hindering & delaying the said cmplnt in the recovery of his said judgments. That Richd N Loker, Wm Glover, & Jos A Ridgeway do not reside in the District of Columbia. The object of the bill is to obtain a full & true disclosure & discovery of the several parties touching the aforesaid conveyances, etc, a decree setting aside the deed for fraud, & the sale, under the direction of the court, of the said property for the purpose of paying the said judgments. The absent dfndnts are to appear at the rules of said court to be held on the 1st Mon of Feb, 1858, next, to answer said bill, or otherwise the same will be taken proconfesso against them.
–Jas Dunlop, Ch J -John A Smith, clerk -John C Brent, Solicitor for cmplnt

Orphans Court of Wash Co, D C. In the case of the administration of Saml Baldwin, deceased, the Orphans Court of Wash Co, D C has appointed Oct 6 for the final settlement of the said estate. –Ed N Roach, Reg/o wills

Isaac N Robertson, who lived in Charlotte Co, Va, died on Aug 22, & left a will emancipating about 75 slaves, & dividing his real estate & other property among them. Provision is made in the will for their removal to Liberia.

On Fri, at Phil, Mr Edw Genay, of the firm of Genay & Co, tobacconists, lost his life. The deceased, with 3 friends, was out gunning. John Ellison, his friend, accidentally shot & killed Mr Edw Genay, when he raised his gun to fire at a flock of birds. The unfortunate man died instantly.

Orphans Court of Wash Co, D C. In the case of John McDermott, exc of Mary O'Reilly, deceased: the executor & Court have appointed Oct 6 next for the final settlement of the personal estate, of the assets in hand. –Ed N Roach, Reg/o wills

Died: on Sep 11, of typhoid fever, Horatio C Scott, jr, of Upper Marlborough, Md, in his 21st year.

Died: on Sep 5, in Fred'k City, Md, of cholera infantum, Mary Virginia, youngest child of C M & Mary A Keys, of Wash City, aged 6 months & 10 days.

TUE SEP 15, 1857
Carriages, buggies, carryalls, harness, & horses at auction, on Oct 1, at the Livery Stables of Messrs Webber & Blake, on 8th st, near the Navy Yard. -A Green auct

We learnt yesterday that Hon Thos H Benton was lying in a state of dangerous if not hopeless illness at his residence in Wash City. He is suffering an organic intestinal disease of several years' standing, which, within a week past, assumed so very serious a condition as to threaten his life. Surgical skill afforded yesterday at least temporary relief. He is attended by those eminently skillful practioners, Messrs Hall & May.

David Allman, charged with passing counterfeit money, & Thos E Day, charged with robbing the mail, have been tried before the U S District Court of Western Va, & acquitted.

Mr Philip Clark, formerly of Iowa city, returned to that place a day or two since from Calif, after an absence of 8 years. He left a wife, children, & a valuable farm when he went to Calif. He finds, on his return, that his wife has long since married, having first secured a divorce & a decree giving her the farm for her support. The farm has been sold & is now in other hands, & his former wife is in some other part of the country. -Albany statesman

Orphans Court of Wash Co, D C. In the case of Benj L Jackson, adm of Geo W Bowie, deceased, the administrator & Court have appointed Oct 6 next, for the final settlement of the personal estate of the deceased, with the assets in hand.
-Ed N Roach, Reg/o wills

Died: on Sep 13, at **Walnut Grange**, PG Co, Md, at the residence of her mother, Mrs Mary Virginia Hunter, wife of Cmder Thos T Hunter, U S Navy, & daughter of the late Hon John C Herbert, of Md.

Died: on Sep 10, in Gtwn, James, infant son of J D B & Caroline DeBow, aged 1 year.

Suicide at Niagara Falls. Clifton House, Sep 11. A man, registering the name of W T Allen, New England, threw himself from the Table Rock this afternoon.

N Y, Sep 14. Andrew Jackson, jr, who visited this city to present his father's gold box, declines to give it up, on the award of the military commission, to Maj Dyckman. He returns to Tenn tomorrow.

WED SEP 16, 1857
At the residence of Maj Keys, in Phillips Co, Ark, a few days ago, a man named Norwood, of Aberdeen, Miss, son-in-law of Maj Keys, assaulted Mrs Keys with a bowie-knife, & inflicted wounds which proved fatal in a few days. When stabbed Mrs Keys was endeavoring to prevent Norwood from attacking a man named Watson, her husband's overseer, who at the time was confined in her house suffering from wounds inflicted upon him by a negro man. The misunderstanding between Watson & Norwood grew out of the difficulty between Watson & the negro. Great excitement prevailed, & Norwood would have been immediately lynched had he not made good his escape. –Nashville Gaz, Sep 6

New Orleans Courier: The infant daughter of Mr Gunnegle, box door-keeper at the Gaiety Theatre, on Sunday morning, was found to have fallen into the space between the side-post of the bedstead & the wall, & suffocated. The mother & father were horror-stricken when they found their infant.

N Y, Sep 14. Some sensation has been created in religious circles by the ordination of Rev Geo H Doane, son of the Episcopal Bishop of N J, as a priest of the Roman Catholic Church in St Patrick's Cathedral, Newark, N J. Dr Doane has recently returned from Rome, where he became a convert.

It is stated that Richd Yeadon, of the Charleston Courier, has proceeded to the North for the purpose of having the remains of Hon Hugh S Legare transferred from Boston to his native State, where a monument is to be erected to the memory of the gifted statesman & orator.

Letter in the Richmond Dispatch, dated Amelia Co, Va, Sep 8, says an epidemic is prevailing in this county which has proved very fatal. It is a malignant form of dysentery. Of Mr A Tinsley's family of 9 children, 5 were taken sick at one time, & have since died. After their death two more were carried to the grave with the same disease. The wife of Mr Tinsley is now lying in a critical condition.

Circuit Court of Wash Co, D C-Mar Term, 1857. In the case of the petition of the heirs of Wm Phillips for a division of his real estae, the Court has passed the following order: The com'rs report that they have sold the real estate of Wm Phillips as follows: the farm & 8 & 7/8 acres, at $132 per acre, to S F & J H Burrows, $2,503.87. Home-place to Louisa Phillips, $1,000. One-seventh Robey's estate to Danl Lightfoot, $240, & the purchasers have complied with the terms of the sale.
-John A Smith, clerk

Mrd: on Sep 15, in Wash City, at Capitol Hill M E Church, by Rev Robt R S Hough, Mr Alfred H Marlow to Miss M Evaline Stanford, daughter of Wm H Stanford, all of Wash City.

Mrd: on Sep 15, in Wash City, by Rev J B Byrne, Wm Henry Palmer to Anna Maria, daughter of A T Kieckhoeper, of Wash City.

Died: on Sep 15, in Wash City, William Ruff, aged 2 years, 11 months & 15 days, son of Mary Ann & William Garner. His funeral will be tomorrow at 4 o'clock P M.

THU SEP 17, 1857
Household & kitchen furniture at auction on Sep 18, at the late residence of Michl Keller, deceased, on G, between 2nd & 3rd sts west. –R Eichhorn, exc -A Green auct

Household & kitchen furniture at auction on Sep 22, by order of the Orphans Court of Wash Co, D C; on K st, between 8th & 9th sts, the residence of the late John T Towers, deceased. –W G Palmer, Wm Towers, admx -Jas C McGuire, auct

Chancery sale of valuable real estate known as the *Nat'l Theatre*, by decree of the Circuit Court of Wash Co, D C, made in the cause No 1,094, in chancery between Jas A Lenman & John T Lenman, as cmplnts, & Wm H Winder & others as dfndnts: public auction on Oct 13, on the premises, the whole of lot 4, & part of lot 3, in square 254, fronting 88 feet 10½ inches on north E st, between 13th & 14th sts west, by 159 feet deep, to a 30 foot alley, with improvements, which consist of the remaining walls of the burnt Nat'l Theatre, containing several hundred thousand brick suitable for use in building. –Chas S Wallach, Walter D Davidge, trustees -Jas C McGuire, auct

At a convention of Delegates appointed by the Democratic & Anti-Know-Nothing electors in the several election districts of PG Co, held in Upper Marlborough on Sat last, the following were nominated candidates for the Genr'l Assembly & for the several county ofcs, viz: for the State Senate, John B Brooke; for the House of Delegates, Edw H Wyville, Edw W Belt, & John Contee; for Clerk of the Circuit Court, John Henry Sansbury; for Register of Wills, Wm A Jarboe; for Sheriff, John W Webster; for County Surveyor, Walter Bowie; for Com'rs of Tax, Isaac Scaggs, Richd N Darnall, Robt W G Baden, Jas P Kerby, & David Barry.

Offered for private sale, the beautiful residence called **Summer Hill**, in Va, on the turnpike road leading from Wash City, D C, to Alexandria, 3½ miles from either city; with 150 acres & a new comfortable dwlg-house & out bldgs. Apply to John F Callan, at the Drug Store corner of 7th & E sts, in Wash, or at the Law Ofc of Brent & Kinzer, in Alexandria.

Trustee's sale of Mill Property: by deed of trust from John J Peabody, dated May 25, 1856, recorded amongst the land records of Fairfax Co, Liber X, No 3, folio 335. I shall sell, at public auction, on Oct 19, the property known as ***Sugar Land Mills***, together with 20 acres of land attached thereto. This property lies 1½ miles from Dranesville, Fairfax Co, Va. Mr Wm H Bates, residing in the vicinity, will show the property. –Robt W Bates, trustee

A Hong Kong correspondent of the London Times states that an American pirate, Eli Boggs, a young man, was tried at Hong Kong on Wed last for piracy & murder. He was acquitted of murder, but found guilty of piracy. He was sentenced to be transported for life.

Died: on Sep 15, Wm Hunt, in his 47th year. He was a native of England, but for the last 20 years a resident of Wash City, & in all the relations of life a valued citizen.

Died: on Sep 14, of acute dysentery, Henry Martyn, infant son of John Carder Pedrick, of Wash City.

Died: on Sep 16, in Wash City, Sophia E, daughter of Wm & S E Douglas, aged 3 years & 9 months. Her funeral will be this afternoon at 3 o'clock, from the residence of her father, on H st, between 4th & 5th sts.

Died: on Sep 15, in Wash City, Jas Cook, aged 25 years. His funeral will be this afternoon at 3 o'clock, from his late residence, 362 E st.

FRI SEP 18, 1857
Appointments by the President: 1-Wm R Calhoun, of S C, to be the Sec of Legation at Paris, vice O Jennings Wise, of Va, resigned. 2-A M Jackson, of Miss, to be Sec of the Territory of New Mexico, vice Wm W H Davis, resigned.

Balt Patriot: yesterday, in Balt, the boiler of the Telegraph Telegraph Steam Flour Mill exploded. Three dwlg houses on Slemmer's alley were demolished, & a 3½ year old child of Mrs Malloy was killed. Mr Henry Brown, the head miller, was so severely scalded, that it is thought he will not recover. The engineer, Thos Schofield, escaped unhurt.

Orchard Lake, which is the usual resort for pleasure parties, was made on Fri last the scene of a most distressing occurrence. One of the largest companies of the season gathered there yesterday. A large scow which was in tow of several boats was sunk & the following drowned: Mrs Eliz Newell, aged 62 years; Miss Mary A Colvin, aged 16; Miss Jane Herrington, aged 20; & Mr John Owens, aged 21 years, all residents in this vicinity. –Detroit Advocate of 12th. [Sep 19th newspaper: the names of those drowned are: Mr John Owens, Mrs Eliz Newell, Miss Calvin, & Miss Harrington.]

Died: on Sep 16, at Warren Springs, Mrs Louisa Wadsworth, relict of Cmdor A S Wadsworth, of the U S Navy.

Col Benton has continued steadily to improve & is now announced by his physician to be much better.

Telegraphic dispatch from Charleston brings the news of the loss of the Calif mail steamer **Central America**, formerly the steamer **George Law**. She left Havana for N Y on Sep 8, with several hundred passengers, the Calif mails of Aug 20, & about $1,500,000 in specie. Apprehensions for her safety have existed for several days. The dispatch states that the steamship **Thomas Swann**, from N Y, arrived at Charleston yesterday. She reports that on the 15th she spoke the Norweigan barque **Eloise**, 15 miles north of Cape Hatteras, with 40 passengers of the **Central America** on board. The passengers reported that the **Central America** foundered at sea on the 12th instant, with 500 passengers, beside her crew, & that only 60 of the whole number on board were saved.

Marshal's sale: by writ of fieri facias, issued by the Clerk's Ofc of the Circuit Court of Wash Co, D C, I shall expose to public sale, for cash, on Oct 13 next, before the Court-house door: all the right, title, & interest of a tract of land called *Meridian Hill*, with all the dwlg houses, farm house, barn, stables, bldgs, rights of way privileges, seized & levied upon as the property of Gilbert L Thompson, & will be sold to satisfy Judicials No 139, to Oct term, 1857. Corcoran & Riggs, use of Wm A Bradley vs Gilbert L Thompson. –Jonah D Hoover, Marshal for D C.

SAT SEP 19, 1857
On Aug 7 Mr John O'Byrne, a compositor in the ofc of the Democrat, at Santa Fe, New Mexico, was killed by lightning while working at his case.

Excellent household & kitchen furniture at auction on: Sep 24, at the residence of Wm H Gilman, 485 D st, between 1st & 2nd sts. -Jas C McGuire, auct

The late hurricane at the South: the storm which occurred on the Southern Coast towards the close of last week was the most violent that has been recorded for many years, & has been especially disastrous to the steamers plying between Northern & Southern ports. Two of them, the steamer **Central America** & the Norfolk, were totally lost. The **Central America** was commanded by Lt Wm L Herndon, of the U S Navy, favorably known as the head of an expedition to the Amazon, a gallant & skillful ofcr, who sealed with his life his devotion to duty. The other ofcrs were Chas M Van Rensselaer, first ofcr, Jas M Frazer, second ofcr, [saved] Chas A Myers, third ofcr, E W Hull, purser, W H Hull, ship storekeeper, brother to the purser.

Champlin M Fletcher, of Orwell, Vt, committed suicide at Stanwix Hall, Albany, on Sunday, by taking chloroform. Losses at the race track is supposed to be the cause.

Mrs Robinson, of Richmond, Macomb Co, Mich, was instantly killed by lightning last week.

Geo Wilson, a young man, was tending a saw-mill in Ottawa district, Canada, last week, & accidentally got caught in the machinery and was killed.

W H Greenman, a lawyer, committed suicide on Sat, at the Canton Hotel, in Canton, Pa, by cutting his throat, while laboring under a fit of delirium tremens. On seeing the corpse of Mr G, the proprietor of the hotel, Mr Spaulding, fell in a fit & died immediately.

Mr McLoskey, a gentleman worth some $150,000, dying in Paris, left $6,000 to a niece in Dubuque, Iowa. The niece or legatee died on the same day as the testator. If the hour of her death preceded his, the legacy lapsed; if it succeeded his, the legacy is invested in her. The difference may have to be determined by the difference between solar & true time.

Improved Morning-Star Cook Stoves: Jas Skirving, 267 Pa ave & 11th st.

Md Politics. In PG Co Richd W W Bowie is an independent candidate for the Senate, E Pliney Bryan for the House, & Shelby Clark for Clerk of the Circuit Court.

The Balt Patriot of last evening announces the death of Gen Geo Rust, of that city, formerly a prominent citizen of Va, & for several years Superintendent of the Nat'l Armory at Harper's Ferry.

Mr Wm Boulden, a farmer, residing near the Manor Church, Cecil Co, Md, while attending a thrashing machine on Sat, had his arm torn to pieces to the elbow. The accident occurred in the morning & by 2 o'clock death put an end to his sufferings.

At Ellensville, Ulster Co, N Y, on Sep 10, 3 young ladies, Sarah D Otis, daughter of Dr Abijah Otis; Harriet Hunt, daughter of S A Hunt, of Ellenville, & Anna Bartlett, daughter of Dudley Bartlett, of Poughkeepsie, were bathing at Houk Falls, & were swept away by the undercurrent & all drowned. They were young ladies of great promise.

For sale or rent: the east half of lot 22 in square D, fronting on Maine ave, between 4½ & 6th sts, with a 2 story brick house, recently occupied by Joshua V Dulin as a blacksmith & machine shop, with all the tools & fixtures. –E Owen, 212 Pa ave.

Chesly Boatwright, convicted of the murder of Evans some time since was executed at Camden, S C, in the jail yard, on Friday last; a large concourse of people present.

Beautiful Va Farm for sale: the subscriber offers his farm at private sale; contains 520 acres, with a fine stone dwlg of 6 rooms, stone barn, & out bldgs. Address, Buckland, Prince Wm Co, Va. –Wm H Hite

Mrd: on Sep 17, in Wash City, by Rev B F Bittinger, Mr Jacob Rowles to Miss Nancy Hicks.

Died: on Sep 18, in Wash City, Mrs Abigail Barnhill, aged 74 years. Her funeral is today, at 3½ o'clock, from her late residence on N Y ave, between 4th & 5th sts.

Died: yesterday, in Wash City, Jesse Jenkins, a native of Balt, but for the last 16 years a resident of Wash City. Gifted with strong practical sense, & scrupulously honest, he commanded the esteem & respect of all who knew him.

Norfolk, Sep 18. The Norwegian barque **Eloise** has just arrived in Hampton Roads, with 50 passengers of the ill-fated steamer **Central America**, including 26 females. All the ofcrs, including Capt Herndon, were lost, except Frasier. The chief engineer, Ashby, is reported to have taken a boat & deserted the ship. Two millions of specie were lost.

+

Savannah, Sep 18. The barque **Saxony** has just arrived with 5 passengers of the steamer **Central America**. The **Saxony** reports the total loss of the steamer, treasure, & mails, & about 500 passengers & crew. Men, women, & children, numbering 40 to 50, were saved by the brig **Marine**, of Boston. There was a heavy sea at the time, & this was all the brig could do. Forty-nine others committed themselves to the sea, &, after 6 to 12 hours, were picked up by the barque **Ellen**, which made for some port on the coast. Those saved are, H H Childs, of the firm of Childs & Dougherty, N Y; Jabez Howes, of the firm of Geo Howes & Co, San Francisco; Geo W Cook, of Maine; & Adolph Fredericks, of San Francisco.

+

Norfolk, Sep 18. The brig **Marine** recovered 26 females & 20 men. The chief engineer deserted the ship an hour before going down. The Norwegian barque **Ellen**, from Belize, Honduras, bound to Falmouth, England, rescued Capt Thos W Badger, A Y Easton, R L Brown, O Harvey, J Birch, J A Forrester, O P Malone, J V Clark, John D Eneu, H T O'Conner, J Stetson, F A Walls, G Bruin, J H Rose, T McNeish, W A Osborn, L W Tollus, W Chase, J C Taylor, C Aquele, H Holland, W F Fletcher, W Ede, Chas A Vose, R Casey, Jno W Crafts, Henry A Rummel, Jacob Juencer, Henry Hartman, John M Collier, S Calwell, Benj Sawyer, J George, E Moore, B M Lee, Jas Jackson & Chas Reid. On board the brig **Marine**, bound for Boston, are Mrs Badger, Mrs Eaton, Mrs Browne, Mrs Harvey, Mrs Birch, & Mrs Conner. Of the crew saved are Jas M Frazier, 2nd ofcr; Henry Keefor, 2nd assist engineer; ___ Jones, fireman; Jas McCarty, ditto; A R Halcumbe, H Hardenburg, & Tim McKugh.

Died: on Sep 7, in Westmoreland Co, Va, Jas Jett, in his 78th year, one of the oldest & most respected citizens of the county.

MON SEP 21 1857
The names of those lost on the ill-fated steamer **Central America** cannot be known until the next arrival from Calif. The following are some of them: Lt Wm L Herndon, U S Navy, cmder of the steamer; Chas M Van Rensselaer, 1st ofcr; Jas T Tennison, surgeon; John V Dobbin, late Purser in the U S Navy, & brother of the late Sec of the Navy, North Carolina; Wm Lee, Canada; Benj Colt, Hancock Co, Ill; Hanson & John Home, Missouri; Richd Wilton, Quincy, Ill; Jas E Birch, Fall River, U S contractor; Gabriel Brush, baggage master, N Y; Chas Taylor, North Carolina; Saml Shreves, San Francisco; Dr Fanni, San Francisco; Dr Gibbs, Calif; Mr Marvin, Calif; Mr Parker, San Francisco; Mr Boker, Boston; Mr White, Sacramento; Purser Hull [of the ship] & brother, N Y; Mr Serony, San Francisco.
The following are names of passengers who were saved & carried into Norfolk by the Norwegian barque **Ellen**, most of whom have since been conveyed to N Y: Capt Thos W Badger, San Francisco, Calif; A J Gaston, do; R F Brown, Sacramento; O Harvey, Placerville; Wm Birch, San Francisco; J A Forrester, Murphy's, Calif; Oliver P Manlove, Grant Co, Wisc; J B Clark, Polk Co, Mo; John D B Ements, Oregon City, Oregon Territory; H T O'Conner, Albany, N Y; Julius Stetson, Shaw's Flat, Calif; T A Wells, Leyden, Mass; Geo Bryan, Ulster Co, N Y; Jas H Ross, Mohoning Co, Ohio; Thos McNeish, Grass Valley, Calif; Wm N Osborne, Isthmus of Panama; J N Falleno, Cincinnati, Ohio; Wm Chase, Michigan; J C Taylor, Albany Co, N Y; E Ayulo, Lima, Peru; Henry Halcon, Montreal, Canada; W F Fletcher, Bloomfield, Maine; Wm Irde, Wisc; R Casey, Ark; J M Casey, Ark; John N Crafts, Maine; Henry Runnel, Ill; Jacob Quener, Watertown, N Y; Henry Hartman, Ill; Jacob Quener, Watertown, N Y; Henry Hartman, Bremen, Germany; John B McCable, N Y; S Caldwell, N Y; Benj Sage, St Louis; John George, England; Edw Moore, Boston; B M Lee, Plattsburgh, Pa; Jas Jackson, Mo; Chas Reid, N Y.
+
The following are the 5 persons who were transferred from the barque **Ellen** [Capt A Johnson,] to the barque **Saxony**, & carried into the port of Savannah: Henry H Childs, of N Y; Jabez Howe, San Francisco; Geo W Loot, of Maine; Adolph Frederick, San Francisco; & Robt Ridley.
+
The brig **Marine** [Capt Hiram Burt,] arrived at Norfolk on Sat. List of persons saved on her: Women saved: Mrs Adie Mills Easton, San Francisco; Mrs Jane A Badger, do; Mrs Adie Sawley & 2 children, wife of F S Sawley, hardware merchant, supposed to have been lost, San Francisco; Mrs M V Burch, San Francisco, wife of A T Birch, supposed to be lost; Mrs Harriet Lockwood, San Francisco, wife of R A Lockwood, supposed lost; Miss Rose Alice Lockwood, Miss Harriet Lockwood, & Master R C Lockwood, son & daughters of R A Lockwood; Mrs Amanda Marvin, Sacramento, wife of W H Marvin, supposed lost; Mrs Angeline Bowley & 2 children, San Francisco, wife of J McKinnon Bowley, supposed lost; Mrs Cynthia

Ellis & 4 children, San Francisco, wife of A Ellis, suppose lost; Mrs Anne McMill, [perhaps McNeill;] Mrs Mary Ann Travis & 2 children, Alvarado; Mrs H Van Harper & child, Nevada Co, wife of J A Van Harper, supposed lost; Mrs B B Thayer & 2 children, San Francisco; Mrs Rosalie Hand, & 3 children, San Francisco; Miss Frances A Thomas, San Francisco; Mrs Almira A Killidge, San Francisco; Mrs Eliza G Carthers, Placer Co, Calif; Mrs Ann Redding, N Y; Mrs Ann Small & child, Newburyport, Mass-her husband died at Panama on his way to Calif; Miss Eliza Smith, Tuolumne Co, Calif; Mrs Eleanor O'Conner, San Francisco, whose son is supposed lost; Mrs Jane Fell & 2 children; Mrs Jane Harris & child, San Francisco; Miss Winifred Fallow, [brother Jas & father supposed lost;] Louis Bennett, a child, in charge of Mrs O'Conner; Mrs Athronsahu, of Ureka, son & husband supposed lost; Mrs Mary Swan & child, wife of Saml P Swan, Nevada City, husband supposed lost; Mrs Mary Seeger & 2 children, wife of Benj Seeger, Calaveras Co, supposed lost; Mrs Mary Ann Rudwell, wife of John Rudwell, Grass Valley, Calif; Mrs Mary Bailey, Alamado Co, Calif; & Mrs Caroline Shaw, Amanda Co.

Men saved: Hiram Burt, Sacramento; A C Monson, do; Theodore Rayne, San Francisco; Albert Priest, Sacramento; Chas McCarty, San Francisco; Frank Johnes, Sacramento; Auge Rich, Belgian Consul; Wm H Adams, Placer Co, Calif; Robt Hutchinson, Nevada City, Calif; John Cummer, Sierra Co, Calif; Henry Kimball, Sacramento Co, Calif; M L McCoy, Sacramento City, Calif; Douglas Butterford, Yuba Co, Calif; Jos Glay [or Clay] Eldorado Co, Calif; Wm Bliss, Naper Valley, Calif; Gilam Thesto, San Francisco, Calif; Thos Bride, Yuba Co, Calif; Alex'r Gardner, Jas Gallagher, & Thos Fryer, three of the crew of the ship **Vespasian**, condemned on Old Providence island.

Ofcrs of the steamer **Central America** saved: Geo Ashby, chief engineer; John Black, boatswain; Finlay Frazier, quartermaster; David Raymond, quartermaster; Robt Long, quartermaster; & Wm Jackson, quartermaster.

Seamen saved: Jas Clark, Richd Reed, Fred'k Reed, Fred'k Brougham, John Davidson, Jas Travis, Edw Brown, Jas McClean, & Edw Higgins.

Firemen saved: Morgan Badgley, Henry Hethington, John Clark, & Geo Stewart.

Waiters saved: Michl Dwyer, Wm Garrison, Lucy Dawson, & Susan P Etorcell. The latter's husband supposed lost.

Hon Chas Fenton Mercer has been for several days sojourning in Wash City, at Mr Maddox's, 4½ st & Pa ave. He has chosen to avoid observation during this visit, because the purpose of it was to have a sarcomatous ulcer removed from his lip. Dr May skillfully performed the operation. Mr Mercer is now nearly 80 years old.
-States

Fire on Sat at Mr Henry Blunt's whiskey rectifying establishment, on Water st, Gtwn, between Market & High sts was the result of an accident. A candle dropped into one of the vats containing some highly inflammable fluid. All the property was consumed to the value of about $4,000. The property of Mr Thecker stored in the bldg was lost.

Died: on Aug 21, at **Greenbrier** White Sulphur Springs, Va, in his 49th year, Gwyn Page, late of San Francisco, Calif. Mr Page was a native of Va, a grandson of Mr Mann Page, of **Rosewell**, Gloucester Co. When very young he removed with his parents to Ky, where he was educated, & spent the greater portion of his life. Mr Page leaves an only sister, with whose grief a stranger dare not intermeddle. He was all to her that a brother could be, & in him were all her affections centered. -R

U S Patent Ofc, Wash, Sep 17, 1857. Ptn of Jonathan Ball, of Elmira, N Y, praying for the extension of a patent granted to him on Nov 15 next, for an improvement in coating water pipes, for 7 years from the expiration of said patent, which takes place on Dec 30, 1857. –J Holt, Acting Com'r of Patents

Calif: The Settlers' Convention adjourned on Sep 5, nominating Edw Stanly for Govn'r, Nathl Bennett for Supreme Court Judge, A A Sargeant for Atty Genr'l, & P M Randall for Surveyor Genr'l.

TUE SEP 22, 1857
Sale of the **Whiton farm**; the best in the State, was sold yesterday; it lies on the east bank of the Pemigewasset, 1 mile east of Plymouth village, & contains 217 acres. Ex-Pres Pierce bid $17,000, a New Yorker $17,500, when the Englishman added $500 more, & took the farm for $18,000. He also bought **Fairmeadow**, a tract of 25 acres, at $100 per acre. –Manchester [N H] American

Incidents of the wreck of the steamer **Central America**. As Theodore Payne, of San Francisco, was leaving the steamer to go to the barque **Marine**, Capt Herndon gave him his watch, with the request that he would deliver it to Mrs Herndon should he fortunately be saved. Mr Payne was saved, with the watch in his possession, & the request of the captain will be faithfully complied with. Capt Thos W Badger, of Va, one of the rescued, lost $16,500 in gold eagles, which sum was in a carpet-bag in his state-room. Mrs Birch, had a beautiful canary bird which she left in a cage in a state-room. Before she left the ship she took it from its cage, &, placing it in her bosom, brought it safe to the brig. Her husband secured jewelry of great value about his own person. Mr Wm N Osborne, formerly of Tenn, but whose relatives now reside in Sullivan Co, Indiana, was one among the rescued. In giving a statement of his experience on board he says: "During the whole time Capt Herndon was in all parts of the ship, with an anxious face, cool, calm, & deliberate, & without the least apparent excitement, he gave his orders, which were promptly obeyed. Mr Chas McCarty, chief engineer of the steamer **Golden Gate**, states that he was in the boat with the chief engineer, Mr Ashby, & had cognizance of his conduct before leaving the ship. The going out of the fires was entirely beyond his control, & he did everything possible for the safety of the ship & passengers.

Closing-out sale of Dry Goods at the store of Noxon & Son will be concluded this day. -Jas C McGuire, auct

Mrd: on Sep 15, in Wash City, at Trinity Church, by Rev Dr Cummins, Jas G Scott, of Onslow Co, N C, to Mary J, daughter of E French, of Wash City.

Mrd: on Sep 17, in St Luke's Church, Bladensburgh, Md, by Rev Wm Pinckney, D C, Dr J B Gibbs to Miss Bettie Boyd Wright, daughter of Robt Wright, of PG Co, Md.

Died: at **Walnut Grange**, PG Co, Md [her late residence,] Mary Herbert, relict of the late Hon John C Herbert, of Md, in her 73rd year. She was as a wife devoted & self-sacrificing, as a mother fond & anxious, as a neighbor kind & charitable, & as a Christian humble though hopeful. [No death date given-current item.]

New Agricultural & Machine Warehouse, 558 7th st, south of Pa ave, opposite Centre Market. —J P Bartholow

For sale, the estate on which I reside, being nearly one half of each of the tracts given by Col Ed Carter, of **Blenham**, to his sons, John Champ & Hill Carter, containing 1,670 acres, on both sides of Piney river, the county line between Amherst & Nelson Counties. Also, slaves, [100,] stock, [50 horses,] 100 cattle, including 20 yoke work steers. —Danl Warwick, Amherst, Rose Mills P O.

Marshal's sale: by writ of fieri facias: all the right, title, claim, & interest in part of lot 12 in square 729, in Wash City, seized & levied upon as the property of Benj E Green, & will be sold to satisfy judicials No 156 to Oct Term, 1857, in favor of Nathl Carusi. —J D Hooer, Marshal for D C.

Orphans Court of Wash Co, D C. Letters of administration on the personal estate of Sarah Thruston, late of Wash Co, deceased. —Thos W Thruston, adm

We learn that Mr J B Ements, of Oregon city, who is reported amongst the saved from the steamer **Central America**, is Lt John D Dement, whose family are of Washington & its vicinity.

WED SEP 23, 1857
The last Congress formed a new Territory under the name of **Dacotah**. It includes a great part of the valley of the Sioux, the valleys of the James & Vermillion rivers, & large tracts of beautiful bottom lands lying on the Missouri. It has an unusually healthy climate.

Amongst the visiters at present in Wash City is Col J B Bryant, of Louisville, & formerly of the U S Army, who is stopping at the residence of his friend & relative, Col Benton. The health of the venerable ex-Senator, we regret to add, continues precarious.

Statement of Frank A Jones, a passenger in the steamer **Central America**, who was saved in the brig **Marine**, says: the brig Marine had suffered severely by the storm; her mizzenmast was gone, & she was otherwise so disabled as to have lost all command of herself. Capt Herndon ordered the boats to be lowered; the first 3 were successfully launched, but the other 2 were stove in the attempt to launch them from the upper decks. The Captain ordered the men to fall back to allow the ladies & children preference. They immediately obeyed. The first boat was commanded by Mr Black, the boatswain; the 2nd by Mr Frazier, the quartermaster, & the 3rd by Mr Ashby, the chief engineer. Mr John Black, a boatswain of the **Central America**, returned a third time to the **Central America**, but, on nearing her, was told to keep off, as the steamer was about to sink. He did so, & about 10 minutes afterwards she went down. Mr Black could see in the distance the heads of the drowning men, looking like blackbirds on the water, but no inducement could prevail on his men to approach them. Mr Ashby implored his men & offered them $100 apiece, but all to no purpose. They were unwilling to risk their lives again, with the exception of Mr Raymond.

Steen de Bille, who was for more than 25 years Charge d'Affaires from his Majesty the King of Denmark in the U S, sailed, with his estimable family, from N Y on Sat last for Havre. Although constantly at Washington when his public duties required it, his domestic residence was in this city. His son, Torbin de Bille, who was educated at the Univ of Pa, & who was appointed about 2 years ago successor to his father as Charge to this country, has recently been promoted by the King of Denmark to the grade of Minister to the Courts of Hague & Brussels. Mr de Bille & his son, as well as his wife & daughters, carry with them the kind feelings of all who had the pleasure of knowing them. –Phil American

Geo W Kendall, who owns a ranch in Texas, has been very successful in raising the Chinese sugar-cane. My friends are saving the seed to plant for bread, & are making sirup & sugar of the juice of the stalk; they re feeding it out as good fodder & saving it for dry. No part of it is wasted; cattle, horses, sheep, & hogs eat it clean, from the ground upwards, when the stalk is ripe, & gain strength & grow fat upon it.

Danl S Morrison, of Hot Springs Co, became lost & bewildered in his immense growth of corn, & wandered 3 days, subsisting during that time on green corn. His negroes found him on the 4th day. –Little Rock [Ark] Gazette of Sep 8.

The undersigned, having 300 acres of land in his farm, will dispose of from one to two hundeed acres, in lots to suit purchasers. Said land is in Alexandria Co, Va.
-S B Corbett

Mrd: on Sep 17, in Portsmouth, Va, by Rev Isaac W K Handy, John M Covert, M D, to Miss Gussie Lamar Pendleton, youngest daughter of Henry Pendleton, all of Portsmouth.

Collector's sale on Dec 17, at the Town House, in Gtwn, D C, for taxes due on the year annexed, [all 1856] with assessments & taxes; to the Corp of Gtwn, D C.
Jas Clagett's heirs, lot 29, $175, taxes $1.40.
Wm Crawford, jr's heirs, subdivision lot 5, $185, $1.48.
Gabriel Duvall's heirs, lot 281, $300, $2.40.
Do, pt Threlkeld's square, $500, $4.00.
Do, pt of Threlkeld's square, front foot tax, $90.
Chas Gordon, part of lot 177,
Do, part of lot 177, $1,500, $12.00
John Hoyes' heirs, lot 39, $200, $1.60.
Chas King's heirs, lot 224, $350, $2.80.
R B Lloyd, part of lot 99 & part of lot 100, $750, $6.00.
John Laurence's heirs, part lot 81, $900, $7.20.
Mrs Sarah Munro, part of lot 72, $350, $2.80.
Do, pt of lot 72, front foot tax, $6.40.
Henry Reintzel's heirs, lot 170, $900, $7.20.
Do, lot 170, front foot tax, $6.84.
Basil & Ignatius Waters, part of lot 221, $295, $2.36.
Elijah Walker's heirs, part of lot 22, $400, $3.20.
John A Grimes, part of lot 59, front foot tax, $6.40.
Hannah Bargey & others, part of lot 44, 2-5ths of $4,000, $12.80.
Do, pt of lot 44, front foot tax, $25.24.
Brooke Mackall, lot 200, $750, $6.00.
Co, lot 227, $350, $2.80.
Do, lot 9, $500, $4.00.
Do, part of lot 89, $1,200, $9.60.
Do, part of lot 111, $250, $2.
Do, part of 111 & 112, $300, $2.40.
John Lee, part of lot 24, $200, $1.60.
Do, part of lot 25, $300, $2.40.
Do, part of lot 32, $350, $2.80.
Do, part of lot 33, $300, $2.40.
Gtwn, D C, Sep 22, 1857 -C F Shekell, Collector

For sale-handsome residence on the Heights of Gtwn. The property comprises an entire square of ground. The dwlg house is large & room, having a front of 95 feet, [with the wings,] & commands one of the finest views of the Potomac river & country around. It is heated by a furnace, lighted with gas, & contains bath firxtures for hot & cold water, a large cistern, kitchen range, & almost every convenience for a first-class house. Apply to Saml C Edes, Trustee, at Pairo & Nourse' Banking House, opposite Treasury Dept.

Died: on Sep 21, in Wash City, Annie Cass, 2nd daughter of G Peyton & Martha E Page, aged 5 years & 8 months. Her funeral will take place on Sep 23, at 3½ o'clock, from their residence, 525 Va ave, near 4th st east.

Died: on Sep 22, in Wash City, Mrs Ann C Kearon, in her 58th year. Her funeral will take place this afternoon, at 4 o'clock, from her late residence, 330 8th st.

The following Military Land Warrants, transmitted from this city by mail of Jul 23, 1857, addressed to Rev Joshua Webster, Hilton, Canada West, have not been received by Mr Webster, viz: No 70,03 for 160 acres, with name of Pitkin Gross; & No 69,779 for 160 acres, in the name of Stephen Blanchard. After 6 weeks, application will be made to the Com'r of Pensions for duplicates of the same, should the original not sooner come to hand. –Michl Nourse

THU SEP 24, 1857
From Europe: Dr Aichtenstein, the celebrated Prussian professor of natural history, is dead. [No date-current item.]

The Minnesota Democratic Convention met at St Paul on Thu & made the following nominations: for Govn'r-H H Sibley; for Lt Govn'r-W Holcomb; for Reps to Congress-Geo L Becker, W W Phelps, J M Cavanaugh. For Delegate to Congress-W W Kingsbury.

Shocking tragedy at Bangor, Me on Sunday, in a school-boy quarrel between Wm Crosby, son of Wm C Crosby, & Chas Lowell, son of John Lowell. Young Lowell was stabbed by Crosby with his pocket knife, & died within 10 minutes. They were both about 15 years old, & attended school in the same bldg.

Loss of the steamer **Central America**: a Lady's statement: Mrs Fred'k S Hawley, daughter of Chas de Forest, of Bridgeport, Conn. Her husband is among the lost. She was with her 2 children, an infant of 5 months & another 2 years old, both boys. Her narrative: we left the steamer in the second boat, in company with Mrs Easton, Mrs Badger, Mrs Thayer, Mrs McNeil, Miss Winifred Fallon, Mrs Thayer's nurse, [Susan,] & Miss Smith. The last I saw of my husband he stood on the wheel-house & kissed his hand to me as the boat pulled away from the ship. The children did not cry, except when the salt water came over us & flew in their faces. We were all without clothing or bonnets, except the thin dresses we had on. Capt Herndon & Mr Hull, the purser, were active in directing about getting the women & children into the boats. Capt Herndon said to the boatmen, Tell the captain of the brig for Heaven's sake to lay by us all night. Capt Burt & mate stood with open arms & willing hearts to receive us. He took my little Willy, & the mate received De Forest, playfully saying as he passed him over the side, "He is all gold." My heart was lighter when I saw my children safely on board the brig. We were immediately placed in the cabin, where we were made as comfortable as the circumstances would permit. Capt Burt opened his chest & handed out his own clothes, which we put on, & soon made ourselves very warm & comfortable. Another boat load came bringing, among them, Mr Priest, [an old gentleman;] Judge Munson; the colored boy Garrison, the captain's servant. Capt Herndon, when he saw him going away in the boat, upbraided him sharply for deserting his post. We began to despair for the safety of our husbands who were yet on board. At daylight on Sunday morning the doomed vessel had disappeared.

+

A fearful night on the waves. Mr George was one of the hundreds who had supplied themselves with life-preservers, pieces of plank, & preferred to await the ship's going down to leaping over-board in anticipation of her fate. He was sucked in by the whirlpool caused by the ships' swift descent. God moves in mysterious ways. He saw the lights of the barque **Ellen** & shouted, & was taken up.

+

Capt Herndon when last seen. Mr Easton, now in N Y, went down with Herndon, & rose near him & Van Rensselaer. He spoke to him after he rose. Herndon had on a good cork life-preserver, as is known to several passengers-Mr Jones, one of the survivors, seeing him with it on. Mr Van Rensselaer was devoted to Herndon, sunk & rose with him, & declared he would not leave him. Herndon, it is believed, was seen on a piece of wreck some time after he was separated from Easton. The Savannah News says: "Capt Herndon was last seen by Mr Childs [one of the rescued] about 4 hours after the sinking of the steamer. About 12 o'clock on Sat night, Mr Childs was drifted near Capt Herndon, hailed him, & received an encouraging answer. He never saw him again."

+

The following gentlemen were received on board the steamer **Central America** at Havana: Ancho Richon, bearer of a desaptch to Paris & Belgian Consul at Lima; Jose Seguin, Peruvian Minister to the U S, & his Sec, Nicholas Tirado; Adolphus Ollague, Richd Ollague, & Enirique Quolo, of Lima, all from Lima, & supposed to be lost.

Wash Corp: 1-Cmte on Finance: Bill for the relief of Michl Guista: passed.

Pleased to announce: Wm Henry Thomas, of St Mary's, as an independent candidate for Congress in the 6th Congressional District. –Voters of St Mary's Co.

Central Academy, corner of E & 10th sts, will be opened on Sep 1.
–Silas Merchant, A M, Principal.

Mrd: on Sep 21, in the Wesley Chapel, by Rev Mr Krebs, J Wm Morsell to Mary Ellen Collison, all of Wash City.

Mrd: on Sep 16, at Hopeton, by Rev E Kingsford, D D, F H Stickney to Libbie E, daughter of J C Lewis.

Mrd: on Sep 22, in Balt, by Rev L H Johns, Wm P Ingle to Eliza, daughter of the late Edw A Crimmer, of Balt, Md.

Died: on Sep 22, in Alexandria, Va, J W Lugenbeel, M D. His funeral will take place this afternoon, at 3 o'clock, from the residence of Mr Davy.

Died: on Sep 20, at Rahway, N J, Jas Prentiss, of N Y, in his 77th year.

Died: on Sep 23, Catherine, daughter of Mary & W P Mohun, aged 19 months. Her funeral will take place from the residence of her parents, 322 Third st, Sep 24, at 4 o'clock.

Three days from Europe. 1-Capt Roberts, who was convicted of the murder of a sailor on board a ship, was hung at Liverpool on Sep 12. The 2 mates were respited. 2-The submarine telegraph between Europe & Africa was successfully laid on Sep 9.

FRI SEP 25, 1857

N Y Mirror of Sep 23. Miss Juliana May's first concert was last evening in the American Concert Room. She has a mezzo soprano voice, pure silvery, round firm, & powerful.

Capt Wm Lewis Herndon of the steamer **Central America**, went down on Sep 12. He was born in Fredericksburg, Va, in 1813; entered the U S Navy as midshipman in 1828, & for the next 10 or 12 years was almost constantly afloat in the ship **Guerriere** in the Pacific, in the sloop-of-war **Constellation** in the Mediterranean, & afterwards on the coast of Brazil in the frig **Independence**. At the outbreak of the Florida war he volunteered for service, & was appointed to the command of a brig in Indian Key, remaining in that service for upwards of 2 years. For 3 years he was then actively employed in the Nat'l Observatory, under his distinguished brother-in-law, Lt Maury. Finding his health unequal to his duties at the Observatory, Herndon resigned, & when the Mexican war broke out we find him again employed in command of the steamer **Iris**, until the end of the war. After another year's service at the Observatory he was appointed to the ship **Vandalia**, on the Pacific station, whence, in 1850, he was detached on special duty, to explore the valley of the Amazon. His scientific attainments & his accurate knowledge of the Spanish language eminently qualified him. He again went to sea in the frig **San Jacinto**, & after his return in 1854-5, he was appointed to the command of the ill-fated steamer **Central America**, then known as the steamer **George Law**. -Journal of Commerce

Hon John Henderson died at his residence at Pass Christian, Miss, on Sep 16. He was formerly a prominent Senator in Congress from the State of Miss, & has since devoted himself to the practice of the law. For the last few months he had been quite ill. He died in the 62nd year of his age.

Trustee's sale of valuable improved real estate known as the **Kirkwood House**: by deed of trust from Thos Y Conly & wife to me, dated Jul 31, 1847, recorded in Liber W B No 136, folios 14 thru 18, of the land records for Wash Co, D C. Public auction on Oct 31, on the premises, situated at 12th & Pa ave: all those parcels of ground known as parts of lots 2 & 3 in square 322, & designated as lots C, D, & E, of the subdivision made by John McClelland, of said lots numbered 2 & 3.
–Thos J Semmes, tustee -Jas C McGuire, auct

Trustee's sale of valuable real esate: by deed of trust from Geo Page & wife, dated Jul 9, 1853, recorded in Liber J A S, No 67, folio 209; public auction on Oct 29 next, on the premises, all that part of square 472 owned by said Geo Page, comprising nearly the whole of said square, which fronts 289 feet 10 inches on 6th st west, 479 feet 4 inches on south L st, 314 feet 3 inches on Water st, & 357 feet 3 inches on south M st with the 3 story brick bldg known as McKenna's Warehouse.
-John T Fenwick, Wm Van Reswick, trustees -Jas C McGuire, auct

The brig **Marine**, of Boston, which rescued so many passengers from the steamer **Central America**, is 215 tons register, & was built at Catine, Maine, about 7 years ago. Her gallant cmder, Capt Burt, did not hesitate a moment to bring his vessel by the wind & relieve those in distress. The **Marine** is owned by Elisha Atkins, of this city. A year ago last winter she fell in with the ship **Seaman**, of Balt, on fire, & took off all on board, about 35, & landed them safely. The owner of the **Seaman** never wrote a line of thanks to those who had saved the people who manned his ship. Perhaps he forgot all about the crew, & remembered only that his vessel was insured.
-Boston Traveller

The report of the Experts, Messrs Brantz Mayer & Theodore G Hunt, who were appointed to make a partition of the John McDonogh estate between the cities of New Orleans & Balt, has been submitted to the City Councils. The valuation placed upon the estate is $1,465,680. There is pending in court a claim of $100,000, as an alleged legacy to F Pena. The claim of the heirs of S Greenwood for a like sum has been denied by the Supreme Court of Louisiana. –Balt American

The son of Cmdor Cole, of N Y, recently died in Florence. He was a promising youth of 19 years, & had been a student of the arts during the past year. The family went to Florence a few weeks ago from Paris, & was scarcely established in a fine residence, when he was taken off with the fever of the country, after an illness of 10 days. After a typhoid prostration of some 2 or 3 days, he suddenly opened his eyes, called for his parents by name, & remarked, with deliberation & emphasis, "I am journeying to a strange country; but, oh, how beautiful!" & expired humming a favorite Spanish air.

New Grocery Store. The subscriber has taken the store at 42 La ave, between 7th & 8th sts. –H M B McPherson

It has been stated that Hon S H Sullivan, the British Minister at Lima, in Peru, had been assassinated by some unknown person, when he was sitting down to dinner with Mr & Mrs Cheeseman. The assassin entered the dining room abruptly, encountering Mr Sullivan, discharged a blunderbuss directly in the groin, saying "now I am revenged," & made his escape. Mr Sullivan was still alive at last accounts, but could not possibly survive.

The stage was standing at the Gen Post Ofc whilst the driver was delivering the mail, when the horses took fright & ran away at full speed. A passenger, since discovered to be Miss Yonson, attempted to escape & in doing so bruised herself fearfully. He parents live in the 7th Ward & visited her yesterday. Miss Yonson continues in a comatose state, quite unable to recognize any body. [Sep 28th newspaper: Miss Yonson was reported yesterday something better; as very weak, & thus not yet considered out of danger.]

Rapphannock land for sale. As atty for the heirs of John Seymour Taliaferro, I offer for sale the desirable estate known as *Hays*: situated in King George Co, Va, bounded by the land of Mr Wm Wallace on one side, & Mr J Parke Corbin on the other. 1st: *Hays* proper contains about 1,000 acres. 2nd: *Water Grist Mill* tract contains 351 acres. 3rd: *Bloomsberry* contains 750 acres. In my absence the property will be shown by Mr Lee, manager of the estate. –W R Mason

Mrd: on Sep 1, by Rev Mr Graham, Mr Chas E Worthington, of Md, to Maria L, 2nd daughter of Lloyd Logan, of Winchester, Va.

Mrd: on Sep 17, in Shepherdstown, Va, by Rev C W Andrews, Mr Jas A Buchanan, of Davenport, Iowa, formerly of Balt, to Miss Rosa Parran, daughter of the late Dr Richd Parran, of Jefferson Co.

Wm Pettibone, Book-binder & Blank Book Manufacture, has removed to the south side of Pa ave, between 13th & 13 ½ sts. –Wm Pettibone

Hon Wm Davison, who represented the Charlotte, N C district in Congress 2 terms, died on Sep 16, from injuries received a few days previous by his horse taking fright & running off with the vehicle in which he was riding. He was 80 years of age.

SAT SEP 26, 1857
The N Y papers announce the death of Cornelius S Bogardus, for a long period Deputy Collector, & subsequently Naval Ofcr at this port, & well known as a leading Democrat. He died on Monday, of consumption, in his 46th year.

Orphans Court of Wash Co, D C. Letters of administration, with the will annexed, on the personal estate of Ignatius N Clements, late of Wash Co, deceased.
–Mary Ann Clements, admx, will annexed

The Coos Country; letter from our friend & townsman, Mr Chas Lanman. Glen House, White Mountains, Jul, 1857. The word Coos is of Indian origin, & is said to signify "the pine country.' Walter Neale is the first white man who explored these mountains in 1631; Darby Field is said to have been the first European who, with 2 Indians, in 1642, visited the summit of what is now called *Mount Washington.* Forty rods from the top of Mt Washington stands a little monument of stone. There, on Sep 14, 1855, the body of Lizzie Bourne, daughter of E E Bourne, of Kennebunk, Me, was found. The day before she had started from Glen House, with her uncle Geo W Bourne, & his daughter, to walk to the top of Mt Washington. Later in the walk, Lizzie complained of being sleepy. It was well known that inaction would be certain death. Her uncle & his daughter aided Lizzie, but after a short distance she breathed her last. In Aug, 1856, an old man, Benj Chandler, of Wilmington, Dela, left Glen House to visit the mountain top. He was in his 70th year, & scorned the idea of taking a guide. A few days ago his fate was unknown, until his skeleton was found about a mile from the spot. His son searched for him in vain last autumn. He is expected at arrive by train to receive the still sacred remains of his father. On Oct 24, 1856, B L Ball left Glen House for a ramble to the summit of Mt Washington. He became lost, & when found was perfectly helpless, half frozen, & very nearly dead. He was taken down the mountain with care & in the course of 2 weeks was quite well again.

U S Patent Ofc, Wash, Sep 24, 1857. Ptn of Luther Boardman, of East Haddam, Conn, praying for the extension of a patent granted to him on Dec 15, 1843, for an improvement in buff for polishing spoons, etc, for 7 years, which takes place on Dec 15, 1857. –J Holt, Com'r of Patents

The Life of John Fitch, the Inventor of the Steamboat, by Thompson Westcott, 1 vol, $1.25. –Franck Taylor

Mr Payne, of Calif, to whom Capt Herndon left his watch, to be handed by him to his wife, in case of his death, has just executed that painful duty, & the watch is now in Mrs Herndon's possession, the last said relic of her heroic husband. –N Y Express
+
The sword & several boxes containing effects belonging to Lt Herndon were placed by him, before he left Wash City, in the keeping of Mr Jas C McGuire, auctioneer. -Union

Judge Probasco, law partner of Gov Corwin, & a distinguished practioner of the bar, died at Lebanon, Ohio, on Fri. He was attacked with bilious fever, which terminated in typhus.

Died: on Sep 20, in Fredericksburg, Mrs Mary Botts, relict of Gen Thos H Botts.

Ordination: Rev C C Meador will be ordained for the Gospel Ministry next Sabbath. Services at the Island Hall, Island, 3:30 P M. Rev J G Binney is expected to preach the sermon.

Augusta, Sep 25. Col Dell, Collector at Jacksonville, Fla, died suddenly on Sunday of disease of the heart.

Wheeling Female Seminary, in charge of The Sisters of the Visitation, B V M. Letters to be addressed "Directress of the Academy of the Visitation, Wheeling, Va.

MON SEP 28, 1857
Wash, Sep 22, 1857. I propose to my countrywomen that a meeting be called in each city & village in the U S, & that funds be collected & transmited to Geo W Riggs, banker, in Washington, to be invested for the wife & daughter of Capt Herndon, late of the U S Navy. Let us do something to show our gratitude to one who in time of trouble sacrificed himself to his duty & to woman. Your countrywoman, Sarah Magruder [To the Women of the U S.]

Mr W F Fletcher, of Bloomfield, Maine, a passenger in the steamer **Central America**, who was rescued by the barque **Ellen**, states that the schnr **El Dorado** did not lay by the **Central America**, but kept on her course after having hailed her. Mr Fletcher thinks it very strange that Capt Stone, if he remained near the place where the **Central America** went down did not discover any of the scores of men who were floating in the water during the night. Mr Fletcher was not rescued until the next morning, being the last but two of those picked up. At that time a schooner was in sight at a great distance. -Traveller

The U S M steamship **Baltic**, for Liverpool, took out 52 passengers; among them Beverley Tucker, U S Consul at Liverpool. [No date-current item.

On Sunday, Sep 13, Mr Horace Taylor & wife & father were riding to church in Grafton, Vt, when the harness became disengaged, & the horse started to run & overturned the carriage. Mr Taylor died almost immediately; his wife had both of her arms broken, besides other injuries; the old gentleman was so much hurt as to preclude all hope of his recovery.

Mr David Paul Brown, a distinguished lawyer of Phil, in attempting to get upon the train as it moved, fell beneath the first step of the car, & every one thought that he was certainly killed. Fortunately, he did not fall upon the track, & the entire train passed over the crown of his hat. –Charlottesville [Va] Advocate

The Lotteries of Saml Swan & Co are chartered by the State of Georiga. Tickets are $10; halves $5; & quarters $2.50. Prizes vary from $2 to $60. Address plainly, & direct to S Swan & Co, Augusta, Ga.

Revolutionary document: the Portsmouth [N H] Gaz published the following: To the Selectmen & Cmte of the town of Portsmouth: Colony of N H. In Cmte of Safety, Apr 12, 1776. In order to carry the underwritten resolve of honorable Continental Congress into execution, you are requested to desire all males about 21 years of age [idiots, lunatics, & negroes excepted] to sign to the declaration on this paper; &, when so done, to make return thereof, together with the name or names of those who shall refuse to sign the same, to the Genr'l Assemby or Cmte of Safety to this Colony. –M Weare, Chairman

Albert Patterson was recently indited at Boston for Bigamy for having married one Eliz Adkins under the name of Eli Merrill. He was positively identified by the clergyman & other parties, & was detained in jail 2 weeks, when he succeeded in producing the bona fide Eli Merrill in court, who testified to his own identity & the fact of his marriage, & Patterson was thereupon released.

The Naval Courts of Inquiry: since the reopening of the 3 courts on Sep 7 the cases of the following ofcrs have been up for consideration: Cmders J R Jarvis, T G Benham, John Calhoun, & Lockwood; Lts G G Williamson, J J Glasson, Geo R Gray, J M Watson, Chas Hunter, & J F Abbott; Passed Midshipmen J H March & Chas Gray. On Sat last the cases before the first, second, & third courts respectively were as follow: Lts P Turner, S B Bissell, & R B Riell.

On Sat, south of Benning's bridge, Mr Eugene Burr, a young man, second son of Mr David H Burr, of Wash City, late Surveyor General of Utah, lost his life. He was returning from shooting with 2 young friends, Henry Robbins & Wm McLean, & was taking his gun from the skiff, when the gun exploded. His companions stuffed a handkerchief into the wound to keep down the gushing blood. Drs Lindsly, May, Richards, & Middleton were in attendance, but the case was beyond remedy, & he died in full possession of his senses. He would have been 18 years of age in Jan next. His parents, Mr & Mrs Burr, have been spending some time on Staten Island, but were yesterday telegraphed of the dreadful event.

Mrd: on Sep 24, at St John's Church, by Rev Thos G Addison, Henry D J Pratt to Louisa, daughter of Danl D Addison, all of Wash City.

Died: on Sep 27, in Wash City, Maj Geo F Lindsay, U S Marine Corps. His funeral is tomorrow at 3 o'clock from his late residence, corner of K & 12th sts. The ofcrs of the Army, Navy, & Marine Corps are also respectively invited to attend.

Mrs Cecilia Young will resume her lessons in Vocal Music, either in classes or private pupils, on Oct 1. Apply at 468 10th st, between D & E sts. [Sep 30th newspaper: Mrs Young is the daughter & grand-daughter of famous old-world musicians, & inherits her special gifts of voice & style.]

Orphans Court of Wash Co, D C. Letters testamentary on the personal estate of Chas Frailer, late of Wash Co, deceased. –Catherine Frailer, excx

Orphans Court of Wash Co, D C. Letters testamentary on the personal estate of John Mountz, late of Wash Co, deceased. –Jos Mountz, exc

Orphans Court of Wash Co, D C. Letters of administration on the personal estate of Fidel Hirst, late of Wash Co, deceased. –M Hirst, admx

TUE SEP 29, 1857
Household & kitchen furniture at auction on Oct 2 next, at the residence of Wm C Rawlings, 310 8th st, between L & M sts, in the Northern Liberties. -A Green auct

Excellent household & kitchen furniture at auction on Oct 5 next, at the residence of Mrs Campbell, 32 4½ st, near Pa ave. -A Green auct

The trial of Jas P Donnelly for the murder of Albert S Moses, at the Sea View House, on Aug 1st last, terminated at Freehold, N J, on Sat, & resulted in the conviction of the prisoner of murder in the first degree, as charged in the indictment. [Oct 19th newspaper: Jas P Donnelly will be hung on Jan 8 next. A writ of error was given yesterday & the execution postponed, to allow time for the action of the Supreme Court. That hearing will take place on the first Tues in Nov, at Trenton.
–Newark Daily Advertiser]

In Florence, Nebraska, on Sep 5, while the friends of Judge Ferguson were firing a salute in honor of his election to Congress, the cannon burst, injuring Dr A H Hardcastle so severely that he died the next day. He was a graduate of the Univ of N Y, & served as surgeon & captain in Walker's army in Nicaragua.

Mrd: on Sep 27, by Rev W H Chapman, Mr John W Sinclair to Miss Olivia A Robinson, all of Wash City.

Died: on Sep 27, in Wash City, Miss Eliza Watterston. Her funeral will be from the residence of her mother, on Capitol Hill, at 12 o'clock tomorrow, Wed.

Died: on Sep 27, Eugene B Burr, aged 17 years. His funeral will take place this day, at 3 o'clock P M, from the residence of his father, David H Burr, 364 C st. [Sep 30th newspaper: the funeral of Mr Eugene B Burr took place yesterday; services were conducted by Rev Dr Cummins]

Died: on Sep 26, in Wash City, John Kirby, infant son of Rev Wm C & Mary E Stout, of Marshall Co, Miss, aged 6 months & 23 days.

WED SEP 30, 1857

In the pocket-book of Hon Stephen Allen who was drowned several years ago by a seamboat disaster on the Hudson river, was found a printed slip, apparently cut from a newpaper, of which the following is a copy: Keep good company or none. Never be idle. Always speak the truth. If any one speaks evil of you, let your life be so that none will believe him. When you speak to a person, look him in the face. Drink no kind of intoxicating liquors. Make no haste to be rich, if you would prosper. Never play at any game of chance. Earn money before you spend it. Do not marry until you are able to support a wife. Never speak evil of any one. Save when you are young, to spend when you are old. Read the above maxims at least once a week.

N Y Times: Capt Stone acknowledges he saw the rockets & the ship [steamer **Central America**] when she sunk. Had he shook out his reefs & made all sail, which he could easily do, there being little wind, he could probably have rescued many of those lost from their watery grave. A number of us survivors saw his lights & him after we were in the water. They, however, shortly after disappeared. Signed: H H Childs, 20 East 32nd st; T W Badger, 20 East 32nd st; S J Eaton, Metropolitan Hotel; & D O Harvey, Metropolitan Hotel.

The Alabama Journal, published at Montgomery, announces the death on Sep 22, of Maj John C Bates, its senior editor & proprietor.

Fire broke out in a brick dwlg house on Jefferson st, Gtwn, & was not put out before its 2 immediate neighbors were likewise consumed. The middle bldg was the property of Mr Philip T Berry, that on its left belonged to the estate of the Foxhall's heirs, & the one on the right is owned by Mr Chas De Selding, of Wash. They were all insured at probably about their value.

Obit-died: on Sep 27, at the Fauquier *White Sulphur Springs*, in his 88th year, Gen Moses Green, formerly of Culpeper Co, Va. In early life he was a volunteer in some of the Western expeditions; subsequently a member of the State Legislature for several years, & Adjutant Genr'l. In the war of 1812 he commanded an independent advanced corps, & was every ready to serve the State in time of need. Of a large frame, 6 feet 4 inches in height, weighing nearly 300, he was active in person & mind; a warm friend, a generous & chivalrous opponent; liberal & hospitable to all. A widely extended family connexion attested his worth in all the relations of life.

Mrd: on Sep 29, at Wesley Chapel, by Rev W Krebs, Richd Griffin to Cecelia J Hawkins, both of Wash City.

Died: on Sep 26, in Gtwn, George Allan, infant son of A M & Mary E *Hofgar, aged 15 months. [*Paper is creased-this is what is appears to be.]

THU OCT 1, 1857
Among the persons to be promoted in the British peerage is the Marquis of Lansdown, who is to be made Duke of Kerry. 51 years ago the Marquis, then Lord Henry Petty, was Chancellor of the Exchequer in the Ministry of Fox & Grenville. Among the companions of Earl Strongbow, who invaded Ireland in the 12th century, was Wm Fitzgerald, whose son Raymond married Strongbow's sister, from which union came a son name Maurice, who was the father of Thos Fitzmaurice, first Baron of Kerry. From him were descended the Earls of Kerry. The first Earl's young son, in 1751, changed his patrician & Norman name of Fitzmaurice for the plebeian & Saxon one of Petty. An uncle of Young Fitzmaurice was the son of Sir Wm Petty, the famous political arithmetician of the 17th century. Wm Petty was born at Romsey in 1623. His father was a clothier & dyer-that is, he dyed the cloths which he sold. The boy had an absolute genius for making money. His fortune produced an income of 15,000 pounds in 1685. His daughter Anne was married to the first Earl of Kerry, & both his sons died childless, Henry, the second son, & the Earl of Shelburne, dying in 1751. He bequeathed his property to his sister's second son, John Fitzmaurice, who assumed the surname of Petty, & who was created Viscount Fitzmaurice; & subsequently he was made Earl of Shelburne. These were Irish titles, but he was made a Peer of Great Britain by the title of Baron Wycombe in 1760. His son was that Earl of Shelburne who played so prominent part in English politics for a short time after the fall of Lord North, but whom the younger Pitt managed to cut out. The Earl was created Marquis of Lansdowne in 1781. On his death the title went to his eldest son; but the second Marquis dying without issue, his brother, Lord Henry Petty, succeeded to the title & estates in 1809. In 1818, on the death of Earl of Kerry, without children, the old Irish titles of the elder branch of the Fitzmaurices fell to the Marquis of Lansdowne, whose eldest son's courtesy title was Earl of Kerry. That son died in 1836. By becoming Duke of Kerry, the Marquis will cause his present title to sink to one of mere courtesy, though it had been so honorably borne for more than 70 years. The descendant of the tradesman of Romsey has now risen as high as any British subject can ever look to reach.
–Boston Traveller

Liquors & teas at auction on Oct 5, at the store of Jas Patterson, on 4½ st, near Md ave. -Jas C McGuire, auct

Trustee's sale under decree of the Circuit Court of Wash Co, D C, pronounced in a casue wherein Jos Libby is cmplnt & Jas B Phillips & others are dfndnts, being No 1,062 in equity, the subscriber, as trustee, will expose to sale at auction, on Oct 27, lots S, T U, V, in subdivision of lots Nos 1 thru 4, & 10 & 11 in square 452, Wash City, fronting on Mass ave near 6th st, with improvements.
–Wm R Woodward, trustee -A Green auct

Sgt Thos P Monroe, U S Army, was killed at *Fort Myers*, Fla, on the 6th ult by Lt Myers, of the volunteer service.

An incident at sea. On Aug 27, as the ship **Illinois** was steaming towards Havana, having got off the reef the previous night, we met the steamer **Central America**, with her myriad of passengers bound to Aspinwall. She passed on the port side within 100 yards. The engines of both ships were quiest. Upon the wheel-house stood Capt Herndon; near by Van Renssalaer, the first ofcr; Purser Hull, Dr Tennyson, & a number of gentlemen easily recognized & known. When directly opposite, Capt Herndon hailed Capt Boggs in that distinct & gentlemanly tone of voice that so distinguished him. "Good morning Capt Boggs! Can I render you any assistance?" Capt Boggs replied, :We are all right, & bound for Havana." The wheels again moved & the ships separated. We all stood & gazed after the **Central America**; & as the foam dashed upon her quarters & stern rendered the sight imposing, we exclaimed, how beautiful! My friend Church, the celebrated artist of N Y, he who transferred Niagara Falls to canvass, stood at my elbow. That last sight of the **Central America** will not be lost to him, nor ever effaced from my memory, as it was the everlasting adieu to a noble ship, & many kind & respected friends among her officers. —Correspondence of the Boston Traveller

Capt Jeremiah Thurlow, accompanied by Capt Edw Beal, Misses Sarah & Helen J Thurlow, & a daughter of Capt Thurlow, [name not given,] started on Sep 15, headed for n w harbor of Deer Island, Me, in the open boat **Ellsworth**. At Burnt Point they took on board 2 gentlemen passengers, supposed to belong to N Y. About half-past one the boat was struck by a squall & capsized. The Journal says: Capt Thurlow became utterly exhausted, & the last Capt Beal saw of him his fingers gradually slid off the boat, &, with his daughter still clinging around his neck, he sunk to rise no more. After this Capt Beal & the young girl Helen remained in the water another hour, making 2½ hours from the time of the disaster. They were picked up by Capt Geo Bousey, of the schnr **Spartan**. One of the gentlemen of N Y sunk some time previous, with one of the ladies [Sarah,] in his arms. The other gentleman was not seen after the boat capsized.

A son of Dr Kelly, of Mobile, who had just returned home from the Univ of Va, was drowned a few days ago while bathing near the city with his father. He was 17 years of age. He sunk so suddenly that it is supposed he was seized by an alligator, & probably devoured, as his body could not be recovered. He had been in the water but a moment when he exclaimed, 'Father, father!" & disappeared beneath the surface.

The passengers of the steamer **Central America** who were taken on board the steamer **Empire City** from the brig **Marine** have presented Capt McGowan with a handsome gold chronometer watch & highly wrought chain, as a token of their esteem for his able & humane conduct during the late destructive hurricane.

On the 19th ult the entire stock of 8 fine blooded ewes on the farm of Mills Roberts, of Gates Co, N C, which he purchased from Mr T A Hardy, of Norfolk Co, were killed by a stroke of lightning.

In reply to several survivors of the steamer **Central America** the pilot of the schnr **Eldorado** says it was an impossibility for that schnr to lay by the steamer. She is a large flat-bottomed schnr, drawing only 7 feet water, & would inevitably have drifted to leeward, without any possibility of getting back. She could easily have accommodated all on board the steamer, but her only chance of succoring them was to have made fast to the steamer. The captain, when he approached the steamer, fully expected they would throw him a line to which he could make fast, but there was but a moment in which he was near enough for this, & that precious moment was lost without any attempt made on board the steamer for this purpose. The Norfolk Argus is informed by the captain of the brig **Marine** that he also rounded to close under the stern of the steamer, & expected to find a boat out with the end of one of her large hawsers on board, which he might easily have secured & held on by, but to his dismay found none in readiness, & in a minute more he was drifting rapidly away, & in so disabled a condition that he could not get back.

Wm Vaughn, the last surviving Revolutioanry soldier residing in Sumter district, S C, died last week. He served under Marion & Sumter.

Mr Bartless, the alleged defaulter in a bank at Charleston, has been arrested at Wilmington, N C, & $53,000 of the missing $60,000 recovered.

Mr Robt Bowie, of the wholesale dry goods store of Messrs J S & L Bowie was accidentally killed on Sat last. His sleeping room was on the 3rd floor, & it is supposed he took a seat in the window for the purpose of smoking, &, being overcome by fatigue, dropped asleep, & fell to the pavement. He was a young man of fair promise & bright prospects. –Charleston Mercury

Louisville Journal of Sat. Gwynn Page died at White Sulphur Springs, in Va, on Sep 1, after a lingering illness, surrounded by friends & a few near relatives. Mr Page was several times honored with a seat in the State Legislature, & discharged the duties of Speaker of the House of Reps with eminent gracefulness & ability. A few years ago he determined to seek his fortune in Calif. He left from Louisville & returned a few months ago broken in health.

A young man, Geo Wilkins, residing with Mrs O'Connor, on West Fayette st, Balt, was badly burnt when filling a lamp with oil whilst the wick was burning. We have recorded more accidents from explosive fluids than from gunpowder.

Mrd: on Wed, by Rev John C Smith, Horace J Frost, of Detroit, to Miss Mildred C Walker, of Wash City.

Mrd: on Sep 29, by Rev S P Bachus, Richd P Thomas, formerly of Montg Co, Md, to Harriet, daughter of S P Cowman, of Balt City.

Mrd: on Tue, by Rev B F Bittinger, Mr Geo Dixon to Miss Joanna Gates.

Norfolk, Sep 30. The brig **Edward H Titler**, from Phil, bound to Savannah, is ashore on Currituck beach. She will prove a total loss.

The undersigned have this day, Oct 1, formed a partnership, under the name of Murray & Randolph, 55 La ave, Wash City. They have in hand from Thirty to Forty Thousand Dollars of Securities on real estate in Wash City, bearing 6% interest, good beyond all doubt. Persons wishing to invest in such securities can do so by calling at 55 La ave. –Stan's Murray, Wm M Randolph

FRI OCT 2, 1857
The Boston papers record the death at Brookline, of John Eliot Thayer, in his 53rd year. He was a son of Rev Nathl Thayer, D D, of Lancaster, Mass, & a lineal descendant of Rev John Cotton, the first minister of Boston. He began life with no inheritance except a good name, he engaged in active pursuits before he was 21 years old, & at his death was at the head of a banking-house second to none in the country, & the possessor of a most ample fortune. He had elegant mansions in town & in the country.

Trustee's sale of very valuable improved property at public sale, on Nov 6, on the Navy Yard: by deed of trust from W D Acken, made Mar 16, 1857, & duly recorded: sale of part of lot 2 in square 952, fronting 47 feet on 9th st east, & 108 feet on M st south, with a good 3 story brick store & dwlg. –W L Wall, trustee
-Wall & Barnard aucts

Five cattle among a herd of 20 were struck by lightning on Saml Keller's farm, near West View, Augusta Co, Va, on Sat last, & instantly killed. The cattle were on the summit of a high & bare hill, remote from timber of any kind.

We announce the defalcation of Mr Fred'k W Porter, who has for 30 years held the post of Corr Sec of the American Sunday School Union. He has issued notes & acceptances for his private purposes, without the knowledge or authority of the board, of officers, to the amount of $88,883.00. Mr Porter is well advanced in years, of quiet habits, & a member of the church vestry for many years.
-Phil Evening Bulletin

Shooting match at St Louis near the city last week. Trial of skill between Capt Paul, of St Louis, & John Travis, of N Y, who are said to stand as the champion pistol shots of the world. Friday: up to the 19th shot the chances were in Capt Paul's favor; but on the 20th & last shot he lost, the pistol discharging before he took proper aim. On Saturday: Mr Travis did not shoot the 4th round, from the fact that he could not win.

A young lady, residing in Chas City Co, Va, playfully snapped a gun at her lover, Saml Throg, on Wed last, supposing it to be empty. It happened to be loaded, & Throg was killed instantly.

A man by the name of Hornsby, residing about 13 miles from Brunswick, charged with stealing his neighbors' stock, had been notified by them to leave the settlement by Tue last. Not complying, several men set out for his house to force him to leave. They were fired on by inmates in the house, & Mr Rumph was killed, & an old man-Radcliffe & his son, were both wounded. Fire was returned & Mr & Mrs Hornsby both were killed. A child in the mother's arms was badly wounded, & it was thought would die. A wounded man is not expected to recover. –Savannah News, Sep 21

Mrd: on Oct 1, in Gtwn, D C, by Rev B N Brown, Saml M Brooks, of Balt, to Laura Virginia, daughter of Henry King, of Gtwn.

Died: on Oct 1, in Wash City, Mary Jane, daughter of John & Jane C Kearon, in her 7th year. Her funeral will take place this afternoon, at 4 o'clock, from the residence of her parents, 137 E st, between 20th & 21st sts.

Died: on Sep 17, in Charlotte, N C, Hon Wm Davidson, in his 80th year. He represented Mecklenburg Co many years in the State Senate, & was a member of the 15th & 16th Congress from the Mecklenberg district.

Boston, Oct 1. Messrs John A Lowell, Benj Howard, Richardson, Kendall & Co, & Peter C Jones have failed.

N Y, Oct 1. Last evening the boiler of the Knickerbocker plaster works, West st, exploded, destroying the factory & 2 adjoining brick dwlgs occupied by 200 Irish & Germans. Catharine Dogan, aged 19, was killed, & 17 were seriously wounded. [Oct 3rd newspaper: The only dead body found was that of Catharine Duganne.]

SAT OCT 3, 1857
Richmond "South". Since the death & burial in 1836 the mortal remains of Ex-Pres Madison have been quietly reposing at **Montpelier**, Orange Co, about 9 miles from Gordonsville, on the Va Central railroad. A monument was procured, & it was conveyed to Montpelier on Sep 15 & placed in position. It is of James river granite, in form an obelisk & the gross weight of the entire monument is about 32,000 pounds. The inscription is simple:
MADISON
Born March 16, 1751,
Died June 28, 1836.

Appointments: The Com'r of Patents had made the following appointments in his ofc, with the approval of the Sec of the Interior: Dr Henry King, of Mo, & Jas S French, of Va, examiners of patents. Salaries $2,500 each.

Our desirable farm for sale: **Indiantown**, Chas Co, Md, about 940 acres; on Nanjemoy Creek; dwlg house & every necessary out-bldg, some new. The property will be shown by B M & W L Campbell, Balt, or Fred'k Stone, Port Tobacco, Md.

The partnership under the firm of Cripps & Waller is this day dissolved by mutual consent. Wm McL Cripps, A B Waller [A B Waller will sell the stock of seasoned lumber at reduced prices. He will continue the business at the old stand.]

A meeting has been called by Mrs Sally Pendleton & other ladies, of Berkley Co, Va, to carry out the suggestion of Mrs Magruder, of Wash City, for the women of America to raise funds for the support of the widow & daughter of the late Capt Herndon.

Wm S Williams, son of a grocer at Wheeling, was arrested there on Tue last, charged with being the person who, a few days since, obtained, through a young man named McLain, the contents of the Post Ofc bag of the Manufacturers' & Farmers' Bank of Wheeling. He was held to bail in the sum of $2,000. He was arrested while sitting at the breakfast table, & only an hour or two after his marriage with a respectable young lady, & was on the point of starting his wedding tour. Is it said that although apparently not over 21 years of age he has been married once before, & had served out a term in the penitentiary at Albany, N Y.

House for sale: corner of E & 4th sts: 3 stories high. –C E Walker, Carpenter & Builder

Orphans Court of Wash Co, D C. In the case of Maria E Harvey, excx of Jas F Harvey deceased: the excx & Court have appointed Oct 20th next, for the final settlement of the personal estate of the deceased, of the assets in hand.
–Ed N Roach, Reg/o wills

Mr John Long has just completed walling up a well at his residence near Macomb, Ill, when he accidentally dropped his hammer into the well. A boy was sent down to recover it, but when about 10 feet down, fell to the bottom. Mr Long then descended, gave an alarm he was suffocating, & before aid was furnished he too fell lifeless to the bottom. Both bodies were recovered several hours afterward.

Mrd: Oct 1, by Rev John C Smith, D D , Jos S Wright, of Va, to Miss Debbie F, daughter of John Y Bryant, of Wash City.

Mrd: Oct 1, in Christ Church, Easton, Md, by Rev Dr Mason, Wm Shepard Bryan, of Balt, to Lizzie Edmundston, daughter of the late Wm H Hayward, of Talbot Co, Md.

Balt, Oct 2. Geo Braden was today convicted of murder in the 2nd degree, for killing Wm Walters, in May last, at the Nat'l Garden.

MON OCT 5, 1857

For sale: a beautiful Farm of about 50 acres, with a good house, about 2 miles from Wash City. A small Farm, of 24 acres, about 5 miles from Wash City. Also, some desirable houses. Apply to Arthur W Fletcher, 430 F st, between 6th & 7th sts.

Two weeks more. We shall continue selling off for 2 weeks more, & beg all who really want bargains to call & secure them, as every thing we have on hand must be sold out at some price. We have yet a large stock of fine goods unsold. Persons who buy to sell again will find it to their advantage to give us a call, as we promise them great bargains. –H J McLaughlin & Co, 20, between 8th & 9th sts.

Obit-died: on Sep 17, in Balt City, Gen Geo Rust, many years a resident of this county, where he amassed a large property, & was generally esteemed for his integrity of purpose & uprightness of character. During the war of 1812 he was one of the volunteer defenders of Balt. He represented Loudoun Co in the Legislature of Va, & was also during the Administration of Gen Jackson superintendent of the nat'l armory at Harper's Ferry. A few months ago he disposed of his beautiful estate in this county, & removed to Balt City, where he connected himself with the banking firm of Messrs Appleton & Co, of which he was a member at the time of his death. The deceased was in his 70th year. –Loudoun Mirror

Died: on Oct 3, at the residence of her brother, Capt Carbery, Mrs Martha Catalana. Her funeral will take place this evening at 3 o'clock.

Died: on Oct 3, in Wash City, Ida, infant child of Jos A & Eliz A Deeble, aged 4 months & 21 days.

Died: on Oct 1, Eva Mary, youngest daughter of Saml L & Amelia Ann Housewright, aged 16 months.

Died: on Oct 3, at N Y, John W Nelson, aged 37 years, eldest son of Mr Justice Nelson, of the U S Supreme Court. He was late clerk of the U S Circuit Court for the Southern District of N Y. He resigned his ofc to make a tour of Europe.

Died: on Oct 4, in Wash City, Mary Ann Clark, daughter of Thos & Margaret Clark, in her 38th year. Her funeral will take place tomorrow at 3½ o'clock, from the residence of her parents, 405 G st, between 6th & 7th sts.

Orphans Court of Wash Co, D C. Letters of administration on the personal estate of Julia A Carroll, late of Wash Co, deceased. —Thos Johnson, adm

The ship **Star of the West** brings only a list of the passengers of the steamer Central **America** who were from the Isthmus. The following were passengers, & are supposed to have been lost, unless they stopped at Havana: F M B Smith, Wm Graffus, Capt W G Dyer, J Sellaner, N M Tirato, W Watson & son, Otis Barlow, Jas O'Neil, Mr Olfero, C W Griffiths, Thos Maloney, Frank Carpenter, Wm Hemmell, Wm Plass, A Amour, T J Morris, & F Griffith.

TUE OCT 6, 1857
Chancery sale: by decree of the Circuit Court of Wash Co, D C, made in the case of Wm Bird et al, vs H R Maryman, exc of Hazel et al, No 886 equity: public auction Oct 29, on the premises: the east half of lot 3 in square 728, on the north side of East Capitol st, between 1st & 2nd sts; also, part of lot 3 in square 784, fronting about 30 feet on Md ave, running back about 80 feet. —Walter S Cox, trustee -A Green auct

Panama Herald of Sep 18. Hon Wm E Venable, U S Minister to Gutemala, died on Sep 22, from cholera, shortly after his arrival at the seat of gov't, which will be received with regret by all parties in the U S, & prove a deep blow to his family. He left Panama in the steamer **Columbus** in July for his official post, & it appears suffered much from sea sickness & the fatigues of the land journey, so that when attacked by the fatal epidemic he soon became its easy victim. He was a native of N C, but a resident of the State of Tenn. He was buried in the ***Protestant burial ground*** of Gutemala on Sep 23, the funeral service being read by Chas Lenox Wyke, her Britannic Majesty's Charge d'Affaires. He died at the residence of Henry Savage, who has been & still remains in charge of the U S Legation. Another of the victims to the cholera here, has been the Sra Dona Petrona Garcia de Barrera, the lady of the Pres of this Republic, who died on Sep 17, after an illness of a few hours. Her remains were kept in state until Tue, when they were deposited in the family vault in the cathedral. Dr Don Quirino Flores, & 2 other physicians have also died of the cholera.

Com'rs sale of a valuable farm, by decree of the Circuit Court of Fauquier, pronounced on Sep 18, 1857, in the Chancery cause of Saffell vs Carter: public auction, on the premises, on Oct 15, of the farm belonging to the heirs of Landon L Carter, deceased, containing 112½ acres in upper Fauquier; with a comfortable dwlg house, & the necessary out-bldgs. —Rice W Payne, Com'r

Two vacancies have occurred by death in the Indiana Congressional delegation during the present year-by the death of Hon Jas Lockhart in the 1st district, & of Hon Saml Brereton in the 10th. In the 10th district the Republicans have in the field Chas Case, & the Democrats Judge Worden.

Excellent household & kitchen furniture at auction on: Oct 13, at the residence of Mrs Hamilton, on Indiana ave. -Jas C McGuire, auct

To the children & heirs of Eliz Coffman, [wife of John Coffman,] formerly Eliz Crowbarger, & one of the children of Geo Crowbarger, deceased, late of Augusta Co, Va. There is in my hands, subject to the control of the Circuit Court of Augusta Co, the sum of $677.50, to which you are entitled as heirs of Geo Crowbarger, deceased. You are notified to come forward & furnish satisfactory proof of your heirship, so as to entitle you to receive said fund. –Nich G Kenney, Receiver of Cir Court of Augusta.

Washington-new Board of School Trustees:

Wm B Randolph	Wm P Young	Chas Wilson
Thos P Morgan	Wm F Price	J E Willett
Roger B Ironsides	Jno D Brandt	Robt Ricketts
Peter F Bacon	Aaron W Miller	Valentine Harbaugh
Erasmus Chapin	S York AtLee	

Mr W J Stone, for many years well known as one of our principal Washington engravers, was yesterday riding in his carriage on 14th st, near the dwlg of his son, Dr Robt Stone, when he was suddenly attacked by a fit of apoplexy. Happily his son & Dr Thos Miller who was very near at the time, & by rendering immediate assistance & the use of the lancet, was enabled to arrest the perilous progress of this disease.

N Y, Oct 5. The Bremen barque **Bremen** arrived here this morning, with J Tice, the 2nd engineer, Alex'r Grant, fireman, & G W Dawson, a passenger of the steamer **Central America**, who were rescued by the British brig **Mary**, from Cardenas, bound for Queenstown, & transferred therefrom to the **Bremen**. Mr Tice states that he drifted on a plank 72 hours. On the 4th morning after the disaster he drifted up to a boat, & succeeded in getting into it. On the 5th day he picked up Grant, who had been 5 days on a part of the hurricane deck. The two then pulled for the hurricane deck, & took from it Dawson. There had been 10 other men on this part of the wreck, viz: Geo Buddington, 3rd engineer; John Bank, coal-heaver; Patrick Card, do; Evers, fireman; & 6 passengers, whose names were unknown, all of whom had died. Tice, Grant, & Dawson were 8 days without water or provisions, with the sea making a breach over them. On the 2nd day after the steamer went down they saw a number of passengers on pieces of the wreck, but could not assist them. The rescued are in sad condition, badly bruised, & covered with boils. [Oct 7th newspaper: John Tice makes a statement. Alex'r Grant's statement names those who were with them & died: Geo Buddington, 3rd assist engineer; Patrick Carr, fireman; John Banks, coal passer; Jas Kenelty, coal passer; Evers, coal passer, & Richd Gilbert, colored, engineer's messman.]

Mrd: on Jul 23, at Astoria, Oregon Territory, by Rev Dr McCarty, Lt Wm T Welcker, U S Army, to Miss Katy Adair, daughter of Gen John Adair.

Geo W Dorrance, formerly one of the principals of the Central Academy, has opened a Select School for Boys at 361 C st, between 4½ & 6th sts. Limited to 25.

WED OCT 7, 1857

Geo E Parmelee, a merchant doing business at 25 Murray st, N Y, was arrested on Wed, charged with having during the past 2 years, robbed the store of Messrs H E Dibblee & Co, occupying the first floor of the same bldg, of silks, satins, & other costly goods to the aggregate value of $30,000. Mr Parmelee confessed & said he always performed his work on Sunday & got rid of his plunder before the store was opened on the following morning. He used a rope ladder to descend from his own store to that of Dibblee & Co.

Capt D J Sutherland, the Assist Quartermaster of the Marine Corps, has been appointed Quartermaster, vice Lindsay, deceased. Capt Wm A T Maddox, of the corps, has been appointed Assist Quartermaster, to fill the vacancy caused by the promotion of Capt Sutherland.

Orphan's Court Sale: by order of the administrators of the late Maj Wm B Scott, deceased: sale on Oct 14, at the farm near Tenallytown, the personal effects thereon: 2 good working horses, 2 horse wagon & harness; market wagon & harness; horse cart & gearing; ploughs, cultivators, harrows, & tools. –Barnard & Buckey, aucts

John B Robertson, cashier of the Eagle Bank, has been indicted at Rochester, by the grand jury, for attempting to destroy the life of his wife by poison. Rumor says that of 21 jurors only 2 were opposed to a bill. Robertson gave bail on Sat morning.

The venerable Rembrandt Peale, of Phil, now in his 80th year, is sojourning near Boston. This distinguished artist is the only painter now living to whom Washington sat for his portrait. Mr Peale's first visit to Europe was made in 1809, when he painted Thorwaldsen.

Mr Richd Yeadon, a distinguished citizen of South Carolina, passed on to the South this week with the remains of the late Hugh Swinton Legare, which are to be deposited in *Magnolia Cemetery*, near Charleston. In 1843 Mr Legare was the Atty Gen of the U S, during the administration of Mr Tyler, & visited Boston in company with the Pres, in order to take part in the celebration of the anniversary of the battle of Bunker Hill. On the morning of the anniversary, Jun 17th, he was attacked by disease, & unable to take part in the ceremonies. He died on Jun 20th & was buried in *Mount Auburn Cemetery*. –Richmond Dispatch

Household & kitchen furniture at auction on Oct 8, at the residence of Mr Forrest, Va ave & 8th st, near the Navy Yard. -A Green auct

We have received intelligence by a late European steamer of the death of Auguste Comte. France has lost one of her most remarkable men & the world one of the acutest intellects. He was at one time a professor of mathematics in the Ecole Politecnique of Paris. He lived a very secluded life, & died in his 60th year.

Last Wed 4 men put out from Wilder's Point, on Lake Canandaigua, in a light skiff, for the purpose of boarding a steamer. The skiff capsized in about 15 feet of water, & all drowned. They were supposed to be Mr Wager, an aged clergyman, & Messrs Perryman, Green, & Wood.

THU OCT 8, 1857
Public auction, by authority of deed of trust, executed by Thos H Havenner & Mary Cornelia, his wife, recorded in Calhoun Co, Va. Sale at the auction house of Jas C McGuire, in Wash City, on Nov 10 next, of 1,000 acres of land in Calhoun Co, Va, on the west fork of Little Kanawha river, it being a moiety of the tract of land conveyed by Norval Wilson & Cornelia S Wilson, his wife, to Thos H Havenner & Edmund H Wilson, by deed dated Oct 4, 1852, recorded in Gilmer Co, Va. The title to this land is believed to be indisputable. –S S Baxter, trustee -Jas C McGuire, auct

<u>Candidates admitted to the Naval Academy, having passed the preliminary examinations for admission, & have received appointments as Acting Midshipmen in the Navy:</u>

Roswell E Morey, Maine
Geo Albert Sleeper, Maine
Odillon B Hobbs, N H
Frank Augustus Platt, Vt
Jas Edgar Fisk, Vt
Fra's J Higginson, Mass
Ochran H Howard, Mass
Geo P Ryan, Mass
Alfred Titus Snell, Mas
John F Churchill, Mass
Geo Henry Conklin, Mass
Nathl W Thomas, Mass
Lym'n P Hempstead, Conn
Edgar C Merriman, N Y
Wm Piercy Lee, N Y
Morgan Lewis Ogden, N Y
Douglas Lodge, N Y
Wm Thos Sampson, N Y
Henry C Tallman, N Y
Thos P Farrington, N Y
Chas Edmund McKay, N Y
Wm Barker Cushing, N Y
Lloyd Phoenix, N Y
Patton Jones Yorke, N J
Robt Boggs, N J
Chas Polhemus, N J
Rufus King Duer, N J
Eugene B Sturgeon, Pa
Wm Fra's Stewart, Pa
Chas Gordon Foster, Pa
John McFarland, Pa
Chas J Smyser, Pa
John Weidman, Pa
John F McGlensey, Pa
Henry F Picking, Pa
Saml Swift, Pa
Francis Smith, Pa
John W Haverstick, Pa

Jas P Robertson, Pa
Geo Paine Lord, Del
Frederic Rogers, Md
Franck Munroe, Md
Robt L Meade, D C
Albert G Hudgins, Va
John Kerr Connally, N C
Thos L Moore, N C
Theodore Sturdivant, N C
Benj Franklin Perry, S C
Thos H Frierson, Geo
Thos Wm Hooper, Geo
Richd F Armstrong, Geo
Clifford B Walker, Geo
Jos David Wilson, Fla
Andrew Jeff'n Clark, Ala
Napoleon J Smith, Ala
Sardine G Strong, Ala
Crawford M Jackson, Ala
Chas S Keeney, Miss
Thos Quitman Munce, Miss
Wm Anderson Hicks, Miss
Wm Van Comstock, La
Jno Feeney Holden, Tenn
Chas Dunlap Cooney, Tenn
Jas Fullerton Fuller, Ky
Henry Withers, Ky
John Henry Rowland, Ky
Danl Talbott, jr, Ky
Geo Stidger Lester, Ohio
Howard Grimes, Ohio
Adolphus Dexter, Ohio
Tecumseh Steece, Ohio
Emery Malin, Ohio
Thos Corwin Bowen, Ohio
Christopher H Orth, Ohio
Robt L McKinley, Ohio
John Nune, Indiana
Wm Henry Marsh, Ill
Louis Kempff, Ill
Jas D Graham, Ill
Hiram McVeigh, Mo
Sylvanus Backus, Mich
Wm B Martin, Mich
Geo Wash Hayward, Wis
Horace E Mullen, Kansas
B J Cromwell, Neb

Jas Copeland, was convicted & sentenced to death after 10 years' imprisonment, a couple days ago at Augusta, Miss. He was charged with killing Jas A Harvey, & has been found guilty twice before by the juries of the country; yet, by resorting to the technicalities of the law, he has been enabled to gain trial after trial to the present time. He is ordered to be executed-hung, on Oct 30th.

Law Partnership: Saml Chilton & A B Magruder, late of Va, will practice in the Courts of Wash City, the Court of Claims, & the U S Supreme Court.

By virtue of 2 executions issued by Jas Cull, a Justice of the Peace for Wash Co, D C, at the suit of Saml R Turner, against the goods & chattels of Richd Brooks, to me directed, I have seized & taken in execution all the right, title, & interest of said Richd Brooks in & to one frame dwlg-house, on a part of lot 11 in square 1,000, on 11th st: public auction of this house, on the premises, on Oct 15, 1857.
-H R Maryman, constable

Mrd: on Thu last, in Wash City, by Rev Mr Samson, Mr John H Holtzclaw, of Fauquier Co, Va, to Miss Eliz Sinclair, of Wash City.

Mrd: on Oct 6, in Wash City, by Rev John Lanahan, Chas H Lane to Sue Ellen, daughter of the late Richd Dement, of Wash City.

Mayor's Office. Gtwn, D C, Sep 29, 1857. The subscriber will receive sealed written proposals until Oct 10 next, for furnishing about 60 cords of oak wood, in such quantities as may be required from time to time during the ensuing winter, for the use of the destitute residents of the town. –Richd R Crawford, Mayor

FRI OCT 9, 1857
Trustee's sale of very valuable improved property: by deed of trust to me, from Benj E Green, dated Sep 2, 1856, recorded in the land records of Wash Co, in Liber J A S No 121, at folios 465, I shall sell, on the premises, on Nov 2 next, parts of lots 12 & 13 in square 729; being that portion of the said lots upon which the dwlg-houses stand numbered 2 & 3 Carroll Place, on Capitol Hill. –Wm B Webb, Trustee -Jas C McGuire, auct [This property was sold on Dec 17, 1855, & the purchaser at such sale failed to comply with the terms of the sale. –Johnson Hellen, Jas Adams, trustees]]

Appointments by the President:
Jas M Cutts, 2nd Comptroller of the Treasury.
Thos Crockett, Collector at Yorktown, Va.
Dr Thos P Bagwell, Surveyor at Accomac.
Zachary Herndon, Surveyor at Velasco, Texas.
Thos Ledwith, Collector at Jacksonville, Fla.

The barque **Jerome Knight**, of Boston, foundered at sea on Sep 23. Capt Perkins, his wife, & 2 children, one of them an infant of 9 weeks, & 7 of the crew, were 5 days lashed to the rigging & on the wreck, without food or water, much of the time suffering horribly. They were all saved & taken to N Y by the brig **Alteevelta**.

Col Ichabod B Crane, 1st Artl, died at Port Richmond, Staten Island, N Y, on Oct 5, of paralysis.

Mrd: on Oct 6, at Brooklyn, N Y, by Rev Geo Jones, U S N, Thos Bergden, of Wash, D C, to Laura, daughter of Gold S Silliman, of Brooklyn.

Died: on Oct 8, of pulmonary consumption, John P Stallings, in his 41st year. His funeral will be from his late residence, 440 F st, near 6th, today at 3 o'clock P M.

Died: on Sep 30, at Jacksonville, Fla, Mrs Eliz Drew, wife of the late Solomon Drew, a native of Cornwall, England, but for the last 37 years a resident of Wash City, aged 72 years.

The vacant Collectorship at Gtwn has been supplied by the appointment of Mr Jno McHenry Hollingsworth, late Assist Collector.

Hon Louis McLane died on Wed, at his residence in Balt, in his 72nd year. He was the son of Allan McLane, a distinguished ofcr in the Revolutionary war, & was born in the village of Smyrna, Kent Co, Delaware, on May 28, 1794. In 1798, at age only 14 years, he served with great credit as a midshipman on board the frig **Philadelphia**, then on her first cruise, & under the command of Stephen Decatur, the father of Cmdor Decatur. In 1801, yielding to the desire of his family, he left the navy. He completed his education at Newark College, in his native State; & began to study law, in 1804, under Jas A Bayard, of Delaware. He was admitted to the bar in 1807. In the war of 1812 he was a volunteer in a company commanded by Caesar A Rodney, who had been the U S Atty Genr'l under Mr Jefferson, & marched with the company to the relief of Balt when it was threatened by the British. He was elected in 1816 to the House of Reps from Delaware & remained a member of that body until 1827, when he was chosen by the Legislature a U S Senator. He was president of the Balt & Ohio Railroad Co, &, removing to this State, discharged the duties of this office until 1847. In 1850 he resided in Cecil Co, Md. –Balt Sun

SAT OCT 10, 1857

American minister in France: Judge Mason is alleged to have committed the impropriety of putting his arm upon the chair of the Empress. It is unquestionably false. For some reason or other Judge Mason, during his residence in France, has been visited with an unusual share of misrepresentation & abuse. –N Y Times

Promotions in the Marine Corps. W L Shuttleworth to be captain, vice Maddox promoted. John L Broome to be 1st lt, vice Shuttleworth promoted.

Mr Edw Shaw, of Conn, has been appointed to be an assistant examiner in the Patent Ofc, salary $1,600 per annum.

The illustrious Alex'r Von Humboldt celebrated his 82nd birthday on Sep 14. A number of deputations called upon him to offer him their congratulations.

Trustee's sale of valuable country garden land: by deed of trust from Michl Byrnes, dated Nov 16, 1855, recorded in Liber J A S 117, folios 216, of the land records for Wash Co, D C: public sale on the premises, on Oct 26, 1857, of the south half of lot 13, in plat of resurvey made by Lewis Carbery, formerly known as *Bayley's purchase*, containing 26 acres & 14 perches, more or less. The said tract is about a mile beyond Benning's bridge, on the road to Marlboro, improved by a good frame dwlg, market garden, & orchard of young fruit trees. –Richd H Clarke, Danl Ratcliffe, trustees -A Green auct

For sale, a good cook, a slave for life. Apply to W A Waugh, at the Jail.

By an order of distrain for house rent due to Wm A Bradley by Danl Wells, I will expose at public sale on the Analostan Island, opposite Gtwn, in Wash Co, D C, on Oct 21, 1857, for cash, the goods, chattels, & crops of said Danl Wells.
–H R Maryman, constable

Signor Blitz & his learned Canary Birds will give a pleasant entertainment this afternoon at the Odd Fellows' Hall, commencing at 3½ o'clock.

When the aged are stricken down in death we are apt to regard the event as the common lot of humanity. But when those in the prime of intellect & attractiveness bow down, we are more struck with awe & emotion. In the recent death of Miss Eliza Watterston these sentiments have been emphatically manifested. She was an affectionate daughter, a fond sister, a kind neighbor, & a devoted friend. She was ever ready to pour forth a song on her favorite instruments for the amusement of family & friends. For many a long month she had borne with patience the privations of ill health. She departed at the morn of twilight of a Sabbath like an infant in sleep. –A [Death notice in Sep 29th newspaper. Miss Warrenton died on Sep 27th.]

Mrd: on Oct 6, by Rev Dr Spotswood, Chas H Hammond, of Balt, Md, to Julia, daughter of the late Chancellor Johns, of Newcastle, Del.

Mrd: on Oct 7, in N Y, at the Church of the Ascension, by Rev Dr Bedell, Wm Brisbane, of S C, to Sarah, daughter of Wm Hogan, of N Y.

Mrd: on Oct 6, at **Pleasant Grove**, near Hagerstown, by Rev Mr Heck, John C Noerr, of Wash City, to Malinda M, daughter of Geo Beard, of the former place.

Died: on Oct 9, in Wash City, after a lingering illness, Mrs Mgt Ferriss, aged 63 years. Her funeral will be tomorrow at 4 o'clock, from her late residence, F st.

Died: on Oct 8, in Wash City, after a protracted illness, Mrs Eliz Campbell, wife of P Campbell, in her 43rd year. Her funeral will take place from the residence of her husband, on F, between 13th & 14th sts, this afternoon at 3 o'clock.

MON OCT 12, 1857
Two little boys, Geo Willard, aged 7 years, & Francis Barnaby, aged 2½, have been missing from their home, Court & Atlantic sts, Brooklyn, since Wed noon. They were not discovered until Sat, when they were found lying dead under a pile of mattresses in the rear of an upholstery store. It is supposed that they climbed on the top of the pile of mattresses, which toppled over, burying them under it.

A large number of citizens of Guilford Co, N C, met on Sep 18 last, to institute a plan to erect a suitable monument to the memory of Gen Nathl Greene.

It becomes our painful duty to announce the decease of the venerable Geo Washington Parke Custis, the last of the members of the family of Washington. Mr Custis died at Arlington, near Wash City, after a brief illness, on Oct 10th, in his 77th year. Born amid the great events of the Revolution, by the death of his father, [Col Custis, of the army, & a son of Mrs Washington by a former marriage,] which occurred near the close of the war, he found his home during childhood & youth at **Mount Vernon**, where his manners were formed after the noblest models. He pursued his classical studies at Princeton, &, when deprived by death of his great guide & father, [& soon after of his revered grandmother,] he devoted himself to literary & agricultural pursuits on his ample estate of ***Arlington***, the gift, by will, of that illustrious man. He was early united in marriage to Miss Mary Lee Fitzhugh, of Va, a lady of unsurpassed excellence in all the relations of life, & whose irreparable loss, 3 years ago, he continued with sorrow & affectionate admiration, to his final day, profoundly to deplore. One daughter, [Mrs Lee, wife of Col Robt Lee, of the army,] & several grandchildren survive him. Long a believer in the great truths of Divine Revelation, Mr Custis turned to these for consolation in his last days, & died in communion with the Protestant Episcopal Church.

The steamer **Niagara**, at Boston, when off Boston Light, on Oct 8, struck the schnr **Harriet Maria**, from Boston for New Orleans, & sunk her. The latter had 18 passeners on board, one of whom, Danl Higgins, of New Orleans, was killed in the collision. The remainder were taken on board the **Niagara**.

The Kingston [Jamaica] Dispatch of Aug 24 contains an account of the destruction of the British schnr **Endeavor**, Capt Anthony Durant, & the murder of the greater portion of her crew by Indians. The vessel arrived off the Indian coast on Jul 8, & anchored at Bay Honna, where the 3 Indians on board belonged. The next morning about 15 Indians boarded & lined the gangway. Not imagining any danger, the captain was speaking to one of the seamen, when some 7 of the Indians simultaneously drew their knives & assassinated him; killed the cook; in the gallery, & attempted to murder the mate, Mr Maduro, who jumped overboard, & made for the shore, with other crew members. Capt Durant was a trader to the Spanish Main for upwards of 30 years, & was so intimate with the natives that he had never apprehended danger.

Died: on Oct 10, at ***Arlington House***, Va, Geo Washington Parke Custis, in his 77th year. His funeral will be on Tue next at Arlington, at 12 o'clock.

Died: on Oct 11, Willard T Drake, in his 23rd years. His funeral is today at 3 o'clock, from the residence of his father, Mr Willard Drake, 11th st, between E & F.

Fall & Winter Millinery: Mrs L Allen, 305 Pa ave, between 9th & 10th sts. [Ad]

Wash City Ordinance: 1-Act for the relief of Chas F McCarthy, assignee of Richd M Harrison: that the sum of $6.75 be refunded, the amount of taxes erroneously paid on 3 slaves by R M Harrison; said slaves were emancipated by said Harrison in Nov last. Approved, Oct 8, 1857

Jas Madison Cutts has been appointed Second Comptroller of the Treasury. He has been employed in the office for many years. This ofc was created on Mar 3, 1817. The first appointment under the act, by Pres Monroe, was that of Hon Richd Cutts, of Maine, father of the present incumbent, who had been a Rep in Congress for many years. Though a large ship-owner, he voted in Congress for the restrictive measures which precede the war, & for the war itself, although this policy not only impaired, but almost destroyed his private fortune. He was removed by Pres Jackson, 1829, to make room for Hon Isaac Hill, of N H, who was rejected by the Senate. The office has since been successively held by Jas B Thornton, Albion K Parris, Hiland Hall, Ed J Phelps, & John M Brodhead. –A B

It appears that the late John E Thayer, of Boston, in addition to his bequest of $50,000 to Harvard College, left $10,000 to his friend, Rev Geo Putnam, of Roxbury; $5,000 to Rev Rufus Ellis, of the First Church in Boston, where the legator worshipped, & $1,000 a year to Dr Jas Jackson as long as he lives, & to be continued to his wife if she survives him. [Oct 17th newspaper: Mr Thayer also leaves $5,000 to Mrs Kebler, his cousin; $2,000 to Miss Bebson; to Rev N L Frothingham, a valuable piece of silver plate; $5,000 to Rufus Ellis; $30,000 in trust, the income to inure to the testator's sister, Mrs Marston, & her children; $39,000 in trust, the income to inure to his brother, Rev Christopher T Thayer; $50,000 in trust, the income to inure to the testator's mother & unmarried sister. To his wife $500,000 is left in trust, with the right of disposing of $100,000 by her will. To Dr Jas Jackson, $1,000 per annum is left as long as he shall live, & the same to his wife if she shall outlive him. The balance of his estate goes to his son. The whole of it is valued at $3,000,000.]

Lumber! Lumber! Lumber! F Wheatly, Yard 37 Water st, Gtwn. [Ad]

TUE OCT 13, 1857
Boots, Shoes, & Gaiters, will be sold at auction, at the store of W Clendenin, 516 7th st, on Oct 15. The entire stock. -A Green auct

Dr Chase, dentist, & Mr Hill, stage coachman, exchanged pistol shots & used knives in a street rencontre in Raymond day before yesterday, which resulted in the death of Mr Hill. Dr Chase, who was shot through the knee & & neck, was supposed to be dying. An affair of others caused the action. –Vicksburg Sentinel, Oct 1.

Mrd: on Sep 26, at **Fort Gibson**, Col Wm H Garrett, U S agent for the Creek tribe of Indians, to Miss Mary, daughter of Col Jas Logan, of Scott Co, Ark.

A gentleman of Va, has sent us a letter addressed in 1778, by Richd Henry Lee to his sister, Mrs Hannah Corbin, of Richmond, Va, which has never been previously published. It was written from Chantilly, Westmoreland Co, Va, the country seat & residence of the illustrious Revolutionary statesmen, & appears to have been in reply to a communication from his sister in which she had suggested or enforced the political right of Widows, either to exemption from taxation or to a share in the election of the people's reps.

+-Reply:
Chantilly, Mar 17, 1778. My Dear Sister: I am illy able by letter to give you the satisfaction I could wish on the several subjects of your letter. I should have no doubt about giving you perfect content in a few hours' conversation.
-Richd Henry Lee P S: Dr Steptoe & myself returned last night from a 10 days' confinement at *Belleview*, where our Brother [MS, defaced]   very great danger of losing his life...[MS. Defaced]. I have the pleasure to inform you ... [MS defaced.].....danger. R H L

Coroner Perry held an inquest at N Y on Thu on the body of Ellen Powers, a child, who died from the effects of morphine. The druggist put up the wrong cough mixture that the physician had prescribed, in mixing Magendie's solution of morphine for U S solution of sulphate of morphine.

The Rockingham Register says that our townsman, Jos H Shue, raised a pumpkin this season which weighed 103 pounds. Mr Jacob Shank, living near Harrisonburg, brought us a pumpkin which weighed 123½ pounds.

The undersigned, special com'rs of the Circuit Court of Stafford, will offer for sale, at public auction, on Nov 10 next, the real estate, the plate, & household & kitchen furniture belonging to the estate of the late Judge John Coalter. This estate, the residence of the late Judge Coalter, known as *Chatham*, contains about 712 acres, on the Rappahannock river, immediately opposite the town of Fredericksburg; the dwlg is of brick & in good repair, & has 10 spacious rooms; there are all also all necessary out-houses, farm bldgs, & a valuable grist mill, withing a quarter of a mile of the town, on this estate. Refer to Messrs Fitzhugh & Little, attys-at-law, of Fredericksburg, Va. –John R Bryan, H B Tomlin

Valuable mining property in Buckingham Co, Va, for sale at public auction: by decree of the Circuit Court of Buckingham, in the case of Dueson & others against the Buckingham Iron Manufaturing Co & others: public auction, in New Canton, Buckingham Co, on Dec 15 next: contains about 3,500 acres. Mr David J Woodfin, who resides in New Canton will show the property. Inquiries addressed either to Edw W Sims or the undersigned at Ca Ira, Cumberland, will be promptly answered.
–Geo H Matthews, com'r

Book & Job Printing. Lemuel Towers has purchased the interest of the late John T Towers in the Book & Job Printing establishment lately conducted by John T & Lemuel Towers, 6th & La ave.

Three days later from Europe: N Y, Oct 12. The Collins steamer **Atlantic**, from Liverpool on Sep 30th, has arrived. She has 120 passengers, including Chas S Spence, bearer of the ratified commercial treaty with Persia; F Schroeder, late Minister to Sweden; & W R Osborn, Pres of the Illinois Central Railroad.
2-An English officer reports that he saw Nena Sahib & his family swamped in a boat on the Ganges & all drowned.

WED OCT 14, 1857
Sale in the country of horses, cattle, wagons, & implements: on Oct 16, at the farm of Mr Curtis, [formerly McKelden's,] on the Rockville road, about 3 miles above Gtwn. We will sell the entire personal effects. –Barnard & Buckey, aucts

Stock of a wholesale & retail grocery at auction, on Oct 19, at the store of Mr W S Jones, on Water st, Gtwn, the entire stock & fixtures. –W S Jones
-Barnard & Buckey, aucts

A private letter, dated London, Sep 25, tells of the death of old Mr Sinclair. He has been failing with gout for a long time, & just lasted long enough to know & rejoice at his daughter's success on the London boards. He died on the 22nd. He was 75 years old, & died tranquilly.

The funeral of the late Geo Washington Parke Custis took place yesterday at *Arlington*. Besides the family & their particular friends, officers of the army & navy, distinguished gentlemen of the legal profession, residents of Wash, Gtwn, & Alexandria, as well as the neighbors of the deceased for many miles around thronged the parlors & hall. The Association of the Survivors of the War of 1812 of D C, a delegtion of the Jamestown Society of D C, field & staff officers of the volunteer regt, & the Wash Light Infantry, & a delegation of the officers of the Pres' Mounted Guard, traveled a distance of 6 miles to unite in the solemn testimonials of respect. The pall-bearers appointed were Wm W Seaton, Philip R Fendall, Cassius F Lee, Bushrod W Hunter, Henry Daingerfield, & Wm B Randolph. The religious services were conducted by Rev Dr Dana, of Christ Church, Alexandria, according to the usages of the Protestant Episcopal Church. The interment took place in a beautiful grove a short distance from the mansion.

Hon Wm Pitt Preble died on Oct 11th, at his residence in Portland, Maine, after only 3 days' illness. He was about 74 years of age. -Union

$100 reward on the detection & conviction of the incendiary who fired 2 separate stacks of grain on the lot attached to my Printing ofc on Sat last. –C Wendell

Millinery & Fancy Goods, Mrs J G Robinson, 439 7th st, between G & H sts. [Ad]

Mrd: on Oct 5, by Rev Wm B Edwards, of Balt, Mr John A Edwards, son of the officiating Clergyman, to Miss Rosa E Edwards, daughter of Enoch Edwards, all of King Geo Co, Va.

Died: on Oct 12, Mrs Mary Knott, wife of J Harrison Knott, aged 46 years. Her funeral will be this afternoon at 3 o'clock, from her late residence, 525 G st, & 15th.

Otto Scior. His friends & acquaintances are requested to attend his funeral this afternoon at 2 o'clock, from his residence, 264 South L st, between 3rd & 4th sts.

N Y, Oct 18. Today up to 2 o'clock, 15 city banks had suspended. Wall st was crowded with an anxious mass of people. The steps of all the banks were blocked up by persons forcing their way into the banks. At the American Exchange Bank David Leavitt addressed the crowd, assuring them that the bank would pay all to the last dollar. The run on the Brooklyn Savings Bank was renewed today, with less vigor than yesterday. The bank paid promptly.

Boston, Oct 13. 1-Messrs Geo T & W P Lyman, china merchants, have suspended. 2-Francis Skinner & Co, the largest dry goods & commission merchants, have suspended.

Petersburg, Va, Oct 13. Thos H Hardenburg, Cashier of the Branch Bank of Cape Fear at Washington, N C, committed suicide yesterday by shooting himself. He leaves a large family & is universally respected. There is no cause assigned. [Oct 19th newspaper: T H Hardinburg, cashier of the branch of the Bank of Cape Fear at Wash, N C, committed suicide by blowing out his brains with a pistol during the night of Oct 10th. It is reported that a love affair was the exciting cause.]

Orphans Court of Wash Co, D C. Letters testamentary on the personal estate of Wm Hunt, late of Wash Co, deceased. –Sarah A Hunt, excx

THU OCT 15, 1857
Household & kitchen furniture at auction on: Oct 17, belonging to the estate of the late Wm Bigly; also an excellent Family Carriage, suitable for 1 or 2 horses.
-T C Donn, Thos J Fisher, trustee -Jas C McGuire, auct

Postmaster Genr'l Hon A V Brown left Wash yesterday for a short visit to N Y. He is expected to return in about a week. During his absence Horatio King will discharge the duties of his position as Acting Postmaster Genr'l.

Gen Henderson, of the Marine Corps, accompanied by his son, D Henderson, as his aid-de-camp, passed through this city yesterday on their way to Washington. Both the father & the son have done good service to the country, the former in the war of 1812 & the latter in the Mexican war. –Phil Inquirer

Dentistry: Dr Wm P McConnell, continues the practice of his profession. Ofc at his residence, south side of N Y ave, between 8th & 9th sts.

I have an excellent house which I will sell, part check on Pairo & Nourse, remainder in Virginia money. –Arthur W Fletcher, 430 F st, between 6th & 7th sts.

R C Stevens, dealer in French Millinery & Fancy Goods, removed to 336 Pa ave, between 9th & 10th sts. [Ad]

Orphans Court of Wash Co, D C. Letters testamentary on the personal estate of G F Lindsay, late of the U S Marine Corps, deceased. –Margaret F Lindsay, excx

Mrd: at Newport, R I, by Very Rev Dr O'Reilly, & afterwards at Emanuel Church, by Rev Mr Brewer, Ancelis Edouard de Vaughrigneuse, of the French Legation, to Sarah Morris, only daughter of the late Aquila G Stout, of N Y C. [No marriage date given-current item.]

Mrd: on Oct 13, by Rev Wm H Chapman, Wm Biddle to Miss Rebecca J Richardson, all of Wash City.

Riot in Balt, Oct 11. The police have captured a quantity of muskets at Jackson Hall. Police officer Jordan was killed, & others were wounded. [Oct 16th newspaper: Sgt Jourdan was shot & expired in a few minutes. Police officer Thomas received a shot in the left hand & may have to have 2 fingers amputated. A young man, Jos Emmert, was shot in the left thigh, just above the knee, & amputation of the limb is thought to be necessary. Arrested: John Fossitt, John Ryan, Michl Dougherty, John Bruns, Jas Murray, Geo Bradley, Michl Cox, Michl J Grady, John Carrigan, Patrick Fitzpatrick, & a man named McFarland. John Burns was arrested on the charge of attempting to shoot officer Thos Dennison from a window of Jackson Hall. McFarland was arrested on the charge of attempting to shoot police officer Wm Pindel. The others were held without bail for the killing of Sgt Jourdan.]

FRI OCT 16, 1857
Accident at Leeds, Northampton, Pa, last Thu. Mr Alex'r Berry & his wife were sitting at a table while he was at work over a loaded pistol, when it suddenly exploded, sending the ball through the right breast of Mrs Berry to the shoulder blade, where it lodged. She was living at last accounts, though but little hope was entertained of her recovery.

The trial of John Fellinger, an aged German, charged with burglary in the 1st degree, was concluded in N Y on Fri, the jury rendering a verdict of guilty. He was sentenced to imprisonment in the State prison at hard labor for the term of his natural life.

Ice Cream & Water Ices, at $1.50 per gallon, at the Phil Ice Cream Depot, corner 12th & F sts, Wash. –J Fussell

$100 reward for runaway negro man Saml Williams, about 54 years of age. His wife belongs to Mr Clement D Hill, of PG Co. –Robt W W Bowie, living near Buena Vista Post Ofc, PG Co, Md.

On Tue evening, a young man, Jacob Miexell, son of Jacob Miexell, former magistrate of the 12th Ward, was accidentally shot by falling upon his own pistol whilst running along Mulberry st to a fire which prevailed at the time. The ball entered the front part of the right thigh, & embedded itself in the bone. He was removed to his home, where he was attended by Dr Knight, who took the limb off above the wound.

Mrd: on Oct 13, in the Presbyterian Church, Charlestown, Jefferson Co, Va, by Rev Septimus Tustin, D D, Wm H Deitz, of Wash City, to Mary, daughter of John Reed, of the former place.

Mrd: on Oct 14, in Balt, by Rev Mr Williams, Henry Thorn, of Wash, to Marion Stockdale, of Balt.

Died: on Oct 14, in Wash City, after a long & severe illness, Mrs Ephy Price, in her 57th year. Her funeral will take place at her late residence, on north B st, between 3rd & 4th sts, this afternoon, at 2 o'clock.

Died: on Oct 11, at Augusta, Ga, Joseph P Brenner, aged 4 years & 11 months, son of John A & Catherine Brenner.

SAT OCT 17, 1857
Col Nicholas Goldsborough, a prominent citizen of Talbot Co, Md, died last week.

At a special term of the Monmouth Court, N J, Jas P Donnelly was sentenced to be hung on Jan 8 next, for the murder of Albert S Moses, at the Sea-view House, Highlands, N J. The prisoner addressed the Court in an emphatic & eloquent manner, asseverating his innocence.

Dr W C Williams, of Manchester, who lost $10,000 by the Ohio Life & Trust Co, hung himself in a barn on Oct 6th.

The Calais Advertiser says that a man named John Frazer, who resides on the Old Ridge, a few miles out of St Stephen, N B, had both of his eyes destroyed, & one of his hands blown off, while blasting rocks in St Stephen, on Thursday. He is not expected to live.

We have received by the Northern Light a full list of the passengers who were on board the lost steamship **Central America**, including those comprised in the supplementary way-bill & those taken on board at Aspinwall.

First Cabin:
Judge Manson
F S Hawley, wife, & 2 infants, nurse & servant
Mrs J McKim Bowley & 2 infants
Mrs Lockwood, daughter, & 2 children
Mrs B Thayer, child, infant, & servant
Mrs Pahud, 2 children & infant
J N Van Hagan, wife & infant
A B Smith, wife, child, & 3 infants
Dr J Travis, wife, & 2 infants
Albert Priest
Mr Farmer
A J Easton & wife
Wm McNeil & wife
Capt F W Badger & wife
Mrs F A Thomas
E Kirshfield
M Lasiski
G G Ridgway
Peter Brown
Wm Birch & wife
T O'Neil
Jabez Howes
J A Foster
N Montgomery
S F Parker
Mrs Eliza Carothers
Saml S Shreve
J V Dobbin
Mrs Eliz Smith
J Pell, wife & 2 infants
C A Low
Second Cabin:
D B Raassi
Chas Blum
D Levick

G C Farnhjam
S D Dement
H H Childs
M White
F Jones & servant
Jas E Birch
F A Bokee
Dr O Harney
A J Alston
N Sawyer
Chas Gibb
D Yanney
C Moore
A Doud
S Aker
Theodore Paine
H D Beach
E M Williams
Mr Saroni
Mrs Dr Kittridge
Chas A Vose
R T Brown

L Fallon, daughter & infant
G N Gaul
M Gitterman

Robt Edmann
J F Reed
J W Tompkins
Isaac N Tompkins
Geo Manott
S G Wheelwright
E Strauss
P Holler
L Dorsey
J O Stevens
G W Hutchinson
Steerage:
B Segur, wife, & infant
Mrs E O'Conner & son
G Hahn, wife & son
S B Swan, wife & infant
W B Van Natter
E Ford
A W Eastman
F Henry
L A Follins
A P Manlove
W P Deshond
J Vanhorn
C Simon
T Sigel
G Narramore
D H C Chapman
J Boynton
C McCormick
P Moran
D Moran
J Morris
B Sheldon
W Young
W Delyan
J McLelland
R C Farnham
J Keer
J H Foster
P Kron
Mr McGrenary
C Berks
J Callakran

J C Clow
Peter McChardy
J H Adams
H B Kent
Mr Barchman
Geo Lee
J Bassford
J W Mullen
Noble Fish
R Richman
J N Munger

B L Smith
J Schmendmann
A Stakl
H M Fish
J Mangold
H Stinchfield
W Newman
J Chapman
Mr Spaulding
E Wells
T Willett
Mr Maynard
J C Mitchell
T Hicks
H Runnell
E Hibs
R Short
H Frank
C Zimmerlin
W Falconer
D D Smith
H Hutchinson
W Stevens
R Reese
R Wilton
D H Ridley
H A Berry
F G Van Waldheim
Mr Bactendzorff
Mrs Bull
T Ryan
B Loring

J Sawin	N P Sanborn
S Christman	W N Kendrick
W S Eaton	W Bell
J H Ragland	W Weige
F Simmons	W Lee
W R Fenner	W Gorley
M I Montaguon	W Chase
R J White	D Buckway
D Willett	G Ceyello
J Schuber	F Festu
T R Hughes	D Casta
H Sibbot	L Daley
A Closer	B W Bagwill
L Miller	A Moseley
W G Berry	D Young
J Bround	B Casey
P Lean	J M Casey
Mr Pullen	A Crist
Mr Thomas	L Gushee
Mr Guild	E Crider
Mr Johnson	B Palmer
Mr Steward	S B Murch
Thos R Blanton	W Geary
Mr Blanton	C Gilkey
Mr Querpon	W J Reese
H H Bedell	J Quencer
P Pomery	G Simon
M D Spaulding	J Woodworth
V Mitchell	C Kilburn
Mr Haag	J George
John Harris	D Howe
R Hodge	J Chort
C McGugan	W Ede
R Hutchinson	L Davis
T Ravenna	D Beaver
R E Roberts	R L Garrison
W Van Reed	R H Horn
E Spohn	J N Horn
W Flangan	B P Colt
S Caldwell	S L Gahn
John P Chaillan	H Hoadley
H Frank	H Beashler
F Ash	W C Owings
A Mack	C H Tuck

Chas Lagan
H Hart
Mr Villat
Mr Fletcher
Mr Shaw
Mr Morse
F A Wells
E Meron
M Murphy
J Stevens
E Luckeman
M Crimins
P Ball
F Mathy
H Hallard
J Rodwell & wife
G Lebse
P S Smith
J Powell
W Burns
J E Jones
E F Jones
H F Hoadley
J H Strohm
R P Lugden
Mr Danberg
J Denman
G Bruyn
O McGuire
John O'Conner
A Strueve
R Burdick
E Condos
J F Hoagland
Danl Mahoney
B M Lee
J N Harrell
D Clark
B A Anderson
E Wiley
J H Blackman
Mr Carter
J Wiley
S Richards

Jas Whalan
F Barr
S Durett
N Barr
J Leech
Jas Sullivan
W Browning
Mrs Shaw
H W Crohn
H Adams
R Reed
J Stetson
J Tanner
J D Horne
R Wade
A F Crowen
I Wood
J Emond
L Murray
F Murray
A Thebergo
G Pope
H Hastings
J Kubbe
J Kius/Klus
W Prohert
N Lepper
L M Young
E H Burt
M L McCloy
P Finnigan
G W Brainard
A Greenlee
S Look
P S Look
C Reed
P Butler
J W Cross
G D Sheppard
H D Porter
T Barber
E Kirk
D Fisher, Jr
J W Sanborn

J Kay	P Dugan
J L Weeks	J R Cheeney
J L Buchanan	D Keer
Mr Pool	W G Thomas
John Taylor	D W Foust
J Meyer	L A Wells
J B Wells	Chas Taylor
H G Anderson	J Christie
H H Miller	G F Goodenow
Mary Garnet	T McNash
Benj Hassey	J Lowenthal
Jas Smith	J Wallace
Mr Anthony	C Pritchard
John Kelly	M Fredt
J B Guerher	R W Ogden & bro
D Rutherford	H Y Cabell
Thos Brade & bro	D F Shipman
H Kimball	E R Merry
Mr Robertson	T B Ball
E Frederick	J W Anderson
J Rubb	R Taylor
J Forrest	A J Goastree

Tickets sold at Aspinwall:
Senor Jose Seguin, Consul-Genr'l for Peru, in N Y
Nicholas Tirado, his Secretary
Adolfo Oitagne & brother, of Peru
Senor A Richon, Consul of Belgium at Lima, partner in the house of Montane & Co, Paris, from Peru for N Y
J A Thune, for N Y
Senor Escurda, for N Y
A De la Cova, infant & nurse, for Havana
Dr Corpancho, for Havana
Santiago Olivia, for Havana
C de Lasola, for Havana
Chas Taylor, for N Y
J McCarthy, for N Y
F M B Smith, for N Y
Wm Graffus, for N Y
Capt Walter G Dyer, for N Y
J Sellamer, for N Y
Geo Ganie, for New Orleans

Steerage:

Otis Barlow, N Y	E Flinada, Havana
Jas O Neil, N Y	M Bertrand, New Orleans

Frank Carpenter
W Hemmel
Wm Piasso
Mr Olfur
A Amm

C W Griffeths
T J Morris
Wm Osborn
F Griffith
Thos Maloney

A general Court Martial is hereby appointed to meet at *Fort Leavenworth*, [K T] on Nov 1st next, for the trial of Col Edwin V Sumner, 1st Regt of Cavalry, & such other officers as may be brought before it. Detail for the Court:
Bvt Brig Gen Wm S Harney, Col 2nd Dragoons
Bvt Col C A May, Major 2nd Dragoons
Bvt Col J Monroe, Lt Col 4th Artl
Col H Wilson, 7th Infty
Col F Lee, 2nd Infty
Bvt Lt Col W Hoffman, Major 6th Infty
Bvt Lt Col H Brooks, Capt 2nd Artl
Bvt Lt Col M Burke, Major 2nd Artl
Lt Col Pictairn Morrison, 7th Infty
Lt Col G Andrews, 6th Infty
Lt Col G H Crosman, Deputy Quartermaster Gen'l
Bvt Maj G D Ramsey, Capt Ordnance Dept
Bvt Maj H J Hunt, Capt 2nd Artl
Judge Advocate-Capt W F Barry, 2nd Artl.
By order of Bvt Maj Gen P F Smith
Richd C Drum, Lt & Aid-de-Camp, Act'l Asst Adjt Gen

In 1856 Col Saml Colt, of Hartford, went to Russia, & soon after his return entered into a contract to deliver a large quantity of Minnie rifles at certain points in Russia. They were not delivered, & he imputed the fault to that Gov't, & claimed a large sum as damages. The Russian Gov't consented to submit the matter to arbitrators, to be chosen among his own countrymen, & to have the case tried at Hartford. Col Cooper, of the U S Army, Hon L P Waldo, one of the Judges of the Superior Court of Conn, & Hon Geo S Hillard, of Boston, were agreed upon as arbitrators. R A Chapman, of this city, was counsel for the Russian Gov't, & Wm W Eaton, of Hartford, was counsel for Colt. The hearing was finished on Wed last, & on Thu the arbitrators made an award against Col Colt. –Springfield Republican

On Sep 14 Mrs Hill, a widow, residing near Berlin, Ark, & a negro woman, were murdered by negroes, who then fired the house & burnt the bodies. A few days after 2 negroes confessed to having committed the deed, & were taken by the citizens & burnt alive.

Mrd: on Oct 8, at Brownville, N Y, by Rev A Oliver, Dr John C Fairfax, of D C, to Mary, daughter of the late Col E Kirby, of Brownville.

Mrd: on Oct 15, at ***Mount Arat***, the residence of Robt C ___gett, PG Co, Md, by Rev Mr Rolfe, John W Lyons, of Gtwn, D C, to Miss Amelia J Dorsett, of Anne Arundel, Co. Md. [Ink blot on first 3 letters.]

Murder in Somerset Co, Md. Mgt Stewart was brutally murdered near Princess Anne, Md, last week, by the negro John Gorvens. Her right hand, which the wretch deliberately cut from her body, has since been found near where the murder was perpetrated. The villain is in jail.

Syracuse, Oct 16. Railroad disaster: the Central railroad was thrown off the track west of his city last night, the road being washed away. Miss Brown, of Toronto, C W, was drowned; Mr Bronson, of New Britain, Conn, was badly injured, & died today.

Public sale of valuable real estate, water power, & mill site, in Alexandria Co, Va; by a decree of the Circuit Court of Alexandria Co, Va, rendered at the May term, 1857, in the suit of John Marbury, Trustee, against Geo Hill & others. Public sale on Oct 31, of a tract of land, containing 15 acres, more or less, in said county, near the Little Falls Bridge, at the junction of Pimet Rum with the Potomac river. Some bldgs have already been erected. –Francis L Smith, Com'r

Circuit Court of Wash Co, D C-in Chancery. Isaac Vandovender against Wm D Bell, Mary Bell, John W Bell, Mary V Bell, Sarah Bell, Wm P Brook, & Wm Z Bell & others. The cmplnt obtained 2 judgments against Wm D Bell, each for $3,000 & interest & costs; that he has been unable to obtain payment; that said Bell is the owner of 2 acres of land, part of ***Mount Pleasant***, on the borders of the city, with improvements thereon; that he caused the same to be conveyed to one Jas Colburn upon a secret trust for himself, & subsequently procured a conveyance from him to his [Bell's] wife & children; & the object of the bill is to set aside such deeds & have the property sold for the payment of said judgments; & because the dfndnts are not residents of this District, they are to appear on the first Monday of Mar next & answer said bill. –Jas S Morsell, Ass't Judge

MON OCT 19, 1857
Calif item: Chief Justice Hugh C Murray died at Sacramento on Oct 18 of disease of the lungs.

The Wilmington [N C] Herald records that Mr Geo Southall, of that town, on Wed, prepared a small vial of a chemical composition, of which nitric acid was the principal ingredient. This vial exploded scattering the corrosive fluid into his face, & a portion of it entered one of his eyes, instantly depriving it of sight.

Died: on Oct 17, at Newburgh, N Y, of paralysis, Mrs Amanda E, the wife of John M Gilbert, of Wash City.

Mr Lefevre, a wealthy sugar planter of Lafourche, died recently without issue, his wife having preceded him to the grave. His estate was appraised at about $700,000. He left the whole of his possessions to be divided equally between 2 gentlemen of this city, one a nephew to his wife, & the other the broker who had transacted his business in this city. The broker renounced the whole legacy making it over in favor of the relatives of the deceased in France, some 20 or 30 nephews & nieces. The old man had previously made a will in which his French relatives were handsomely remembered, but on returning from a visit to them, not long ago, for some reason known only to himself, he tore the will to pieces, & wrote this new one. He had come to this country when young, a poor hatter; but prospering in his business, & finally marrying a lady of wealth, he went into the sugar culture, & in a few years was made a millionaire. –N O Crescent

Died: on Oct 18, after a lingering illness, in his 30th year, Andrew Jackson Parker. His funeral will take place from the residence of his mother, on G, between 18th & 19th sts, this afternoon at 3½ o'clock.

Obit-died: on Oct 3, at Lawrenceport, Indiana, Mrs Minerva Elton, wife of Alfred N Bullitt, formerly of Louisville, Ky. In all the relations of wife, mother, & friend, she was the pride of all to whom she was known. -F

TUE OCT 20, 1857
Paul Leidy, Democrat, has been elected to Congress by a large majority over Smith B Thompson, opposition, in the 12th district of Pa, to fill the vacancy occasioned by the death of Mr Montgomery.

Saml Archibald, of the Steam Engineer Corps, has received the appointment from the Sec of the Navy of Engineer-in-Chief of the U S Navy, in place of Mr Martin.

Mrd: on Oct 15, at the First Presbyterian Church, Brooklyn, by Rev Jesse T Peck, Thos I Gardner, of Wash, to Miss Mary G Burnett, of Brooklyn.

Teachers' Association meeting on Oct 20. –Chas B Young, Rec Sec

Boston, Oct 19. 1-Henry L Sutton, in an affray, killed John Hilton, & also stabbed John Donovan supposed mortally. Sutton was captured, but with a desperate resistance, after stabbing Jacob Todd seriously. 2-Policeman Hodgson was killed by a pistol shot while arresting a suspected burglar.

N Y, Oct 19. John Swenson was killed on Sat, by 3 rowdies, while walking the street accompanied by his wife. The murderers have escaped.

WED OCT 21, 1857
Public sale of horses, cattle, carriages, corn, fodder, & farming implements; household & kitchen furniture, on Oct 26, at the farm of Mrs Mgt S A Cummings, on Rock Creek road, 1½ miles from Rock Creek Church. -A Green auct

Gen Wm Walker, the Man of Destiny, announces to you that he is now prepared to return to Central America to establish himself as the rightful President of that Republic, which position he was compelled to vacate for awhile, through the combination of the surrounding States-the influence of gold, the treachery of the notorious Spencer, & the improper & illegal interferences of the presumptuous English.

Meeting to be held on Oct 22 to take steps to demostrate our gratitude for the noble conduct of the late Cmder Herndon to save the women & children on board the ill-fated steamer **Central America**, in behalf of his widow & daughter. Signed:

Mrs Sarah Magruder
Mrs H C W Shubrick
Mrs Mary S Clymer
Mrs Mary H Wilkes
Mrs B Page
Mrs John W Maury
Mrs Aulick

Mrs L M Goldsborough
Mrs Geo C Ames
Mrs Chas H Hall
Mrs Col Abert
Mrs Col Irwin
Mrs Seaton

Chicago, Oct 20. Terrible conflagration on Oct 19 in Chicago. The following bodies have been found under the ruins of a devastating fire: John A Raymond, formerly of Worcester, Mass; D C Emerson-painter, Lawrence, Mass; Mr Marsh, Marcus D Grant-fireman, John Farr; Auguste Wolfe-fireman; B Mussey, Dudley C White-clerk, H T Bradley, Jean Junger-a German, & John High, jr-retired merchant. Killed by the falling of a wall: John B Dickey-fireman, Peter Kenvan, fireman; Mr Ezra H Barnum, proprietor of a variety store of the firm of Barnum & Brothers; & Mr E Romeyn Clark-merchant, of the firm of Metz & Clark, stove & tinware dealers. Several others are missing. [Oct 26th newspaper: persons killed by the falling of a wall: {including some of those above named,} H S Bradley-dealer in jewelry; John Tar-gasfitter; Mathius Mensh-clerk; Lawrence Griebel-German sailor; John Keegan-formerly of Port Clinton, Pa; Timothy Buckley-fireman; A H P Corning-clerk; & A Bogart-silver plater.]

Mrd: on Tue, by Rev John C Smith, John H Bartlett to Miss Louisa M Barnhill, all of Wash City.

Died: on Oct 14, in Morganton, N C, Catherine Lawrence, infant daughter of Rev Henry F Greene & Alice G Greene.

St Louis, Oct 20. Drowned when the steamer **Tropic** sunk: Wm Hoster & Joel Cross, Co B, 2nd Artl, a son of Mr Stephens, of Ky, & a negro belonging to the same gentleman. A number of deck hands were also lost. 150 passengers were on board, 12 or 15 of whom are supposed to have been lost. [Oct 23rd newspaper: The steamer **Tropic** sunk in the Missouri river, near Waverley, on Oct 15. Wm Wester & Joel Cross, of Co B, 2nd Artl, are known to have been drowned; also, a son of Mr Stephens, of Ky.]

THU OCT 22, 1857

At Point De-la-Hache, near New Orleans, Father Savelli was assassinated by a gang of ruffians, who inflicted upon him 28 wounds with a poniard. Dominique Ormea, who has been arrested, has made a full confession, criminating about a dozen others.

At the house of Mr Harris, in Barley st, Phil, a lad, Wm Spriggs, shot a colored boy, Dempsey, killing him instantly. An old grudge existed between the boys.

On Oct 14 Mary Ridgley was struck upon the head by a man who claimed to be her husband, & she died in the Pa hospital on Friday.

At Gay Head, **Martha's Vineyard**, on Oct 10, an Indian boy, Anthony Cole, stabbed Rachel Anthony, an Indian girl, in the abdomen, because she undertook to prevent him from pulling her brother off from a horse. He had just threatened to kill the brother. She was not expected to live.

On board the steamer **Gazelle**, near Mound city, in an affray between the cook & some passengers, the cook & Gilbert Moseau were killed & Abram Clemens & a Mr Hudson were dangerously wounded.

At St Louis, on Oct 15, a desperate prisoner of the workhouse, Jack Smith, refused to obey the commands of his guard, who shot him dead.

Hiram Cole was arrested recently in St Louis charged with the murder of his wife last month at Bainbridge, Ohio, by poisoning. Ofcrs have followed him through a dozen states.

At Boston on Sat Henry L Sutton, of N Y, but recently of Calif, got into a quarrel with John Donovan, residing in High st, & stabbed him with a dirk. Donovan is in a critical state. Sutton fled to Liverpool, where he was followed by Donovan's cousin, John Hilton, a well-known pugilist. Word ensued, & Sutton killed Hilton with the same dirk. Sutton was captured after a desperate resistance, during which he wounded seriously Mr Jacob Todd, a well known citizen. On the same morning Policeman Ezekiel Hodgon arrested a man suspected of burglary, when an accomplice of the fellow shot him through the head. Hodgon died in about 5 hours. The murderer fled.

Dr D T Smith, who is said to have killed Dr Blackburn, in Cairo, Ill, some months since, was arrested on Oct 13, at Bolivar, Tenn. He swallowed poison, but was recovered by an antidote.

A gentleman named Johnson, recently moved to Fentonville, with his family, a wife & 3 children, the oldest but 8 years of age. Not having got all his beds up, the wife remained at the hotel over-night, while Mr Johnson went to his house with the children, & was accompanied by a boy named Geo Colwell, about 17 years of age. About 8 o'clock 2 young men came in, asking for Mr Johnson, saying that they were going tohis father's house the next morning, a short distance from there. During the night Colwell & one of the little girls were killed; the other little girls are doing well; & the son is not expected to recover. The father himself received 2 blows on the head & a badly cut hand. Mr Johnson had about $400, & the two men took this means of gaining possession of it. -Detroit Daily Advertiser

Massacre of 4 missionary families of the Presbyterian board at Futtehgurgh in India. Gen Havelock arrived there to rescue them & found but one white person as saved. Her name was not given. Freeman, Campbell, Johnson, & Mc Mullen, & their wives, & 2 children of Mrs & Mrs Campbell, have fallen victims to the awful insurrection in India. Rev John E Freeman went out in 1838, & has been a faithful missionary for about 19 years. Rev David A Campbell was from Wisconsin, & his wife from Ohio. Rev Albert O Johnson & wife are both from Western Pa. Rev Robt McMullen was from Phil, & his wife was Miss Pierson, from Paterson, N J. Their loss is a blow to their work. $100,000 worth of property in India was destroyed. -N Y Observer

The Stamford [Conn] Advocate says that P T Barnum is again on his legs; that he is today a richer man than he was before his connexion with the Jerome Clock Co. He is now refurnishing & refitting *Iranistan* in good style for his future permanent residence.

European News: 1-Catherine Hays, the singer, was married in London to Mr Bushnell, of N Y. 2-The King of Prussia was feared to be dying.

Philip R Fendall, jr, of Calif, has been appointed a 2nd lt in the Marine Corps. -Star

The subscriber desires to dispose of a very profitable small farm & pleasant residence, in the parish of Washington & county of Westmoreland, Va, at a fair price. The homestead proper contains 315 acres; with a small tract detached containing 170 acres; no bldgs on the smaller place. The homsestead dwlg is built of brick, with 9 rooms, & the out bldgs are good & new. I will show the premises & will sell them a bargain, but will answer no letters. -Henry T Garnett, *Ingleside*, near **Oak Grove**, Westmoreland, Va.

The Annapolis [Md] Republican states that Deputy Sheriff J W Parkinson captured, on Thu morning last, the schnr **Wren**, for an alleged violation of the oyster law.

Teacher wanted: Trustees of Primary School No 3, in the 2nd election district of Kent Co, desire engaging the services of a competent Teacher for the ensuing year. Salary $400 per annum. Danl Jones, Thos C Kennards, Jas W Webb, Sewell Hepbron, John Wilson. -Harmony, Kent Co, Md.

Circuit Court of Wash Co, D C, in Equity, No 1317. Alexander C H Darne & Mary A his wife, [formerly Mary A Gassaway,] John H Gassaway, Geo Peter, jr & Eliza L his wife, [formerly Eliza L Gassaway,] Jane A Gassaway, & Wm A & Laura Gassaway, by Geo Peter, jr, their next friend, cmplnt, vs Wm H Barnaclo, Sam S Williams, & Susan Jackson, dfndnts. The cmplnts, the Gassaways, are the devisees & heirs-at-law of the late Amelia Thomas & Hanson Gassaway, & as such entitled to part of lot 5 in square 288 in Wash City. The dfndnt Sam S Williams was the administrator with the will annexed of the said Amelia Thomas, &, as such, & also as agent & trustee of the cmplnts, the devisees & heirs aforesaid, leased the said lot & premises to the dfndnt Wm H Barnaclo at a monthly rent of $8 a month, he, the said Barnaclo, agreeing out of said rent to pay all the charges, including the taxes, arising or to arise against said lot & premises. That said Barnclo, though in arrear for rent to an amount exceeding said taxes & charges, fraudulently permitted said taxes to remain unpaid & the lot to be sold by the corporate authorities of said city for the taxes so unpaid. That said Barnaclo fraudulently became the purchaser at such tax sale, & obtained a deed from the Mayor of said city, & afterwards sold said premises to the other dfndnt, Susan Jackson, who is now in possession & claims title thereto under said Barnaclo. The bill prays to set aside said tax purchase by said Barnclo & said tax deed to him as fraudulent & void, & also to set aside the sale by said Barnclo to Susan Jackson, the other dfndnt, & that the possession & enjoyment of the premises may be decreed to the cmplnts. The bill also states that 2 of the cmplnts, Wm A & Laura Gassaway, are minors, & entitled by the charter of Wash City to redeem said property, which they are ready & willing & pray to be allowed to do. Barnaclo does not reside in this District. He is to appear on the 1st Monday of March, 1858. –John A Smith, clerk -W L Dunlop, for cmplnt

Mrd: on Oct 20, in Wash City, at the residence of the bride, by Rev Dr Doggett, Saml H Latimer to Rebecca R, daughter of the late Richd I Morsell, of Wash City.

Circuit Court of Wash Co, D C-in Chancery. Selden, Withers & Co against John F Callan & Somerville Nicholson, administrators of Aug A Nicholson, & said Somerville & others, his heirs at law. By order of the Courr I am directed to state an account of the personal estate of said A A Nicholson, & of the debts due from him, & of his real estate; & to ascertain whether it is necessary to sell the latter in aid of the personal payment of his debts. Meeting on Oct 31 in the City Hall, Wash, Auditor's room. –Walter s Cox, Special Auditor

Select Family Boarding School for Small Boys, at Claymont, Delaware. Number limited to 10. Solid, refined, Christian education; $300 per annum, payable semi-monthly. Address Rev John B Clemson, D D, Claymont, Delaware.

FRI OCT 23, 1857

Fort Smith [Ark] Herald, of Oct 3: Col McKissick, the newly appointed agent to the Wichita Indians, a tribe inhabiting the country beyond that of the Choctaws & Chickasaws, had left *Fort Smith* for the purpose of visiting those Indians, & with the view of fixing upon a suitable place for the location of the agency. Col McKissisk is the first agent that has ever been sent to this tribe, who live near the mountains that bear their name. The Western Superintendency is now under the direction of Maj Rector, at *Fort Smith.*

Fatal accidents. 1-A young man, Chas Thrash, attempted to get upon a train at South Acton, on the Fitchburg road, last Sat, but he lost his balance, was thrown under the wheels, has his right arm cut off, & died of his injuries at the South Boston Hospital the same night. 2-Jas Durfee, aged 15, was shot by the premature discharge of his companions gun while the 2 were hunting near Taunton last Sat. 3-Mr Cornelius Terhune, of N Y, was thrown out of a carriage in which he was riding on Sat & died on Sunday. 4-Two lads named Hayes & Robinson went out gunning at Manchester, N H, last Fri, when Robinson's gun accidentally discharged in poor Hayes' breast. The lad died in about an hour. 5-Chas Holman, of Lancaster, Pa, was bitten on the lip by a spider during the night, & died from the poison in a week. His face severely swelled, followed by insanity, & finally mortification.

Miss Mgt Coffren, of Nottingham district, in this county, was burnt on Friday last, at the residence of her father, Mr Francis Coffren. While stooping over the hearth the skirt of her dress took fire, & in a few moments her garments were in a blaze. She expired on Sat evening or Sunday morning. –Marlboro Gazette

Last evening Patrick Collins became involved in a difficulty, but, being separated from those with whom he quarreled, started for home. He was later found badly wounded, having a severe wound upon the neck, the ball passing through his neck. He was conveyed to his residence & medical aid called in. –Balt Clipper

Counterfeiters. Wm Stanley, his wife, & Johnny McGraw, have been arrested in Wmsburg, N Y, charged with passing counterfeit bills. $12,000 in counterfeit money was found about them.

Children to bind out. Several healthy children, of both sexes, from 1 to 5 years of age, will be bound on application to the Com'rs of the Wash Asylum. -Geo W Emerson, Geo Mattingly, Jacob Gideon, Com'rs

For Rent: Desirable brick dwlg, 485 D st, lately occupied by W H Gilman, apothecary. Gas & water in the house. –Z W McKnew, at Jackson Hall.

Mrd: on Oct 15, at *Oaklawn*, PG Co, Md, by Rev P B Leneghan, Pembroke A Brawner, of Chas Co, Md, to Matilda, daughter of Dr B I Semmes.

Died: on Oct 19, in Wash City, Mr John Galpin, of Conn, aged 41 years, an Assist Examiner in the Patent Ofc.

Health Report: Ofc of the Com'r of Health, Wash, Oct 21, 1857. Monthly report of deaths in Wash City for Sept, 1857: 94. –Chas F Force, Com'r of Health.

SAT OCT 24, 1857
Henry Shaw, a former resident of Lanesboro, Mass, & from 1817 to 1821 a member of Congress from the western district of that State, died at Newburgh, N Y, on Oct 16, at the age of nearly 70 years. In 1843 he removed to N Y C, where he was elected to several offices.

The late fire at Chicago on Monday; 9 bldgs occupied as stores were consumed. The following is a list of the dead whose bodies have been rescued from the ruins & identified: John B Dickey, foreman Liberty Hose, aged 24 years; Dudley C White, clerk for Jos Fisk & Co, aged 22 years; Auguste Wolfe, fireman, aged 18 years; E Romeyn Clark, from Utica, N Y, aged 30 years, married; H S Bradley, leaves a wife & 2 children, aged 55 years; Jean Jungers, or Youngards, German; John Farr, gasfitter; John A Raymond, clerk, formerly of Worcester, Mass; C Emerson, supposed to be a painter, from Lawrence, Mass; Israel H Barnum, of Barnum Brothers; John High, jr, late High & Magie.

Synod of Va. Appointments for preaching on the Sabbath:
Assembly's Church: Rev A H H Boyd, D D; Rev T D Bell
First Presbyterian Church: Rev C H Read, D D; Rev L P Ledoux
Fourth Presbyterian Church: Rev J D Mitchell; Revs Dr Boyd & Mitchell.
Sixth Presbyterian Church: Rev J O Sloan
Western Presbyterian Church: Rev L P Ledoux; Rev J J McMahon
F st Presbyterian Church: Rev E H Cumpston; Rev R Gray
Bridge st Church, Gtwn: Rev J J McMahon; Rev H R Smith
Seventh st Presbyterian Church: Rev J W K Handy; Rev J L Fracy
E st Baptist Church: Rev P Fletcher; Rev C H Read, D D
Wesley Chapel: Rev T D Bell; Rev A H H Boyd, D D
English Lutheran Church: Rev R Gray; Rev J O Sloan
Gorsuch Chapel: Rev J W McMena
Union Chapel: Rev G W Leybour; Rev J W McMena

Richd Taylor, only son of the late Pres Taylor, is the Democratic candidate for the Senate of Louisiana in the St Charles district.

Orphans Court of Wash Co, D C. In the case of John E Neale, executor of Priscilla Neale, deceased: the executor & Court have appointed Nov 14 next, for the final settlement of the personal estate of said deceased, of the assets in hand.
-Ed N Roach, Reg/o wills

Mrd: on Oct 22, in Wash City, by Rev Dr Cummins, Oscar F Bullock, of Spottsylvania Co, Va, to Miss Catharine E Kyle, of Alabama.

Mrd: on Oct 22, at Carlisle, Penn, by Rev Dr McClintock, Mr Chas W Carrigan to Miss Lizzie C K Seymour.

Died: on Oct 1, in Goochland Co, Fabius M Lawson, formerly Treasurer of the State of Va, in his 52nd year.

Died: on Oct 23, suddenly, in Wash City, Albert Gabriel, infant son of Nicholas & Christina V N Callan. His funeral is tomorrow at 2 o'clock.

Died: on Oct 19, at the residence of his father, in Chas Co, Md, John Richard, infant son of Ruel K & Rachel Compton, aged 1 year, 3 months & 9 days.

Chicago, Oct 23. The propeller **Reindeer**, running between this city & Montreal, went to pieces on Point-au-Sable on Monday. All hands except two were lost.

MON OCT 26, 1857
Died: on Oct 19, in Staunton, Va, at the residence of her son-in-law, Cmder T T Craven, U S Navy, Mrs Anna Maria Henderson, wife of the late Dr Thos Henderson, U S Army, & daughter of Cmdor Thos Truxton, aged 65 years. Thus the life of wife, mother, & friend have been brought to a close. Her last sickness was soothed by the affectionate attention of nearly all her large family of children, who hastened to her side to render this labor of love to an honored mother. They followed her remains to Lexington, & laid them, in compliance with her own request, beside her husband.

Appointments by the Pres: 1-Jos Ganahi, U S Atty for the district of Georgia.
2-John M Harrell, U S Atty for the eastern district of Arkansas.

Died: on Sep 12, at his residence in Calvert Co, Md, in his 30th year, Dr Thos Chesley Hance. It is but a few months since that we recorded the death of his young & lovely wife; & now the devoted husband has followed her whom he so sincerely mourned, leaving 2 lovely little girls.

Obit-died: Cornelius Thornton, of Phil, came to his death by falling beneath the cars at Balt on Oct 3. He was an affectionate son, a kind brother, & a sincere friend. He was on his way to visit his widowed mother, residing in Phil, when the accident occurred. -C

Mr Edw Young was shot & instantly killed near Jackson, in this county, on Sat last, by Mr John Linkenhoger, who was firing at a mark, 50 yards distant. The shooting was of course purely accidental. –Fincastle [Va] Whig, Oct 23.

Valuable farm for sale at auction today, on the premises, the farm of Maj G Tochman, on the Alexandria & Wash turnpike & railroad. The dwlg house is large & comfortable. -Jas C McGuire, auct

TUE OCT 27, 1857
Mrd: on Oct 20, by Rev A W Wayman, Wm H Thomas to Anna V Tilghman, daughter of Henry H Tilghman, all of Wash.

Died: on Oct 26, Mrs Eliz Thompson, aged 62 years, wife of Geo Thompson. Her funeral is today at 3 o'clock, from her late residence, 5th st, between F & G sts.

Marshal's sale: by virtue of 2 writs of fieri facias: public auction, for cash, on Nov 28, lots 1, 37, 38, & the east half of lot 2 in reservation A, in Wash City, with the improvements. Seized & levied upon as the property of David A Hall, & will be sold to satisfy Judicials Nos 3 & 6 to Dec term, 1852, in favor of the U S.
–Richd Wallach, late Marshal, D C

C Miller, Cupper & Leecher. A good supply of Swedish & Russian Leeches always on hand. Ofc 427 6th st, between F & G sts.

Copartnership: we have associated Mr Bushrod Robinson with us in the clothing business, which will be conducted under the firm of Wall, Stephens & Co. from this date, Oct 27. Wall & Stephens, 322 Pa ave.

WED OCT 28, 1857
Superior matched gray carriage horses, phaeton, & buggy, & harness, at auction on Oct 31, the personal property belonging to the estate of the late Maj Geo F Lindsay, U S Army.

Circuit Court of D C-in Equity, No 1,269. Wm W Hough, vs Eleanor Hines, widow, Christian M Hines, adm, Enoch G Hines, & others, heirs at law of Abraham Hines, deceased. Chas S Wallach, the trustee, reported to the Court that, on Sep 17, 1857, he sold the property named in the decree of sale, to Geo J Johnson for $1,376, & that Geo J Johnson has complied with the terms of sale. –Jno A Smith, clerk

By the steamer **Baltic** we have received the intelligence of the death of our distinguished countryman, Thos Crawford, sculptor, who died at the early age of 43. He had been laboring under a disease for the last few months. He was born in N Y C Mar 22, 1814. Encouraged by his father, he was placed with Mr Frazee & Mr Lawnitz, from whom he acquired the art of modeling in clay. In 1834, at 20 years of age, he was sent to Italy, & established himself in Rome, where he gained admittance into the studio of Thorwaldsen, to whose instruction & friendship he became indebted for much of his subsequent success. He executed busts of the late Cmdor Hull, Mr Kenyon, the English poet, Sir Chas Vaughan, formerly Minister at Washington; Josiah Quincy, Pres of Harvard Univ, & many others. Mr Crawford was married some years ago to Miss Ward, of this city, a sister of Mrs Saml G Howe, of Boston, the author of Passion Flowers, & the World's Own. He has left several children, who are now living with his wife's sister, Mrs Maillard, at Bordentown, N J. For the last year or 2 he has been the victim of a dreadful disease, which has deprived him almost entirely of sight, & caused him to renounce his art entirely. A malignant tumor made its appearance in his left eye, &, in spite of every effort of his physicians, increased to such an extent that the eye protruded almost out of its socket, while the agony, which was intense, seemed beyond the aid of art. The disease penetrated to the brain, &, after months of anguish, he was relieved of his sufferings by death. His wife had attended him with untiring solicitude during his whole illness. –N Y Evening Post

Hon Theodore Frelinghuysen, of N J, was lately married to Miss Harriet H Pumpelly, of Owego, N Y.

Old English funeral. In 1466, upon the death of Sir John Pastor, which was celebrated at Bromholm Priory, Norfolk Co, the funeral feast lasted 3 days.

Balt: last night at the High St Hotel of Mr Thos Dukehart, on High st, Balt, Mr Jerome White was shot to death, by Mr John Clagett. Clagett was arrested. No cause given. Mr White died in a few minutes, & was taken to his residence in High st. His wife & children endured grief that touched all hearts. –Balt Sun

Orphans Court of Wash Co, D C. Letters of administration on the personal estate of Stephen Cassin, late of the U S Navy, deceased. –W Redin, Walter S Cox, Wm P Maulsby, adms

Mrd: on Oct 27, by Rev J G Butler, Christian G Schneider to Miss Mary Amelia Myers, both of Wash.

Mrd: on Oct 22, at Union, Loudoun Co, Va, by Rev Mr Lipscomb, Mr Geo W Bohrer, of Gtwn, D C, to Miss Maggie V Torreyson, of Union, Loudoun Co, Va.

THU OCT 29, 1857
Trustee's sale of a house & lot: by deed of trust from Edw Lycett to me, dated Sep 26, 1854, recorded in Liber J A S No 87, folios 241, of the land records of Wash Co, D C: public auction on Nov 12, of parts of lots 1 thru 4 in square 351, with the 2 story frame dwlg & other improvements thereon.-Wm R Woodward, trustee
-A Green auct

On Oct 21 there were 3 desperate affrays in Memphis, Tenn. A man named Keene was killed by Dr F Gibbes; another named Puckett was shot accidentally by ofcr Butler, who fired at a fellow named Lewis. The latter had attacked Puckett, when Butler interfered. In the other affray Dr J J Hooks was shot & dangerously wounded by D Cockrell.

Phil, Oct 28. An affray occurred yesterday in the cars near Chambersburg between Mr McKibbin, member of Congress from Calif, & Isaac Craig, his brother-in-law. The latter had incurred the enmity of the whole family by a criminal act, committed several years ago. The parties met accidentally in the cars for the first time since the occurrence. Pistols were used, & Craig was wounded, but not seriously.

Pleasant M Coleman, convicted of the murder of Mrs Bagby, at the last term of the Logan Circuit Court, was hung on Friday last, at Russelville, Ky.

Mrd: on Oct 27, in Wash City, by Rev B F Bittinger, Mr _ G Singles to Miss Phebe J Rodgers, of Pa.

Mrd: on Oct 20, in Wash City, at St John's Church, by Rev Chas H Hall, Mr Edw C Eddie to Miss Ellen Hammond, both of Wash City.

Mrd: on Oct 22, in Gtwn, by Rev Mr Murray, Mr John Berry to Miss Martha A, 2nd daughter of Geo Hill, jr, of the former place.

Mrd: on Oct 1, by Rev Jas A Harrold, Mr Jas H Gilmore, of Va, to Miss Estelle Derrick, of Wash City.

Died: on Oct 27, Saml J Potts, in his 63rd year. His funeral will take place from his late residence, 497 7th st, this morning, at 10½ o'clock.

Died: Oct 28, Miss Honora Griffin, aged 75 years. Her funeral will take place from the residence of Mrs Catherine Hill, on 5th, between G & H sts, at 3:30, on Oct 29.

FRI OCT 30, 1857
Died: last evening, after a protracted illness, Wm J McCormick, in his 62nd year. His funeral will take place tomorrow at 3 o'clock, from his late residence, on 1st st east, Capitol Hill.

The late Senator Rusk: was the son of an Irish emigrant, who settled in S C, & without the aid of fortune or friends, he educated himself, studied law, & at an early day married in Ga & settled in Texas, then a province of Mexico, & at the time of her declaration of independence we find him Sec of War. Rusk joined the army under Gen Houston. He captured in single combat the most gallant of the Mexican generals, Gen Almonte, & received his sword. In all the relations of life, as husband, father, neighbor, friend, warrior, or statesman, entirely exemplary towards others. He had his faults, & fell by his own hand in a temporary fit of insanity, produced by excessive grief for the loss of his devoted wife, a lady or rare excellence & piety, who had married him early in life, & followed his fortunes with pride & devotion in all his struggles to fortune & fame. Senator Rusk died on Jul 29 last. –San Jacinto

The late Col Crane: Col I B Crane, of the 1st Regt U S Artl, whose decease on Oct 5 was announced, was born in Elizabethtown, N J, on Jul 18, 1787, & was the son of Gen Wm Crane, of that place, a highly meritorious officer of the Revolutionary army. His 2 brothers, Judge Crane of Ohio, & Cmdor Wm M Crane, U S Navy, died a few years since. In Jan, 1809, he was appointed a 2nd Lt in the Marine Corps, & in May of the same year promoted a 1st Lt, & served in the frig **United States** for upwards of 2 years under command of Cmdor Decatur. In Apr, 1812, he was transferred to the army as a Capt of the 3rd Regt of Artl, commanded by Col Alex Macomb, afterwards Maj Genr'l commanding the army. He marched with his regt to Sackett's Harbor for the protection of the fleet about being formed there, & in May following embarked with his company on board the fleet & proceeded to Little York, [now Toronto,] Upper Canada, & assisted in the capture of **Fort George** & the town of Newark. He served under Maj Gen Brown's command on the Niagara frontier; was stationed at different posts in New England, & at the Artl School of Practice at **Fort Monroe**, Va; was in command of N Y harbor; served, in 1832, on the Black Hawk expedition, & during the Florida war in 1835 thru 1837; during the Mexican wwar he was superintendent of the general recruiting service in N Y C, & afterwards as Govn'r of the Military Asylum in Wash City. His last service was in command of his regt at **Fort Monroe**, Va. In 1854, after 45 years of continuous service, he was attacked by a disease which incapacitated him from further duty, & which suddenly terminated his life. He was a kind father, a generous refined & courteous gentleman, an honest, upright & conscientious man. To his family his loss is irreparable.

Mrd: on Thu, in Wash City, by Rev John C Smith, Mr Jas E Cook to Miss Mary Ellen Williams, both of PG Co, Md.

A great stampede of slaves took place at Cambridge, Md, on Sat night last. No less than 30 made their escape-15 belonging to Saml Pattison, 7 to Miss Jane Carter, 3 to Richd Keene, 1 to W V Brannock, 1 to Reuben E Phillips, 1 to the estate of Wm D Traverse, deceased, & 2 free negroes. Messrs Pattison, Phillips, & Brannock have offered a reward of $3,100 for the apprehension of their slaves. -Sun

Richmond, Oct 29. John C Haley was stabbed at the fair grounds this afternoon by Nimrod Dickinson, a well known citizen, & killed instantly.

The Canadian steamer **Reindeer** was wrecked near Big Point Sable, on the Michigan coast, & only 2 firemen out of her crew of 23 men were saved. There was a severe gale on Lakes Michigan & Superior last Monday week. She was formerly the ship **Commerce**, & was run into & sunk in Lake Erie some 8 years ago when transporting some companies of British troops. A great many lives were lost.

SAT OCT 31, 1857
Army order: 1-Lt R E DeRussy to take charge of the works at *Fort Monroe*, Va, & other works now under the control of Brvt Col J L Smith. 2-Brvt Col J L Smith to take charge of the operations at Sandy Hook, N Y. 3-Brvt Maj J G Larnard relieved temporarily from the charge of the works in & about N Y harbor, & to take charge, temporarily, of the works about Mobile Bay, Ala, now under the control of Capt D Leadbeater, who has tendered his resignation. 4-Capt G W Cullon relieved from the works in Charleston harbor, S C, including lighthouses, & to assume the charge of the work at Willitt's Point, N Y. 5-Capt H W Benham to take charge of the engineer operations at *Fort Adams*, Rhode Island, in addition to his present duties. 6-Lt G B Fant assigned to the charge of *Fort Taylor*, Key West, Florida, relieving Capt D P Woodbury therefrom. 7-Brvt Capt J G Foster relieved from the temporary measures preliminary to the commencement of the fort at Willit's Point, N Y, & to take charge of the works about Charleston harbor, Charleston, S C, under the superintendence of Capt G W Cullum, including his lighthouse duties. 8-1st Lt P E Prime to take charge of the works about Mobile bay, Ala, relieving Brvt Maj J G Barnard. 9-1st Lt J B McPherson relieved from duty as assistant on the works under the charge of Brvt Major J G Barnard, & to take charge of the works on Alcatrasy island, San Francisco Bay, Calif. 10-2nd Lt M D McAleston relieved from duty as assistant to the Board of Engineers, & to report for duty as assistant on the works now under the charge of Brvt Maj J G Barnard, in & about the harbor of N Y.

The Port Tobacco [Md] Times announces the death of Rev Mr Woodley, the pastor of St Thomas [Catholic] Church, near that village. He was a native of Va, & during the prevalence of the yellow fever at Norfolk, in the summer of 1855, was one of the few who, from a sense of duty, regardless of self, visited that plague-stricken city & administered to the sick & dying.

A man named John Fee, living near Bullock's Creek, Ala, in a fit of anger shot his horse & some cattle, & on Sunday week set fire to his house, which he had previously locked. His 3 motherless children, from 5 to 14, are supposed to have perished in the flames. He has been arrested.

N Y, Oct 30. A fight occurred at the City Hall today between 2 Democratic politicians. One, named Conner, was beaten to death by Teddy Donovan, a custom-house officer.

Obit-died: Mrs Dr Rush, of Phil, we learn from Saratoga, died there on Friday. The proximate cause was erysipelas. She went to Saratoga in June last, as has been her custom for many years, to drink the waters & enjoy the air & society of this great watering place; but early in Sept, the usual time of her return, she was taken ill, & has been there confined ever since, in that vast, but now lone establishment, the U S Hotel. Mrs Rush was about 60 years of age. She was a Miss Ridgway, of Phil, & a large fortune was left her by her father. –N Y Express

Mrd: on Thu, in the Fourth Presbyterian Church, by Rev J C Smith, John A Borland to Miss Mary Jane Connell; &, on the same evening, by the same, Bernard Sears to Miss Mary E, daughter of the late David Miller, all of Wash City.

Mrd: on Wed last, at Trinity Church, by Rev Dr Cummin, Warden W Sperry, of Winchester, Va, to Miss Fannie P Fairbanks, of Tuscaloosa, Ala.

Died: on Thu last, after a protracted illness, Wm J McCormick, in his 62nd year. Early in life, by the death of his father, he was left in charge of a large & rather helpless family, but he proved himself equal to the responsible task. He was truly exemplary as husband, father, & brother. For 18 years he was elected to the ofc of Postmaster of the House of Reps, & subsequently was elected for 2 terms as Register of Wash City. His funeral will take place at 3 o'clock this afternoon, from his late residence on Capitol Hill.

Died: on Oct 29, of typhoid pneumonia, John Aylmer Golden, in his 50th year. He was a native of Dublin, & a resident of this city for the last 18 years. His funeral is this afternoon at 1 o'clock, at his late residence on 8th st, near the Navy Yard.

Died: on Oct 29, Geo H Payne, aged 30 years, a native of Wash City. His funeral is this afternoon, at 3 o'clock, from the residence of his brother-in-law, John P Dennis, on 6th st, between D & E Sts.

Notice. All person indebted to me are requested to come forward at once & settle their accounts, as it is absolutely necessary that my books should be settled up at once. –F L Moore

MON NOV 2, 1857
A son of J J Winter, of Clarksburg, Va, returned home the other day after an absence of 3 years. His father had difficulty recognizing him, & called to two of his daughters. The young ladies did not at first recognize their brother, but almost instantly the eldest recognized him & sank instantly to the floor, dead.

By deed of trust from Albert J Webb & wife to Andrew Wylie, dated Aug 14, 1854, recorded in liber J A S No 84, folios 51 thru 53, of the land records for D C, the undersigned will offer for sale on Nov 16, lots 1, 2, 23, & 24, & that part of lot 22, in square 780, which remains after deducting so much of said lot 22 as was conveyed by Zephaniah Farrell to Jas Anderson by deed dated Sep 8, 1815, recorded in liber A J, No 34, folio 474. –Andrew Wylie, trustee -Jas C McGuire, auct

In the case of Wm H Pollard vs the N Y & New Haven Railroad Co decided before the Supreme Court of N Y C on Thu, the plntf, on Mar 20, 1854, was injured when one train violently struck his car. Verdict of $3,000 for the plntf.

Providence Journal of Friday. Boiler explosion at Providence, in the India rubber works of Nathl Hayward, took place yesterday. Injured: Mr F E Hewes, superintendent of the shoe dept; Elijah Ormsbee, engineer; Danl Higgins, heel-cutter for shoes-recovery doubtful; & Eliz Millan. The house which the boiler struck was occupied by Michl Drury & Michl H McGwin, in the upper story; Jas Faulkner & Mrs Catharine McElry, in the basement. Mrs Faulkner was with her child in the rocking chair & received a few bruises. Mr McGwin's mother & sister had just finished breakfast. The front side of the room was demolished.

Alex'r Veal has been sentenced to 18 years in the penitentiary for the murder of Robt S Saunders, in Loudoun Co, Va.

From the Raleigh Register of Oct 31. Obit-died: on Thu last, at his residence in this city, in his 84th year, Wm Hill, Sec of the State of N C. He was a native of Stokes Co. According to Wheeler's History, he came to Raleigh in 1795 as clerk to Jas Glasgow, who went out of ofc in 1798, & was succeeded by Wm White. On Mr White's death, in Oct, 1811, Mr Hill was eleced Sec of State, & filled the ofc to the day of his death, a period of 46 years. He died in communion with the Methodist Church, at peace with God & man.

Richmond, Oct 31. Govn'r Wise has sent 3,000 muskets to Balt, in compliance with the request of Govn'r Ligon, of Md.

Sat night in the neighborhood of 7th st & Mass ave, firemen returning from Gtwn got into a conflict with a party of the police. Ofcr Benj Klopper was shot in the right eye; Mr Davis, shoemaker, was shot in the leg & arm. Dr Eliot extracted both bullets. They proceeded to the tavern on 7th & G sts, kept by Mr John T Halleck, where they commenced a work of spoliation & demolition. Nearly a dozen arrests were made of the party in the Northern Liberties, of whom John Fay & Thos Venable alone are held for trial & have been committed to jail. Jefferson Taylor has been held to bail for further trial on Oct 10.

TUE NOV 3, 1857
Local Matters. The Mayor nominated to the Board of Aldermen last night 25 additional police officers, for night service. Their names are as follows:

David Lucas	Washington Wallingsford
John Angerman	John Browers
Thos Lomax	Richd Evans
W B Maxwell	Peter Goodyear
J F Carter	Henry Nash
J B Conway	Jacob Ash
Jas Collins	Jas Kavanaugh
Jas F Edwards	Jas Powers
Patrick Gormley	David A Harrover
Jas Belt	Robt King
Jas H Irvine	David G McComb

Regular meeting of the Missionary Society in aid of St Andrew's Mission [Rev Mr Harrold's] will meet on Wed at the residence of Mrs E Hamilton Holly, H st.

For sale, a good saddle horse, well gaited, would suit a lady or gentleman. Inquire of Wm McL Cripps, 499 11th st.

Sale of furniture, crockery, glassware, stoves, & ironware, this morning, at the house-furnishing establishment of Messrs Garner & Lease, at 9th & Pa ave: the entire stock. –Wall & Barnard, aucts

Female Academy at Albany, N Y, will open on Nov 18, under the direction of Rev E S Stearns, A M, & a full corps of accomplished professors & assistants. Trustees:

Hon A J Parker, L L D, Pres	Rev J N Wyckoff, D D
*Hon W L Marcy, L L D	Maj Gen J F Cooper
Hon W Olcott	Marcus T Reynolds
Hon Ira Harriss, L L D	Jos H Armsby, M D
Hon J Q Wilson	Harmon Pumpelly
Rev W B Sprague, D D	Rev Eben S Stearns, A M
Jos W Naughton, M D	

*Vacancy not filled.

Vigilance Cmte in Michigan appointed by the citizens to check the lawlessness & violence which has been exhibited in Flint & other towns in Genesee Co, Mich. Some of the recent exploits: the death of Mr Seavers shot in Grand Blanc; the horsestealing after the fair; the murders in Mr Johnson's family in Fentonville; attempts to rob the house of Hon W M Fenton; & the burglary of Mr Belcher's house on Tue night, foiled by the intrepidity of the maid.

The only Half-price Music store in the U S. –Jno Marsh, 1302 Chestnut st, 2nd door above 13th, [formerly 358,] Phil. –G D Korponay, Book-keeper

$10 reward for the recovery of a lady's Fur Victorine, lost on 6th st on Sep 27. –C W Hinman, 393 C st

Mrd: on Oct 22, in the Presbyterian Church, Havre de Grace, Md, by Rev Septimus Tustin, D D, Edw T Rigney, of Phil, Pa, to Miss Ann G, daughter of Wm Poplar, of the former place.

Augusta, Nov 2. Mr Bell, agent of Douglas & Co, of N Y, [of the Commercial Agency,] killed Jas Allen, of Yorkville, S C, on Sat. Bell had communicated information injurious to Allen. Bell was arrested.

WED NOV 4, 1857
A promising youth named Thornton Clarke, aged 16 years, son of the late Mason E Clarke, formerly of Upper Marlborough, was thrown from a horse, whilst riding a race, near Centreville, Chas Co, Md, on Oct 23. His head struck a stump as he fell, which gave the fatal blow. Drs Edelen & Dent rendered medical assistance, but the poor boy died in less than an hour after the fall. –Marlboro Gaz

Brvt Maj Jefferson Van Horne, captain in the 3rd infty, U S Army, died at Albuquerque, New Mexico, on Sep 28 last.

The decisive measures of Pres Buchanan to maintain the authority of the Federal Gov't in Utah Territory have proved how insincere were the professions of the Mormon leaders that they were loyal to the Federal Gov't. Their game of deception having failed at Washington, they now display their true colors, & openly avow their treasonable purposes. They are cunning enough to perceive that if the political power is take from Gov'r Brigham Young [their chief,] his influence over the people will be greatly diminished, as they will no longer fear him when his power to punish is taken away. –N Y Sun

Mrd: on Oct 20, in Balt, by Rev Mr Dunning, of Balt, John H Harding, jr, of Northumberland Co, Va, to Miss Louisa Willis, of Balt.

The colonization ship **M C Stevens** sailed from Balt yesterday for Liberia, touching at Norfolk. She takes out 40 emigrants from Md, 30 of whom were liberated & provided for by Mrs Riggen, of Balt. There are also several from Ky & a family from Providence, R I. At Norfolk she will take on board 100 additional emigrants, all from Va, & 70 of whom were liberated with the proviso that they would go to Africa.

Died: on Oct 30, in Phil, in his 23rd year, Michl Quinn, of consumption. He was a native of Ireland, but for the last 15 years a resident of Wash City.

The brig **Walborg**, Capt Lund, having on board Crawford's equestrian statue of Washington, has arrived at Richmond. It will be conveyed to the Capitol Square, where, some future day, it will be erected. –Richmond Enquirer

Geo Cowee, clerk, Jacob Stanton, hotel keeper, & Edw Price, a prize fighter, are implicated in the matter of the forgeries of the unsigned bank bills stolen from the New England Bank Note Co at Boston. Price handed the notes to Stanton unsigned, Stanton delivered them to Cowee, who forged the names of the presidents & cashiers of the banks on which the bills were & returned then to Price. The amount exceeds $60,000.

The American shipmasters at Liverpool have subscribed for a handsome piece of plate to be presented to the Vice-Consul at that port. Inscribed: "To Samuel Pierce, on his retirement from the office of Vice-Consul of the United States, after nearly forty years of faithful service; a testimony of high respect from American shipmasters. Liverpool, Oct 12, 1857." The plate comprises a claret jug, salver, & two goblets of silver.

A young man, Geo Bradley, arrived at Chambersburg, Pa, on Fri last, & walked into the jewelry store of John Hutton, unseen, picked up several watches, valued at $386, & made off, but was pursued & arrested. On Mon he was convicted & sentenced to the penitentiary for 21 months. He said he had a family in Pittsburg, but that he was formerly a clerk in a commission house at Balt.

Winter Millinery: Miss E E McDonald, showrooms, 71 Bridge st, Gtwn. [Ad]

Obit-died: on Oct 8, at ***Otwell***, the seat of his fathers for several generations, Col Nicholas Goldsborough, in his 71st year. He frequently contributed to the various journals of the day, but more particularly did he lend his assistance to Mr Skinner when he commenced the American Farmer, & greatly contributed to the success of that valuable paper. Col Goldsborough left a large family.

THU NOV 5, 1857
Annual communication of the M W Grand Lodge of Free & Accepted Masons of D C: list of the following ofcrs elected for the ensuing year: G Whiting, M W Gr Master; T P Page, R W D G Master; S T Shugert, R W S G Warden; Hopkins Lightner, R W J G Warden; G Schwarzman, R W G Sec; C Cammack, R W G Treasurer; W M Smith, W G Visiter & Lecturer; Rev W M Ferguson, W G Chaplain; Grafton Powell, W G Marshal; J E Holmead, W S G Deacon; A G Fowler, W J G Deacon; S B Erwin, W G Sword Bearer; E Alexander, W G Pursuivant.

Hon Robt M Stewart was inaugurated as Gov'r of Missouri at Jefferson City on Oct 22, in the presence of both Houses of the Legislature & a large crowd of auditors.

Mrd: on Nov 3, in Wash City, at St Mary's Church, by Rev Mr Alig, Mr Anton Ruppert to Miss Anna Shwing, all of Wash City.

Died: yesterday, in Wash City, of consumption, Miss Hester Maria Wroth, in her 45th year. Her funeral is this evening at 3 o'clock, from the residence of her brother-in-law, [E B Robinson,] 856 D, between 9th & 10th sts.

St John's, N B, Nov 2. Last evening Breen & Slavin, & his son, the supposed murderers of the Mackenzie family of 6 persons, on Oct 24, were arrested at their camp in the woods & brought to the city & placed in jail. They offered no resistence. The coroner's jury had returned a verdict of willful murder against the above parties.

Phil, Nov 4. Richd Carter, Pres of the Anthracite Bank at Tamaqua, was shot dead this evening in a parlor of the St Lawrence Hotel by Thos Washington Smith, of Cecil Co, Md. Carter was a middle-aged man, of a wealthy family. Smith was laboring under great excitement when he committed the deed. He was arrested.

FRI NOV 6, 1857
Mr Patrick Dillon, Consul-General & Charge d'Affaires of the French Gov't to Hayti, has just died at Paris, after a lingering illness, contracted during his residence as consul to San Francisco.

A house occupied by Mr Hoever, in Kirkland, Ohio, was destroyed by fire last Thu. Mr H perished in the flames. He was much intoxicated, & had just turned his family out of doors that night, & then perished miserably.

Died: on Nov 5, in Wash City, Rachel Weeks, in her 84th year, a native of Harford Co, Md, near *Belle-Air*, formerly of Balt, but for the last 13 years a resident of Wash City. She was a member of the Orthodox Friends, [Quakers.] Her funeral is this afternoon, at 2:30 o'clock, from the residence of Mr Benj C Wright, 497 I st north.

Household & kitchen furniture at auction on: Nov 6, at the residence of F M Ewell, 13th st, between L st & Mass ave. -Jas C McGuire, auct

Orphans Court of Wash Co, D C. In the case of Mary Mudd, administratrix of Ignatius Mudd, deceased: the administratrix & Court have appointed Dec 1 next, for the final settlement of the personal estate of said deceased, of the assets in hand. -Ed N Roach, Reg/o wills

SAT NOV 7, 1857
The following ia an aggregate statement of the votes cast for Govn'r in the State of Ohio at the late election:

Salmon P Chase: 160,568　　　　　T B McCormick: 185
Henry B Payne: 169,065　　　　　　Philaelphus: 142
Philadelphus Van Trump: 9,263　　Scattering: 109
Peter Van Trump: 823　　　　　　　Govn'r Chase's plurality 1,503.

Balt Sun: affray on Wed resulted in the death of one of the participants, Parker White, who was stabbed & died yesterday. The assailant, Patrick Kelley, who was himself shot after inflicting the fatal wound, still lies at the Lombard st infirmary in a state of semi-unconsciousness. The physicians have pronounced his case hopeless.

U S District Court, Judge Halyburton presiding, Chas Cowlan, charged with robbing the U S mails, was put upon his trial yesterday & plead guilty, throwing himself upon the mercy of the jury, & pleading his youth & inexperience in extenuation of his offence. He is 19 years of age. The jury returned a verdict of guilty; & his term of confinement in the penitentiary, as fixed by law, is not less than 10 nor more than 20 years. He was defended by Farewell Taylor. –Norfolk Herald

A Liverpool paper states that the immense estate of the Jennens family has been formally taken possession of by Jos Martin, heir-at-law. As a portion of the property was purchased from the Daniels' family by Robt Jennens, the father of Wm "the rich," &, as the latter died intestate, it descends to Mr Jos Martin, as an heir-loom. The other portions of the estate are strictly entailed, & pass to Mr Martin under wills which have been duly proved.

Mrd: on Nov 5, by Rev W Krebs, Geo W Graves to Mary Ann Mack, both of Wash City.

Mrd: on Nov 5, at Gtwn, D C, by Rev Thos Mullady, J Johnson Smith to Virginia, daughter of the late Cmdor Stephen Cassin, U S Navy.

The copartnership existing between Topham & Norflet is this day dissolved by mutual consent. –Jas S Tophan, Thos Norflet. [Jas S Tophan will continue the same at the old stand, 499 7th st, the Saddle, Harness, & Trunk business.]

MON NOV 9, 1857
Hon Isham G Harris was duly installed into office on Nov 3 as Govn'r of the State of Tenn for the ensuing 2 years.

Household & kitchen furniture at auction on: Nov 14, at the auction rooms; the personal estateof the late Stephen Cassin. By order, Wm Redin, Walter S Cox, Wm P Maulsby, adms -Jas C McGuire, auct

The long protracted Chas Morey negotiation has been decided, & the French Gov't has made the liberal allowance to the widow of 76,000 frs, about $15,000. This is a handsome indemnity, & does honor to the liberality of the French Gov't. It was the sum fixed between the widow & the American Minister, & was accepted without a murmur after other preliminaries had been got rid of. Mr Mason has been indefatigable in the prosecution of this claim, & deserves the highest praise.

A letter from Rome of Oct 12 announces that <u>Cardinal Francisco</u> de Medici was struck with apoplexy the preceding evening while paying a visit to Monsignor Guiseppe Stola, private camerist of his holiness. He died in the evening. The Cardinal was born at Naples Nov 28, 1808, & received the purple on Jun 16, 1856.

Lines: on the death of the venerable John D Catlin, of Dayton, Ala, & affectionately inscribed to his son, J D Catlin, of Louisiana, by Sallie Ada Reedy. [4 stanzas.] –Glenada, La, Oct, 1857

Died: on Fri, Oct, 1857, at St Louis, Mo, Stephen Keane, aged 63 years, for a long period a resident of Wash City. [*Copied as written-no day number noted.]

Select Boarding School for Young Ladies. English & French: 309 F st, between 11th & 12th sts. Under the personal superintendence of Prof Donald Macleod & the Ladies of his family, with assistants of ability & experience.

Orphans Court of Wash Co, D C. Letters of administration on the personal estate of Geo McNeir, late of Wash Co, deceased. –Thos S NcNeir, adm

U S Patent Ofc, Wash, Nov 7, 1857. Ptn of Josiah Copeland, of Weymouth, Mass, praying for the extension of a patent granted to him on Jan 20, 1844, for an improvement in boot crimps for 7 years from the expiration of said patent, which takes place on Jan 25, 1858. –Jos Holt, Com'r of Patents

TUE NOV 10, 1857
Mr Haskell, of Jamesport, Long Island, with 3 of his boys, all young, went out in a skiff to visit their eel-pots last Mon, when by accident the boat upset & the father & children all drowned. Mr Haskell leaves a wife, & a child only one month old.

Seneca Co, Ohio. A few days since, Horace Fleming was sentenced to the penitentiary for burglary; whereupon his wife, Mary Jane, plead guilty of an attempt at arson & received a like sentence. She did this for the purpose of accompanying her husband into his place of confinement.

Norman Van Buren, of Ballston, Saratoga Co, shot himself accidentally several days ago, while cleaning his gun. He staggered a few steps & fell dead. Mr Van Buren was to have been married the same evening.

Mr Jas Norton died in Nicholas Co, Ky, on Oct 21 at the advanced age of 96 years. In early life he enlisted as a private soldier in the ranks of the army of the U S, & was present & took an active part in many of the battles of the Revolution. He afterwards participated in the war with the Indians in the Northwest.

Mr Ebenezer Robinson, of South Reading, Vt, died on Oct 31. He was 92 years of age, was a soldier of the Revolution, & during that war was for some time held as a prisoner by the British.

Died: on Nov 7, Augustine H Hill, in his 23rd year. His funeral will take place from the residence of his mother, Mrs Catherine Hill, on 5th st, between G & H sts, this evening at 3 o'clock.

Died: on Nov 3, at the residence of her brother-in-law, J Wilson Iglehart, in Anne Arundel Co, Md, Pamelia R, wife of Rev Saml Kepler, of the Methodist Episcopal Church, & sister of Mr John Davidson, of Gtwn, D C.

Probable assassination of a Washingtonian. We have perused a letter written by Mr Lewis A Franklin, at San Diego, Oct 7, to Mrs Henry H Whaley, of this city, informing that lady that on Oct 3 her husband had been unprovokedly & wantonly assailed by a drunken man named Rube Le Roy, & so injured with a knife that his left arm had to be amputated; that mortification had supervened; & that the life, of Mr Whaley was, at the date of this letter, regarded as in imminent peril. The kindness of Maj Ringgold & others is spoken of in terms of warm commendation by the writer. Mr Whaley is well known to many of our city readers. -State

WED NOV 11, 1857
Valuable farm, stock, crop, & farm utensils at auction, in PG Co, Md, on Nov 20: a handsome farm on the road leading from Balt turnpike, between Scaggs' & Brown's White House, to the Paint Chapel. The farm contains 140 acres, more or less, it being the farm lately occupied by Jos Owens. The improvements are a frame dwlg, barn, & stables. -A Green auct

During the past year Henry Wood, of Christy & Wood's Minstrels, purchased lots 561 & 563 Broadway, N Y; lots together are 50 feet on Broadway by 100 feet deep, & in addition Mr Wood leased the back lot on Prince st, giving him a depth of about 150 feet, with a Broadway front of 50 feet. On this land he has erected *Wood's Bldgs*, a handsome white marble edifice, which contains 2 fine stores on Broadway already occupied, a deep & spacious basement, to be leased for a first-class restaurant, & a spacious & elegant theatre, with seats for 2,000 auditors. The whole cost of the edifice & land is $178,000, & it will undoubtedly be as profitable an investment as it is a fine ornament to this part of Broadway. The theatre was duly inaugurated on Oct 16.

Wanted, a Manager on the estate of the late Roderick McGregor, in PG Co, Md. Inquire of N M McGregor, exc, 530 7th st, Wash. [Wanted, 20 dry cows.]

Balt Sun: arrests have been made of persons transgressing the law by carrying weapons in the street. Geo Ogle was arraigned before Justice Webb by Ofcr Caulk, charged with carrying firearms through the street & resisting him in the discharge of his duty. Committed for court. Jas Fredell was brought up on several charges of assaulting his wife & carrying deadly weapons. Committed to court. Martin Owen, charged with carry firearms in the street was held for a further hearing. Timothy Clark, Chas Spear, & Lewis Febron were arrested by ofcrs Gardner, Groves, & Reed, all charged with firing pistols in the street contrary to ordinance. The first were fined $6, & the latter $3.33, with costs.

The Pension Bureau has advices of the conviction of John E Ballow, of Carthage, Tenn, at Nashville, for forging papers to obtain bounty-land warrants. His sentence is 8 years' confinement in the penitentiary or State prison. He is a well connected young man, about 25 years of age. –Star

Miss Christie Johnson, Teacher of Elocution: residence-Miss Harrover's [formerly Miss English] Female Seminary, Washington & Gay sts, Gtwn. Apply at Blanchard & Mohun's Bookstore, Pa ave & 11th sts.

Mrd: on Nov 3, at Christ Church, Winchester, Va, by Rev Mr Walker, Mr Geo R Page, of Clark Co, to Miss Margaret P Cabell, daughter of the late P H Cabell, of Lynchburg, Va.

Mrd: on Nov 10, by Rev J G Butler, Geo B Scaggs, of Montg Co, Md, to Ruth Clark, of Wash City.

Died: on Tue, Harriett Wethered Clymer, daughter of Dr Geo Clymer, U S Navy. Her funeral will take place on Thu, at 10 o'clock, from the residence of Cmdor Shubrick.

THU NOV 12, 1857
Miss Cline, about 16 years of age, while lighting candles at a tomb in the **Gretna Cemetery**, on Sunday, had her dress accidentally ignited, & she died in an hour. Her father was badly burnt trying to extinguish the flames. –N O Picayune

Cummings, who embezzled the funds of the Bank of Upper Canada, has been sentenced to 5 years imprisonment in the penitentiary. Saml D Ross, who was found guilty of robbing the mails in the cars between Montreal & Toronto, has been sentenced to imprisonment for life.

On Tue telegraph cable was layed down between Phil & Camden in about 21 minutes; the length of the cable very nearly 3,000 feet. The wires were tested by the aid of a battery & found to be perfect.

Orphans Court of Wash Co, D C. Letters of administration on the personal estate of Jos L Peabody, late of Wash Co, deceased. –W H Ward, adm

Orphans Court of Wash Co, D C. Letters testamentary on the personal estate of Eliz Talbot, late of Wash Co, deceased. –John R Holt, exc

Died: on Nov 10, in Wash City, Estelle Fillmore, infant daughter of Benj C & Martha S Wright, aged 15 months & 21 days. Her funeral is this evening, at 2½ o'clock, from the residence of her parents, 497 I st north.

FRI NOV 13, 1857

On Nov 4 Mr Butterfield Varnum & his wife, a venerable pair, who for 57 years have lived happily together in Dracut, Mass, died under somewhat singular circumstances. Mrs Varnum, who has for nearly a year past been in failing health, has frequently expressed the wish that her life might be spared as long as that of her aged partner; &, as if Heaven had answered her prayers, she expired on the same day in less than 5 hours after he breathed his last. Mrs Varnum was 78 years of age, & had been for many years an exemplary member of the First Congretional Church. Mr Varnum was born in Dracut upont the same estate upon which he died, & upon which he had passed his life. He was 82 years of age at the time of his decease, & till within a few months had been actively engaged upon his farm.

Mail robbers, L C Griswold, David Lochbaum, & Solomon Lochbaum, were arrested on Thu last, charged with robbing the U S mail. Griswold was arrested at Galesburg, one of the Lochbaums at Knoxville, & the other at Elmwood, Peoria Co, Ill.

A man named Jones, convicted at Columbus, Ohio, of shooting Cyrus Beebe, has been sentenced to the penitentiary for life.

Brownsville Flag Extra of Oct 24. On Friday last, fire & explosion at the establishment of Messrs Galvan & Co. Mr Frank North, of the firm of Woodhuse & Co, expired; Mr J Moritz was killed; Mr Allsbach & Mr Portilla were wounded.

Before the Court of Common Pleas for Worcester Co, Thos Graham, for breaking into & robbing the house of Ethan Allen, of that city, was sentenced to hard labor in the State Prison during his natural life. Graham was armed at the time of the robbery. –Boston Journal

Mrd: on Nov 10, at the residence of the bride's brother, by Rev Danl Motzer, Mr Alex'r Peter to Miss Jennie Gassaway, all of Montg Co, Md.

SAT NOV 14, 1857

Public sale of valuable farm: public auction on Nov 20, his tract of land in Stafford Co, Va, containing about 500 acres; with a dwlg, stable, corn-house, fish-house, & servants' house, all new. –John L Marye, Fredericksburg, Va

New Store & New Goods: Fancy Millinery Goods, Toys, Perfumery, & Hosiery: 502 11th st, [old stand.] -Wm P Shedd

$150 reward for runaway negro man Jerry Ogle, age about 50. –J W Lyons, Gtwn

Mrd: on Nov 12, at the Assembly's Church, by Rev Andrew G Carothers, Mr C Isaac Beers to Miss Ann E Duvall, both of Wash City.

Mrd: on Oct 20, at Montville, King Wm Co, Va, by Rev MrTravers, Dr Patrick H Cabell, of Selma, Ala, to Pattie, daughter of the late Gen Philip Aylett, of Va.

Mrd: on Nov 3, in Hillsboro, Va, by Rev Mr Beard, Mr Saml T Brown, of Waterford, Va, to Miss Mary H Shaw, of Gtwn, D C.

Mrd: on Tue, at St Mary's Church, by Rev Fr Vicinanzi, J Wm Bowling, of Alexandria, Va, to Mary Julia, eldest daughter of the late Dr F Boarman, of Chas Co.

Mrd: on Nov 11, at the residence of her father, in Upperville, Fauquier Co, Va, by Rev O A Kiusching, J Welby Armstrong to Bettie O G, daughter of W A Stephenson.

One week later from Europe: Gen Cabaignac died suddenly of disease of the heart. [No other information.]

MON NOV 16, 1857

Household & kitchen furniture at auction on: Nov 19, at the residence of the late Mrs Lenox, E st, between 10th & 11th sts. -Jas C McGuire, auct

Household & kitchen furniture at auction on: Nov 17, by virtue of a distrain for house rent from Jno F Clark against A Thompson, deceased; also, a distrain from P A Beall against E Willigman, deceased. –Jas Ginnatty, Bailiff -Jas C McGuire, auct

Ex-Pres Pierce, it is stated, has accepted the invitation tendered him some time since by Pres Buchanan, offering himself & wife a passage to Madeira in the steamer **Powhatan**. They will sail somewhere about the last of the month.

Valuable work horses, wagon, buggy, & carriage at auction on Nov 20, at Hagel's stables, on Beall st, near High. –Barnard & Buckey, aucts, Gtwn

By the New Orleans papers we see that the contract for the statue to be erected in that city to the memory of Henry Clay has been signed, & the sculptor is Mr Joel T Hart, who will be assisted in casting the statue by Mons Miller, of Munich, who is reported to be the most eminent caster in Europe. The Monument Association agree to pay the artist for this work $14,000-$6,000 on the completion of the model & its readiness to be cast in bronze, & the remaining $8,000 on the delivery of the statue to the cmte. The artist gives a hope that the statue will be ready for inauguration on Apr 12, 1859.

It is not Wm D Rogers, late of the Univ of Va, but his brother, Henry D Rogers, who has been elected Professor of Natural Science in the Univ of Glasgow, Scotland.

Mrd: on Nov 10, in Hampton, Va, by Rev E H Harlow, John Critcher, of Westmoreland, to Lizzie, 2nd daughter of Kennon Whiting.

Died: on Nov 12, at Balt, Alex'r Montgomery Hamilton, aged 58 years, brother of Mrs R Patten. Mr Hamilton was connected with the U S Navy for upwards of 40 years.

Died: on Nov 1, at the residence of his father, in Leonardtown, Md, Robert, youngest son of Robert Ford, aged 19 months.

New Orleans, Nov 14. J P Henderson & J W Hempell are elected to the U S Senate from Texas.

TUE NOV 17, 1857
Extract from a letter of Chief Justice Echols, of Utah, dated at Camp on Sweet Water, 21 miles east of South Pass, Oct 13, 1857. An express has just arrived from Green river, & reports that on Oct 5 a train of 26 wagons was captured by the Mormons, 25 miles from the Pacific Spring. At the same time 2 other trains were taken near Green river, in all 78 wagons & loading. The Mormons said they had 700 men there & 1,500 more at Salt Lake City. Col Alexander is encamped on **Ham's Fort**, 30 miles in advance of the front train, which is destroyed. He sent Capt Marcy with 400 men back to Green river to enable the teamsters to collect their cattle. The Mormons killed no one, for the reason that no resistance was made.
+
Camp Sweet Water, Oct 13. Col Smith, of the 10th infty, with a portion of his command, consisting of about 65 men, rank & file, are encamped here for the night. Lt J T Lee, with 50 men, were left at Laramie to escort Govn'r Cumming on, when he comes that far. Our camp is 35 miles east of Pacific Springs. An express has just reached us from Grand river, bringing news to us as unexpected as it is important; & I avail myself to a halt to give you a succinct statement for the public. The Mormon problem is solved at last.

Balt: 1-On Nov 6 Mrs Mgt Weyhing was wounded by a slug fired at her while she was standing at her door, Bond & Shakespeare sts. Dr Dashields extracted the slug, but to no avail. She died on Saturday. 2-Jas McAllister, age 25 years, accidentally shot himself in the thigh with a pistol. His left leg was amputated, but he died.

Convictions under the new "Arms' Ordinance: on Sat Chas Hurdle, D C, was arrested by watchman Donelly for carrying a double-barrel pistol, of rather singular make, found in his possession. Hurdle was fined $20 & costs; upon which Hurdle appealed to the Circuit Court.

N Y, Nov 16. P H Burnett is appointed Justice of the Supreme Court in Calif, vice Judge Murrray, deceased.

An affray occurred in Huntsville, Texas, on Oct 26, in which Wm Leach, who had attempted to procure a divorce from his wife, was attacked by his 2 step-sons. One of the sons was killed & the other mortally wounded.

Circuit Court: 1-Wm M Cripps vs E A Edmonston. The plntf not having produced his witnesses in Court, suffered a non pros. 2-Robt S Patterson vs Saml Devaugh. Plntf complained of damage done to his property by the improperly constructed sewer of dfndnt. Verdict for plntf for $276.26. 3-Benj Crane vs Anthony Buckley, adm of Ann E Marcellus. Verdict for the plntf for $805.86 & interest from Apr 21, 1851. 4-Wm M Cripps vs Melvine Frye. This was a case on an appeal from a magistrate's decision in favor of dfndnt. Verdict for plntf $29. 5-Chas H Brown vs Andrew Schwartz. This was a case in which there was no buying or selling, but a simple exchange, or what is properly styled a swop; one of the parties refusing to stick to his bargain. It had not been decided when we left the Court.

N Y, Nov 16. P H Burnett is appointed Justice of the Supreme Court in Calif, vice Judge Murrray, deceased.

T S Verdi, M D, Homoeopathic Physician & Surgeon: 442 15th st, & N Y ave. [Ad]

WED NOV 18, 1857
N Y Courier: Sir Wm Gore Ouseley, the newly appointed British Minister to Central America arrived in that city. He will leave this morning for Washington, for the purpose of consulting with Lord Napier.

New Orleans papers: Died-Hon Dennis Prieur, of that city, aged 66 years. He was formerly mayor of New Orleans & Collector of the Port. [No death date given- current item.]

Catharine Marvine died from burns received from the explosion of a camphene lamp on Thu. –N Y Post

Headquarters of the Army, N Y, Nov 13, 1857.

1-On Feb 17, 1856, Capt Jas Oakes, with a part of his company, C, 2nd Cavalry, from **Fort Mason**, Texas, after a pursuit of 6 days, & on the 9th day from his post, overtook a party of 7 more Indians; killed & wounded several others, capturing all their animals & other property; Sgt Reis & private Kuhn severely wounded.

2-Lt August V Kautz, 4th Infty, [wounded,] & Lts Robt H Davis & David B McKibbin, 9th Infty, are commended for their gallantry in the engagement with the Indians on White river.

3-In Mar, 1856, Sgt M Kelley, Co H, 4th Infty, with 8 men, gallantly defended a small block-house & protected all the public property at the Cascades, Wash Territory, for 2 days against a body of 50 Indians. He had one man, private L Rooney killed, & privates F Bernaud & O McManus, wounded, the latter since dead of his wounds.

4-Apr, 1856. A detachment of 30 dragoons, commanded by 1st Lt Isaiah N Moore, 1st Dragoons, with 2nd Lt Horace Randal, sent out by Brvt Lt Col D T Chandler, 3rd Infty, from the force under his command, near the Almaigre Mountains, New Mexico, came upon & charged a band of Gila Apaches in a canon, killed one, wounded several others, of whom 3 died, & captured their prisoners, baggage, sheep, horses, & mules. Pvt Allen, of Co I, severely & dangerously, & private Fox, of Co D, 1st Dragoons, severely wounded.

5-Apr 7, 1856. A detachment of 108 men from the 1st & 2nd Artl, commanded by Brvt Maj Lewis G Arnold, 2nd Artl, with Capt Saml K Dawson & 2nd Lt Loomis L Langdon, 1st Artl, & 2nd Lt Geo G Garner, 2nd Artl, were attacked by a large assembled force of Seminoles in the **Big Cypress** Swamp, Florida. The Indians were repeatedly charged & driven from the strong positions they successively occupied in the swamps & hammocks, but with what loss is not known. Private John Simons, Co L, 2nd Artl, was killed; Capt Jos Carson & privates Geo Muller, John Strobell, Co C, 2nd Artl, & private Thos Newton, Co L, 1st Artl, severely, & privates Silas M Watkins & Wm Abbott, Co C, 2nd Artl, slightly wounded.

6-On Apr 13, 1856, a party of 55 Indians was overtaken on the head waters of the Nueces by detachments from companies B & D, Mounted Riflemen, & F, 1st Artl, from **Fort McIntosh** & **Fort Duncan**, Texas, under the command respectively of Capt Thos Claiborne, jr, & Brvt Capt Gordon Granger, Mounted Riflemen, & 2nd Lt Geo H Elliot, 1st Artl. One Indian killed & 4 made prisoners, their camp & all their animals captured. The troops marched 350 miles in 8 days in pursuit of the Indians. The Mayor of Loredo, Sr Don Santos Benevidas, Mr Edw Jordan, & some 25 other citizens of that place participated in this pursuit, & are represented as having rendered valuable service.

7-Nov 25, 1856, Capt Wm R Barfute, with a detachement of 19 men of his company G, 2nd Cavalry, from **Fort Mason**, Texas, after a march of 8 days came upon & surprised a party of Comanche Indians, near the head of the main Concho, killing 4, wounding several. In the conflict private John Curtis was severely wounded.

8-Dec 22, 1856. Capt R W Johnson with 25 men of Co F, with 2nd Lt A P Porter, all of the 2nd Cavalry, after a march of 7 days from **Camp Colorado**, Texas, came upon a part of Saneco's band of Comanche Indians, near Concho; charged upon & drove them into the chaparral. In this sharp conflict bugler Campion & private Lamb were killed by arrow shots through the heart, & Sgt Gardnier & private McKim slightly wounded.

9-Mar 9, 1857. Brvt Capt Alfred Gibbs, Mounted Riflemen, commanding a detachment of 16 men of Co G, same regt, from *Fort Fillmore*, New Mexico, attacked a party of Mimbris Apache Indians. Brvt Capt Gibbs received a severe wound in the body from a lance.

10-Mar 11, 1857, 2nd Lt Lawrence S Baker, Mounted Riflemen, with a small detachment from Co B, same regt, from *Fort Thorn*, New Mexico, after a hot pursuit, came upon a party of Indians supposed to be Mescalero Apaches or Kioways: recaptured stolen animals, as well as those belonging to the Indians, with their other property. His loss was private Patrick Sullivan, killed, & private Bernard Dougherty mortally wounded, [since dead,] Sgt P Duggan, Cpl John Brady, & musician Thos Reed, wounded.

11-Jun 27, 1857. The southern column, commanded by Lt Col Dixon S Miles, of the Gila expedition under Col B L E Bonneville, 3rd Infty, composed of detachments from Companies B, D, G, & K, 1st Dragoons, B, G, & K, Mounted Riflemen, C, F, & K, 3rd Infty, & B & I, 8th Infty, with a company of guides & Mexicans, of Puebla Indians, & Capt __; came upon a band of Coyotero & Mogollon Apaches, killed 24. Wounded: 1st Dragoons, 2nd Lt Benj F Davis, Cpl Anderson, & Pvt Donelly, Co G. 3rd Infty, 2nd Lt Alex'r E Steen, Sgt Jas Heron, Co K, & Pvts Johnson & McNamara, Co C. Special mention is made by the superior cmders of Capt Richd S Ewell, 1st Dragoons, in planning the action & breaking the enemy. Col Bonneville gives much credit to 2nd Lt A McD McCook, 2nd Infty, for the admirable manner in which he managed his Puebla Indians. Great credit is also given by their cmders to the following named ofcrs & men:

Medical Staff: Assist Surgeon John M Haden.

1st Dragoons: 1st Lt I N Moore; 2nd Lt Alfred B Chapman & Benj F Davis; Sgt N Pishon, Co B; Cpl J Anderson & Pvts Donelly & R Walsh, Co F; Lance Cpl W Lambert & Pvt N Brewer, of Co D.

Mounted Riflemen: Capt Thos Caliborne, jr, & 2nd Lt J V D Dubois.

3rd Infty: 1st Lt Wm D Whipple & 2nd Lt A E Steen, Sgt J Heron & Pvt John S Harper, Co K; Pvts Thos McNamara, Thos P Morris, & John Brown, Co C; Sgts Dooling & Morrison, Cpl Maloney, Pvts Giles, Moore, McCardle, Quinn, Woodsman, Weis, & Zinzinhoffer, Co F.

8th Infty: 2nd Lt Henry M Lazelle, Cpl John O'Donnel & W Robinson, Co B; Sgt C Wolpent & Pvt Mckay, Co I.

12-Jul 20, 1857. A detachment of 24 men of Co G, 2nd Cavalry, commanded by 2nd Lt John B Hood, from *Fort Mason*, Texas, came upon a body of 50 Comanche & Lipan Indians, near Devil's river, San Pedro, & after severe hand to hand conflict, forced them to retire, with a loss of 9 of their number [one a chief] killed & 10 to 12 wounded. Pvt Thos Ryan, killed; 2nd Lt John B Hood, Pvts John Davit Wm W Williams, Thos E Tirrell, & John J Kane, wounded. Pvt Wm Barry missing, supposed to have been mortally wounded.

13-Col E V Sumner, 1st Cavalry, commanding expedition against the Cheyennes, with Companies A, B, D, E, G, & H of his regt, & Companies D, D, & G, 6th Infty, after a march of more than 1,000 miles, came upon some 300 Cheyenne warriors on Solomon's fork of the Kansas, in Kansas Territory, drawn up in battle array to oppose his march. The Indians were all well mounted & well armed. They were pursued 7 miles, with a loss of 9 killed. Col Sumner's loss: Pvt Martin Lynch, of Co A, & Geo Cade, Co G, 1st Cavalry, killed; 1st lt Jas E B Stuart, 1st Cavalry, severely, though not dangerously, wounded; 1st Sgt Geo C McEowen, Co D, Pvt Franz Piot, Co B, & Jas M Cooke, Co G, dangerously; 1st Sgt Henry B Robinson, Co H, Pvts Francis F Freer, Co B, Rolin Taylor, Co E, & Thos Wilson, Co D, severely; & Pvt Alex'r Wilkey, Co B, slightly wounded. -By command of Brvt Lt Gen Scott: Irvin McDowell, Assist Adj Gen

San Bernardino, Oct 4, 1857. An entire train of emigrants, on their way from Missouri & Arkansas to this State, via Great Salt Lake City, about 130 men, women, & children, were massacred, at the Mountain Meadows, near the Rim of the Great Basin, by the Indians. The emigrants sent out a flag of truce borne by a little girl, & gave themselves up to the mercy of the savages, who immediately rushed in & slaughtered all of them, with the exception of 15 infant children, that have since been purchased with much difficulty by the Mormon interpreters. –J Ward Christian

Jas Copeland, one of a notorious clan which for a long time infested the border counties of Alabama & Mississippi, was hanged at Augusta, Perry Co, Miss, on Oct 30, for the murder of Jas Harvey, some 10 years ago. The culprit was 31 years of age, & had passed 11 years of his existence in prison.

Mr Jas Morrison, one of the wealthiest merchants of London, is dead. The value of his property is estimated at nearly four million pounds sterling, a considerable portion of which is invested in securities in the U S. [No death date given-current item.]

The funeral of Gen Cavaignac took place at Paris on Oct 31, in the Church of St Louis d'Antin. He was interred in the cemetery of Montmartre.

The practice ship **Plymouth** arrived yesterday in the Potomac, last from England; all well on board. List of ofcrs: Cmder, John A Dahlgren; Lts, C Ap R Jones, Geo B Balch, Saml Edwards, W A Webb, O C Badger, Wm T Truxtun; Surgeon, J D Miller; Assist Surgeon, A M Vedder; Purser, W Brenton Boggs; Boatswain, Chas W Smith; Gunner, R H Cross; Carpenter, T C Terrall; Sailmaker, Mr Brayton; Cmder's Clerk, Mr Sengstack; Purser's Clerk, L J O'Toole.

On Mon, 2 men, one originally from Balt, Eugene Lanahan, the other latterly, G W Hook, were walking on Pa ave. When they arrived between Tiber bridge & 1st st they went into a restaurant kept by Jos E Birch, but soon left. As they walked a few steps from the door Hook & Lanahan were struck by some person. Words ensued between the opposing parties, one of whom was Birch; who in reply to Lanahan fired a pistol wounding Lanahan in the right breast. He is lying in a perilous condition. Birch & Hook were arrested by officers Brewers & Gormley, & brought before Justice Donn. Jos Codderick, the timer for Vanderwerken's omnibuses, testified that the person who fired the pistol was one of 2 persons who came along the avenue. Lanahan distinctly asserts that it was Birch who shot him. Birch was refused bail.

Calif: There is no local news of interest. 1-*Hock Farm*, the residence of Gen John A Sutter, has been redeemed, & the old pioneer says that he now sits under his own vine & fig tree. 2-The telegraph is to be extended northward from Marysville to Shasta, Weaverville, & Yreka. 3-F V Moore, who was under the sentence of death for the crime of murder, committed suicide in the Navada jail, by taking strychnine, on the night previous to the day on which he was to be executed. 4-Hon P H Burnett has been appointed as Supreme Court Justice, vice Murray, deceased. Stephen J Field, Justice elect, has been appointed in place of Burnett, who was appointed vice Heydenfeldt, resigned.

Mrd: on Nov 12, at Calvary Church, N Y, by Rev Dr Hawks, Thos Aston Coffin, of Charleston, S C, to Miss Sarah Heyward Cruger, daughter of the late Henry N Cruger, of N Y C.

Died: on Nov 14, at Cumberland, Md, Caroline, daughter of Geo M Kendall, & widow of the late Rev S W Price, aged about 22 years. Her disease waas inflamed sore throat, & her decease sudden & painful; but her Christian hope, entertained from earliest childhood, was strong in death. Her funeral will be at the residence of her father, on Md ave, between 4½ & 6th sts, today, at 12 o'clock.

Died: on Nov 17, of water on the brain, Richard W, son of Dr Wm P & Eliza McConnell, aged 9 years & 10 months. His funeral will take place on Nov 19, at 2 o'clock, from the residence, 9 N Y ave, between 8th & 9th sts.

THU NOV 19, 1857
Died: at his residence, Capitol Hill, Mr John L Wirt, in his 47th year. His funeral will take place on Nov 19, at 3 o'clock. [No death date given.]
+
I O O F. Members of Central Lodge, No 1, are requested to attend the funeral of Brother John L Wirt. –Robt W Middleton, sec.]

Died: on Nov 2, at his residence, in Windsor, Conn, Martin Ellsworth, aged 74 years, eldest son of Oliver Ellsworth, the 2nd Chief Justice of the U S.

The New Orleans papers announce the death of Gen Casimir Lacoste, a native of Louisiana, & a veteran of the last war with Great Britain. For many years past he discharged the duties of Quartermaster-Genr'l of the State, & also frequently served in the Legislature. He died on Nov 10th from a sword wound in the side which he received several days previously in a duel.

New Orleans, Nov 18. The mail steamship **Opelousas**, from Berwick Bay to Galveston, Texas, came in collision with the steamer **Galveston**, of the same line on Nov 15. The **Opelousas** sunk almost immediately, & from 20 to 25 persons were lost, among whom was Gen Hamilton, of S C. All the ofcrs & crew were saved. [Nov 28th newspaper: Gen Hamilton was born at Charleston, S C, in 1789. His maternal grandfather, Thos Lynch, not only signed the Declaration of Independence, but was the author of the first address & remonstrance to the British House of Commons in the first Congress of the Colonies after the passage of the stamp act. His father, the late venerable Maj Hamilton, of the old continental line, was a favorite aid of the great Washington; commanded one of the regts of Wayne's brigade, & was gallantly distinguished in almost every important battle of the Revolution. In the war of 1812 Gen [then Major] Hamilton served with great distinction throughout the Canadian campaigns. At the termination of the war he returned to the practice of the law in Charleston, in copartnership with the late eminent Judge Huger. In 1824 he was successor to the great Wm Lowndes, who had been one of his dearest friends, & whose death he most deeply deplored.]

Trustee's sale of valuable real estate: by decree passed on Nov 6, 1857, by the Circuit Court for PG Co, sitting as a Court of Equity, in a cause wherein Mgt S A Cumming, next friend to Edmund B Cumming & others, is cmplnt, & Edmund B Cumming & others are dfndnts, the undersigned, as trustee, will expose at public sale on Dec 10, all that valuable real estate in said county, which was heretofore conveyed to Hon Thos U Cumming [now deceased & intestate] by Martin Buel & Lucy Ann, his wife, in fee simple, containing 177½ acres, more or less. The country road to Washington by way of 7th & North Capitol sts is a boundary one one side; it is within 2 miles of Soldiers' Home; adjoins the property of the late Stephen Markwood, the Messrs Wingerd, Diggs, Clarke, & others. –Danl C Digges, trustee, Upper Marlboro, Md.

The recently erected Lutheran Church, [German language,] corner of 4th & E sts, will be dedicated to Almighty God on Nov 22. Rev E W Keyl, of St Paul's Church, Balt, will officiate in the morning; Rev W Summer in the afternoon; & Rev Mr Gross, of Richmond, in the evening.

FRI NOV 20, 1857
The will of the late Mrs Dr Rush, of Phil, in effect makes her husband her sole & absolute legatee. The estate is estimated at one million dollars.

In the Circuit Court of Bedford Co, Va, last week, Miss Elmira W Wingfield obtained a verdict of $27,000 damages from Wm Stein for breach of marriage contract. The lady is about 34 & the gentleman about 80. This was the second trial of the case; a former jury having given a verdict of $650 for the plntf, which was set aside on motion of the dfndnt. –Harrisburg [Pa] Telegraph, Nov 13

The Newark [Ohio] Advocate contains the notice of the death of Mr Zachariah Albaugh, who died on Nov 8, aged 109 years. He was born in Md in 1748, where he resided until the commencement of the Revolutionary war, when he entered the army as a private soldier, & remained in it until the close of that struggle. He soon became an ofcr, & was in the battle of Germantown, Oct 3, 1777. After the close of the war Mr Albaugh removed to Westmoreland Co, Pa, where he lived in the vicinity of the residence of Gen St Clair, [one of the Revolutionary veterans,] until 1817, the period of his removal to Licking Co, Ohio. Here he lived in a comparative retirement during the last 40 years of his life, being known to but a small circle of friends. He has long been the recipient of a pension from his country, whose freedom he assisted in establishing. Until within a short period of his death he retained to a remarkable degree his mental faculties. He died in full possession of a Christian's hope.

The Phil Bulletin of Tue states that Eliz Fleck, living in Spring Garden st, was badly burnt, the night before, by the exploision of a fluid lamp.

Whirlwind in Mississippi, in Tunica Co, on Nov 8, blew down the dwlg of Emerson O'Neal. His wife was killed, & her mother was also fatally injured.

Mr Jas Blakely, a worthy mechanic at the Navy Yard, was seriously injured yesterday whilst assisting in lifting a heavy weight in the new ordnance shop. His thigh was broken & several ribs fractured. A rafter broke from which the weight was suspended.

Mrd: on Nov 19, at Trinity Church, by Rev Mr Cummin, Malcolm Seaton to Jane, daughter of the late Benj Sprigg, all of Wash City.

Mrd: on Nov 17, in Wash City, by Rev Mr O'Toole, Edw T Mathews to Miss Jane E Faherty, both of Wash.

Navy Dept, Nov 19, 1857. Sealed proposal: endorsed Proposals for Steam Machinery for Screw Propeller Sloop-of-war, will be received at this Dept until Dec 13 next, for the complete construction of the steam machinery & appendages, & placing it on board a screw propeller ship-of-war building in the U S navy yard at Phil. -Isaac Toucey, Sec of the Navy

New Orleans Picayune of Nov 13. Before this reaches you, Gen Walker will have left the U S on his way back to Nicaragua, with the 1st division of emigrants; about 350 men, over 200 of whom left New Orleans. The ofcrs are as follows:
Aide to the Gen: Maj J V Hooff & Capt A Brady
Assist Surgeon Gen: Dr Kellum
Cols: Frank P Anderson, Bruno Natzmer, Thos Henry
Lt Cols: S T Tucker, A Swingle
Capts: C Fayssoux & Kennedy, [Navy,] J S West, J V Cook, B F Whittier, McChesney
Lts: Wm A Rhea, McMichael, R G Stokely, Winn
Civil Ofcrs: F Belcher, Jacob Colmus
Soldiers & Citizens:Chas Brogan, John Tabor, [editor Nicaraguense,] Fred Romer, John Rutter, J M West, M Cavanagh, R V C Richards, W H Hunter, John Yates, Tom Moore. Col Anderson, Maj Hooff, Capt Kennedy, Chas Brogan, & Jacob Colmus were among the original 56 who left San Francisco with Gen Walker in 1855, in the brig **Vesta**.
+
Mobile, Nov 12. Last night some 50 or more went aboard the steamer **Dick Keys**, which immediately left for the lower harbor, where she took Gen Walker on board today.

SAT NOV 21, 1857
Last week Joel Schoonhozen, 100 years of age, was discharged from Sing Sing State Prison, having been pardoned by the Govn'r. He was committed for life for arson. He is a native of Orange Co, & in prison reached the age of a century on Jul 4 last. He saw Washington at Newburg during the war.

The Portland [Me] Argus of Nov 18 says that Breen & the elder Slavin have confessed the murder of the McKenzie family, at St John, N B, on Oct 24. The younger Slavin was found guilty of complicity in the crime, but recommended to mercy. They have been sentenced to be executed on Dec 11.

Constable arrested. It seems that Constable H R Maryman, unable to effect an execution on the goods & chattels of Mich O'Brien during daylight, waylaid the house, &, with his 2 sons & 2 others to aid him, threatened to break into the house after dark. O'Brien secured the protection of the Auziliary Guard, who arrested the assailing party & brought them before Justice Donn. The Justice decided against the legality of Maryman's course, held to bail to answer at the next term of the criminal Court, & fined the 4 others $20 each for carrying dangerous weapons. It is said that appeal will be made to the Circuit Court in the matter of the fines.

The death of the distinguished French Gen Eugene Cavaignac. He fell dead of aneurism of the heart, while out shooting, & was buried at Paris on Oct 30. He was born at Paris, Dec 15, 1802.

MON NOV 23, 1857
Household & kitchen furniture at auction on Nov 27, by order of the Orphans Court of Wash Co, D C; at the late residence of the late Wm Holmead, in rear of Columbia College, on Pine Branch road. –Mary A Holmead, admx -Jas C McGuire, auct

Auction of stock of Family Groceries, on Nov 27, at the store of Francis Miller, 12th & F sts, his entire stock. -J C McGuire, auct

N Y: Dr Alex'r B Mott, son of the celebrated Dr Mott, was attacked on Thu night, on his return from a sick call, but by a vigorous use of a revolver repelled his assailants.

Arrival of the steam frig **Niagara**, Capt Hudson, from Plymouth, England, arrived at N Y on Fri. She left Plymouth on Nov 5, thus making the passage in 14 days & 4 hours. List of her ofcrs: Wm L Hudson, Capt; Alex M Pennock, Cmder; Jas H North, Lts: Joshua D Todd, John Guest, Wm D Whiting, Edw Y McCauly, Beverly Kennon; Jas C Palmer, Surgeon; Jos C Eldridge, Purser; Jabez C Rich, Capt Marines; Wm S Boyd, Lt, do; Arthur M Lynch, Passed Assist Surgeon; H W H Washington, Assist Surgeon; Wm E Everett, Chief Engineer; John Faron, 1st do; Thos A Shock, 1st do; Mortimer Kellogg, 2nd do; John W Moore, 2nd do; Alex Green, 3rd do; Jackson McElwell, 3rd do; Geo F Kutz, 3rd do; Theo R Ely, 3rd do; John W Hudson, Capt's Clerk; Edw Willard, Purser's Clerk

Dissolution of copartnership under the firm of Haslup & Weeden, by mutual consent. -Lewis Haslup, Henry H Weeden

Orphans Court of Wash Co, D C. Letters testamentary on the personal estate of Jane Goldsborough, late of Wash Co, deceased. –R Goddard, exc

Four days from Europe: Delhi was in complete possession of the British on Sep 21. Gen Nicholson died of his wounds. The King of Delhi had surrendered. His life was spared, but his 2 sons were shot.

I hereby certify that Enoch Ward brought before me, as strays, 2 spayed heifers. –Thos C Donn, J P [Owner is to come forward, prove property, pay charges, & take them away. –Enoch Ward, 10th & E sts, south, Island]

Ofcrs of the Utah Expedition:
Col A S Johnston, 2nd Cavalry, commanding; Maj Fitzjohn Porter, Assist Adj Gen; Capt J H Dickerson, Assist Quartermaster; Capt H F Clarke, Commissary of Subsistence; Dr Madison Mills, Surgeon; Dr A T Ridgeley, Assist Surgeon; Dr J Moore, Assist Surgeon; Dr J C Bailey, Acting Assist Surgeon; Dr R Barthelow, Assist Surgeon; Dr E J Bailey, Assist Surgeon; Maj T E Hunt, Paymaster.

Artillery: Capt J W Phelps, 4th Artl, commanindg light field battery; Lts R V Howard, 4th Artl; G Tallmadge, do; J A Kensel, do; Capt J L Reno, Ordnance Corps, commanding heavy field battery.

2nd Dragoons [8 Companies.] Lt Col P St Geo Cooke, commanding regt; Maj M S Howe; Lt J Pegram, Adj; Lt J Buford, Regimental Quartermaster; Maj H H Sibley; Capt J M Haws; Lts W D Smith, C H Tyler, J P Holliday, T Hight, J B Villepigue, G A Gordon, J Mullins, F C Armstrong, H B Livingston, J Green, E Gay, Jackson, Ferguson.

Fifth Infty: Lt Col C A Waite, commanding; Lt A Chambers, Adj; Lt W W Burns, Regimental Quartermaster; Capt & Brvt Lt Col W Chapman; Capts R B Marcy, J C Robinson, H R Seldon, T H Neill; Lts S Archer, W H Lewis, H C Bankhead, W A Webb, C J Lynde, A T Torbert, R C Hill, J F Ritter, H B Bristol, A W Shipley, L L Rich.

Tenth Infty: Col E B Alexander, commanding; Lt Col C Smith; Maj & Brvt Lt Col E R S Canby; Lt H E Maynadier, Adj; Lt P T Swaine, Regimental Quartermaster; Capts F Gardney, A Tracy, J A Gore, J Dunovant, J L Tidball, & B E Bee; Lts C Grover, W Clinton, N A M Dudley, J H Forney, L A Williams, J Deshler, W Kearney, J H Hill, C E Bennett, J L Thompson, F S Armistead, S E Carroll, A S Cunninghan, H B Kelly, J McNab, A Murry, T J Lee.

There are 4 ladies with the army, viz: Mrs Gov Cummings, Mrs Col Canby, Mrs Lt Tyler & Mrs Lt Burns.

Died: on Nov 21, aged 89 years, Mrs Susan Griffing, relict of Christopher Griffing, late of New London, Conn. Her remains will be buried this afternoon at 3 o'clock, from the residence of her son-in-law, Thos P Trott, at 586 N J ave, Capitol Hill.

Died: on Nov 21, at his late residence, 369 9th st, our venerable & highly esteemed fellow citizen, Geo Crandell, in his 79th year. He was a native of Anne Arundel Co, Md, & settled in Wash City in 1803 or 1804. For more than half a century he has met among us with great fidelity the responsibilities of husband, father, friend, & citizen. Christian hope will inscribe upon the tablet of his grave, he is not here, but gone before.

Died: on Oct 26, at his late residence in Kent Co, Md, Peregrine Wetherell, aged 83 years.

TUE NOV 24, 1857
News from India: London, Nov 11. The old King of Delhi, said to be 90 years of age, surrendered to Capt Hodgson about 15 miles south of Delhi. He was accompanied by his chief wife, & their lives were spared. Two of his sons & grandson were captured by Capt Hodgson about 5 miles from Delhi. They were shot on the spot.

The Balt Patriot mentions the sudden death, near that city yesterday, of Judge Alex'r Nesbit, in his 80th year.

Free lovers arrested. Sandusky [Ohio] Register: on Monday a descent was made on the Free Love establishment at Berlin, Erie Co, & E S Tyler, A W Smith, Mary Dame, *Mary Lewis, Sophronia Powers, Thos Homer, & Thos Wright were brought before the Mayor of Sandusky, on charge of adultery preferred against them.
*Mrs Mary Lewis is 42 years of age, the wife of a gentleman of high respectability; the mother of 3 children the youngest a little fellow of 5 years, who accompanied her before the court. E S Tyler had stayed at the house of her husband, & while there had made her a convert. The father & husband of Mrs Lewis urge her to come home again, but she persistently refuses to accompany them.

N Y, Nov 22. 1-Mr Waters, a resident of Port Jefferson, Long Island, entered his dwlg where his wife, her daughter, & her daughter's husband, Mr Sturdevant, were partaking of breakfast. Armed with a heavy bar of iron, Waters attacked the party, killing his wife & Mr Sturdevant almost instantly, & wounding Mrs Sturdevant so seriously as to render her recovery very doubtful. Waters proceeded to the barn & hanged himself. Mrs Waters was formerly the wife of Mr Darling, a shipbuilder, of repute at Port Jefferson. 2-Jas Rodgers, convicted of killing John Swanston while walking peaceably with his wife, was sentenced to be hung on Jan 15.
3-Young Donnelly, of Wash City, the murderer of Moses, at the Sea View House last summer, has been refused a new trial by the N J court, & will suffer the extreme penalty of the law on Jan 8, in accordance with the sentence passed upon him.

Died on Nov 21, at Middlebury, Hon Horatio Seymour, for 12 years a Senator in Congress from Vt.

Capt Walter Coles, for many years a Rep in Congress from the Lynchburg district of Va, died at his residence in Pittsylvania Co, on Nov 9, after an illness of some 4 or 5 days. He was about 68 years old. During the war of 1812 he held the ofc of Capt of Dragoons, & served upon the Northern frontier, under Gen Wade Hampton, of S C.

Danl Lynch, a laboring man, took passage from N Y on Thu at Rondout on the steamer **North America**, & having drank freely he wandered into the engine room. He was caught in the machinery & his head cut clear from his body.

Distressing accident on Nov 17 to the packet **Cataract**, Capt O'Neil, which resulted in the death of Wm Brace, Hartford, Ct; ____ Blackburn, Cass Co, Mo; Barney Kelley, barkeeper; & McDonald, express messenger. Lee Jones, 2nd engineer, lost. Thos Hutchins, Kelso, Woodbridge, Loring, & 5 deck hands & fireman, names not known, scalded. –St Louis Republican

Verdict of the Coroner's Jury in the case of the killing of Michl Murphy on Sat last, Nov 21. At the house of Mrs Catherine Hughes, G & 2nd sts, where he resided, a party of men, 8 or 10, entered the house with muskets & pistols and began firing. We believe that Wm Wilson, alias Mahoney, & Patrick McCarthy, formed a portion of the party & were committed for trial at the next term of the Criminal Court.

Jos Cunningham & Isaac Lambert were identified by Mr Polton as the men who robbed & burnt his premises, on the Island, in Sep last. Cunningham was captured, but Lambert fled.

Mrd: on Nov 19, by Rev Dr DeCharms, Mr Albert W Johnson to Miss Margaret Clark, daughter of M B Clark, formerly of Phil.

Mrd: on Nov 17, by Rev Wm H Chapman, Fred'k Albright to Miss Mary F McKenney, all of Wash.

Mrd: on Nov 17, at Foundry Church, by Rev Mr Lanahan, Mr Henry Prince, of Winchester, Va, to Miss Agnes H Ricketts, of Wash City.

Died: on Sat last, in Wash City, Mrs Harriet Simms, wife of Sampson Simms, in her 57th year. Her funeral will take place today at 1 o'clock, from their residence, 486 L st.

Died: on Nov 23, in Wash City, Jos M Lauck. His funeral will be tomorrow at 3 o'clock, from his late residence on G st, between 12th & 13th sts.

We learn from Paris of the death of Mr Camille A Fleischmann, only son of Mr Chas Fleischmann, our late Consul at Stutgardt, & for several years an esteemed resident of Wash City. His respected parents have the sincere sympathy of a large number of friends in our community. [No date death given-current item.]

WED NOV 25, 1857
Executor's sale of desirable stock of lumber, by order of the Orphan's Court for Balt City: the undersigned execs of Chas B White, deceased, will sell, on Nov 30, at his lumber yard, on Light st Wharf, Balt, the very large stock of well seasoned panel, common, & select white & yellow pine, belonging to the estate of the deceased.
-Rebecca B White, Saml Kirby, excs -Gibson & Co, aucts, Balt

In Equity, No 1,269. Wm W Hough against Eleanor, Christian M, Enosh G, Abraham F, Eliza J, John B, Christiana E K, & Philip Hines. The parties above named, as widow, administrator, & heirs of Abraham Hines, & his creditors, & trustees, are to attend at my ofc in City Hall, Wash, on Dec 17 next, when a statement of the trustee's account will be made & the funds in his hands distributed.
-W Redin, auditor

On board steamship **Galveston**. Nov 17, 1857. On Nov 15 the steamship **Galveston** came in contact with the steamship **Opelousas**, striking the **Opelousas** nearly amidship, causing her to sink in about 20 minutes. The **Galveston** received little damage, & saved the following passengers, & all of the ofcrs & crew. –John McNair, Clerk steamship **Galveston**. List of those known to be lost:
Gen J Hamilton, S C
Judge John C Cleland, New Orleans
Mr Smith, mother, & young lady, St Louis
Miss Lucy Williams, Lavaca
C W Wilmot, Hardin Co, Ky
One child of C W Wilmot, Ky
Miss Mary Pettway, Nashville, Tenn
McFarlane, late mate steamship **Jasper**
Two children of Geo Williams, Columbia, Texas
One child of Mrs Fontes, Buchanan Co, Mo
August Mendell, Dewitt Co, Texas
Dunn, Navarro, Texas
One negro girl belonging to Mr Hushbergh
One negro boy, third cook on **Opelousas**
We find on the passenger list of the **Opelousas** the following names not included in the published lists of the saved & lost. We fear that they must be included among the latter: Mr H Trainer, Mr G Hardney, Mr E Hill, Mr A J Hollis, Mr Wyeth & lady.

Edw T Nichols, cousin of Phineas T Barnum, plead guilty to forgery. In Ohio 20 years is the shortest term allowed by law for forgery. The trial just terminated in Cleveland, Ohio.

Circuit Court of Wash Co, D C-No 1,179, Equity. Pairo & Nourse against Chas H Van Patten, R H Chew, & others. W Redin, trustee, reported that on Jun 26 last he sold part of the lots decreed in said cause; that he sold the same according to a subdivision made thereof & of other lots by said Van Patten; that Chas W Pairo & Wm Nourse were the purchasers of lots 1, 2, 6 thru 13, in square 144, the same being a part of the original lots nos 10 thru 16, at the price for the whole, of $1,867.66; that Geo Lautner was the purchaser of lots 4 & 5 in same square for $317.42. The purchasers have complied with the terms of the sale. –Jno A Smith, clerk

Mrd: on Nov 24, in Wash City, by Rev Father Clarkson, John Sinon to Margaret Robinson, both of Wash City.

Mrd: on Nov 24, in Wash City, by Rev John B Meek, Wm S Payne, of King Geo Co, Va, to Columbia Newton, eldest daughter of Lt Otway H Berryman, U S Navy.

THU NOV 26, 1857
The Grand Jury of Norfolk have found 2 true bills against Wm M Pannel-one for embezzlement of money from the Farmers' Bank of Va at that place, of which he was a long time teller; & another for an attempt to poison the President.

The U S frig **Niagara** arrived at this port yesterday from Plymouth, England. Before their departure they received an anonymous letter, informing them that in one corner of the old churchyard at Plymouth laid the remains of Lt Wm Henry Allen, the cmder of the U S brig-of-war **Argus**, at the time of her capture in the English channel, during the war of 1812, & who received a fatal wound during the hard-fought contest. The ofcrs of the **Niagara** took this opportunity to renew the face of the tombstone, which tells that he whose remains lie beneath, died bravely in defence of his country's flag. "Sacred to the memory of William Henry Allen, aged 27 years, late Commander of the United States Brig **Argus**, who died August 18, 1813, in consequence of a wound received in action with H B M Brig **Pelican**, August 14, 1813. Also, in remebrance of Richard Delphy, Midshipman, aged 18 years, U S Navy, killed in the same action, whose remains are deposited on the left. Here sleep the brave." "Repaired by the officers of the U S ships **Susquehanna and Niagara**, Sep, 1857". –N Y Mirror

The dwlg of Wm Quin, near Alliance, Ohio, was burnt down on Tue, together with 3 of his children. Mr Quin was absent, & Mrs Quin had gone to town on an errand, shutting the children in the house, fearing some accident might befall them upon the railroad, which was close by. She extinguished the coal upon the hearth, & no fire was left in the bldg. The eldest, who escaped death, said the little ones found matches & in playing with them ignited the bed. The oldest had counted but 7 summers. Two, a boy & a girl, were twins.

Donation to the Smithsonian Institute. Chas S Spence showed us a rare & beautiful work of art entrusted to his care whilst in the East by Miss Eliz B Koutaxaki, of Crete, to be presented to the Smithsonian Institute. It is entitled the Classical Bouquet, & was executed by that lady & her assistants, [all native Greeks,] as a contribution to the Universal Exhibition at Paris, in 1855. Though solicited by the Queen of Greece to place it in the museum of Athens, so great is Miss Koutaxaki's admiration of the U S that she determined to send it to this country.

The equestrian statue of Washington was placed in its proper place in Capitol square, in front of the monument, on Tuesday. It will remain covered until Feb 22, when there will be a grand inauguration. –Richmond, Va

Mrd: on Nov 24, at *Leinwood*, PG Co, Md, by Rev Mr Gordon, Leonard Huyck, of N Y, to Minnie, youngest daughter of the late S E Scott, of Gtwn, D C.

Mrd: on Nov 24, at Trinity Church, by Rev Geo D Cummins, Dr Chas H Nichols to Ellen G, daughter of the late John W Maury, all of Wash City.

SAT NOV 28, 1857
Wm Wilcox, a young man, of Balt, was fatally injured on Sat by the bursting of his gun-barrel whilst out hunting.

Hon Esbon Blackman, a prominent citizen of Newark, Wayne Co, N Y, committed suicide on Thu last by drowning himself in a spring or shallow well in the cellar of his house. On Monday last he was compelled to yield to the prssure of the times & make an assignment. His pecuniary liabilities were very large, but his assets would have been ample to meet them in ordinary times. His depressed sprits caused him to commit self-destruction.

Jos Hadsall, a young man, residing near Wash, Adams Co, Miss, accidentally shot himself with a fowling-piece on Nov 13. He died soon afterwards.

The pulpit of the South Church, Salem, Mass, on Sunday last, was occupied by 2 venerable brothers, Rev Reuben Emerson, of South Reading, & Brown Emerson, D D, of Salem, the former being in his 87th year & the latter in his 80th year. They have been settled pastors within 9 miles of each other about 53 years.
–Boston Courier

The sale at **Blenheim** on Tue & Wed last, by N H Massie, exc of A Stevenson, deceased, was well attended. A miniatur of Napoleon, by Isabee, brought upwards of $400. A full length portrait of Marshal Soult, by Healy, presented to Mr Stevenson while Minister to England by Marshal Soult himself, brought $415. The paintings alone brought $4,900. –Charlottesville paper

Capt Foxhall A Parker, on the furlough list of the U S Navy, died at Phil on Monday last. He was a native of Va, & entered the navy in 1805.

The Hannah More Female Academy, near Reistertown, took fire on Tue & was burnt to the ground. All the inmates escaped, but they lost most of their wardrobe. -Sun

Died: on Nov 25, of consumption, in her 16th year, Julia C Schneider, eldest daughter of L H & J Schneider.

Mrd: on Nov 25, by Rev Mr Eckard, Cmder John Rodgers, of the U S Navy, to Miss Annie Eliz, daughter of Wm L Hodge, of Wash City.

Mrd: on Nov 16, by Rev Francis Hillyard, in St Paul's Church, Edenton, N C, Dr Edw Warren to Bettie C, daughter of Rev Saml J Johnston.

On Nov 21 the steamer **Rainbow**, Capt Holcraft, on her way from New Orleans to Louisville, with a full cargo of sugar & coffee, & with about 150 souls on board, about 10 miles above Napoleon, was discovered to be on fire, & the ofcr on the deck, Mr C Whitlow, at once gave the order to run her on shore, which was immediately executed by Mr Lamb, the pilot at the wheel, but by that time the entire boat was enveloped in flames. The loss of human life cannot be less than 75 human beings. The boat **Sovereign** was near by & succeeded in picking up several passengers. A few hours after the ship **James E Woodruff** came up & took the crew & remaining passengers saved, on board, with the exception of a few who stayed to look for the remains of their lost friends. A majority of the passengers were returned Californians, with their treasures of gold & their families, coming back to their fader land. Mr Wheatly, from Calif, with wife & child, jumped from the stern, but the wife, having $2,400 in gold on person, soon sunk to rise no more; the father, with his infant in his arms, battled for life, but being numbed from cold the child slipped & was lost; the father was saved by those on shore who had witnessed his brave struggle. He had $3,500 in the safe of the boat, which was recovered & placed in his hands. He remained at the wreck to recover, if possible, the remains of his lost companion & child. Mr Maddox, a traveling agent of Phil house, lost $20,000 worth of jewelry. Mr J B Flunery, of Ark, S R Arnold, of Bowling Green Ky, & N M Lee, of Richmond, Va, told all to go to the store at Lacona, & to clothe themselves, & they would foot the bill; which was done. Capt Rogers, of the ship **James E Woodruff**, took all some 100 persons to Memphis free of charge, & the crew of the **Rainbow** to Cairo on the same terms. List of some of the lost & missing: McGoffin, of Scott Co, Ky; Leake, of Ark; Ingraham, of New Orleans; Mrs Wheatly & child; Mrs Lamrock; Brochear, of West Point; 3 children of Mrs Whittaker; blind man, wife & child. –St Louis Republican

The Local Spy, printed at Wallingford, Vt, announces the death at South Wallingford, on Nov 14, of Jerathiel Doty, a soldier of the Revolution, & the last survivor of the body-guard escort of Lafayette to his native country. Mr Doty was born in Rhode Island in 1764, & was 93 years of age. He enlisted in the continental army when only 15 years old, & served throughout the 7 years' struggle. Again, in 1812, he volunteered in his country's service & took part in the operations at Plattsburg. The deceased was buried on Nov 18, with public honors. Ebenezer Robinson, another Revolutionary veteran, died at South Reading, Vt, Oct 31, aged 92 years & 8 months.

Mrd: on Nov 24, by Rev B Villeger, at ***Ellen Dale***, Wm E Hamilton, of Wash D C, to Nannie M, eldest daughter of Capt Geo H Willson, of Kent Co, Md.

Mrd: on Nov 26, by Rev Mr Dana, of Christ Church, Alexandria, at the residence of Mr Milton Garrett, of Wash City, Dr John B Johnson, of Alexandria, to Miss Mary Arnette Garrett, of Jefferson Co, Va.

Valuable Albemarle estate for sale: intending to change my location, I offer for sale my farm, **Holkham**, containing 1,200 acres; 5½ miles from the Univ of Va. Call on me, near Woodville Depot, Albemarle Co, Va, John R Woods.

MON NOV 30, 1857
U S District Court-Judge McCaleb. A Van Horne Ellis, late master of the steamer **Opelousas**, was this morning arraigned & held to bail in the sum of $10,000 till Nov 25, & from that day to day thereafter until finally discharged by due course of law. He of course pleaded not guilty to the charge of manslaughter contained in the indictment against him & others. The others arrested: Thos Beacker, 1st mate; J W Jewell, 2nd mate; & John R Young, pilot. All are in prison, & will be brought up for arraignment on Monday. J W Brown, the quartermaster, has not yet been arrested. The above all belonged to the **Opelousas**. Those belonging to the **Galveston**, against whom indictments were also found, have not yet been arrested, the **Galveston** not having arrived.

From the Oregon papers we learn that Col Backenstos, formerly of Illinois, committed suicide by drowning himself in the Williamettee river on Sep 26. He was formerly sheriff of Hancock Co, Ill, & as such ofcr was prominent in the Mormon troubles in the State in 1835. In the fall of that year, at the head of a posse, he gave an order to fire upon a body resisting his authority. A Capt Morrell was killed. Col Backenstos was indicted for his murder, & tried in Peoria Co, & acquitted. He went to Mexico, served through that war, & in 1849 went to Oregon.

Jas G Birney died at Eagleswood, near Perth Amboy, N J, on Tue. He was born in 1798, at Danville, Ky. He was widely known as the anti-slavery candidate for the Presidency in 1844. His death was caused by paralysis, aggravated by heart disease.

Equity, No 1,116. Thos R Bird against Jas C McGuire, adm, & Rebecca C Brown, widow, & Jos Brown, heir at law of John D Brown & of Alice Brown. Trustee's account will be stated on Dec 23 next, at my ofc in City Hall. –W Redin, auditor

The Society of Stonecutters, joined by many other persons, yesterday attended the funeral of Michl Murphy, who died of the wound inflicted upon him by some unknown hand on Nov 21.

Appointments by the Va Conference of the Methodist Protestant Church, last week in session at Petersburg, for the neighborhood of Wash, are as follows: Wash District, W W Bennett, P E; Wash City, J C Granberry; Alexandria, J Manning; Fairfax, T J Bayton; Potomac, S V Hoyle; Loudoun, T A Ware, H C Cheatham; Warrenton, W G Cross, A J Beckwith; Leesburg, W L Dalby; Clarke, W G Williams; Rock Creek & Howard, P F August; Prince Wm, [one to be supplied,] J Crown; Springfield, J E Potts; Patterson Creek, W Fitzpatrick; Berlin, J H Amiss; Richmond District, D S Doggett, P E; Trinity, J A Duncan; Centenary, N Head.

Mrd: on Thu, by Rev John C Smith, Chas A Huntress, of Brooklyn, N Y, to Miss Eliz, daughter of Benj Williamson, of Wash City.

Mrd: on Nov 26, by Rev Mr Boyle, Mr Saml L Brown to Miss Ellen P Harbaugh, all of Wash.

Mrd: on Nov 25, at Harrisonburg, Va, by Rev W Krebs, Alex'r M Hamilton to Virginia B Smith.

Mrd: on Nov 12, at *Prospect Hill*, by Rev N Young, Jos Manning to Mary E, youngest daughter of Robt Brooke, all of PG Co, Md.

Died: on Nov 28, Mr Chas S West, formerly of Phil, in his 60th year. His funeral will be today at 1 o'clock, from his late residence at K & 14th sts.

Died: on Nov 29, Jos Whyte, a native of England, in his 20th year.

Died: on Nov 27, in Wash City, suddenly, Henry K, the youngest son of Lt Henry K Davenport, U S Navy, aged 4 years & 1 month.
+
On Friday a fine young son of Lt Davenport, U S Navy, was so badly burnt while left alone by his nurse that he died, after having lingered in agony about 2 hours. He was between 4 & 5 years of age.

In Chancery, 1,169. Thos R Bird against Jas C McGuire, adm, Rebecca C Brown, & Jos Brown, widow & heir of Jno D Brown & Alice C Brown. Chas S Wallach, trustee, reported that he sold lot 3 in square 226 to Jos Abbott, for $1,211.25; & the east half of lot 4 in square 226, to John Plant, for $605.63. & they have complied with the terms of sale. –John A Smith, clerk

Calif: Mr Harasthy, the late refiner in the Mint, has been indicted for embezzling $150,000.

TUE DEC 1, 1857
Complete list of the ofcrs of the U S steam frig **Powhatan**, to sail from Norfolk in a few days for the Pacific: Capt, Geo F Pearson. Lts: Lt J D Johnston; 2nd, S D Trenchard; 3rd W W Roberts; 4th Thos Roney; 5th, A A Semmes; 6th, A W Habersham. First Surgeon, W A W Spotswood; Passed Assist, do, C H Williamson; Assist do, John W Sanford; Purser, B F Gallaher; Master, Robt Boyd; Captain Marines, A S Taylor; Boatswain, Edw Kenney; Gunner, ___ Fitzosborn; Carpenter, R G Thomas; Sailmaker, A A Warren; Chief Engineer, W H Shock; 1st Assists, W H Rutherford, R C Potts; 2nd do, G W City; 3rd do, King, Dungah, Archer, & Bright.

N Y, Nov 29. The death of Geo R Gliddon, formerly U S Consul at Cario, Egypt, & distinguished for his contributions to antiquarian lore, will be a subject of deep regret to the votaries of science in every part of the world.

A young man named John Zimmerman, barkeeper of Hoffman's Union House, in Harrisburg, Pa, was accidentally shot in the breast & dangerously wounded a few evenings ago, by a boarder who was carelessly handling a pistol.

Mr W H Robinson, of Phil, on Fri night at the Carolina Hotel, Wilmington, N C, where he had taken lodgings, in the night raised the window & leaped to the pavement below, a distance of upwards of 50 feet, killing himself instantly. Mental derangement, it is supposed, caused the commitment of the rash act.

On Thu, Thanksgiving Day, Mr Wm Rhinehart proceeded to the country with his children. During the day, whilst he was handling a gun, it prematurely discharged, taking effect in the body of his son George, a fine active lad of some 12 or 13 years, & wounded him mortally. He lingered until Sat, when death released him of his sufferings. –Balt Sun

Mrd: on Nov 28, by Rev S D Finckel, Mr Florian Hitz to Miss Susanna Dolf, all of Wash City.
+
Mrd: on Nov 28, by Rev S D Finckel, Mr Geo Hitz to Miss Lucy Wetzel, all of Wash City.

Mrd: on Nov 24, at St Matthew's Church, by Rev E Q S Waldron, Stephen C Clements, of Gtwn, D C, to Isabella M, daughter of John F Boyle, of Wash City.

Mrd: on Nov 26, Thanksgiving Day, by Rev Mr Lanaghan, Dr Saml A Mudd to Miss Sallie Frank, youngest daughter of the late Thos Dyer, all of Chas Co, Md.

Died: on Nov 29, in her 80th year, Mrs Anna Maria Mason, widow of the late Gen John Mason, of Clermont, Fairfax Co, Va. The funeral solemnities will be conducted at the house of her son, Gen John Mason, [the late residence of the deceased in this city,] 23 Pa ave, at 10 o'clock this morning. The interment at the graveyard of <u>Christ Church</u>, Alexandria, Va.

Died: on Nov 29, in Wash City, Mr Perrin Washington, aged 65 years. He was a native of Va, but for the last 25 years a resident of Wash City. As a husband & father who shall speak of him except those to whom he stood so fondly related. The last few years of his life were spent on a bed of suffering, where he clearly illustrated the faith & fortitude of the Christian. His funeral will be this afternoon, at 3 o'clock, at his late residence, on 11th st, between G & H sts.

Died: on Nov 22, in the Reserve, Lauderdale Co, Ala, Mr Isaac Winston Beckwith, eldest son of the late Dr Jonathan Beckwith.

WED DEC 2, 1857
By deed of trust, made by Wm Morgan to the subscriber, I shall sell, on Dec 7, on the Navy Yard Hill, opposite the residence of Gen Henderson, that handsome leasehold property on Lot 1 in square 926, with a 2 story frame house, with a back bldg, on ground rent of $20 per annum. –John L Smith, trustee
-Baden & Lownds, aucts

On Mon, Mr R P Lemon, wine merchant of Bath, who was one of the deacons at Argyle Chapel, was at the prayer meeting & died while praying. –English paper

The Richmond [Va] Whig says that P P Winston, sheriff of that county, is a defaulter to the amount of $25,000.

Miss Julia Armstrong, daughter of the late Col Robt L Armstrong, residing in Woodbury, N J, was so dreadfully burnt last Wed, by the upsetting of a fluid lamp, that she died the next morning.

Washington Academy of Music, 11th & Pa ave, Mr F Nicholls Crouch, Composer & Lecturer & Musical Editor of Godey's Lady's Book. To secure admission early application must be made.

Obit-died: on Nov 16, at Panama, Geo R Gliddon, the well-known Egyptian archaeologist. He was born in England in 1807, & at an early age went to Egypt, where his father was the American Consul, an ofc which Mr Gliddon himself afterwards held. He was on his return to the U S when he died. His disease was pulmonary congestion; his age 50 years. –N Y Post

Mrd: on Dec 1, in Wash City, by Rev John C Smith, Mr Edw O Bell to Miss Permela Prather, both of PG Co, Md.

Died: on Nov 24, at Newport, R I, Mrs Mary Cranston, wife of Hon Henry Y Cranston.

Died: on Nov 19, near Newport, Mrs Esther R Lawrence, wife of Hon Wm B Lawrence, & daughter of the late Archibald Gracie, of N Y.

Springfield, Mass, Nov 30. W T Tuckerman, who was formerly Treasurer of the Eastern Railroad Co, was arrested at New Haven last night, on the charge of mail robbery. He confesses his guilt.

THU DEC 3, 1857
Small farm near Washington at public auction: on Dec 9, at the auction rooms, the tract known as *Chillan Castle Manor*, containing 62 acres, more or less, lying partially in Wash & PG Counties. –Jas C McGuire, auct

Trustee's sale of frame house & lot 10 in square 818, on Dec 14, by deed of trust from T H Lucas, dated Dec 17, 1856, recorded in Liber J A S, No 127, folios 190 thru 193, of the land records of Wash Co, D C. –Geo S Donn, trustee -A Green auct

The young Countess Maria Dorethee de Castelline has just been united to Prince Frederic de Radziwill, a Prussian officer. [Late from Europe.]

Col Claudius Crozet was yesterday appointed Principal Assist Engineer on the Washington Aqueduct, & was duly installed in ofc. He is the father of the civil engineering profession, having been the chief engineer of the State of Va for more than a quarter of a century. –Star of yesterday evening.

Lewis Lewis, alias Richd Harvey, who recently fled from England a defaulter to the amount of $30,000, has been traced to N Y C, where he has been overhauled, & nearly $4,500 recovered on him. The crime alleged against him does not come under the extradition treaty, & the ofcrs could not arrest him. A civil action is to be commenced against him for the recovery of the rest of the money.

Nicholas Masters has recovered a verdict of $3,500 against the town of Warren, Conn, on account of the insufficiency of a bridge belonging to the town.

There was recently a public sale of lots in Ceredo, Va, the site chosen by Eli Thayer, of Mass, for his proposed settlement. Purchasers are required to build on them within 2 years.

Orphans Court of Wash Co, D C. Letters of administration on the personal estate of Hyppolite Bezian, late of the State of N Y, deceased. –J H Goddard, adm

Circuit Court of Wash Co, D C, in Chancery, No 1,001. Jas W Strange, Jos C Hawke, & Mgt Hawke, vs Mgt Strange, Robt Strange, & French Strange. Wm B Webb, trustee, reports that he sold lot 8 in square 702 to A & T A Richards, for $40; & lot 7 in square 127 to F & A Schneider, for 46 cents per square foot, amounting to $3,152.84. –Jno A Smith, clerk

FRI DEC 4, 1857
Capt Thos R Gedney, U S Navy, died yesterday, at the residence of a relative in Charleston city, where he has been confined by disease for some time. We learn that his body is to be removed to Washington. –Charleston News

Wm S Tuckerman, the embezzler, is in trouble again. Some time ago, while Treasurer of the Eastern railroad, he appropriated $250,000 of the company's funds to his private use. He has been in the habit of taking the Sunday night train from N Y to Boston, carrying with him a large trunk, in which placed a carpet bag filled with clock weights, to make it appear heavy, & while the mail man's back was turned Tuckerman would withdraw the carpet bag & conceal a mail bag in the trunk. It seems strange that a man who had confessed the robbery of $217,000, & who had been convicted of larceny of $7,000, should be suffered to enjoy the freedom of the baggage train.

River improvements-Gtwn, Wash City, & Alexandria. Affidavit made in 1856 by Mr Thos A Lazenby, late deputy collector of the port of Gtwn, before Justice Reaver, testifies to the unvaried opinion of the masters of vessels trading to Gtwn as to the Potomac bridge being a most dangerous & inconvenient obstruction to the navigation of the river. Mr Jas A Magruder, a merchant of Gtwn, in Jun, 1855, in attempting to pass the bridge, had a hole knocked in her bow, which caused her to sink. Mr Henry Lewis, for 15 years master of vessels trading to Gtwn, on Apr 4, 1856, testifies that even with a fair wind there is difficulty & danger in attempting to get through the draw in the Long Bridge. Mr Chas Wilson deposes to the danger & detention to vessels often caused by the Long Bridge. Mr Wm E Beall, captain of a trading vessel, who also for 7 years had been acting as mate & captain of the steamer **Salem**, states that about 6 years ago, he was towing the schnr **Industry**, & during a high wind, she struck the wind, & was much injured & sunk within an hour. Mr Joshua N Fearson makes affidavit of his being on board the schnr **Adventure**, on her way from Alexandria to Gtwn, & that, it being almost dark, on passing the Long Bridge, the schnr struck a pier violently, & at the same time the concussion threw his brother Wm Fearson, overboard, who was immediately crushed to death between the vessel & pier.

Mr Henry Lingo, of Merer Co, Pa, one day last week swallowed buckwheat cakes & at that time partially swallowed a needle, that stuck in his throat. Every effort was made to extricate it, but without success, & he died a day or two after.

Franklin Holden, a good looking merchant of Pen Yan, N Y, has been sentenced at Albany to 5 years in the State prison for forgery.

Hon Robt J Walker, the Govn'r of Kansas, reached Phil yesterday, & is the guest of his relative, St Geo Tucker Campbell. –Phil Press, Wed

Foreign News: The Espana says that Mr Dodge, U S Minister at Madrid, has sent in his resignation on account of the health of his family & other private considerations.

Jas B Dickens, Atty at Law: Patent, Claim & Genr'l Agency. Ofc: 7th & F sts. [Ad]

Mrd: on Dec 3, by Rev G W Samson, Mr Wm H Fenton, of Fairfax Co, Va, to Miss Cordelia, 2nd daughter of the late John Walker.

Died: on Oct 7, in Tacna, near Arica, Peru, of pulmonary consumption, Mr Andrew Fenelon, formerly of Cincinnati, Ohio, in about his 30th year.

Died: on Nov 29, in Gtwn, D C, after a long & painful illness, Mary E, wife of Timothy Remisk, in her 45th year.

SAT DEC 5, 1857
Scene in the First District Court at New Orleans. Hon T G Hunt. Geo W Stovall was arraigned yesterday for the murder of Mary Rey Durand. He said: "I am guilty: but I would request the court to grant me time to arrange my wordly business." Judge Hunt asked him, "are you aware that your plea condemns yourself to death?" He replied that he thought he was, so very strangely, that the lawyers began to suspect he was insane. The Judge asked him if he desired to order the plea not to be entered for the present, & he consented, thanking the Judge. Stovall, after the murder, jumped head foremost into a well, from which he scrambled out again. He confessed to the murder at the time it was committed. –Bee, 28th

Mr McGill, boarding at Harper's Hotel, was in his room loading a pistol, & the 7 year old daughter of Mr Harper, being in the room at the time, by some mishap the pistol exploded taking effect in her side. Very little probability of her recovery. -Weldon [N C] Patriot [Dec 8th newspaper: The little daughter of Mr Harper has since died.]

A young man, John B Brough, of Hamilton, Ohio, has been arrested for stealing a draft for $200 from the post office. He had a good character, & much interest is felt in his case.

Michl Rigley, of N Y C, accidentally shot & killed his own little girl, age 6 years, on Tue, while preparing his revolver for the purpose of taking part in the election.

Andrew Mathieu, who came into this country from France with Count de Grasse, died in Davis Co, N C, recently, at age 96 years. He was present at Yorktown when Cornwallis surrendered & afterwards served his country in the East Indies & in the battles of Napoleon. He was a witness of the Marat, Danton, & Robespierre saturnalia, "when France got drunk on crime to vomit blood." On one occasion when returning from the post ofc, with a letter in his hand, some one asked him the news. Very good news, he innocently replied, my mudder in France is dead, & leaves me $10,000; & the Frenchman danced for joy. –Columbus [Geo] Enquirer

MON DEC 7, 1857
A letter has been received by the San Antonio [Texas] Ledger, from El Paso, under date of Oct 24, by which it appears that Col Leach, the Superintendent of the **Fort Yuma** & El Paso wagon road, had arrived at El Paso with part of his train. The ox train is a long way behind, & will not reach here in much less than a month.

At a late meeting of the Philodemic Society of Gtwn College, the death of Rev Geo Fenwick was announced. –Edw H Welch, S J, Pres Philodemic Society

Mrd: on Dec 1, at Cedar Valley, in Granville Co, N C, by Rev Mr Hines, Jennings Pigott, of Wash, to Mrs Eliza A Mosely, of the former place.

Mrd: on Dec 3, by Rev B F Bittinger, Mr Wm H Branson to Miss Mary Tippett.

Died: on Dec 3, in Wash City, Ada Thrift, youngest daughter of Edw & Maria Louisa Swann, aged 1 year, 6 months & 3 days.

Died: on Oct 24, near Warrenton, Miss, of typhoid fever, Frisby A Freeland, in his 33rd year.

TUE DEC 8, 1857
On Tue Dennis Wilkinson, a resident of Blairsville, Pa, was run over on the Pa railroad, near that town, & instantly killed. On Wed Robt Buchanan, a coal digger, was run over & killed near Steubenville, Ohio, on the Steubenville & Indiana railroad. It is thought he intended to commit suicide.

Mr Allen T Burton, of Caswell Co, N C, while out hunting on Tue last, was killed when his gun exploded, killing him almost instantly.

Mr Andrew Gilmore, a civil engineer, was found dead at Gtwn, S C, on Dec 2.

The Balt Patriot announces the death in that city yesterday of Col Jacob G Davies, in his 62nd year, a prominent & respected citizen, who filled faithfully at different periods the offices of Mayor & Postmaster of the city. The military, of which he was always an efficient member, intend paying suitable honors to his memory tomorrow.

Died: on Nov 28, at Troy, N Y, Mrs Martha P H, widow of the late Gen Henry Robinson, of Vt, in her 57th year.

Died: on Dec 6, suddenly, in Montg Co, Md, Kate, beloved daughter of Fred'k A & Eliz A W Tschiffely, aged 11 years & 10 days.

Died: on Dec 7, after a lingering illness, in his 57th year, Richd G Briscoe. His funeral will take place on Dec 9 at 10 o'clock, from Mr Fitzgerald's, Pa ave, between 4½ & 3rd sts.

Supreme Court of the U S, Dec 7, 1857, present:
Hon Roger B Taney, Chief Justice
Associate Justices:
Hon John McLean
Hon Jas M Wayne
Hon John Catron
Hon Peter V Daniel
Hon Saml Nelson
Hon Robt C Grier
Hon John A Campbell
No 28-U S, appellants, vs Juan Pacifico Ontiveras
No 29-U S, appellants, vs John C Gore
No 38-U S, appellants, vs Juan Perez Paceco
No 101-U S, appellants, vs Geo C Yount
No 106-U S, appellants, vs John B R Cooper
No 131-R S, appellants, vs Anastasio Chaboya
No 143-U S, appellants, vs Anastasio

Local: the Criminal Court commenced yesterday before Hon Judge Thos H Crawford. The following are the members of the Grand Jury:

Wm Gunton, foreman	Thos H Parsons
Hamilton Loughborough	A W Miller
Wm Thompson	John P Pepper
John F Coyle	Judson Mitchell
Benj Ogle Tayloe	Thos Brown
Saml Drury	Richd Jones
Danl B Clarke	Enos Ray
Peter M Pearson	Jeremiah Orme
Hudson Taylor	Selby Scaggs
Francis Mohun	Edw M Linthicum
Chas L Coltman	John Costigan
Edw C Dyer	Chas B Belt

Criminal Court-Wash-Yesterday. The case of John James & John Campbell charged with keeping a gambling establishment last year, the evidence to convict being quite insufficient, the Court ordered an acquittal.

House of Reps: 1-Ptn of Jos Day, Hon John Pettit, & 300 other citizens of White & Tippecanoe Counties, Indiana, praying that the benefits of the act of 1818, granting pensions of $100 per year during life to the ofcrs & soldiers of the Revolutionary war & their surviving children, may be extended to those who were orphan children thereof at that time, or that bounty land may be granted to them.

John Tiner shot W W Burns in Bibb Co, Ala, 2 weeks ago, wounding him mortally. Burns then seized Tiner & literally cut his neck in two, killing him instantly.

Wash-The following constitutes the panel of the Petit Jury:

David W Oyster	John A Cockwell	Jonathan Cathell
Richd Abbott	Leoanrd Harbaugh	Isaac Marshall
Benj Sothoron	John H A Wilson	Paul Stevens
Theodore F Boucher	B J Fenwick	Geo W Garrett
Bernard Brien	Chandler Craig	Chas M Skippon
Alex Paul	Henry Barron	Wm Sanderson
Natthy Moreland	Jas Handley	Alfred Ray
Wm Bond	Lewis Brooks	Geo W Talbert
Jas W Coombs	Henry M Hurdle	Thos Brown
John Lowrie	Price Shoemaker	Edw Tolson

Columbia Typographical Society of Wash City. Officers elected yesterday for 1858:
Pres: John H Thorn   Cor Sec: Wm R McLean
V Pres: Thos Rich   Treas: M Caton
Rec Sec: H S Bowen

Law Partnership: Geo M Bibb, Edw Swann, & Robt G Swift: ofc 26 La ave, Wash, D C. [Ad]

Mrd: on Dec 8, in Wash City, by Rev W Krebs, Wm Gihon to Mary A Rutherford.

Murder in our city Mon night. Mr Edw A Lutts was shot by Jas Powers, in the tavern of Jas McColgan, on Pa ave. They had no controversy, but about 3 years ago they had a difference at an excursion. Lutts was living last night, but reported by the attending physicians as sinking fast. His mother & sister arrived by train last evening from Balt. [Dec 10th newspaper: death was caused by being shot. He died at the Infirmary on Dec 8; the jury find deceased left no property. John Adamson was held to bail in the sum of $2,000 for his appearance as a witness, &, in default of finding bail, was committed to jail.]

Cincinnati, Dec 8. On Sunday Frank S McClure went into the store of Messrs Beattie & Anderson to talk business matters with Mr Beattie. About an hour afterwards McClure was seen to fall from the front step of the store, & when picked up it was found his skull had been fractured. He died last night. Beattie was arrested last night on the affidavit of Saml Mitchell, accusing him of having killed McClure by striking him on the head with an iron bar. Beattie was held to bail in $4,000. The parties were well known & highly respectable.

Norfolk, Dec 8. The ship **Eva Dorothea**, Capt Gatyear, from Bremen, bound to Balt, is ashore near Cape Henry. She had on board 260 passengers, & together with the crew, all were saved. The vessel & cargo will probably prove a total loss.

Marshal's sale: by 2 writs of fieri facias: auction on Jan 11 next, all the dfndnt's right, title, claim, & interest in & to lots 1, 37 & 38 & the east half of lot 2, in reservation A, in Wash City, with improvements. Seized & levied upon as the property of David A Hall, & will be sold to satisfy Judicials 3 & 5 to Dec term, 1852, in favor of the U S. –Richd Wallach, late Marshal D C

THU DEC 10, 1857

Wm E Coleman, age 14 years, has been convicted at Richmond, Va, of stealing from the post ofc a letter containing $163. He is the only son of a widowed mother. The jury signed a petition to the Pres, asking him to pardon the prisoner. The brothers Danl & Solomon Lochbaum, arrested some weeks since for a mail robbery in Knox Co, Ill, were indicted for embezzlement, & sentenced to 10 years' imprisonment in the penitentiary. They, too, are sons of a respectable widow lady. –Richmond Enq

Obit-died: on Monday last, at his residence in Lexington, Hon C H Williams. He was one of the first settlers in West Tenn, & one of the most distinguished men in the State. He was emphatically the leader of the Clay party in Tenn. He died from a paralytic attack on the Friday preceding his death. –West Tenn Whig of Nov 27.

Senate: 1-The heirs of John J Bulow had leave to withdraw their papers, no adverse report having been made in the case.

Mrd: on Nov 24, at Balt, by Rev Mr Foley, Outerbridge Horsey, of Needwood, Fred'k Co, Md, to Anna, daughter of Geo R Carroll.

Mrd: on Dec 8, in Wash City, at the Church of the Ascension, by Rev Wm Pinckney, Geo W Tubman, of Chas Co, Md, to Laura, youngest daughter of Richd Dement.

Died: on Fri last, in Wash City, after a protracted illness, G H Jones, aged 50 years. He was a native of Petersburg, Va, but for a number of years back a resident of this place, during which time he has held several important positions under Gov't; among others, that of Sec to the late Hon W R King, Pres of the Senate, & at the time of his death was Sec to the Pres to sign land patents. His wife & children have lost a devoted husband & father.

An affray at West Point, Ark, on Nov 22 resulted in the death by shooting of Dr C C Webb & Isaac Felsenthrall. They had threatened each other with extermination.

Died: on Dec 9, Dr Robt Taylor Wilson, aged 25 years. He died of a protract illness of many months. His funeral will take place on Dec 11, from his father's residence, 395 18th st, whence the remains will be taken to the **Gtwn Cemetery** for interment.

Died: on Nov 29, in Wash City, Mrs Lucy Brockenbrough, widow of the late Arthur S Brockenbrough, of the Univ of Va, in her 62nd year.

Died: on Dec 9, in Wash City, Mary, infant daughter of Geo T & Lucretia R Smallwood, aged 17 months & 10 days. Her funeral is this afternoon at 2 o'clock, from the residence of her father, 410 D st, between 6th & 7th sts.

Trinity Church pew for sale: Pew No 83, in the Episcopal Church, corner of 3rd & C sts. Inquire of the Sexton, or J C Gibson, 34 Market Space, between 7th & 8th sts.

I certify that Cornelius Brook & John Francis brought before me a Roan Horse, a light spring wagon, containing 3 barrels of apples: found on M st, between 16th & 17th st, Wash, where they had been standing for about 16 hours before being taken into their possession. –Thos Donn, J P [Owner is come forward, prove property, pay charges. Cornelius Brook, John Francis]

U S Patent Ofc, Wash, Dec 9, 1857. Ptn of Silas C Durgin, of Holyoke, Mass, praying for the extension of a patent granted to him on Mar 9, 1844, for an improvement in machine for measuring & folding cloth, for 7 years from expiration of said patent, which takes place Mar 9, 1858. –Jos Holt, Acting Com'r of Patents

FRI DEC 11, 1857
Telegraphic dispatch at the War Dept yesterday announced the death of Col Wm Turnbull, of the Corps of Topographical Engineers, a gallant soldier & a noble gentleman. He was chief of his corps under Gen Scott in Mexico in 1848, & was twice brevetted for gallant & meritorious conduct, first in the battles of Contreras & Churubusco, & secondly in the battle of Chapultepec. He was a graduate of West Point, & at the time of his decease had been in the military service 40 years. He had suffered much from impaired health during the last year, & died suddenly at Wilmington the day before yesterday. [Dec 18th newspaper: Col Turnbull was a native of Pa. By his sudden death, a loving consort, a large family of children, & numerous relatives & friends have been plunged in the deepest affliction.]

By decree of the Circuit Court of Wash Co, D C, in Chancery, in the case where Thos Reddin is cmplnt, John Ratrie & Jas Havelin dfndnts, I shall sell on Jan 6, in front of the premises, lot 1 in square 881 in Wash City, with improvements, & lots 2 & 4 in square south of square 990. –Chas Walter, trustee -A Green, auct

Died: on Dec 7, at Balt, after a long & painful illness, of cancer, Sallie, the beloved wife of John B Carroll, & daughter of the late Capt John D Ross, of Alexandria, Va.

Senate: 1-Court of Claims: favorable decisions in the following cases:

Jane Martin	Lydia Clapp
Melinda Durkee	Eliz Morgan
Sarah Weed	Phoebe Polly
Mary Pierce	Nancy Mary Grant
Ann B Johnson	Jas McIntosh
Hannah Menzies	Neal Smith
Rebecca Nourse	Charner T Scaife
Anna Hill	Wm H Russell
Polly Booth	Ferdinand Coxe
Sarah Eaton	Benj L McAfee & J E Eastham
Temperance Childress	
Eliz King	

2-Court of Claims: adverse opinions in the following cases:

Fred'k Griffing	Jas Thompson
Francis Picard	J H King
Danl Van Winkle	T S J Johnson
Jos Loranger	Abraham King
Henry G Curtiss	Llewellyn Jones
Philip Lamoy	Robt S Garnett
Ezra T Marnay	Robt C Thompson
Henry Miller	Ann W Butler
Stephen C Hayden	Christiana Dener
David Noble	Stephen C Phillips
Jos Stokely	Ellen Martin
Jeremiah Williams	Abraham R Woolly
Arnold Harris	Ralph Richardson
E B Chamberlain	Nathl Williams
Eliza Shaffer	Hugh Hughes
Auguste Demers	R L Page
Alex'r H Cooke	Robt Harrison
Joshua R Jewett	Letitia Humphreys
John M Thorne	Michl Musy & Andre Galtier
J C Buckles	Geo W Dow & John H Ditmas

Col E V Sumner, of the First Cavalry, recently on trial at a general court martial held at **Fort Leavenworth**, has been suspended from rank & pay for 4 months, & to be reprimanded by the Genr'l-in-Chief. We understand that the Commanding Gen [Gen Scott] has confirmed the sentence of the court, but has remitted the penalty. The charges on which Col Sumner was tried were preferred by Maj Geo Deas, Assist Adj Gen -St Louis Republican

Leesburg Mirror: Dr Nathan Janney died on Tue last, Nov 30, by injuries received some days previous by being thrown from his buggy. He was a prominent physician of Loudoun Co, beloved by all who knew him. He was about 40 years of age.

Arrest was made last evening on Archy McCleish, by officers McHenry & Suit, at the tavern of G Springman, on Pa ave, where he & others were engaged in riotously destroying the furniture there. He was committed to jail; & was one of the party of McColgan's when Lutts was shot. McCleish & his companions are from Balt. [Dec 12th newspaper: Jas Roach & Francis McDevitt have also been arrested; McDevitt was carrying a deadly weapon.]

SAT DEC 12, 1857
American & English Missionairies known to have been killed since the commencement of the mutiny in India:
Rev W H Haycock: Cawnpore: Propag Soc
Rev H Cockey: Cawnpore: Propag Society
Rev J E Freeman: Futteghur: Am Pres Mis
Rev D E Campbell: Futteghur: Am Pres Mis
Rev A O Johnson: Futteghur: Am Pres Mis
Rev R Macmullin: Futteghur: Am Pres Mis
Rev T Mackay: Delhui: Bapt Mis Soc
Rev A R Hubbard: Delhi: Propag Soc
Rev D Sandys: Delhi: Propag Soc
Rev R Hunter: Sealcote: Scotch Kirk
Rev J Maccalum: Shahjehanpore: Addit Clergy
Ladies & children killed:

Mrs Haycock	Mrs Macmullin
Mrs Cockey	Mrs Hunter
Mrs Freeman	Miss Thompson
Mrs Johnson	Miss Grace Thompson

Mrs Campbell, with 2 children
Mrs Thompson, of Delhi, widow of Rev T Thompson

Hon Wm A Richardson, of Ill, has been appointed by the Pres & Senate Govn'r of the Territory of Nebraska, vice Mark W Izard, resigned.

On Nov 14 three children of Jos Brotte, in Willow Creek, on Lake Huron, Mich, strayed from their father's shanty into the surrounding woods; two girls of 8 & 6, & a boy of 4. After 2 days & 2 nights they were found alive. The little boy died in his mother's arms.

The funeral of the late Col Wm Turnbull, U S Topographical Engineers, will take place this day, at 12 o'clock, from his late residene on F st.

St Andrew's Society: elected as office bearers for the incoming year: Gilbert Cameron, Pres; R B McFarland, 1st V Pres; John Smith, 2nd do; Wm Ballantyne, Treasurer; Jas A Brown, Rec Sec; John Reekie, Cor Sec. Managers: Andrew Small, Danl Dewer, John Brown, Henry Bruce Todd, Thos Spence, Alexr McKerrechar.

Criminal Court-Wash-yesterday: 1-John Thompson, colored, guilty of grand larceny: sentenced to the penitentiary for 1 year. 2-W H H Butterbaugh, a youth, found guilty of petty larceny. 3-Matthew Butler, colored, guilty of grand larceny: sentenced to the penitentiary for 1 year. 4-Geo Jenkins, colored, guilty of petit larceny: sentenced to 6 months in jail & fined $1. [Dec 15th newspaper: 1-Butterbaugh found not guilty. 2-Hilleary Hutchins, Gtwn, guilty of assault & battery on Michl Maginnis: fined $5 & costs.]

Mrd: on Dec 3, by Rev Dr Ridley, J B Kilebrew, of Clarksville, Tenn, to Miss Kate Wimberley, of Montg Co, Md.

Died: on Dec 5, at Jacksonville, Fla, of fever, at the residence of Columbus Drew, Mr Jas Wimer, printer; a native of Pa, but recently & for many years a resident of Wash City. [Dec 17th newspaper: Mr Wimer was for many years Foreman of Mr G S Gideon's printing establishment in Wash City. He leaves his aged parents & relatives.]

MON DEC 14, 1857

Thos J Mackey was recently called before the U S Com'r in this city, to be examined upon the charge of violating the neutrality laws in recruiting soldiers & fitting out an expedition for Nicaragua, destined for the service of Gen Walker. The matter terminated in the dfndnt being bound over in a bond of $8,000, to appear & answer at the Jan term of the U S District Court. –Charleston News, 8th

The Wayne Co Republican says that Mr H G Hotchkiss, of Lyons, N Y, is the greatest producer of peppermint in the world. He has from two to three hundred acres under cultivation, & sells to the amount of $75,000 to $100,000 worth of oil annually.

Died: on Dec 12, at his residence at *Ellaville*, near Washington, Brvt Capt Wm L Young, U S Marine Corps. His funeral is this afternoon at 2 o'clock, from Christ Church, near the Navy Yard.

Died: on Oct 27 last, in Cincinnati, Mrs Ellen Browning, relict of the late Lt R L Browning, of the U S Navy, who was lost with a surveying party on the Pacific coast in attempting to effect a landing. She passed many winters in Wash City, & attracted a large number of warm & admiring friends.

Died: on Dec 8, in Morris Co, N J, aged 21 years, Ann Estelle, daughter of Hon A C M Pennington, late a Rep in Congress.

Com'rs appointed in the several counties of the Territory of Kansas:
Doniphan: S P Blair, C B Whitehead, B O'Driscoll
Atchison: J T Hereford, Eli C Mason, Jas Adkins
Leavenworth: Oliver Diefendorf, Robt Thompson, Marion Todd
Johnson: J H Danforth, A J Campbell, Jas Evans
Lykins: Henry M Peck, Jas Beets, L D Williams
Bourbon: Thos B Arnett, Saml A Williams, John H Little
McGee: W A Frazier, J C Head, Wm Hinton
Dorn: Jas M Linn, John Lemons, W J Godfrey
Linn: Briscoe Davis, Willis M Sutton, C S Fleming
Shawnee & Richardson: Edmund L Yates, John Martin, Jas Gordon
Davis: C L Sanford, Fox Booth, Robt Reynolds
Douglas: John Spicer, Wm S Wells, Parish Ellison
Breckinridge & Wise: A J Baker, Wm Grimsley, H W Fisk
Anderson: Saml Anderson, Jas H Howser, Ephraim Coy
Franklin: Jos Merritt, Jesse B Way, Jacob Marcello
Coffee: Hiram Hoover, John Woolman, Hardee McMahon
Madison, Butler, & Hunter: G D Humphries, C Bunch, S G Brown
Allen & Greenwood: B W Cowden, T H Bashaw, J Johnson
Riley: George Montague, S B White, J S Randolph
Pottowattomie: A J Chapman, G W Gillespie, Robt Wilson
Calhoun: Saml Boydson, John Christy, Henry D Owden
Jefferson: H A Lowe, Jas Haddox, Geo M Dyer
Marshal, Washington, & Arapahoe: F J Marshall, Peter Valentine, J P Miller
Nemaha: Cyrus Dolman, David M Locknane, A Brown
Brown: Henry Smith, T Whitehead, Sam Brown

Orphans Court of Wash Co, D C. In the case of Alex'r Lee, adm, with the will annexed, of Hanson Barnes, deceased: the administrator & Court have appointed Jan 5 next, for the final settlement of the personal estate of the deceased, with the assets in hand. –Ed N Roache, Reg/o wills

On Sat Robt Parkhill, Edw Barron, & John Barron, were arrested & brought to the guard-house on a charge of shooting & rioting on Va ave. Parkhill was fined $30 & costs; Edw Barron fined $25; J Barron was fined $5. The first two were fined under the Corp ordinance-carrying deadly weapons.

Criminal Court-Wash-Sat: 1-John Baptist found guilty of petty larceny. 2-Wm Nicholson, of Gtwn, tried for stabbing Jas Moore, [since deceased,] in Gtwn, on Jul 22 last. The jury found for the assault & battery simply, without the intent to kill.

TUE DEC 15, 1857
Senate: 1-Announcement of the death of Hon A P Butler, late a Senator from S C. [No other information given.] 2-Ptn of Gottleib Schurer, praying for a release of the judgment obtained by the U S against him as surety of Jos Hill. 3-Ptn of Paul D Delano & others, of Maine, soldiers of the war of 1812, asking that a pension may be granted the ofcrs & soldiers of that war & of the Indian wars during the same period.

St Geo Randolph, a nephew of John Randolph, of Roanoke, died in Charlotte Co, Va, on Dec 4. He was born deaf & dumb, but was highly educated in France. On returning home to Va in 1814 he heard of the hopeless illness of his brother at Harvard College, & immediately became deranged. From that time to the day of his death he is said never to have known a lucid interval.

Mrd: on Dec 10, in Trinity Church, Portsmouth, Va, by Rev John H Wingfield, Lt Richd H Ridick, 1st Cavalry U S Army, to Miss Texana Eugenia, the only daughter of the late John Clarke, of Nansemond Co, Va.

Died: on Dec 14, James Madison, son of Thos M & Emily Wall, aged 14 years,1 month & 14 days. His funeral is today at 3 o'clock P M, 3rd & D st, Capitol Hill.

Circuit Court of Wash Co, D C-in Chancery. Alex'r H Mechlin against Henry Breathitt, Wm Carroll & Eliza Carroll his wife, heirs of John H Eaton, & Mgt Eaton, his admx. The bill, amended bill, & bill or reviver in the above cause state that the late John H Eaton purchased on May 17, 1854, of the cmplnt, lot 21 in square 127, in Wash City, for $3,427, & paid one third thereof or thereabouts, & was to have given his two notes in equal sums, payable at 6 & 12 months from said day, with interest, to be satisfactorily secured; but he departed this life after the expiration of the said period, without having given said notes or paid the said residue of the said purchase money & interest or any part thereof. That he died leaving a will, by which he gave all his property to his widow, the said Mgt Eaton, & who hath obtained letters testamentary on his estate, & possessed herself of personal property of the said John H Eaton sufficient to pay the said residue of said purchase money & interest. That the heirs at law of said John H Eaton are Henry Breathitt & Eliza Carroll, the wife of said Wm Carroll. That the said residue of said purchase money & interest has not been paid. The object of the said bill is to obtain a specific execution of the said contract for the purchase of said lot, & payment of the residue of the purchase money & interest; & because the said Henry Breathitt & Wm Carroll, & Eliza his wife, do not reside in this District, but beyond the jurisdiction of this Court, they are to appear in this Court in person or by solicitor, on or before the first Monday in May next.
-Jno A Smith, clerk

Circuit Court-Wash: 1-The Court yesterday heard the case of A E L Keese, a constable of this county, charged with malfeasance in ofc. He was suspended from the functions of his ofc for 6 months.

House of Reps: 1-Hon Andrew Pickens Butler, late a Senator from S C, died on May 25, 1857, at *Stonelands*, his residence, in Edgefield district, S C. He was born on Nov 18, 1796, in Edgefield district, S C. His father rendered distinguished services to the Whig cause in the war of our Revolution, & his mother was a woman of great strength of mind & unusual force of character. 2-Ptn of Jos Plummer, guardian of Jos M Plummer & Mary R Plummer, minor children of Capt Saml M Plummer, late of the U S Army, deceased.

Criminal Court-Wash-yesterday: 1-Geo Krouse was found guilty for assault & battery, with intent to kill, on John Hilleary in Gtwn in Feb.

Miss Cornelia Thomas, daughter of Dr Thomas, living on 15th st, near Pa ave, was severely injured when she passed too near the parlor grate & her dress caught fire. Her mother & 2 sisters, running to her assistance, likewise burnt their hands & arms quite badly. Medical aid was rendered as speedilyas possible, & it is hoped that all will soon recover. [Dec 19th newspaper: The suffering ladies in the family of Dr Thomas were reported yesterday as all much better, & hopes are entertained of their safe, if not very speedy recovery.]

New Orleans, Dec 14. The steamboat **Colonel Edwards** was destroyed by fire on the Red river on Sat. The vessel & cargo are a total loss. She had on board 1,100 bales of cotton. Fifteen to twenty persons perished. [Dec 23rd newspaper: Among the victims lost were J J Varner, of Ga; U A Brooks, of San Antonio, Texas; B Turner, of Prussia, & a Baptist preacher, name unknown. T R Garrett, of Hopkins Co, Ky, lost nearly 60 head of cattle & cash in all about $2,000.]

N Y, Dec 15. The brig **E Drummond** recently arrives at Aspinwall, bringing 42 Peruvian Llamas. 70 were originally shipped, but 29 died on the passage.

THU DEC 17, 1857
The Queen of Spain has conferred upon Capt Jose Bosch, of the Spanish brig **Jacinto**, the first-class cross of the Order of Beneficencia, for his humanity in picking up at sea & restoring to their ship the 3 whale-boats containing the capt & most of the crew of the American barque **Alto**, of New Bedford, on Jul 22 & 23 last.

Thos J Semmes, formerly of Wash City, has been confirmed by the Senate as U S Atty for the Eastern District of La, vice F H Clack, removed.

Fred'k W Lincoln, jr, was elected Mayor of the city of Boston on Mon by a majority of nearly 4,000 over Chas B Hall.

Orphans Court of Wash Co, D C. Letters of administration, with the will annexed, on the personal estate of Louisa J Wadsworth, late of Wash Co, deceased.
–J B H Smith, adm

Col Francis M Wynkoop, late U S marshal of the Eastern district of Pa, came to his death a day or two ago, near Tamqua, from a wound received from a gun in the hands of a hired man, with whom the colonel was engaged hunting pheasants. He commanded one of the Pa regts in Mexico during the war with that Republic, & won the commendation of his superiors for bravery & the love of his men for the kindness always shown them. He was at the capture of the city of Vera Cruz & at the battle of Cerro Gordo, & other numerous skirmishes.

Capt Van Vleit, U S Army, arrived in this city Sat, breakfasted, & was off again for the West, on the Pacific cars. He was just from Washington. He may be the bearer of instructions to Gen Denver, the Sec, or to Gen Harney, in command of the U S troops in Kansas Territory. –St Louis Republican of Monday

Harding Johnson, a retired merchant of Cincinnati, committed suicide on Dec 7 by drowning himself. Mr Johnson some years since became security for a friend, & he was reduced to poverty by having to meet his demand. In addition to this his house was recently destroyed by fire.

Wm F Wightman, Editor of the North Carolinian, & another young man, M S Elliott, were found dead in one bed in the Shemwell House, in Fayetteville, on Dec 11. They left a note stating that they had taken nitric acid for the purpose of committing suicide.

Mr Martin Rickhert, a native of Germany, died recently at the North Mountain House, above Clearspring, Wash Co, Md, at the advanced age of 106 years & 11 months. He came to America at the close of the Revolutionary war, & cast his first vote for Washington. He was accustomed, when 100 years of age, to walk to Clearspring, 4½ miles.

Theodore Tucker, age 14 years, in endeavoring to get on one of the cars of the 8th ave line in N Y, was run over & killed.

Died: on Dec 15, at Alexandria, Rev Job Guest, in his 73rd year. He was attached to the Balt Conference of the Methodist Episcopal Church, & had been a faithful minister for 42 years, having joined the conference in 1806. He has left a name without reproach to his descendants.

House of Reps: 1-Ptn of Fred'k Zaracher, for payment of expenses incurred by him during the riots in Christiana, Lancaster Co, Pa.

FRI DEC 18, 1857
Mrd: on Dec 15, at the Southern Methodist Church, by Rev Mr Granberry, Wm T Johnson, of Montg Co, Md, to Miss Eliza J Murphy, of Rappahannock Co, Va.

Mrd: on Dec 9, at Oakwood Plantation, La, by Rev Mr Trader, Dr Paul S Carrington to Mary M Roy, adopted daughter of P Lansdale Cox.

Mrd: on Dec 15, at Coombe Cottage, Prince Wm Co, Va, By Rev T B Balch, Arthur Ashton, of Ashley, to Anne Carter, daughter of the officiating minister.

Died: on Dec 14, in N Y, after a long & painfull illness, Agnes Macleod, daughter of the late John Macleod, formerly of the Genr'l Post Ofc Dept in Wash City. Her funeral will be from the residence of her nephew, W C Bestor, D st, between 2nd & 3rd sts, this afternoon, at 2 o'clock.

Died: on Dec 17, Emma Gurley, infant daughter of Mr & Mrs J Hackett, aged 8 months & 2 days. Her funeral will be today at 3 o'clock, at 327 9th st, between L & M sts.

Died: on Dec 9, at her residence in PG Co, Md, Mrs Mary Berry, in her 78th year.

Criminal Court-Wash-yesterday. 1-Jas Williamson was convicted of stealing a money-drawer & 2 gold dollars: sentenced to 5 months in jail. John M Cuen, tried for participation in the same offence, was found guilty & had the same sentence. 2-Anthony Grey was acquitted of a charge of stealing $25 in gold.

House of Reps: 1-By Mr Phillips, of Pa. 2-Ptn of Mrs D Minis, praying the passage of a law authorizing the payment to her of certain amounts of loan.

$10 reward for runaway mulatto servant Jane, about 17. –Chr Grammer, of excs of G C Grammer. Ofc north side of D st, between 5th & 6th sts.

SAT DEC 19, 1857
Senate: 1-Bill introduced to confirm the title in a certain tract of land in Missouri to the heirs & legal reps of Thos Maddin, deceased.

In the recent trial of Col Edwin V Sumner, 1st Regt U S Cavalry, by a general court martial at **Fort Leavenworth**, Col Henry Stanton, 7th infty, was Pres. Col Sumner was put upon his trial on 2 charges: one neglect of duty, & the other conduct unbecoming an ofcr & gentleman. On the first charge he was found guilty; on the second charge he was found not guilty. Gen Scott remits the whole of the sentence: to be reprimanded; suspended from rank & from command, & to forfeit his pay proper for 4 months.]

M B Lamar, of Texas, was on Thu confirmed by the Senate as U S Minister to Central America.

Saml F Jones, jr, late cashier of the Colchester Bank, Conn, was recently arrested in N Y, charged with having embezzled from the bank about $75,000; but owing to the want of power on the part of the authorities to detain him without a requisition from the Govn'r of the State he was set at libery; & after the requisition was procured he could not be found. Jones is well connected, is married, & has a family residing n Arkansas. He is about 30 years of age.

Died: on Dec 18, in Wash City, Edwin G Evens, son of Benj Evens, in his 31st year. His funeral will be on Dec 20, at 2 o'clock, from his father's residence, 601 H st.

Orphans Court of Wash Co, D C. Letters testamentary on the personal estate of Geo H Jones, late of Wash Co, deceased. –Frances Jane Jones, excx

MON DEC 21, 1857
Her Britannic Majesty' Legation, Wash, Dec 15, 1857. I am instructed by the Earl of Clarendon to place in your hands the accompanying medals which her Majesty's Gov't desire to present to the ofcrs & men engaged in the several expeditions which have been fitted out in the U S for the recovery of Sir John Franklin & his companions. A list of the persons to whom these marks of gratitude are offered is enclosed herewith, & should there be any errors or omissions in the roll of names, I beg they may be indicated for the information of her Majesty's Gov't. –Napier
Expedition to the Artic ses in search of Sir John Franklin, under the command of Lt DeHaven, U S Navy; sailed from N Y May 26, 1850, returned Sep 30, 1851. The brig **Advance**: Lt commanding, Edwin J DeHaven; acting master, Wm H Murdaugh; passed assist surgeon, Elisha Kent Kane; midshipman, Wm W Lovell. All-U S navy.
Men: Wm Morton, ship's steward; Jas Smith, ordinary seaman; John Brennen, sailmaker's mate; Louis Coster, armorer; Edw Wilson, seaman; Thos Dunnin, boatswain's mate; Edw C Delano, seaman; Henry Derockle, ship's cook; Wm Holmes, ordinary seaman; Gibson Caruthers, carpenter's mate; Chas Berry, seaman; Wm Weast, boatswain's mate.
The brig **Rescue**: Acting master, Saml P Griffin; acting master, Robt R Carter; assist surgeon, Benj Vreeland; boatswain, Henry Brooks. –All-U S navy.
Men: Rufus C Baggs, ordinary seaman; John Williams, quartermaster; Robt Bruce, armorer; Harman G Willie, carpenter's mate; Wm Benson, ordinary seaman; Wm Lincon, boatswain's mate; Wm J Kuner, ofcrs' steward; Jean A Knauss, cook; Smith Benjamin, seaman; David Davis, sailmaker's mate; Jas Johnson, seaman; Jas Stewart, ordinary seaman; Alec'r Daly, seaman.
Ofcrs & men of the expedition to the Artic seas in search of passed Assist Surgeon E K Kane, under the command of Lt H J Hartstene, U S Navy; sailed from N Y Jun 4, 1855, returned Oct 11, 1855.
The barque **Release**: Lt commanding, H J Hartstene, U S navy; acting master, Wm S Lovell, do; passed midshipman, Jos P Fyffe, do; assist surgeon, Jas Laws, do; boartswain, Van Rensselaer Hall, do; Capt's clerk, Chas Lever; purser's steward, Thos Franklin; surgeon's steward, Richd M Clarke.

Men: John Blinn, boatswain's mate; Wm Smith, boatswain's mate; Wm Carey, gunner's mate; John Haley, gunner's mate; Wm Phinney, quartermaster, John Smith, quartermaster; Chas Williams, carpenter's mate; Wm Harry, ship's cook; Francis Taylor, capt of the hold; Chas Johnson, capt maintop; David Batey, capt fortop; Geo Devys, Thos Ford, Lawrence Lewis, Andrew Larcen, Jos Morris, Byron Potter, & Geo Price, seamen.

The propeller **Arctic**: Lt commanding, C Simms, U S navy; acting master, Watson Smith, U S navy; acting assist surgeon, John K Kane; 1st assist engineer, Harmen Newell, U S navy; acting 3rd assist engineer, Wm Johnston; purser's steward, Jas Van Dyke; surgeon's steward, Abraham W Kendall; acting boatswain, Saml Whiting; acting carpenter, Wm Richardson.

Men: Robt Bruce, boatswain's mate; John Bidwold, boatswain's mate; Wm Grover, quartermaster; Walter Wilkinson, quartermaster; John Thompson, carpenter's mate; Jos Brown, ship's cook; Richd Hartley, capt of the hold; Jas Botsford, seaman; John Brown, seaman; John Fox, 2nd class fireman; Geo Tyler, 2nd class fireman; John Gilbert, 2nd class fireman.

Passed Assist Surgeon E K Kane, & the following named persons belonging to his party returned with Lt Hartstene's expedition:
John W Wilson, Amos Bensall, J J Hays, Augustus Sontag, Henry Goodfellow, Geo Stephenson, Thos Hickey, Jas McGary, Geo Riley, Wm Godfrey, Chas Blake, Geo Whittle, John Huzzy, Christian Olsen, Peter Schubert, Jefferson Temple.

Last winter Chas E Sage, about 19, was missing from his home in Cornwell, near Middleton, Conn, & that an Irishman, Patrick Nugent, was arrested on a charge of murdering the lad & putting his body under the ice in the Conn river. A few months later a body believed to be that of the missing boy was found in the river without a head. Thus the matter rested until a few weeks ago, when the cousin of the missing boy, living in Ithica, N Y, received an anonymous letter from Pa, which he showed to his father, Mr Williams. Mr Williams answered the letter & asked the postmaster to watch for the person who called for the letter & describe him. The postmaster did so. Mr Williams left for Pa, & found the person was his nephew, Chas E Sage, the identical missing boy! Nugent was liberated. There is no indentity of the body that was found & buried as that of the boy Sage.

On Tue Mrs Conrad Garber & Mrs Ream were murdered in the house of the former, near Lancaster, Pa, by two negroes, Alex'r Anderson & Wm Richards, who were soon after found in the vicinity, having in their possession money stolen from Mrs Garber's house.

Mr Robt Welsh, of Clearfield, Pa, a silversmith, a few days ago drank by mistake from a tumbler which contained cyanide of potassium, which he had been using in his business, from the effects of which he died in a few minutes.

A skiff which left Kansas City on Dec 9, containing Fr Durand, of the Catholic Mission, D J F Smith, of Leavenworth, Mr Patterson, of Nebraska, Mr Sears, of Indiana, & another gentleman, from Belfast, Maine, when about 25 miles from Kansas City, struck a snag & capsized, throwing the entire party into the river. All were lost except Mr Smith & Mr Sears, who held onto the boat. Fr Durand was a prominent gentleman at the Mission, & was highly respected. –St Louis Democrat

Five men under sentence at N Y to suffer the extreme penalty of the law early in the ensuing year: Jas Gallagher sentenced in Brooklyn last Thu to be hung Feb 5 for stabbing Hugh Kelly in a porter-house. Jas Rogers for the murder of John Swanston & Michl Cancemi for the murder of policeman Anderson, sentenced to be hanged on Jan 15. Jas P Donnely, convicted of the murder of Albert S Moses, at Naversink, N J, sentenced to hung on Jan 8; & Jas Shepherd, convicted of murder in the 1st degree, will be sentenced today.

Iranistan, the residence of P T Barnum, near Bridgeport, Conn, was totally destroyed by fire on Thu night. The cost of the bldg was over $100,000. It was erected 8 years ago. The insurance on the house was between $30,000 & $40,000, & on the furniture $1,000, all held by mortgagees. Mr Barnum was preparing to re-occupy the premises, & the fire is supposed to have been occasioned by the carelessness of workmen engaged in refitting & repairing.

Yesterday the body of a man was found in the Canal between 9th & 10th sts, which proved to be Mr David Newland, of Wisconsin, but formerly of N C, in which latter State he once ran for Rep to Congress & took his seat, but, it being contested, & he was unseated. The jury came to the conclusion that the death was caused by accidental drowning. He was about 58 years of age. The body was yesterday taken possession of by the Masonic Order here, of which Order the deceased was a member, & will be buried by them.

Mrd: on Dec 15, at the residence of Jno D Thorne, by Rev Robt O Burton, Mr Saml J Clark, of La, to Miss Tempie D Thorne, of Halifax Co, N C.

TUE DEC 22, 1857
Senate: 1-Hon Jno C Breckinridge, Vice Pres of the U S, took his seat this morning as presiding ofcr of the Senate. 2-Ptn from Isaac Swain, asking that he may be paid a balance of his claim for damages in consequenece of the loss of the ship **Ellen Brooks** & cargo, which claim was rejected by the Court of Claims.

Died: on Dec 15, Mrs Ann Power, in her 67th year.

Died: Dec 18, at his residence, near Bladensburg, Md, John Eversfield, in his 68th year.

Criminal Court-Wash-Mon: 1-Edw Mahoney & Chas Brown charged with grand larceny in stealing a revolver. 2-Chas Nicholls charged with stealing a book valued at $4 from Alfred Hunter: not guilty. 3-Robt Squibs & Chas Hurdle on trial for a riot on Oct 14 last, at the time a haystack was burnt. Witnesses for the U S were ofcrs Klopfer & McHenry, & for the defence Chas Prather, H Luckett, Capt Mills, & Ignatius Knott. 4-Jefferson Payne, colored, found guilty of assault. 5-Jas Cowen found guilty of larceny. 6-Warren Wallace, found not guilty of petty larceny. 7-Thos Richards, colored, convicted of stealing a pair of boots. [Dec 23rd newspaper: Chas Hurdle acquitted. Catharine O Rose was convicted of stealing $63, & sentenced to 2 years in the penitentiary. Edw Mahoney & Chas Brown were both convicted of stealing a revolver from Hilleary Hutchins: each sentenced to one year in the penitentiary.]

Navy: List of Ofcrs of the Navy whose cases have been investigated by Courts of Inquiry, & who have been nominated to the Senate for restoration to the active list.
Capt Jos Smith, from leave pay.
Cmders:
J R Jarvis, from leave
Jas Glynn, from leave
Robt Ritchie, from leave
C Ringgold, fom leave
J S Sterrett, from leave
Robt D Thorburn, from leave
Saml Lockwood, from leave
W S Ogden, droped
John Colhoun, dropped
Murray, Mason, furlough
Lts:
Wm E Hunt, furlough
M F Maury, leave
Jas S Palmer, leave
Robt Henry, furlough
Henry Walke, furlough
Lewis C Sartori, furlough
Fabius Stanly, furlough
*Thos H Stevens, dropped
J N Maffit, furlough
A D Harrell, dropped
A Murray, furlough
Van R Morgan, furlough
Abner Read, dropped
Geo A Stevens, dropped
Masters: A McLaughlin, dropped; W W Low, leave
Passed Midshipmen:
J Howard March, dropped
Jas S Thornton, dropped
Ed C Grafton, furlough
List of Ofcrs who were dropped who have been placed on the reserved list:
Lts:
W A C Farragut, leave
R W Meade, furlough
Thos Brownell, furlough
Master: Julius S Bohrer, leave
Passed Midshipman: N T West, leave
List of Ofcrs on reserved list on furlough pay who have been placed on leave pay:
Capts:
Jesse Wilkinson
Thos M Newell
W K Latimer
John H Graham
W Inman

Cmders:
Chas T Platt			Henry Bruce			Chas H Jackson
Lts:
Peter Turner			Henry A Steele			E C Bowers
G G Williamson			Wm Chandler			Augustus S Baldwin
Simon B Bissell			Jas M Gilliss			Wm B Whiting
John J Glasson			John P Parker			M C Marin
Master R Clarendon Jones
Passed Midshipman Saml Pearce
[*Lt Thos H Stevens was picked up through a correction in the Dec 24th newspaper.]

WED DEC 23, 1857
Senate: 1-Ptn from Horace E Dimick, asking an appropriation for the purpose of testing his improvement of the rifle cannon for throwing solid shot & shells. 2-Ptn from A W McPherson, asking to be remunerated for fitting up & furnishing rooms for the use of the district court of the U S at San Francisco. 3-Ptn from Jas Page & others, citizens of Phil, asking that the Post Ofce in that city may be located on the site of the present custom-house, & the custom-house transferred to the site selected for the post ofc. 4-Ptn from G A Breast, asking to be pensioned on account of injuries received while employed in the service of the U S at Wash City navy yard. 5-Cmte on Foreign Relations: bill for the relief of Aler's J Atocha. Same cmte: bill for the relief of Geo P Marsh, with a report recommending its passage.

A Legacy. Rev Robt Gray, a Presbyterian minister at Burt, near Londonderry, Ireland, died lately leaving considerable property to his nephew, John Gray, who is supposed to be in the U S.

Petersburg, Dec 22. Henry Potter, Judge of the U S district court for N C, died on Sun last at Fayetteville, aged 93 years. [Dec 29th newspaper: Hon Potter died on Dec 20; he was born in Michlenburg, Va, in 1765, & appointed District Judge by Mr Jefferson in 1801. He was a contemporary of Caswell, Davie, Alexander, Taylor, Hill, & others, distinguished in their day in N C, & was the last survivor of those who signed the original Constitution of the Grand Lodge in that State in 1787. Judge Potter was in Phil & was present & heard Gen Washington deliver his first message to the Congress that convened after his election to the Presidency.]

Cyclopidia of Wit and Humor of America, Ireland, Scotland, & England; by Wm E Burton, Comedian. Embellished with upwards of 600 engravings of original design, & a portrait on steel of the author. 3 vols, price $6. –Blanchard & Mohun

Mrd: on Dec 22, by Rev Andrew G Carothers, Mr Robt Gibson to Miss Lucinda Baker, both of PG Co, Md.

St Louis, Dec 22. A letter in the St Louis Democrat says that Gen Lane was shot at Lecompton by a Gov't official on Dec 15 during a political discussion. Much excitement prevailed. Mr Stanton was still acting as Govn'r on Dec 19th apparently with the approbation of Mr Denver. Gen Harney had dispatched 2 companies of cavalry, upon Stantons' requisition, to suppress rebellion at **Fort Scott**, where several lives were sacrificed. Gen Harney had also posted troops at Leavenworth, Lecompton, & other points.

THU DEC 24, 1857
Thos C Johnson & Saml M Colman, Law & Land Agency Ofc, 46 Chestnut st, St Louis, Mo. [Ad]

The murder of Chas W Littles causes great excitement in Rochester. Mrs Littles & her brother Ira Stout swear positively that they know nothing about the transaction, & account, the one for her wrist & the other for his arm being broken by saying that leisurely returning home from the house of a friend on the night of the murder, they each sustained a fall from a plant walk. [Dec 25th newspaper: On Sunday the body of Chas W Little, a lawyer of Rochester, N Y, was found in the Genesee river, below the falls, shockingly mangled, which, together with the evidences on shore of a murderous conflict having taken place near the spot, point to the fact that Mr Little is the victim of an assassin. His wife, her brother, Ira Stout, & several of her relatives have been arrested on suspicion of having committed the crime. Articles belonging to Mrs Little & Ira Stout, were found on the ground. Mrs Little & her brother each had a left arm broken. Mr & Mrs Little separated a year ago, but for the last 2 months have lived together.]

Since the death of Capt Paige, Maj Mordecai Myers, of Schenectady, Gen Wool, of the U S Army, & Dr John McCall, of Utica, are the only surviving ofcrs of the 13th Regt in the war of 1812.

Col Chas L Thompson was killed by an accident on the Mississippi railroad on Dec 11. He was a native of Va.

The Star says that on Mar 3 last the Pres placed Capt H B Sawyer, who had been furloughed by the Retiring Board, on the leave list.

At Oakhill, near Pottsville, Pa, on Sat, Jas Holland, aged 19, killed his own mother by kicking her. He was drunk. He has disappeared.

Senate: 1-Bill for the relief of Wm K Jennings & other: introduced & referred. 2-Bill for the relief of Eliz Montgomery, heir of Hugh Montgomery: introduced & referred.

Restoration of the "Resolute to Queen Victoria:" this interesting picture by Simpson represents the scene which took place on Dec 6, 1856, on board the ship **Resolute**, when the Queen & her suite came on board & Capt Hartstene & his ofcrs received her Majesty, & the Capt made that admirable speech to which she is here represented as replying, "Sir, I thank you." The grouping is of the Queen & Prince Albert, Adm Seymour, & Capt Hartstene as the central group, & behind the Queen, the Princess Royal, the Prince of Wales, Princess Alice, & others of the Queen's household. The Queen looks a little younger in the picture than out of it. This painting cannot fail to interest Americans, all who are not so far removed as not to feel a throb of emotion when in the presence of the loved <u>Queen of England</u>. –P S

Mrd: on Dec 22, at the Assembly's Church, by Rev Andrew G Carothers, Mr Chas T Smith to Mrs Mary F Jones, daughter of Chas L Coltman.

Died: on Dec 22, in Wash City, Mary D B, 2nd daughter of Edw & Maria L Swann, aged 6 years, 8 months & 22 days. Her funeral is today at 12 o'clock, from the residence of her parents, 26 La ave.

Died: on Dec 23, Edw Lochrey, in his 35th year. His funeral is on Christmas Day, at 3 o'clock, at his late residence, 441 13th st, to St Patrick's Church.

Trenton, N J, Dec 23. The Court of Pardons has declined to pardon Donnelly, now under sentence of death.

St Patrick's-Christmas Day-Masses: The first, a High Mass, will commence at 5 o'clock; then 3 in immediate succession, at all of which Holy Communion will be administered. The usual Masses at 9 & 11 o'clock; 11 o'clock Mass, the last, will be a High Mass. Four o'clock P M Vespers, followed by Benediction. The first bell in the morning will be rung at 4½ o'clock. Please be prepared to hand in your contributions at the doors.

U S Patent Ofc, Wash, Dec 23, 1857. Ptn of Henry McCarty, of Pittsburgh, Pa, praying for the extension of a patent granted to him on Mar 16, 1844, for an improvement in suspending, opening, & closing lock gates, for 7 years from the expiration of said patent, which takes place on Mar 16, 1858. –Jos Holt, Com'r of Patents

FRI DEC 25, 1857
Jos Eaches, formerly Mayor of Alexandria, & Collector of that port, & at the time of his decease a President of the Alexandria Canal Co, which ofc he had held for a number of years, departed this life on Sat last, after a lingering illness. Mr Eaches was a native of Loudoun Co, but for a long time a resident of this city.
-Alexandria Gaz

Wickliffe Hutchinson, Postmaster at Charlottesville, Va, died very suddenly in the cars on Fri, between that place & Gordonsville. He appeared in his usual good health a moment before his death.

Lt Sackeld, of the Bengal engineers, who gallantly blew up the Cashmere Gate on the day that Delhi was informed by the English, died of his wounds on Oct 19th.

The friends of Rev Dr Danforth, on the eve of his departure for Delaware, have presented him with a rich service of plate as a parting testimonial of that Christian love & affection which has so long existed between them. –Alexandria Gaz

Geo W Cockrell, a young man, son of Mrs Jane Cockrell, residing on the Leesburg Turnpike, in Fairfax Co, was found on Friday in a ditch, between his mother's residence & Col Wm Minor's, dead. He had left home on Thu, to attend a party at Col Minor's, & the night being very dark, it is supposed he lost his way, as the ditch into which it is supposed his horse fell, throwing him off, & killing him instantly, was some 50 feet from the road. This affair has thrown a deep gloom over the family of the deceased. –Alexandria Gaz

Richd W Jacobs, age 22 years, of South Danvers, Mass, who had been unwell for a few days, was on Fri seized with severe pains, with all the symptoms of hydrophobia, which continued through the day until his death sometime during the night. He had been bitten by a dog some 15 years ago, while living in Ill, & the deadly virus it is supposed must have been lurking in his system ever since.

Died: on Dec 23, Florence B R, daughter of Jas W & Sarah A R Barker, aged 11 months & 4 days. Her funeral is today at 2 o'clock.

A correspondent of the Silver Creek Mirror says that Col Jacob Carrol, of Texas, is the largest planter in the U S. He owns 250,000 acres of land in that & adjoining counties. His home plantaion contains about 8,000 acres, along the Guadalupe river. He has a force of about 50 field hands. His annual income from the sale of stock amounted to from $5,000 to $10,000; & from the sale of cotton to from $15,000 to $20,000.

Man buried with a belt full of gold around him. About a month ago the body of Nicholas Wertner, of Maseoutha, St Clair Co, was found in the water near Jersey City, & it was interred at Bergen. Justice Bedford addressed a letter to Maseoutha, relating the occurrence, & a day or two since the widow of the deceased made her appearance in Jersey City, & stated that her husband had a considerable amount of gold with him, which he carried in a belt about his waist. Justice engaged an undertaker to examine the remains, & the result was the finding of the belt about the body containing $1,600 in gold. –Boston Courier

J Milton Clapp, associate Editor of the Charleston Mercury, died on Wed. He had long been an invalid. The Charleston papers render a sincere tribute to his memory as a man of marked worth.

MON DEC 28, 1857

All persons indebted to me, either by notes, past dues, due bills, or open accounts, are hereby notified that I shall expect them to pay the cash on or before Jan 1, 1858. -Wm M Cripps, Wholesale & Retail Grocer, 61 La ave, between 6th & 7th sts.

Jas A Partridge, of Balt, has been tendered by Gov Hicks the ofc of Sec of State of Md, & he has accepted the trust.

The public are cautioned against purchasing certain lots, purporting to be owned by one Geo T Massey, & to have been conveyed to said Massey by David A Hall, no consideration having been paid therefore. And caution is also given against buying any notes payable to the order of the said Maasey, & signed by D A Hall. As no consideration has been given for these notes the payment thereof will be contested. [Not signed.]

Death of an Old Tar. Thos Penny died at the Naval Asylum, near Phil, on Monday, aged 81 years. This gallant tar was one of the crew of Cmdor Perry's flagship **Lawrence**, & fought most nobly on board that vessel until, owing to her disabled condition, it was determined that Cmdor Perry should go on board the ship **Niagara**, when Penny was selected as one of the crew of the boat that was to convey his brave cmder. The passage was effected amid a storm of round shot & grape, which splintered many of the oars & so shattered the boat that when it reached the **Niagara** it was in a sinking condition. The character of the fight on board the **Lawrence**, in which this heroic seaman, Penny, acted his part with cool & determined courage, may be gathered from the fact that out of crew of 103 fit for duty, 22 were killed & 63 wounded.

The Raleigh Register has announced the sudden death of Jas Meban, a prominent citizen of North Carolina.

Circuit Court of Wash Co, D C-in Chancery, No 1,217. Sarah B French & others vs Junius French & Rose French. The trustees in this cause report that on Dec 17, 1857, they made sale of part of lot 16 in square 437, in Wash City, to Nathl M McGregor at & for the sum of $7,500. –Jno A Smith, clerk

The residence of Hon Horace F Clark, on 13th & K sts, was entered some time on Sat night or Sun morning, & sundry acticles taken. We do not have any clue to the actors in this burglary.

Mrd: on Dec 24, by Rev Wm H Tyrce, Mahlon A Hensley, Principal of Meadesville Academy, to Miss Mattie A Tompkins, all of Halifax Co, Va.

Died: on Dec 27, Mrs Kitty E Gassaway, eldest daughter of the late Dr Hendley Barron, of Prince Wm Co, Va, in her 59th year. Her funeral will be from her late residence, on D st, this day at 2 o'clock.

Died: on Dec 25, Miss Mary Magruder, eldest daughter of the late Jas A Magruder.

Died: on Fri, in his 16th year, Thomas, son of the late Col Thomas Corcoran.

Died: on Dec 26, in Wash City, J R Sutton, in his 41st year.

Died: on Dec 22, at Brook Grove, PG Co, Md, Jos H Wilson, in his 66th year.

N Y, Dec 27. Among the passengers by the mail steamer **Northern Light** is Gen Wm Walker, prisoner on parole. Walker had captured *Fort Castillo* & 4 steamers, when he himself & 150 of his men were captured by Cmdor Paulding, of the frig **Wabash**. The men were sent in the ship **Saratoga** to Norfolk, & Gen Walker has been permitted to proceed to N Y on parole. Walker's force was captured by 350 men, landed from the frig **Wabash**. Col Anderson & 50 Americans still held *Fort Castillo* & the River San Juan. The Costa Ricans had sent 400 men against them.

TUE DEC 29, 1857
The Galveston News announced the death of Rev Danl Baker, of Austin, an eminent divine, & the founder of the Austin College. [No death date given-current item.]

Greenbury O Mullenix was hung at Greencastle, Indiana, on Friday last for the murder of his wife.

Prof C W Schuermann, late from the Academy of Music, Leipzig, Germany, continues to give instructions on the Piano, in Vocal Music. Residence: 402 16th st, 1½ squares north of Lafayette Square.

City Academy, 483 10th st, established in 1832, will resume Jan 4, 1858.
-Prof J Fill, Principal

Criminal Court-Wash-Monday. 1-Dennis McGhee guilty of resisting Ofcr Daw in the discharge of his duty: sentenced to 2 months in jail & $10 fine. 2-Jas Digges, colored, guilty of petty larceny in stealing 4 whips: sentenced to 11 months in jail. 3-Benj McGraw was convicted of riot at the house of David B Jenkins on Nov 1. Not yet sentenced. 4-Jos E Birch, indicted for an assault & battery with intent to kill Eugene Lanahan on Nov 17 last, is set for trial tomorrow.

Died: on Dec 27, Eleanor Frances, wife of T M Triplett, & daughter of the late Henry Howard, in her 24th year. Her funeral will take place from the residence of her husband, on Mass ave, between 14th & 15th sts, this day, at 2½ o'clock P M.

N Y, Dec 28. Gen Walker delivered himself to Marshal Rynders, who had made arrangements to accompany the prisoner to Washington tomorrow to ascertain the intentions of the President.

WED DEC 30, 1857
On Wed night, in Clark Co, Indiana, Miss Prather was married to a cousin at her father's residence. The bride being on horseback, to go to the home of the bridegroom, the animal becoming frightened, threw the bride off, & she had her neck broken, causing instant death.

An itinerant lecturer, O P Prescott, recently committed suicide at Indianapolis, Ia, by taking morphine. He writes that his only regret is leaving his dear loving wife.

Criminal Court-Wash-Tue: Jos Cunningham was found guilty of stealing, on Dec 8, 8 hats, the property of John Maguire. He again was put upon trial for stealing boots & shoes, the property of Thos Spates, on Sep 10, at the time of the burning of the house of Mr Poulton, on the Island, in which Mr Spates resided. He was found guilty on the second charge also. The indictment for arson has been abandoned.

Jas Charles, alias Simms, who was shot on Wed last by Chas Willey, was reported to be in a dying condition.

Orphans Court of Wash Co, D C. Letters of administration on the personal estate of Lewis Dorr, late of Wash Co, deceased. –Eliz Dorr, admx

Died: on Dec 29, in Wash City, John Goldin, in his 70th year. His funeral will be on Thu at 2 o'clock, from his late residence on D st, between 7th & 8th sts.

Madame A Nourrit, 716 Walnut st, below 8th, Phil. Importer of French Flowers, Head-Dresses, Bonnets, & Fine Millinery. [Ad]

THU DEC 31, 1857
The undersigned propose to conduct in Lynchburg, commencing on Jan 4, 1858, a Boarding & Day School for Young Ladies. Mr Williamson will lecture on Ancient & Modern Languages, & on Mathematics. He does not propose to abandon his profession of law. –Mrs M R Williamson, Mrs S E Page

Orphans Court of Wash Co, D C. Letters of administration on the personal estate of Wm J McCormick, late of Wash Co, deceased. –Eliz B McCormick, admx

Died: on Dec 27, in Uniontown, Pa, Thos Greer, 2nd son of Rev T G & Virginia A Clayton, in his 17th year. His funeral will take place today, at 3 o'clock P M, from his father's residence on K, near 7th st.

Collector's & Distributors for the Ladies' Union Benevolent Society.

Geo W Emerson	Mrs W H Baldwin
Miss Julia W Parris	T J Magruder
S L Loomis	Mrs J F Webb
Mrs S P Hill	L Perry
J W Easby	Mrs J O Mahon
Miss Emma M Steiger	O C Wight
T F Harkness	Mrs Wm Cox
Mrs L Maynard	A Thos Bradley
Z Richards	Mrs Noble Young
Mrs M C Lammond	Dr Jas Grimes
John Ott	Mrs John Houston
Mrs J A Harrold	Dr Jas Grimes
H Beard	Mrs John Underwood
Mrs P D Gurley	Mrs Seth Eliot
G W Hall	Mrs E B Mills
Mrs D Ratcliffe	Mrs Em L Ellis
F H Stickney	Mrs Abel David
Mrs J R Eckard	Dr Jas McKim
J W Clarke	J T Given
Mrs L B Gilliss	Mrs A Holmead
Dr Jas Wilson	R M Pierson
Mrs J C Harkness	Mr Brawner
Walter Johnson	Dr J E Willet
F Magruder	Mrs Wheeler
Mrs Chas Fowler	Chas S Allen
B Milburn	Mrs R B Clark
Mrs W B Todd	Wm Ballantyne

A

A'Beckett, 306
Abbegil, 344
Abbot, 100, 276, 279
Abbott, 97, 103, 132, 145, 257, 347, 350, 385, 444, 460, 468
Abell, 148
Abenel, 282
Abercrombie, 192
Abert, 51, 418
Aberthney, 337
Aby, 104
Accardi, 29
Acken, 153, 391
Adair, 108, 397
Adams, 6, 9, 13, 21, 28, 29, 69, 95, 100, 104, 107, 151, 153, 182, 208, 213, 224, 233, 250, 254, 261, 262, 282, 308, 309, 311, 323, 327, 352, 373, 400, 411, 413
Adamson, 273, 468
Addison, 121, 201, 385
Adkins, 385, 474
Adler, 83, 208
Agamemon, 326
age of 108, 27
Ager, 297, 299
Agg, 133, 160
Aichtenstein, 378
Aiken, 4, 62
Ailcock, 213
Ainsworth, 312
Aker, 410
Albaugh, 449
Albert, 350
Albrecht, 108
Albright, 343, 454
Alcott, 64
Aldie Mill, 123
Aldie Mills, 123
Aldrich, 297

Alexander, 16, 78, 164, 170, 225, 232, 234, 246, 270, 280, 297, 352, 434, 442, 452, 483
Alig, 54, 435
Alison, 306
Allcock, 15
Allen, 7, 31, 53, 56, 64, 73, 96, 109, 140, 174, 175, 189, 203, 208, 233, 236, 240, 254, 273, 295, 309, 365, 387, 403, 433, 440, 444, 456, 490
Alley, 224
Allman, 365
Allmand, 206, 274
Allnutt, 193
Allock, 18
Allsbach, 440
Allston, 207, 281
Almonte, 428
Almy, 350
Alsten, 207
Alston, 410
Altemus, 52
Althrop, 305
Alvord, 58, 72
Ambler, 63
Ament, 115
Ames, 230, 253, 361, 418
Amiss, 459
Amm, 415
Ammen, 45
Amour, 395
Ampere, 341
Anacosta, 190
Anastasio, 467
Anderson, 44, 53, 76, 100, 124, 164, 168, 174, 188, 222, 233, 234, 236, 242, 250, 254, 275, 280, 287, 309, 354, 413, 414, 431, 445, 450, 468, 474, 480, 481, 488
Andre, 349
Andrews, 100, 254, 283, 382, 415
Aneya, 88

Angel, 283
Angel Gabriel, 13
Angell, 171
Angerman, 432
Anguera, 336
Ankeny, 28
Anthony, 414, 419
Apperson, 151
Appleby, 31, 72
Appleton, 52, 132, 394
Applewhaite, 22
Appointments by the Pres, 9, 93, 97, 100, 108, 109, 110, 111, 114, 115, 117, 119, 121, 124, 130, 132, 134, 135, 141, 148, 149, 152, 187, 207, 209, 217, 226, 258, 283, 336, 360, 424
Aquele, 371
Arbaca, 254
Arbuckle, 317
Archduchess Sophia, 259
Archer, 23, 116, 314, 348, 452, 460
Archibald, 310, 417
Arguello, 25
Arlington, 403, 406
Arlington Estate, 148
Arlington House, 403
Armistead, 452
Armsby, 432
Armstrong, 25, 26, 35, 68, 77, 87, 88, 92, 112, 135, 175, 359, 399, 441, 452, 462
Arnal, 28
Arnett, 474
Arnold, 34, 56, 188, 219, 220, 290, 444, 458
Arth, 292
Arthur, 320
Ash, 412, 432
Ashburton, 194
Ashby, 232, 371, 373, 374, 376
Ashley, 67, 74
Ashmore, 174
Ashton, 328, 478

Askey, 266
Asnon, 299
Athronsahu, 373
Atkins, 49, 238, 381
Atkinson, 115, 314
Atlantic Telegraph, 326, 331, 332, 334
Atlee, 154, 262
AtLee, 109, 396
Atocha, 22, 51, 483
Attarnelli, 281
Audubon, 30
August, 459
Auld, 213
Aulick, 339, 418
Ausman, 64
Austill, 72, 86, 92, 216
Austin, 65, 87, 109, 255
Avent, 254
Averill, 293, 294
Avery, 238
Aye, 86
Aylett, 441
Aylott, 36
Aymar, 49
Ayres, 287
Ayulo, 372

B

Babbitt, 45, 72, 77
Babcock, 188
Baccus, 274
Bachus, 390
Backenstos, 459
Backus, 194, 260, 399
Bacon, 1, 85, 116, 229, 230, 285, 300, 315, 396
Bactendzorff, 411
Baden, 267, 367, 462
Badey, 309
Badger, 107, 371, 372, 374, 378, 387, 410, 446
Badgley, 373
Bagby, 133, 221, 244, 427

492

Baggot, 206
Baggott, 79, 295, 298
Baggs, 479
Bagley, 253
Bagnam, 237, 324
Bagwell, 400
Bagwill, 412
Bailey, 37, 49, 51, 65, 74, 87, 91, 100, 103, 164, 169, 210, 213, 217, 222, 225, 281, 306, 310, 311, 373, 451
Bailhache, 352
Bailie, 308
Baily, 203
Bain, 342
Bainbridge, 208, 219, 220, 227
Baird, 1, 42, 105, 211, 312
Baker, 50, 73, 82, 107, 111, 164, 167, 223, 244, 248, 300, 309, 344, 349, 445, 474, 483, 488
Balch, 119, 234, 248, 446, 478
Baldwin, 17, 18, 57, 58, 60, 62, 87, 91, 132, 174, 175, 236, 364, 483, 490
Balestier, 182
Balk, 289
Ball, 105, 122, 141, 255, 281, 288, 289, 310, 322, 374, 383, 413, 414
Ballantyne, 303, 473, 490
Ballard, 199
Ballinger, 200
Ballman, 298
Ballow, 439
Baltzell, 15, 18, 49, 82, 90
Bampton, 189
Bancroft, 309
Bangs, 133, 319
Banister, 113
Bank, 396
Bankhead, 156, 224, 452
Banks, 132, 159, 205, 317, 396
Bankston, 16
Baptist, 474
Barbarin, 66
Barber, 413

Barbour, 70, 270
Barchman, 411
Barclay, 178, 249, 284
Barfute, 444
Bargey, 377
Bargy, 86
Baring, 194, 292
Barker, 51, 117, 120, 134, 240, 275, 338, 486
Barlow, 341, 395, 414
Barnaby, 402
Barnaclo, 144, 421
Barnard, 19, 74, 83, 86, 112, 222, 237, 277, 345, 429
Barnes, 224, 230, 244, 474
Barney, 42, 269
Barnhill, 371, 418
Barnum, 418, 420, 423, 455, 481
Baron Alphonse, 118
barque **A G Cochran**, 32
barque **Alto**, 476
barque **Ann Elizabeth**, 46, 51, 84
barque **Bremen**, 396
barque **Chester**, 32
barque **Ellen**, 371, 372, 379, 384
barque **Eloise**, 369, 371
barque **H Crapo**, 116
barque **Jerome Knight**, 400
barque **Marine**, 374
barque **Monasco**, 313, 319
barque **Sarah**, 18, 20, 62
barque **Saxony**, 371, 372
barque **Tedesco**, 32
barque **William & Anne**, 205
Barr, 254, 413
Barret, 7, 99
Barrett, 298
Barrington, 174
Barron, 159, 180, 230, 350, 364, 468, 474, 488
Barrow, 3, 363
Barrows, 186
Barry, 105, 199, 209, 322, 337, 344, 367, 415, 446

Barteau, 282
Bartell, 67
Bartelson, 310
Barth, 242, 348
Barthelow, 451
Bartholomew, 261
Bartholow, 203, 280, 375
Bartle, 276
Bartless, 390
Bartlett, 51, 98, 180, 254, 370, 418
Barton, 66, 82, 99, 102, 119, 239, 287
Bartow, 254
Bartt, 350
Basham, 119
Bashaw, 474
Bashford, 146
Basnett, 289
Bassett, 143
Bassford, 411
Bassler, 301
Bastianelli, 288
Batchell, 139
Batchellor, 174
Bates, 58, 102, 122, 130, 144, 324, 346, 368, 387
Batey, 480
Batson, 110
Battersby, 11
Battin, 243
Baugh, 353, 354
Baughman, 187
Baxter, 1, 257, 398
Bayard, 55, 401
Bayley's purchase, 401
Bayliss, 92, 112, 230
Baylor, 49, 100, 222, 234, 280
Bayly, 85
Bayman, 4
Baynard, 197, 213
Bayne, 1, 129, 204
Bayton, 459
Beach, 189, 222, 234, 236, 280, 410
Beach Hill, 255
Beacker, 459

Beal, 168, 204, 389
Beale, 67
Beall, 2, 22, 116, 186, 211, 243, 244, 246, 247, 259, 285, 320, 441, 464
Beam, 68
Beamer, 214
Beames, 180
Bean, 37, 87, 92, 209, 217, 331
Bear, 30
Beard, 183, 402, 441, 490
Beashler, 412
Beattie, 468
Beatty, 46
Beauchamp, 275
Beaver, 412
Bebb, 86, 210
Bebson, 404
Beck, 154, 333
Becker, 29, 378
Beckett, 213, 231
Beckwith, 459, 462
Bede, 130
Bedell, 178, 402, 412
Bedford, 486
Bedini, 210
Bee, 157, 172, 452
Beebe, 440
Beecher, 169
Beedle, 343
Beekmann, 219
Beelen, 74
Beers, 1, 6, 41, 56, 57, 75, 83, 213, 441
Beeson, 110
Beets, 474
Behan, 258
Beidleman, 164
Belair, 27
Belcher, 254, 432, 450
Belden, 55, 72, 90, 216
Belger, 35, 42, 90
Belknap, 30
Belknapp, 69

Bell, 6, 21, 40, 61, 64, 69, 85, 109, 172, 196, 200, 206, 218, 259, 309, 324, 337, 348, 412, 416, 423, 433, 462
Belle-Air, 435
Belleview, 405
Bellevue, 99
Bellinger, 30, 45
Bellmonte Estate, 311
Bellows, 38, 169
Belmont, 207
Belt, 367, 432, 467
Belton, 279
Belyea, 252
Bemas, 11
Bender, 4, 92, 212
Benevidas, 444
Benford, 4, 14
Benham, 33, 385, 429
Beninger, 349
Benjamin, 68, 115, 479
Benners, 287
Bennet, 46
Bennett, 3, 16, 60, 93, 101, 184, 188, 194, 254, 268, 271, 296, 317, 373, 374, 452, 459
Bensall, 480
Benson, 69, 479
Benthall, 109
Bentley, 293
Benton, 45, 70, 72, 365, 369, 375
Beranger, 305
Berard, 115, 166
Bergden, 400
Bergman, 236
Berkeley, 123
Berks, 411
Bernard, 113, 353
Bernaud, 444
Berne, 120
Bernhisel, 53
Berrell, 130, 132
Berrett, 179
Berrington, 164

Berry, 37, 52, 59, 61, 85, 105, 106, 124, 137, 201, 222, 234, 247, 248, 280, 298, 313, 316, 322, 324, 338, 387, 408, 411, 412, 427, 478, 479
Berryman, 48, 49, 242, 455
Bertrand, 414
Bertron, 320
Bestor, 87, 478
Betaneourt, 341
Bettinger, 361
Beveridge, 103
Beyer, 298
Beylard, 318
Bezian, 463
Bibb, 123, 242, 468
Bicknell, 172
Bidder, 51
Biddle, 104, 152, 210, 408
Biddleman, 206
Bidly, 142
Bidwold, 480
Bier, 260
Big Cypress, 19, 119, 444
Bigelow, 35, 42, 67, 82, 91, 103, 293
Bigham, 262
Bigler, 76, 109
Bigly, 318, 407
Bignon, 270
Bille, 376
Bills, 118
Bindon, 35
Binney, 244, 328, 384
Binns, 308
Birch, 109, 122, 255, 278, 371, 372, 374, 410, 447, 488
Birchard, 336
Birchett, 6
Birckhead, 206
Bird, 137, 191, 395, 459, 460
Birkhead, 27, 312
Birney, 459
Biscoe, 15, 37
Bishop, 36, 110, 115, 141, 171, 275
Bishop of Exeter, 173

Bissell, 33, 239, 385, 483
Bittinger, 98, 371, 391, 427, 466
Biven, 252
Black, 36, 89, 135, 152, 224, 261, 373, 376
Blackbeard, 178
Blackburn, 152, 420, 453
Blackman, 413, 457
Blackstone, 287
Blackwell, 267
Blades, 339
Blagden, 96, 209, 288
Blair, 176, 281, 474
Blaisdell, 7
Blake, 232, 234, 239, 253, 308, 343, 365, 480
Blakely, 265, 449
Blakemore, 119
Blanchard, 109, 378, 439, 483
Bland, 183
Blanderman, 254
Blandford Cemetery, 54
Blandon, 288
Blanton, 412
Bleak Half, 120
Bleakwood, 327
Blenham, 375
Blenheim, 43, 290, 457
Blew, 155
Blinn, 480
Bliss, 373
Blitz, 402
Blondhaem, 347
Blood, 144, 289
Bloodgood, 100, 173
Bloomfield, 327
Blooms' Grove, 120
Bloomsberry, 382
Blossom, 9
Blount, 330
Blue, 82, 91
Blue Ridge Tunnel, 84
Blum, 410
Blunt, 263, 373

Boardman, 383
Boarman, 77, 171, 236, 441
boat **Dragonet**, 352
boat **Ellsworth**, 389
boat **Newton**, 310
boat **Sovereign**, 458
Boatwright, 370
Bocock, 114, 223
Boden, 55
Bogardus, 382
Bogart, 418
Boggs, 281, 368, 389, 398, 446
Bohrer, 81, 162, 230, 426, 482
Boisseau, 52
Bokee, 410
Boker, 372
Bolling, 357
Bollman, 148
Boman, 308
Bonaparte, 305, 327, 340
Bonaparte Estate, 231
Bond, 87, 88, 92, 122, 193, 468
Bonham, 153
Bonling, 324
Bonneville, 445
Bonnycastle, 27
Bontz, 143
Boomer, 56, 82, 91, 215
Boon, 266
Boone, 42, 340
Booth, 27, 471, 474
Boots, 6
Borland, 5, 430
Borremans, 203
Borrows, 298
Boroughs, 205
Bosch, 476
Boschke, 77
Boscow, 81
Bosket, 309
Boss, 180, 237, 295, 297, 325
Bostick, 199
Boston, 117
Boswell, 308

Boteler, 25, 80, 96, 118, 136, 138, 149, 152, 166, 182, 183, 190, 201, 219, 222, 269, 344, 348
Botsford, 480
Bottle paper, 154
Botts, 361, 383
Boucher, 270, 468
Bouck, 43
Boulanger, 79
Boulden, 370
Bourne, 383
Bousey, 389
Bowden, 113
Bowdon, 270
Bowen, 121, 122, 135, 169, 193, 297, 325, 399, 468
Bowers, 40, 483
Bowie, 5, 147, 193, 346, 365, 367, 370, 390, 409
Bowler, 213
Bowley, 372, 410
Bowling, 265, 325, 441
Bowman, 224
Bowne, 45
Bowyer, 52, 235, 271
Boyce, 69, 83
Boyd, 176, 290, 330, 340, 423, 451, 460
Boyden, 134
Boydson, 474
Boyer, 275, 289
Boyle, 3, 32, 110, 148, 203, 207, 210, 221, 310, 360, 460, 461
Boylston, 287
Boyne, 272
Boynton, 411
Bozarth, 287
Brace, 453
Bracely, 26
Brackett, 288
Brade, 414
Braden, 394
Bradford, 52, 184, 267, 337

Bradley, 14, 63, 125, 154, 160, 218, 230, 259, 310, 311, 313, 326, 348, 369, 402, 408, 418, 423, 434, 490
Bradshaw, 157
Brady, 148, 167, 175, 337, 445, 450
Bragelow, 282
Braiden, 118
Brainard, 413
Braman, 223
Branch, 249
Brandt, 298, 396
Brangan, 281
Brannen, 257
Brannock, 428
Branson, 466
Brant, 78, 141
Brashears, 121, 363, 364
Brasher, 273
Brawner, 423, 490
Bray, 86
Brayman, 329
Brayton, 446
Breast, 483
Breathitt, 475
Breck, 27
Breckenridge, 83, 88
Breckinridge, 1, 3, 76, 145, 255, 265, 289, 481
Breen, 435, 450
Brenan, 254, 281
Brenham, 220
Brennan, 254
Brennen, 479
Brenner, 409
Brent, 30, 36, 106, 121, 364, 367
Brenton, 129, 446
Brereton, 165, 279, 318, 320, 335, 395
Breslin, 232, 244
Brett, 342
Brewer, 322, 408, 445
Brewers, 447
Brewster, 362
Bride, 373
Bridge, 152

Bridgman, 281
Briebach, 4, 5
Brien, 18, 25, 77, 86, 175, 281, 468
brig **Advance**, 78, 479
brig **Alteevelta**, 400
Brig **Argus**, 456
brig **Dolphin**, 210
brig **E Drummond**, 476
brig **Edward H Titler**, 391
brig **Ellen**, 166
brig **General Pierce**, 200, 362
brig **Geneva**, 32
brig **Jacinto**, 476
brig **King Brothers**, 328
brig **L Gillis**, 319
brig **Marine**, 371, 372, 376, 381, 389, 390
brig **Mary**, 396
Brig **Pelican**, 456
brig **Rescue**, 479
brig **Sully**, 342
brig **Vesta**, 450
brig **Walborg**, 434
Briggs, 110, 167, 194
Brigham, 155, 170, 262
Brigham Young, 78
Bright, 141, 189, 326, 460
Brightwell, 86, 188
brig-of-war **Argus**, 456
Brinckley, 254
Brinkerhoof, 253
Brinley, 130
Brinly, 104
Brisbane, 402
Briscoe, 232, 270, 332, 467
Bristol, 225, 452
British peerage, 388
Broadhead, 209
Broadie, 64
Broadis, 65
Broadnax, 23
Brochear, 458
Brochim, 174
Brockenbrough, 470

Brodhead, 39, 49, 119, 404
Brodie, 49, 86, 87, 91
Broeck, 306
Brogan, 450
Brom, 174
Bromley, 141
Bromwell, 276
Bronson, 416
Brook, 344, 416, 470
Brooke, 52, 62, 73, 104, 164, 173, 185, 190, 209, 316, 348, 367, 460
Brookes, 3
Brookeville Academy, 329
Brooks, 3, 30, 41, 61, 114, 123, 136, 160, 173, 174, 229, 230, 259, 270, 275, 284, 289, 347, 354, 360, 392, 399, 415, 468, 476, 479
Broom, 77, 209, 275
Broome, 19, 170, 401
Brosnahan, 297
Brotte, 472
Brough, 465
Brougham, 373
Bround, 412
Broussard, 64
Brow, 68
Browers, 432
Brown, 2, 3, 5, 6, 7, 20, 24, 33, 41, 43, 47, 67, 72, 78, 86, 89, 100, 104, 105, 109, 111, 126, 130, 143, 147, 148, 159, 166, 171, 174, 180, 188, 219, 220, 224, 248, 253, 264, 281, 293, 294, 310, 322, 323, 325, 334, 340, 348, 362, 368, 371, 372, 373, 384, 392, 407, 410, 416, 428, 438, 441, 443, 445, 459, 460, 467, 468, 473, 474, 480, 482
Browne, 2, 86, 272, 371
Brownell, 11, 482
Browning, 205, 228, 241, 283, 328, 413, 473
Broyinton, 175
Bruce, 148, 240, 254, 479, 480, 483
Bruckner, 8

Bruin, 371
Brumidi, 273
Brun, 148
Brunley, 34
Bruns, 408
Brush, 87, 372
Bruyn, 413
Bryan, 2, 3, 20, 35, 49, 85, 90, 108, 151, 154, 221, 234, 248, 257, 298, 370, 372, 394, 405
Bryant, 248, 375, 393
Buchanan, 1, 3, 20, 40, 51, 76, 78, 81, 83, 88, 89, 154, 167, 201, 233, 262, 288, 382, 414, 433, 441, 466
Buchey, 135
Buck, 13, 96, 208
Buckey, 277
Buckingham, 209
Buckler, 314
Buckles, 471
Buckley, 148, 334, 418, 443
Buckner, 14, 82, 182
Buckway, 412
Buddington, 396
Budlong, 237
Buel, 448
Buffington, 164
Buford, 452
Bull, 51, 104, 411
Bullard, 262
Bullitt, 417
Bullock, 424
Bulow, 469
Bunce, 232, 323
Bunch, 97, 474
Bunker, 233
Bunting, 105
Burch, 158, 361, 372
Burdell, 48, 66, 87, 91, 170, 333
Burden, 264
Burdick, 413
Burditt's Rest, 332
Burdsall, 67
Burdsau, 70

Burford, 274
Burger, 18
Burgess, 130, 236, 246
Burgher, 15, 20
Burgoyne, 192
Burke, 48, 114, 148, 224, 279, 415
Burkhardt, 188
Burley, 193
Burnap, 47
Burnett, 242, 417, 443, 447
Burney, 218
Burnley, 194
Burns, 11, 124, 151, 158, 209, 297, 349, 408, 413, 452, 468
Burnt Mills, 168
Burr, 110, 211, 217, 218, 301, 385, 386
Burritt, 346
Burroughs, 308
Burrows, 107, 366
Burt, 247, 281, 309, 372, 373, 378, 381, 413
Burton, 466, 481, 483
Busey, 105, 292
Bushnell, 137, 420
Buskirk, 64
Butler, 22, 41, 65, 77, 80, 117, 150, 164, 188, 197, 221, 230, 234, 284, 297, 311, 413, 426, 427, 439, 471, 473, 475, 476
Butt, 138, 188
Butterbaugh, 473
Butterfield, 281
Butterford, 373
Butterworth, 89
Butts, 254
Byer, 240
Byrne, 96, 138, 149, 155, 170, 367, 369
Byrnes, 281, 401

C

Cabaignac, 441
Cabell, 61, 206, 414, 439, 441

Cabury, 352
Caddington, 250
Cadwell, 281
Cahil, 198
Cahill, 271
Caile, 231
Caillard, 340
Calder, 213
Caldwell, 36, 49, 53, 64, 139, 144, 197, 313, 412
Calhoun, 136, 179, 182, 368, 385
Calhouns, 252
Caliborne, 445
Callahan, 175, 253, 308
Callakran, 411
Callan, 108, 228, 270, 367, 421, 424
Calmos, 254
Calvert, 73, 120, 177, 278
Calvin, 368
Calwell, 120, 371
Cameron, 95, 98, 473
Cammack, 193, 434
Camp, 225
Camp Colorado, 444
Campau, 110
Campbell, 25, 30, 45, 73, 141, 151, 281, 283, 290, 299, 307, 310, 337, 341, 347, 350, 386, 393, 402, 420, 464, 467, 472, 474
Camper, 308
Campion, 445
Canas, 255
Canby, 452
Cancemi, 481
Canel, 123
Canfield, 254
Canino, 340
Canning, 339
Cannon, 190
Cansby, 254
Canson, 270
Cantatore, 360
Cantrell, 309
Capen, 217

Capers, 174
Capert, 325
Caperton, 51, 96, 120
Caranagh, 281
Carbery, 50, 201, 230, 394, 401
Card, 396
Carder, 368
Cardinal Francisco, 437
Carey, 480
Carimill, 146
Carleton, 176
Carlisle, 52, 108, 209, 225, 322
Carll, 346
Carman, 9
Carne, 137
Carother, 146
Carothers, 7, 14, 31, 89, 142, 229, 322, 326, 343, 347, 410, 441, 483, 485
Carpenter, 52, 329, 395, 415
Carr, 156, 185, 279, 396
Carrell, 165
Carrigan, 53, 408, 424
Carrington, 133, 221, 293, 478
Carrison, 233
Carrol, 152, 486
Carroll, 32, 41, 51, 75, 115, 133, 162, 229, 343, 395, 452, 469, 470, 475
Carson, 105, 142, 253, 254, 266, 309, 444
Carswell, 203
Carter, 2, 22, 69, 74, 119, 124, 140, 143, 152, 188, 206, 208, 235, 314, 375, 395, 413, 428, 432, 435, 478, 479
Carter's, 284
Carthers, 373
Caruana, 170
Carusi, 261, 322, 345, 375
Caruthers, 3, 109, 479
Carver, 157
Casady, 142
Casali, 273, 288
Case, 51, 115, 395

Casey, 15, 19, 92, 225, 371, 372, 412
Casfang, 63
Caskie, 223
Cass, 78, 89, 378
Cassady, 38, 67, 87, 92
Cassel, 345
Cassidy, 99
Cassin, 106, 145, 339, 340, 426, 436
Casta, 412
Castel, 147
Castle, 203, 309
Caswell, 483
Catalana, 394
Cathcart, 144
Cathell, 468
Catholic Burying ground, 339
Catlett, 6
Catlin, 437
Caton, 236, 468
Catron, 467
Caulfield, 346
Caulk, 16, 439
Cavaignac, 446, 450
Cavalo, 341
Cavana, 308
Cavanagh, 450
Cavanaugh, 378
Cavarrugras, 109
Cazelar, 25, 45
Cazencuve, 28
Cazenove, 58
Cedar Hill Villa, 339
Central Academy, 379
Cerachi, 245
Cessford, 287
Ceyello, 412
Chaboya, 467
Chace, 175
Chadwick, 271
Chaillan, 412
Chalien, 284
Chamberlain, 471
Chambers, 2, 188, 452
Champ, 375

Champion, 16, 52, 105, 196, 236
Champney, 108, 120
Chandler, 208, 383, 444, 483
Chaney, 74
Chapdelaine, 28
Chapin, 396
Chaplin, 152, 199, 233
Chapman, 22, 53, 105, 130, 134, 140, 151, 160, 183, 218, 222, 241, 246, 250, 259, 295, 302, 320, 331, 334, 345, 360, 386, 408, 411, 415, 445, 452, 454, 474
Chappell, 131
Charlsby Farm, 250
Charlten, 148
Charpenning, 31
Chase, 3, 37, 39, 55, 72, 221, 224, 234, 371, 372, 404, 412, 436
Chatard, 25
Chatfield, 152
Chatham, 405
Chauncey, 41
Chauncy, 42
Cheatham, 226, 459
Cheeney, 414
Cheeseman, 382
Cheever, 55, 100, 104, 179, 340
Cheevis, 56, 65
Chelsea, 325
Chene, 310
Cheney, 119
Chester, 36, 175, 290
Chestnut Hill, 299
Cheves, 252
Chew, 207, 276, 455
Chickering, 151, 177
Chief of the Pilgrims, 362
Childress, 471
Childs, 83, 189, 371, 372, 379, 387, 410
Chillan Castle Manor, 463
Chillon Castle Manor, 73, 204, 330
Chilton, 21, 67, 107, 118, 201, 276, 399

Chip Oaks, 249
Chipman, 166, 276
Chisholm, 213
Chisholn, 164
Chisom, 77
Choate, 180
Choice, 265
Chorpenning, 92, 216
Chorpenny, 86
Chort, 412
Christ Church, 72, 461
Christian, 244, 277, 290, 446
Christie, 414
Christman, 412
Christy, 438, 474
Chronise, 291
Chubb, 3
Chunn, 184
Church, 18, 34, 157, 222, 389
Churchill, 26, 35, 46, 90, 398
Ciampi, 106
Cilley, 15, 18, 92
Cisne, 29, 36
City, 460
Clack, 476
Claflin, 222, 234, 280
Clagett, 37, 208, 230, 245, 343, 377, 426
Claiborne, 444
Clapham, 222
Clapp, 471, 487
Clare, 265
Clark, 2, 6, 17, 33, 52, 82, 91, 92, 122, 141, 144, 172, 179, 183, 213, 220, 222, 230, 236, 286, 289, 315, 343, 350, 365, 370, 371, 372, 373, 394, 399, 413, 418, 423, 439, 441, 454, 481, 487, 490
Clarke, 42, 59, 63, 76, 98, 104, 108, 160, 179, 220, 225, 254, 262, 270, 286, 304, 309, 401, 433, 448, 451, 467, 475, 479, 490
Clarkson, 21, 31, 455
Clary, 27

Claviaccord, 291
Clawson, 292, 346
Claxton, 51
Clay, 15, 92, 122, 193, 199, 212, 235, 242, 250, 265, 373, 442, 469
Clayton, 100, 149, 297, 331, 490
Cleary, 55, 270
Cleaveland, 220, 314
Cleland, 455
Clemens, 39, 223, 419
Clement, 132, 213
Clements, 39, 44, 58, 87, 97, 225, 268, 270, 277, 349, 382, 461
Clemson, 422
Clendenin, 404
Cleveland, 193, 220
Clever, 174
Cliffe, 314
Clifford, 335
Clifton farm, 99
Cline, 439
Clinton, 452
Clitherall, 132
Clokey, 235
Cloquet, 349
Close, 35, 135
Closer, 412
Cloud, 43
Cloutier, 115
Clow, 115, 411
Clumph, 254
Cluney, 308
Cluskey, 52, 184
Clutter, 285, 296
Clymer, 418, 439
Coakley, 7, 98, 101
Coale, 184
Coalter, 61, 350, 405
Coates, 233
Cobb, 78
Coburn, 112
Cochlin, 141
Cochran, 25, 79, 269, 339
Cochrane, 64, 97, 216

Cockey, 472
Cockrell, 12, 427, 486
Cockwell, 468
Codderick, 447
Coe, 105, 254
Coffin, 351, 447
Coffman, 396
Coffren, 422
Coghlin, 164
Cohen, 102
Coit, 16
Colbert, 65, 309
Colburn, 288, 416
Colburne, 229
Colclazer, 313
Colcock, 108
Cole, 254, 381, 419
Coleman, 53, 113, 174, 229, 255, 283, 303, 309, 427, 469
Colemen, 303
Coles, 355, 453
Coley, 208
Colhoun, 482
Collard, 209
Collier, 371
Collingwood, 160, 199
Collins, 97, 104, 167, 173, 177, 252, 263, 298, 422, 432
Collison, 7, 379
Colman, 484
Colmen, 174
Colmus, 450
Colt, 80, 372, 412, 415
Coltman, 85, 116, 179, 298, 467, 485
Colton, 107
Columbia College, 178
Columbus, 149
Colvin, 63, 368
Colwell, 420
Combe, 127, 128
Combs, 11, 321
Commodore, 139
Compton, 184, 424
Comte, 398

Condos, 413
Cone, 222, 223, 234, 280, 337
Congressional Burying Ground, 38, 295
Congressional Cemetery, 41
Conklin, 174, 309, 398
Conlan, 297, 324, 325
Conley, 132
Conly, 381
Connally, 399
Connell, 430
Connelly, 115
Conner, 52, 115, 152, 222, 234, 280, 297, 371, 372, 411, 413, 430
Connolly, 1
Connor, 181
Conrad, 222, 234, 280, 284
Contee, 338, 367
Continental Congress, 10
convicts, 324
Conway, 26, 80, 175, 192, 289, 303, 432
Cook, 24, 41, 52, 63, 82, 91, 168, 214, 264, 328, 342, 368, 371, 428, 450
Cooke, 47, 446, 452, 471
Cool Spring Farm, 222
Coolidge, 106, 270, 282
Coombs, 86, 105, 143, 284, 468
Cooney, 399
Cooper, 27, 60, 134, 158, 180, 281, 309, 361, 415, 432, 467
Copeland, 399, 437, 446
Copley, 304
Corbett, 376
Corbin, 382, 405
Corcoran, 41, 136, 141, 190, 369, 488
Corcorn, 282
Corlace, 68
Cornack, 86
Cornell, 220
corner-stone, 265
Corning, 264, 418
Cornwallis, 465
Corpancho, 414

503

Corry, 49
Cortelyou, 233
Corwin, 383
Corwine, 25, 92, 212
Coster, 237, 479
Costigan, 171, 467
Cottage Hill, 47
Cotterill, 293
Cotton, 75, 391
Couchman, 13
Coudon, 14
Coul, 309
Couney, 122
Count de Flahault, 181
Count de Grasse, 465
Countryman, 133
Courtney, 141
Cousins, 124
Coutts, 261
Cova, 414
Covert, 376
Cowden, 331, 474
Cowdery, 22
Cowee, 434
Cowen, 482
Cowlain, 241
Cowlan, 436
Cowley, 220
Cowling, 163
Cowman, 390
Cox, 16, 29, 36, 43, 87, 92, 126, 127, 163, 204, 216, 242, 244, 267, 276, 331, 341, 395, 408, 421, 426, 436, 478, 490
Coxe, 229, 278, 360, 471
Coxuiga, 328
Coy, 194, 474
Coyle, 52, 110, 176, 179, 255, 467
Cozens, 134
Crabb, 252, 277
Crabbe, 211, 219, 228, 233
Crafts, 371, 372
Cragin, 148
Craig, 15, 18, 67, 92, 154, 225, 254, 309, 427, 468
Crain, 233
Crambo, 309
Crandall, 15, 20, 90, 212, 346
Crandell, 452
Crane, 400, 428, 443
Cranston, 462
Cratz, 349
Craufurd, 247
Craven, 242, 424
Crawford, 97, 164, 213, 214, 230, 248, 271, 302, 318, 377, 400, 426, 434, 467
Creamer, 24
Creedo, 344
Crelie, 253
Crenshaw, 179
Crider, 412
Crimins, 413
Crimmer, 380
Crimmins, 19
Cripps, 145, 363, 393, 432, 443, 487
Crist, 412
Critcher, 442
Crittenden, 224, 278, 362
Crocket, 266
Crockett, 400
Crohn, 413
Croker, 339
Cromwell, 184, 399
Cronin, 189, 297
Cronyn, 66
Crook, 87, 175
Crooks, 239
Cropper, 172, 261
Cropsey, 101, 248
Crosbie, 97
Crosby, 64, 68, 378
Croskey, 207
Crosman, 415
Cross, 5, 19, 46, 175, 257, 281, 282, 305, 312, 350, 413, 419, 446, 459
Crossfield, 19, 89

Crossman, 224
Crouch, 462
Crouse, 68, 270
Crowbarger, 396
Crowder, 260
Crowell, 361
Crowen, 413
Crown, 14, 15, 92, 104, 215, 231, 459
Crozet, 463
Cruger, 447
Cruit, 162, 363
Crutchet, 138
Cubies, 174
Cuddy, 175
Cudlipps, 274
Cuen, 478
Culbert, 175
Cull, 298, 399
Cullon, 429
Culloni, 270
Cullum, 429
Culver, 52
Cumingham, 281
Cummer, 373
Cummin, 250, 430, 449
Cumming, 442, 448
Cummings, 16, 176, 332, 418, 439, 452
Cumminns, 103
Cummins, 27, 40, 79, 173, 186, 200, 229, 246, 361, 375, 386, 424, 457
Cumpston, 423
Cundiff, 211
Cunningham, 23, 40, 44, 62, 66, 100, 119, 124, 170, 176, 209, 222, 234, 271, 280, 315, 333, 337, 454, 489
Cunningham's Garden, 193
Cunninghan, 452
Curran, 52, 89, 130
Curren, 282
Curry, 45
Curson, 141
Curtain, 141
Curtis, 19, 54, 85, 346, 406, 444

Curtiss, 155, 471
Cury, 175
Cushing, 136, 361, 398
Cushman, 100, 103
Cusick, 297
Custis, 187, 261, 301, 403, 406
Cutler, 289
Cutter, 36, 54
cutter **Hamilton**, 48
cutter **Washington**, 166
Cutts, 234, 400, 404
Cyclops, 326

D

D'Aram, 166
D'Oremieux, 224
D'Unger, 259
Dacey, 254
Dacotah, 375
Dahlgreen, 271
Dahlgren, 199, 446
Dailey, 37
Daily, 19, 85
Dainese, 35
Daingerfield, 248, 311, 406
Dake, 309
Dalby, 459
Dalecarlia, 126
Daley, 412
Dallam, 110, 166
Dalton, 17, 122
Daly, 69, 82, 479
Dame, 453
Dameron, 109
Dammond, 218
Dana, 406, 458
Danberg, 413
Dandridge, 23
Danforth, 115, 336, 474, 486
Daniel, 5, 6, 39, 70, 73, 124, 280, 467
Daniels, 52, 134, 258, 348, 436
Dankworth, 271
Danl Boone, 42
Danton, 465

Darden, 256, 316
Dardenne, 74
Darger, 186
Darien, 202
Darling, 453
Darnall, 367
Darne, 421
Dart, 36
Dasher, 16
Dashields, 443
Dashiell, 104
Dauterive, 8
Davenport, 69, 460
David, 490
Davidge, 126, 127, 367
Davidson, 3, 9, 31, 72, 91, 95, 126, 163, 176, 215, 373, 392, 438
Davie, 483
Davies, 119, 170, 466
Davis, 1, 3, 28, 36, 39, 51, 55, 56, 61, 71, 72, 76, 81, 87, 92, 104, 110, 122, 141, 151, 179, 180, 190, 202, 217, 230, 246, 256, 270, 275, 289, 298, 301, 327, 329, 333, 342, 346, 351, 358, 368, 412, 431, 444, 445, 474, 479
Davison, 382
Davy, 342
Daw, 298, 488
Dawes, 2, 222
Dawson, 42, 347, 373, 396, 444
Day, 104, 145, 232, 365, 467
Dayman, 326
Dayton, 1
de Barrera, 395
de Bille, 376
de Castelline, 463
de Cramer, 256
De Cramer, 278
de Forest, 378
De Forrest, 60
De Krafft, 150
De Louville, 168
de Medici, 437

de Neuville, 258
De Ridley, 55
De Russey, 216, 231
De Sanno, 189
De Saules, 262
De Selding, 387
de Stoeckl, 61
De Zeyk, 96
Deal, 105
Deale, 112
Dean, 176
Dearth, 317
Deary, 152
Deas, 185, 471
Death, 293
DeBow, 365
Debree, 34
DeCamp, 27, 183, 307
Decatur, 4, 258, 275, 286, 401, 428
DeCharms, 454
Deeble, 177, 394
Deeton, 347
Deford, 47
Degenhard, 327
Degges, 129, 179, 206
Deguid, 355
DeHaven, 479
Deitz, 194, 409
Delafield, 44
Delaigle, 270
Delane, 326
Delaney, 9, 299
Delano, 18, 475, 479
Delaroche, 159
Delarouche, 339
Dell, 121, 384
Dellavaine, 174
Dellett, 2
Delphy, 456
Delyan, 411
Dement, 375, 400, 410, 469
Demers, 471
Deming, 221, 234
Dempsey, 281, 419

Dener, 471
Denham, 179
Denman, 24, 92, 212, 413
Denmann, 309
Dennis, 97, 430
Dennison, 220, 408
Denny, 136
Dent, 101, 106, 433
Denver, 57, 58, 82, 91, 148, 149, 477, 484
Derby, 136
Derockle, 479
Derrick, 276, 288, 427
DeRussy, 234, 429
Desaules, 263
DeSaules, 275
Deseret, 182
Deshield, 309
Deshler, 452
Deshond, 411
Desloude, 148
Desmak, 26
Desmarres, 318
Desponniers, 339
Devaugh, 443
Devauroux, 310
Devine, 298
Devit, 37, 38, 42, 66, 82, 90
Devlin, 52, 86, 348
Devys, 480
Dewer, 473
Dewey, 108
Dexer, 282
Dexter, 323, 399
Dey, 178
Deyoe, 119
Dibble, 114, 191
Dibblee, 397
Dice, 105
Dick, 25, 32, 45, 64, 135, 327
Dickard, 172
Dickens, 243, 464
Dickerson, 451
Dickey, 418, 423

Dickins, 28
Dickinson, 9, 41, 179, 429
Dickson, 105, 115, 119
Diefendorf, 474
Dietz, 94, 134
Digges, 52, 194, 201, 248, 265, 300, 324, 448, 488
Diggs, 324, 448
Dignan, 213
Dikraff, 125
Diller, 114, 207, 287
Dillon, 68, 280, 435
Dimick, 483
Dimitry, 3, 276
Dirickson, 283
Dishman, 328
Disney, 101, 123
Ditmas, 471
Divine, 230
Dix, 228, 338
Dixon, 176, 218, 220, 228, 301, 391
Doak, 124
Doane, 366
Dobbin, 311, 336, 372, 410
Dobbins, 282, 283
Dobbs, 151
Dobbyn, 324
Dobyns, 41
Dodd, 22, 281
Dode, 230
Dodge, 1, 51, 95, 140, 162, 464
Dodson, 85, 115, 208, 217
Dogan, 392
Doggett, 147, 153, 421, 459
Dolan, 16, 255, 281
Dold, 23
Dolf, 461
Dollfus, 347
Dolman, 253, 474
Donaldson, 94, 107, 284
Donelan, 3, 182, 250
Donelly, 443, 445
Donelson, 1, 35, 66
Doniphan, 64

Donn, 142, 206, 218, 221, 237, 295, 318, 361, 363, 364, 407, 447, 450, 451, 463, 470
Donnell, 347
Donnelly, 306, 360, 362, 386, 409, 453, 485
Donnely, 348, 481
Donner, 281
Donoho, 119, 236
Donohoe, 179
Donohoo, 295
Donovan, 56, 253, 417, 419, 430
Dooling, 445
Dorethee, 463
Dorion, 132
Dorman, 336
Dorn, 52
Dorothy, 347
Dorr, 489
Dorrance, 30, 397
Dorsett, 15, 236, 363, 416
Dorsey, 112, 115, 127, 128, 259, 293, 299, 411
Dosser, 47
Doty, 60, 458
Doubleday, 164
Doud, 410
Dougal, 3
Dougherty, 110, 167, 265, 268, 270, 309, 371, 408, 445
Doughtery, 331
Doughty, 265
Doughty's Row, 244
Douglas, 141, 218, 297, 304, 328, 351, 368
Douglass, 123, 221, 295, 298, 312
Dove, 230, 235, 236
Dow, 471
Dowd, 310
Dowell, 101
Downer, 124
Downes, 281
Downing, 6, 66, 134, 179, 312
Downson, 278

Doyle, 12, 99, 254
Dozier, 337
Drain, 16
Drake, 273, 403
Drane, 160
Drant, 84
Draper, 58, 127, 284
Drayton, 31, 251
Dred Scott, 132
Drew, 22, 400, 473
Driggs, 249
Drinker, 269
Drinkhouse, 309
Drinkwater, 335
Driscoll, 220, 474
Driver, 27
Drought, 274
Drout, 26, 92
Drum, 415
Drummond, 185, 229
Drury, 85, 86, 179, 291, 298, 431, 467
Dry Meadow, 131
Dryden, 24
Du Pont, 159
Dubois, 5, 445
Duchess of Gloucester, 173, 185
Duchess of Kent, 251
Duckwood, 309
Dudley, 452
Dueincker, 281
Duer, 398
Dueson, 405
Duffey, 300
Duffield, 137
Duffy, 297
Dugan, 167, 414
Duganne, 392
Duggan, 445
Duhamel, 52
Duke, 193
Dukehart, 426
Dulaney, 31
Dulany, 1, 103
Dulin, 370

Dull, 49
Dunawin, 305
Dunbar, 273
Duncan, 35, 37, 38, 49, 54, 79, 88, 90, 199, 200, 265, 320, 459
Dundas, 13, 39
Dungah, 460
Dunington, 104
Dunkle, 117
Dunlap, 51
Dunlop, 294, 315, 364, 421
Dunmire, 213
Dunn, 17, 191, 360, 455
Dunnawin, 298
Dunnican, 253
Dunnin, 479
Dunning, 30, 433
Dunnington, 100, 136, 154, 168, 314
Dunovant, 41, 452
Duplaine, 189
Dupont, 150, 152, 199, 331
Dupuy, 293
Durand, 465, 481
Durant, 403
Durett, 413
Durfee, 422
Durgin, 470
Durham, 235
Durkee, 471
Durrett, 289
Duryee, 203
Dutton, 224
Duval, 93, 258, 314
Duvall, 63, 84, 97, 153, 168, 245, 273, 322, 377, 441
Duveyrier, 271
Dwight, 32
Dwyer, 373
Dyckman, 366
Dye, 36
Dyer, 85, 179, 209, 277, 324, 342, 395, 414, 461, 467, 474
Dykeman, 313
Dyson, 190, 278, 332

E

Eaches, 485
Eakin, 105
Eanes, 359
Earl of Clarendon to, 479
Earl of Ellesmere, 89
Earl of Fife, 141
Earl of Kerry, 388
Earl of Sandwich, 194
Earl of Shelburne, 388
Early, 8, 220
Earthman, 309
Easby, 14, 16, 57, 58, 63, 73, 75, 87, 91, 160, 161, 216, 490
Easby's ship yard, 161
Eastern Shore of Md, 275
Eastham, 471
Eastlake, 243
Eastland, 354
Eastman, 224, 411
Easton, 38, 371, 372, 378, 379, 410
Eaton, 41, 104, 186, 224, 371, 387, 412, 415, 471, 475
Eby, 266
Eccleston, 201
Echardt, 66
Echols, 442
Eckard, 87, 457, 490
Eckart, 34
Eckel, 66, 170
Eckles, 277
Eckloff, 363, 364
Eckman, 240
Eddie, 113, 427
Ede, 371, 412
Edelen, 106, 324, 433
Edelin, 122, 127, 128, 298
Edes, 267, 377
Edgar, 235, 309
Edgehill, 302
Edgeworth, 317
Edie, 48
Edings, 213
Edmann, 411

Edmondson, 233, 312, 319, 362
Edmondston, 86
Edmonson, 164
Edmonston, 122, 297, 443
Edmundson, 3, 41
Edmundston, 223, 394
Edwards, 43, 50, 51, 71, 72, 73, 104, 105, 130, 142, 145, 188, 193, 252, 345, 348, 350, 360, 407, 432, 446
Effinger, 200
Egan, 282
Egerton, 94
Eggleston, 67, 105, 300
Egleston, 54
Eichhorn, 367
Eickhon, 116
Elder, 141, 168, 287
Elderkin, 221, 234
Elders, 108
Eldred, 111
Eldridge, 74, 215, 289, 326, 451
electric telegraph, 341
Eliason, 83, 184
Elicott, 49
Eliot, 147, 172, 252, 431, 490
Elkins, 335
Ellar, 267
Ellaville, 473
Ellen, 95
Ellen Dale, 458
Ellery, 343
Ellet, 226
Ellicot, 87, 91
Ellicott, 64, 86
Ellinder, 175
Ellington, 274
Elliot, 266, 281, 444
Elliott, 4, 26, 70, 73, 84, 88, 91, 112, 231, 242, 289, 361, 477
Ellis, 48, 61, 154, 174, 179, 275, 282, 297, 309, 346, 373, 404, 459, 490
Ellison, 100, 103, 364, 474
Ellsworth, 447
Elmer, 36

Elmwood, 300
Elphinstone, 181
Elrod, 289
Elton, 417
Elward, 115
Elwood, 225
Ely, 275, 451
Emanuel, 177
Ements, 372, 375
Emerick, 287
Emerson, 115, 298, 418, 422, 423, 457, 490
Emery, 34, 64, 86, 87, 92, 146, 215, 295
Emmert, 408
Emmet, 272
Emmons, 49, 100, 103
Emond, 413
Emory, 72, 124, 147
Empson, 83, 92
Emrich, 290
Enclosure, 247
Endlich, 336
Eneu, 361, 371
Engle, 111
English, 64, 69, 102, 183, 209, 251, 322, 328, 439
English Hill, 178
Ennis, 6, 179
Enniscorthy burying grounds, 43
Enright, 139, 297
Entrée, 156
Entwisle, 39
equestrian statue, 456
Erben, 100, 104
Erickson, 63
Erwin, 434
Escurda, 414
Esinhart, 309
Eskridge, 334
Espey, 52
Essex, 31, 271
Estey, 350
Etheridge, 203, 238

Etlet, 276
Etorcell, 373
Etter, 220
Eubank, 244
Eudy, 190
Evans, 38, 59, 97, 122, 134, 152, 180, 192, 233, 277, 295, 351, 370, 432, 474
Evening Paper, 111
Evens, 158, 479
Everett, 169, 253, 301, 312, 451
Evergreen Cottage, 207, 210
Evers, 396
Eversfield, 481
Ewell, 435, 445
Expedition to the Artic, 479
Ezell, 220

F

Fabens, 283
Faber, 254
Fabris, 210
Fagan, 309
Faherty, 276, 449
Fairbanks, 346, 430
Fairfax, 415
Fairland Estate, 84
Fairmeadow, 374
Falconer, 411
Falleno, 372
Fallon, 169, 378, 410
Fallow, 373
Fambro, 115
Fanell, 206
Fangamon, 281
Fanni, 372
Fannin, 65
Fanning, 8, 298
Fant, 72, 429
Farish, 220
Farley, 77
Farmer, 410
Farnham, 30, 229, 285, 411
Farnhjam, 410

Farnsworth, 350
Faron, 451
Farquhar, 50
Farr, 418, 423
Farragut, 482
Farrall, 270
Farrand, 222, 234, 280
Farrard, 337
Farrell, 431
Farribault, 65
Farrington, 398
Farris, 10
Fathers of Mercy, 28
Faulkner, 223, 240, 431
Faulknew, 256
Fauquier White Sulphur Springs, 18, 223
Fausse, 50
Favier, 204, 360
Fay, 431
Fayssoux, 450
Fearson, 464
Febron, 439
Fee, 429
Felch, 34, 55, 72
Felder, 205
Felix, 308
Fell, 248, 373
Fellinger, 409
Felsenthrall, 469
Felton, 260
Fendall, 154, 168, 406, 420
Fenelon, 465
Fenimore, 301
Fenner, 412
Fenton, 110, 206, 432, 465
Fenwick, 86, 92, 98, 329, 381, 466, 468
Feodore, 251
Fergosson, 301
Ferguson, 222, 234, 280, 351, 386, 434, 452
Fergusson, 3
Ferieira, 340

Ferries, 278
Ferriss, 402
Fessenden, 291
Festu, 412
Fewell, 164
Fichlin, 219
Ficklin, 220
Fiedler, 46
Field, 26, 30, 73, 383, 447
Fieldstop, 237
Fife, 278
Fill, 488
Fillmore, 1, 346, 440
Finch, 135
Finckel, 137, 461
Fingler, 290
Finisch, 138
Finkle, 229
Finley, 14, 121
Finn, 220
Finnegan, 98
Finnigan, 413
Finotti, 255
Fischback, 34
Fischer, 258
Fish, 64, 95, 181, 222, 234, 280, 411
Fishburn, 197
Fisher, 3, 33, 51, 70, 77, 142, 168, 194, 204, 318, 324, 330, 331, 343, 355, 407, 413
Fisk, 398, 423, 474
Fitch, 153, 383
Fitman, 31, 86
Fitzgerald, 35, 81, 100, 297, 306, 388, 467
Fitzhugh, 100, 103, 182, 320, 326, 403, 405
Fitzmaurice, 388
Fitzosborn, 460
Fitzpatrick, 194, 208, 309, 310, 322, 325, 335, 408, 459
Flack, 274
Flagg, 276
flagship **Lawrence**, 487

Flaherty, 363
Flandrau, 276
Flandreau, 283
Flanegan, 66
Flangan, 412
Flanigan, 186
Flanner, 117
Fleck, 449
Fleehiman, 195
Flehatfield, 309
Fleischmann, 454
Fleming, 4, 6, 30, 90, 104, 212, 242, 437, 474
Fletcher, 30, 74, 111, 122, 139, 236, 240, 302, 314, 369, 371, 372, 384, 394, 408, 413, 423
Fleurot, 207
Flinada, 414
Flinn, 53, 119, 265
Flint, 168, 175, 224
Flood, 8
Flores, 119, 395
Flournoy, 23, 163
Flowen, 175
Floyd, 56, 75, 78, 80, 89, 96
Flume House, 288
Flunery, 458
Flynn, 175, 296
Foaren, 66
Foley, 79, 270, 350, 469
Folk, 172
Follins, 411
Font Hill, 274
Fontaine, 97, 102, 253, 329
Fontes, 455
Foote, 68, 69, 269, 292, 313
Forbes, 117
Force, 66, 85, 116, 155, 287, 423
Ford, 22, 40, 98, 178, 246, 289, 349, 411, 442, 480
Forest, 378
Forest of PG Co, 247
Forman, 141
Formosa, 328

Forney, 149, 336, 452
Fornshil, 347
Forrest, 30, 127, 246, 310, 312, 340, 398, 414
Forrester, 371, 372
Fort Adams, 429
Fort Brooke, 19
Fort Brown, 5
Fort Castillo, 488
Fort Chadbourne, 332
Fort Dallas, 107
Fort Defiance, 140, 162
Fort Denaud, 337
Fort des Moines, 142
Fort Des Moines, 171
Fort Dodge, 157, 171, 172, 242, 360
Fort Duncan, 444
Fort Fillmore, 167, 445
Fort George, 428
Fort Gibson, 198, 404
Fort Jackson, 214
Fort Kearny, 8, 218, 267, 329
Fort Laramie, 8, 218
Fort Leavenworth, 167, 236, 415, 471, 478
Fort Madison, 227
Fort Mason, 444, 445
Fort McIntosh, 444
Fort Meyers, 246
Fort Monroe, 216, 428, 429
Fort Myers, 119, 337, 344, 388
Fort Reiley, 94
Fort Ridgeley, 157
Fort Ridgely, 172, 276
Fort Riley, 236
Fort Scott, 484
Fort Smith, 47, 422
Fort Snelling, 157, 167, 352
Fort Sullivan, 303
Fort Taylor, 429
Fort Thorn, 200, 445
Fort Thorne, 167
Fort Washington, 6, 47
Fort Wayne, 114, 129

Fort Yuma, 466
Fortress Monroe, 47
Forward, 64
Foss, 63, 238
Fossitt, 408
Foster, 55, 82, 175, 186, 274, 290, 363, 364, 398, 410, 411, 429
Fouble, 24
Fouche, 206
Four Holes Swamp, 132
Foust, 414
Fowble, 86
Fowle, 314
Fowler, 25, 89, 114, 147, 184, 223, 225, 246, 434, 490
Fox, 46, 104, 112, 311, 331, 336, 388, 444, 480
Foxhall, 387
Foy, 14
Fracy, 423
Frailer, 386
Frailey, 51, 194
Frame, 322
Francis, 317, 318, 345, 470
Frank, 411, 412, 461
Frank Cemetery, 32
Frankenberger, 302
Franklin, 22, 173, 217, 279, 298, 337, 341, 344, 349, 438, 479
Franklin row, 136
Franklin Row, 98
Frantz, 24
Fraser, 135
Frasier, 371
Frazee, 426
Frazer, 225, 282, 369, 410
Frazier, 143, 263, 371, 373, 376, 474
Fredell, 439
Frederic, 270, 271
Frederick, 372, 414
Fredericks, 371
Fredt, 414
Freeland, 466

Freeman, 109, 119, 213, 229, 270, 420, 472
Freer, 446
Frelinghuysen, 426
Fremont, 1
French, 146, 164, 201, 375, 393, 487
Frere, 300, 312
Frick, 199
Frickland, 220
Friend, 141, 220
Frierson, 399
frig **Cumberland**, 206
frig **Independence**, 308, 380
frig **Merrimac**, 106, 150
frig **Minnesota**, 159, 232
frig **Mississippi**, 271
frig **Missouri**, 40
frig **Niagara**, 451, 456
frig **Philadelphia**, 401
frig **Powhatan**, 460
frig **Roanoke**, 150, 308
frig **San Jacinto**, 68, 69, 326, 380
frig **St Lawrence**, 340
frig **Susquehanna**, 20
frig **United States**, 428
frig **Wabash**, 488
frig-**Minnesota**, 150
Frinch, 172
Friry, 281
Frisbee, 220
Frisbie, 220
Frontman, 100
Frost, 30, 390
Frost's, 350
Frothingham, 404
Fry, 132, 162
Fry Property, 229
Frye, 443
Fryer, 373
Fugitt, 112
Fulbright, 115
Fulkerson, 303
Fullalove, 53, 122, 230
Fuller, 75, 149, 284, 399

Fullerton, 132
Fulton, 254
Fultz, 300
Furlough, 281
Furnace Tract, 162
Furtner, 329
Fussell, 38, 409
Fyffe, 479

G

Gage, 102
Gahn, 412
Gaiennie, 297
Gaines, 68
Gale, 29, 87, 91, 169
Gallagher, 89, 122, 281, 373, 481
Gallaher, 173, 182, 267, 460
Gallant, 179, 298
Gallaudet, 267
Galligan, 19
Galloway, 134, 234
Gallup, 39, 309
Galpin, 423
Galt, 168, 179, 184, 230, 340
Galtier, 471
Galvan, 440
Galwin, 175
Gamble, 74
Gammon, 87, 88
Ganahi, 424
Ganie, 414
Gant, 305
Gantt, 5, 26, 49, 79, 82, 91
Ganz, 237
Garber, 480
Garcia, 119, 395
Garden Hammock, 119
Gardener, 20
Gardere, 74
Gardiner, 28, 45, 105, 122, 246, 276, 298, 324, 325
Gardner, 37, 39, 57, 58, 108, 111, 137, 153, 157, 160, 169, 172, 242, 254, 334, 373, 417, 439

Gardney, 452
Gardnier, 445
Garland, 100, 104
Garlinger, 269
Garman, 4, 14
Garner, 112, 186, 283, 315, 367, 432, 444
Garnet, 414
Garnett, 38, 51, 53, 190, 223, 240, 420, 471
Garretson, 297
Garrett, 42, 117, 195, 404, 458, 468, 476
Garrison, 220, 243, 373, 379, 412
Garrity, 9
Garsa, 237
Gaskell, 134
Gaskins, 176
Gaslights, 320
Gassaway, 115, 125, 127, 128, 170, 421, 440, 488
Gaston, 280, 308, 372
Gates, 391
Gatewood, 362
Gatyear, 469
Gaul, 410
Gauss, 342
Gautier, 28, 110
Gaveny, 346
Gavioli, 291
Gay, 87, 92, 116, 215, 226, 452
Gaynor, 68
Geary, 99, 121, 412
Gedney, 463
Gee, 113
Geer, 188
Genay, 364
Genois, 97
George, 52, 281, 371, 372, 379, 412
George III, 139
Gere, 226
Gerhard, 226, 268, 271, 274, 276
Germon, 179
Gerrald, 309

Gerretson, 167
Gerrish, 223
Gerry, 253
Gettings, 81
Getty, 173
Gibb, 410
Gibbes, 427
Gibbon, 13
Gibbons, 68, 104, 262
Gibbs, 167, 200, 336, 372, 375, 445
Gibson, 60, 76, 77, 208, 224, 232, 244, 318, 320, 350, 454, 470, 483
Giddings, 67
Gideon, 229, 230, 298, 422, 473
Gift, 111
Gigon, 205
Gihon, 468
Gilbert, 15, 18, 34, 67, 71, 87, 91, 132, 213, 216, 217, 246, 250, 323, 349, 396, 416, 480
Gildemeister, 83
Giles, 61, 310, 445
Gilkeson, 5, 258
Gilkey, 412
Gill, 4, 34, 51, 233, 298, 332, 338
Gillaspie, 149
Gillen, 309
Gillespie, 301, 474
Gillett, 172
Gilliam, 268, 271
Gillion, 233
Gilliss, 73, 483, 490
Gillmore, 303
Gilman, 369, 423
Gilmore, 153, 184, 427, 466
Gilpatrick, 281
Ginnatty, 441
Gitterman, 410
Gittings, 230, 301
Given, 490
Gladden, 41
Gladmon, 163
Glantz, 283
Glascock, 119

Glasgow, 130, 431
Glass, 130
Glasson, 25, 69, 385, 483
Glay, 373
Gleason, 195, 289
Glencoe, 150
Gliddon, 461, 462
Glover, 197, 363, 364
Glynn, 195, 482
Goastree, 414
Gobbi, 291
Gobright, 230
Goddard, 42, 79, 163, 179, 206, 211, 295, 298, 451, 463
Goddin, 151
Godey, 103, 462
Godfrey, 474, 480
Godfroy, 26, 49, 82, 91
Godman, 269
Goff, 308
Gohen, 104
Goldborough, 308
Golden, 114, 430
Goldin, 489
Goldizen, 188
Goldsborough, 239, 409, 418, 434, 451
Goldsmith, 6
Gonzales, 220
Good, 66, 70, 240
Goode, 223, 279
Goodenow, 414
Goodfellow, 480
Gooding, 81
Goodloe, 238
Goodrich, 37
Goodwin, 54, 79, 271
Goodyear, 37, 432
Gordon, 25, 45, 72, 151, 190, 312, 323, 377, 452, 456, 474
Gore, 443, 452, 467
Gorgas, 97
Gorley, 412
Gorman, 44

Gormley, 270, 432, 447
Gorsuch, 250
Gorton, 39
Gorvens, 416
Gosnell, 187
Goss, 110
Gott, 331
Gould, 11
Gouley, 134
Gove, 238
Gracie, 462
Grady, 408
Graffenried, 53
Graffus, 395, 414
Graftenich, 193
Grafton, 482
Graham, 14, 16, 32, 36, 68, 86, 92, 97, 180, 215, 238, 309, 313, 320, 382, 399, 440, 482
Grammar, 110
Grammer, 25, 44, 251, 478
Granberry, 459, 477
Granes, 254
Granger, 157, 172, 444
Grant, 41, 45, 78, 299, 310, 320, 396, 418, 471
Grassmere, 194
Graveraet, 109
Graves, 80, 133, 232, 254, 353, 436
Gray, 26, 27, 56, 115, 117, 134, 151, 187, 258, 270, 303, 350, 385, 423, 483
Greeland, 344
Green, 4, 17, 18, 21, 30, 52, 64, 82, 113, 123, 134, 204, 253, 261, 297, 308, 309, 323, 350, 358, 375, 387, 398, 400, 451, 452
Green's Row, 248
Greenbrier, 120, 374
Greene, 29, 141, 145, 402, 418
Greenleaf, 191
Greenlee, 413
Greenman, 6, 370
Greenwold, 351

Greenwood, 381
Greenwood Cemetery, 233
Greer, 490
Gregg, 19
Gregory, 260
Grenville, 388
Gretna Cemetery, 439
Grey, 16, 308, 478
Grice, 23
Griebel, 418
Grier, 467
Griffen, 260
Griffeths, 415
Griffin, 22, 122, 150, 163, 167, 179, 193, 253, 309, 351, 387, 427, 479
Griffing, 452, 471
Griffith, 45, 105, 152, 395, 415
Griffiths, 395
Griffore, 152
Griggs, 15, 18, 20, 79, 88, 322
Grigsby, 61
Grimes, 41, 240, 242, 255, 338, 377, 399, 490
Grimshaw, 135
Grimsley, 474
Grinder, 208, 209
Griswold, 210, 236, 440
Grockett, 153
Grodon, 180
Groome, 299
Groomes, 26
Gross, 38, 223, 378, 448
Grouard, 291, 307
Grove, 236
Grover, 4, 92, 211, 219, 220, 309, 452, 480
Groves, 439
Grubb, 122
Grumby, 241
Gtwn Cemetery, 470
Guerher, 414
Guest, 35, 90, 154, 212, 271, 451, 477
Guibert, 139
Guild, 238, 412

Guista, 379
Gunnegle, 366
Gunnel, 289
Gunnell, 310
Gunter, 140
Gunton, 467
Gurley, 32, 54, 57, 322, 343, 478, 490
Gushee, 412
Guthrie, 9, 43, 44, 69, 80
Guy, 110, 167, 335
Gwinn, 52
Gwynn, 265, 324

H

Haag, 412
Habersham, 460
Hackett, 52, 478
Haddock's Hills, 247
Haddock's Hills Farm, 63
Haddox, 474
Haden, 445
Hadley, 132
Hadsall, 457
Hagan, 124, 309, 410
Hagel, 441
Hagerty, 66
Hagner, 2, 3, 5, 25
Hahn, 411
Haight, 26, 56, 82, 91
Hail Columbia, 263
Haile, 218
Halcon, 372
Halcumbe, 371
Halderman, 343
Hale, 16, 111, 276, 317
Haley, 429, 480
Haliday, 12, 155
Hall, 7, 26, 35, 60, 73, 115, 135, 137, 203, 211, 226, 229, 267, 278, 286, 295, 305, 308, 310, 314, 328, 344, 347, 361, 365, 404, 418, 425, 427, 469, 476, 479, 487, 490
Hall Farm, 300
Hall's Bottom, 283

Hallard, 413
Halleck, 41, 431
Haller, 263
Hallet, 109
Hallowell, 114, 218
Halsey, 64, 131, 164
Ham's Fort, 442
Hamacker, 246
Hamar, 245
Hambright, 115
Hambrooks, 147
Hamburg lime kilns, 161
Hamer, 57
Hamill, 2
Hamilton, 9, 11, 25, 43, 46, 47, 83, 104, 107, 111, 175, 190, 220, 225, 237, 309, 310, 311, 339, 396, 448, 455, 458, 460
Hammond, 141, 402, 427
Hampden, 91
Hampton, 12, 453
Hance, 186, 424
Hancock, 22, 23, 83, 245, 277
Hand, 31, 373
Handley, 468
Handy, 51, 66, 132, 143, 237, 312, 376, 423
Hanlon, 12
Hann, 157
Hanna, 59
Hannahan, 213
Hannay, 158, 235
Hanson, 64, 122, 201, 242, 247, 360, 372
Hanway, 254
Hararzthy, 249
Harasthy, 460
Harbaugh, 85, 179, 301, 396, 460, 468
Harcum, 221
Hardcastle, 386
Hardee, 43, 337
Hardenbrook, 147
Hardenburg, 371, 407
Hardin, 70, 90, 213, 258

Harding, 7, 244, 433
Hardney, 455
Hardy, 151, 158, 178, 266, 282, 389
Hare, 308
Hargrove, 148
Harilland, 40
Harkin, 309
Harkness, 29, 39, 68, 236, 490
Harlan, 282, 310
Harlow, 442
Harman, 121
Harmell, 253
Harney, 33, 107, 267, 410, 415, 477, 484
Harp, 162
Harpe, 233
Harper, 123, 136, 208, 257, 274, 347, 445, 465
Harralson, 97
Harrell, 413, 424, 482
Harrelson, 132
Harriet, 172
Harrington, 211, 368
Harris, 6, 51, 64, 87, 99, 123, 131, 141, 174, 175, 281, 331, 337, 373, 412, 419, 436, 471
Harrison, 41, 58, 60, 113, 211, 230, 253, 266, 275, 313, 404, 471
Harriss, 432
Harrold, 427, 432, 490
Harrover, 15, 150, 322, 432, 439
Harry, 210, 480
Harsham, 172
Harshman, 188
Hart, 52, 98, 115, 189, 213, 220, 237, 253, 309, 413, 442
Harte, 24, 26
Hartley, 480
Hartman, 371, 372
Hartshorn, 200
Hartstene, 82, 86, 479, 480, 485
Harty, 271
Harvey, 41, 115, 174, 371, 372, 387, 393, 399, 446, 463

Harwell, 254
Hascall, 217
Hasey, 310
Haskell, 218, 437
Hasker, 176
Haskins, 36
Haslup, 190, 451
Hassey, 414
Hastings, 26, 413
Hatch, 53, 97, 155
Hatcher, 184
Hatfield, 29
Hathaway, 130, 246
Hatton, 324
Havelin, 470
Havelock, 420
Havener, 218
Havenner, 80, 180, 340, 398
Havens, 54
Haverstick, 398
Haverty, 19
Haw, 46, 52
Hawk, 340
Hawke, 463
Hawkins, 136, 158, 162, 233, 387
Hawks, 447
Hawley, 100, 104, 165, 378, 410
Haws, 452
Hawthorne, 336
Hay, 287
Hayard, 65
Haycock, 472
Hayden, 306, 471
Hayes, 64, 422
Haymes, 26
Haynes, 16, 93, 124
Hays, 65, 87, 88, 91, 174, 223, 250, 382, 420, 480
Hayward, 328, 394, 399, 431
Haywood, 184
Hayzell, 248
Hazard, 8, 14, 60, 64, 86
Hazel, 265, 271, 395
Hazlewood, 313

Head, 474
Health Report, 66, 423
Healy, 346, 457
Heap, 36
Heard, 35
Hearsey, 253, 254
Heath, 52, 254, 320
Hecht, 310
Heck, 402
Hedrick, 56
Hegnrick, 82
Heileman, 104, 199
Heine, 72
Heiskell, 238
Heiss, 111
Hellen, 3, 67, 323, 338, 400
Hely, 291
Hemmel, 415
Hemmell, 395
Hempell, 442
Hempstead, 398
Henderson, 11, 52, 146, 168, 231, 238, 322, 325, 380, 408, 424, 442, 462
Hendley, 165
Hendrew, 49
Hendricks, 52, 233, 309
Hendrickson, 236
Hening, 322
Henley, 22
Henly, 216
Henn, 246
Hennick, 349
Henning, 121, 328
Henrie, 165
Henry, 56, 110, 111, 134, 144, 147, 196, 293, 295, 308, 341, 342, 346, 411, 450, 482
Henry VII, 149
Henshaw, 180
Hensley, 488
Hepbron, 421
Hepburn, 122, 230
Herbert, 174, 314, 338, 365, 375
Herckenrath, 249

Hereford, 474
Herlihy, 297
Hern, 342
Hernandez, 186, 275, 285
Herndon, 369, 371, 372, 374, 376, 378, 379, 380, 383, 384, 389, 393, 400, 418
Heron, 271, 445
Herrick, 133
Herriman, 1
Herrington, 368
Herrisse, 144
Herrmann, 223
Herron, 190, 258
Herty, 128
Hertz, 254
Hervey, 305
Hess, 110
Hesselius, 39
Hessey, 9
Hesslinger, 9
Hester, 361
Heston, 175
Heth, 146, 225, 281
Hethington, 373
Hetzel, 68
Hewes, 309, 431
Hewett, 184
Hewlett, 358
Hewling, 188
Heydenfeldt, 447
Hibler, 256
Hibs, 411
Hickey, 51, 190, 268, 271, 480
Hickman, 89
Hicks, 371, 399, 411, 487
Higdon, 325
Higgins, 46, 104, 107, 164, 309, 310, 373, 403, 431
Higginson, 398
High, 418, 423
Hight, 452
Hildebrand, 207
Hildt, 18, 30

Hill, 6, 23, 46, 60, 77, 90, 105, 150, 184, 191, 211, 229, 246, 256, 263, 265, 281, 310, 315, 320, 404, 409, 415, 416, 427, 431, 438, 452, 455, 471, 475, 483, 490
Hillard, 415
Hilleary, 476
Hiller, 281
Hillery, 46
Hilliard, 46
Hillyard, 457
Hillyer, 121
Hilton, 32, 417, 419
Hine, 48, 84, 233
Hines, 41, 81, 98, 179, 190, 203, 258, 262, 330, 425, 454, 466
Hinkley, 30
Hinman, 433
Hinton, 63, 154, 204, 474
Hirst, 105, 386
Hiscock, 183
Hite, 265, 371
Hitrick, 105
Hitz, 75, 461
Hoadley, 412, 413
Hoagland, 68, 330, 413
Hobbs, 183, 398
Hock Farm, 447
Hodge, 140, 314, 412, 457
Hodges, 15, 331
Hodgkinson, 56
Hodgon, 419
Hodgson, 202, 417, 452
Hoe, 86
Hoever, 435
Hoffman, 42, 114, 209, 285, 309, 323, 331, 415, 461
Hofgar, 387
Hogan, 276, 296, 402
Hogs & Geese, 79
Hohenhausen, 233
Holcomb, 378
Holcombe, 132
Holcraft, 458

Holden, 179, 308, 399, 464
Holgate, 67, 74
Holiday, 105
Holkham, 459
Holladay, 233
Holland, 64, 236, 250, 371, 484
Hollenbush, 280
Holler, 411
Holliday, 452
Hollingshead, 268
Hollingsworth, 401
Hollis, 455
Hollman, 18
Hollohan, 14, 52
Holly, 432
Holman, 16, 87, 422
Holme's Hole, 352
Holmead, 76, 83, 230, 345, 434, 451, 490
Holmes, 3, 81, 87, 253, 254, 272, 325, 334, 351, 479
Holohan, 31
Holt, 222, 229, 234, 242, 280, 352, 374, 383, 437, 440, 470, 485
Holtzclaw, 399
Holtzman, 42, 98
Holy, 360
Home, 372
Homer, 453
Hood, 51, 83, 445, 446
Hooe, 90, 134, 253, 254
Hooer, 375
Hooff, 450
Hook, 30, 447
Hooker, 35, 84, 92
Hooks, 427
hoop skirts, 178
Hooper, 191, 399
Hooton, 11
Hoover, 105, 118, 150, 153, 171, 206, 239, 261, 284, 298, 300, 312, 369, 474
Hope, 168

Hopkins, 100, 148, 169, 203, 223, 303, 346, 352
Hopkinson, 263
Hoppen, 122
Hopper, 2
Horn, 169, 342, 412
Horne, 35, 92, 212, 270, 413, 459
Horner, 39, 123
Hornor, 327
Hornsby, 289, 392
Horsemann, 115
Horsey, 469
Horstkamp, 82
Horton, 154, 288
Hoskins, 18, 48
Hoslep, 141
Hosmer, 319
Hoss, 47
Hoster, 419
Hotchkiss, 473
Houdon, 245
Hough, 46, 105, 190, 203, 330, 367, 425, 454
Houk, 3, 221, 234
House, 25, 64, 157, 328, 342
Houser, 26
Housewright, 394
Houston, 52, 189, 236, 248, 350, 428, 490
Hovey, 16
How, 204
Howard, 67, 93, 98, 279, 309, 392, 398, 452, 489
Howe, 17, 151, 172, 192, 372, 412, 426, 452
Howell, 27, 52, 89, 133, 188
Howes, 172, 371, 410
Howison, 189
Howle, 233, 282, 288, 317
Howlett, 193
Howley, 219, 220, 261
Howser, 474
Hoyes, 377
Hoyle, 459

Hoyt, 134, 189, 233, 265
Hubbard, 18, 45, 72, 93, 218, 228, 356, 357, 358, 472
Hubbell, 39
Hubble, 122
Hudgins, 399
Hudine, 17
Hudson, 419, 451
Huesten, 243
Huey, 35, 76
Huff, 35, 49, 82, 214
Huger, 448
Hugg, 91
Huggins, 272
Hughes, 38, 68, 81, 135, 206, 219, 220, 232, 299, 312, 317, 321, 342, 358, 412, 454, 471
Hugle, 165
Hugon, 69
Hull, 86, 171, 174, 211, 300, 369, 372, 378, 389, 426
Humbert, 205
Hume, 90, 107, 120
Humphrey, 26
Humphreys, 40, 77, 208, 471
Humphries, 333, 474
Hunnicut, 52
Hunnycut, 254
Hunsberger, 103
Hunt, 36, 119, 186, 199, 224, 227, 231, 323, 331, 368, 370, 381, 407, 415, 451, 465, 482
Hunter, 8, 22, 52, 53, 100, 103, 104, 117, 175, 176, 258, 276, 294, 339, 365, 385, 406, 450, 472, 482
Hunter Farm, 28
Huntington, 314
Huntress, 460
Hurdle, 124, 270, 283, 300, 443, 468, 482
Hurlburt, 346
Hurlbut, 271
Hurt, 218
Hushbergh, 455

Hussey, 148
Huston, 96, 224
Hutch, 35
Hutchins, 45, 98, 189, 239, 453, 473, 482
Hutchinson, 52, 76, 117, 180, 229, 289, 292, 373, 411, 412, 486
Hutchison, 182
Hutton, 182, 434
Huyck, 456
Huzzy, 480
Hyatt, 106, 211
Hyde, 63, 75, 160, 161, 179, 200, 258, 338
Hyerman, 110
Hylawder, 165
Hynes, 281, 282

I

Iddins, 180, 295
Iglehart, 438
Iliff, 45
Imboden, 143
Immaculate Conception, 38
In, 247
Indiantown, 393
Ingalls, 152
Ingersoll, 168, 338
Ingle, 66, 201, 230, 257, 298, 380
Inglee, 328
Ingleside, 343, 420
Ingraham, 458
Ingram, 184, 223
Inham, 242
Inkamp, 190
Inman, 482
Innmen, 282
Iranistan, 420, 481
Irde, 372
Ireland, 8, 229
Irish, 16, 57, 58, 60, 87, 91
Iron Duke, 133
Ironsides, 396
Irvin, 177

Irvine, 432
Irving, 31, 270, 303
Irvy, 271
Irwin, 51, 53, 136, 226, 418
Isabee, 457
Isherwood, 222
Israel, 104, 180, 295, 312
Iverson, 262
Ives, 101, 279
Ivy, 270
Izard, 207, 472

J

Jackson, 12, 130, 140, 153, 160, 174, 240, 242, 281, 286, 290, 300, 301, 313, 365, 366, 368, 371, 372, 373, 394, 399, 404, 421, 452, 483
Jackson Hill, 352
Jacob, 309
Jacobs, 42, 72, 117, 486
Jacques, 202
James, 9, 26, 56, 66, 67, 79, 83, 309, 344, 467
Jameson, 218, 325
Jamestown Society, 136, 154, 168
Jamiszkiewiez, 4
Janeway, 316
Janney, 15, 169, 472
Janon, 280
Jaquet, 139
Jarboe, 367
Jardin, 204, 360
Jarrett, 326
Jarvis, 385, 482
Jay, 349
Jefferson, 51, 276, 401, 483
Jeffries, 86
Jemell, 254
Jenkins, 20, 55, 57, 58, 62, 70, 72, 88, 114, 124, 126, 127, 132, 136, 195, 213, 223, 289, 290, 298, 325, 349, 371, 473, 488
Jenks, 175
Jennens, 436
Jennings, 36, 93, 175, 304, 484
Jero, 26
Jerold, 243, 251
Jerrold, 243
Jeserun, 283
Jessop, 99
Jett, 119, 278, 372
Jewell, 86, 92, 127, 162, 254, 299, 459
Jewett, 24, 128, 170, 242, 471
Jickerson, 254
Jillard, 269
Jogan, 281
Johnes, 373
Johns, 122, 131, 283, 356, 380, 402
Johnson, 13, 14, 15, 18, 23, 26, 33, 36, 48, 54, 68, 70, 82, 98, 100, 119, 127, 136, 142, 147, 163, 168, 175, 180, 186, 189, 194, 224, 232, 242, 253, 257, 258, 269, 271, 273, 276, 283, 284, 287, 297, 298, 299, 300, 309, 310, 317, 333, 342, 344, 351, 352, 363, 364, 372, 395, 412, 420, 425, 432, 439, 444, 445, 454, 458, 471, 472, 474, 477, 479, 480, 484, 490
Johnston, 36, 61, 66, 72, 86, 92, 298, 337, 339, 342, 451, 457, 460, 480
Joise, 208
Jones, 3, 17, 38, 41, 45, 51, 52, 65, 78, 85, 88, 91, 93, 100, 116, 124, 130, 141, 179, 196, 199, 202, 208, 209, 213, 217, 220, 227, 230, 236, 238, 246, 259, 262, 269, 278, 283, 298, 300, 309, 310, 317, 324, 325, 347, 359, 360, 371, 376, 379, 392, 400, 406, 410, 413, 421, 440, 446, 453, 467, 469, 471, 479, 483, 485
Jordan, 52, 124, 152, 243, 309, 336, 408, 444
Jordon, 264
Joseph, 327
Joslin, 31
Jourdan, 408
Joy, 81

Joyce, 28, 185, 323, 328
Joynes, 353, 359
Juencer, 371
Juncker, 165
Junger, 418
Jungers, 423
Justice, 22

K

Kaibel, 236
Kake, 34
Kalufsowski, 83
Kane, 22, 49, 78, 93, 100, 152, 162, 446, 479, 480
Kanghi, 328
Kara Protestant cemetery, 16
Karn, 309
Karnasch, 193
Karnbacher, 254
Kaufman, 233
Kautz, 444
Kavanaugh, 432
Kavenaugh, 291
Kay, 414
Kayser, 253
Keane, 437
Kearney, 309, 312, 452
Kearny, 247, 267
Kearon, 378, 392
Keating, 324, 347
Kebler, 404
Keech, 314
Keef, 72
Keefor, 371
Keegan, 270, 418
Keenan, 146, 270
Keene, 284, 427, 428
Keeney, 399
Keep, 39, 55
Keer, 411, 414
Keese, 95, 96, 143, 184, 344, 475
Keeth, 98
Kehler, 324
Keiger, 52

Keilay, 95
Keiley, 253
Keith, 18, 21, 94, 162, 181, 188, 243, 252, 309
Keitt, 3
Keleher, 325
Keley, 188
Kellen, 291
Keller, 116, 367, 391
Kelley, 252, 274, 283, 436, 444, 453
Kellogg, 451
Kellum, 450
Kelly, 4, 41, 62, 174, 190, 204, 232, 253, 270, 297, 331, 389, 414, 452, 481
Kelsey, 71
Kemble, 156
Kemmel, 233
Kempff, 399
Kendall, 4, 6, 34, 39, 82, 91, 153, 214, 230, 246, 267, 376, 392, 447, 480
Kendrick, 26, 139, 140, 225, 351, 360, 412
Kenelty, 396
Keneman, 83
Kennard, 176, 327
Kennards, 421
Kennedy, 15, 30, 47, 52, 57, 58, 63, 65, 72, 84, 86, 87, 92, 96, 124, 164, 182, 220, 230, 236, 244, 260, 275, 312, 450
Kennerly, 42, 82, 214
Kenney, 47, 63, 396, 460
Kennon, 98, 451
Kenny, 5, 265
Kensel, 222, 234, 280, 452
Kent, 135, 156, 193, 411
Kenton, 42
Kenvan, 418
Kenyon, 426
Kepler, 438
Keplinger, 268
Kerby, 338, 367

Kerr, 26, 53, 67, 81, 87, 174, 218, 254, 326
Kessler, 193
Ketterman, 312
Kettlewell, 121
Key, 2, 52, 75, 126, 268
Keyl, 448
Keys, 114, 267, 365, 366
Khingsohr, 282
Kibbey, 127, 170, 188
Kid, 189
Kidder, 109, 217
Kidwell, 270
Kieckhoeper, 367
Kilburn, 412
Kilby, 23, 353
Kilebrew, 473
Kilgour, 45
Killburn, 92
Killidge, 373
Killmon, 180
Kilts, 174
Kilty, 96
Kimball, 15, 18, 60, 88, 124, 334, 373, 414
Kimbel, 195
Kimbrough, 82
Kimmel, 47, 52, 222, 234, 280
Kincannon, 153
King, 5, 7, 45, 51, 57, 62, 63, 70, 75, 77, 91, 102, 112, 114, 117, 118, 122, 155, 160, 161, 163, 176, 178, 184, 189, 197, 202, 230, 233, 246, 249, 259, 268, 281, 303, 363, 377, 392, 393, 407, 432, 460, 469, 471
King of Delhi, 451
King of Prussia, 420
Kingman, 51
Kingsbury, 176, 378
Kingsford, 379
Kinney, 55, 180, 186, 300
Kinny, 72
Kinsey, 269
Kinzer, 120, 367

Kip, 2, 280
Kirby, 26, 67, 91, 151, 415, 454
Kirchner, 172
Kirk, 52, 413
Kirkland, 69, 337, 340
Kirkman, 271
Kirkpatrick, 347
Kirkwood House, 381
Kirshfield, 410
Kirwan, 204
Kiss, 16
Kissick, 118
Kittridge, 410
Kius, 413
Kiusching, 441
Kleisendorf, 134
Klinehanse, 296
Klingle, 345
Klingshor, 281
Klopfer, 206, 298, 334, 482
Klopper, 295, 431
Klus, 413
Knapp, 344
Knapper, 274
Knauss, 479
Knickerbocker, 339, 392
Knight, 86, 98, 127, 154, 184, 270, 409
Knott, 80, 407, 482
Knowles, 16, 86, 87
Knowlton, 312
Knox, 25, 45
Knoxville, 98
Kobbe, 310
Koones, 103, 153
Koons, 284
Koran, 13
Korponay, 433
Kosciusko, 15
Koss, 30
Koutaxaki, 456
Krebbs, 165, 183

Krebs, 7, 43, 105, 123, 130, 163, 206, 235, 245, 246, 314, 317, 379, 387, 436, 460, 468
Kres, 233
Kron, 411
Kros, 281
Krouse, 122, 476
Kubbe, 413
Kuhn, 444
Kuner, 479
Kunkel, 56
Kunkle, 345
Kuntz, 236
Kursted, 199
Kurtz, 126, 127
Kutz, 451
Kyle, 355, 424

L

La Blas, 309
La Motte, 224
Lacey, 123, 289
Lacoste, 448
Lacy, 236
Lafayette, 60, 349, 458
Lafever, 24
Lagan, 413
Lago, 310
Lake, 68, 271, 307
Lakeman, 311
Lamar, 283, 478
Lamarue, 233
Lamb, 254, 445, 458
Lambell, 201
Lambert, 284, 445, 454
Lambeth, 105
Lamki, 175
Lammond, 490
Lamontague, 272
Lamoy, 471
Lamrock, 458
Lanaghan, 461
Lanahan, 105, 238, 400, 447, 454, 488
Lancaster, 52, 98, 166, 265, 270

Land, 114, 136
Lander, 152, 158
Landman, 175
Landon Seminary, 17
Landseer, 243
Landstreet, 65, 105
Lane, 77, 252, 289, 400, 484
Laney, 104
Langdon, 444
Langhorne, 48, 175
Langley, 15, 18, 79, 88, 108, 281, 336
Lanman, 383
Lansdale, 15, 123
Lansing, 164
Lapoint, 242
Lappan, 93
Larcen, 480
Larcombe, 259
Largo, 247
Larkin, 103
Larnard, 429
Larned, 229, 274
Larner, 145, 230, 297, 346
Lasiski, 410
Lasola, 414
Latham, 1, 15, 18, 109, 180, 182
Lathan, 257
Lathrop, 22, 42, 56, 91, 309
Latil, 79
Latimer, 89, 358, 421, 482
Latrobe, 47
Latta, 289
Lauck, 454
Laurence, 377
Laurens, 61
Laurie, 72, 219
Laury, 310
Lautner, 455
Lavaca, 220
Lavainway, 26, 30
Lavalette, 314
Lavender, 137
Law, 153, 208
Lawnitz, 426

Lawrence, 45, 102, 128, 142, 318, 333, 345, 462
Lawrenson, 235, 236, 298
Laws, 479
Lawson, 200, 424
Lawton, 42, 166
Lay, 179, 224
Layne, 329
Layton, 289
Lazelle, 445
Lazenby, 464
Le Case, 51
Le Caze, 8
Le Merle, 251
Le Roy, 438
Lea, 72
Leach, 443, 466
Leachman, 44
Leadbeater, 429
Leake, 355, 458
Lean, 412
Lease, 432
Leavenworth, 83
Leavitt, 124, 407
Lebby, 264
LeBlanc, 43
Lebse, 413
Leckel, 310
Leclerc, 287
Leclere, 11
Lecompt, 95
Lecompte, 270, 312
LeCompte, 268
Ledoux, 423
Ledwith, 400
Lee, 4, 20, 47, 48, 90, 101, 107, 110, 120, 142, 168, 207, 222, 234, 247, 280, 282, 292, 315, 323, 336, 337, 371, 372, 377, 382, 398, 403, 405, 406, 411, 412, 413, 415, 442, 452, 458, 474
Leech, 105, 413
Leesburg Academy, 327
Lee-Sic, 140

Lefevre, 165, 417
Leffer, 34
Legare, 124, 366, 397
Legg, 69
Leggett, 254, 281, 352
Lehman, 316
Lehmann, 279
Leidy, 417
Leinhart, 309
Leinwood, 456
Leishear, 142
Leitch, 23
Lemon, 105, 312, 462
Lemons, 474
Lendig, 206, 207
Lendram, 47
Leneghan, 423
Lenman, 367
Lennox, 139
Lenox, 3, 51, 105, 312, 343, 441
Lenox's Wharf, 343
Leonard, 64, 253, 337
Leopard, 326
Lepper, 413
Lepreux, 205
Lesage, 341
Leslie, 36, 47, 267, 272
Lester, 109, 113, 175, 254, 399
Letcher, 223
Letendre, 188
Letzinger, 148
Leutze, 55
Lever, 479
Levering, 236
Levey, 309
Levick, 410
Levin, 223
Levitical degree, 21
Levouse, 310
Levy, 122
Lewell, 309
Lewellener, 171
Lewis, 22, 31, 51, 62, 69, 89, 113, 115, 154, 198, 208, 233, 236, 242,

243, 246, 260, 262, 363, 379, 427,
452, 453, 463, 464, 480
Leybour, 423
Leyburn, 300
Libaher, 282
Libbey, 145, 264
Libby, 388
Lighter, 188
Lightfoot, 28, 229, 230, 366
Lightner, 51, 434
Ligon, 354, 357, 431
Lilly, 57, 58, 80, 87, 92
Limantour, 21
Limbecker, 174
Lincoln, 254, 476
Lincon, 479
Lindsay, 17, 25, 29, 51, 221, 234, 241, 317, 385, 397, 408, 425
Lindsley, 301
Lindsly, 173, 385
Lindsuy, 254
Lines, 68
Lingley, 252
Lingo, 464
Lining, 148
Linkenhoger, 425
Linkens, 3
Linkins, 54
Linn, 474
Linthicum, 83, 105, 144, 269, 467
Linton, 361
Lippincott, 362
Lippitt, 326
Lipscomb, 105, 426
Littig, 189
Little, 82, 102, 110, 130, 236, 327, 405, 474, 484
Littlefield, 30
Littlejohn, 191
Littles, 484
Lively, 287
Livingston, 97, 100, 103, 254, 452
Livingstone, 11, 13, 348
Liza, 26

Llangollen, 151
Lloyd, 115, 221, 298, 324, 377
Lochbaum, 440, 469
Locher, 201
Lochrey, 65, 485
Locke, 30
Locker, 248
Lockey, 130
Lockhart, 351, 395
Locknane, 474
Lockridge, 174
Lockwood, 350, 372, 385, 410, 482
Locust Grove, 329
Locust Hill, 72
Locust-Grove Academy, 218
Lodge, 398
Loefner, 288
Loeser, 224
Logan, 30, 174, 382, 404
Loisel, 26
Loker, 363, 364
Lomax, 80, 192, 432
Lomond, 341
Loncairne, 51
Long, 45, 54, 57, 179, 188, 326, 373, 393
Long Old Fields, 201, 248
Longfellow, 253
Longhurst, 344
Longstreet, 45, 72
Look, 413
Loomis, 98, 254, 490
Loot, 372
Loranger, 471
Lord, 30, 72, 230, 280, 297, 324, 399
Lore, 281
Loring, 224, 411, 453
Lothrop, 337
Loughborough, 85, 116, 467
Love, 238
Lovejoy, 97
Lovelace, 138
Lovell, 202, 479
Lovering, 189

Low, 410, 482
Lowe, 474
Lowell, 97, 132, 253, 378, 392
Lowenthal, 414
Lown, 254
Lowndes, 148, 448
Lownds, 227, 462
Lowrey, 12, 213
Lowrie, 468
Lowry, 97
Loyall, 100, 103
Lozier, 199
Lucas, 6, 25, 45, 122, 134, 205, 282, 284, 432, 463
Luce, 172
Luckeman, 413
Luckett, 142, 482
Ludlan, 309
Ludlow, 343
Lugden, 413
Lugenbeel, 380
Luke, 254
Lullay, 265
Lumpkin, 154, 168
Lumsden, 105
lunatics, 144
Lund, 434
Lusby, 86
Lutheran Church, 448
Lutts, 468, 472
Lycett, 175, 427
Lyddane, 5
Lyle, 263
Lyles, 312
Lyman, 407
Lynch, 54, 100, 103, 122, 328, 336, 344, 446, 448, 451, 453
Lynde, 452
Lyndhurst, 304
Lynn, 182, 309
Lyon, 174, 185, 320
Lyons, 4, 80, 81, 126, 134, 209, 309, 416, 441

M

Mabee, 268
Macall, 168
Macann, 174
Maccaboy, 63
Maccalum, 472
Macdonald, 124
MacDonough, 360
Macfarland, 61, 120
Machen, 195, 309
Mack, 412, 436
Mackall, 377
Mackay, 213, 472
Mackenzie, 435
Mackey, 361, 473
Mackie, 276
Mackin, 68
Macleod, 108, 251, 437, 478
Macmullin, 472
Macomb, 230, 428
Macon, 281
Macrae, 280
Madden, 52
Maddin, 478
Maddox, 97, 112, 162, 334, 373, 397, 401, 458
Madison, 58, 221, 224, 233, 266, 392, 475
Maduro, 403
Maffit, 482
Magan, 26
Magee, 76, 143
Maghee, 207
Magie, 423
Magilton, 279
Maginnis, 473
Maglenen, 72
Magnolia Cemetery, 397
Magraw, 158
Magruder, 59, 63, 88, 145, 154, 201, 222, 234, 248, 262, 273, 280, 384, 393, 399, 418, 464, 488, 490
Maguire, 98, 131, 184, 232, 270, 282, 283, 314, 339, 343, 351, 489

Magull, 205
Maher, 34, 92, 334
Mahomet, 13
Mahon, 490
Mahoney, 124, 413, 454, 482
Mahony, 274
Maicke, 282
Maier, 114
Maillard, 426
Majors, 188
Makin, 11
Malacher, 270
Malbon, 270
Malcolm, 339
Malin, 399
Mallet, 8, 51
Malley, 281
Mallon, 24
Mallory, 46
Malloy, 368
Malone, 371
Maloney, 9, 395, 415, 445
Maney, 60, 67
Mangold, 411
Mangum, 163
Manlove, 372, 411
Mann, 118, 198, 270, 347
Manner, 313
Manning, 14, 222, 249, 459, 460
Manott, 411
Manson, 410
Mante, 192
Manypenny, 149, 286
Maple, 252
Marat, 465
Marbury, 126, 128, 156, 247, 416
Marcello, 474
Marcellus, 443
March, 105, 361, 385, 482
Marche, 6, 41
Marcy, 89, 178, 262, 264, 276, 432, 442, 452
Margioli, 309
Marin, 483

Mario, 261
Marion, 265, 390
Markham, 157
Markoe, 276
Markriter, 156
Marks, 7, 130, 151, 222, 292, 295
Markwood, 448
Marlow, 367
Marmaduke, 222, 234, 280
Marnay, 471
Marochetti, 159
Maron, 179
Marquis, 271
Marquis of Lansdowne, 388
Marrs, 316
Marsh, 12, 72, 299, 308, 309, 399, 418, 433, 483
Marshal, 242
Marshall, 8, 21, 25, 41, 116, 209, 254, 264, 279, 360, 468, 474
Marshek, 148
Marston, 404
Marten, 130
Martgan, 101
Martha's Vineyard, 419
Martin, 6, 26, 41, 46, 52, 57, 58, 79, 87, 91, 101, 104, 122, 152, 199, 254, 259, 295, 399, 417, 436, 471, 474
Martis, 175
Marts, 175
Maruel, 157
Marvin, 115, 372
Marvine, 443
Marye, 303, 441
Maryman, 361, 395, 399, 402, 450
Masi, 32, 33, 75, 230
Masloor, 282
Mason, 2, 7, 17, 37, 60, 61, 73, 88, 101, 109, 117, 121, 154, 176, 192, 213, 242, 243, 249, 264, 303, 316, 382, 394, 401, 437, 461, 474, 482
massacred, 446
Masseo, 50

Massey, 185, 487
Massie, 168, 290, 457
Masters, 463
Mastin, 42, 268
Mather, 241
Mathews, 80, 182, 212, 270, 449
Mathieson, 208
Mathieu, 465
Mathy, 413
Matteson, 71
Matthews, 24, 49, 50, 53, 92, 150, 152, 196, 213, 324, 405
Mattingly, 45, 52, 137, 244, 258, 298, 422
Mattock, 157, 172
Maud, 174
Maulsby, 426, 436
Maupin, 68, 233, 244, 346
Mauro, 125
Maury, 52, 79, 154, 296, 380, 418, 457, 482
Maximilian, 225
Maximillian, 319
Maxwell, 14, 24, 36, 61, 76, 97, 100, 104, 120, 131, 238, 432
May, 54, 100, 104, 113, 129, 167, 195, 208, 298, 362, 365, 373, 380, 385, 415
Maybee, 270
Mayer, 381
Mayers, 142
Mayflower Pilgrim, 304
Mayhew, 47
Maynadier, 452
Maynard, 238, 411, 490
Mayo, 124, 357
Mc_ann, 287
McAdams, 36
McAleston, 429
McAllister, 281, 443
McArthur, 93
McAuley, 344
McBain, 277
McBlair, 106

McBride, 278
McCabe, 35, 90, 309
McCable, 372
McCaeny, 347
McCaffrey, 52, 197
McCaleb, 459
McCall, 117, 484
McCalla, 154
McCalmont, 53
McCardle, 445
McCarthy, 16, 287, 404, 414, 454
McCarty, 64, 219, 271, 371, 373, 374, 397, 485
McCauly, 451
McCeney, 230
McChardy, 411
McChesney, 450
McClafferty, 331
McClanahan, 97
McClean, 30, 373
McCleery, 350
McCleish, 472
McClellan, 224
McClelland, 23, 381
McClenden, 142
McClintock, 424
McCloud, 95
McCloy, 413
McClure, 4, 6, 34, 82, 87, 91, 215, 309, 468
McCluskey, 138
McColgan, 468, 472
McComb, 432
McConnell, 4, 6, 34, 52, 72, 82, 91, 213, 316, 408, 447
McCook, 445
McCormick, 16, 24, 36, 97, 115, 141, 411, 427, 430, 436, 489
McCoun, 233
McCoy, 98, 373
McCrea, 100, 104
McCreary, 43, 44
McCree, 164
McCuffey, 262

McCulley, 174
McCulloch, 52, 185
McCullom, 52
McCullough, 156, 308
McDaniel, 21, 315
McDanniel, 84
McDermot, 179
McDermott, 6, 150, 169, 364
McDevitt, 472
McDonald, 253, 257, 258, 281, 434, 453
McDonnel, 22
McDonnell, 40
McDonogh, 381
McDonough, 175, 316
McDougal, 79, 100, 103, 104
McDougall, 213
McDowall, 159
McDowell, 63, 110, 233, 446
McElderry, 16
McElfresh, 206
McElry, 431
McElwell, 451
McEnery, 122
McEowen, 446
McEwen, 47
McFadden, 259
McFales, 278
McFarland, 154, 279, 346, 398, 408, 473
McFarlane, 455
McFaul, 233
McFerran, 224
McGanity, 281
McGarr, 324
McGary, 265, 480
McGee, 12, 188, 208, 310
McGhee, 488
McGill, 291, 310, 465
McGilvroy, 253
McGlensey, 398
McGlue, 221
McGoffin, 458
McGowan, 249, 389

McGowen, 52
McGraw, 37, 233, 422, 488
McGreery, 151
McGreevy, 68
McGregor, 91, 175, 439, 487
McGrenary, 411
McGriff, 175
McGuffey, 176
McGugan, 412
McGuiggan, 183
McGuire, 7, 51, 73, 176, 267, 281, 367, 383, 398, 413, 459, 460
McGunnegle, 90, 211
McGunnelge, 90
McGunnigle, 337
McGwin, 431
McHatton, 111
McHenry, 298, 401, 472, 482
McHugh, 252
McIlveen, 154
McIlwaine, 249
McIntosh, 68, 100, 103, 224, 471
McKaig, 32, 134, 285
Mckay, 258, 445
McKay, 134, 254, 309, 398
McKean, 320
McKee, 203
McKeever, 103
McKelden, 19, 85, 406
McKenna, 122, 298, 381
McKenney, 126, 148, 151, 171, 454
McKenny, 260, 284
McKenzie, 450
McKerrechar, 473
McKessack, 97
McKesson, 309
McKibben, 107
McKibbin, 111, 427, 444
McKierman, 296
McKim, 47, 141, 189, 286, 410, 445, 490
McKine, 329
McKinley, 399
McKinney, 191, 254, 281

McKinnon, 372
McKinstry, 154
McKissick, 422
McKneeh, 309
McKnew, 230, 296, 423
McKnight, 106, 122, 184, 230
McKree, 200
McKugh, 371
McLain, 24, 328, 393
McLane, 224, 401
Mclaughlin, 276
McLaughlin, 240, 265, 394, 482
McLaurine, 354, 358
McLean, 198, 297, 299, 324, 385, 467, 468
McLees, 309
McLelland, 411
Mcleod, 156
McLeod, 150, 213, 259, 265, 271, 286, 325, 337, 340, 344, 350
McLoskey, 370
McLure, 167
McMahan, 264
McMahon, 17, 101, 423, 474
McMahony, 264
McManus, 220, 444
McMasters, 182, 193, 278
McMena, 423
McMichael, 450
McMill, 373
McMillan, 254
McMullen, 420
McMullin, 105, 201
McMurtrie, 162
McNab, 452
McNabb, 281
McNain, 45
McNair, 52, 232, 294, 455
McNairy, 272
McNamara, 445
McNantz, 21
McNash, 414
McNeil, 33, 49, 234, 378, 410
Mcneill, 280

McNeill, 26, 222, 322, 337, 353, 373
McNeir, 11, 84, 206, 228, 233, 437
McNeish, 371, 372
McNerhaney, 55
McNerhany, 3, 52
McNew, 269
McNiel, 72
McNutt, 224
McPhail, 180
McPherson, 225, 241, 258, 381, 429, 483
McRae, 103, 145, 336
McRea, 168
McReynolds, 73
McSherry, 3
McTavish, 350
McVeigh, 399
McWilliams, 270
McWillie, 197
Mead, 172, 236, 350
Meade, 94, 127, 128, 222, 234, 237, 261, 280, 283, 299, 399, 482
Meador, 244, 384
Meadows, 328
Meagher, 299
Means, 317, 359
Mears, 175
Meban, 487
Mechlin, 475
Medary, 87, 91, 170
Medill, 117
Medland, 304
Meek, 455
Meek's Adventure, 332
Meeker, 288
Meggett, 213, 214
Melrose, 73
Melson, 297
Melvin, 68, 140
Menard, 8
Mendell, 455
Mendenhall, 218
Menefee, 278
Mensh, 418

Menzeisheimer, 7
Menzies, 471
Mercer, 28, 34, 105, 373
Merchant, 232, 279, 314, 379
Meridian Hill, 293, 369
Meron, 413
Merrick, 40, 55, 106, 247, 260, 265
Merrifield, 306
Merrill, 281, 297, 385
Merriman, 398
Merritt, 360, 474
Merry, 414
Mervine, 62
Metropolitan Female Institute, 218
Metternich, 335
Metz, 418
Meyer, 46, 414
Michaux, 355, 356
Michell, 49, 332
Mickle, 11, 121
Micon, 309
Middleton, 56, 59, 76, 100, 103, 130, 166, 172, 188, 209, 259, 319, 385, 447
Miexell, 409
Mignault, 37
Mikell, 213
Milburn, 256, 490
Miles, 165, 236, 253, 324, 333, 445
Milhouse, 220
Millan, 431
Millandon, 45
Millaudon, 25
Miller, 7, 31, 32, 36, 39, 42, 51, 52, 53, 115, 129, 164, 182, 186, 196, 208, 220, 231, 232, 233, 237, 238, 253, 254, 262, 274, 298, 306, 309, 310, 317, 327, 396, 412, 414, 425, 430, 442, 446, 451, 467, 471, 474
Millet, 51
Millett, 4, 64, 91
Millholland, 286
Millhouse, 220
Mills, 152, 220, 232, 268, 309, 312, 315, 451, 482, 490
Millson, 104, 223
Milsop, 281
Milstead, 129
Miner, 169
Mines, 17
Ming, 64
Minge, 49, 86, 87, 91
Minis, 478
Minnigerode, 68
Minor, 52, 228, 241, 271, 302, 338, 486
Minot, 29
Miorton, 70
Mirick, 303
Mitchell, 4, 50, 68, 91, 114, 119, 130, 185, 208, 213, 220, 263, 267, 272, 277, 281, 301, 332, 411, 412, 423, 467, 468
Mix, 124
Mockabee, 241
Moffall, 213
Mohan, 69
Mohler, 221
Mohun, 179, 252, 380, 439, 467, 483
Moise, 244
monks at St Onotrio, 210
Monroe, 26, 45, 224, 313, 388, 404, 415
Monson, 346, 373
Montague, 53, 474
Montaguon, 412
Montane, 414
Montey, 37
Montgomery, 20, 33, 45, 56, 72, 86, 90, 106, 150, 156, 161, 224, 280, 308, 310, 410, 417, 484
Monti, 282
Monticello, 95
Montpelier, 221, 266, 392
Montreal, 335
Montserrat, 1
Moody, 18, 20, 26, 62

Mooers, 20
Moon, 174, 221
Mooney, 17
Moor, 8, 283
Moore, 21, 22, 23, 27, 70, 98, 123, 135, 145, 175, 197, 244, 268, 270, 281, 295, 299, 309, 337, 345, 371, 372, 399, 410, 430, 444, 445, 447, 450, 451, 474
Moran, 107, 139, 281, 411
Morant, 56
Mordecai, 77
More, 457
Morehead, 265
Morel, 37
Moreland, 131, 468
Moreno, 152
Morey, 37, 398, 437
Morfit, 269
Morfitt, 221, 234
Morgan, 24, 103, 105, 183, 222, 230, 234, 235, 244, 260, 280, 284, 298, 356, 396, 462, 471, 482
Moriarty, 12
Moritz, 440
Mormon, 156, 186, 198, 433, 446, 459
Mormons, 275, 442
Morrell, 459
Morrill, 81, 257
Morris, 55, 100, 103, 119, 164, 200, 240, 242, 279, 309, 314, 339, 347, 357, 358, 395, 411, 415, 445, 480
Morrisen, 315
Morrison, 4, 6, 42, 44, 82, 86, 91, 109, 214, 286, 352, 376, 415, 445, 446
Morrissy, 120
Morrow, 49, 67, 92, 152, 289
Morse, 271, 272, 342, 413
Morsell, 151, 229, 379, 416, 421
Morson, 61
Morton, 28, 83, 141, 293, 351, 479
Moseau, 419
Moseley, 23, 412
Mosely, 117, 466

Moses, 13, 213, 293, 306, 386, 409, 453, 481
Mosher, 52, 121, 137
Mostyn, 181
Mothershead, 133
Mott, 451
Motzer, 440
Moulder, 57
Moulgomer, 309
Moulton, 289
Mount Airy, 120
Mount Arat, 416
Mount Auburn, 333
Mount Auburn Cemetery, 124, 397
Mount Hebron Cemetery, 99
Mount Hope, 325
Mount Hope Cemetery, 202, 289
Mount Pleasant, 81, 94, 101, 352, 416
Mount Vernon, 6, 141, 187, 245, 403
Mount Vernon Association, 301
Mount Washington, 383
Mount Welby, 6
Mountain View, 252
Mountz, 186, 302, 386
Moxley, 270
MrTravers, 441
Muckenfuss, 303
Mudd, 35, 82, 91, 324, 435, 461
Mueller, 320
Mugford, 26
Muir, 99
Mulholland, 164, 174
Mullady, 436
Mullen, 9, 68, 254, 309, 399, 411, 420
Mullenix, 488
Muller, 444
Mullikin, 338
Mullinix, 176
Mullins, 452
Mullony, 263
Mulloy, 52
Mumford, 36
Muncaster, 311, 348
Munce, 399

Munck, 259
Munford, 293
Munger, 411
Munro, 229, 299, 377
Munroe, 19, 166, 224, 399
Munson, 379
Murch, 412
Murdaugh, 479
Murdoch, 246
Murdock, 98
Murphy, 86, 97, 105, 180, 207, 259, 340, 349, 413, 454, 459, 477
Murray, 69, 85, 87, 88, 91, 96, 164, 179, 184, 204, 213, 276, 299, 311, 326, 346, 347, 391, 408, 413, 416, 427, 447, 482
Murrell, 217
Murrray, 443
Murry, 452
Musgrove, 310
Musser, 328
Mussey, 173, 418
Musy, 471
Muzzy, 174
Myers, 53, 54, 61, 104, 112, 206, 361, 369, 426, 484

N

Nacogdoches, 307
Nairn, 101, 268, 290
Nalation, 318
Nalle, 213, 271
Nally, 101, 146, 183
Nance, 119, 220
Nantucket, 351
Napier, 35, 139, 443
Naples, 358
Napoleon, 205, 305, 327, 340, 457, 465
Napoleon I, 328
Narramore, 411
Nash, 36, 87, 92, 432
Nason, 30, 72
Nat'l Theatre, 367

Natick, 282, 284
National Theatre, 56
Natzmer, 450
Naughton, 195, 432
Naylor, 138, 149
Neal, 20, 46
Neale, 15, 230, 265, 270, 282, 324, 325, 329, 383, 424
Neel, 167
Neely, 1, 112, 232
Neil, 414
Neill, 225, 254, 317, 452
Neilson, 36
Nellis, 309
Nelson, 38, 47, 53, 100, 152, 156, 246, 299, 394, 467
Nesbit, 453
Nesmith, 97
Neuislein, 184
Nevins, 38, 276
Nevitt, 111
new Catholic church, 196
New Seat, 59
Newbold, 56
Newell, 57, 58, 63, 92, 350, 368, 480, 482
Newland, 481
Newman, 165, 199, 270, 411
Newton, 146, 179, 208, 229, 230, 281, 295, 320, 444, 455
Ney, 139
Niagara, 326
Nichol, 164
Nicholas, 12, 124, 362
Nicholl, 79, 310
Nicholls, 482
Nichols, 333, 455, 457
Nicholson, 1, 40, 51, 166, 191, 421, 451, 474
Nicklin, 278
Nicolay, 231
Nicols, 84, 231
Niemeyer, 77
Niles, 15, 92, 212, 268

Nisbet, 115
Nixon, 148
Noble, 25, 75, 86, 87, 157, 172, 174, 217, 276, 303, 471
Noddall, 326
Noerr, 402
Nokes, 89, 147, 297, 312
Nolan, 175, 281
Noland, 48
nomenclature, 59
Noonan, 130, 296
Norcross, 189, 329
Norflet, 436
Norman, 254
Norris, 101, 107, 114, 278
North, 347, 388, 440, 451
Northbridge, 253
Norton, 117, 246, 281, 303, 438
Norwood, 263, 366
Norwood Cemetery, 243
Nourrit, 489
Nourse, 18, 65, 207, 327, 377, 378, 408, 455, 471
Noxon, 374
Noyes, 7, 66, 130
Nugent, 248, 263, 480
Nune, 399
Nutt, 76
Nye, 14, 24, 217

O

O'Brien, 72, 297, 450
O'Callaghan, 138
O'Connell, 98
O'Conner, 373
O'Connor, 296, 297, 390
O'Donnel, 445
O'Donnoghue, 179, 235, 270
O'Fallon, 169
O'Flynn, 98
O'Hara, 224
O'Keefe, 98
O'Meara, 101
O'More, 248

O'Neal, 449
O'Neale, 298
O'Neil, 271, 299, 395, 410, 453
O'Neill, 69
O'Toole, 70, 306, 446, 449
Oak Grove, 120, 420
Oak Hill Cemetery, 6, 169, 197
Oakes, 444
Oakey, 29
Oaklawn, 423
Oakley, 104, 181, 182
Oaks, 281
Oakwood farm, 99
Oatman, 16
Ocean encroachments, 159
Ochiltree, 307
Odell, 35, 88
Odenhammer, 289
Offley, 225
Offutt, 81, 230, 282
Ogden, 54, 55, 82, 268, 300, 398, 414, 482
Ogle, 27, 148, 439, 441
Oglethorpe, 85, 266
Oitagne, 414
Oken-stan-tah, 140
Olcott, 432
Old English funeral, 426
Old Fields, 130
Old Gas Works, 362
Old Trinity Church, 143
oldest book, 256
oldest engine, 317
Oldham, 13
Olds, 107
Olfero, 395
Olfur, 415
Olive Hill, 331
Oliver, 26, 30, 77, 87, 92, 216, 415
Olivera, 111
Olivia, 414
Ollague, 379
Olmstead, 24, 56, 65, 310
Olney, 152

Olsen, 480
Oney, 57, 58, 87
Ontiveras, 467
Orme, 298, 467
Ormea, 419
Ormsbee, 431
Orr, 72, 162
Ort, 344
Orth, 399
Osborn, 93, 108, 371, 406, 415
Osborne, 334, 372, 374
Ostrander, 277
Oswald, 11
Oswalt, 354
Otero, 53
Otis, 370
Ott, 122, 125, 200, 230, 490
Otterback, 52
Otto, 138
Otwell, 434
Ould, 51
Ourand, 184, 320
Ouseley, 443
Ousley, 228
Owden, 474
Owen, 79, 105, 119, 143, 175, 208, 358, 370, 439
Owen's Mills, 117
Owens, 86, 114, 195, 206, 253, 295, 300, 324, 368, 438
Owings, 412
Owner, 52, 283
Oxen Hill, 338
Oxley, 233
Oxnard, 147
Oyster, 298, 468

P

Pace, 272
Paceco, 467
packet **Cataract**, 453
Packwood, 69
Page, 1, 8, 19, 23, 25, 30, 39, 62, 72, 120, 222, 239, 261, 310, 337, 362, 374, 378, 381, 390, 418, 434, 439, 471, 483, 489
Pahud, 410
Paige, 21, 224, 484
Paine, 69, 71, 223, 224, 410
Painter, 42, 51, 64, 90, 330
Pairo, 207, 377, 408, 455
Pakenham, 133
Palfrey, 142, 222, 234, 280
Palmer, 62, 67, 267, 272, 331, 367, 412, 451, 482
Palmetto, 41
Palmiter, 180
Palms, 142
Pannel, 456
Panson, 343
Pantony, 68
Pardon, 241, 251
Parish, 35, 67, 309
Parke, 39
Parker, 3, 52, 104, 121, 134, 145, 230, 233, 238, 293, 336, 344, 363, 364, 372, 410, 417, 432, 457, 483
Parkhill, 337, 474
Parkinson, 421
Parkison, 105
Parks, 132, 310
Parlin, 124
Parma, 254
Parmelee, 397
Parmer, 254
Parran, 382
Parris, 62, 404, 490
Parrish, 87, 91, 186
Parrot, 289
Parry, 20, 169
Parson, 175
Parsons, 93, 308, 309, 467
Partlow, 284
Partridge, 487
<u>Passionist order</u>, 133
Pastor, 426
Patch, 318
Patrick, 141, 148

Patten, 14, 117, 352, 442
Patterson, 23, 52, 79, 135, 141, 149, 165, 194, 213, 225, 230, 312, 317, 385, 388, 443, 481
Pattieson, 213
Pattison, 428
Patton, 209
Paul, 79, 391, 468
Paulding, 38, 72, 253, 349, 488
Paulk, 150
Payne, 99, 148, 224, 252, 271, 292, 297, 309, 360, 374, 383, 395, 430, 436, 455, 482
Paynter, 165
Peabody, 5, 47, 100, 293, 320, 321, 368, 440
Peace, 252, 275
Peake, 185
Peale, 245, 397
Pearce, 2, 44, 483
Pearson, 460, 467
Peaslee, 109
Peck, 95, 152, 206, 222, 234, 280, 345, 417, 474
Peden, 117, 283
Pedrick, 368
Peel, 185
Pegg, 92, 212
Pegram, 452
Peirce, 131, 230
Pelfesser, 287
Pelham, 304
Pell, 410
Pellerin, 8
Pellet, 350
Pelot, 100, 104, 176
Peltro, 186
Pembertons, 107
Pena, 381
Pendergast, 11, 55, 72
Pendleton, 250, 290, 376, 393
Penix, 166
Penman, 324
Penn, 85, 195

Pennell, 309
Pennie, 152
Pennington, 94, 102, 474
Pennock, 100, 103, 451
Penny, 240, 487
Penrose, 135
Peoples, 174
Pepper, 2, 303, 467
Peretz, 36
Perkins, 17, 171, 188, 233, 400
Perley, 187
Perrie, 211, 258, 271
Perry, 35, 58, 148, 208, 233, 360, 399, 405, 487, 490
Perryman, 398
Peruvian Llamas, 476
Pestelle, 206
Peter, 47, 352, 421, 440
Peterkin, 240
Peterman, 316
Peters, 75, 205, 231, 270, 274, 310, 363
Petherbridge, 23
Petigru, 114, 118
Petit, 270
Petriken, 188
Petro, 68
Pettet, 199
Pettibone, 52, 208, 382
Pettit, 152, 268, 467
Pettway, 455
Petty, 388
Peugh, 363
Peugnet, 141
Peyton, 3, 139, 242
Phair, 118
Phelan, 227
Phelps, 34, 35, 67, 72, 87, 91, 105, 110, 220, 221, 234, 344, 378, 404, 452
Philips, 88, 329
Phillips, 15, 18, 38, 57, 58, 82, 87, 91, 122, 131, 152, 154, 177, 188, 256, 289, 366, 388, 428, 471, 478

Phinney, 480
Phinny, 117
Phoenix, 64, 398
Piasso, 415
Piatt, 91, 215
Pic, 52
Picard, 471
Pickens, 26
Pickett, 238
Picking, 398
Pickman, 179
Pickrell, 53, 85, 270, 320
Pico, 111
Picton, 223
Pierce, 55, 88, 89, 95, 143, 193, 264, 311, 345, 361, 374, 434, 441, 471
Pierson, 336, 420, 490
Piertle, 145
Pigott, 466
Pike, 283
Pilcher, 185, 202
Piles, 300
Pillans, 213
Pilling, 122, 127
Pinckney, 375, 469
Pindel, 408
Pine, 245
Piney Point Pavilion, 228
Pinkham, 18, 79
Pinkney, 346
Piot, 446
Piozzi, 181
Piper, 89
Pishon, 445
Pistole, 333
Pitt, 192, 388
Pittman, 6, 30, 58
Pitts, 309
Pizzini, 268, 270, 271
Place, 37
Plain Dealing, 352
Plant, 179, 349, 460
Plass, 395
Platt, 398, 483

Pleasant Grove, 402
Pleasants, 46
Plowden, 268, 270
Plug-Uglies, 206
Plumbe, 263
Plumer, 132
Plummer, 476
Poague, 290
Poe, 268, 270
Pohick, 105
Poindexter, 197
Poisal, 104
Poland, 310
Polhemus, 139, 398
Polk, 109, 140, 154, 162, 264, 276
Polkinhorn, 1, 243
Pollard, 201, 310, 347, 431
Pollock, 123, 189, 337
Polly, 471
Polton, 454
Pomery, 412
Ponts, 292
Pool, 15, 18, 414
Poole, 49, 82, 91
Poor, 23
Pope, 102, 210, 320, 337, 413
Popes creek estate, 187
Poplar, 433
Porteous, 283
Porter, 11, 38, 97, 141, 168, 222, 233, 254, 256, 267, 272, 358, 391, 413, 444, 451
Porterfield, 55, 72
Portilla, 440
Portland Manor, 156
Portman, 31, 72
Posey, 292
Post, 207, 346
Potomac Furnace, 162
Potomac Iron Furnace, 162
Potter, 17, 186, 191, 253, 254, 325, 480, 483
Potts, 16, 53, 225, 427, 459, 460
Pouder, 187

Poultney, 187
Poulton, 489
Powell, 52, 171, 223, 239, 301, 413, 434
Power, 481
Powers, 405, 432, 453, 468
Prather, 236, 462, 482, 489
Pratt, 47, 100, 198, 276, 385
Pratz, 109
Preble, 406
Precise, 44
Prenot, 6
Prentice, 289, 323
Prentiss, 25, 349, 380
Prescott, 250, 489
President's Mansion, 55
Presley, 282
Preston, 109, 213, 301
Pretty Prospect, 352
Prettyman, 105, 329
Preuss, 79
Previtt, 283
Price, 98, 180, 226, 254, 281, 319, 396, 409, 434, 447, 480
Price Luigi, 50
Prichett, 232
Priest, 373, 379, 410
Prieur, 443
Prigmore, 114
Prime, 429
Primmett's Run, 202
Prince, 454
Prince Albert, 143
Prince Frederick, 2
Princess Charlotte, 319
Princess of England, 251
Pritchard, 414
Pritchett, 232
Probasco, 383
Prohert, 413
propeller **Arctic**, 480
propeller **Edinburgh**, 332
propeller **J N Harris**, 323
propeller **Reindeer**, 424

Prospect Hill, 460
Protestant burial ground, 395
Prout, 230
Provost, 3, 51
Prudhomme, 271
Pryer, 21
Pryor, 88, 250, 254, 353
Pucci, 113
Puckett, 16, 45, 427
Pulaski, 15
Pullen, 412
Pumpelly, 426, 432
Pumphrey, 52, 79
Purcell, 165, 345
Purdy, 24, 164, 209, 251
Purrington, 61, 222
Pursell, 80
Purviance, 100, 103
Putnam, 222, 234, 267, 280, 404
Pyne, 60, 148, 189, 229

Q

Quackenbush, 29
Quakers, 435
Quantrill, 236
Quarles, 233
Quattlebaum, 222, 234, 280
Queen, 52, 84, 247, 295, 300, 347
Queen Isabella, 139
Queen of England, 485
Queen Victoria, 159, 167, 177, 185, 335
Queens, 300
Quencer, 412
Quener, 372
Querpon, 412
Quin, 456
Quincy, 281, 426
Quinichett, 113
Quinn, 144, 199, 434, 445
Quintana, 139
Quitman, 213
Quolo, 379

R

Raassi, 410
Radcliffe, 51, 392
Radford, 224
Radziwill, 463
Ragan, 225, 297
Ragland, 412
Railey, 235, 357
Rainbow, 51, 53, 312
Raincock, 113
Rainey, 254
Rains, 224
Rainsford, 255
Rainy, 270
Ralston, 346
Ramsay, 100, 313, 337, 339
Ramsey, 6, 97, 415
Rand, 314
Randal, 444
Randall, 34, 38, 72, 74, 90, 130, 227, 309, 374
Randolph, 61, 171, 174, 193, 233, 297, 302, 391, 396, 406, 474, 475
Rankin, 242, 310
Ransom, 195
Ranson, 1, 124
Rapphannock, 382
Ratcliff, 66
Ratcliffe, 259, 325, 401, 490
rate of pay, 10
Ratrie, 40, 470
Ravenna, 412
Ravenswood, 5
Rawland, 298
Rawlings, 244, 269, 386
Ray, 141, 188, 230, 467, 468
Rayburn, 255
Raymond, 11, 107, 346, 373, 376, 418, 423
Rayne, 373
Raynolds, 279
Raynor, 275
Read, 119, 221, 229, 234, 293, 423, 482

Ready, 95, 238
Ream, 480
Reams, 281
Reany, 317
Reaver, 464
Record, 37
Rector, 65, 422
Red Land District of Albemarle, 290
Redd, 206
Reddall, 276
Reddin, 40, 470
Redding, 108, 373
Redfield, 115
Rediman, 195
Redin, 1, 176, 426, 436, 455
Redpath, 324
Reed, 22, 30, 49, 101, 119, 174, 188, 199, 202, 234, 326, 332, 343, 373, 409, 411, 412, 413, 439, 445
Reeder, 110
Reedy, 437
Reekie, 473
Reeley, 51
Reese, 101, 117, 259, 309, 411, 412
Reeside, 6, 20, 56, 80, 176, 212
Regester, 105
Regger, 175
Register, 73, 184
Reid, 76, 167, 371, 372
Reidhead, 343
Reidy, 332
Reilly, 52, 56, 364, 408
Reily, 151
Reinecker, 35
Reinhart, 175
Reintzel, 176, 377
Reis, 444
Reiser, 341
Reklewski, 4
Remisk, 465
Remshaw, 152
Renau, 254
Reneau, 254
Renneau, 20, 33

Renner, 24
Reno, 280, 452
Renshaw, 199
Reppe, 165
Revolutionary document, 385
Revolutionary Reliques, 261
Reyburn, 97
Reymert, 134
Reynard, 63
Reynold, 349
Reynolds, 79, 93, 209, 271, 432, 474
Rhea, 254, 450
Rhees, 147
Rheinhardt, 60
Rhind, 136
Rhinehart, 461
Rhoads, 169
Rhodes, 72, 86, 87, 92, 216, 324
Rian, 172
Rice, 17, 49, 51, 60, 74, 87, 91, 136, 141
Rich, 64, 179, 235, 246, 373, 451, 452, 468
Rich Point farm, 202
Richard, 77
Richards, 4, 250, 385, 413, 450, 463, 480, 482, 490
Richardson, 23, 99, 187, 207, 262, 310, 392, 408, 471, 472, 480
Richey, 105, 150
Richman, 411
Richon, 379, 414
Rickard, 52
Rickets, 102
Ricketts, 396, 454
Rickhert, 477
Riddle, 52
Ridenour, 141, 239, 271
Rider, 66
Ridgaway, 360
Ridgeley, 15, 246, 451
Ridgely, 115, 138, 194, 274
Ridgeway, 156, 363, 364
Ridgley, 419

Ridgway, 32, 300, 410, 430
Ridick, 475
Ridley, 372, 411, 473
Ridout, 331
Riecker, 138
Riell, 385
Riggen, 433
Riggles, 42, 86, 327
Riggs, 39, 51, 84, 104, 230, 267, 369, 384
Rigley, 465
Rigney, 433
Riker, 35
Riley, 68, 85, 125, 208, 233, 312, 480
Rillieux, 192
Rind, 53
Ring, 23
Ringgold, 438, 482
Riordan, 27
Risque, 270
Ritchie, 71, 72, 199, 305, 312, 482
Rittenhouse, 72
Ritter, 246, 452
Rivels, 282
Rives, 52, 61, 113, 132
Rixey, 44
Roach, 20, 223, 472
Roache, 53
Road, 49
Roan, 15, 18, 82, 90
Roane, 225
Roars, 254
Robb, 65
Robbin, 5
Robbins, 385
Robedeau, 6, 69, 88
Robedeaux, 4
Robert, 222, 234, 273, 280
Roberts, 7, 16, 33, 98, 152, 154, 191, 200, 310, 333, 380, 389, 412, 460
Robertson, 175, 349, 353, 354, 364, 397, 399, 414
Robespierre, 465
Robey, 130, 131, 366

Robins, 5, 130, 314
Robinson, 23, 51, 61, 68, 74, 89, 95, 98, 144, 151, 160, 183, 222, 226, 234, 246, 257, 264, 280, 281, 282, 295, 298, 307, 317, 325, 356, 370, 386, 407, 422, 425, 435, 438, 445, 446, 452, 455, 458, 461, 466
Robson, 292, 324
Rockwell, 25
Roddy, 24, 67, 175
Rodgers, 3, 76, 254, 337, 427, 453, 457
Rodinski, 306
Rodman, 146, 357
Rodney, 401
Rodwell, 413
Roemle, 182
Rogers, 20, 24, 45, 49, 64, 72, 105, 132, 146, 309, 317, 337, 350, 399, 442, 458, 481
Rogy, 174
Rohdenberg, 199
Rohon, 281
Rohrer, 35
Rolfe, 416
Rolinson, 67
Rollins, 49, 328, 330
Roman, 152
Romer, 450
Romeyn, 288
Ronalds, 341
Roney, 460
Rooney, 8, 134, 164, 444
Roose, 60, 84
Root, 100, 290, 350
Roots, 247
Rose, 21, 28, 90, 277, 371, 482
Rose Cottage, 149
Rosenthal, 7, 44
Rosewell, 374
Rosner, 262
Ross, 239, 270, 286, 295, 298, 312, 336, 340, 345, 372, 439, 470
Rosser, 30

Rost, 265
Roszel, 105
Roten, 349
Rothrock, 164
Rothschild, 118
Rothweiler, 210
Rothwell, 78
Rousseau, 170
Rouston, 328
Roux, 340
Rowan, 23, 103
Rowe, 144, 276
Rowland, 1, 83, 399
Rowles, 371
Rowzie, 22, 23
Roy, 316, 478
Royal, 36, 46
Royston, 255, 354
Rozenthall, 131
Rozier, 349
Rubb, 414
Rucker, 109
Rudd, 135, 226
Rudwell, 373
Ruff, 112, 224, 367
Ruffin, 302
Ruffner, 196
Ruger, 173
Ruggles, 349, 363
Rumery, 15, 18
Rummel, 371
Rumph, 392
Rumsey, 77
Runnel, 372
Runnell, 336, 411
Runnells, 26
Ruppel, 265
Ruppert, 435
Rurth, 337
Ruse, 64
Rush, 430, 448
Rusk, 52, 307, 428
Russel, 49
Russell, 16, 53, 69, 99, 246, 309, 471

Rust, 41, 370, 394
Ruth, 3
Rutherford, 268, 414, 460, 468
Ruthven, 293
Rutledge, 232, 233
Rutter, 308, 450
Rutton, 233
Ryan, 157, 222, 234, 280, 281, 309, 310, 398, 408, 411, 446
Ryland, 105, 203
Ryley, 42, 87, 90
Rynders, 115, 489
Ryon, 135, 270

S

Sabine, 304
Sackeld, 486
Sackett, 258
Saffell, 395
Sage, 6, 372, 480
Sahib, 406
Saledine, 261
Salter, 36
Salusbury, 181
Samain, 309
Sampson, 398
Sams, 282
Samson, 44, 57, 206, 229, 248, 399, 465
Samstag, 211, 237
Sanborn, 412, 413
Sanders, 121, 253, 254, 265, 279, 324
Sanderson, 114, 188, 283, 468
Sandford, 57, 148, 174
Sands, 141, 326
Sandy Point, 335
Sandys, 472
Saneco, 445
Sanford, 16, 135, 176, 219, 220, 273, 460, 474
Sanger, 282
Sansbury, 367
Santa Anna, 65
Sanzeneau, 100

Sapp, 29
Sargeant, 119, 374
Sargent, 343
Saroni, 410
Sartori, 482
Sasscer, 325
Satone, 310
Saunders, 4, 15, 17, 82, 92, 120, 128, 215, 269, 308, 431
Sav_ry, 341
Savage, 107, 179, 189, 229, 238, 395
Savelli, 419
Saward, 324
Sawin, 412
Sawley, 372
Sawyer, 30, 186, 312, 371, 410, 484
Saxton, 209
Sayre, 15
Scaggs, 85, 188, 367, 438, 439, 467
Scaife, 471
Scales, 134
Scanlon, 297
Scannell, 281
Schaefer, 324
Schaeffer, 296
Schaffer, 309
Scharpff, 220
Schell, 115, 178
Schellinger, 82, 91, 214
Schenck, 87
Schermerhorn, 253, 254
Schiemer, 234
Schilling, 342
Schillird, 283
Schley, 189
Schlicht, 164
Schmendmann, 411
Schmering, 341
Schneider, 426, 457, 463
schnr **Adventure**, 464
schnr **Bonetta**, 32
schnr **El Dorado**, 384
schnr **Eldorado**, 390
schnr **Elizabeth**, 216

schnr **Endeavor**, 403
schnr **Eudorus**, 195
schnr **Falcon**, 25
schnr **Garnet**, 16, 87
schnr **Granada**, 120, 202
schnr **Granite State**, 32
schnr **Harriet Maria**, 403
schnr **Hassler**, 333
schnr **Industry**, 464
schnr **Nenuphar**, 27
schnr **Panama**, 32
schnr **Pearl**, 251
schnr **Spartan**, 389
schnr **St Lawrence**, 18
schnr **Two Brothers**, 38
schnr **Wren**, 421
Schoeffler, 135
Schofield, 368
Schoolfield, 113
Schoonhozen, 450
Schroeder, 280, 283, 406
Schuber, 412
Schubert, 480
Schucking, 1
Schuermann, 488
Schulte, 268
Schultze, 276
Schulze, 52
Schurer, 475
Schussler, 338, 344
Schusssler, 265
Schuyler, 25, 64, 192, 216, 289, 339
Schwartz, 147, 443
Schwartze, 268, 271
Schwarzman, 194, 243, 434
Scior, 407
Scofield, 109
Scollay, 29
Scott, 23, 25, 51, 64, 99, 100, 101, 103, 104, 126, 132, 137, 144, 154, 174, 204, 218, 221, 231, 254, 269, 270, 273, 279, 300, 314, 330, 339, 365, 375, 397, 446, 456, 470, 471, 478

Screven, 73
Scrivener, 130
Scrivenner, 86
Scrivner, 327
Scrope, 192
Scudder, 249
Scully, 309, 312
Seabrook, 77, 82, 91, 213
Sears, 64, 80, 96, 208, 251, 346, 430, 481
Seaton, 59, 233, 236, 406, 418, 449
Seavers, 432
Seeger, 373
Seeley, 227
Seely, 232, 309
Seguin, 379, 414
Segur, 411
Seibert, 250
Seiler, 254
Seinney, 254
Selden, 1, 5, 52, 146, 191, 246, 350, 354, 421
Seldner, 53
Seldon, 452
Sellamer, 414
Sellaner, 395
Semken, 83
Semmes, 85, 101, 179, 236, 241, 270, 381, 423, 460, 476
Sengstack, 59, 446
Serf, 175
Sergeant, 152
Serony, 372
Serrin, 179
Sessford, 143, 236
Sestini, 344
Settle, 336
Seven Oaks, 200
Sewall, 104, 148, 272
Seward, 18
Sewell, 104, 165, 336
Sexton, 297
Seydel, 205

Seymour, 270, 271, 282, 424, 453, 485
Seys, 107
Shackelford, 18, 21
Shackleford, 65
Shaeffer, 330
Shaffer, 54, 471
Shandley, 214
Shaney, 148
Shank, 405
Shannon, 69
Sharp, 227, 249
Sharpe, 242, 253
Sharpstein, 130
Shattuck, 59
Shaw, 11, 16, 22, 27, 33, 38, 49, 51, 58, 72, 82, 90, 114, 214, 263, 277, 351, 373, 401, 413, 423, 441
Shea, 309
Sheckels, 295
Shedd, 179, 441
Sheehan, 24
Sheek, 330
Sheesy, 296
Sheffey, 332
Shekell, 246, 377
Shekells, 250
Sheldon, 132, 152, 199, 411
Shelton, 30, 31
Shepard, 69, 220
Shephard, 223
Shepherd, 36, 481
Shepley, 124
Sheppard, 50, 219, 413
Shepperd, 100, 104
Sherburne, 152
Sheriden, 281
Sheriff, 184
Sherman, 167, 176
Sherrard, 99
Sheves, 12
Shewannuc, 92
Shiding, 257
Shields, 51, 177

Shigley, 157
Shilley, 9
Shimer, 221
ship **Cahawba**, 78
ship **Caleb Grimshaw**, 18, 20, 62
ship **California**, 30
ship **Cathedral**, 168
ship **Commerce**, 429
ship **Cyane**, 202, 206, 253
ship **Ellen Brooks**, 217, 481
ship **Eva Dorothea**, 469
ship **Frolic**, 13
ship **Geo Washington**, 156
ship **Grampus**, 356
ship **Guerriere**, 380
ship **Illinois**, 389
ship **James E Woodruff**, 458
ship **Java**, 29
ship **M C Stevens**, 433
ship **Malacca**, 50
ship **Mary Caroline Stevens**, 185
ship **Neptune's Car**, 14
ship **Niagara**, 487
ship **Orissa**, 32
ship **Plymouth**, 446
ship **Portsmouth**, 68
ship **Rambler**, 195
ship **Resolute**, 485
ship **Roanoke**, 258
ship **Saratoga**, 488
ship **Seaman**, 381
ship **St Mary's**, 215
ship **Star of the West**, 395
ship **Steamer of America**, 72
ship **Vandalia**, 380
ship **Vespasian**, 373
ship **Wabash**, 202
ship **Welsford**, 29
Shipley, 280, 452
Shipman, 414
ships **Portsmouth, San Jacinto, & Levant**, 68
ships **Susquehanna and Niagara**, 456
Shirk, 100, 104

Shirley, 211
Shirley Female Institute, 77
Shirley Female Seminary, 311
Shivers, 163
Shock, 451, 460
Shoemaker, 5, 121, 131, 136, 314, 352, 468
Short, 411
Shorter, 223
Shoultz, 242
Showalter, 104
Shreve, 339, 410
Shreves, 372
Shroeder, 199
Shubrick, 418, 439
Shucking, 52
Shue, 405
Shugert, 307, 316, 344, 434
Shulte, 226
Shultz, 117, 190
Shulze, 340
Shumate, 2
Shuster, 208
Shuttleworth, 401
Shweatt, 36
Shwing, 435
Sibbot, 412
Sibley, 163, 176, 224, 246, 378, 452
Sibour, 38
Sichel, 318
Sierra, 121
Sifford, 100
Sigel, 411
Silliman, 346, 400
Sillis, 309
Simes, 281
Simmes, 52, 234
Simmons, 117, 257, 338, 412
Simms, 23, 179, 199, 326, 454, 480, 489
Simon, 309, 411, 412
Simonds, 53
Simons, 72, 226, 444
Simonton, 72

Simpson, 69, 79, 123, 255, 485
Sims, 23, 69, 152, 405
Sinclair, 184, 222, 234, 280, 336, 386, 399, 406
Siner, 348
Singles, 427
Sing-Sing prison, 178
Sinon, 96, 455
Sir John Franklin, 217
Sistere, 164
Sisters of Mercy, 262
Sisters of the Visitation, 384
Sitlington, 300
Skidmore, 46
Skillman, 335
Skinker, 240
Skinner, 107, 144, 236, 407, 434
Skippon, 122, 468
Skipwith, 8
Skirving, 370
Sknaggs, 275
Slack, 97
Slade, 89, 245
Slasinger, 309
Slatford, 283, 300
Slattery, 162, 206
Slavin, 82, 91, 435, 450
Sleeper, 398
Slemmer, 368
Sliney, 281
Slinker, 310
Sloan, 423
Slocum, 52
Sloo, 33, 79
sloop **Falmouth**, 340
sloop of war **Dale**, 176
sloop-of-war **Constellation**, 16, 32, 580
sloop-of-war **Cumberland**, 242
sloop-of-war **Falmouth**, 337
sloop-of-war **Levant**, 68
sloop-of-war **Plymouth**, 295, 350
sloop-of-war **Portsmouth**, 68, 313
sloop-of-war **St Mary's**, 202

Slough, 49
Small, 121, 253, 373, 473
Smalley, 52
Smallwood, 160, 470
Smedes, 238
Smith, 2, 7, 9, 17, 24, 26, 28, 29, 37, 44, 45, 47, 49, 52, 53, 54, 63, 65, 67, 69, 70, 72, 74, 75, 79, 81, 82, 86, 89, 97, 98, 100, 105, 111, 112, 116, 123, 126, 130, 131, 138, 141, 143, 145, 146, 147, 148, 157, 158, 160, 161, 175, 183, 184, 199, 209, 217, 218, 220, 221, 222, 223, 224, 226, 227, 229, 234, 236, 238, 243, 245, 249, 262, 265, 266, 270, 272, 273, 274, 275, 278, 280, 288, 292, 296, 298, 304, 307, 308, 309, 314, 315, 323, 339, 344, 352, 362, 364, 366, 373, 378, 390, 393, 395, 398, 399, 410, 411, 413, 414, 415, 416, 418, 419, 420, 421, 423, 428, 429, 430, 434, 435, 436, 442, 446, 452, 453, 455, 460, 462, 471, 473, 474, 476, 479, 480, 481, 482, 485
Smith's Virginia House, 292
Smithson, 57, 58, 87, 92, 216
Smithsonian Institute, 456
Smithsop, 69
Smithwick, 223
Smoot, 46, 98, 151, 363
Smyser, 398
Smyth, 220, 281, 318
Snell, 398
Snipes, 105
Snodgrass, 66
Snow, 124, 319, 357
Snowden, 84, 90, 171, 182, 231
Snyder, 157
Soares, 362
Society of Stonecutters, 459
Sohl, 324
Soldiers' Home, 448
Somers, 33, 206, 308
Sontag, 480

Soper, 289
Sothoron, 122, 230, 297, 468
Soulard, 35
Soule, 320
Soult, 457
Southall, 22, 41, 416
Southard, 260
Southgate, 23, 283, 292
Southwick, 199
Southworth, 107
Sowders, 31
Sowers, 351
Spalding, 2, 55, 58, 165
Spanks, 281
Sparkman, 337
Sparks, 3
Sparrow, 112
Spates, 334, 489
Spaulding, 98, 370, 411, 412
Spazzina, 291
Spear, 175, 439
Spears, 357
Speed, 145
Speir, 134
Speirs, 281
Spence, 406, 456, 473
Spencer, 52, 63, 86, 118, 121, 159, 166, 206, 283, 305, 336, 353, 357, 418
Sperry, 192, 281, 430
Spicer, 474
Spirit Lake, 157, 172
Spofford, 155
Spohn, 412
Spotswood, 402, 460
Spottswood, 30
Spradlin, 351
Sprague, 432
Sprigg, 46, 449
Spriggs, 419
Spring Grove, 58
Springer, 187, 270, 287
Springfield estate, 201, 248
Springman, 315, 472

Squibs, 482
St Clair, 28, 90, 212, 449
St James' College, 150
St Palais, 165
St Patrick's, 485
St Patrick's Catholic Church, 188
St Patrick's Church, 179
Stabler, 218
Stacy, 112
Staffordshire estate, 187
Stakl, 411
Staley, 214
Stalker, 203
Stallings, 21, 235, 400
Stambaugh, 51
Stanard, 209
Stanford, 203, 367
Stanley, 37, 58, 79, 142, 167, 422
Stanly, 271, 374, 482
Stansberry, 262
Stanton, 52, 68, 100, 121, 190, 434, 478, 484
Starbuck, 296
Stares, 296
Starke, 9
Starkweather, 109
Starr, 167
Start, 105
Starwood, 49
Staubly, 340
Steadman, 26
steamboat **Colonel Edwards**, 476
steamboat **Danl Boone**, 66
steamboat **Montreal**, 256
steamboat **Red Wings**, 47
steamer **America**, 334
steamer **Arctic**, 242
steamer **Atherton**, 196
steamer **Atlantic**, 406
steamer **Avon**, 262
steamer **Baltic**, 426
steamer **Baltimore**, 165
steamer **Belvidere**, 335
steamer **Carolina**, 33
steamer **Central America**, 369, 371, 372, 373, 374, 375, 376, 378, 379, 380, 381, 384, 387, 389, 390, 395, 396, 418
steamer **Columbus**, 395
steamer **Dardanelles**, 140
steamer **Dick Keys**, 450
steamer **Dr Kane**, 299
steamer **Empire City**, 174, 389
steamer **Engineer**, 18
steamer **England**, 116
steamer **Europa**, 305
steamer **Falls City**, 161
steamer **Forest Rose**, 140
steamer **Fulton**, 350
steamer **Galveston**, 208, 448
steamer **Gazelle**, 419
steamer **General Rusk**, 135
steamer **Geo Law**, 154
steamer **George Law**, 369, 380
steamer **Georgia**, 336
steamer **Golden Gate**, 374
steamer **Gray Cloud**, 337
steamer **Havana**, 147
steamer **Iris**, 380
steamer **Iturbide**, 27
steamer **John Hancock**, 42
steamer **John Simonds**, 161
steamer **Louisiana**, 227, 228
steamer **Metropolis**, 323
steamer **Michigan**, 22
steamer **Minnesota**, 33, 152, 242
steamer **Missouri**, 67
steamer **Montreal**, 251, 272, 278
steamer **Niagara**, 332, 403
steamer **North America**, 453
steamer **Northern Light**, 488
steamer **Opelousas**, 459
steamer **Powhatan**, 61, 441
steamer **Rainbow**, 458
steamer **Reindeer**, 429
steamer **Salem**, 464
steamer **Scott**, 164
steamer **St Nicholas**, 335

steamer **Statesman**, 197
steamer **Texas**, 211
steamer **Tropic**, 419
steamer **Vixen**, 82, 86
steamer **Water Witch**, 62, 242
steamer **Wilson Small**, 180
steam-frig **Minnesoto**, 199
steam-frig **Wabash**, 253
steamship **America**, 246
steamship **Baltic**, 384
steamship **Central America**, 410
steamship **Empire City**, 202
steamship **Galveston**, 219, 455
steamship **Illinois**, 170
steamship **Jasper**, 455
steamship **Louisiana**, 208, 219, 220
steamship **Mississippi**, 232
steamship **Opelousas**, 448, 455
steamship **Persia**, 94
steamship **San Francisco**, 16
steamship **Tempest**, 165
steamship **Thomas Swann**, 369
steamship **Winfield Scott**, 16
Stearns, 282, 293, 294, 432
Steece, 399
Steede, 156
Steedman, 52
Steel, 281, 309, 357
Steele, 4, 6, 57, 58, 65, 82, 91, 103, 214, 362, 483
Steen, 333, 445
Steiger, 490
Stein, 449
Steiner, 244
Stell, 209
Stelle, 14, 241
Stephen, 196
Stephens, 41, 119, 179, 238, 309, 337, 419, 425
Stephenson, 233, 258, 300, 441, 480
Steptoe, 309, 405
Sterrett, 194, 274, 482
Stetson, 371, 372, 413
Stettinius, 303

Steuart, 72, 87, 90
Steuckrath, 322
Stevens, 1, 15, 18, 28, 46, 73, 82, 87, 92, 158, 226, 227, 236, 239, 271, 308, 408, 411, 413, 468, 482, 483
Stevenson, 23, 26, 43, 57, 86, 119, 242, 290, 457
Steward, 412
Stewart, 13, 15, 18, 22, 23, 26, 34, 36, 76, 80, 83, 86, 92, 117, 157, 163, 168, 172, 180, 215, 242, 248, 253, 278, 283, 300, 309, 312, 317, 335, 337, 350, 373, 398, 416, 435, 479
Stick, 76
Stickney, 149, 267, 379, 490
Stienhiel, 342
Stiles, 217, 226, 336
Stillman, 109
Stinchfield, 411
Stinson, 135, 337
Stirges, 46
Stirman, 52
Stith, 113
Stoball, 175
Stockdale, 360, 409
Stockett, 84, 112, 231, 331
Stockton, 100, 104
Stoddard, 146, 255
Stokely, 450, 471
Stokes, 72, 327, 358
Stola, 437
Stone, 42, 54, 57, 58, 68, 80, 81, 87, 88, 94, 138, 185, 230, 260, 286, 298, 309, 384, 387, 393, 396
Stonelands, 197, 476
Stonestreet, 246, 270
Storer, 296, 320
Storm, 38
Storrow, 107
Stott, 126, 230
Stouffer, 118
Stoughton, 66, 152
Stout, 227, 386, 408, 484
Stovall, 23, 465

Stover, 298
Stowe, 169, 272
Stowell, 64
Strahn, 324
Strain, 202, 206
Strange, 181, 311, 463
Stras, 303
Stratton, 353, 354, 356, 357
Strausbuug, 309
Strauss, 411
Street, 3, 73, 99
Streeter, 47
streets lighted, 144
Stribbling, 170
Strobel, 213
Strobell, 444
Strohecker, 115
Strohm, 413
Strong, 9, 130, 204, 222, 234, 265, 280, 330, 399
Strongbow, 388
Strother, 11
Strueve, 413
Stuart, 99, 151, 245, 275, 301, 446
Stubbs, 112, 179, 276, 362
Stuck, 134
Stucken, 220
Studer, 7
Studs, 189
Stueckrath, 40
Stump, 199, 347
Stupp, 174
Sturdevant, 453
Sturdivant, 399
Sturgeon, 100, 341, 398
Sturgess, 293
Sturgis, 57, 58, 60, 87, 91
Suddards, 351
Sudler, 72
Sudley Springs, 332
Sudley View, 332
Sue, 326, 340
Suezy, 30
Sugar Land Mills, 368

Suit, 137, 298, 472
Sullivan, 17, 136, 138, 167, 178, 197, 220, 297, 309, 382, 413, 445
Sumby, 12
Sumer, 236
Summer, 448
Summer Hill, 367
Summer residence for the Pres, 202
Summers, 30
Sumner, 267, 415, 446, 471, 478
Sumter, 390
Sunderland, 21, 25, 164, 173, 218, 229, 267
Surghnor, 332
Surratt, 77, 324
Susquehanna, 326
Suter, 40, 238, 312
Sutherland, 11, 191, 258, 287, 397
Sutter, 447
Sutton, 102, 152, 417, 419, 474, 488
Sutz, 64
Swain, 57, 58, 63, 87, 92, 217, 306, 481
Swaine, 452
Swampoodle, 263
Swan, 26, 77, 353, 373, 384, 411
Swann, 47, 222, 353, 354, 355, 356, 357, 359, 466, 468, 485
Swanston, 453, 481
Swartwout, 64
Swarzman, 52
Sweat, 114
Swedish emigrants, 313
Sweeney, 72, 334
Sweeny, 48, 72, 97, 122, 143, 179, 201, 270
Sweet, 9, 28, 109, 179, 355
Sweney, 281
Swenson, 417
Swift, 398, 468
Swingle, 254, 450
Swinton, 214, 397
Swiver, 157
Sylvester, 122

552

Symington, 320
Symons, 145
Syple, 308
Szymanoske, 144

T

Tabbs, 39
Taber, 272
Tabler, 7, 68
Tabor, 450
Taft, 255
Taggart, 149
Tait, 6
Talbert, 243, 468
Talbot, 22, 131, 277, 440
Talbott, 135, 242, 399
Talburt, 52
Taliaferro, 65, 86, 91, 116, 224, 382
Tallmadge, 100, 282, 452
Tallman, 398
Talty, 179
Taney, 335, 467
Tanner, 413
Tappan, 115, 153, 323
Tar, 418
Tardy, 168
Tarpley, 354
Tasso, 210
Tate, 143
Tatham, 169
Tatine, 133
Tattnall, 97
Tatum, 346
Tayloe, 148, 156, 229, 467
Taylor, 15, 22, 37, 40, 42, 43, 51, 53, 56, 61, 66, 67, 81, 95, 96, 100, 104, 110, 121, 129, 130, 133, 144, 145, 146, 157, 158, 160, 167, 184, 199, 223, 225, 230, 231, 233, 237, 238, 249, 250, 276, 293, 297, 298, 302, 335, 347, 371, 372, 383, 384, 414, 424, 431, 436, 446, 460, 467, 480, 483
Teasdale, 34, 260

Tebbs, 140, 182
Tecumseh, 182
Teel, 254
Tees, 26
telegraph, 380
telegraph cable, 440
Teller, 254
Temple, 25, 45, 174, 480
Templeton, 39
Temps, 220
Tennessee Historical Society, 140
Tenney, 143
Tennison, 372
Tenny, 4
Tennyson, 389
Terhune, 422
Terrall, 446
Terrett, 152, 199, 207
Territt, 199
Terry, 140, 232
Test, 73
Tewksbury, 264
Thackaray, 175
Thackeray, 243
Thaler, 152
Thatcher, 157, 172
Thaw, 52
Thayer, 214, 344, 373, 378, 391, 404, 410, 463
The Lodge, 255
The Plains, 241
The Refuge, 106
The Times, 111
Thebergo, 413
Thecker, 271, 373
Thesto, 373
Thistle, 26
Thom, 203
Thomas, 16, 105, 108, 121, 132, 146, 157, 164, 172, 176, 185, 232, 263, 281, 305, 330, 373, 379, 390, 398, 408, 410, 412, 414, 421, 425, 460, 476
Thompkins, 123

553

Thompson, 7, 22, 24, 26, 29, 42, 64,
  68, 72, 78, 89, 94, 107, 140, 141,
  146, 158, 159, 176, 180, 188, 197,
  208, 220, 221, 229, 253, 254, 266,
  273, 274, 293, 308, 309, 353, 358,
  369, 417, 425, 441, 452, 467, 471,
  472, 473, 474, 480, 484
Thomson, 207
Thorburn, 314, 482
Thorington, 96, 129
Thorn, 86, 274, 284, 324, 409, 468
Thorne, 471, 481
Thornton, 65, 86, 91, 100, 229, 238,
  292, 336, 404, 425, 482
Thorwaldsen, 397, 426
Thrale, 181
Thrash, 422
Threlkeld, 377
Thrift, 466
Throg, 392
Thrush, 104
Thruston, 3, 215, 333, 375
Thune, 414
Thurlow, 389
Thurston, 25, 41, 82, 90
Thyson, 291
Tiber, 14
Tiber bridge, 447
Tice, 396
Tidball, 452
Tigil, 167
Tilden, 164
Tilford, 109
Tilghman, 46, 62, 425
Till, 239
Tillner, 278
Tillotson, 217
Tilton, 339
Timmons, 165
Tiner, 468
Tingle, 111
Tinsley, 366
Tippett, 466
Tirado, 379, 414

Tirato, 395
Tirrell, 446
Tisdale, 352
Tison, 152
Titus, 309
Tobin, 186
Tochman, 425
Todd, 8, 23, 34, 45, 72, 79, 103, 111,
  224, 230, 232, 417, 419, 451, 473,
  474, 490
Tola, 309
Toledano, 297
Tollus, 371
Tolson, 86, 122, 200, 468
Tomlin, 405
Tomlinson, 30
Tompkins, 224, 253, 411, 488
Tompson, 214
Tongue, 105
Topham, 436
Torbert, 452
Torrence, 92
Torreyson, 426
Toshman, 153
Totten, 286
Toucey, 78, 89, 295, 449
Towers, 31, 154, 168, 214, 319, 331,
  367, 406
Towle, 209
Towner, 209
Townley, 329
Townsend, 213, 214
Tozer, 233, 277
Tracy, 273, 452
Trader, 478
Trafton, 86
Trail, 70
Train, 168
Trainer, 455
Tranchard, 82
Trapp, 253, 254
Trappe, 332
Traveller's Rest, 187
Travers, 220

Traverse, 428
Travis, 22, 373, 391, 410
Traylor, 43
Treadway, 293
Treadwell, 64
Treat, 93
Tree, 94, 110
Trenchard, 86, 460
Trevitt, 224
Tricon, 310
Trimmer, 118
Triplett, 71, 489
Tripp, 79, 88
Trist, 148
Tritton, 292
Trone, 105
Trott, 452
Trotter, 35
Trousdale, 283
Trowbridge, 254
True, 201
Trueheart, 77
Truesdell, 309
Trumbull, 245
Truxton, 424
Truxtun, 446
Tryon, 253
Tschaeke, 220
Tschiffely, 466
Tubman, 469
Tuck, 412
Tucker, 6, 30, 52, 87, 168, 183, 233, 274, 336, 347, 384, 450, 464, 477
Tuckerman, 462, 464
Tudor Place, 334
Tuell, 180
Tuley, 299
Tull, 332
Tungate, 195
Tuomey, 138
Turk, 148
Turnbull, 470, 472

Turner, 2, 31, 37, 38, 68, 90, 100, 105, 122, 159, 163, 181, 194, 202, 225, 241, 302, 308, 385, 399, 476, 483
Turney, 318
Turpin, 66, 142
Tustin, 18, 409, 433
Tuthill, 115
Tutt, 15
Tuttle, 360
Tweedy, 260
Twiggs, 108
Tyland, 244
Tyler, 3, 23, 51, 53, 69, 149, 164, 167, 168, 219, 250, 253, 288, 295, 312, 324, 397, 452, 453, 480
Tyrce, 488
Tyson, 5, 75, 241, 285
Tyssowski, 133, 134, 142
Tyssowsky, 158

U

Ulum, 93
Underwood, 74, 102, 152, 242, 490
Undine, 17
Unseld, 200
Upham, 97
Uphan, 196
Upperman, 149
Upshur, 22, 51, 164, 238
Upton, 314
Urquart, 99
Ustrick, 284
Utah Expedition, 451
Utermahle, 103

V

Vache, 331
Vail, 52
Vald, 72
Vale, 131
Valentine, 352, 474
Valk, 41
Valle, 8
Valley Forge, 313

Valley View Farm, 230
Valuable Table, 85
Van Bibber, 148
Van Buren, 182, 231, 437
Van Buskirk, 16
Van Camp, 195
Van Comstock, 399
Van DeWalker, 109
Van Dyke, 33, 480
Van Harper, 373
Van Horne, 433
Van Lear, 164
Van Natter, 411
Van Patten, 158, 339, 455
Van Pelt, 35, 67, 87, 91, 216
Van Renssalaer, 389
Van Rensselaer, 35, 339, 369, 372, 379
Van Reswick, 137, 230, 381
Van Trump, 436
Van Vleit, 477
Van Vliet, 329
Van Waldheim, 411
Van Wert, 349
Van Winkle, 471
Vanderlin, 245
Vandirer, 84
Vandorne, 233
Vandovender, 416
Vanfossen, 17
Vanhorn, 411
Vanhouten, 68
Vanover, 309
Vanzant, 65
Varden, 236
Varez, 21
Varnell, 52
Varner, 476
Varnum, 194, 440
Vass, 23
Vattier, 26, 49, 82, 91
Vaucluse, 164
Vaughan, 426
Vaughn, 87, 88, 92, 229, 390

Vaughrigneuse, 408
Veal, 431
Veche, 228
Veddar, 97
Vedder, 276, 446
Velpeau, 318
Venable, 100, 129, 163, 395, 431
Verbiski, 20, 45
Verdi, 443
Verges, 38
Vernet, 78
Vernon, 142
Versted, 341
vessel **Lee**, 87
Vial, 166
Vicinanzi, 441
Vickroy, 205
Vidocq, 220
Viers, 328
Vigal, 101
Villard, 28
Villat, 413
Villeger, 458
Villepigue, 279, 452
Villiers, 181
Villiger, 235, 344
Vincent, 8, 51
Vineyard, 133, 160
Vinton, 350
Vogel, 131, 348, 351
Vogelsang, 351
Volgen, 164
Volger, 336
Von Humboldt, 401
Voorhees, 109
Vosburg, 273
Vose, 371, 410
Voss, 57, 196, 298, 299, 361
Vreeland, 16, 479
Vroom, 207

W

Wabbott, 337
Wacaser, 64, 65, 87, 88, 92

Waddell, 197, 271
Wade, 257, 413
Wadsworth, 103, 369, 476
Wager, 398
Waggaman, 360
Waggner, 263
Waggoner, 260
Wagner, 26, 52, 132, 138, 141, 148, 346
Wagonseller, 118
Wagstaff, 309
Wailes, 180
Wainwright, 26, 326
Wait, 152
Waite, 237, 452
Wakefield, 187
Walbach, 225
Walbridge, 52, 343
Walden, 152
Waldo, 415
Waldron, 78, 461
Wales, 49
Walke, 482
Walker, 7, 23, 25, 30, 57, 86, 97, 104, 111, 121, 134, 135, 143, 160, 174, 176, 185, 186, 202, 220, 222, 234, 238, 253, 258, 280, 281, 282, 298, 308, 312, 313, 338, 348, 352, 356, 377, 386, 390, 393, 399, 418, 439, 450, 464, 465, 473, 488, 489
Wall, 19, 112, 222, 237, 281, 391, 425, 475
Wallace, 23, 86, 117, 238, 335, 382, 414, 482
Wallach, 3, 12, 52, 158, 203, 219, 237, 297, 330, 367, 425, 460, 469
Waller, 309, 393
Walling, 135
Wallingsford, 432
Wallington, 309
Walls, 371
Walnut Grange, 365, 375
Walsh, 263, 298, 445
Walter, 108, 182, 221, 238, 284, 470

Walters, 70, 119, 189, 220, 394
Walton, 35, 77, 87, 90
Wampum, 195
Wangler, 267
Wankowietez, 77
Wann, 117
War of 1812, 236
Ward, 42, 49, 50, 58, 100, 104, 138, 141, 148, 179, 183, 191, 229, 235, 246, 253, 254, 269, 270, 321, 325, 426, 440, 446, 451
Wardell, 340
Warden, 52
Ware, 119, 331, 459
Warfield, 182
Waring, 63, 270
Warington, 152
Warmick, 309
Warner, 71, 72, 109, 199, 222, 234, 280, 287
Warnock, 255
Warren, 119, 237, 261, 265, 281, 324, 457, 460
Warrenton Male Academy, 317
Warrington, 189, 350
Warwick, 63, 375
Washburn, 96
Washburne, 15, 18, 77, 87, 92
Washington, 42, 109, 160, 167, 187, 193, 194, 199, 231, 245, 253, 261, 301, 325, 339, 397, 403, 434, 448, 450, 451, 456, 461, 477, 483
Washington Crossing the Delaware, 55
Washington Monument, 154
Washington Resigning, 209
Washington University, 169
Water Grist Mill, 382
Waterman, 86, 88, 91
Waters, 62, 271, 325, 328, 377, 453
Watkins, 121, 133, 230, 265, 293, 311, 320, 348, 359, 444
Watmough, 69

557

Watson, 58, 63, 79, 110, 196, 271, 295, 298, 341, 366, 385, 395
Watt, 281
Watterston, 386, 402
Watts, 164, 233, 281
Waugh, 105, 401
Waveland, 24
Way, 49, 125, 474
Way Side, 294
Wayman, 425
Wayne, 284, 448, 467
Weare, 385
Weast, 479
Weaver, 236, 243
Webb, 59, 63, 73, 160, 181, 186, 232, 233, 294, 400, 421, 431, 446, 452, 463, 469, 490
Webber, 14, 281, 365
Weber, 65, 292, 342
Webster, 57, 95, 143, 173, 182, 203, 255, 308, 361, 367, 378
Wederstrandt, 110
Weed, 154, 254, 331, 471
Weeden, 190, 451
Weeks, 8, 26, 222, 234, 280, 414, 435
Weems, 283
Weer, 100
Weidman, 398
Weige, 412
Weigert, 197
Weightman, 57, 269
Weigle, 4
Weil, 220
Weirman, 262
Weis, 445
Welch, 3, 71, 80, 83, 148, 152, 174, 298, 466
Welcker, 397
Weld, 350
Wells, 12, 54, 73, 174, 219, 240, 254, 372, 402, 411, 413, 414, 474
Welsey, 104
Welsh, 65, 142, 480
Wemly, 174

Wendell, 1, 198, 407
Wentworth, 83, 93
Werner, 160
Wertmuller, 245
Wertner, 486
Wescoat, 214
West, 7, 147, 174, 208, 218, 254, 255, 350, 450, 460, 482
West Point Academy, 221
West Point Military Academy, 222
Westcott, 107, 115, 383
Wester, 419
Westerlo, 339
Western, 310
Westmoreland Co, Va, 187
Weston, 34, 48
Wetherby, 109
Wetherell, 452
Wetherspoon, 281
Wetmore, 178
Wetzel, 461
Weyhing, 443
Wezell, 245
Whalan, 413
Whaley, 213, 214, 438
Whallon, 9
Wharton, 8, 73, 121, 352, 356
Wheat, 347
Wheatley, 235, 352
Wheatly, 52, 404, 458
Wheatman, 144
Wheaton, 60, 167, 242
Wheatstone, 342
Wheelan, 265
Wheeler, 31, 220, 339, 431, 490
Wheelock, 174
Wheelwright, 411
Whelan, 165
Whidden, 130
Whippe, 118
Whipple, 445
White, 4, 6, 8, 14, 16, 26, 43, 53, 74, 85, 100, 105, 109, 116, 124, 133, 135, 150, 152, 209, 212, 225, 229,

253, 281, 297, 312, 328, 372, 410, 412, 418, 423, 426, 431, 436, 454, 474
White Sulphur Springs, 18, 21, 120, 208, 243, 252, 335, 387
Whitehead, 337, 474
Whiteman, 315
Whitemen, 102
Whitfield, 53, 124
Whiting, 29, 160, 216, 309, 434, 442, 451, 480, 483
Whitlocke, 331
Whitlow, 458
Whitman, 33, 62, 315, 346
Whitney, 64, 65, 80
Whiton farm, 374
Whittaker, 458
Whittemore, 77, 254
Whitten, 15, 18
Whittier, 97, 253, 450
Whittingham, 314
Whittington, 142
Whittle, 22, 480
Whittlesey, 28, 96, 117
Whyte, 315, 460
Wick, 135
Wickham, 68
Wickliffe, 258
Wierman, 147
Wietzell, 148
Wiggin, 354
Wight, 490
Wightman, 477
Wigle, 14
Wilcox, 22, 26, 98, 233, 242, 290, 457
Wild Cat, 269
Wilder, 233, 289
Wilderick, 234
Wildrick, 222, 280
Wile, 40
Wiley, 97, 115, 413
Wilhoit, 55
Wilkes, 351, 418
Wilkey, 446

Wilkie, 69
Wilkin's Point, 303
Wilkins, 23, 161, 390
Wilkinson, 23, 213, 214, 225, 336, 466, 480, 482
Willard, 177, 337, 402, 451
Willemin, 205
Willet, 490
Willett, 328, 396, 411, 412
Willey, 489
Williams, 26, 40, 46, 49, 57, 61, 82, 85, 97, 106, 143, 152, 157, 168, 172, 174, 175, 183, 188, 209, 217, 230, 236, 248, 253, 254, 255, 262, 271, 281, 284, 288, 308, 323, 346, 347, 349, 393, 409, 410, 421, 428, 446, 452, 455, 459, 469, 471, 474, 479, 480
Williamson, 7, 169, 174, 295, 298, 354, 385, 460, 478, 483, 489
Willie, 33, 479
Williman, 441
Willis, 121, 282, 433
Willits, 135
Wills, 170, 206, 220, 249, 324
Willson, 184, 458
Wilmer, 175
Wilmot, 455
Wilsey, 250
Wilson, 13, 22, 23, 26, 27, 46, 76, 80, 86, 90, 92, 94, 100, 104, 105, 115, 164, 169, 175, 181, 182, 184, 185, 187, 215, 232, 233, 250, 255, 278, 281, 282, 283, 298, 309, 324, 358, 370, 396, 398, 399, 415, 421, 432, 446, 454, 464, 468, 470, 474, 479, 480, 488, 490
Wiltberger, 85, 86
Wilton, 372, 411
Wimberley, 473
Wimberly, 88, 92, 215
Wimer, 473
Wimmer, 36, 70
Winder, 2, 45, 72, 235, 367

Window, 175
Winfrey, 195
Wingate, 151, 246
Wingerd, 76, 448
Wingfield, 23, 119, 449, 475
Wingo, 309
Winkler, 341
Winn, 46, 144, 450
Winner, 121, 253
Winniford, 174
Winship, 72, 74, 90
Winslow, 4, 6, 25, 90, 304
Winslows, 304
Winston, 462
Winter, 258, 430
Winters, 309
Winton, 281
Wirt, 38, 74, 120, 447
Wise, 21, 51, 89, 90, 103, 114, 144, 167, 180, 187, 249, 265, 296, 297, 340, 368, 431
Witcher, 263
Witherow, 32
Withers, 1, 191, 308, 399, 421
Witherspoon, 256
Woelfer, 309
Woeslin, 242
Wolfe, 49, 205, 418, 423
Wolff, 105, 281
Wollard, 17
Wolpent, 445
Wonderly, 98
Wood, 4, 8, 26, 40, 49, 57, 67, 81, 97, 135, 157, 165, 172, 189, 206, 213, 233, 237, 259, 272, 277, 287, 341, 398, 413, 438
Wood's Bldgs, 438
Woodbridge, 453
Woodbury, 35, 88, 109, 124, 429
Woodcock, 350
Woodeard, 206
Woodell, 76
Woodfin, 405
Woodford, 3
Woodhuse, 440
Woodley, 3, 52, 429
Woodmorton, 175
Woodruff, 205
Woods, 77, 224, 225, 233, 312, 344, 459
Woodsman, 445
Woodson, 121, 124, 310
Woodward, 77, 216, 289, 307, 324, 352, 388, 427
Woodworth, 26, 412
Woody, 358
Wool, 108, 484
Woolly, 471
Woolman, 474
Worcester, 11
Worden, 395
Wore, 249
Worrel, 257
Worrell, 190
Worsham, 113
Worthington, 297, 326, 331, 382
Wray, 65, 86, 90, 215
Wren, 283
Wright, 31, 53, 56, 70, 72, 108, 118, 132, 176, 179, 188, 207, 238, 337, 375, 393, 435, 440, 453
Wroth, 435
Wyatt, 194
Wyckoff, 432
Wycombe, 388
Wydick, 174
Wyeth, 455
Wyke, 395
Wylie, 1, 44, 240, 269, 431
Wynkoop, 53, 477
Wysong, 105
Wyvill, 149
Wyville, 367

Y

yacht **Rambler**, 205
Yancey, 159, **188**
Yanney, 410

Yates, 232, 450, 474
Yeadon, 366, 397
Yeatman, 298
Yell, 119
Yonson, 382
York, 16, 164
Yorke, 398
Yost, 107, 115, 142
Young, 15, 36, 38, 39, 55, 72, 77, 93, 104, 135, 142, 165, 168, 207, 210, 211, 218, 219, 233, 236, 238, 255, 276, 291, 321, 385, 396, 411, 412, 413, 417, 425, 433, 459, 460, 473, 490
Youngards, 423
Yount, 467
Yulee, 138

Z

Zantzinger, 18, 258
Zaracher, 477
Zeilen, 295
Zeilin, 312
Zenaide, 327
Zimmerlin, 411
Zimmerman, 99, 461
Zinzinhoffer, 445
Zollicoffer, 238, 275, 286

Other Heritage Books by Joan M. Dixon:

National Intelligencer *Newspaper Abstracts*
Special Edition: The Civil War Years
Volume 1: January 1, 1861-June 30, 1863

National Intelligencer *Newspaper Abstracts*
Special Edition: The Civil War Years
Volume 2: July 1, 1863-December 31, 1865

National Intelligencer *Newspaper Abstracts 1858*
National Intelligencer *Newspaper Abstracts 1857*
National Intelligencer *Newspaper Abstracts 1856*
National Intelligencer *Newspaper Abstracts 1855*
National Intelligencer *Newspaper Abstracts 1854*
National Intelligencer *Newspaper Abstracts 1853*
National Intelligencer *Newspaper Abstracts 1852*
National Intelligencer *Newspaper Abstracts 1851*
National Intelligencer *Newspaper Abstracts 1850*
National Intelligencer *Newspaper Abstracts 1849*
National Intelligencer *Newspaper Abstracts 1848*
National Intelligencer *Newspaper Abstracts 1847*
National Intelligencer *Newspaper Abstracts 1846*
National Intelligencer *Newspaper Abstracts 1845*
National Intelligencer *Newspaper Abstracts 1844*
National Intelligencer *Newspaper Abstracts 1843*
National Intelligencer *Newspaper Abstracts 1842*
National Intelligencer *Newspaper Abstracts 1841*
National Intelligencer *Newspaper Abstracts 1840*
National Intelligencer *Newspaper Abstracts, 1838-1839*
National Intelligencer *Newspaper Abstracts, 1836-1837*
National Intelligencer *Newspaper Abstracts, 1834-1835*
National Intelligencer *Newspaper Abstracts, 1832-1833*
National Intelligencer *Newspaper Abstracts, 1830-1831*
National Intelligencer *Newspaper Abstracts, 1827-1829*
National Intelligencer *Newspaper Abstracts, 1824-1826*
National Intelligencer *Newspaper Abstracts, 1821-1823*
National Intelligencer *Newspaper Abstracts, 1818-1820*
National Intelligencer *Newspaper Abstracts, 1814-1817*
National Intelligencer *Newspaper Abstracts, 1811-1813*
National Intelligencer *Newspaper Abstracts, 1806-1810*
National Intelligencer *Newspaper Abstracts, 1800-1805*

www.ingramcontent.com/pod-product-compliance
Lightning Source LLC
Chambersburg PA
CBHW052135300426
44115CB00011B/1398